MW01221842

# Archaeology of Culture Contact and Colonialism in Spanish and Portuguese America

Pedro Paulo A. Funari
Maria Ximena Senatore
Editors

# Archaeology of Culture Contact and Colonialism in Spanish and Portuguese America

 Springer

*Editors*
Pedro Paulo A. Funari
Campinas
São Paulo
Brazil

Maria Ximena Senatore
Buenos Aires
Argentina

ISBN 978-3-319-08068-0          ISBN 978-3-319-08069-7 (eBook)
DOI 10.1007/978-3-319-08069-7
Springer Cham Heidelberg New York Dordrecht London

Library of Congress Control Number: 2014953959

Printed on acid-free paper

Springer is part of Springer Science+Business Media (www.springer.com)

*To the memory of my parents*

P.P.A.F.

*To my parents*

M.X.S.

# I Foreword

For a very long time, historical archaeology has been the archaeology of the European expansion in the former British colonies (USA, Caribbean, Canada and Australia) and its consequences: the Atlantic trade, the fur trade, slave plantations, colonial conflicts, creolization, urbanization and industrialization. Iberia has played rather a secondary role in the narratives of historical archaeology, except in those areas of the USA that were once part of the Spanish Empire (such as Florida, California or Texas). During the last couple of decades, however, historical archaeology has grown vigorously in many Latin American countries, most notably Argentina and Brazil, and has expanded to other regions where pre-Columbian archaeology used to ring the tune, as in Ecuador or Colombia. This can be noticed in the growing presence of Latin American contributions to international journals and books.

However, a monographic volume like the present one was much needed. First, it was necessary to display the richness and diversity of the archaeologies of Iberian colonialism. With the inclusion of Scandinavia, Africa and Latin America, historical archaeology is becoming truly global and, therefore, more balanced in geographical and cultural terms. It would be wrong, however, to consider that including Latin America in the wider picture is just an issue of increasing diversity: in fact, the second reason why a volume like this is crucial for the development of historical archaeology is that there can be no archaeological understanding of modernity and capitalism (whatever these concepts mean) without Latin America. As decolonial thinkers, such as Aníbal Quijano and Enrique Dussel, have made abundantly clear, the regions conquered by Spain and Portugal are not just another area colonized by Europe; they are the cradle of coloniality. The place where all began: from racism to predatory capitalism and also novel forms of challenging or evading colonial power.

Decolonial thinkers insist—and this is of paramount importance for archaeologists—that the imperial practices developed by Spain and Portugal (genocide, slavery, concubinage, racism or economic depredation) are not independent of the development of modernity, but actually an essential part of the modern episteme itself. While archaeologists may have a hard time identifying the philosophical categories of modernity as such in the archaeological record, they are excellent at locating politico-economic and cultural practices, which are so vital in the decolonial definition of colonial modernity. The coloniality of power is strongly material as the contributors to this volume eloquently show. It has to do with political economy, including trade, technology, markets, anti-market strategies and tribute, the body, which materializes racial hierarchies and performs gender, ethnic and class differences and controlling the land and the sea through seafaring, ports, forts and outposts. The present volume covers all these issues.

These issues are in turn related to another phenomenon in which archaeology excels: documenting the creation of cultural diversity through *mestizaje*, creolization, transculturation or hybridity—terms that have been all developed outside archaeology but to which archaeology has much to contribute. The case studies presented in this book help disrupt the grand narrative of colonialism, which is another product of the coloniality of power. They do so by scrutinizing the manifold local interactions made possible by the colonial encounter/conflict, from the fisheries of Canada to the Spanish settlements in Patagonia. In these local contexts, myriad histories and a wealth of cultural practices developed which have often passed unnoticed to conventional historiography—more concerned with cities, revolutions, large industrial centres and global missionary projects.

Archaeology thrives in "small things" as James Deetz famously put it: minimal things that have been neglected by history, often because they were ephemeral, like Fort San José in Florida, or because they were a failure, like the sugar and gold industries in Concepción de la Vega, or the settlement of Floridablanca. Of all ephemeral times, perhaps that of the early contact is the most fascinating. Some of the chapters contained in this volume open a window into the short but eventful time of the first encounter, and there is something uncanny, and at the same time, deeply archaeological in it. Perhaps because this ephemeral time is so flimsy and fragile, but had such extremely solid, material consequences. Or perhaps because it is an infinite time of possibility. Failed things are equally irresistible. In small, failed things, we can grasp the nature of history and, perhaps more poignantly, the history of modernity, which tends to portray itself as grand, progressive and successful. In local interactions between the colonizers and the colonized, we see asymmetries and violence, and also the contradictions and weaknesses of imperial power, whose attempts at fully mastering reality were often thwarted, or at least had unforeseen outcomes. Much of the hybridity that we can detect in the archaeological record is witness to this failure of colonial regimentation.

Archaeology is of course not limited to the ephemeral and unsuccessful. It also has an unrivalled ability to document the long term and the remote past. In the case of the colonization of the Americas, this ability is of enormous relevance: many of the historical trajectories and cultural practices that we document during the colonization are impossible to understand without a look at the deep history of the continent. Several of the chapters of this book take a long-term perspective in order to reclaim indigenous agencies and reveal the ways in which colonial power imposed itself in a foreign land, often in a very physical way. If failed outposts speak of the inconsistencies of imperial power, the long-term resilience of indigenous practices, which several of the contributors tackle in their chapters, speaks of success—the secret victory of the subaltern.

During the last decades, archaeologists have been more and more concerned with recent times and with the effects of the past in the present—not the least through the concept of cultural heritage. The effects of the colonial past in contemporary societies are perhaps nowhere clearer than in Latin America. In Cuba and Brazil, slavery left a vibrant cultural heritage and a bitter legacy of social asymmetry. From the deep past to the very present, this book shows the strengths and potentialities of archaeology to unravel the colonial experience of the Americas under Iberian rule.

For a long time, theoretically guided research has been regarded as the preserve of Anglo-Saxon academia. This overlooks the fact that Latin American archaeologists have consistently developed theoretical approaches to their rich material, both prehistoric and historical. The present volume, by bringing together scholars from Latin America, Iberia and the USA, goes a long way in redressing another epistemic imbalance of coloniality—in this case, regarding the geography of knowledge production on coloniality itself. The volume offers a unique opportunity to have a glimpse of the varied and sophisticate interpretations of Iberian colonialism that have been put forward in recent years in the North as well as in the South. Hopefully, colleagues from other countries and intellectual traditions will pay heed and engage with the many dialogues that this book now opens.

Institute of Heritage Sciences Spanish                        Alfredo González-Ruibal
National Research Council (Incipit-CSIC)

# II Foreword

At a time when grand narratives of all kinds are being discarded, this volume, archaeology of culture contact and colonialism in Spanish and Portuguese America, both skillfully deconstructs the triumphalist myth of European colonization in the western hemisphere and builds a firm, empirical foundation for an emerging twenty-first century alternative. Readers of this volume will see precisely how the tide is turning: from binary cultural oppositions to cultural interactions. In the physical and psychic violence of the European arrival and colonization of the Americas, all participants were profoundly changed. Beyond the overt acts of domination and resistance, more subtle changes took place in the everyday life and working landscapes of all peoples involved. And as the material culture and archival materials show, those changes—so incremental that they were almost invisible to the participants—were far more influential than theological and territorial claims in determining the historical evolution of the Americas.

Indeed one of the great values of this volume lies in its sheer geographical scope. In framing the great transformation through the lenses of archaeology, material culture studies, anthropology and political economy, the contributors to this volume have together presented the commonalities as well as the regional specificities of Euro-American culture contact in an area stretching all the way from the Basque fishing stations of Eastern Canada to the Spanish Enlightenment-inspired utopian colony of Floridablanca in Patagonia. In place of the timeworn binary oppositions of Europeans and native peoples, the essays in this volume show how profound were the local, improvised and creative responses to alien understandings of gender, faith, race, and social hierarchy. Moreover, the authors' empirical evidence from the contact period clearly contradicts the belief that history proceeded in only one direction with the Europeans' arrival. In the colonial encounter, all peoples were shaped by, and participated in the profound reshaping of landscapes and social environments.

In contrast to the traditional historiography of Spanish and Portuguese colonization, whose interpretive goal was the othering of the native peoples, and the more recent narratives of victimhood and resistance of the native peoples to European colonization, this volume presents the more complex process of Mestizaje in both a genealogical and cultural sense. Though the violence, enslavement, and genocide performed on native peoples by the European colonizers have been extensively discussed, the unconscious assumption of the essential separateness between the colonizers and the colonized has only recently been challenged effectively. This volume certainly makes an important contribution to that discussion, in moving beyond essentialist distinctions of "us" vs. "them"—even in an ideologically projected Saidian "orientalist" sense. Cultural purity and segregation have always been ideological objectives attempted but never fully realized, in the period of euro-American cultural contact and colonization no less than in the current era of neoliberal globalization.

Indeed, because of this contemporary relevance, this volume should be of great interest to heritage professionals as well as archaeologists and social historians, for it provides the outlines of a new framework for public heritage interpretation in which actions and behaviours sometimes (often) differ sharply from what is being said. Ethnic essentialism has been and continues to be an ideology that promotes inequality and justifies structural violence. Yet this essentialism is a chimera as the empirical evidence presented here clearly shows. Though it still serves as a basis for the selective preservation of certain historical and archaeological sites by national governments and UNESCO World Heritage list nominations, the new perspectives presented here have the potential of more deeply engaging the culturally diverse public and raising the significance of cultural diversity in the public's historical consciousness.

The construction of an inclusive public discourse about the past—in the Americas, as elsewhere—is arguably of equal importance to the academic interests in collecting data to fill gaps in specialist knowledge and the refinement or discarding of theoretical paradigms. This volume represents a generational turn in the understanding of contact period archaeology in the Americas. More than that, it is deeply relevant to the wider field of contemporary public heritage and identity making in the western hemisphere.

The contributors and editors of this volume are to be congratulated for their collection, compilation and analysis of a vast body of data from the contact and initial colonization eras that offers new insights into the entangled relations of globalization, nationalism, scholarship, gender, race, and, ultimately, contemporary cultural heritage policies in the Americas. The link between past and present in former Spanish and Portuguese colonies in the "New World" remains unbroken. Yet this volume powerfully rearticulates that trans-historical connection by challenging traditional narratives of binary opposition and replacing them with a more sophisticated understanding of how complex processes of cultural interaction and hybridization are still deeply felt in the evolving culture and consciousness of the region in the twenty-first century.

University of Massachusetts Amherst                                    Neil Asher Silberman
Coherit Associates

# Acknowledgements

In the first place, we would like to thank all of the contributors of this book for their very valuable and instrumental ideas and research.

We also acknowledge the book proposal reviewers for their influential suggestions back when this book was only a project as well as the suggestions from Mary Beaudry and Barbara Voss, which contributed to improve and widen the contents of this book. We are grateful to Teresa Krauss, Springer senior editor of archaeology and anthropology, and we would also like to thank Hana Nagdimov for assisting us in the manuscript submission process.

We specially thank Barbara L. Voss who generously agreed to write an insightful final commentary for the volume. Special thanks also to Alfredo González-Ruibal and Neil A. Silberman for their valuable words in the forewords introducing and framing the book proposal into its wider context.

We must also mention the institutional support from the Universities of Campinas and Buenos Aires, the Brazilian National Science Foundation (CNPq), São Paulo Science Foundation (FAPESP) and the National Scientific and Technical Research Council of Argentina (CONICET). The responsibility for the volume is our own and we are solely responsible for it.

# Contents

# Contributors

**Agustin Azkarate** Cátedra Territorio, Paisaje y Patrimonio, Grupo de Investigación en Patrimonio Construido, GPAC (UPV-EHU), Centro de Investigación Lascaray Ikergunea, Vitoria-Gasteiz, Spain

**Paulo Fernando Bava de Camargo** Department of Archaeology, Federal University of Sergipe, Laranjeiras, SE, Brazil

**Joana Bento Torres** Faculdade de Ciências Sociais e Humanas, CHAM, Lisboa, Portugal

**José Bettencourt** Faculdade de Ciências Sociais e Humanas, CHAM, Lisboa, Portugal

**Horacio Chiavazza** Departamento de Historia, Instituto de Arqueología y Etnología, Facultad de Filosofía y Letras, Universidad Nacional de Cuyo, Mendoza, Argentina

**Diana DiPaolo Loren** Peabody Museum of Archaeology and Ethnology, Harvard University, Cambridge, MA, USA

**Lourdes Domínguez** Oficina del Historiador de la Habana and Academia de la Historia, Havana, Cuba

**Sergio Escribano-Ruiz** Cátedra Territorio, Paisaje y Patrimonio, Grupo de Investigación en Patrimonio Construido, GPAC (UPV-EHU), Centro de Investigación Lascaray Ikergunea, Vitoria-Gasteiz, Spain

**Pedro Paulo A. Funari** Department of History and Center for Environmental Studies, University of Campinas, Campinas, SP, Brazil

Departamento de História, IFCH, Unicamp Laboratório de Arqueologia Pública Paulo Duarte (LAP/Nepam/Unicamp) UNICAMP Cidade Universitária Zeferino Vaz, Campinas, SP, Brazil

**Denise Maria Cavalcante Gomes** Departamento de Antropologia, Museu Nacional, Universidade Federal do Rio de Janeiro, São Cristóvão, RJ, Brazil

**Susan Kepecs** Department of Anthropology, University of Wisconsin-Madison, Madison, WI, USA

**Pauline Martha Kulstad-Gonzalez** Doral, FL, USA

**Ana María Navas Méndez** Caracas, Venezuela

**Guido Pezzarossi** Department of Anthropology, Stanford University, Oakland, CA, USA

**Rita Juliana Soares Poloni** Pós-doc LAP/NEPAM—Unicamp, Campinas, São Paulo, Brazil

**Enrique Rodríguez-Alegría** Department of Anthropology, University of Texas, Austin, Texas, USA

**Nan A. Rothschild** Barnard College, Columbia University, New York, NY, USA

**Julie Rogers Saccente** Next Generation Cultural Services, Inc., Clearwater, FL, USA

**Franz Scaramelli** Pittsburg, CA, USA

**Kay Scaramelli** Pittsburg, CA, USA

Departamento de Arqueología y Antropología Histórica, Escuela de Antropología, Universidad Central de Venezuela, Caracas, Venezuela

**Maria Ximena Senatore** IMHICIHU Instituto Multidisciplinario de Historia y Ciencias Humanas, CONICET Consejo Nacional de Investigaciones Científicas y Técnicas, Universidad Nacional de la Patagonia Austral & Universidad de Buenos Aires, Argentina, Ciudad Autónoma de Buenos Aires, Argentina

CONICET, Consejo Nacional de Investigaciones Científicas y Técnicas, IMHICIHU Instituto Multidisciplinario de Historia y Ciencias Humanas & Universidad de Buenos Aires, Ciudad Autónoma de Buenos Aires, Argentina

**Luís Cláudio Pereira Symanski** Departamento de Sociologia e Antropologia, Universidade Federal de Minas Gerais, Belo Horizonte, Brazil

**André Teixeira** Faculdade de Ciências Sociais e Humanas, CHAM, Lisboa, Portugal

**Barbara L. Voss** Department of Anthropology, Stanford University, Stanford, CA, USA

**Nancy Marie White** Department of Anthropology, University of South Florida, Tampa, FL, USA

# About the Editors

**Pedro Paulo Abreu Funari** is a professor of historical archaeology at the University of Campinas, Brazil, former World Archaeological Congress secretary, author and editor of several books, such as Historical Archaeology, Back from the edge (London, Routledge, 1999), Global Archaeological Theory (New York, Springer, 2005), Memories from Darkness, the archaeology of repression and resistance in Latin America (New York, Springer, 2009), with fieldwork in Brazil, England, Wales, Spain and Italy (several in each country). Funari is member of the editorial boards of several journals, notably the International Journal of Historical Archaeology (New York), Journal of Material Culture (London), Public Archaeology (London, UCL) and is referee in several other journals, like Current Anthropology. Funari has published papers in most prestigious journals, such as Historical Archaeology, Current Anthropology, Archaeologies, Révue Archéologique, Antiquity, American Antiquity, American Journal of Archaeology, and has edited archaeological encyclopedias.

**Maria Ximena Senatore** is a national researcher at CONICET (National Council of Scientific and Technological Research), Argentina. Professor of historical archaeology and heritage at University of Buenos Aires and National University of Patagonia Austral. Senatore has a degree in archaeology (University of Buenos Aires, 1995) and PhD in History (2003, University of Valladolid, Spain). She is running research projects on Spanish Colonialism in South Patagonia, and capitalism expansion to Antarctica. Senatore has published papers in several journals such as International Journal of Historical Archaeology, Historical Archaeology, Polar Record and 3 books in Argentina and Brazil.

# Chapter 1
# Introduction: Disrupting the Grand Narrative of Spanish and Portuguese Colonialism

Maria Ximena Senatore and Pedro Paulo A. Funari

## 1.1 Introduction

The edited volume aims at exploring contact archaeology in the modern era. Archaeology has been exploring the interaction of peoples and cultures from early times, but only in the last few decades have cultural contact and the material world been recognized as crucial elements to understanding colonialism and the emergence of modernity (Gosden 2004).

Impressive literature on colonialism has been produced on a worldwide scale which shows that shared attributes in colonial situations around the world and throughout time have been identified (Fitzhugh 1985; Given 2004; Gosden 2004; Liebmann and Murphy 2011; Stein 2005, inter alios). In this sense, the Gosden's typology of colonialism as a "grand scheme" approach intended to apply to colonialism at all times and places, based on general and wide categories, and has been proved significant. Nevertheless, the question of the need to develop more granular approaches to studying colonialism and colonial projects in either a regional or more limited time scale has been posed.

Latin America would thus be an interesting contribution to the study of colonialism and cultural contact in this respect and for a good reason: Its diversity is particularly daunting for social theorists and archaeologists. The fact that hybridism, transculturation, and *métissage* have been developed as interpretative tools to understand cultural mixture in Latin America is no coincidence: Cultural contact in

M. X. Senatore (✉)
IMHICIHU Instituto Multidisciplinario de Historia y Ciencias Humanas CONICET Consejo Nacional de Investigaciones Científicas y Técnicas, Universidad Nacional de la Patagonia Austral & Universidad de Buenos Aires, Argentina, Cornelio Saavedra 15 5th Floor, C1083ACA Ciudad Autónoma de Buenos Aires, Argentina
e-mail: mxsenatore@gmail.com

P. P. A. Funari
Departamento de História, IFCH, Unicamp Laboratório de Arqueologia Pública Paulo Duarte, (LAP/Nepam/Unicamp) UNICAMP Cidade Universitária Zeferino Vaz, Campinas, SP 13083-970, Brazil
e-mail: ppfunari@uol.com.br

© Springer International Publishing Switzerland 2015                                                    1
P. P. A. Funari, M. X. Senatore (eds.), *Archaeology of Culture Contact and Colonialism in Spanish and Portuguese America*, DOI 10.1007/978-3-319-08069-7_1

Spanish and Portuguese America has meant that the lives of European, native and African peoples and cultures became intertwined and therefore shaped new social and material realities. It is noteworthy that other specialized fields, such as classical archaeology, have been using Latin American mixtures as a way of interpreting ancient material culture processes in the Ancient Mediterranean.

This volume has been designed comprehensively including authors from different intellectual traditions from Spanish- and Portuguese-speaking Latin American countries, which resulted in a highly diverse "native perspective," added to the contributions of authors from Spain, Portugal, and English-speaking countries.

## 1.2   Main Ideas

The contents and the organizational scheme of the volume reflect three broad areas of discussion: Sect. I—posing questions in cultural contact and colonialism, Sect. II—local histories: diversity, creativity, and novelty, and Sect. III—new realities and material worlds. As a result, this book offers a view that encompasses histories that question the idea of homogeneity in Latin America, as it appears in the master narrative of the Iberian colonization.

Modern colonialism studies pose questions in need of broader answers. This volume explores these answers in Spanish and Portuguese America, comprising mainly present-day Latin America and former Spanish territories now part of the USA. This initial map has widened to include spaces on the Atlantic coast of current Canada and of Portugal beyond the ocean. Contributions span different geographies, landscapes, and material contexts, within a temporal range extending from the past to contemporary times.

Colonialism had enough unity to be understood within a single comparative framework, but it also had deep variations in different times and places: It had its own local histories (Gosden 2004, p. 24). The volume stresses the importance of local context (Funari et al. 1999). The contributors address studies of the particular features of Spanish-Portuguese colonialism, as well as the specificities of Iberian colonization, including hybridism, religious novelties, medieval and modern social features, all mixed in a variety of ways unique and so different from other areas, particularly the Anglo-Saxon colonial thrust. Cultural contact studies offer particularly an in-depth picture of the uniqueness of Latin America in terms of its cultural mixture.

Colonialism created new worlds through the meeting, clash, and sometimes mergence of varying values. We need to explore the variety of these worlds and the processes, whereby the contacts between social logics put existing values at risk, including some of those we mostly take for granted (Gosden 2004, p. 23). The edited volume creates a dual view conjugating particularities and generalities, as well as expressing the unity and diversity of Latin America. This volume particularly highlights local histories, revealing novelty, diversity, and creativity in the conformation of the new colonial realities, as well as presenting Latin America as a multicultural arena, with astonishing heterogeneity in thoughts, experiences, practices, and material worlds.

### 1.2.1 Contribution of This Volume

The case studies presented in this volume examine the Spanish and Portuguese co-lonial projects in a wide variety of contexts. The chapters included in Sect. I show different approaches to posing questions about colonialism. In Chap. 2, Teixeira et al. investigate the Atlantic expansion and the Portuguese material culture in the early modern age (Portugal). Azkarate and Escribano-Ruiz, in Chap. 3, question the historiographical representation of the early colonization of the Rio de la Plata Basin (Argentina). Rodríguez-Alegría et al., in Chap. 4, examine technological transformations comparing two different colonial settings (Mexico and Venezuela). In Chap. 5, Pezzarossi analyzes market engagement in Colonial Guatemala. In Chap. 6, Kepecs considers the complex relationships between indigenous ideology and the economy of the northern lowlands Maya of Yucatan (Mexico). In Chap. 7, Dominguez and Funari present a reassessment of archaeology of cultural contact in Cuba.

Local histories in specific social contexts are examined in the contributions in Sect. II. In Chap. 8, Loren aims at obtaining a fuller understanding of the complete colonial body in eighteenth century Spanish Texas. Scaramelli and Scaramelli, in Chap. 9, investigate the commercialization of wild resources articulating the global and local perspectives in the Orinoco frontier (Venezuela). Rosthchild, in Chap. 10, investigates in different social contexts the women's role in the Spanish colonial world. Symansky and Gomes, in Chap. 11, study social segmentation and mes-tizage between Portuguese and indigenous people in northern Brazil. Senatore, in Chap. 12, presents novelty as part of social interaction in eighteenth-century Pata-gonic Atlantic Coast Spanish colony (Argentina).

New realities and material worlds are primary themes addressed in Sect. III. In Chap. 13, Escribano-Ruiz and Azkarate investigate Basque fisheries in eastern Canada. In Chap. 14, Chiavazza presents the sixteenth-century Spanish occupation of the lowlands of Central South America (Bolivia). In Chap. 15, Camargo studies maritime landscapes in sixteenth-century Brazil. Saccente and White, in Chap. 16, present an archaeological view of a remote Spanish outpost in eighteenth-century Northwest Florida. In Chap. 17, Kulstad-González examines the economic activity at Concepción de la Vega settlement. In the final chapter, Poloni discusses the role of archaeology in the emergence of the concept of heritage and national culture in modern Brazil.

## 1.3 Disrupting the Master Narrative of Iberian Colonialism

The volume—as a whole—contributes to disrupt the grand old narrative of cul-tural contact and colonialism in Spanish and Portuguese America in a wide and complete sense. We understand master narrative as a concept rooted in Lyotardian thoughts (Lyotard 1984) introduced in the field of historical archaeology by Johnson (1999). In this case, we refer to the normalized and the standard view of Spanish and Portuguese colonization, which works as a cultural message as well as a framework of knowledge and interpretation.

The different chapters question master narrative in their multiple dimensions: the theoretical dimension, the methodological one, and a further dimension related to the sources of information used. They also question the spatial and temporal scales applied to the study of colonial experiences. This questioning may be either explicit or not, but it becomes evident in the proposal of alternatives, and it is shaped in the widening and diversification of the ways of looking at, analyzing and thinking over the cases presented in this book. Moreover, there is a questioning of the colonial discourse, which has been naturalized in the shape of individual stories, explanations of cultural change, historiographical discourse, or legacies of colonialism in the present time.

### 1.3.1  Ideas and Theoretical Concepts

Theoretical concepts are reviewed with different degrees of depth. Some of them are more or less widened or else new, different or alternative concepts are presented to contrast them. Thus, categories which have been naturalized both in colonial discourse and by scholars working on cultural contact are questioned.

Along this line mestizaje and cultural change become relevant as key concepts. Mestizaje is used both in multiple theoretical-methodological-analytical dimensions and from experience. Rothschild questions "mestizaje today is valued but naturalized, and masks a great deal of variation, some of which is strongly linked to class differences and would have been present in the past." Symanski problematizes it following Gruzinski's when he refers to mestizaje as "the mixtures between human beings, imaginaries, and lifeways," and states it as a process which "is as much objective, being observed in several kinds of sources, as subjective, implying the consciousness that these past actors had about what was going on." Poloni uses the concepts "mestiçagem or miscegenation" in a central and structuring way in her analysis of colonialism legacy. Dominguez and Funari interpret it as experience. These multiple approaches contribute to the theoretical debate of the scope and the analytical limitations of the concept of mestizaje as well as to the understanding of its multiple interpretative dimensions.

Another immensely rich concept is that of cultural change that appears in this book as linked to the use of different analytical scales. Hence, cultural change is studied in different and complementary spatial scales, for instance, regional scales in Rodriguez et al., Scaramelli and Scaramelli, and Kepecs's chapters. Teixeira et al.'s contribution offers some clues for the global understanding of the impact of the relations developed with people bordering the opposite sides of the Atlantic Ocean (Brazil and Portugal).

Also the studies of cultural change are set forth on different temporal scales. Rodriguez et al.'s chapter presents research in which change is considered through a wide temporal scale so that the indigenous history—previous and subsequent—may be linked to the articulation of the colonial power. Scaramelli and Scaramelli's contribution follows recent propositions concerning the examination of long-term contact histories, and stresses the importance of multidimensional contextual analysis for comparative purposes on a larger geographical scale. In a complementary way, other chapters also deal with cases of contact that stretched along several centuries. Escribano-Ruiz and Azkarate from another standpoint contribute to think of the process of change considering the causal nature of early colonialism, underscoring the random nature of its development.

The contribution made by the authors previously mentioned regarding cultural change must be highlighted. In previous papers, misrepresentations of aspects of change and continuity (Lightfoot 2005; Silliman 2010) were considered as a serious deficit in the studies of colonialism in America: "Simply put, scholars cannot do justice to understanding long–term native histories if they neglect the periods immediately preceding, and even those within the twentieth century" (Silliman and Witt 2010, p. 46). In her review of the archaeology of Spanish colonialism studies in the Americas, Van Buren states that there are some issues that "require a change in scale to include the broader socioeconomic fields in which colonial groups participated. Although the sheer size of the Spanish Empire makes this a daunting task, archaeologists can broaden their scope in a variety of ways" (Van Buren 2010, p. 179).

Other specific concepts are reviewed such as the idea of freedom and capitalism. Further examples of this are Dominguez and Funari's ideas of freedom in the context of Colonial Cuba. They state that "freedom is no natural concept, for it depends on specific historical conditions," in consequence, "there are degrees of freedom, not absolute enslavement or freedom." Capitalism is another concept the questioning of which turns into new proposals. Pezzarossi uses the concept "antimarkets—heterogeneous assemblages of humans, discourse, and things that structured and manipulated the relations of production and exchange for the purpose of wealth/capital accumulation—as an experiment in moving beyond the baggage-laden concept of capitalism."

Material culture as a concept is widened and integrated to other dimensions of the lived experience as from the concept of materiality. Loren's chapter is a good example of a broad and integral look from the concept of materiality. She understands that "lived experience is constituted with and through material culture, leaving residues of experiences in texts, objects, and space." In her chapter, she brings attention to the corporeal predicament of colonialism through interpretations of the physicality and materiality of the human body afforded by a perspective on embodiment. The body is "viewed as a totality: Physicality, health, and spirituality are constituted in daily practice with material culture."

This book presents theoretical perspectives, which have discarded essentialism and the dichotomy colonizer/colonized as a way of conceiving colonial society (Liebmann 2008) and this has direct implications in the ways of organizing the material world. Analytical alternatives are proposed to the essentialist organization of the material world, structured in the indigenous-Spanish/Portuguese-Spanish/indigenous categories traditionally used in the study of Spanish colonialism in historical archaeology.

Symanski and Gomes's chapter is an example of this. They state that the recognition of colonial configurations as products of the agency of all actors involved in this process is indeed, a great advance over the theoretical models that highlight only the perspective of the politically dominant. In contexts of multicultural interaction, multiple identities emerged which cannot be purely reduced to the colonizer-colonized dichotomy. Another example of this perspective is Senatore's chapter, which explores the heterogeneity of the "newly arrived" colonizing group. She is interested in exploring novelty as part of different choices and decisions made by individuals in everyday life. Therefore, the idea of a homogenous response on the part of the Spanish colonizing group is left aside and there appears the possibility of understanding differences and similarities in the multiple choices that arose. She presents an analytical proposal in which the interpretation of the meanings that certain objects/resources acquire in specific contexts is essential.

### 1.3.2   Times and Spaces

The master narratives of the Spanish and Portuguese presence in America in general tend to overlook the temporal depth it had. In many histories, colonization times seem to have a synchronic and homogeneous character. This becomes evident in the scope of the term "contact" or "period of contact" when referring to several centuries of interaction. This general perspective tends to darken the variety of and changes in ideas, practices, experiences and contexts that centuries of colonialism carry not only in America, Spain and Portugal but also in the rest of the world. It also diminishes the relevance of the changes, which took place in material culture and in the shapes of graphic and written representations throughout time. Therefore, that homogenizing and synchronic look works against the possibility of understanding the deep changes taking place in the diverse geographic contexts throughout time (Silliman 2005). Change tends to be presented as the inevitable result of the Euro-American clash or of the expansion of capitalism (Senatore and Zarankin 2002). Consequently the "how," the "why," and the "how far" of every situation and every moment are not explained.

In this book, cases are presented that help understand the extension and diversity of the times of the Spanish and Portuguese colonization in America. Chronologically this book covers a large temporal range. The cases analyzed focus on contexts extending from the end of the fifteenth century along the sixteenth, seventeenth, eighteenth, nineteenth and twentieth centuries and up to the present time. It is important to point out that the authors of several chapters have successfully faced the challenge of studying change and continuity of the contexts studied. Thus, we can find indigenous stories previous to the European arrival as in the contributions of Rodríguez-Alegría et al., Kepecs, Pezzarossi, and Scaramelli and Scaramelli can therefore say that the topics approached in this book do not start with Columbus' arrival in 1492. Other chapters such as those written by Poloni and Dominguez and Funari from the standpoint of the present, deal with the fact that colonialism and its legacies have outlived the past. For example, Dominguez and Funari state "cultural contact is not only a recent epiphenomenon of imperialism, but a genuine constituent of the Cuban way of life."

The master narrative of the history of colonization tends to focus on the cases which have lasted through time. As Azkarate and Escribano-Ruiz state, the settlements, which did not last or did not develop, were given very little importance in historiographical representations. In this sense, it is interesting to point out the place certain authors give to what is considered ephemeral. For instance, Chiavazza considers that "the ruins of an ephemeral city represent the acceptance of the colonial defeat," and Saccente and White state that "even the smallest of outposts can play an important role in the larger stage of globalization, immigration (or in this case, colonization), and transformation."

Another recurrent aspect in this book is the place devoted to the analysis of specific short-lasting cases. Escribano-Ruiz and Azkarate present the case of the establishment of European fisheries in Newfoundland in which the European presence was intermittent. Other cases must be added to theirs, in which European presence was permanent but these colonial settlements only worked for a very short time. For instance, Kulstad-González presents Concepción de la Vega settled from 1495 to 1564 in the Cabao valley now in the Dominican Republic. Chiavazza analyzes the 40 years Santa Cruz de la Sierra (1561–1604) lasted in land that now belongs to Bolivia. Saccente and White refer to the history of Fort San José in Northwest Florida briefly occupied—late 1701 and reoccupied from 1719 to 1721. Another case is the 50-year settlement of Presidio Los Adaes (1729–1770) located in Spanish Texas dealt with in Loren's chapter. Senatore presents that the Colonia de Floridablanca settled on the Atlantic coast of Patagonia, which worked only 4 years from 1780 to 1784. Azkarate and Escribano-Ruiz present the case of Sancti Spiritus (1527) in Río de la Plata region. For them, this example "calls for alternative accounts to be incorporated into the discourse on the colonization of the Americas, highlights the importance that specific local contexts had in its development." This idea may encompass the other settlements mentioned and therefore contribute to wonder and at the same time question why they were excluded of the master narratives of colonial history due to their short duration in time.

Regarding spaces, this book seeks to widen the view we usually have of the map of the Spanish and colonial experience in America (Fig. 1.1). The chapters mainly refer to the diverse landscapes of the territories formerly dominated by Spain and Portugal along and across the continent. This look is complemented with three chapters, which focus in contexts not usually included in the master narratives.

Teixeira et al.'s chapter is centered in Portugal. They are now beginning to produce the first archaeological contributions to the understanding of the Portuguese expansionist phenomenon, namely assessing the impact of this process on the Portuguese society. Camargo in his chapter looks towards the sea. The author highlights "the difficulty of most researchers in transcending the dominance of the

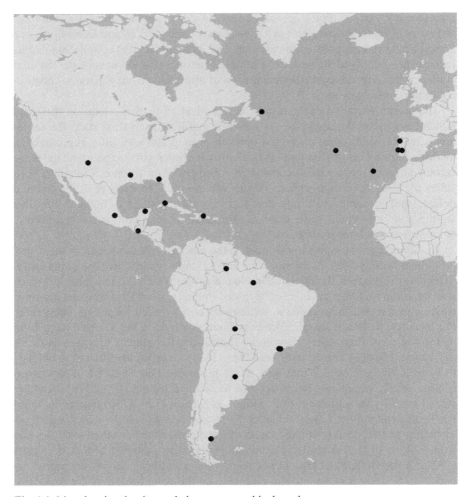

**Fig. 1.1** Map showing the sites and places presented in the volume

land-centered views that built History or Archaeology." The chapter presents the study of the "seascapes" of the coast of Sao Paulo in Brazil making clear that he "approached the coastal environments not only as a physical interface between the land and the sea, but also as a mediator between societies and cultures." Escribano-Ruiz and Azkarate move their look away from the map of Spanish and Portuguese political domination towards the coast of Newfoundland (currently Canada). The study of the Basque fisheries overseas "stresses the importance of individual actions in the colonial process."

These looks outside the "usual map" contribute to understand the amplitude and diversity of the spaces of colonial experience and invites us to look beyond the limits imposed by the master narrative.

### 1.3.3 Methodology, Sources, and Material Culture

The methodology used in the study of cultural contact and colonialisms is another field for questioning, widening, and proposals. All in all, the master narratives about the Spanish and Portuguese colonization in America were built on the basis of written narratives: Material culture was not relevant. This is the case not only in America but also in the different spaces colonized by the Western World (Senatore and Zarankin 2014). In every chapter of this book, material culture breaks in and allows other histories to be told.

It must be emphasized that the analysis cases used a rich and diverse variety of material and written sources. Yet many different sources have been used in addition to these. For instance, in her chapter, Kepecs uses "late pre-Hispanic iconography, colonial-era Spanish sources, secondary works based on these sources, the native-written books of Chilam Balam, sacred Christian art still visible in the region's sixteenth century Spanish churches, and diachronic archaeological evidence from the territory the Maya of the transitional epoch called Chikinchel, in the northeast corner of Yucatan state." On the other hand, the sources of oral tradition become important as in Rothschild and Scaramelli and Scaramelli's chapters. The inclusion of "immaterial" evidence such as linguistics that we find in Escribano-Ruiz and Azkarate's contributions is also new. They also used a wide range of sources of evidence, such as archaeological remains, written documents, language, toponymy, cartography, or testimonies from people present at the time that the events took place.

One of the great challenges in historical archaeology research is how to articulate and integrate the diverse sources used (Funari et al. 1999). In this sense, Rothschild presents a way marked in advance to integrate the diverse sources of information. She proposes the concept "archive" as a source of information available. "Each archive represents a specific perspective on a particular target for reasons of that moment," and she adds, "The various archives which yield different components of information allow us to piece together a somewhat more complete picture."

Regarding questioning in the methodological field, Rothschild's chapter also appears of great interest. She questions the reliability and neutrality of historical archives expressing, "They are neither as reliable nor neutral as sources of data as had once been assumed." She follows the thoughts of anthropologists examining post-colonial phenomena. From this perspective, archives are seen as "cultural agents of 'fact' production, of taxonomies in the making, and of state authority" (Stoler 2002, p. 1). The key point in her reflection is that historic archives "objectify individuals and groups, recording them according to specific parameters." Later Rothschild says, "These attributes, ephemeral and subjective, once created, leave traces and acquire an existence that is independent of things, people or even themselves and are used, at the time and later, by colonial government agents and scholars, as if the attributes were real."

This book presents several looks over the material world. Another central topic marking the methodological layout in the chapters which form part of this book is the role of material culture in the different instances of research. The variety of proposals in this book integrates new approaches to the artifactual sets and categories that have been studied before from different approaches. On the other hand, some authors present analytical proposals on other kinds of resources that had not been considered up to the moment.

Several objects and raw material as metal artifacts had been traditionally considered as a proof of the incorporation of European artifacts to indigenous contexts. Rodríguez-Alegría el al.'s chapter focuses on technologies that European colonizers and traders introduced, which were largely foreign to indigenous peoples, to explain technological change among indigenous people after their contact with Europeans. What is new here is the methodological and comparative proposal—considering economic factors among the many relevant causes of change—that allowed them to explain how the locals then incorporated the new technologies into their own systems of production and exchange differently in each region studied.

In their chapter, Teixeira et al. focus their attention on the presence of exogenous material culture in the Portuguese archaeological contexts, regarding elements such as sugar, tobacco, timber, vegetables, animals, cotton and ivory. What is new here is not only the objects studied but also the contexts in which their presence becomes significant. For these authors, "Europe enforced socio-economic exploitation systems, models of political organisation and sets of values and beliefs over vast regions bordering the Atlantic, on the other hand, it underwent profound changes as a result." These objects allow them to review the impact of these exchanges in Portugal through archaeology.

The Scaramellis' chapter changes completely the focus of analysis. They explore the commercialization of wild resources but they do not focus on the legendary commerce in cacao, coffee, cotton, sugarcane and leather. They analyze the role of "uncommon commodities," and demonstrate that these local resources were fundamental items for exchange prior to and following the European colonization.

Different authors recognize the material world as a crucial element to understanding colonialism and the emergence of modernity, and they studied how material culture challenged traditional values, impacting on everyone involved in the colonial process. As a whole, these approaches to material culture offer new perspectives, which help understand the very diverse and heterogeneous ways in which material culture played a central role in colonialism.

### 1.3.4   Colonial Discourse

In this book, certain authors question colonial discourse overtly. However, these discrepancies offer a variety of ways to achieve and of topics to question or review. Historiographical representations as part of a meta-narrative of Spanish imperialism are a topic of discrepancy in Azkarate and Escribano-Ruiz's chapter. Following postcolonial theories, they claim: "Conventional literature and historiography reflect and represent the colonial ideal, whereas archaeology documents colonial actions and goes into the nature of 'contact' in greater depth." Within this frame they present the colonial settlement of Sancti Spiritus as "a rare example that enables further exploration of the nature of the colonization of the Americas and its discursive strategies."

Simple and mono-causal explanations can be dismantled as from the case presented by Rodríguez-Alegría et al. They study technological transformation among indigenous people in two distant colonial settings. Deep and extended analysis allows them to demonstrate that "technological change in both regions was far from a simple story of progress and civilization." Another type of questioning is aimed at specific stories. Kulstad-González states that preliminary research into the archaeological assemblage at the Concepción de la Vega site seems to contradict the "official" history's depiction of a site, which went bust after a gold boom period. This chapter shows an extended standpoint in historical archaeology which reviews "historical accounts" as from its lack of concordance with the results of archaeological research.

Ultimately, a different example is the one questioning the legacies of colonialism in the present time. Poloni analyzes how the construction of a discourse about the past acquires its political dimension. In her chapter, she thrives to understand the development of a national discourse around the idea of *mestiçagem* or miscegenation in both its racial and cultural aspects and in direct connection with national identity. Thus, she evaluates the role of archaeology in shaping the Brazilian concepts of national culture and heritage.

### 1.3.5   Spanish and Portuguese Colonialism in a Wider View

The contents of this book complement the perspectives developed in the research of other analytic cases from different regions of the American continent already published (Thomas 1989, 1990, 1991; Deagan 2003, see reviews by Schaedel 1992; Van Buren 2010; Zarankin and Senatore 1996). For example, the main themes of Portuguese colonialism such as plantations and slavery (Agostini 2002; Funari 2006; Orser and Funari 2001; Guimarães et al. 2013; Torres de Souza 2002, 2013, inter alios) and the themes researched in Spanish colonial experiences such as urban centers (Charlton and Fournier 1993; Fowler 2011; Rodríguez-Alegría 2005; Rovira and Martin 2008, inter alios).

The map of colonial experience presented in the volume could be widen, for example, with the research developed in the Andes region (DeFrance 2003; Jamieson 2005; Rice 2011; Van Buren 1999, inter alios), Mesoamerica and the Caribbean (Curet 2011; Deagan 1995; Deagan and Cruxent 2002; Hauser 2009; Gasco 2005; Rovira and Gaitan 2010, inter alios), and former Spanish territories of North America (Atherton and Rothschild 2008; Deagan 1983; Loren 2000; McEwan 1993, 2000; Pavao-Zuckermann and La-Mota 2007; Voss 2000, 2008) and South America (De Nigris et al. 2010; Navarrete 2014; Scaramelli and Scaramelli 2005; Senatore 2008; Senatore et al. 2014, inter alios).

Furthermore, this book offers perspectives complementary to those focused on specific themes such as resistance (Liebmann and Murphy 2011), ethnogenesis (Voss 2008), or comparative studies in colonialism (Lightfoot 2005; Rothschild 2003; Voss and Casella 2012, inter alios). The volume offers multiple views to explore the meaningful differences and similarities between Hispanic and Portuguese America from a comparative archaeology (see Fournier 1998; Funari 2005). Ultimately, it complements the theoretical contributions connecting the past and present of Spanish and Portuguese colonialism and revise its legacy (Sunseri 2010; Haber 2007; Haber and Gnecco 2007; Silliman 2001, 2010; Verdesio 2008, inter alios).

The volume thus contributes to a more nuanced and complex discussion of the material world of cultural contact and colonialism in Spanish and Portuguese America. We will be happy if the readers will be enticed to further looking for the materiality of colonial encounters and contacts in the Spanish and Portuguese American experience.

# References

Agostini, C. (2002). Entre senzalas e quilombos: "comunidades do mato" em Vassouras do oitocentos In: A. Zarankin & M. X. Senatore (org.). Arqueologia da Sociedade Moderna (pp. 19–30). Buenos Aires: Ed. del Tridente.

Atherton, H., & Rothschild, N. (2008). Colonialism, past and present, in New Mexico. *Archaeologies, 4*(2), 250–263.

Charlton, T., & Fournier, G. P. (1993). *Urban and rural dimensions of the contact period.* In J. D. Rogers & S. D. Wilson (Eds.), *Ethnohistory and archaeology: Approaches to postcontact change in the Americas* (pp. 201–220). New York: Plenum Press.

Curet, A. (2011). Colonialism and the History of Archaeology in the Spanish Caribbean. In L. R. Lozny (Ed.), *Comparative archaeologies: A sociological view of the science of the past* (pp. 641–672). New York: Springer.

De France, S. (2003). Diet and provisioning in the high Andes: A Spanish colonial settlement on the outskirts of Potosí, Bolivia. *International Journal of Historical Archaeology, 7,* 99–125.

De Nigris, M. E., Palombo, P. S., & Senatore, M. X. (2010). Craving for hunger: A zooarchaeological study at the edge of the Spanish empire. In P. Crabtreey, A. Choyke, D. Campana (Eds.), *Anthropological approaches to zooarchaeology: Colonialism, complexity and animal transformations* (pp. 131–138). Oxford: Oxbow Books.

Deagan, K. A. (Ed.). (1983). *Spanish St. Augustine: The archaeology of a colonial Creole community.* New York: Academic Press.

Deagan, K. (Ed.). (1995). *Puerto real: The archaeology of a sixteenth-century town in Hispaniola.* Gainesville: University Press of Florida.

Deagan, K. (2003). Colonial origins and colonial transformations in Spanish America. *Historical Archaeology, 37*(4), 3–13.

Deagan, K., & Cruxent, J. M. (2002). *Archaeology at La Isabela: America's first European town.* New Haven: Yale University Press.

Fitzhugh, W. (Ed.). (1985). *Cultures in contact: The European impact on native cultural institutions in Eastern North America, A.D. 1000–1800.* Washington: Smithsonian Institution Press.

Fournier, P. (1998). *Arqueología del colonialismo de España y Portugal: imperios contrastantes en el nuevo mundo.* Boletín de Antropología Americana, *32,* 89–96.

Fowler, W. (2011). *Ciudad Vieja: Excavaciones, arquitectura y paisaje cultural de la primera Villa de San Salvador.* El Salvador: Editorial Universitaria.

Funari, P. P. A. (2005). The Comparative Method in Archaeology and the Study of Spanish and Portuguese South American Material Culture. In Funari et al. (Eds.), *Global archaeological theory, contextual voices and contemporary thoughts* (pp. 97–106). New York: Kluwer Academic/Plenum Publishers.

Funari, P. P. A. (2006). Conquistadors, plantations, and Quilombo: Latin America in historical archaeological context. In M. Hall & S. W. Silliman (Eds.), *Historical archaeology: Vol. 9. Blackwell studies in Global archaeology* (pp. 209–229). Malden: Blackwell Publishing.

Funari, P. P. A., Hall, M., & Jones, S. (Eds.). (1999). *Historical archaeology, back from the edge*. London: Routledge.

Gasco, J. (2005). Spanish colonialism and processes of social change in Mesoamerica. In G. Stein (Ed.), *The archaeology of colonial encounters: Comparative perspectives* (pp. 69–108). Santa Fe, NM: School of American Research Press.

Given, M. (2004). *The archaeology of the colonized*. London: Routledge.

Gosden, C. (2004). *Archaeology and colonialism: Culture contact from 5000 BC to the present*. Cambridge: Cambridge University Press.

Guimarães, C. M., Fernandes de Morais, C., & Ladeia, A. L. (2013). Escravismo, arqueologia e capitalismo: Transição e conexão entre dois mundos (Brasil, séc. XIX/XX) Vestigios 7 (pp. 107–143).

Haber, A. (2007). This is not an answer to the question "Who is Indigenous?". *Archaeologies, 3*(3), 213–229.

Haber, A., & Gnecco, C. (2007). Virtual forum: Archaeology and decolonization. *Archaeologies, 3*(3), 390–412.

Hauser, M. W. (2009). Scale locality and the Caribbean historical archaeology. *International Journal of Historical Archaeology, 13*, 3–11.

Jamieson, R. (2005). Colonialism, social archaeology, and lo andino: Historical archaeology in the Andes. *World Archaeology, 37*, 352–372.

Johnson, M. (1999). Rethinking historical archaeology. In P. Funari, M. Hall, & S. Jones (Eds.), *Historical archaeology. Back from the edge* (pp. 23–36). London: Routledge.

Liebmann, M. J. (2008). Introduction: The intersections of Archaeology and postcolonial studies. In M. J. Liebmann & U. Z. Rivzi (Eds.), *Archaeology and the postcolonial critique* (pp. 1–20). Lanham: Altamira Press.

Liebmann, M., & Murphy, M. S. (Eds.). (2011). *Enduring conquests: Rethinking the archaeology of resistance to Spanish colonialism in the Americas*. Santa Fe: SAR Press.

Lightfoot, K. G. (2005). *Indians, missionaries, and merchants: The legacy of colonial encounters on the California frontiers*. Berkeley: University of California Press.

Loren, D. D. (2000). The intersections of Colonial policy and colonial practice: Creolization on the 18th-century Louisiana/Texas Frontier. *Historical Archaeology, 34*(3), 85–98.

Lyotard, J. F. (1984). *The postmodern condition: A report on knowledge*. Minneapolis: University of Minnesota Press.

McEwan, B. (Ed.). (1993). *The Spanish missions of La Florida*. Gainesville: University Press of Florida.

McEwan, B. (2000). The spiritual conquest of Florida. *American Anthropologist, 103*, 633–644.

Navarrete, R. (2014). Palenques and Palisades: A revision of social complexity issues in contact-period eastern Venezuela. In C. Gnecco & C. Langebaek (Eds.), *Against typological tyranny in archaeology* (pp. 43–56). New York: Springer.

Orser, C., & Funari, P. (2001). Archaeology and slave resistance and rebellion. *World Archaeology, 33*, 61–72.

Pavao-Zuckerman, P., & La-Motta, V. M. (2007). Missionization and economic change in the Pimería Alta: The zooarchaeology of San Agustín de Tucson. *International Journal of Historical Archaeology, 11*(3), 241–268.

Rice, P. (2011). Order (and Disorder) in Early colonial Moquegua. *Peru International Journal of Historical Archaeology, 15*(3), 481–508.

Rodríguez-Alegría, E. (2005). Consumption and the varied ideologies of domination in colonial Mexico city. In S. Kepecs & R. T. Alexander (Eds.), *The postclassic to Spanish- era transition in Mesoamerica: Archaeological perspectives* (pp. 35–48). Albuquerque: University of New Mexico Press.

Rothschild, N. A. (2003). *Colonial encounters in a native American landscape: The Spanish and Dutch in North America*. Washington, D. C.: Smithsonian Institution Press.

Rovira, B., & Gaitán, F. (2010). Los búcaros. De las Indias para el mundo. *Canto Rodado, 5*, 39–78.

Rovira, B., & Martín, J. (2008). Arqueología histórica de Panamá. La experiencia en las ruinas de Panamá Viejo. *Vestigios, 2,* 7–33.

Scaramelli, F., & Tarble de Scaramelli, K. (2005). The roles of material culture in the colonization of the Orinoco, Venezuela. *Journal of Social Archaeology, 5,* 135–168.

Schaedel, R. P. (1992). The archaeology of the Spanish colonial experience in South America. *Antiquity, 66,* 216–242.

Senatore, M. X., & Zarankin, A. (2014). Against the Domain of Master narratives: Archaeology and Antarctic history. In C. Gnecco & C. Langebaek (Eds.), *Against typological Tyranny in archaeology* (pp. 121–132). New York: Springer.

Senatore, M. X. (2008). Morir en Nombre de Jesús. Escenas de ambivalencia en los confines del mundo colonial. In F. A. Acuto & A. Zarankin (Eds.), *Sed Non Satiata II. Acercamientos sociales a la arqueología latinoamericana* (pp. 241–258). Córdoba & Catamarca: Encuentro/ Humanidades.

Senatore, M. X., De Nigris, M., & Rigone, R. C. (2014). Una arqueología del colonialismo español en el extremo sur de Sudamérica. La ciudad del Nombre de Jesús (Estrecho de Magallanes, siglo XVI). Publicación del Seminario Internacional de la Red Iberoamericana de Investigación del Urbanismo Colonial (RII_UC) "Primeros asentamientos españoles y portugueses en la América Central y Meridional S. XVI y XVII". Santa Fe: FADU-UNL y el Ministerio de Innovación y Cultura.

Senatore, M. X., & Zarankin, A. (2002). Leituras da Sociedade Moderna Cultura Material, Discursos e Práticas. In A. Zarankin & M. X. Senatore (Eds.), *Arqueologia da Sociedade Moderna na America do Sul* (pp. 5–18). Buenos Aires: Ediciones del Tridente.

Silliman, S. W. (2001). Theoretical perspectives on labor and colonialism: Reconsidering the California Missions. *Journal of Anthropological Archaeology, 20*(4), 379–407.

Silliman, S. W. (2005). Culture contact or colonialism? Challenges in the archaeology of native North America. *American Antiquity, 70,* 55–74.

Silliman, S. W. (2010). Indigenous traces in colonial spaces. Archaeologies of ambiguity, origin, and practice. *Journal of Social Archaeology, 10*(1), 28–58.

Silliman, S. W., & Witt, T. (2010). The complexities of comsumption: Easter Pequot Cultural Economics in Eigtheenth-Century New England. *Historcal Arcaehology, 44*(4), 46–68.

Stein, G. (2005). Introduction. The comparative archaeology of colonial encounters. In G. Stein (Ed.), *The archaeology of colonial encounters. Comparative perspectives* (pp. 1–31). Santa Fe: SAR Press.

Stoler, A. L. (2002). Colonial archives and the arts of governance. *Archival Science, 2,* 87–109.

Sunseri, J. (2010). (Re)Constructing la Tierra de la Guerra: An Indo-Hispano Gendered Landscape on the Rito Colorado Frontier of Spanish Colonial New Mexico. In S. Baugher & S. M. Spencer-Wood (Eds.), *Archaeology and preservation of gendered landscapes* (pp. 141–164). New York: Springer.

Thomas, D. H. (Ed.). (1989). *Columbian consequences: 1. Archaeological and historical perspectives on the Spanish Borderlands West.* Washington, D. C.: Smithsonian Institution Press.

Thomas, D. H. (Ed.). (1990). *Columbian consequences: 2. Archaeological and historical perspectives on the Spanish Borderlands East.* Washington, D. C.: Smithsonian Institution Press.

Thomas, D. H. (Ed.). (1991). *Columbian consequences: 3. The Spanish Borderlands in Pan-American perspective.* Washington, D. C.: Smithsonian Institution Press.

Torres de Souza, M. A. (2002). Entre práticas e discursos: a construção social do espaço no contexto de Goiás do século 18. In A. Zarankin & M. X. Senatore (Eds.), *Arqueologia da Sociedade Moderna* (pp. 63–85). Buenos Aires: Editorial del Tridente.

Torres de Souza, M. A. (2013). Arqueologia da diaspora africana no Brasil. Vestigios 7 Special Edition.

Van Buren, M. (1999). Tarapaya: An elite Spanish residence near colonial Potosí in comparative perspective. *Historical Archaeology, 33*(2), 108–122.

Van Buren, M. (2010). The archaeological study of Spanish colonialism in the Americas. *Journal of Archaeological Research, 18,* 151–201.

Verdesio, G. (2008). From the erasure to the rewriting of indigenous pasts: The troubled life of archaeology in Uruguay. In H. Silverman & W. Isbell (Eds.), *The Handbook of South American archaeology* (pp. 1115–1126). New York: Springer.

Voss, B. L. (2000). Colonial sex: archaeology, structured space, and sexuality in Alta California's Spanish-colonial missions. In R. A. Schmidt & B. L. Voss (Eds.), *Archaeologies of sexuality* (pp. 35–61). London: Routledge.

Voss, B. L. (2008). *The archaeology of ethnogenesis: race and sexuality in colonial San Francisco*. Berkeley: University of California Press.

Voss, B. L., & Casella, E. C. (2012). (Eds.). *The archaeology of colonialism: Intimate encounters and sexual effects* (pp. 1–10). Cambridge: Cambridge University Press.

Zarankin, A., & Senatore, M. X. (1996). Reseña crítica del desarrollo de la arqueología histórica colonial en Argentina. Páginas sobre Hispanoamérica Colonial, 3, pp. 123–141.

# Part I
# Posing Questions in Cultural Contact and Colonialism

# Chapter 2
# The Atlantic Expansion and the Portuguese Material Culture in the Early Modern Age: An Archaeological Approach

André Teixeira, Joana Bento Torres and José Bettencourt

## 2.1 Introduction

The Portuguese expansion in the Atlantic was undoubtedly one of the pioneering highlights of early modern Europe, along with the Spanish exploration of America. Once this was the world's region with least communications, the extensive contact with the Iberian navigations led to interchanges in almost all dimensions of human life. In this chapter, we review the impact of these exchanges in Portugal through archaeology. The attempt is to determine the presence of exogenous products among Portuguese everyday life material culture and the changes carried out in the country to enable this colonial enterprise. The Atlantic is approached as a whole, given the exchanges and complementarities here occurred during the Early Modern Age, although with particular focus on Brazil, for the hegemonic weight that it quickly acquired within this framework.

This is a field of research that has been developed in Portugal from written sources and artistic objects (Trnek and Silva 2001; Henriques 2009). These approaches reflect the consumptions and the spaces of the elites and hence do not show the extent of the contact, in a broader sense, in the Portuguese society. The ones with a more global approach demonstrate an important penetration of material culture elements from the overseas in small coastal villages. This is the case of Vila do Conde (Fig. 2.1), where wills, inventories, and other records of the sixteenth century attest the presence of dyeing products, spices, sugar, precious stones, porcelain, silks, and other fabrics, as well as "brazilwood spindles." Documentation from later

A. Teixeira (✉) · J. Bento Torres · J. Bettencourt
Faculdade de Ciências Sociais e Humanas, CHAM, Avenida de Berna, 26C, 1069-061 Lisboa, Portugal
e-mail: texa@fcsh.unl.pt

J. Bento Torres
e-mail: joanabtorres@gmail.com

J. Bettencourt
e-mail: jbettencourt.cham@gmail.com

© Springer International Publishing Switzerland 2015
P. P. A. Funari, M. X. Senatore (eds.), *Archaeology of Culture Contact and Colonialism in Spanish and Portuguese America*, DOI 10.1007/978-3-319-08069-7_2

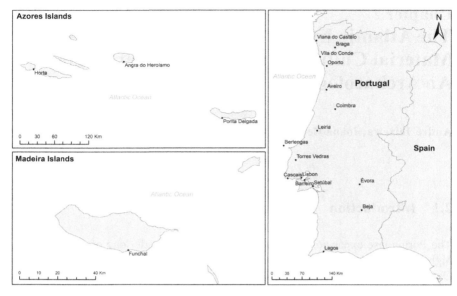

**Fig. 2.1** Places mentioned in the text

on extends the range and quantity of American products, reducing the presence of oriental goods, thus, following the decrease of travels flow undertaken from this port, from Atlantic islands and the Indian Ocean to Brazil (Polónia 2007, pp. 174–181 and 448–451).

In fact, the Early Modern Age archaeology in Portugal is underdeveloped, so its contribution in these issues has been limited. The multiple field works within the urban archaeology do not match an identical volume of publications and research projects. This is the result of contract archaeology circumstances and the faded presence of this field in the Portuguese academia (Sousa 2010, pp. 10–15).

The archaeological studies of contact material culture in Portugal have been centered in Asia, for the prestige of the orientalism, but also for its expression in the archaeological record. Porcelain and other eastern ceramics were brought in large quantities to Europe, resulting in a significant, continued, and progressive presence in Portuguese contexts, from the wealthy classes to the common population, even though synthesis studies are still lacking. Other Asian products have a more residual occurrence, such as spices, fabrics, or precious stones, present mostly in shipwrecks of the sea route to India, namely the presumed remains of the Nossa Senhora dos Mártires, wrecked at the entrance of Lisbon in 1606 (Brigadier 2002). Also note the cowrie shells, gastropod molluscs with important currency and symbolic functions in Africa and Asia, frequently present in the archaeological record. We highlight the cargo aboard the ships of the return trip from the Indian Ocean, as exemplified by the Nossa Senhora da Luz, foundered in 1615 near Horta, Azores (Bettencourt 2006). The study of India sea route logistics is also more consolidated than that of the Atlantic ones, since it was managed by an institution based on the ground floor of the royal palace in Lisbon (Costa 1997; Caetano 2004).

At the same time, note the scarce visibility of Brazilian goods in the archaeological record, including sugar, tobacco, woods, fruits and other vegetables, animals (alive or in furs), or cotton, mostly due to its perishable condition. We exclude the gold or diamonds, with a turnout during the eighteenth century, by its enormous monetary value. The same is valid with goods brought from Africa, such as ivory, fabrics, chilli pepper, or even slaves. Also, the logistic structures of this trade came to light more recently, through urban archaeology. Thus, the text here presented is mainly a starting point for the study of this issue, looking to provide some clues for a global understanding of the impact, in the Portuguese everyday life, of the relations developed with people bordering the Atlantic, especially Brazil.

## 2.2   Sugar: The Industrial Ceramics and the Sweet Consumption

Sugar was the main drive for the Portuguese expansion in the Atlantic, regardless of its production in southern Europe during the Middle Ages, including Portugal. It was first experimented in Madeira with great accomplishment, and then took to the Cape Verde and São Tomé and Príncipe archipelagos, the latter with thriving success. In the second half of the sixteenth century, the sugarcane and its mills expanded to Brazil, with remarkable production volumes in the following century. These inhibited other local economic activities and flooded the European markets with sugar. The consumption was no longer a prerogative of the most favored groups, wide-spreading to society in general. After crossing the Atlantic packed in wooden boxes as the bulk of the cargo on the route between Brazil and Portugal, sugar was unloaded in Lisbon, but also with great expression in Oporto or in Viana. The connections to the American colony became the main destination of the trading activity of these ports, even in times of crisis or war. The product was later sold in Portugal or shipped to other Atlantic European cities, by Portuguese as well as foreign merchants (Mauro 1997; Costa 2002). The importance of sugar in Early Modern Portuguese economy is demonstrated in archaeology by two factors: the ceramics designed for its production and the objects related with its consumption.

In the first case, we speak mainly of the so-called sugar moulds, a conical vessel with an orifice in the bottom to purge the product (Mauro 1997, pp. 265–277). So far, there were two main production centers recognized in Portugal. The first, with a known production in the fifteenth and sixteenth century, was located on the left bank of the Tagus estuary, facing Lisbon, in a space that for centuries served as the industrial area of the capital. At the time, it was integrated in a structure complex meant for the overseas expansion, such as the biscuit factory or shipyards (Torres 1990; Barros et al. 2006; Silva 2012). The second, operating in the sixteenth and seventeenth centuries, was located in Aveiro lagoon (Fig. 2.2), a region of salt production, not just for domestic consumption but also for export to northern Europe,

**Fig. 2.2** Sugar moulds from the Aveiro B-C archaeological site. (Inês Pinto Coelho 2012)

and of intensive fishing activity, both coastal and deep sea (Coelho 2012; Morgado et al. 2012).

The dissemination of these ceramic forms is poorly known. In Portugal, they were detected and associated to a monastery from the first half of the sixteenth century in the Berlengas islands, suggesting that the sugar loaves contained in those forms were given as payment for supplies during a port of call (Lourenço and Bugalhão 2006). In Madeira archipelago, the link between the forms from Aveiro and the sugar production was already established to the sixteenth and seventeenth centuries. It is clear that these islands imported them in order to solve their lack of clays, as they would do with other ceramic forms (Sousa 2011). The same thing would have happened in Azores, despite the lesser importance of this product, and in the Canary Islands, which imported these and other ceramics from Aveiro even though it was a Spanish colony. The dissemination of red micaceous pottery from this region is, in fact, attested in a wide area including the western European front and North America (Bettencourt and Carvalho 2008). However, it is not clear if there was a supply of sugar moulds to other Atlantic sugar production centers, namely in the primitive Brazilian mills, such as in São Jorge dos Erasmos (Andreatta 1999).

Concerning the sugar consumption, at start, it was used for mainly therapeutic purposes, found in apothecaries as an ingredient for medicinal solutions. Apothecaries could either be in a specific room in the house or a more indistinctive area where its objects were gathered. In this set, there were conserved fruit, marmalades and candied fruit peel (usually of citrus fruit), as well as rose and violet sugar, frequently acting as an energy supplement, and sometimes used to fight scurvy or even fever (Nunes 2002, p. 160; Algranti 2005, p. 42). Regarding the stocking of these preparations, it is clear that the type of containers is basically the same throughout the early modern age, both in documentation and iconographic representations, as well as in the archaeological record.

The marmalades were usually kept in wooden boxes, namely visible in the still lifes of Juan van der Hamen y León, Josefa de Óbidos (Fig. 2.3), Francisco de Zurbarán, or Luís Meléndez, therefore hard to find in archaeological contexts. But this product is also present in small glass containers, such as small jugs or bowls, or in small clay basins. With the second half of the seventeenth century, came a

**Fig. 2.3** Caixa com potes, Josefa de Óbidos, c. 1660. (Museu Nacional de Arte Antiga, 1875)

new ceramic form, the *covilhete* (Fig. 2.4), a "small vase of clay with a concave surface," specifically associated to sweets packing and consumption (Bluteau 1712, v. 2, p. 594). This type has a more systematic presence in archaeological contexts. On one hand, in convent spaces, as São Francisco de Lisboa (Torres 2011), Salvador de Évora (Mangucci 2007), Santana de Leiria (Trindade 2013), or Bom Jesus de Setúbal (Almeida 2012). On the other, in civil buildings, like the Casa do Infante, in Oporto (Barreira et al. 1995, pp. 145–184), or in the Paços do Concelho of Torres Vedras (Luna and Cardoso 2006, pp. 99–112). Its production in Lisbon is documented in the second half of the seventeenth century (Batalha et al. 2012).

In the specific case of conserved fruit and of rose and violet sugar, written sources mention the general use of glazed pots and pans (Fig. 2.5). These containers are present in several Portuguese and Brazilian archaeological sites of the seventeenth century, especially in convents. As an example, note São Francisco de Lisboa (Torres 2012), Nossa Senhora da Piedade de Cascais (Cardoso and Rodrigues 2002), but also the aforementioned Paços do Concelho of Torres Vedras (Luna and Cardoso 2006, pp. 99–112). Its production is established for the fifteenth and sixteenth century in the industrial area of Barreiro (Carmona 2005). Not being an exclusive item of religious background, the presence of this kind of objects is more frequently observed in places belonging to socially favored strata. Coated with lead glaze with shades of green, yellow, and brown, they possess a spherical form, usually with an inverted rim with an outer thickening, under which we find a set of incised lines marking a slight narrowing on the body. According to the paintings of Josefa de Óbidos, these vessels were covered with a cloth and sealed with a small string, which would easily fit those lines. In the upper part of the body, there was a handle on each side, horizontal or vertical.

Throughout the sixteenth and seventeenth century, there was a widespread of these products' consumption associating fruit and sugar, becoming increasingly part of the regular meals, even though they were still kept in or near the apothecaries. Sugar also became a condiment used in small portions while cooking meals, as shown by the coeval recipes, where there is a clear taste for the contrast between the sweet and salty (Scully 1995). It is also used in large quantities as the key ingredient

Fig. 2.4 Covilhetes from São
Francisco convent in Lisbon

in confectionery, as in the making of *fartéis*, comfits, and blancmange, the most popular of the time. This incorporation of sugar in the food habits happened mostly in the higher strata of the Portuguese society, continuously replacing the use of honey as a natural sweetener.

These changes initially took place in the apothecaries of the main noble houses, highlighting the role of the women who specifically make the conserves within those who worked at those places. It is interesting to note that, contrary to what happened in most apothecaries, managed by a male apothecary, in these nobiliary environments these spaces are generally related to the feminine universe, falling to the apothecary only the making or delivering of medicines (Dias 2007). This relation

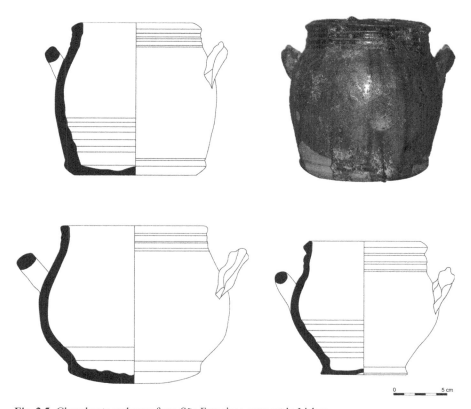

**Fig. 2.5** Glazed pots and pans from São Francisco convent in Lisbon

was strengthened throughout the seventeenth and eighteenth centuries, becoming even clearer because of the connection between the confectionery and women, particularly in feminine convents, a fact that had major repercussions in the culinary and food habits of the time. Finally, the sugar will eventually become increasingly ubiquitous, being served at the table in sugar bowls, whose characteristics are difficult to determine for these chronologies.

## 2.3  Tobacco and Smoking Pipes

The introduction of tobacco in Portugal through Brazil is dated from the 1530s or 1540s. It was tried by early settlers in South America, curious about the habit of the Amerindians of consuming tobacco and its alleged medicinal effects. It was initially purchased locally, and afterwards became extensively grown. In Lisbon, there are references to the habit of chewing tobacco among the sailors as early as 1558. Its consumption by inhalation was accounted in documentation from Brazil in the 1580s (Silva and Guinote 1998, p. 87). In the early seventeenth century it was already the second most exported good originating from those lands into Portugal, right after sugar, leading to the laying of a strict and profitable regal monopoly. Its use became socially widespread, reaching a large percentage of the adult population by the end of that century (Caldeira 2000). Tobacco use was also disseminated through Europe of the seventeenth century, a time where it was also in high demand in Africa, even reaching the shores of the Indian Ocean. It left a remarkable archaeological record during the early modern age by the frequent presence of ceramic pipes.

In Portugal, there are still no systematic studies of these artefacts, preventing the analyses of tobacco diffusion in chronological, spatial and socioeconomic terms. This obstacle is further increased by the peninsular habits, where tobacco would be preferably consumed as snuff. Unlike other European countries, the use of the pipe and smoking was socially less prestigious in Portugal until the end of the eighteenth century, when compared for example, to inhalation (Caldeira 2000). Being the trading of Brazilian tobacco evidently clear in Portuguese historiography, this difference appears to be confirmed by the archaeological record, where no pipes for the early seventeenth century are known. These are common, for example, in the British Isles and in the Netherlands, or in the colonial spaces under their influence in the American continent, such as Jamestown (Straube and Luccketti 1996, pp. 26–27). Note also the frequent presence of pipes in English and Dutch shipwrecks operating in the Atlantic from the early seventeenth century, as the English ship *Sea Venture* of 1609, found in the Bermuda (Wingood 1986, p. 152), or the presumably Dutch ship from mid-seventeenth century of Monte Cristi, surveyed in the Dominican Republic (Hall 2006). Sometimes massive presence of pipes contrasts with an absence or scarce expression in coeval Iberian contexts.

In any case, the presence of pipes occurs in Portuguese archaeological sites, mostly of North European kaolin productions, but also from the Mediterranean and of pre-discoveries tradition, connected with the consumption of other substances. There is discussion about a possible manufacture in Lisbon, in earthenware, which also appears in Cascais (Silva and Guinote 1998, p. 89; Rodrigues et al. 2012, pp. 872–874). The North European pipes are mostly in deposits of the second half of the seventeenth century or of the eighteenth century, excavated in Lisbon (Calado et al. 2003; Pinto et al. 2011), Cascais (Rodrigues et al. 2012), Porto (Pereira 2000), or in Madeira island (Sousa 2011). Most are fragments sorted from landfill materials without precise socioeconomic reference. They are, however, also found in archaeological contexts: military, such as the forts of São João Baptista and of São José in Madeira island (Sousa 2011); from hospitals, like the All Saints in Lisbon; from prisons in São Jorge castle from Lisbon (Calado et al. 2003); or from households, such as the Casa dos Bicos in the capital's riverside (Silva and Guinote 1998, p. 89). The frequent presence of pipes in the main Portuguese ports, in anchorage areas, is also an interesting aspect. Such is the case of Lisbon[1], Aveiro (Coelho 2012), or Angra (Bettencourt and Carvalho 2010).

---

[1] See the report directed by one of us (José Bettencourt) about Boavista 1 and Boavista 2 ships, recovered in Lisbon in 2012, presented to Direcção Geral do Património Cultural.

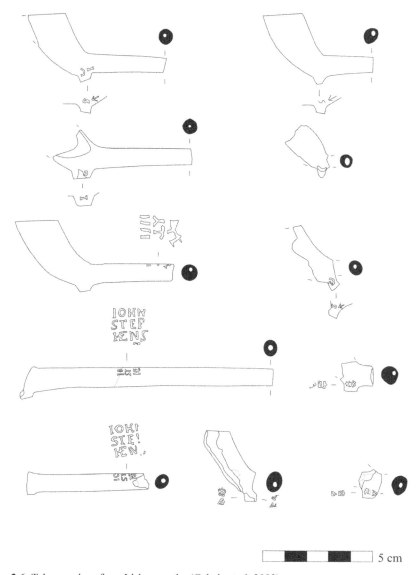

5 cm

**Fig. 2.6** Tobacco pipes from Lisbon castle. (Calado et al. 2003)

The pipes are mainly from several production centres of the British Isles or the Netherlands. For example, among the pipes of the São Jorge castle (Fig. 2.6), the brands identified were mostly Dutch from Gouda, but also from Harlem or Contrai, and British, from Hartlepool, London, Newcastle, or Bristol (Calado et al. 2003). The same diversity was registered in the Mercado da Ribeira, also in the capital (Pinto et al. 2011), or in the Casa do Infante, in Oporto (Pereira 2000). It is from these cities, the Portuguese main ports, that we find the largest collection published so far in Portugal, even though in small numbers, with less than a thousand fragments, mostly stems.

## 2.4  The Wood: From Dyes and Furniture to Shipbuilding—Mutations in Lisbon's Seascape

The trading of tropical timber acquired from the Amerindians was the first economic driving force of the Portuguese presence in Brazil during the first half of the sixteenth century. At this stage, the several types of brazilwood therein were overwhelmingly predominant in the cargo volume transported to Europe. This tree species, once grounded, was used in the production of red dyes. The gross profit of this trade in regal revenues grew throughout that century and the beginning of the following, although its share in the whole Brazilian income had been quickly overtaken by sugar. Yet, timber kept being amply exploited, given the considerable profits made by the settlers, even fearing for its extinction. The brazilwood was then transported to Portugal in logs as ballast of sugar shipments and thence to European textile industries. Other secondary uses for this and other Brazilian timber were documented in written sources, such as construction and shipbuilding and the manufacture of boxes and furniture (Mauro 1997, p. I, pp. 166–200). Nevertheless, it is found that, at least until the end of the eighteenth century, the exploitation and export of dye-producing wood greatly surpassed in quantity and profit, that which was used for furniture (Valente 2007, p. 235).

Given the perishable nature of these materials, part of these objects can only be found in art collections. See the case of the Arraiolos tapestries of the Museu Nacional Machado de Castro, in Coimbra, dated from the seventeenth century, whose red wool thread was demonstrated to be coloured with a brazilwood dye (Marques 2007). In terms of furniture made with wood from Brazil, there are no known archaeological evidences, remaining only studs, plates, locks, handles, or metal chains, which may indicate their types (Torres 2012). In art collections, we find several furniture specimens made with Brazilian wood, such as the yellow pequia, the red *angelim* (*Dinizia Excelsa Ducke*), the *sucupira* (*Pterodon emarginatus*), the *pau-rosa* (*Aniba rosaeodora*), the *pau-santo, pau-preto,* or *jacarandá* (*Dalbergia nigra*), the *freijó* (*Cordia goeldiana*), the *gonçalo-alves* (*Astronium fraxinifolium*) (Pinto 2005; Mendonça 2008, pp. 15–29). Among them, we find chairs with various shapes from Oporto, Viana do Castelo, or Braga, a sewing table from Beja, another table from Ponta Delgada, a cabinet from Viana do Castelo, another one from Braga and two from Lisbon, two trunks from Lisbon and two from Vila do Conde, an inkstand from Viana do Castelo and a writing cabinet from Évora, all of which were from ancient religious buildings and with variable chronologies ranging from the late fifteenth century to the eighteenth century (Pinto 1987, pp. 45–50, 57–59, 73–74).

American wood is found in other aspects of the material culture connected to the overseas expansion logistics, even though with very scarce occurrences. Consider the presence of tropical timber in the structure of ship Ria de Aveiro F, from the sixteenth century, with features similar to ships built mostly in the Mediterranean space. The studies, although still not fully conclusive, point to the non-exclusive use of common species especially in South America, in territories now belonging to Brazil, Venezuela, Guyana, Peru, or Bolivia (Lopes 2013, p. 48). This fact suggests the ship could have been built in Europe or in a colonial shipyard and afterwards repaired in several ports of its operative area, including the South Atlantic (Hutter 1985). This hypothesis is particularly interesting as the ship Ria de Aveiro F shares some characteristics of Mediterranean origin with the ship Boavista 1, recently discovered in Lisbon in the area occupied by the headquarters of the trading with Brazil, where there have been archaeological surveys in the last few years.

In fact, the growing importance of Brazilian trading led to significant changes in the riverside landscape of the Portuguese capital, which underwent an urban growth to the west. From the areas of the Royal Palace and the *Ribeira das Naus*, the port city extended to the neighbourhoods of São Paulo and Santos, in the second half of the sixteenth century, and especially in the following century. There, a number of buildings and warehouses were built with similar architectural features, arranged in a row along the river (Caetano 2004, pp. 111–124). The *Companhia Geral de Comércio do Brasil* was rooted here, a monopolistic mercantile enterprise created to streamline the connections to that South American colony between 1649 and 1720 (Costa 2002). The company purchased land here in the 1670s, creating the so-called *Ribeira da Junta do Comércio*, an area of shipbuilding and repair (Castilho 1893, p. 537). This activity would use the wooden slipway recently found in archaeological excavations on the site (Fig. 2.7), with 315 m$^2$, composed of about three hundred wooden joists, also reusing nautical pieces, in three overlapping layers, with a slope of half a meter and 2.75 % incline. This feature is part of several archaeological remains related to maritime activities, as anchorage and beaching areas, docks, or the fort of São Paulo, displaying the potential of these riverside areas to better understand the logistics aspects of the Atlantic maritime trade in the Early Modern Age (Sarrazola et al. 2014).

## 2.5   Fruits, Plants and Animals: The Journey of the Species

One of the most deep and long lasting aspects of the exchange rendered by the Portuguese sea voyages is the transfer of plant and animal species between continents (Ferrão 1992). It is a subject of which, once again, we have information about transportation, dates of the first experiments and its consumption by the elites, but still lacks a full assessment of its geographic, social, and cultural diffusion. Regarding America, it should be noted that the Iberian people were responsible for introducing their products in Europe, although it is not always clear which of

**Fig. 2.7** Wooden slipway from São Paulo quarter in Lisbon

the initiatives excelled or had greater influence. Naturally, these products have a little impact in the archaeological record. The Early Modern Age archaeobotanical and archaeozoological studies undertaken in Portugal are still recent and limited, although with promising results.

Maize (*Zea Mays*) was one of these goods, brought by the Portuguese and Spanish from America during the first half of the sixteenth century. The former are also responsible for its diffusion in the Atlantic islands and western African coast, where maize progressively replaced the less efficient pre-existent cereals. In archaeological terms, the oldest finds reports to the ancient medieval monastery of Santa Clara-a-Velha, in Coimbra, one of the main Franciscan female establishments in Portugal (Fig. 2.8). The remains were detected in a layer of silts directly over the cloister brick courtyard and the galleries slabs, deposited between the late sixteenth and early seventeenth century. It was a first stage of the convent flooding, even before the collapse of the ceilings and part of the structures, therein forming a natural stagnant waters lake, a process repeated over the centuries. The presence of maize in this context does not prove its cultivation within the convent grounds, but for sure in the surroundings of the religious complex, on the left bank of the Mondego river. It is one of the oldest findings of this cereal in Portugal, introduced in the sixteenth century, precisely in the fields of this river (Queiroz et al. 2006).

**Fig. 2.8** Cloister of Santa
Clara-a-Velha convent in
Coimbra

Also in the centre-north of Portugal, but this time closer to the shore, the presence of maize was found in two ponds dated from the eighteenth century or early nineteenth century (Danielsen 2008).

Among the new fruits from overseas, we find the coconut (from the coconut tree, *Cocos nucifera L.*) from Asia, which the Portuguese spread to the African west coast and Brazil. It was extensively cultivated in these regions, with its fruit exported back to Portugal, since it was impossible to cultivate it here. The findings of the aforementioned Santa Clara-a-Velha convent are the earliest, demonstrating the consumption of milk and the seed's edible part, perhaps in culinary preparations and particularly confectionery (Queiroz et al. 2007). Among the first recipes of coconut desserts, we find the culinary book of Francisco Borges Henriques from the first half of the eighteenth century (Braga 2004).

The macro-remains recovered from moist environments of Lisbon's riverside area related to the navigation and trade with Brazil in the seventeenth and eighteenth century are most likely of Brazilian origin. The amount of coconuts recovered from the slipway or from the remains of Boavista 2 ship is particularly significant. In fact, the coconut is considered by eastern people as "a providential plant", since it can supply food, clothing, building, and medicine. The Portuguese have used them as practical and effective mean to transport fresh food and water aboard, considering the great ease of conservation (Ferrão 1992, pp. 173–179). The coconuts could also be reused as everyday objects, usually as liquid containers. In the ship *Nossa Senhora dos Mártires,* it was also registered as a container to carry pepper (D'Intino 1998, p. 223). Note that coconuts were also used in nautical activities, since their fibres were used as raw material for cables and caulking ships (Carvalho 2008, p. 141).

The fascination for the exotic, present almost everywhere in Europe with the dissemination of the "cabinets of curiosities", enhanced the taste for the gathering of these foreign objects, often acknowledging the healing and apotropaic abilities of this fruit. Sometimes, these objects were mounted in precious metals, boosting its aesthetic and monetary value (Trnek and Silva 2001). The Duke of Braganza, the most important nobleman in Portugal after the King, had five coconuts in mid-sixteenth century, two of which were mounted in silver.[2]

Lastly, consider the common bean from America (*Phaseolus vulgaris L.*), coming to Portugal in the sixteenth century from Brazil, where it was part of the Amerindians diet, and also reaching the African shores, where it replaced other kinds of beans. Aside from its high nutritional value, it was also known by its diuretic and cleansing properties. In Portugal, it was firstly cultivated along with maize (Ferrão 1992, pp. 94–95). In the aforementioned convent in Coimbra, a grain from this plant was identified, in a dump deposit among plenty of archaeobotanical findings, assumed as the nuns diet leftovers (Queiroz et al. 2007).

In terms of fauna, we highlight the domestication and consumption of American species, mainly the turkey, brought to the Iberian Peninsula at the brink of the sixteenth century. These birds are mentioned in inventories from various strata of the nobility of the sixteenth century, not just for consumption, but already intended for breeding.[3] Its dissemination to the general public is harder to assess. So far, in Portugal, there are only two records of this species in an archaeological context.

The first is once again the Santa Clara-a-Velha convent. The turkey vestiges were detected in two dump deposit of the seventeenth century, next to the cloister vertices, where near 5000 faunal remains were exhumed, predominantly domestic animals and a significant percentage of young animals, especially chickens, and plenty of eggshells. These are the earliest findings of turkey in a stratigraphic context in the Iberian Peninsula so far, representing nonetheless a percentage of less than 1 % of all the faunal remains, indicating a still limited penetration (Moreno-García and Detry 2010, pp. 45–55). The second site where turkey was detected was the Palácio Centeno, in Lisbon, built by Queen Catarina de Bragança between the late seventeenth and early eighteenth century. The bones exhumed from a context of the 18th–19th century were from young animals, suggesting that their breeding was already implemented in Portugal (Davis 2009, p. 242).

## 2.6 Slaves: Skeletons and Ceramics

The intense transatlantic traffic of African slaves during the Early Modern Age was dramatically directed to the American continent in order to supply manpower. Despite the reduction to slavery of important indigenous contingent, Brazil absorbed globally 44 % of this movement, becoming the destination of nearly 90 % of the black people carried by Portuguese and Brazilian ships. During the same period, between the early sixteenth century and mid-nineteenth century, Europe absorbed only 1 % of the slaves, with the percentage aboard Portuguese slavers being lower,

---

[2] See the inventory of Duke Teodósio I, of the research project *All his Worldly Possessions. The Estate of the 5th Duke of Bragança, D.Teodósio I* (PTDC/EAT-HAT/098461/2008).

[3] The turkeys are mentioned, for example, in the inventory of the Duke D. Teodosio I in 1564, or of Joana Pereira, daughter of the Arraiolos *alcaide-mor*, in 1572.

even though it might be undervalued (Caldeira 2013).[4] However, the importance of the presence of African slaves in Portuguese territory during the Early Modern Age is undeniable, proved by various historical elements. In almost all southern Portuguese towns and small villages, there are records of slaves between the sixteenth and seventeenth century. This region had the most expressive numbers, especially around Lisbon and Algarve, the main entry ports in Portugal. In fact, this distribution is demonstrated by genetic studies made to the current population of these regions. The overall percentage of slaves ranged from around 3 % in the countryside villages and 10 % accounted in certain coastal towns and, although its expression has decreased by a reduced influx, the numbers have more than doubled in those centuries, as a result of reproduction (Fonseca 2002, pp. 17–29).

In archaeological terms, we highlight the recent finding of 155 skeletons of African slaves (99 adults and 56 sub-adults), discarded in a vast dump deposit in Lagos. This village, from where the first discovery expeditions departed into the Atlantic, kept an important slavery activity and a significant slave population over the centuries. The dump deposit was located in the space immediately outside the walls, in the valley of a stream. A considerable amount of fauna and ceramics, some of it African, was found in the countless deposits associated to the skeletons. Radiochronometric results for the earlier stratigraphic layers point to the fifteenth century. The individuals were buried in various positions and with very diverse orientations, part of them randomly, others apparently tied up, others still carefully buried with objects associated. Despite these later examples, indicating a somewhat more valued social context, perhaps associated to a brotherhood of slaves, the lack of care taken with the majority of these individuals at death and the absence of Christian rituals is clear. The findings of Lagos attest to the practice of discarding deceased slaves to specific areas in the urban spaces, in the so-called "wells", as indicated by the written documentation and the toponymy (Neves et al. 2011). These are also a testament to the importance of this element to the Portuguese population in the Early Modern Age.

The presence of African people in Portugal has also been demonstrated by the ceramic findings, especially in Lisbon region and in contexts of the second half of the seventeenth century and early eighteenth century (Fig. 2.9). These are objects of coarse pastes, with a fully manual moulding and reducing firing, some of them with burnished decoration, including mostly globular containers with globular body and horizontal handles. With fragments detected in three places in the outskirts of the capital, some consider that they were manufactured in the region or imported, being assigned to African craftsmanship, given the similarities with the traditional pottery of this continent (Barros and Cardoso 2008).

The overwhelming majority of slaves in Portugal in the sixteenth and seventeenth centuries was African, although there were also North Africans and Asians. It is difficult to classify those mentioned in the documentation as "Indians," a very small percentage, but probably some were Amerindians (Fonseca 2002, pp. 29–34).

---

[4] Values taken from the database of *The Trans-Atlantic Slave Trade,* directed by David Eltis and Martin Halbert from the Emory University, Atlanta, Georgia, USA.

Fig. 2.9 African type
ceramics from Lisbon region.
(Barros and Cardoso 2008)

In this regard, note the reference to the presence of a Tupi Amerindian serving in the apothecary of Queen Catarina de Áustria, as well as other Amerindian slaves who worked in her house (Jordan 2005, p. 162).

## 2.7 Ivory

The transatlantic trafficking of African slaves was associated to the trade of elephant ivory since the sixteenth century. Once again, the ongoing study of osteological remains of the early modern period has not allowed for the identification of ivory in Portuguese contexts, even though they were quite common in other European port cities, such as Amsterdam (Rijkelijkhuizen 2009). In Europe, ivory was used in the manufacture of several everyday life objects, including combs, knife handles, or furniture, as documented by archaeological records and written and iconographic sources.

However, the Portuguese trading of African ivory in tusks had a transoceanic dimension, with a part of this raw material entering the kingdom being redistributed to the Asian continent through the sea route to India, as attested by the elephant tusks found in the wreck of Oranjemund (Namibia), which is presumed to be the remains of a Portuguese ship sailing to India in the first half of the sixteenth century (Chirikure et al. 2009, pp. 44–45).

## 2.8 Final Remarks

Early Modern archaeology in Portugal only recently got an incipient institutional and scientific recognition. We are now beginning to produce the first archaeology contributions to the understanding of the Portuguese expansionist phenomenon, namely assessing the impact of this process in Portuguese society.

Of all the goods coming from or largely exploited in the Atlantic colonies, mainly Brazil, sugar is the one that left the most important marks in the material culture, both in the manufacture of ceramics to its production as well as the several containers designed to store and serve sweet foods. Tobacco generated a limited presence of pipes in the Portuguese archaeological contexts, especially when compared with other European countries, which can be related with different habits of consumption. The trail of dye plants is harder to follow as well as furniture, but recent findings show us that American timber could meet logistical needs of naval activities. Fauna and flora remains show us the global dissemination of species from different origins and its slow introduction in everyday life. The traces of African slaves in Portugal support the notion that this phenomenon was not only Afro-American, as men and women were also brought to Europe along with ivory and other products, inscribing their genes among the people of the old continent. Anyway, the Atlantic adventure of the Portuguese led to the transformation of the country's landscape itself, namely in urban contexts as Lisbon, brightening an intensive port activity.

The shortage of archaeological samples available in all cases hinders a more comprehensive study about the introduction of Atlantic products in Portugal. This is a field of research that could dramatically benefit from the systematic publication of countless contexts which have been recently detected within the urban archaeology. Therefore, rather than a finishing point, what we have written here is first and foremost a work program for the next decades, in which we hope to provide some input.

# References

Algranti, L. M. (2005). A Alimentação, Saúde e Sociabilidade: A arte de conservar e confeitar os frutos (séculos XV–XVIII). *História: Questões & Debates, 42*, 33–52.

Almeida, M. (2012). *Convento de Jesus (Setúbal): Arqueologia e História: Faiança decorada.* Unpublished MA dissertation. Universidade Nova de Lisboa, Lisbon.

Andreatta, M. D. (1999). Engenho de São Jorge dos Erasmos: prospecção arqueológica, histórica e industrial. *Revista da Universidade de São Paulo, 41,* 28–47.

Barreira, P., Dórdio, P., & Teixeira, R. (1995). *200 anos de cerâmica na Casa do Infante: do século XVI a meados do século XVIII. Actas das 2.as Jornadas de Cerâmica Medieval e Pós-medieval: métodos e resultados para o seu estudo* (pp. 145–184). Tondela: Câmara Municipal.

Barros, L., & Cardoso, G. (2008). Cerâmicas manuais dos séculos XVI a XVIII de Almada, Cadaval e Cascais. *Revista Portuguesa de Arqueologia, 11*(2), 347–360.

Barros, L., Cardoso, G., & González, A. (2006). As Formas de Pão de Açúcar da Olaria de S. António da Charneca—Barreiro. In E. Sousa (Ed.) *A Cerâmica do Açúcar em Portugal na Época Moderna* (pp. 34–45). Machico: Centro de Estudos de Arqueologia Moderna e Contemporânea.

Batalha, L., Campôa, A., Cardoso, G., Neto, N., Rebelo, P., & Santos, R. (2012). Vestígios de um centro produtor de faiança dos séculos XVII e XVIII: dados de uma intervenção arqueológica na Rua de Buenos Aires, n° 10, Lisboa. In A. Teixeira & J. Bettencourt (Eds.) *Velhos e Novos Mundos: Estudos de Arqueologia Moderna* (pp. 951–962). Lisboa: Centro de História de Além-Mar.

Bettencourt, J. (2006). Os vestígios da nau Nossa Senhora da Luz, resultados dos trabalhos arqueológicos. *Arquipélago—História, 2s, 9–10,* 231–273.

Bettencourt, J., & Carvalho, P. (2008). A carga do navio Ria de Aveiro A (Ílhavo, Portugal): Uma aproximação preliminar ao seu significado histórico-cultural. *Cuadernos de Estudios Borjanos, 50–51,* 257–287.

Bettencourt, J., & Carvalho, P. (2010). Arqueologia marítima na baía de Angra (Angra do Heroísmo, Terceira): Enquadramento e resultados preliminares do projecto PIAS. *Arqueologia Moderna e Contemporânea, 1,* 69–91.

Bluteau, R. (1712). Vocabulario Portuguez & Latino. http://www.ieb.usp.br/online/index.asp. Accessed 27 Sept 2013.

Braga, I. D. (2004). *Do Primeiro Almoço À Ceia: Estudos de História da Alimentação.* Sintra: Colares Editora.

Brigadier, S. (2002). *The artifact assemblage from the Pepper Wreck: An early seventeenth century Portuguese East-Indiaman that wrecked in the Tagus River.* Unpublished MA dissertation. Texas A & M University.

Caetano, C. (2004). *A Ribeira de Lisboa na Época da Expansão Portuguesa (Séculos XV a XVIII).* Lisboa: Pandora.

Calado, M., Pimenta, J., & Silva, R. B. (2003). Cachimbos de cerâmica provenientes da escavação do Caminho de Ronda no Castelo de São Jorge em Lisboa. *Património e Estudos, 5,* 83–95.

Caldeira, A. M. (2000). O tabaco brasileiro em Portugal: Divulgação e formas de consumo durante o Antigo Regime. In Portugal-Brasil: Memórias e Imaginários. Congresso Luso-Brasileiro. Actas, vol. I. Lisboa: Grupo de Trabalho do Ministério da Educação para as Comemorações dos Descobrimentos Portugueses, 567–586.

Caldeira, A. M. (2013). *Escravos e Traficantes no Império Português. O comércio negreiro português no Atlântico durante os séculos XV a XIX.* Lisboa: Esfera dos Livros.

Cardoso, G., & Rodrigues, S. (2002). Conjunto de peças de cerâmica do século XVII do Convento de Nossa Senhora da Piedade de Cascais. In Actas do 3º Encontro Nacional de Arqueologia Urbana (pp. 269–288). Almada: Câmara Municipal de Almada.

Carmona, R. (2005). *Olaria da mata da Machada: Cerâmicas dos séculos XV-XVI.* Barreiro: Câmara Municipal do Barreiro.

Carvalho, P. (2008). *Os estaleiros na Índia portuguesa (1595–1630).* Unpublished MA dissertation. Universidade Nova de Lisboa, Lisbon.

Castilho, J. (1893). *A Ribeira de Lisboa. Descripção historica da margem do Tejo desde a Madre-de-Deus até Santos-o-Velho.* Lisboa: Imprensa Nacional.

Chirikure, S., Sinamai, A., Goagoses, E., Mubusisi, M., & Ndoro, W. (2010). Maritime archaeology and trans-oceanic trade: A case study of the Oranjemund shipwreck cargo, Namibia. *Journal of Maritime Archaeology, 5,* 37–55.

Coelho, I. P. (2012). Muito mais que lixo: A cerâmica do sítio arqueológico subaquático Ria de Aveiro B-C. In A. Teixeira & J. Bettencourt (Eds.) *Velhos e Novos Mundos: Estudos de Arqueologia Moderna* (pp. 757–770). Lisboa: Centro de História de Além-Mar.

Costa, L. F. (1997). *Naus e Galeões na Ribeira de Lisboa: A construção naval no século XVI para a Rota do Cabo.* Cascais: Patrimónia.

Costa, L. F. (2002). *O transporte no Atlântico e a Companhia Geral do Comércio do Brasil, 1580–1663.* Lisboa: Comissão Nacional para as Comemorações dos Descobrimentos Portugueses.

D'Intino, R. (1998). Objectos do quotidiano. In *Nossa Senhora dos Mártires: A Última Viagem* (pp. 219-227). Lisboa: Pavilhão de Portugal Expo98 and Verbo.

Danielsen, R. (2008). Palaeoecologial development of the Quiaios–Mira dunes, northern-central littoral Portugal. *Review of Palaeobotany and Palynology, 152,* 74–99.

Davis, S. (2009). Animal remains from an 18th–19th century AD pit in the Palácio Centeno, Lisbon. *Revista Portuguesa de Arqueologia, 12*(2), 239–250.

Dias, J. P. S. (2007). *Droguistas, boticários e segredistas: Ciência e Sociedade na Produção de Medicamentos na Lisboa de Setecentos.* Lisboa: Fundação Calouste Gulbenkian.

Ferrão, J. E. M. (1992). *A aventura das plantas e os descobrimentos portugueses.* Lisboa: Comissão Nacional para as Comemorações dos Descobrimentos Portugueses.

Fonseca, J. (2002). *Escravos no Sul de Portugal: Séculos XVI-XVII.* Lisboa: Vulgata.

Hall, J. L. (2006). The Monte Cristi «Pipe Wreck»'. In R. Grenier, D. Nutley, & I. Cochran (Eds.) *Underwater cultural heritage at risk: Managing natural and human impacts* (pp. 20–22). Paris: ICOMOS.

Henriques, A. C. (Ed). (2009). *Portugal e o Mundo nos Séculos XVI e XVII*. Lisboa: Smithsonian Institution and Instituto dos Museus e da Conservação.

Hutter, L. M. (1985). A madeira do Brasil na construção e reparos de embarcações. *Revista da Universidade de Coimbra, 33*, 413–430.

Jordan, A. (2005). Images of empire: Slaves in the Lisbon household and court of Catherine of Austria. In T. F. Earle & K. J. P. Lowe (Eds.) *Black Africans in renaissance Europe* (pp. 155–180). New York: Cambridge University Press.

Lopes, G. C. (2013). *Ria de Aveiro F (Ílhavo): um naufrágio de época moderna na laguna de Aveiro*. Unpublished MA dissertation. Universidade Nova de Lisboa, Lisbon.

Lourenço, S., & Bugalhão, J. (2006). As Formas de Pão de Açúcar da Ilha da Berlenga. In E. Sousa (Ed.) *A Cerâmica do Açúcar em Portugal na Época Moderna*. (pp. 48–61) Machico: Centro de Estudos de Arqueologia Moderna e Contemporânea.

Luna, I. & Cardoso, G. (2006). *Nota preliminar sobre as cerâmicas provenientes do Poço dos Paços do Concelho de Torres Vedras*. In *Actas do III Seminário do Património da Região Oeste* (pp. 99–112). Cadaval: Câmara Municipal do Cadaval.

Mangucci, A. C. (2007). Da louça ordinária e não tão ordinária que se fazia em Lisboa, em 1767. Cenáculo: Boletim online do Museu de Évora, 1. Évora: Museu de Évora

Marques, R. (2007). *A História e Técnica dos Tapetes de Arraiolos*. Unpublished MA dissertation. Universidade Nova de Lisboa, Lisbon.

Mauro, F. (1997). *Portugal, o Brasil e o Atlântico*. (Vol. 2) Lisboa: Estampa.

Mendonça, I. M. (2008). *O mobiliário religioso de António Vaz de Castro, «entalhador e ensamblador de Sua Magestade»*. In *Mobiliário Português. Actas do 1º Colóquio de Artes Decorativas* (pp. 15–29). Lisboa: ESAD.

Moreno-Garcìa, M., & Detry, C. (2010). The dietary role of hens, chickens and eggs among a 17th-century monastic order: The Clarisse of Santa Clara-a-Velha, Coimbra (Portugal). In W. Prummel, J. T. Zeiler, & D. C. Brinkhuizen (Eds.), Birds in archaeology, Proceedings of the 6th Meeting of the ICAZ Bird Working Group. Groningen: Groningen Institute of Archaeology, (pp. 45–55) (Groningen Archaeological Studies, 12).

Morgado, P. J., Silva, R. C., & Filipe, S. J. (2012). A cerâmica do açúcar de Aveiro: recentes achados na área do antigo bairro das olarias. In A. Teixeira & J. Bettencourt (Eds.) *Velhos e Novos Mundos: Estudos de Arqueologia Moderna* (pp. 771–782). Lisboa: Centro de História de Além-Mar.

Neves, M. J., Almeida, M., & Ferreira, M. T. (2011). História de um Arrabalde durante os séculos XV e XVI: o Poço dos negros em Lagos (Algarve, Portugal) e o seu contributo para o estudo dos escravos africanos em Portugal. In A. T. Matos & J. P. O. Costa (Eds.) *A Herança do Infante* (pp. 29–46). Lisboa: Câmara Municipal de Lagos, Centro de Estudos dos Povos e Culturas de Expressão Portuguesa and Centro de História de Além-Mar.

Nunes, N. (2002). *O açúcar de cana na ilha da Madeira: do Mediterrâneo ao Atlântico. Terminologia e tecnologia históricas e actuais da cultura açucareira*. Unpublished PhD thesis. Universidade da Madeira, Funchal.

Pereira, A. L. (2000). Cachimbos cerâmicos do século XVII da Casa do Infante (Porto). In Actas das 3ªs Jornadas de Cerâmica Medieval e Pós-Medieval: métodos e resultados para o seu estudo (pp. 253–269). Tondela: Câmara Municipal de Tondela.

Pinto, M., Filipe, I., & Miguel, L. (2011). Os cachimbos de caulino provenientes do Mercado da Ribeira: contributo para a história socio-económica da Lisboa Moderna. *Apontamentos, 7*, 41–48.

Pinto, M. H. M. (1987). *Os móveis e o seu tempo: mobiliário português do Museu Nacional de Arte Antiga, séculos XV–XIX*. Lisboa: Instituto Português do Património Cultural.

Pinto, P. (2005). *Móvel de Assento Português do século XVIII*. Lisboa: Mediatexto.

Polónia, A. (2007). *A expansão ultramarina numa perspectiva local: O porto de Vila do Conde no século XVI*. Lisboa: Imprensa Nacional Casa da Moeda.

Queiroz, P. F., Mateus, J. E., & Ruas, J. P. (2007). Santa Clara-a-Velha, o quotidiano para além da ruína: Frutos e sementes recolhidos nos trabalhos de escavação arqueológica (1996–2001). Trabalhos do CIPA, 111. http://www.terra-scenica.pt/PDFs/TC_111TOTAL_PROT.pdf. Accessed 25 Oct 2013.

Queiroz, P. F., Mateus, J. E., Pereira, T., & Mendes, P. (2006). Santa Clara-a-Velha, o quotidiano para além da ruína: Primeiros resultados da investigação Paleoecológica e Arqueobotânica. Trabalhos do CIPA, 97. http://www.terra-scenica.pt/PDFs/TC_97.pdf. Accessed 25 Oct 2013.

Rijkelijkhuizen, M. (2009). Whales, walruses, and elephants: Artisans in ivory, baleen and other skeletal materials in seventeenth and eighteenth century Amsterdam. *International Journal of Historical Archaeology, 13*(4), 409–429.

Rodrigues, J. A. S., Bolila, C., Filipe, V., Henriques, J. P., Ribeiro, I. A., & Simões, S. T. (2012). As cerâmicas da Idade Moderna da Fortaleza de Nossa Senhora da Luz, Cascais. In A. Teixeira & J. Bettencourt (Eds.) *Velhos e Novos Mundos: Estudos de Arqueologia Moderna* (pp. 865–876). Lisboa: Centro de História de Além-Mar.

Sarrazola, A., Bettencourt, J., & Teixeira, A. (2014). Lisboa, o Tejo e a expansão portuguesa: Os mais recentes achados arqueológicos da zona ribeirinha. In A. Silveira (Ed.) *O tempo resgatado ao mar*. Lisboa: Imprensa Nacional Casa da Moeda and Museu Nacional de Arqueologia, 111–116.

Scully, T. (1995). The art of cookery in the middle ages. Woodbridge: Boydell.

Silva, F. G. (2012). As formas de pão-de-açúcar da Mata do Machado, Barreiro. In A. Teixeira & J. Bettencourt (Eds.) *Velhos e Novos Mundos: Estudos de Arqueologia Moderna* (pp. 711-718). Lisboa: Centro de História de Além-Mar.

Silva, R. B., & Guinote, P. (1998). *O Quotidiano na Lisboa dos Descobrimentos: Roteiro Arqueológico e Documental dos Espaços e Objectos*. Lisboa: Grupo de Trabalho do Ministério da Educação para as Comemorações dos Descobrimentos Portugueses.

Sousa, E. (2010). Tanta «arqueologia» para uma-só: Abordagem acrítica e descritiva das arqueologias de âmbito pós-quinhnetista. *Arqueologia Moderna e Contemporânea, 1*, 10–15.

Sousa, E. (2011). *Ilhas Arqueológicas. O quotidiano e a civilização material na Madeira e nos Açores (séculos XV-XVIII)*. Unpublished PhD thesis. Universidade de Lisboa, Lisbon.

Straube, B., & Luccketti, N. (1996). The Association for the Preservation of Virginia Antiquities: 1995 interim report. http://www.apva.org/rediscovery/pdf/96report.pdf. Accessed 1 Nov 2013.

Torres, C. (1990). Um forno cerâmico dos séculos XV e XVI na cintura industrial de Lisboa. In F. Amigues & A. Bazzana (Eds.) *Fours de Potiers et «Testares» Médiévaux en Méditerranée Occidentale* (pp. 131–141). Madrid: Casa de Velázquez.

Torres, J. B. (2012). *Quotidianos no Convento de São Francisco de Lisboa: uma análise da cerâmica vidrada, faiança portuguesa e porcelana chinesa*. Unpublished MA dissertation. Universidade Nova de Lisboa, Lisbon.

Trindade, A. R. (2013). *Convento de Santana de Leiria. História, Vivências e Cultura Material (Cerâmicas dos Séculos XV Leiria. História, Vivências e Cultura Material (Cerâmicas dos Séculos XV Lisbon.*

Trnek, H., & Silva, N. V. (Eds.) (2001). *Exotica: The Portuguese discoveries and the Renaissance Kunstkammer*. Lisboa: Calouste Gulbenkian Museum.

Valente, A. (2007). Apontamentos sobre o uso das madeiras em Portugal no Século XVIII. *Revista de Artes Decorativas, 1*, 229–240.

Wingood, A. J. (1986). Sea venture: Second interim report. Part 2: The artefacts. *The International Journal of Nautical Archaeology and Underwater Exploration, 15*(2), 149–159.

# Chapter 3
# The Early Colonisation of the *Rio de la Plata* Basin and the Settlement of *Sancti Spiritus*

Agustin Azkarate and Sergio Escribano-Ruiz

## 3.1 Introduction: The When, Where, What and Why of Sancti Spiritus?

Sancti Spiritus is the name which Sebastian Cabot gave to the settlement that he ordered to be built in 1527 at the confluence of the rivers Coronda and Caracarañá in the present-day town of Puerto Gaboto (Province of Santa Fe, Argentina). It is important to clarify at the outset that we do not use this name to only refer to the ephemeral Spanish settlement, which comprises a fort and several houses, but also to refer to the earlier settlement upon which all the constructions related to the Spanish expedition were erected. The settlement in which the remains of the first fort built in Argentina were recorded represents a multicultural reality which cannot be understood if only one of the parties involved is taken into account. Accordingly, we view the area that is being studied by archaeologists (Cocco et al. 2011; Azkarate et al. 2012a, b, 2013a) as the historical arena in which a complex network of interaction developed between the societies that had already settled there and the European members of the expedition, who took control of the site temporarily and adapted it to their needs. The ongoing work has focused on the study of these interactions, combining the critical analysis of written documentation with the study of material evidence that they left behind (Fig. 3.1).

---

The original manuscript was written in Spanish and has been translated into English by "Traductores-Intérpretes GDS, S. L."

---

A. Azkarate (✉) · S. Escribano-Ruiz
Cátedra Territorio, Paisaje y Patrimonio,
Grupo de Investigación en Patrimonio Construido, GPAC (UPV-EHU),
Centro de Investigación Lascaray Ikergunea, Avda. Miguel de Unamuno, 3,
01006 Vitoria-Gasteiz, Spain
e-mail: agustin.azcarate@ehu.es

S. Escribano-Ruiz
e-mail: sergio.escribanor@ehu.es

© Springer International Publishing Switzerland 2015
P. P. A. Funari, M. X. Senatore (eds.), *Archaeology of Culture Contact and Colonialism in Spanish and Portuguese America*, DOI 10.1007/978-3-319-08069-7_3

**Fig. 3.1** Geographical
location of Sancti Spiritus
settlement

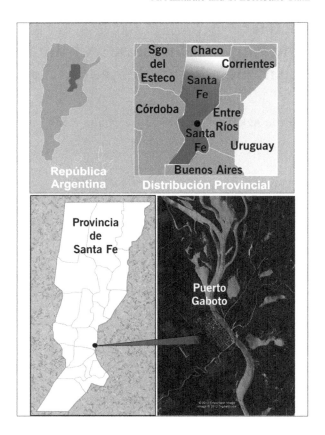

The ephemeral colonial settlement of Sancti Spiritus is a rare example that enables further exploration of the nature of the colonisation of the Americas and its discursive strategies. The episode that we are looking at has certain specificities that make it an example of the diversity that characterised such a dramatic and complex historical process. At the same time, Sancti Spiritus also exhibits many of the characteristics of Spanish colonialism. In spite of this, historiography has overlooked it as a one-off and anecdotal, or even marginal or peripheral, episode in this colonisation process. This chapter will analyse the treatment that this case study has received in accounts of the colonisation of the Americas and evaluate the possible reasons behind it being left on the fringes of the history of colonialism. It will be contextualised under the various definitions of the term "colonialism", taking into account the results obtained in the latest archaeological work. Finally, it will evaluate the epistemological potential of the collection of written sources and materials in the creation of the discourse of European colonialism.

## 3.2    The Position of Sancti Spiritus in the Historiography of the Spanish Colonisation of the Americas

It is now naturally assumed that the discourse of the Spanish colonisation of the Americas is a master narrative (e.g. Buscaglia 2011, p. 59, 69; Bianchi 2012, p. 58). However, both analysing the ways in which it is expressed and studying the mechanisms used are still very recent practices. It is acknowledged that it has been neglected in Hispanic academic fields involved in the history of the Americas (Rodríguez and Martínez 2009). It has also been assumed that archaeology has not given it enough attention, at least until recent times, when importance was attached to post-colonial theory (Liebmann 2008, pp. 4–5).

### 3.2.1    A Quick Assessment

As part of a critical assessment of colonialist discourse, we have analysed how the Sancti Spiritus case was considered in the bibliography in a rather general way. In order to assess its historiographical representation, we have explored and analysed the basic bibliography that is recommended on various Spanish university courses on the history of the Americas (Amores 2006; Bethell 1987; Céspedes 2009; Lucena 1992; Navarro García 1991a; Pérez Herrero 2002). Other works that are international of a synthetic nature or recent publications have also been added (Arjona 1973; Bakewell 1997; González Ochoa 2003; Hernández Sánchez-Barba 2012; Kinsbruner and Langer 2008; Lockhart and Schwartz 1992; Lucena 2005). In the light of their examination, it should be highlighted that there are three main trends concerning Sancti Spiritus: (a) direct omission, (b) its consideration as an episode of exploration or (c) its inclusion in the conquest of the Americas.

a.  As previously mentioned, the majority of texts that address the colonial history of Latin America *do not mention* the Sancti Spiritus episode (Bakewell 1997; Burger 2008; Céspedes 2009; Elliot 1987, 1990; Hernández Sánchez-Barba 2012; Lockhart and Schwartz 1992; Pérez Herrero 2002; Silva 1991). Over half of the sources consulted did not consider it to be a noteworthy event in the context of the colonisation of the Plata River Basin. In contrast, almost all refer to Pedro de Mendoza and relate the origin of the colonisation with the first time that Buenos Aires was founded, a few years later in 1536.

b.  Far fewer authors placed Sancti Spiritus within the *exploration* process of the Plata River Basin (Arjona 1973, p. 83; González Ochoa 2003, pp. 67–68; Lordan and Ward 2008, pp. 162–163). They all consider the settlement to have been a brief anecdote protagonised by Sebastian Cabot, one of the great explorers of the Americas. They, therefore, subordinate the significance of the settlement to the image of its illustrious founder.

c.  Similarly, there are very few sources which consider that Sancti Spiritus was more than mere exploration and which address it as part of the *conquest* of the

Plata River Basin. The vast majority of these regard Sancti Spiritus as incidental (Andreo and Provencio 2006, p. 257; Lucena 2005, pp. 70–71; Paz 2008, p. 249) and only one claims that it was an important event (Ramos 1992, pp. 175–178).

## 3.2.2   Reasoning Its Episodic Consideration

Until very recently the history of the Americas almost exclusively addressed political institutions, major events and the main historical figures. Economic and social issues were treated as secondary. Historical archaeology has also fuelled and encouraged this epistemological viewpoint by studying the colonial past through excavations of colonial outposts or settlements associated with major colonial figures (Jordan 2009, p. 33). Unfortunately, this focus is still characteristic of a significant proportion of North American historical archaeology (Silliman 2005, p. 69) and to a lesser degree in Europe, where the archaeology that deals with the colonisation of the Americas is beset by other serious problems.[1] As we have already shown on another occasion (Azkarate and Escribano 2012), Latin American historical archaeology is very advanced and exemplary both in the way it critically assesses colonialism and considers its implications. However, Latin American archaeological discourse is not yet present in the general sources and guides that address the colonisation of the Americas.

In this respect, it is surprising that despite being connected to one of those major historical figures, Sancti Spiritus is not featured in the discussion in over half of the sources that were consulted and that it was viewed as little more than an anecdote in the rest. We must consider, in the light of the features of historiography outlined above, that this underrepresentation could be related to the importance that was traditionally attached to the history of political institutions when interpreting the colonial process (Cañedo-Arguelles 2006, p. 268; Jordan 2009, p. 33). In this case, the fact that the Sancti Spiritus settlement was not built under orders from the Hispanic monarch but at the initiative of Sebastian Cabot could be the reason behind its underestimation in historiography. It is possible to confirm this, as we have a very clear comparative model, namely the case of the first Buenos Aires, in which involvement by the state is much more evident.

Santa María del Buen Aire was founded by Pedro de Mendoza in 1536, under the instructions of the Castilian monarchy. Apart from this, the experience of Pedro de Mendoza and Buenos Aires is very similar to that of Sebastian Cabot and Sancti Spiritus. Both settlements were developed in the same way: They were destroyed by attacks by the original settlers a few years after they had been founded. However,

---

[1] The archaeology that deals with the gap starting in the sixteenth century is still the least developed in European archaeology, despite enjoying certain dynamism and concerning the period that is most well-represented in the archaeological record. As well as being the time period that has given rise to the lowest amount of historiographical production in European archaeology, its representation in academic works is also minor and even residual. To make matters worse, postmedieval archaeology is currently immersed in an identity crisis, which has resulted in the creation of many labels to refer to archaeology after 1500, such as historical archaeology, recent historical archaeology or archaeology of the recent past.

the first Buenos Aires is considered to be noteworthy in the majority of cases which, paradoxically, do not allude to the Sancti Spiritus episode (Céspedes 2009; Elliot 1987, 1990; Lockhart and Schwartz 1992; Pérez Herrero 2002; Silva 1991). Moreover, all the sources that do mention the Cabot episode consider the first Buenos Aires settlement to be the event which marked the beginning of the colonial process in the Plata River Basin, dismissing Sancti Spiritus as merely episodic. It is clear that in the case of Buenos Aires and Pedro de Mendoza there is a historiographical consensus which is not reached at all in the case of Sancti Spiritus and Sebastian Cabot.

If we look at the contradiction between the historical similarity of the two cases and their different historiographical treatment, it is possible to conclude that historiography attaches greater importance to action that was led by the policy of the Crown. The orders given by the monarch to found Buenos Aires and Sebastian Cabot's apparent personal initiative are the only notable difference in how both cases unfolded. However, besides some exceptions (Pérez Herrero 2002, p. 42; Elliot 1990, pp. 132–133), the majority of the sources consulted reject this idea. Historiography seems to accept that the initial phase of colonialism was characterised by an individualistic attitude and that the central role of the Crown started to develop from the mid-sixteenth century (Hernández Sánchez-Barba 2012, pp. 89–90; Lockhart and Schwartz 1992, pp. 10–20; Muro 1991, p. 29; Navarro García 1991b, p. 7). The very example of Sancti Spiritus negates the existence of a pre-determined colonising policy and shows that the initiative of the crown changed during the course of the events and through improvisation in the first stage of the colonisation of the Americas. It is important to remember that the event directed by Sebastian Cabot completely changed the course of Spanish policy in the Southern Cone, as it confirmed the existence of an inland country in the South and sparked interest in the Spanish courts in continuing to explore and the conquest (Ramos 1992, pp. 177–178).

If the crown's intervention was not decisive, we should still ask why Sancti Spiritus does not feature in the majority of the accounts of the early colonisation and why, in contrast, the first Buenos Aires does. We are of the opinion that the main reason is the "alternative" and different character of Sancti Spiritus, which is an ephemeral event that exemplifies the resistance of indigenous societies to the European occupation. This does not seem to be important for the majority of the authors studied who, to the contrary, prefer to focus on those episodes in which colonisation was successful, even if they were second attempts, as was the case of Buenos Aires. This attitude has deep implications, as by considering Buenos Aires and underestimating Sancti Spiritus a story based on the triumph of the conquest is imposed and colonisation is represented as an inexorable process that minimises the role of the indigenous American societies as it unfolded.

## 3.3    The Sancti Spiritus Settlement, Beyond Colonisation

The example of Sancti Spiritus calls for alternative accounts to be incorporated into the discourse on the colonisation of the Americas, highlights the importance that specific local contexts had in its development (*sensu* Funari et al. 1999, pp. 13–15; Funari 2007, pp. 54–55) and positions itself against the Eurocentric and essentialist attitude of many of the accounts that address this historical process. It does so in various ways, namely by claiming its status as a colonising and colonialist episode, by advocating the need to study the colonised and not only the colonisers (*sensu* Given 2004, pp. 3–4) and by providing an example of collaboration and resistance of the indigenous societies.

### 3.3.1 Sancti Spiritus: A Colonisation Attempt and Example of Colonialism

Despite the dominant opinion in historiography, we maintain that Sancti Spiritus was a clear attempt at colonisation. We do not hesitate to place it in the context of the initial colonisation of the Plata River Basin, as colonising involved above all settling, that is taking possession of a territory (Lamperiere 2004, p. 114).[2] Paradoxically, some of the authors who do not consider our case study worth mentioning put forward a model of action that is identical to the one implemented by Sebastian Cabot in Sancti Spiritus. Rejecting historiographical inertia, we wish to stress that it was the first colonial settlement in the Plata River Basin and that establishing it was clearly intended to support the exploration and conquest of the Plata River. Furthermore, part of its importance in the colonial process is derived from this situation, because exploring meant optimising their operations; Spain was the first colonial country to systematically apply this rule (Todorov 2008, p. 214) (Fig. 3.2).

Moreover, we view the Sancti Spiritus episode as a case of colonialism. We accept the negative connotation and the impartiality of the word colonialism in relation to the events it studies (Lemperiere 2004, pp. 111–112). In fact, we feel identified by the sense of condemnation that the term implies in relation to the process that we are analysing. It is not in vain that the archaeological definitions of colonialism acknowledge that there were relations of domination among the different cultures involved and that the majority of them attach central importance to it in the colonialist process. Addressing this factor, they claim that not all colonisation processes involve colonialism (Jordan 2009, pp. 31–32) and, vice versa, that not all colonialism implies colonisation (Silliman 2005, p. 58; Gosden, pp. 2–3). The way in which it is considered largely depends on the nature of the power relations developed between Europeans and the local communities: If there are relations of domination in a specific case, we will view it as colonialism, and if not, we will refer to the process of colonisation.[3]

---

[2] "Una vez desembarcados, colonizaban una parcela reducida y cuando el territorio ganado a la geografía americana y a las comunidades indígenas resultaban ser insuficientes como consecuencia del aumento demográfico o la llegada de nuevos colonos, se procedía a una expansión del área por medio de una nueva conquista" (Pérez Herrero 2002, p. 62). [*Once they disembarked, they started to colonise a small plot and when the territory won from American geography and the indigenous communities was not enough, as a result of population growth or the arrival of new colonists, a new conquest was started to expand the area*].

[3] While for some definitions the role of intercultural domination is sufficient and defining (Jordan 2009, p. 32), others also view it as necessary to consider its duration (Gasco 2005, pp. 69–70; Stein

**Fig. 3.2** Aerial image of the site. (Photo: Gustavo Frittegotto)

In Sancti Spiritus, we have evidence that suggests that there were relations of domination between the European invaders and the local societies and which reveal a clear will to dominate by the Spanish expedition. The information provided by written evidence is ambiguous, but both its reading and the archaeological results make it possible to discover the colonisers' actual intentions. On the one hand, they reveal that the relations with the local communities were friendly at the outset of their encounter. They talk of a peaceful encounter, which continued over several months and was characterised by intense positive interaction ("...e estuvimos en él más de seis meses de paz e amor con los indios comarcanos..." [...and we were there for more than six months of peace and love with the Indian neighbours...]). On the other hand, they constructed a military structure, a fort, to pacify the land. Whatever the reason behind it,[4] there is no doubt that with the building of this military structure, colonialism took shape in the Spanish settlement.

---

2005, pp. 8–9). In other cases, such as Gosden (2004), the use or otherwise of violence is decisive when classifying the different types of colonialism.

[4] If we accept that the relations were initially friendly, it is clear that the colonisers must have given the native people reasons to resist their demands and for the relations to have become conflictual or vice versa. In this case, colonialism would have emerged during the course of this episode, now on Argentinian soil. If we do not accept their account or if we have doubts about a discourse that seems limited, we could argue that as soon as they disembarked they did so with a will to dominate the local societies.

Archaeology is unambiguous about this situation, by emphasizing the material results of the disagreement and shedding light on the impact that the way in which it was constructed had on the local settlement. The latest excavations have revealed that in order to build the fortress it was necessary to partially destroy a significant part of the original village (Azkarate et al. 2012a, p. 17). We have been able to record how the European desire to dominate get materialised in a military structure, the construction of which entailed both destroying the local settlement and taking over part of the area that it had occupied. Far from reflecting friendly or defensive intentions, these facts demonstrate a clear domineering attitude towards the local societies.

### 3.3.2   Sancti Spiritus: Network of Intercultural Relations and Icon of Resistance

The history of the Americas, especially that which has been written in Europe, has barely showed interest until recently in the societies which were inhabiting the American continent when the first Europeans arrived, nor in their development since the initial encounter. One argument used to justify this lack of attention is the shortage of information about the original settlers of America in written sources, which are the main source of information used to construct that historical narrative. In addition to problems in terms of the quantity of documents available, there are also qualitative issues, especially concerning their arbitrariness. The documents that do exist only provide a European vision, "an ethnification" of the colonised societies.[5] In the case of Sancti Spiritus, there are documents that allude to interaction with the local societies, but they do not provide a lot of information and it is also contradictory. Documents which exclusively refer to the original communities are even scarcer. In this specific case, it does not even mention that the Spanish settlement was built on top of the local village. In stark contrast to this is the study of the material remains, which show the land in all its potential (Fig. 3.3).

Archaeology has made it possible not only to determine the direct impact that the building of the fort had on the original settlers, but also record the coexistence of European and local cultural material in the fort.[6] Through the excavations, we have obtained more information about the local habitation patterns, by exhuming the settlement that existed before the arrival of the Spanish expedition and recording a permanent or semi-permanent habitat made up of wooden huts (Azkarate et al. 2012b, 2013b). It has also been possible to confirm that, at least in the area that was excavated, that the place occupied by the fort was not occupied subsequently in the form of a settlement but was abandoned. It is therefore surprising that the fort is mentioned after it was destroyed (Azkarate et al. 2012b, pp. 47–48) as a recognisable place, as a landmark, as a place that was part of the Europeans' memory and

---

[5] For further discussion of this issue, although concerning another timeframe and geographical area, see Azkarate 2011, p. 246.

[6] The pottery items recovered from a fill level associated with the use of the moat confirm the coexistence of local and European pottery (Azkarate et al. 2013b).

**Fig. 3.3** Underlined in *green* is the earthen wall of the fort; to the *right,* the moat partially excavated; to the *left,* the trench for the wall, cutting the postholes of local huts

that it was noticeable. However, due to the limited area that was excavated, we are unaware if at least one part of Sancti Spiritus remained. Only further progress in the archaeological investigations will clarify this and other fundamental questions, such as the significance that his place could have had for the native settlers once the fort had been destroyed.[7]

Due to the conflict that characterised the interaction between the different cultures that were in contact with each other around the Sancti Spiritus settlement, we have replaced expressions such as *cultural entanglement* or *cultural contact* with expressions such as *cultural conflict* (Azkarate et al. 2013b) during this research. We agree with S. Silliman (2005, p. 57–62) that words such as "contact" or "entanglement" give a neutral connotation to the process, as they allude to a relationship between different cultural units, but they do not define an essential feature of colonialism, namely the asymmetry that underpins these relationships. By emphasising the notion of conflict, we do not intend to encourage the essentialist contrast between the coloniser and the colonised, but rather attempt to highlight the omnipresence of conflict during this episode. In fact, the interaction was much more dynamic than may be assumed. In addition to conflictual relations between the colonisers and those colonised, there were conflicts between the colonisers themselves and the various local societies that were involved, and the partial interaction between them.[8] This is a very complex cultural reality with different colonising agents and

---

[7] This is one of the questions which we are currently working on; we are trying to understand whether the space occupied by the fort became an icon of resistance for the natives, a space for the traumatic memory, or if it was the material actor that sparked the process of cultural hybridisation in the area.

[8] There was well-known controversy between Cabot and Moguer about who had the right to explore in the Plata River, and their later agreement is equally widely known. There is also information about conflict between the Guarani and the other local societies. On top of this, it is assumed that the Spanish expedition members received help from some of the local communities, such as the Guarani, but that the others were opposed to them.

cultural hybridisation on various scales. We trust that continuing the investigations will make it possible for us to analyse the active and passive role that the material culture had in this whole process.

The definitions of colonialism by Gosden (2004), Silliman (2005), Stein (2005) and Jordan (2009) stress the importance in not exclusively examining mechanisms of domination but also analysing creative processes that emerge through the coming together of two cultures: resistance, collaboration, hybridisation, etc. Sancti Spiritus is a good example of the complexity, creativity and dynamism involved in the colonial process in the Americas in the sixteenth century. Although we have just mentioned the simultaneous cohabitation and coexistence in this context, it is resistance which is most clearly reflected in this case study and which, in our opinion, gives Sancti Spiritus a special symbolic importance. This case study highlights that the local communities were not merely passive subjects in the face of colonialism but that they took an active role in its conceptual development and the resulting operational strategies. Recalling what occurred in the Sancti Spiritus settlement not only recovers the voice of those who resisted and highlights their capacity for action, it also reminds us of something very important, that is that the course of history could have been different.

## 3.4   Things and Words, Some Insights on How We Could Make Use of Their Agencies

Sancti Spiritus also gives us the chance to assess the way in which the different sources involved in studying it reflect the colonisation process. In the previous section, we concluded that, in this case, the study of the material sources provided a more direct vision of the Spanish expedition members' colonialist ideal. Archaeology has clarified the ambiguous picture that the written account provides when talking of cultural interaction and it has cast more light on the mechanisms of domination used by the Spaniards. By studying the material remains we have obtained a structural knowledge of the local societies, which had been omitted from the official sources from the era. The reason for the omissions is precisely because those written sources were produced by the colonisers involved and because they could have and did serve their interests.

Observing that the study of the documents written by the colonial elite did not include the subordinate voices has caused some thinkers to adopt pessimistic attitudes (Spivak 1988). It has also meant that, from certain European historiographical viewpoints, there has been a demand for recourse to the narrative autonomy of archaeology. For some years, some European scholars (especially Medievalists) have been starting to openly question the validity of the paradigms that were created using the written sources and to put forward new suggestions mainly by using the material record. It is increasingly clear, in the light of the most recent investigations, that creating quality archaeological records requires that we retain a degree of autonomy and that we analyse the document in the light of archaeological issues.

It cannot be denied that all historical sources (material, written and oral) correspond to different social practices and that, therefore, there are various problems of inference. It also has to be acknowledged that they all have specific information potential, which is worthy of attention and consideration. For this reason, we do not believe that rejecting the use of written documentation when interpreting the archaeological record is as important as ensuring that this process takes place with a critical and reflexive attitude.[9] Another point that should not be forgotten is that only by pooling different sources of evidence and interpreting them simultaneously, it is possible to make suggestions that can answer to the past's many dimensions: If the reality is multidimensional, its treatment can only be transdisciplinary (Azkarate 2010, p. 18). The method used in this case study has involved bringing material evidence to the forefront, critically analysing written documentation and combining both collections of information in the final interpretation.

In the case study of Sancti Spiritus, we have, on the one hand, documents written about the episode led by Sebastian Cabot that say that the fort was built to *pacify* that place. In contrast, the material evidence exhumed from Puerto Gaboto confirms that the fort, which was equipped with a moat and a mud wall, was built over several houses that made up a part of the local settlement. When interpreting this set of information, putting material facts before written ones, we have concluded that the peace that the Spaniards wanted to achieve involved attempting to push the native people into submission. We have not rejected the written information; in fact, to the contrary, including it has helped us to understand and more accurately define the process.

Prioritising facts above words, we have clearly seen that the attempt at colonisation by the Spanish expedition was accompanied by rhetorical discursive mechanisms, with which they tried to conceal their true intentions of domination, minimise the consequences of their heinous actions and justify them. We have not let the ambiguity of the written narrative confuse us and we have been able to confirm that its apparent contradiction corresponds to a euphemism that is inherent to the "discourse of appearances". In the words of T. Todorov (2008, pp. 213–214), this discursive tactic is defined by separating what is *done* from what is *said to be done* and judging the latter to be true. Both oral and written discourse was the main instrument used to bring about this change. What should be dismissed are not the conquests but the word "conquest"; "pacification" is simply another word to refer to the same thing, but we do not believe that this concern for linguistics is to no avail. The reason being that the Spaniards were not asked to be good Christians, but to appear that they were (Todorov 2008, p. 213).

---

[9] In fact, schools of thought as powerful as those derived from the postcolonial theory are exclusively based on this procedure, that is the critical reading of literature produced by the colonial powers. Since, as M. Foucault (1992, p. 5) warns, "in every society the production of discourse is at once controlled, selected, organised and redistributed according to a certain number of procedures, whose role is to avert its powers and its dangers, to cope with chance events, to evade its ponderous, awesome materiality". It is precisely this observation that encouraged Foucault to make discourse a priority subject of study and not to reject it.

Although we did not imagine that this discursive strategy would have been systematically applied to such an apparently peripheral and early case as Sancti Spiritus, the interpretation of material and written sources makes it very clear. They justified building the fort by referring to it as *pacification* of the Indians, and in this way, they avoided revealing details about what was really happening: Houses from the original village were being destroyed, and they were intending to force local societies into submission, namely many of the activities involved in a *conquest*. It is also clear in this case that discourse is not simply that which translates struggles or systems of domination, but is the thing for which and by which there is struggle (Foucault 1992, p. 6).

## 3.5  Final Remarks

This chapter has shown that the role of archaeology is not only essential to representing and understanding the native American societies, a fundamental goal itself, but also to determining the impact that colonisation had on these societies. Furthermore, by showing clearly and without self-interested distortions *what was done*, archaeology plays a key role in deconstructing the discourse of the colonisers, that is *what is said was done*. In this way, it contributes new evidence that helps to identify and invalidate some discursive strategies of colonialism (such as the discourse of appearances) which, to whatever extent, are still active in today's society.

**Acknowledgments**  Our participation in the investigations in Sancti Spiritus was made possible thanks to funding from the Spanish Ministry of Education, Culture and Sport, through the calls for applications for grants for excavation work outside Spain and help from the University of the Basque Country (UPV-EHU). It would not have been possible if the Argentinian team that discovered Sancti Spiritus had not accepted our collaboration or, of course, without the work of our project partners from the UPV-EHU. For this reason, we would like to express our deepest gratitude to Iban Sánchez Pinto and Verónica Benedet as well as to the team led by Guillermo Frittegotto, Fabian Letieri and Gabriel Cocco. Their efforts have made it possible for us to write this chapter, and without their work it would never have been possible.

## References

Amores, J. B. (Ed). (2006). *Historia de América*. Barcelona: Ariel.
Andreo, J., & Provencio, L. (2006). Del Caribe al Pacífico: las grandes conquistas. In J. B. Amores (Ed.), *Historia de América* (pp. 215–259). Barcelona: Ariel.
Arjona, M. (1973). *Historia de América: en cuadros esquemáticos*. Madrid: E.P.E.S.A.
Azkarate, A. (2010). Archeologia dell'architettura in Spagna. *Archeologia dell'Architettura, XV*, 15–26.
Azkarate, A. (2011). Repensando los márgenes circumpirenaicos-occidentales durante los siglos VI y VII d.c.. In E. Baquedano (Ed.), *711. Arqueología e Historia entre dos mundos* (Vol. 1, pp. 241–253). Alcalá de Henares: Museo Arqueológico Regional.
Azkarate, A., & Escribano-Ruiz, S. (2012). La Arqueología de la Colonización española de América. Sobre una historia en construcción, in I Seminario Internacional RII_UC primeros

asentamientos españoles y portugueses en la América central y meridional s. XVI y XVII. Madrid, 20-23 Noviembre de 2012. [In press, in the proceedings of the conference, as: "De la Arqueología Histórica a la Arqueologia del Colonialismo. Una reflexión desde la experiencia europea"].

Azkarate, A., Escribano-Ruiz, S., Sánchez Pinto, I., & Benedet, V. (2012a). Recuperación y puesta en valor del Fuerte Sancti Spiritus, un asentamiento español en la Gran Cuenca del Río de la Plata (Puerto Gaboto, Santa Fe, Argentina). Informes y Trabajos 7. *Excavaciones en el exterior 2010*. pp. 8–21.

Azkarate, A., Escribano-Ruiz, S., Sánchez-Pinto, I., & Benedet, V. (2012b). Recuperación y gestión integral del Fuerte Sancti Spiritus y su entorno (Puerto Gaboto, Santa Fe, Argentina). Balance de actividades y resultados, 2011–2012. Informes y Trabajos 9. *Excavaciones en el exterior 2011*. pp. 42–57.

Azkarate, A., Benedet, V., Escribano-Ruiz, S., & Sanchez-Pinto, I. (2013a). La memoria del pasado, recurso para el presente y el futuro: el caso del proyecto "Fuerte Sancti Spiritus" (Puerto Gaboto, Santa Fe, Argentina). In A. Castillo (Ed.), *Actas del Primer Congreso Internacional de Buenas Prácticas en Patrimonio Mundial: Arqueología. Mahón, Islas Baleares, España, 9–13 Abril de 2012* (pp. 603–612). Madrid: Editora Complutense.

Azkarate, A., Escribano-Ruiz, S., Sánchez-Pinto, I., & Benedet, V. (2013b). First evidences on colonial cultural conflict of Northeast Argentina. Settlement and material culture at Sancti Spiritus, 1527–1529 (Puerto Gaboto, Argentina), in SHA 2013: 46th Annual Conference on Historical and Underwater Archaeology. University of Leicester (UK), January 2013. [To be published as a chapter in A. Teixeira, T. Fraga, J. G. Iñañez (Eds.) Settlement and shipping in the Iberian colonial empires (16–18th centuries)].

Bakewell, P. (1997). *A history of Latin America: empires and sequels 1450–1930*. Malden: Blackwell.

Bethell, L. (1987). *Colonial Spanish America*. Cambridge: Cambridge University Press.

Bianchi, M. (2012). Lo global y lo local en la colonialidad: prácticas cotidianas en la Nueva Población y Fuerte de Floridablanca (San Julián, siglo XVIII). *Intersecciones en Antropología, 13*, 57–70.

Burger, H. (2008). Cabot. In J. Kinsbruner & E. D. Langer (Eds.), *Encyclopedia of Latin American History & Culture* (Vol. 2, pp. 13–14). Detroit: Gale.

Buscaglia, S. (2011). Contacto y colonialismo. Aportes para una discusión crítica en Arqueología Histórica. *Anuario de Arqueología, 3*, 57–76.

Cañedo-Arguelles, T. (2006). Nuevas tendencias historiográficas del americanismo: la historia-problema. *Clío, 171*, 267–282.

Céspedes, G. (2009). *América hispánica (1492–1898)*. Madrid: Marcial Pons.

Cocco, G., Letieri, F., & Frittegotto, G. (2011). El descubrimiento y estudio del Fuerte Sancti Spíritus. *Revista América, 20*, 69–85.

Elliot, J. H. (1987). The Spanish Conquest. In L. M. Bethell (Ed.), *Colonial Spanish America* (pp. 1–58). Cambridge: Cambridge University Press.

Elliot, J. H. (1990). La conquista española y las colonias de América. In Leslie M. Bethell (Ed.), *Historia de América Latina. Parte 1: América Latina Colonial. La América precolombina y la conquista* (pp. 125–169). Barcelona: Crítica.

Foucault, M. (1992). [1970]. *El orden del discurso*. Buenos Aires: Tusquets editores.

Funari, P. P. A. (2007). Teoria e arqueología histórica: a América Latina e o Mundo. *Vestigios, 1*(1), 51–58.

Funari, P. P. A., Jones, S., & Hall, M. (1999). Introduction: archaeology in history. In P. P. A. Funari, S. Jones, & M. Hall (Eds.) *Historical archaeology. Back from the edge* (pp. 1–20). London: Routledge.

Gasco, J. (2005). Spanish colonialism and processes of social change. In G. Stein (Ed.), *The archaeology of Colonial encounters. Comparative perspectives* (pp. 1–129). Santa Fe: SAR Press.

Given, M. (2004). *The archaeology of the colonized*. London: Routledge.

González Ochoa, J. M. (2003). *Quien es quien en la América del descubrimiento (1492–1600)*. Madrid: Acento.

Gosden, C. (2004). *Archaeology and Colonialism. Cultural contact from 5000BC to the present*. Cambridge: Cambridge University Press.

Hernández Sanchez-Barba, M. (2012). *América española. Historia e identidad en un nuevo mundo*. Madrid: Trébede.

Jordan, K. A. (2009). Colonies, colonialism and cultural entanglement: The archaeology of postcolumbian intercultural relations. In T. Majewsji & D. Gaimster (Eds.), *International handbook of historical archaeology* (pp. 31–49). New York: Springer.

Kinsbruner, J., & Langer, E. D. (Eds.). (2008). *Encyclopedia of Latin American History & Culture*. Detroit: Gale.

Lemperiere, A. (2004). El paradigma colonial en la historiografía latinoamericanista. Istor. Revista de Historia Internacional. 19 (Invierno de 2004), pp. 107–128.

Liebmann, M. J. (2008). Introduction: The intersections of Archaeology and postcolonial studies. In M. J. Liebmann & U. Z. Rivzi (Eds.), *Archaeology and the postcolonial critique* (pp. 1–20). Lanham: Altamira Press.

Lockhart, J., & Schwartz, S. B. (1992). *América Latina en la Edad Moderna: una historia de la América española y el Brasil coloniales*. Madrid: Akal.

Lordan, B., & Ward, T. (2008). Explorers and exploration: Spanish America. In J. Kinsbruner & E. D. Langer (Eds.), *Encyclopedia of Latin American History & Culture* (Vol. 3, pp. 161–166). Detroit: Gale.

Lucena, M. (Ed.). (1992). *Historia de Iberoamérica. Tomo II*. Madrid: Cátedra.

Lucena, M. (2005). *Atlas histórico de Latinoamérica*. Madrid: Síntesis.

Muro, F. (1991). El Gobierno de las Indias Españolas. In L. Navarro garcía (Ed.), *Historia de las Américas* (Vol. II, pp. 29–48). Madrid: Alhambra-Longman.

Navarro García, L. (Ed.). (1991a). *Historia de las Américas* (Vol. II). Madrid: Alhambra-Longman.

Navarro García, L. (1991b). Introducción. In L. Navarro garcía (Ed.), *Historia de las Américas* (Vol. II, pp. 1–11). Madrid: Alhambra-Longman.

Paz, G. L. (2008). Argentina: the Colonial Period. In J. Kinsbruner & E. D. Langer (Eds.), *Encyclopedia of Latin American History & Culture* (Vol. 1, pp. 248–256). Detroit: Gale.

Pérez Herrero, P. (2002). *La América Colonial (1492–1763). Política y sociedad*. Madrid: Síntesis.

Ramos, D. (1992). La conquista. In M. Lucena (Ed.), *Historia de Iberoamérica* (Vol. II, pp. 109–199). Madrid: Cátedra.

Rodriguez, I., & Martínez, J. (2009). Introducción. In I. Rodriguez & J. Martínez (Eds.), *Estudios trasatlánticos postcoloniales. I. Narrativas comando/ sistemas mundos: colonialidad/ modernidad* (pp. 7–17). Barcelona: Anthropos.

Silliman, S. W. (2005). Cultural contact or colonialism? Challenges in the archaeology of native North America. *American Antiquity, 70*(1), 55–74.

Silva, H. A. (1991). Las provincias rioplateses. In L. Navarro García (Ed.), *Historia de las Américas* (Vol. II, pp. 519–538). Madrid: Alhambra-Longman.

Spivak, G. C. (1988). Can the subaltern speak? In P. Williams & L. Chrisman (Eds.), *Colonial and postcolonial Theory* (pp. 271–313). Basingstoke: McMillan.

Stein, G. (2005). Introduction. The comparative archaeology of colonial encounters. In G. Stein (Ed.), *The archaeology of Colonial encounters. Comparative perspectives* (pp. 1–31). Santa Fe: SAR Press.

Todorov, T. (2008). [1982, 1987, 2003]. *La conquista de América. El problema del otro*. Buenos Aires: Siglo veintiuno editores.

# Chapter 4
# Technological Transformations: Adaptationist, Relativist, and Economic Models in Mexico and Venezuela

**Enrique Rodríguez-Alegría, Franz Scaramelli and Ana María Navas Méndez**

## 4.1 Introduction

In the past several decades archaeologists have studied technology from a variety of perspectives. Some archaeologists have conceived of technology as an adaptation to the environment. They see technological change as a matter of progress in terms of the efficiency and efficacy of tools. They claim that technology solves practical problems and that it changes as people discover better ways to solve those problems. This perspective has been variously called rationalist (Trigger 1991), the "Standard View" of technology (Pfaffenberger 1992), evolutionary (Neff 2001), a "practical reason" perspective (Dobres 2010, p. 104), and associated with Darwinian theories of evolution (e.g., Loney 2000, 2001; Neff 2001; Ramenofsky 1998).

Other archaeologists have emphasized that technology is a cultural and social construct rather than a mere means of adapting to the environment. This view emphasizes that efficiency is defined culturally, and that techniques and technology are shaped strongly by both material and non-technical considerations, including symbolic, political, economic factors, and a broad variety of others that are not clearly related to efficiency or progress, such as gender (Dobres 2000, 2001; Lemonnier 2002a; Loney 2000, 2001). This perspective is quite varied (Killick 2004) and it has been dubbed romantic (Trigger 1991), constructivist (Dobres 2001; Killick 2004), a "cultural reason" perspective (Dobres 2010, p. 106) and contextual (Loney 2000),

E. Rodríguez-Alegría (✉)
Department of Anthropology, University of Texas, 2201 Speedway C3200, Austin,
Texas 78712, USA
e-mail: chanfle@austin.utexas.edu

F. Scaramelli
42 Atlantic Circle. Apt. 203, Pittsburg, California 94565, USA
e-mail: fscarame@gmail.com

A. M. Navas Méndez
Boulevard Raúl Leoni, Calle El Limón, Residencias Canaima, Piso 11, Apartamento 112,
El Cafetal., Caracas, Venezuela
e-mail: tesisanam@gmail.com

© Springer International Publishing Switzerland 2015                                        53
P. P. A. Funari, M. X. Senatore (eds.), *Archaeology of Culture Contact and Colonialism
in Spanish and Portuguese America,* DOI 10.1007/978-3-319-08069-7_4

and has been associated with the literature on science, technology, and society studies (STS), among other fields and lines of inquiry (Dobres 2000, 2010).

Some archaeologists have begun to transcend the divide between studies that emphasize the material and the social and symbolic aspects of technology (Bayman 2009, pp. 127–157). In part, they see this debate as the result of dichotomies that have structured anthropological thought since the inception of the discipline, such as "culture: nature, symbolic meaning: utilitarian making, style: function," and others (Dobres 2001, p. 47; papers in Lemonnier 2002b). Pierre Lemonnier has argued that the reaction against evolutionary perspectives has tended "to reduce the study of material culture to its symbolic aspects" and that it is necessary to consider the physical aspects of material culture as well as the social and symbolic ones (Lemonnier 2002a, p. 11). Even as archaeologists disagree about many aspects of technological change, there are indications that it is possible to reach a middle ground between studies that emphasize adaptation and studies that emphasize cultural reason.

In this chapter, we foreground a different perspective that is rarely emphasized by archaeologists studying technological change, regardless of their main theoretical inclinations: the economic aspects of technology. We recognize the need to keep in mind the physical aspects of technology as well as the socially constructed definitions of efficiency. Given that tool use, techniques, symbolism, and efficiency have been emphasized in previous archaeological studies of technology, our goal is to draw attention to the economic context in which materials become available to makers and users of tools, in which people manage labor, and in which people have differential access to the products that result from the use of one technology or another. Examining the economic aspects of technological change can advance our understanding of technological change in the past.

To illustrate our main points we present a comparison between aspects of technological change in two regions: central Mexico and southern Venezuela (Fig. 4.1). In both regions, European colonizers and traders introduced technologies—specifically

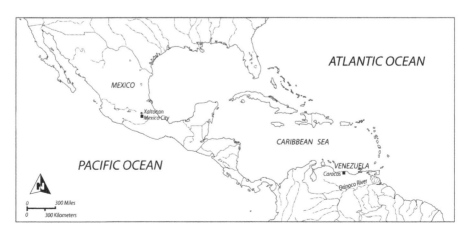

**Fig. 4.1** Map showing the regions discussed in this chapter.

metals for cutting and other utilitarian functions—that were largely foreign to indigenous peoples. Locals then incorporated the new technologies into their own
systems of production and exchange. In spite of these similarities, the two cases
provide important contrasts. Briefly, indigenous people in central Mexico formed
part of the Aztec empire, a highly stratified and politically and economically unified
society. Their exchange systems were partly based on tribute extraction by Aztec
elites, and partly on a complex commercial market system. Tribute extraction and
market exchange continued, albeit transformed, into the colonial period. In contrast,
indigenous people in the tropical lowlands of Venezuela lived in a highly decentralized political system. Status and power were less permanent than in the Aztec case.
Soon after contact with Europeans, these people developed strategies for obtaining
status that depended partly on their ability to exchange goods, on their participation
in ritualized exchange, and on warfare. These two contrasting examples help us see
different ways in which economic factors are involved in technological change.

## 4.2   Central Mexico

The first case study takes place in the Basin of Mexico, the seat of the Aztec empire.
After the conquest of 1521, Spanish colonizers introduced a broad range of technologies into central Mexico, including the use of draft animals, the plow, the wheel,
mills, lead glazing for pottery, and many others (Florescano and García Acosta
2004). The technological drama (sensu Pfaffenberger 2002) that we present here is
that of the introduction of steel cutting tools, including knives, swords, scissors, as
well as nails, and other artifacts. Scholars have had an interest in the introduction of
metal cutting tools by Europeans in colonial contexts, in part because it represents
a meeting of what we conceptualize, correctly or not, as two technological eras:
the Stone Age, represented by indigenous technologies mostly based on the use of
chipped stone tools for cutting and ground stone tools, and the Iron Age, represented
by European colonizers and their steel swords, knives, and other metal tools (e.g.,
Cobb 2003; Rodríguez-Alegría 2008a, b).

Before the Spanish conquered the Aztecs in 1521, indigenous people in
Mesoamerica made objects out of metal, especially copper, copper alloys, silver,
and gold. Production of metal objects was decentralized and none of the varied
polities in the region controlled metallurgy. Until 1200–1300 CE, metallurgy was
confined mostly to the West Mexican region due to the abundance of mineral ores in
the area, but later it spread to other regions as well. Archaeological evidence shows
that people mined ores in hundreds of places and that production was organized in
a wide variety of ways (Hosler 2003, p. 170). Most metal objects in pre-Hispanic
Mexico were not what we consider utilitarian. People fashioned metals into bells
and other objects of display (beads, jewelry, symbolic axes), and axe-money, but did
not produce swords, knives, or cutting tools (Hosler 1994, 2003).

Indigenous people in Mexico satisfied their cutting needs mostly with chipped-
stone tools. Among the different available materials, obsidian was the most widely

**Fig. 4.2** Obsidian artifacts from colonial Xaltocan. From *left* to *right*: informal scraper, blade, prismatic blade, exhausted core.

utilized stone for cutting in Central Mexico. Flakes, blades, scrapers, and projectile points make up the bulk of the chipped-stone tools used in Aztec households (Fig. 4.2), although artifacts also include a variety of ritual and sumptuary objects (Clark 1989; Millhauser 2005; Pastrana 1998, pp. 85–140; Saunders 2001). Flaked obsidian produces extremely sharp edges, which makes it useful in eye, heart, and lung surgery even in modern times (Hernández 1959, p. 407; Schwartz 1981), and made it an effective material for weaponry and everyday needs in the Aztec world. Spanish colonizers admired the sharpness of obsidian, and sometimes requested it for their own use (Clark 1989; Sahagún 1963, p. 223; Saunders 2001). From a strictly utilitarian point of view, obsidian tools satisfied the needs of indigenous people very well, and they were not considered inferior when compared with the steel knives of the Spanish.

Obsidian was also important for symbolic and cosmological purposes. It was associated with Tezcatlipoca, an Aztec deity who was often portrayed with a smoking obsidian mirror, which, in turn, was a metaphor for his power to rule (Saunders 2001, p. 222). Obsidian featured prominently in descriptions of the cosmos, especially in the characterization of the underworld as a place full of obsidian knives (Saunders 2001). Historical sources claim that commoners placed a piece of green obsidian in the mouth of decedents upon burial to animate their bodies in the afterlife (López Austin 1980, p. 373). Its shiny quality and color, often green, made it an important symbolic object in central Mexico. Saunders provides a thoughtful examination of the symbolism of obsidian in the Aztec and colonial worlds (Saunders 2001).

These initial considerations show that obsidian was both efficient from a narrowly utilitarian point of view (as the raw material for cutting and scraping tools), as well as symbolically rich. The economic aspects of obsidian, however, emerge as important in mediating technological changes before and after the Spanish conquest. Two principal factors make obsidian worth examining from an economic perspective. First, it was "the most widely circulated non-perishable good in Mesoamerica" (Braswell 2003, p. 131; Pastrana 1998, p. 22). The analysis of patterns of obsidian exchange through time offers insight into issues of availability of this resource and how people's access to it affected technological change. Second, obsidian tool production could take place in different settings and it could be organized in different ways. Historical sources mention obsidian tool producers who made and sold blades and a range of tools in marketplaces (Clark 1989). Archaeological evidence, on the other hand, has shown that indigenous people had a complex mining industry for the procurement of obsidian (Pastrana 1998), and that people also made stone tools in household contexts and workshops (e.g., Brumfiel 1980; Charlton et al. 1991; Millhauser 2005; Nichols 2004). The varied contexts of tool production could change through time depending on whether mining, tool production, and exchange were controlled by the state, and whether people focused their efforts on other economic pursuits (other than obsidian tool production). Thus, examining production of obsidian tools through time can help understand how technological change and continuity were experienced, and how political and economic processes affected tool production.

Archaeological and ethno–historical research in Xaltocan, a site located approximately 35 km north of Mexico City, has shown that chipped-stone technologies changed through time according to the conditions of domination in the town. Briefly, when Xaltocan was an independent town, beginning around 900 CE, locals enjoyed access to obsidian and they made their own tools from obsidian cores. Xaltocan waged a lengthy war against neighboring Acolhua polities, and lost the war in 1395. The Aztecs subsequently conquered Xaltocan in 1428. In archaeological contexts associated with the time period under Aztec domination, there is little or no evidence of local obsidian tool production in Xaltocan. Instead, the evidence indicates that people were likely obtaining finished tools, mostly prismatic blades, scrapers, and bifacial tools, rather than making them locally (Brumfiel and Hodge 1996; Millhauser 2005). After the Spanish conquest of 1521, the evidence indicates that the people of Xaltocan resumed production of obsidian tools locally, rather than abandoning the use of obsidian altogether (Rodríguez-Alegría 2008a, b). Other scholars have also shown that the use of obsidian continued into the colonial period in Mexico, even after the Spanish introduced steel knives (Cressey 1984; Pastrana 1998; Pastrana and Fournier 1998). Further, preliminary chemical characterization data show that the sources of obsidian under Aztec domination in Xaltocan include only Pachuca and Otumba. In the colonial period, Pachuca and Otumba are still the main sources, but they also include Ucareo, Zacualtipan, and Oyameles-Zaragoza.

The wider range of sources of obsidian in the colonial period suggests that there was an increase in access to raw materials after the fall of the Aztec empire (Millhauser et al. 2011).

The data from Xaltocan are consistent with changes that would be expected if the Aztecs controlled access to obsidian sources and finished products. In periods when Xaltocan was independent and the Aztec empire had not established control over obsidian sources, the people of Xaltocan enjoyed access to obsidian, and produced and used tools independent of state control. When the Aztecs expanded their empire in the fifteenth century, they established control over the most important source of obsidian in Pachuca (Pastrana 1998). During this period, the people of Xaltocan had to obtain finished obsidian tools and apparently could not make their own tools, probably due to a control over production and distribution by the Aztecs. After the Spanish conquest, when the Aztec empire no longer limited access to the obsidian mines in Pachuca, the people of Xaltocan once again obtained access to obsidian raw materials and renewed local production of obsidian tools. Renewed access to raw materials and finished tools stimulated the continuation and renewal of lithic technologies in Xaltocan.

Archaeological contexts have produced little or no evidence of the adoption of metals for cutting tools in Xaltocan during the colonial period. Instead, the data suggest that metals were adopted mostly in the form of religious medals (Fig. 4.3) and nails for construction or for horseshoes. Historical data suggest that indigenous

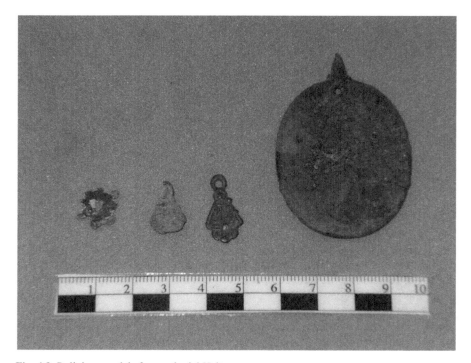

**Fig. 4.3** Religious medals from colonial Xaltocan.

people adopted knives and swords mostly as objects of display, rather than as utilitarian tools in the early colonial period (Rodríguez-Alegría 2010). The pattern of adoption of metals for display is consistent with patterns of use of metals in the pre-Hispanic era discussed above. Other rural sites in central Mexico have not produced significant amounts of metal artifacts either (Charlton et al. 2005). Spanish colonizers were more interested in controlling the availability of metals and metal tools than they were in controlling the availability of obsidian. They were interested in silver for its commercial value, and in controlling knives and swords for their commercial value and use as weaponry. Thus, restrictions on access to raw materials and finished tools of metal technologies conspired with renewed access to the raw materials and tools of lithic technologies.

Alejandro Pastrana (1998) provides a compelling argument to explain how chipped-stone tool technology in central Mexico served to support, rather than compete with metal mining among Spaniards. Spanish colonizers were interested in the rich silver deposits in Mexico. They relied on indigenous labor and mining technologies to extract silver and other metals. Indigenous miners built scaffolds and ladders using rope and leather thongs. They used obsidian tools to obtain vegetal fibers for the rope, to scrape animal hides for thongs and to make containers for the metals they mined. The Spanish even built a Franciscan chapel near the obsidian mines in Pachuca, in part to ensure the conversion and indoctrination of indigenous miners and to guarantee continuity in indigenous technologies that supported the colonizers' hunger for metals (Pastrana 1998, pp. 195–198). Pastrana's research provides a dramatic example in which the commercial interests of Spanish colonizers supported the continuity of indigenous technologies in colonial Mexico.

## 4.3 Economic Factors Affecting Technology Change in the Lowlands of the Orinoco

In this section, we describe the spread of steel technologies as they contributed to the colonial transformations undergone by the indigenous societies of the Middle Orinoco, Venezuela. We make an effort to identify the factors affecting the implementation of steel tools during the initial phase of the encounter (1530–1680) and the relations of dependency and domination that characterized the colonial period (1680–1767), brought about, in part, by the introduction of these tools. A focus on the material and symbolic aspects of the encounter in the Orinoco, as evidenced in archaeological and documentary sources, permits us to examine a broad range of economic dynamics and strategies of action, including varied forms of exchange aimed at increasing native authority and status. In the Orinoco, substantial technological changes took place and variations occurred over space and time. This study offers insights into unforeseen challenges facing indigenous societies when exposed to foreign technologies and goods within the constraints and possibilities of pre-existing relationships of authority and cosmological space.

During the first part of the sixteenth century (1502–1503), European contact in northern South America was limited and circumscribed to the Islands and the

Paria Peninsula on the northeast coast of what is today Venezuela (Romero et al. 1999, pp. 59–64). The early colonial encounter was aimed at establishing a foothold on the coast, to make contact with the local populations, and to exploit slaves for pearl fishing. Although indigenous responses were highly variable, certain Arawak populations initially established friendly relationships with the Spanish. During the early times of the pearl industry, these coastal Indians provided the Spanish with cassava and labor in return for steel tools and possibly weapons (Boomert 1984, pp. 123–188; Lucena Giraldo 1991; Whitehead 1988). Having exhausted their hopes of finding gold or silver and having depleted the pearl fisheries on the nearby islands, European powers became increasingly interested in longer term economic enterprises, such as tobacco and sugar plantations, and the development of certain native products such as hard woods, spices, dyes, gums, and cotton (see Boomert 1984; Whitehead 1988). Slave raids, mistreatment, and exploitation rapidly contributed to the deterioration of the Arawak's attitude toward the Spanish.

By this time, the Spanish were not the only European nation interested in establishing a foothold on the Northeastern Coast. While the Spanish encomienda policy was eroding Spanish/Arawak relations, the Dutch had begun to establish prosperous colonies south of the Essequibo River and were initiating successful trade relations with the Caribs. The Dutch seem to have had a very different attitude toward the indigenous populations. In contrast to the mission and encomienda systems implemented by the Spanish, the Dutch established a system of trading posts primarily conceived to encourage trade in indigenous products such as dyes, tobacco, cotton, hammocks, oils, gums, and fibers, in return for European goods (Whitehead 1988). In order to take advantage of these commercial opportunities, indigenous agents relocated themselves closer to the posts in order to obtain merchandise subsequently used to exchange for other Native products and indigenous slaves further inland. The Dutch appear to have allowed full liberty to the indigenous populations that approached them. In the absence of the constraints imposed by the Spanish in the form of forced labor, tribute, and religious indoctrination, these trading posts promoted Dutch/Carib alliances in the Lower Orinoco that, at times, took the form of violent attacks against the Spanish settlements in the area (Lucena Giraldo 1991).

During the seventeenth century, the consolidation of the Dutch/Carib alliance resulted in the near total monopolization of trade in the Lower Orinoco. This represented a major factor in the spread of technological change among indigenous groups of the whole Guiana Region. The Dutch/Carib alliance provided the Caribs with axes, knives, machetes, shotguns, glass beads, and other desired goods. In return, the Caribs furnished the Dutch with native products, slaves, and services. The Carib groups had initially gained advantage from their proximity to the Dutch colonies, but their trade relations and political influence soon expanded throughout the Lower and Middle Orinoco and beyond. As a result, while the Arawak were forced to move inland to avoid Spanish slave raids, the Carib experienced a spectacular expansion throughout the Orinoco, which lasted for almost 150 years (Gilij 1987; Gumilla 1944; Lucena Giraldo 1991; Rey Fajardo 1974, p. 16; Vega 1974, pp. 3–149).

In the short run, this process involved important innovations in the nature of native leadership. Some types of leadership clearly emerged after contact as a result of a marked increase in warfare and trade. Long distance trade and warfare played a crucial role in the process of status achievement, often involving collective feasts and ritual ceremonies followed by purported cannibalistic activities. This initial period of cultural enhancement, or "develop man" (Sahlins 1992, p. 17–18)[1], promoted the Carib trading expeditions that ranged from the Antilles to the North Coast, and as far as the Guiana Highlands and the Western Llanos of Venezuela and Colombia. These expeditions increased Carib influence throughout the Orinoco, as manifested, among other ways, in the widespread exchange of steel cutting technologies and weapons (Humboldt 1985; Lucena Giraldo 1991).

Certainly the marked increase in warfare and trade, following the Carib alliance with the Dutch, deeply disturbed the whole political economy in the Orinoco. Between 1595 and 1730, the river was subjected to constant raids on the part of Amerindians and rival Europeans (Whitehead 1988, p. 28). Unwilling to lose their economic and political prosperity gained through the monopolization of trade in the Lower Orinoco, the Carib instigated armed resistance and rebellion against the Spanish attempts to colonize the Middle Orinoco. The Carib were also active in the slave trade in the Western Llanos, and the Otomaco and other groups were forming alliances to resist their attacks. The Caribs successfully stayed off the Jesuit attempts to expand their mission base out of the Colombian Llanos throughout the seventeenth century. The four missions that were established in the 1680s were attacked and burnt, and the missionaries killed (Rey Fajardo 1974, p. 154). By the eighteenth century, not many Indians remained on the banks of the Orinoco, having retreated to the hinterland (Gilij 1987, p. 59). When the Jesuits finally gained a foothold, it was due to a concerted military effort to block the Carib access to the Middle Orinoco. Gumilla (1944) described the importance of the Fortín de San Javier de Marimarota, located at a strategic position on the mouth of the Parguaza River, in order to fend off the frequent Carib incursions against the Mapoyo and the Sáliva communities located along the Lower Parguaza River. In the face of this blockade, the Caribs created new trade routes that took them to distant areas of the Upper Orinoco, where they also encountered armed resistance from other powerful Amerindian groups such as the Caverre and the Guipuinave (Gilij 1987; Gumilla 1944).

Over a century of entrepreneurship, territorial increase, and successful opposition to Spanish colonization, the Carib had developed an extended network of marital alliances, trade, and slave raiding. The expansion of Carib slaving brought about a considerable economic inflation across the Orinoco and new standards of value (Gumilla 1944 II, p. 90). By Gumilla's time in the early eighteenth century, the going price for a captive slave obtained by local trade partners for the Carib traders was high [2](Fig. 4.4). To be sure, the "commodity phase" (Appadurai 1986; Kopytoff

---

[1] This process is another example of what Marshall Sahlins has so aptly called "the economics of develop-man," in which foreign trade goods are appropriated into native categories of value with important consequences both in the development of commerce as well as in the sociocultural organization of the native populations. According to Sahlins, "…developman is realized in political organization of unprecedented scale and centralization: the evolution of tribal groupings and confederacies, and the emergence of highly chiefly authorities" (1992: 17–18).

[2] "…box with a key, within which were ten axes, ten machetes, ten knives, ten bundles of strands of beads, a silver pin for the guayuco (men's loin cloth), a mirror for face painting as is their habit, a pair of scissors to cut their hair: all of this is inside the box, besides which they should be paid

**Fig. 4.4** Carib chief distributing European trade goods (Source: Gilij 1987 II: 63).

1986, pp. 64–91)—of persons and goods—was the product of historical events as well as the contingent and open-ended nature of colonialism. To understand it, this process must be examined in the specific cultural context, economic institutions, and temporality of the give and take. In fact, the incorporation of desired items into a highly decentralized political system provoked multiple consequential responses in the face of colonial intervention.

One fascinating example of the varied strategies and reactions of indigenous societies comes from the inland groups of the Upper Orinoco, where native responses to colonial advance have been documented through the analysis of oral history. Between 1953 and 1987, Marc de Civrieux compiled one of the most complete indigenous mythical cycles ever recorded in the area: Watunna (Civrieux 1980, pp. 49–58). With reference to the sacred history of the Ye'kuana (Makiritare) people, a large Carib-speaking group inhabiting the Upper Orinoco, Upper Caura, and the Ventuari Rivers, this cycle is striking not only for its references to the perceived mythical origin of the group but particularly because of its detailed accounts concerning indigenous perceptions of the encounter and the nature of the newly introduced technologies including steel. Defying any simplistic Eurocentric explanation, Watunna makes explicit references to the origin of the Europeans and their technologies as products of celestial powers, and the effects of the desire for

a shotgun, powder and shot, a bottle of firewater, and other sundries such as needles, pins, hooks, etc..." Joseph Gumilla, El Orinoco Ilustrado 1944: II: 90 (translation by K. Scaramelli). See also Felipe Salvador Gilij, Ensayo de Historia Americana 1987: II: 62–63.

European goods on their migrations and relations with other indigenous groups and peoples. As recounted in a series of narratives called the Waities, the migration of the Ye'kuana from the upper Padamo and Cunucunuma rivers to the Ventuari, the Caura, and the Erebato Rivers was the product of new trade possibilities created by the arrival of the Europeans. In 1758, the official border Commission (La Expedición de Límites al Orinoco de 1750–1767) contacted the Ye'kuana while exploring the connection between the Orinoco and the Amazon basin through the Casiquiare River. The encounter initiated a process in which both the Europeans and their material belongings became rapidly incorporated into local schemes of thought. The Ye'kuana considered the Europeans to be a new creation (Iaranavi) of their cultural hero Wanadi and their hard and shiny steel tools began to be perceived as gifts sent from Heaven[3]. With the exchange of goods between indigenous and colonial agents, the Ye'kuana allowed the Iaranavi to establish a village in the Orinoco but their mistreatment soon convinced them that the Iaranavi were under the control of Odosha, Wanadi's ancestral enemy, turning them into Fañuru, a new species from which the contemporary Creole are the descendants. With this in mind, the Ye'kuana attacked the Spanish settlements and migrated east to establish new trade relationships. After an initial period of trade with the Makushi, who apparently charged high prices for the European goods they obtained from the Caribs, the Ye'kuana began to track down the Caribs themselves to see where and how they acquired the various goods. This brought the Ye'kuana into direct contact with the Hurunko (Dutch), Wanadi's preferred people, with whom they initiated an enduring trading relationship.

In practice, the myth illustrates how the introduction of European goods, especially steel tools, produced dramatic transformations in societies that were not even in frequent or direct contact with the Europeans. Among these, settlement patterns, inter-ethnic warfare, and trade were all deeply affected by the desire for these goods. Following their own structures for the classification of people, Watunna reveals aspects of native perception and positioning in relation to the newcomers and their descendents. European items, particularly iron tools, were incorporated into an already existing indigenous system of exchange that placed high value on hard, sharp, and shiny objects (Boomert 1984; Howard 2000; Myers 1977; Scaramelli and Tarble 2005; Whitehead 1990). And the myth also testifies to the dramatic expansion of trade, a practice that became an important source of status among most Amerindian societies in post-contact times. Although the Watunna cycle centers on the oral history of the Ye'kuana, the myth brings to light a variety of processes and transformations that actually serves as a starting point to explore the initial nature of the technological change among the indigenous societies of the Middle Orinoco.

The Middle Orinoco region, in particular, provides multiple examples for the analysis of contact in the face of the missionary presence. In this area the foraging groups were apparently able to subsist through complex "symbiotic" relations

---

[3] Elements of the Orinoco cosmovision, as constructed in different interconnected layers, are widespread in local religious systems, as it has been discussed elsewhere (Tarble and Scaramelli 1999: 27).

that have been characterized as a combined strategy of hunting and gathering and trading with the agricultural populations that were living on more productive lands. At the same time, the agricultural groups often depended on foragers and fishing specialists to obtain game, fish, and wild forest products (Morey 1976, p. 43). As a result, indigenous groups were part of extensive social and commercial networks with people inhabiting geographically distant areas of the Llanos, the Northern and Eastern Coast, the Guayana Highlands, and the Amazon Lowlands (Arvelo-Jiménez and Biord 1994; Coppens 1971, pp. 28–59; Mansutti-Rodríguez 1986, pp. 3–75; Morey and Morey 1973, pp. 229–46; Thomas 1972, pp. 3–37). Among other things, the multiplicity of responses to contact altered, or were the product themselves, of intensified "traditional" patterns of social relations, particularly interethnic relations in the form of trade. That is why the economic factor is so important to the understanding of technological change: the introduction of foreign technologies—embedded with local meanings—into the existing web of interaction produced a sort of disruptive enhancement of the inter-tribal system itself. As far as it can be surmised from historical references, this process contributed to destabilize preexisting relations of power and tended to favor the groups that sought alliance with the Dutch and Portuguese agents engaged in the exchange of goods and slaves.

During the seventeenth century some indigenous factions found themselves in full control of commerce in foreign items, tools, and weapons, provoking profound effects in the Upper and Middle Orinoco, where slave raiding and warfare were rampant (Vega 1974, pp. 3–149). In this context, the missionaries were constantly thwarted in their colonizing endeavor due to the attacks of the indigenous slave raiders, who wanted no obstacles in their profitable business. They supplied the groups of the region with foreign goods in return for local products and slaves, and protected this monopoly by means of alliances with local groups, threats of retaliation, and attacks on colonial and indigenous settlements. In this context, some indigenous groups, such as the Caverre, the Otomaco, and the Guipuinave attacked the missionaries as well as the Carib factions. In the meantime, other groups such as the Wóthuha, Pareca, and the Hiwi had different reactions, at different times, toward the colonial advance, sometimes opting for resistance, retreat or piracy (Gilij 1987, p. 68; Gumilla 1944, p. 68).

Following almost two centuries of denied access to the Upper Orinoco, the Spanish increasingly recognized the potential value of the Middle Orinoco as a strategic fluvial connection between the Eastern highlands of New Granada and the Atlantic coast. The area was considered an important source of coveted tropical products, both wild and cultivated. Moreover, the Spanish Crown feared it would lose control of this crucial axis of communication and potential source of economic benefit and subsequently launched a new program for colonizing the region. This time the colonizing agents were members of different religious orders, including the Capuchins, the Franciscan Observantes and, in the Middle and Upper Orinoco, the Jesuits (Rey Fajardo 1974, pp. 3–149, 154). The missionaries dedicated themselves to the foundation of missions and towns, the consolidation of European presence in the area, and the incorporation of indigenous people into a 'civilized' European way of life, by means of "conversion" to Catholicism. Conversion, however, was but a part of the civilizing project, albeit one with explicit ideological intentions. Trade was a key mechanism that served to initiate and routinize the articulation between the colonizers and the Native peoples who were very much open to trade from the beginning of the colonial encounter. Exercising various modes of decision-making regarding cultural elements, strategies, and political stance, some groups found themselves under mission protection, taking advantage of new opportunities for trade.

Between 1731 and 1767, the Jesuits were able to capitalize on the politically unstable situation, making themselves the suppliers of iron tools and offering protection against the slave-traders. This combined strategy simultaneously converted local groups into a condition of relative dependence on the settlers, either as trade partners or as protectors of the Indians. This method also allowed the missionaries to establish a more permanent relationship with the indigenous populations inhabiting the area, particularly among those who decided to approach the missions on a more regular basis. The protection offered by the missionaries was probably very limited since they already had a hard time protecting themselves. But the offering of tools and other exotic goods was a key means of attraction that allowed the missionaries to create cleavages in the relations among local indigenous groups, and to gain some acceptance among various indigenous factions[4]. The missionaries took advantage of this combination of interests and provided tools and goods as enticement to settlement in the missions and, later, to obtain profits on native production in the form of trade.

Foreign technologies were appropriated by the indigenous societies according to their own interests and forms of action. This appropriation resulted in a generalized process of cultural enhancement facilitated by the availability of trade goods and the political power derived from their circulation without the mediation of intermediaries. However, technological change in the Orinoco was also the product of a particular economic system. Filipo Salvatore Gilij (1987), a Jesuit missionary who spent 17 years in the Middle Orinoco, provides invaluable insights into an aspect of native political economies that contrasts sharply with the one the missionaries were trying to enforce. According to Gilij, the indigenous peoples were very enthusiastic in establishing trade relations with the missionaries. For Gilij, "all the people of Orinoco, some more and some less, hunt and fish; in the same way, all of them partake in trade. Moreover, there is nothing they like more than to acquire things through trade" (Gilij 1987 II, p. 266). The indigenous peoples were especially interested in getting a variety of foreign artifacts such as glass beads, scissors, knives, mirrors, cloth, machetes, and axes in exchange for native products and exotic pets (Gilij 1987 II, p. 266).

It is particularly interesting to note that in the context of the mission, apparently these transactions did not have the explicit purpose of "enriching" the native agents (in the sense of accumulation or maximization). The exchange was more of a social act, a gift involving reciprocity that mobilized social relations, values, or status.

---

[4] On this matter, Gilij comments: "…[the natives accept] an axe, a needle, a pin, or other small gifts offered by the missionaries….with the hope of escaping again to the forest as soon as they receive the gifts. Effectively so, after a month or so among the Christians, some escape and others stay…" Gilij (1987) II: 100.

Although there was a marked emphasis on the circulation of goods, the accumulation of material wealth was not the point of native political economies. In fact, Gilij refers to the process of exchange as a "borrowing" of goods. The borrowing was so common that the missionary became frustrated, talking about this practice as if it were a simple "permutation" of goods; that is, objects circulating among people that never really became the property of anyone—in the way that the missionary was apparently trying to impose (Gilij 1987). Rather, these were all "gift exchange societies" for whom value production was not simply the result of the accumulation of valuables but the product of people's abilities to circulate them[5]. Initial acceptance of these gifts by the natives was seemingly configured by standing structures that once served to connect many autonomous societies into larger systems of interaction. In contrast to other indigenous groups of the Amazon (Viveiros De Castro 1998, pp. 469–488), that seem to place less value on the exchange of material goods, among the indigenous societies of the Middle Orinoco trade was the very foundation of the 'social system' (Scaramelli 2005).

This circulation had the potential to establish or reaffirm social relations, created and maintained through different acts of sociability to extend the "social self" through hospitality, solidarity, generosity, exchange of marriage partners, invitations to intertribal feasting and ceremonies (Turner 1977, 1984). With relatively unrestricted access to resources and means of production, the members of the indigenous communities, including elders, women, and children, were in the position to satisfy their "economic" needs with relative success. As a result, there was very little economic status differentiation, as there was very little individual interest in the accumulation of material wealth (see also Leeds 1960, p. 3; Petrullo 1939). Moreover, political power and leadership was acquired through demonstration of wisdom in speech and practice, trade and warfare, and, particularly, through the production of surplus for redistribution and display (Scaramelli and Tarble 2005, pp. 149–150). In most groups, this surplus depended on the ability of a man to attract a number of wives and in-laws, and therefore to expand the productive potential of the household (Rivière 1983–84). Shamanic and curative knowledge, often possessed by the native headman, provided an alternative way to obtain status and power. In either case, elder males had an advantage over other members of the society in terms of political power, at least for certain forms of leadership.

By offering protection and foreign goods, the Jesuit missionaries were able to attract various native groups from the Middle Orinoco and the Western Llanos, including factions of the Tamanako, Mapoyo, Otomaco, Achagua, Pumé, and Sáliva. This process contributed to the foundation of several missions, among them Nuestra Señora de los Angeles de Pararuma (1733–1767), La Urbana (1733), Carichana (1680–1767) and La Encaramada (1745).

---

[5] For Gilij, the "…custom of exchanging household objects, tools, or even the same clothes they are wearing, never ends. Even those who have grown old in the reductions often make trips to trade the aforementioned things to distant populations; they even go, in spite of the disapproval of the missionary, to the neighboring gentile nations. Rare are those reduced Indians who do not have some friend in the forests who is happy to trade with him" Gilij (1987) pp (translated by Kay Scaramelli).

The foundation and development of the mission system played a key role in the history of technology, especially as revealed in the transition between lithic and metal technologies. The Middle Orinoco region offers a limited assemblage of raw materials for stone tool technology. Chert, obsidian and flint are virtually unknown in the region. Fine-grained rock, such as jasper, was only available through long-distance trade in pre-Colonial times. Quartz, quartzite, and a local fine-grained greenstone were among the more popular raw materials for manufactured tools, whereas pebbles and cobbles were used for multiple purposes as casual artifacts.

A significant shift in tool production can be inferred when we compare the artifact assemblages from pre- and post-contact sites (Gil 2003). The former are characterized by awls, unifacial scrapers, and knives made of crystalline quartz. A few quartz arrowheads have been reported for the area. Fine-grained quartzite was also used to make knives, scrapers, and blades. Cobbles and pebbles, found in riverbeds, were employed as polishing stones, grinding stones, hammer stones, and as anvils for cracking nuts. Beads, spindle whorls, and other decorative objects were made from lignite and jasper. The local coarse-grained granite was used for metates, apparently employed to grind maize. Small flakes of chalcedony and quartzite may have been used in the manufacture of graters to process manioc. Polished celts made of greenstone are frequent in the pre-Hispanic toolkit. Following contact, many of these artifacts continue to appear in the register for the Early and Late Colonial periods, Significantly, manos and metates, unifacial retouched flakes, and nutting stones are common in the Early Colonial period, suggesting that indigenous subsistence practices continued with very few changes. The flakes were likely used to make wooden artifacts and to process vegetal fiber for baskets and cordage. At the same time, polished celts become scarce, while a wide variety of hand wrought and industrial metal tools such as machetes and axes were adopted for the clearing of forests and other agricultural activities. Ethnographic reports indicate that some indigenous groups curated celts as ceremonial objects, even after the adoption of metal axes (Koch-Grünberg in Gil, p. 183). Metal harpoon points, lance points, fishhooks, knives, and machetes are rapidly incorporated into the archaeological record, substituting or complementing stone, bone, or wood equivalents (Gil 2003; Figs. 4.5, and 4.6). By the onset of the Republican period, manos and metates disappear, and small lithic flakes used for manioc graters increase in frequency. Eventually, graters made by punching holes in flattened large cans replace the stone graters. This evidence, along with the increase in ceramic griddles, has been interpreted as a shift in emphasis from maize cultivation to the production of manioc and its byproducts (Tarble de Scaramelli and Scaramelli 2012).

Several types of lithic artifacts appear in the archaeological record following contact, related to the introduction of new technology. Chert gunflints, often showing signs of heavy wear and retouch, are found in mission contexts, but not in contemporary outlying indigenous sites. This may indicate the restricted use of firearms. Stones used to hone metal tools also enter the record with the appearance of metal knives, axes and machetes. At the same time, glass beads and metal coins, perforated to use as pendants, replace the manufacture of stone beads.

At Pararuma, our archaeological investigations permitted the location of a very active blacksmith shop and foundry (Scaramelli 2005). Metal items collected in the

**Fig. 4.5** Fishhooks recovered from the remains of the Jesuit mission of Nuestra Señora de los Angeles de Pararuma (1734–1767).

**Fig. 4.6** Harpoons made in the Jesuit mission of Pararuma (1734–1767).

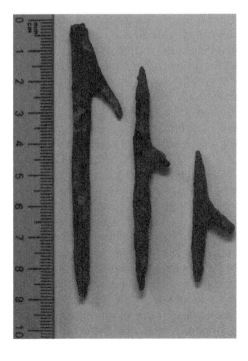

mission include a wide variety of hand wrought and industrial artifacts made out of iron, lead, silver, and copper. Metallurgical analysis of the archaeological evidence allowed us to identify the nature of metal production at the mission (Navas 2012). At the blacksmith shop, the artifacts were manufactured using the direct method of iron production in which the ore is subjected to temperatures between 600 and 1200 °C to release the metal oxides. Iron was obtained as sponge with low carbon content and impurities therein (Navas 2012). The operational sequence of iron production in the Middle Orinoco consisted of two main stages. The first stage was the bloom-smithing process or metal production. The second stage is the forging process, which involves removal of impurities and the formation of bars and artifacts. Metallurgical experts and neophytes worked cooperatively during the operating sequence of iron production. The colonists brought with them the specialized knowledge to transform iron ore to metal; they knew the characteristics of the raw material and fuel, the temperature of the furnace, and the combustion time required. For their part, the natives knew the territory and the mineral and vegetable sources appropriate for the productive process (Navas 2012).

However, despite the relative value of metal artifacts, local communities did not reproduce metallurgical knowledge practiced at the missions. It could be that metallurgical specialists did not transmit the entire operational sequence to the neophytes, especially the knowledge necessary to produce metal. At the same time, local communities apparently preferred to obtain metal goods by trade, rather than learn the metal production process (Navas 2012). When the Jesuits were expelled in 1767, the natives continued to obtain European goods through trade. In the mid-eighteenth century, despite colonial attempts to control and monopolize trade, indigenous agents, brokers, merchants, contrabandists, and free entrepreneurs of diverse origin were circulating along the Orinoco and the Apure river systems, carrying with them merchandise to be offered to the Indians in exchange for local products, including turtle oil, medicines, animal hides, feathers, and pets. These merchants traveled to the region to obtain local products (in exchange for metal tools) and to transport them as far as Angostura, Trinidad, and other emerging markets. The missionaries themselves often depended on these merchants to obtain the food supplies and goods they required in the mission (Vega 1974, pp. 3–149). Although these merchants often charged inflated prices for the merchandise, only goods were used in the exchange with the natives in a barter system. According to Gilij (1987), one could travel throughout the Orinoco using only goods as payment (Gilij 1987, p. 268).

In the context of the mission, the incorporation of metal utensils promoted changes in indigenous social relations of production, and contributed to an important reorientation of labor toward an increasing production of items for exchange, particularly cassava, forest products and game, or the production of similar amounts of agricultural products within a shorter period of time. This process was conducive to an increase in the production of certain cultivated and gathered products and to their commoditization (e.g., cassava and turtle oil) (see Scaramelli and Tarble 2003). The initial native engagement with the missionaries was conducive toward unprecedented forms of communities and economic activities (Scaramelli and Tarble 2005). This restructuring of social and productive relations, introduced by the Jesuits in the early eighteenth century, had a sort of epitomizing effect in native culture history, in the sense that it promoted the selling of native products and labor in return for foreign items and technologies from the outside world. This legacy of the mission persists even while the missions themselves are gone.

In sum, the introduction of foreign technologies in the Orinoco set in motion processes that had profound effects on the indigenous societies of the region, often leading to extinction, submission, or absorption of the neophytes by other groups. Our focus on the intercultural exchange served to illustrate a set of practices showing the clash of different logics of social action and negotiation that were both culturally and historically specific, and the significance of which can only be established in relation to different "regimes of value" (Appadurai 1986) through space and time. Despite the existence of asymmetrical relations of economic and political power, the interaction between the parts cannot be perceived as unidirectional, standardized, and less yet analogous in its aims, purposes, and logics. In order to explore the rationale of the process of interaction in the Orinoco, we have focused on practices and processes that were not necessarily derived from the intentional politics of colonial domination, and that serves to explore the contradictory nature of the interaction between native and colonial agents. Particularly relevant to understand the history of classless societies in the formative period of capitalist global interaction (1730–1800), the case under examination overwhelmingly illustrates strategies of exchange that must be situated and examined in the specific cultural context and rationale of the interaction. To this end we presented examples of the incorporation of certain technologies into native structures of consumption and systems of value, discussing the initial effect of "cultural enhancement," in which native systems of value and status were reinforced and promoted through the involvement in the colonial situation.

It should be noted that colonial strategies designed to create and perpetuate relations of dependency through enticement often articulated with the indigenous strategies intended at enhancing personal status and political power. In both cases, foreign technologies were often the medium through which these different goals were advanced. It must be pointed out, nonetheless, that technological change took place within highly resilient and contradictory structures of economic interaction. These must be treated and analyzed as complex and reflexive processes of multiple clashing strategies for exercising authority. On the one hand, we have recurrent forms of social relationships based on the power of gifts, reciprocity, and constant acts of sociability or social inclusiveness. In this case, power and legitimacy were based on hospitality, kinship, and social action including the ability to create, mobilize, and expand reproductive force. On the other hand, that is, on the side of the colonizers, power was based on the ability to obtain relations of dependency, as well as social and ideological subordination. These aspects are crucial to understand the articulation between local and global structures of culture and power, including the specific mechanisms that contributed to the formation of structures of colonial dependency and domination, and local processes of formation of colonial systems, cultural resilience and defiance.

In this two-fold process, the study of technology and interaction provides insights into different values in action, expectations, and strategies of action concerning material culture, symbolic aspects, social elements, and means of cultural control (Bonfil Batalla 1977, pp. 23–43). In this sense, contrary to conventional assumptions about the growth of capitalism, as a homogenizing cultural process primarily determined at the center of a global economy, what the incorporation of foreign goods into native social life provides are multiple examples of the various ways in which "externalities are indigenized" (Sahlins 1999). As a corollary this study case shows that, in the analysis of technological change, strategy and structure constitute aspects that must be considered simultaneously (Dietler 1998, p. 288; Lightfoot 2004, pp. 380–93; Rodríguez-Alegría 2008a, b; Sahlins 1992, pp. 12–25; Silliman 2001). In the case at hand, the two contributed to a variety of consequences, many of which were absolutely unpredictable from the perspective of the participants.

## 4.4 Comparisons and Conclusion

The processes of technological change in Mexico and Venezuela have some factors in common. In both cases, indigenous people were attracted to metal goods, in part due to their visual properties, specifically, shine. In both regions, indigenous people often used metal goods not just for utilitarian purposes but also for display, whether as decoration for the body or as commodities for exchange. In both regions, indigenous people incorporated metal technologies into their own cultural categories, as has been commonly noted in many colonial contexts.

The processes highlight the markedly different effects that economic variables can have on technological change. In Mexico, we emphasized access to the means of production as a factor that influenced technological change. When indigenous people in Xaltocan had access to obsidian, they used obsidian and made their own tools. They only lost access to obsidian sources and by extension, to production of tools, when the Aztecs controlled obsidian mines and tool production. Once the Spanish conquered the Aztecs and eliminated the direct control over obsidian sources, they resumed production of chipped-stone tools. They even increased the range of sources of obsidian used for tool production, and as access to obsidian increased, they continued using this technology. They adopted the use of metal tools, but often for display, and initially not as a replacement for obsidian. Colonizers may have encouraged the continuation of obsidian tool production because obsidian tools were recognized as sharp, and also because obsidian tools were used to obtain plant fibers and make rope ladders and scaffolds for mining. Given the interest in silver mining among colonizers, they used obsidian as a supporting technology for metal mining. It is interesting that both indigenous people and Spanish colonizers saw the usefulness of obsidian as a tool, and desired metals, whether steel or silver, for their shiny quality.

In Venezuela, the adoption of metal tools was not spurred by simple utilitarian interests either. Although the technology for producing the tools was introduced by the missions, this was not adopted by the Native peoples in the long-term. Instead of wanting to produce metal tools, indigenous people were more interested in trade and exchange, and the prestige this activity brought. Indigenous people obtained machetes, knives, axes, and firearms from European traders, who, in turn, received slaves, local products, and services. The result of the exchange process was not just the adoption of new technologies, but also rather the emergence of new forms of leadership that depended on warfare and trade. Although indigenous people had access to metal tool production, smelting facilities, and techniques of production, as well as instruction in the process of production in the context of the missions, they abandoned metallurgy in favor of exchange. Their economic interests were not in access to production, but rather in exchange, in part for the political gains that resulted from exchange.

Access to the means of production emerges as an important aspect in shaping technological change among indigenous people in central Mexico, but it is not nearly as important in the case of Venezuela. Exchange emerges as an important aspect in Venezuela, but in Mexico, it mostly seems to be a constraint to the adoption of steel tools. This sharp contrast shows the importance of understanding each economic context on its own as well as examining the relationship between economic and political interests and how they relate to the adoption of technology.

In the end, technological change in both regions was far from a simple story of progress and civilization. In both cases, technological change formed part of attempts at obtaining social distinction, and it was an essential aspect of colonial systems of exploitation. In Mexico, colonizers exploited indigenous technologies, mining traditions, and labor in search for metals, especially silver. In Venezuela, trade in metals was an essential ingredient of the slave trade.

Examining economic variables is not enough for understanding technological change. In our attempt to bring attention to the economic aspects of technological change, we have necessarily delved into historical processes that are political, symbolic, and social, and we have also considered utilitarian aspects of tools. But our main point should be clear: economic interests and patterns affected technological change in ways that cannot be explained by efficiency or by symbolic terms alone. Whether due to indigenous attempts at controlling production, to indigenous and colonists' interests in trade, to exploitation of labor, or to people's manipulation of status and the political economy, these examples show that economic variables should be a central part of analysis of technological change in the past.

# References

Appadurai, A. (1986). Introduction: Commodities and the politics of value. In A. Appadurai (Ed.), *The Social Life of Things: Commodities in Cultural Perspective* (pp. 3–63). Cambridge: Cambridge University Press.

Arvelo-Jiménez, N., & Biord, H. (1994). The Impact of Conquest on Contemporary Indigenous Peoples of the Guiana Shield; the System of Orinoco Regional Interdependence. In A. Roosevelt (Ed.), *Amazonian Indians from Prehistory to the Present: Anthropological Perspectives* (pp. 55–78). Tucson: The University of Arizona Press.

Bayman, J. (2009). Technological Change and the Archaeology of Emergent Colonialism in the Kingdom of Hawai'i. *International Journal of Historical Archaeology, 13,* 127–157.

Bonfil Batalla, G. (1987). La Teoría del Control Cultural en el Estudio de los Procesos Étnicos. *Papeles de la Casa Chata, 2*(3), 23–43.

Boomert, A. (1984). The Arawak Indians of Trinidad and Coastal Guiana, ca. 1500–1650. *The Journal of Caribbean History, 19*(2), 123–188.

Braswell, G.E. (2003). Obsidian Exchange Spheres. In M.E. Smith & FF. Berdan (Eds.), *The Postclassic Mesoamerican World* (pp. 131–158). Salt Lake City: University of Utah Press.

Brumfiel, E.M. (1980). Specialization, Market Exchange, and the Aztec State: A View from Huexotla. *Current Anthropology, 21*, 459–478.

Brumfiel, E.M., & Hodge, M. (1996). Interaction in the Basin of Mexico: The Case of Postclassic Xaltocan. In J.R. Parsons, A.G. Mastache, R.S. Santley & M.C. Serra Puche (Eds.), *Arqueología Mesoamericana: Homenaje a William T. Sanders* (pp. 417–438). Mexico City: Instituto Nacional de Antropología e Historia.

Carvajal, Fr. J. de (1956). *Relacion del Descubrimiento del Rio Apure hasta su Ingreso en el Orinoco*. Caracas-Madrid: Editorial Mediterraneo-Ediciones Edime.

Charlton, T.H., Nichols, D., Otis Charlton, C.L. (1991). Aztec Craft Production and Specialization: Archaeological Evidence from the City-State of Otumba, Mexico. *World Archaeology, 23*, 98–114.

Charlton, T.H., Otis Charlton, C.L., Fournier García, P. (2005). The Basin of Mexico A.D. 1450–1620: Archaeological Dimensions. In S. Kepecs & R.T. Alexander (Eds.), *The Postclassic to Spanish-Era Transition in Mesoamerica: Archaeological Perspectives* (pp. 49–64). Albuquerque: University of New Mexico Press.

Civrieux, M. D. (1980). *Watunna: An Orinoco Cycle*. San Fracisco: North Point Press.

Clark, J.E. (1989). Obsidian: The primary Mesoamerican Sources. In M. Gaxiola & J. E. Clark (Eds.), *La Obsidiana en Mesoamerica* (pp. 299–319). Mexico City: Instituto Nacional de Antropología e Historia.

Cobb, Ch. R. (Ed.). (2003). *Stone Tool Traditions in the Contact Era*. Tuscaloosa: Tuscaloosa University.

Coppens, W. (1971). Las Relaciones Comerciales De Los Ye'kuana Del Caura Paragua. *Antropológica, 30*, 28–59.

Cressey, P.J. (1984). *Post-conquest developments in the Teotihuacan Valley*. Mexico: The early colonial obsidian industry. (Occasional Publications in Mesoamerican Anthropology, 8. Greeley: University of Northern Colorado, Museum of Anthropology).

Dietler, M. (1998). Consumption, Agency, and Cultural Entanglement: Theoretical Implications of a Mediterranean Colonial Encounter. In J. G. Cusick (Ed.), *Studies in Culture Contact: Interaction, Culture Change, and Archaeology. Occasional Paper No. 25* (pp. 288–315). Carbondale: Center for Archaeological Investigations, Southern Illinois University.

Dobres, M.-A. (2000). *Technology and Social Agency: Outlining a Practice Framework for Archaeology*. Oxford: Blackwell.

Dobres, M.-A. (2001). Meaning in the Making: Agency and the Social Embodiment of Technology and Art. In M.B. Schiffer (Ed.), *Anthropological Perspectives on Technology* (pp. 47–76). Albuquerque: University of New Mexico Press.

Dobres, M.-A. (2010). Archaeologies of Technology. *Cambridge Journal of Economics, 34*(1), 103–114.

Durbin, M. (1977). A Survey of the Carib Language Family. In E.B. Basso (Ed.), *Carib-Speaking Indians: Culture, Society and Language* (pp. 23–38). Tucson: University of Arizona Press.

Florescano, E., & García Acosta, V. (Eds.). (2004). *Mestizajes Tecnológicos y Cambios Culturales en México*. Mexico City: Centro de Investigaciones y Estudios Superiores en Antropología Social.

Gil, M. (2003). Efectos de la conquista y colonización europea en la industria lítica del Orinoco Medio: Análisis de los cambios del material lítico encontrado en yacimientos arqueológicos post-contacto, localizados entre los ríos Suapure y Parguaza, Estado Bolivar. Unpublished Trabajo Final de Grado para optar al título de Antropólogo, Universidad Central de Venezuela, Caracas (Venezuela).

74                                                                    E. Rodríguez-Alegría et al.

Gilij, F.S. (1987). Ensayo de Historia Americana. Vol. 71–73. Biblioteca de la Academia Nacional de la Historia (3 Vols.). Translated by Antonio Tovar. Fuentes para la Historia Colonial de Venezuela. Caracas: Italgráfica.

Gumilla, J. (1944). *El Orinoco Ilustrado* (2 Vols.). Bogotá: Editorial ABC.

Guss, D.M. (1987). In the absence of gods: The Ye'kuana road to the sacred. *Antropológica, 68*, 49–58.

Guss, D.M. (1989). *To Weave and to Sing: Art, Symbol, and Narrative in the South American Rain Forest*. Berkeley: University of California Press.

Hernández, F. (1959). *Historial Natural de Nueva España* (Vol. 2). Mexico City: UNAM.

Hill, J. (1988). Violent Encounters: Ethnogenesis and Ethnocide in Long-Term Contact Situations. In J.G. Cusick (Ed.), *Studies in Culture Contact: Interaction, Culture Change, and Archaeology. Occasional Paper No. 25* (pp. 146–167). Carbondale: Center for Archaeological Investigations, Southern Illinois University.

Hill, J. (Ed.). (1996). *History, Power, and Identity: Ethnogenesis in the Americas, 1492–1992*. Iowa City: University of Iowa Press.

Hosler, D. (1994). *The Sounds and Colors of Power: The Sacred Metallurgical Technology of Ancient West Mexico*. Cambridge: MIT Press.

Hosler, D. (2003). Metal Production. In M.E. SMITH & F.F. BERDAN (Eds.), *The Postclassic Mesoamerican World* (pp. 159–171). Salt Lake City: University of Utah Press.

Howard, C. (2000). Wrought Identities: The Waiwai Expeditions in Search of the Unseen Tribes of Amazonia. PhD dissertation, Department of Anthropology, University of Chicago.

Humboldt, A. (1985). *Viaje a las Regiones Equinocciales del Nuevo Continente* (5 Vols.). Caracas: Monte Ávila Editores.

Killick, D. (2004). Social Constructionist Approaches to the Study of Technology. *World Archaeology, 36*(4), 571–578.

Kopytoff, I. (1986). The Cultural Biography of Things: Commoditization as Process. In A. Appadurai (Ed.), *The Social Life of Things: Commodities in Cultural Perspective* (pp. 64–91). Cambridge: Cambridge University Press.

Langer, E., & Jackson R. (Eds.). (1995). *The New Latin American Mission History*. Lincoln: The University of Nebraska Press.

Lathrap, D. (1970). *The Upper Amazon. Vol. 70, Ancient Peoples and Places*. London: Thames and Hudson.

Lathrap, D.W., & Oliver, J.R. (1987). Agüerito: El Complejo Polícromo Más Antiguo De América En la Confluencia del Apure y Orinoco. *Interciencia, 12*(6), 274–289.

Leeds, A. (1960). The Ideology of the Yaruro Indians in Relation to Socio-Economic Organization. *Antropológica, 9*, 1–10.

Lemonnier, P. (2002a). Introduction. In P. LEMONNIER (Ed.), *Technological Choices: Tranformation in Material Cultures since the Neolithic* (pp. 1–35). New York: Routledge.

Lemonnier, P. (Ed.). (2002b). *Technological Choices: Tranformation in Material Cultures since the Neolithic*. New York: Routledge.

Lévi-Strauss, C. (1987). El Origen De Las Maneras De Mesa: Mitológicas III. Translated by Juan Almela. 6th ed. México: Siglo XXI.

Lightfoot, K. (2004). Native Negotiations of Missionary Practices in Alta California. *Missionalia, 32*(3), 380–393.

Lightfoot, K., Martínez, A., Schiff, A.M. (1998). Daily Practice and Material Culture in Pluralistic Social Settings: An Archaeological Study of Culture Change and Persistence from Fort Ross, California. *American Antiquity, 63*(2), 199–222.

Loney, H. (2000). Society and Technological Control: A Critical Review of Models of Technological Change in Ceramic Studies. *American Antiquity, 65*(4), 646–668.

Loney, H. (2001). Pots and Evolution: Response to Neff and Schiffer et al. *American Antiquity, 66*(4), 738–741.

López Austin, A. (1980). *Cuerpo Humano e Ideología: Las Concepciones de los Antiguos Nahuas*. Mexico City: UNAM.

Lucena Giraldo, M. (1991). *Laboratorio Tropical: La Expedición de Límites al Orinoco, 1750–1767*. Caracas: Monte Ávila Latinoamericana y Consejo Superior de Investigaciones Científicas.

Mansutti-Rodríguez, A. (1986). Hierro, barro cocido, curare y cerbatanas: el comercio intra e interétnico entre los Uwotjuja. *Antropológica, 65*, 3–75.

Meggers, B. (1975). Aplicación del Modelo Biológico de Diversificación a las Distribuciones Culturales en las Tierras Tropicales Bajas de Sudamérica. *Amazonia Peruana, 4*(8), 7–38.

Millhauser, J.K. (2005). Classic and postclassic chipped stone at Xaltocan. In E. M. Brumfiel (Ed.), *Production and Power at Postclassic Xaltocan* (pp. 267–318). Pittsburgh: University of Pittsburgh.

Millhauser, J.K., Rodríguez-Alegría, E., Glascock, M.D. (2011). Testing the accuracy of portable X-ray fluorescence to study Aztec and Colonial obsidian supply at Xaltocan, Mexico. *Journal of Archaeological Science, 38*(11), 3141–3152.

Montiel Acosta, N. (1993). *Etno Historia del Llanero en Barinas y Apure. Edited by Secretaría Ejecutiva de Investigación UNELLEZ-BARINAS*. Caracas: Editorial Tropykos.

Morey, N.C. (1975). Ethnohistory of the Columbian and Venezuelan Llanos. Ph. D. Dissertation, University of Utah.

Morey, N.C. (1976). Ethnohistorical Evidence for Cultural Complexity in the Western Llanos of Venezuela and the Eastern Llanos of Colombia. *Antropológica, 45*, 41–69.

Morey, N.C., & Morey, R.V. (1973). Foragers and Farmers: Differential Consequences of Spanish Contact. *Ethnohistory, 20*(3), 229–246.

Myers, T.P. (1977). Early Trade Networks in the Amazon Basin. Paper presented at the 42nd Annual Meeting of the Society for American Archaeology, New Orleans, LA.

Navas, A.M. (2012). *Metalurgia y colonización en las misiones religiosas del Río Orinoco, Siglo XVIII. Unpublished Master Thesis*. Caracas: Instituto Venezolano de Investigaciones Científicas.

Neff, H. (2001). We Have Met the Selectionist and It Is Us: Some Comments on Loney's "Critical Review" of Models of Technological Change in Ceramic Studies". *American Antiquity, 66*(4), 726–728.

Nichols, D.L. (2004). The Rural and Urban Landscapes of the Aztec State. In J. Hendon & R. Joyce (Eds.), *Mesoamerican Archaeology* (pp. 265–295). Malden: Blackwell.

Pastrana, A. (1998). *La explotación azteca de la obsidiana en la Sierra de las Navajas. Colección Científica 383*. Mexico City: Instituto Nacional de Antropología e Historia.

Pastrana, A., & Fournier García, P. (1998). Explotación colonial de obsidiana en el yacimiento de Sierra de las Navajas. In E. Fernández Dávila & S. Gómez Serafín (Eds.), *Primer Congreso Nacional de Arqueología Histórica, Memoria 1996* (pp. 486–496). Mexico City: Instituto Nacional de Antropología e Historia.

Perera, M.A. (2003). *La Provincia Fantasma. Guayana Siglo XVII. Ecología Cultural y Antropología Histórica de una rapiña, 1598–1704*. Caracas: Consejo de Desarrollo Científico y Humanístico, Universidad Central de Venezuela.

Petrullo, V. (1939). The Yaruros of the Capanaparo River, Venezuela. *Bureau of American Ethnology Bulletin, Anthropological Papers, 123*(11), 167–290.

Pfaffenberger, B. (1992). Social Anthropology of Technology. *Annual Review of Anthropology, 21*, 491–516.

Ramenofsky, A.F. (1998). Evolutionary Theory and the Native American Record of Artifact Replacement. In J.G. Cusick (Ed.), *Studies in Culture Contact: Interaction, Culture Change, and Archaeology. Occasional Paper No. 25* (pp. 77–101). Carbondale: Center for Archaeological Investigations.

Rey Fajardo, J. del (1971). *Aportes Jesuíticos a La Filología Colonial Venezolana. Edited by Dirección General Ministerio de Educación*. Caracas: Ministerio de Publicaciones, Departamento de Publicaciones.

Rey Fajardo, J. del (Ed.). (1974). *Documentos Jesuíticos Relativos a la Historia de la Compañía de Jesús en Venezuela II* (Vol. 118). Caracas: Biblioteca de la Academia Nacional de la Historia.

Rivière, P. (1983–1984). Aspects of Carib Political Economy. *Antropológica, 59–62*, 349–358.

Rodríguez-Alegría, E. (2008a). Narratives of Conquest, Colonialism, and Cutting-edge Technology. *American Anthropologist, 110*(1), 33–41.

Rodríguez-Alegría, E. (2008b). De la Edad de Piedra a la Edad de más Piedra. *Cuadernos de Arqueología Mediterránea, 17,* 15–30.

Rodríguez-Alegría, E. (2010). Incumbents and Challengers: Indigenous Politics and the Adoption of Spanish Material Culture in Colonial Xaltocan, Mexico. *Historical Archaeology, 44*(2), 51–71.

Romero, A., Chilbert S., Eisenhart, M.G. (1999). Cubagua's Pearl-Oyster Beds: The First Depletion of a Natural Resourse Caused by Europeans in the American Continent. *Journal of Political Ecology, 6,* 57–78.

Roosevelt, A. (1980). *Parmana: Prehistoric Maize and Manioc Subsistence Along the Orinoco and Amazon.* New York: Academic Press.

Sahagun, B. de (1963). General History of the Things of New Spain: Book 11, Earthly Things. Ch. E. Dibble & A.J.O. Anderson (trans). Santa Fe: School of American Research; Salt Lake City: University of Utah.

Sahlins, M.D. (1985). *Islands of History.* Chicago: The University of Chicago Press.

Sahlins, M.D. (1992). The Economics of Develop-Man in the Pacific. *Anthropology and Aesthetics RES, 21*(spring), 12–25.

Sahlins, M.D. (1999). Two or Three Things That I know about Culture. *The Journal of the Royal Anthropological Institute, Vol. 5,* No. 3.

Saunders, N. (2001). A Dark Light: Reflections on Obsidian in Mesoamerica. *World Archaeology, 33*(2), 220–236.

Scaramelli, F., & Tarble de Scaramelli, K. (2003). Caña: The Role of Aguardiente in the Colonization of the Orinoco. In N.L. Whitehead (Ed.), *History and Historicities in Amazonia* (pp. 163–178). Lincoln: University of Nebraska Press.

Scaramelli, F. (2005). Material Culture, Colonialism, and Identity in the Middle Orinoco, Venezuela. Ph. D. Dissertation, The University of Chicago.

Scaramelli, F., & Tarble de Scaramelli, K. (2005). The Roles of Material Culture in the Colonization of the Orinoco, Venezuela. *Journal of Social Archaeology, 5*(1), 135–168.

Schwartz, J. (1981). A Touch of Glass. *Science, 81*(2), 79–80.

Schwartz, S.B. (1978). Indian Labor and New World Plantations: European Demands and Indian Responses in Northeastern Brazil. *The American Historical Review, 83*(1), 43–79.

Silliman, S. W. (2001). Agency, Practical Politics, and the Archaeology of Culture Contact. *Journal of Social Archaeology, 1*(2), 184–204.

Tarble, K. (1985). Un nuevo modelo de expansión Caribe para la época prehispánica. *Antropológica, 63–64,* 45–81.

Tarble, K., & Scaramelli, F. (1999). Style, Function, and Context in the Rock Art of the Middle Orinoco Area. *Boletín de la Sociedad Venezolana de Espeleología, 33* (diciembre), 17–33.

Tarble, K., & Scaramelli, F. (2004). A Brief but Critical Presence: The Archaeology of a Jesuit Mission in the Middle Orinoco (1730–1747). *Missionalia, 32*(3), 419–444.

Tarble, K., & Scaramelli, F. (2012). Cooking for Fame or Fortune: The Effect of European Contact on Casabe Production in the Orinoco. In S. R. Graff & E. Rodríguez-Alegría (Eds.), *The Menial Art of Cooking: Archaeological Studies of Cooking and Food Production* (pp. 119–143). Boulder: University Press of Colorado.

Thomas D.J. (1972). The indigenous trade system of Southeast Estado Bolivar, Venezuela. *Antropológica, 33,* 3–37.

Trigger, B.G. (1991). Early Native North American Response to European Contact: Romantic versus Rationalistic Interpretations. *The Journal of American History, 77*(4), 1195–1215.

Turner, T. (1977). Cosmetics: The Language of Bodily Adornment. In J.P. Spradley & D.W. McCurdy (Eds), *Conformity and Conflict: Readings in Cultural Anthropology* (pp. 162–171). Boston, Toronto: Little, Brown and Company.

Turner, T. (1984). Dual Opposition, Hierarchy and Value: Moiety Structure and Symbolic Polarity in Central Brazil and Elsewhere. In J.C Galey (Ed.), *Differences, Valeurs, Hierarchie: Textes Offertes a Louis Dumont* (pp. 335–370). París: Editions de l' Ecole des Hautes Etudes en Sciences Sociales.

Vega, A. de (1974). Noticia del principio y progresos del establecimiento de las misiones de gen-
tiles en el Río Orinoco, por la Compañía de Jesús (…). In J. del Rey Fajardo (Ed.), *Documentos Jesuíticos Relativos a la Historia de la Compañía de Jesús en Venezuela II* (pp. 3–149). Cara-
cas: Academia Nacional de la Historia.
Viveiros De Castro, E. (1998). Cosmological Deixis and Amerindian Perspectivism. *Journal of the Royal Anthropological Institute, 4*(3), 469–488.
Whitehead, N.L. (1988). *Lords of the Tiger Spirit: A History of the Caribs in Colonial Venezuela and Guyana, 1498–1820.* Dordrecht: Foris Publications.
Whitehead, N.L. (1990). Carib Ethnic Soldiering in Venezuela, Guiana and the Antilles, 1491–
1820. *Ethnohistory, 37*(4), 359–385.
Whitehead, N.L. (1996). Ethnogenesis and Ethnocide in the European Occupation of Native Suri-
nam, 1499–1681. In J. D. Hill (Ed.), *History, Power, and Identity: Ethnogenesis in the Americas, 1492–1992* (pp. 20–35). Iowa City: University of Iowa Press.
Zucchi, A. (1985). Evidencias arqueológicas sobre grupos de posible lengua Caribe. *Antropológica, 63–64*, 23–44.
Zucchi, A., & Tarble, K. (1984). Los Cedeñoides. Un nuevo grupo prehispánico del Orinoco Medio. *Acta Científica Venezolana, 35*(3–4), 293–309.

# Chapter 5
# Tribute, Antimarkets, and Consumption: An Archaeology of Capitalist Effects in Colonial Guatemala

Guido Pezzarossi

## 5.1 Introduction

This chapter seeks to craft an approach to the archaeology of capitalism—in its varied forms and articulations—within Spanish colonial contexts in colonial Guatemala through the archaeology and ethnohistory of a Pacific piedmont, colonial-period Kaqchikel Maya community, San Pedro Aguacatepeque. As part of this, I will sketch out a brief summary of trait-based approaches to identifying and investigating capitalism in colonial contexts—both archaeologically and historically—by highlighting the manifold and inconsistent ways in which capitalism and its relation to colonialism has been defined and investigated in the past. As De Landa (De Landa 1997, p. 48) states, "the conceptual confusion engendered by all the different uses of the world 'capitalism' (as 'free enterprise' or as 'industrial mode of production'…as 'world-economy') is so entrenched that it…has reached the limits of its usefulness."

I propose an alternative approach that draws on the contributions of postcolonial critiques of monolithic models of colonialism (see Croucher and Weiss 2011) and applies them to revealing the unique "hybrid forms of capitalism" through the diversity of relations of production in colonial Guatemala, some of which paralleled "capitalist" relations and their various effects, and some that did not. Having established this diversity, and thus the lack of utility of capitalism as an organizing model or overarching framework for such diverse contexts, I turn to Braudel's (Braudel 1984) and De Landa's (De Landa 1997) neologism of "antimarkets" (i.e., heterogeneous assemblages of humans, discourse, and things that structured and manipulated the relations of production and exchange for the purpose of wealth/capital accumulation) as an experiment in moving beyond the baggage-laden concept of capitalism and turning analyses of capitalism in colonial contexts on their head (see Wallerstein 1991).

G. Pezzarossi (✉)
Department of Anthropology, Stanford University, 824 Erie St Apt 5, Oakland, CA 94610, USA
e-mail: guidopez@stanford.edu

© Springer International Publishing Switzerland 2015        79
P. P. A. Funari, M. X. Senatore (eds.), *Archaeology of Culture Contact and Colonialism in Spanish and Portuguese America*, DOI 10.1007/978-3-319-08069-7_5

A focus on antimarkets shifts the object of analyses of capitalism in colonial contexts away from endlessly and unproductively (re)defining capitalism and determining if capitalism (and thus a claim to modernity) ever bloomed in "feudal" Spanish colonial contexts. Instead, the concept of antimarkets refocuses analytic energies toward identifying the ever-present influence of colonial power in structuring colonial communities' engagement with the emerging global economy (see Quijano 2000) and "local manifestations of the kind of social relations which enabled capital accumulation and growth" in the first place (Hauser 2011, p. 135). In essence, paying attention to antimarkets reorients analyses away from unproductive monolithic abstractions, and toward the entanglements between power, hierarchy, and economic practice as manifested in specific, historically identifiable "antimarket" (or nonfree, manipulated market) processes.

Fernando Coronil's (2007) notion of "imperial effects"—which for the purposes of this chapter I have modified into "capitalist/antimarket effects"—provides the central analytical tool to aid in interrogating colonialism and capitalism/antimarkets (without resorting to monolithic models) "by [focusing on] their effects on the population's subjected to them" (Voss 2012, p. 16). The analysis of effects provides a method for comparative analysis of imperial structures and effects across disparate spatial and temporal contexts. James Scott (1990, pp. x–xi) makes a similar case for the comparative analysis of structures of domination/inequality via a focus on their effects, by arguing that "structurally similar forms of domination will bear a family resemblance to one another...operate in comparable ways...[and] elicit reactions and patterns of resistance that are broadly comparable."

Archaeologically, I will engage with this idea by focusing on the material remnants and documentary mentions of production and consumption at Aguacatepeque, two practices that served as critical vectors for entangling people and things, both near and far, into the types of regional and global connections structured by unequal power relations that that have come to define global capitalism (Tsing 2005). Tracing out the effects of antimarkets stitches together the contributions of Braudel and De Landa with the conceptual method of Coronil, into an effective analytical framework for exploring the role of power in the unfolding of relations of production that tied colonial Guatemala and Maya communities to the emerging global economy, while accounting for the effects on life, experience, and practice that these power-afforded shifts had on subjected Maya communities.

From this theoretical groundwork, I then delve into some specifics of Guatemalan colonial context, with the goal of identifying the complex milieu of colonial power and relations of production that developed there. Drawing on archaeological and documentary research, I explore antecedents of some of these practices in the precolonial Mesoamerican world in order to highlight the fact that "capitalist" practices (e.g., market dependence/consumption, market-based circulation, commodity crop production/specialization, currency economies, etc.) may not be the exclusive domain of capitalism/modernity (see Braudel 1979, p. 581; De Landa 1996; Deleuze et al. 2005). I show that some (but not all) of the iconic capitalist practices active in Colonial Guatemala had deeper histories in the pre-Columbian

Mesoamerican world, and thus represent the persistence of practices that came to be reconfigured through the entanglements with other colonial and capitalist practices.

With this context established, I now draw out the specific genealogy of the development and reconfiguration of these practices and relations, the antimarkets that afforded and sustained them, and their subsequent effects on Aguacatepeque—a multicomponent Kaqchikel Maya community occupied from at least 900–1800 AD (Pezzarossi and Escobar 2011, 2012). In particular, I explore precolonial specialized production and exchange at Aguacatepeque, practices that persisted in a changed manner into the colonial period as a result of Spanish labor and tribute demands. These changes produced a series of effects on the production and consumption practices of Aguacatepeque's residents that in turn afforded a greater reliance on markets for the materials of everyday life. This emerging market dependence, rather than simply being the inevitable outcome of capitalist incursion or the emplacement of capitalist relations onto Maya populations, emerged from the "friction" (sensu Tsing 2005) brought about by Spanish colonial policies, antimarkets, and practices becoming entangled with existing Maya practices and responses to the constraints and emerging opportunities of the colonial and global economy. In sum, the goal is to highlight specifically how colonial power, relations and practices—conceived of as antimarket forces—informed by pre-Hispanic Maya practices, afforded the emergence of new or reconfiguration of existing practices that constituted macro- and microlevel shifts in practices that have been modeled as the effects of a monolithic capitalism and/or colonialism.

## 5.2  Capitalism in Noncapitalist Contexts?

Spanish colonial contexts, in contrast to English and French colonial contexts in North America are unevenly included in archaeological and historical analyses of the emergence and unfolding of the world economic system and its "capitalist" formations. When they are included, the Spanish colonies in Latin America are seen as playing a passive role in the emergence of capitalism as a raw material-producing periphery from which wealth was extracted and made into capital in the metropole (Laclau 1971; Marx 1990, p. 918; Wallerstein 1974). In other analyses, Latin America is considered connected to the capitalist economy, and yet remains excluded from the "modernity" of the emerging capitalist world due to the development and persistence of underdeveloped "feudal" modes of production (Laclau 1971).

The former perspective—associated with World Systems Theory and Analyses—acknowledges the inextricable entanglements and relations of dependence between Spanish colonialism and capitalism and opens the door to simultaneous analyses of both. Yet upon undertaking the excavation of causal genealogies of capitalist relations and effects in the Spanish colonies, one is quickly confronted with the slippages of these monolithic models of capitalism and the slipperiness of defining what exactly is or is not capitalism and when/where (and if) it "appears" in the Spanish colonial world.

While historical evidence lays bare the clear entanglements of colonialism and capitalism in Western colonial projects of the fifteenth to sixteenth centuries (see Harvey 2010, p. 298; Marx 1990, p. 918), scholars are reticent to do so unless a defining practice or all of a variety of practices and set of relations argued to be iconic of capitalism can be identified (e.g., industrialized wage labor, market dependence, commodity production, capital accumulation, etc.). When considering the influence or presence of capitalism in the Spanish colonies, questions quickly arise about their status as either: noncapitalist (but entangled with capitalism) by virtue of its "feudal" or precapitalist relations of production (Laclau 1971); capitalist by connection to the global capitalist economy, regardless of the dominant relations of production (Frank 1967); or as integral but spatially distinct participants of the "periphery" of an emerging capitalist World System constituted by its "variegated modes of production" (Wallerstein 1974).

While insightful, these debates have at times generated more heat than light, as they are variously undergirded by problematic teleological Eurocentric "stages" of development defined by supposedly "dominant" (and thus monolithically conceived) modes of production (i.e., feudalism and coerced labor, capitalism, and free wage labor; see Stern 1993, p. 54). Drawing on these contributions and critiques and applying them to Latin America and the Spanish colonial projects that structured its emergence, Stern (Stern 1988; Stern 1993) has argued for the need to develop models that describe and account for uniquely Spanish colonial hybrid articulations of capitalism and modernity as constituted by a "shifting combination of heterogeneous relations of production in a pragmatic package" (Stern 1993, p. 53). He points out that within the heterogeneous package of relations of production in the Spanish colonies, one finds "approximations of wage labor, complicated tenancy, share and debt-credit arrangements, and forced labor drafts and slavery [as parts of] a single productive process" dictated the politics of production and capital accumulation. This approach then hints at the role of "antimarkets" or extraeconomic power in structuring relations of production in Latin America. (Stern 1993, pp. 54–55).

Despite scholarly attention to the context specific articulations of capitalism, capitalism as a real—though diverse—"thing" persists and is seen to exert a dominant influence to the unfolding of history (for critique see Funari et al. 1999, p. 7). Capitalism comes to dominate interpretations by serving as a model through which changes in practice, tradition, culture, and daily life can be explained (see De Landa 1996; Hauser 2011, p. 212). In turn, capitalism, an abstract concept developed in the nineteenth century (cf. Chiapello 2007) becomes a reified solidity; a real "thing" that is/was internally coherent and contains its own set of internal logics and processes that are seen to exist outside of human practice and the "primary human actors" that carry them out (for parallel argument about globalization of US capitalism see Ho 2005; Mitchell 2002).

In interpretation, archaeologies of capitalism can reify this acculturating, totalizing influence of capitalism by fostering a "muting" or flattening of contextual specificities such that the development and effects of capitalism in any context are known in advance, thus rendering archaeological study practically unnecessary (see Funari 1999, p. 7; Hauser 2011, p. 121; Horning 2011, p. 65). Yet, even with the acknowledgement of the context specific formations and effects of capitalism (see Croucher and Weiss 2011), capitalism as an ambiguous reified "thing" remains an important actor and benchmark to consider in interpreting changes in practices seen archaeologically, without any resolution as to a definition of what exactly capitalism actually is and what its presence consisted of. In these approaches, practices and objects tend to remain divided into capitalist and noncapitalist; which is an ontological division that fuels the reification of capitalism as solidity. Materialists have provided an alternative approach that seeks to avoid this continued reification of capitalism while providing tools for the analyses of the development and effects of power, processes, and practices historically ascribed to capitalism yet present in pre-Hispanic and colonial contexts in Latin America.

## 5.3  Braudel, De Landa, and Antimarkets

Braudel (1979) and De Landa (1997) have offered a broader critique of studies of capitalism and provide an intriguing approach to exploring the mechanisms and processes that constitute capitalism, in a manner with direct applications to Spanish colonial contexts seen as marginal to the emergence and "practice" of capitalism. The first part of their contribution focuses on the history of the term, its valences, and the problems of continuing to work within the confines of the concept of capitalism yet continually stretching its boundaries to account for the continual flow of "negative evidence" that highlights its insufficiencies (De Landa 1997, p. 48). While Braudel argued for the appropriation of the concept/term, De Landa seeks to discard it in favor of Braudel's term: "antimarkets" (De Landa 1997, p. 48). Braudel's critique metaphorically turns the tables on the analysis of capitalism by arguing that capitalism, rather than a system defined by free markets that afford the "free" exchange of commodities, labor, and capital was/is the "system of the antimarket" (Wallerstein 1991, p. 354).

In essence, the argument is that what has been dubbed capitalism is in fact an "effect" (see below for discussion of Coronil 2007) of the operation of antimarkets manipulated by private and state agents and agencies, or "monopolies [that] were the product of power, cunning and intelligence" exploiting through unequal or manipulated forms of exchange (Wallerstein 1991, p. 356). The question is thus posed, shaking classic and neoliberal models of capitalism to their core: "When there was a relationship of force of this kind, what exactly did the terms supply and demand mean?" (Braudel 1979, p. 176; Wallerstein 1991, p. 356).

In this formulation, the traits used to define contexts as feudal and not capitalist (i.e., extraeconomic control, coercion, violence, and power, as opposed to the supposed "free" exchange and markets of capitalism) are in Braudel's conception the very forces and practices of the antimarket(s) that have structured the modern global economy in its current form, which we assuredly define as capitalist. In a sense, it is inequality of power and the coercive, manipulative forces they exert on markets, exchange, and relations of production that constitute the development of antimarkets (and thus capitalism); a perspective acknowledged by Marx through a consideration of the coercive force that underpinned "primitive accumulation" wherein "the treasures captured outside Europe by undisguised looting, enslavement, and murder flowed back to the mother country and were turned into capital there" (Marx 1990, p. 918).

However, in Marx's scheme this overt force made possible by unequal power, fades in capitalist contexts, as the violence that molded capitalist (wage laboring) subjects transitions into what Harvey (2010, p. 296) calls the "silent compulsion of economic relations" and their subtle, unguided disciplining force. Luxemburg (2003, p. 432) provided a corrective to this statement—in an important overlap with the concept of antimarkets—by arguing that capitalism has never left behind primitive accumulation and its coercive, manipulative, and exploitative power relations that are the purview of antimarkets, as "capitalism would long ago have ceased to exist had it not engaged in fresh rounds of primitive accumulation, chiefly through the violence of imperialism" (Harvey 2010, p. 206). These contributions provide further justification for the importance of analyzing the presence of antimarkets, and the coercive and violent power relations that maintained them, in the very colonial/imperial contexts that provided and continue to provide flows of capital critical to our modern, "capitalist" global economy.

By shifting analyses of capitalism away from traits or abstract models and onto "antimarkets" we are able to locate the operation and effects of what would be defined as "capitalist" processes/practices/ideologies in noncapitalist, precapitalist, or heterogeneously capitalist contexts. Underscoring this argument, Braudel makes the point that antimarkets were never unique to the modern world (as a stage on an evolutionary ladder), rather he states: "I am tempted to agree with Deleuze and Guattari that 'capitalism has been a spectre haunting every form of society'—capitalism that is as I have defined it" (Braudel 1979, p. 581).

De Landa concurs: "antimarkets could have arisen anywhere, not just Europe, the moment the flows of goods through markets reach a certain level of intensity, so that an organization bent on manipulating these flows can emerge" (De Landa 1996). Braudel provides three critical conditions that afford the emergence of capitalism as he defines it: (1) a vibrant, expanding market/exchange economy, (2) social inequality and hierarchy, and (3) long-distance, or nonlocal exchange (Braudel 1979, pp. 600–601). These conditions truly do encompass most "complex" societies, and most definitely are present in various forms in precolonial and colonial Mesomaerica (see Smith and Berdan 2003) and in various other contexts subjected to Spanish colonization.

This antimarket approach helps mitigate the problems of talking in terms of capitalist or not capitalist in colonial Latin America, by instead focusing on the emergence and operation of antimarkets in Spanish colonial (and other) contexts and interrogating their effects. The rest of this chapter builds up from this point, as I seek to flesh out what an archaeology of antimarket effects might look like in a Spanish colonial context. The goal is not to carry out a trait list approach to "finding evidence" of capitalism, which is then assigned causal power in interpretation of changes wrought by colonization and the colonial encounter. Rather, I explore the (re)structuring of production, labor, circulation and consumption practices in ways beneficial to those in positions of power able to influence, enact, and maintain such unequal relations of production through threat of force in colonial Guatemala. Through this analysis, the unintended consequences of policies and the unanticipated responses of colonized Maya populations emerge, and it is here, at the points of frictions between people, things, and power that the "hybrid forms of capitalism" (Gaitan-Ammann 2011) unique to Latin American contexts emerge (see also Richard 2011; Stern 1993).

Moving forward from the acknowledgment of the entanglement of colonial power, economy, and daily practice in the Spanish colonial projects in the New World, it becomes possible to move toward a contextual and nuanced analysis of the diversity of formations and experiences of contexts enmeshed in novel combinations of antimarket forces, colonial power, and localized creative formations and responses to these forces and processes. The next section of this chapter explores a conceptual methodology for interrogating the specific effects of these processes and facilitating the cross-context (both temporal and spatial) comparison of antimarkets, the practices they afforded, and their effects on populations subjected to their exploitative potential.

## 5.4 Developing an Archaeology of Capitalist and Antimarket Effects

The previous discussion of antimarkets can be tied to Fernando Coronil's (2007) notion of "imperial effects" by considering the effects of these antimarkets on the people held in their sway. A focus on effects recenters the analysis away from general processes and onto the "significance for subjected populations" and thus onto the ways in which populations were impacted and changed by a set of practices in specific contexts that may or may not be considered part of traditional, academic, and political definitions of imperial, capitalist, or colonial contexts. I argue that what matters is not the manner in which bundles of practices and processes are labeled retroactively by scholars, but rather what the effects of these bundles were, as ways to connect seemingly unrelated phenomena and facilitate their comparative analysis.

From this perspective, I develop and apply an archaeological approach to capitalist or antimarket effects, which is of particular necessity in Spanish colonial contexts, long the object of academic debates on their status as capitalist or non-capitalist. The focus on "effects" provides enough flexibility for diverse "hybrid" formations to be acknowledged, while emphasizing the parallel effects of distinct antimarkets in disparate contexts. In particular, I focus on the development and effects of antimarkets in colonial Guatemala, in terms of the role they played in catalyzing changes in relations of production and consumption practices and influencing shifts in daily practice and community traditions at the Kaqchikel Maya community of Aguacatepeque. Identifying the factors that lead to Aguacatepeque's colonial entanglements (and the relations of production that followed) provides both a specific look at the diversity of early modern production and consumption practices in a colonial Guatemalan Maya context and forwards an argument for the specific causes of their development and persistence without needing to resort to capitalism as an explanatory model.

## 5.5   Background History

The community of Aguacatepeque is located at the transition between the Pacific piedmont and the central highlands of Guatemala, within the confines of the Antigua Valley. It lies within what was in the Late Postclassic (1200–1500 AD) the southernmost territorial boundary of one of the myriad Maya ethnolinguistic groups: the Iximche Kaqchickel. Archaeologists and ethnohistorians have argued that the Kaqchikel established a presence in the central highlands region of Guatemala from at least 1200 AD (Hill 1992, p. 19). In addition to the Kaqchikel, a variety of ethnolinguistic Mayan groups inhabited the region concurrently in the Late Postclassic periods, connected by a complex network of alliances, confederations, and economic relations (Braswell 2003).

In 1524 the initial Spanish incursions into the region began, with the colonial capital, Santiago, eventually established in the Antigua Valley in 1543. Santiago prospered throughout the sixteenth century, and rose to power in the region through its control of Mesoamerican commerce flowing to and from New Spain and Lima, as well as through the regional and global exportation of prized commodities such as cacao (Herrera 2003, pp. 15–32; MacLeod 1973, pp. 80–96). Despite economic depression in the seventeenth century, and the devaluation of cacao in the global market, Santiago remained an important hub of commerce in the Mesoamerican region and the New World that imbedded native people in the colonial structures of the emerging global economy. As a result, the native populations of the Antigua Valley directly impacted the regional and global flow of commodities as producers, consumers, and distributors of local, regional, and global goods.

## 5.6   Archaeological Research

Since 2010, the Highland Maya Colonial Archaeology Project has conducted archaeological research at the multicomponent Kaqchikel Maya community of San Pedro de Aguacatepeque. The site is located on the southeastern portion of the Volcan de Fuego approximately 35 km from Santiago de Guatemala (today Antigua) (Fig. 5.1), within a microclimate that allows for the cultivation of sugarcane and cacao (Pezzarossi and Escobar 2013; Robinson and Pezzarossi 2012). To date, archaeological research has identified extensive community midden deposits associated with the colonial and pre-Hispanic occupations of Aguacatepeque as well as

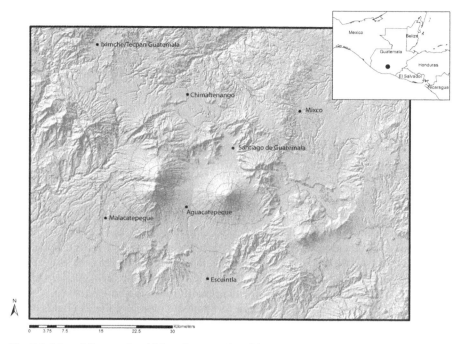

**Fig. 5.1** Map of Guatemala with locations mentioned in text

the remains of a colonial period public space and plaza (see Pezzarossi and Escobar 2011, 2013).

The community of Aguacatepeque is mentioned in a series of documents that show it fluctuating between 50–300 individuals from the early sixteenth century to the early nineteenth century, while archaeological evidence indicates a longer pre-colonial occupation from as early as the Late Classic Period in 900 AD (Pezzarossi and Escobar 2013; Robinson 1990). One of its most prominent mentions appears in a 1768 (Larraz 1958, pp. 287–288) survey of parishes where the community is described as a poverty-stricken subsidiary town of Alotenango of about 120–200 inhabitants living on the margins of the colonial world. However, preliminary archaeological data and other documentary sources (Crespo 1740, p. 9; Vazquez and Lamadrid 1937, pp. 33–67) indicate that Aguacatepeque was intensively engaging the colonial market economy through their production of coveted agricultural commodities and the consumption of colonial material culture (see Pezzarossi and Escobar 2013). A 1688 account by Francisco de Zuaza (Vazquez and Lamadrid 1937, pp. 33–67) supports this contention as he describes the inhabitants of Aguacatepeque as farmers and laborers growing corn, cacao, and sugarcane, the last of which was processed into unrefined sugar loafs (rapaduras) made explicitly for sale at local markets.

The coerced and voluntary participation of the residents of Aguacatepeque in both the regional colonial market economy (as producers and consumers) and in the various tribute-related labor regimes instituted by Spanish colonizers, make this site an excellent candidate for exploring the role that colonial power and early modern antimarkets played in structuring relations of production and influencing material practices and traditions at Aguacatepeque.

## 5.7 Tribute, Labor, and the Repartimiento de Bienes: Antimarkets in Colonial Guatemala

Coerced relations of production in colonial Guatemala were initially overtly violent, especially prior to the 1542 passage of the New Laws that banned the enslavement of native individuals (Hill 1992, p. 110; Sherman 1979, pp. 22–23). While the coercion in later relations of production—such as repartamiento labor drafts—was arguably more subtle, it retained a similar potential for violence (see Borg 1986, pp. 123–124; Sherman 1979, pp. 191–192; de Zorita 1963, pp. 214–216). In effect, colonial policies that leveraged native community leaders and extant native hierarchies as intermediaries and enforcers of Spanish colonial policies (Beals 1967, pp. 453–455) created a situation wherein it could be perceived that colonial coercion had been replaced with the "silent compulsion" of economic and colonial relations that had become "hegemonic" (as used by Scott 1990). However, this silent compulsion must not be overestimated, as the Spanish and native colonial officials, always held the power to discipline recalcitrant colonial subjects (backed by the implicit threat of armed violence; see Baskes 2005; Borg 1986, p. 54; Lokken 2004). This same power and violence underpinned the operation of antimarkets in colonial Guatemala and in effect enforced the policies and practices catalyzing unequal distribution and accumulation through taxes, tributes, and unequal market exchange. These coercive instruments of surplus extraction generated the jolts of "primitive accumulation" upon which early modern antimarkets depended (and continue to depend) on for their emergence and persistence (Harvey 2010, p. 206).

The introduction of Spanish currency was a critical instrument of colonization and antimarkets formation in colonial Guatemala, however currency was not unique to the region, as Spanish currency coexisted for a time with the pre-Hispanic cacao bean currency of the region (see Millon 1974, pp. 204–210; Pugh 2006, p. 372; Reents-Budet 2006, p. 220). Part of the process of establishing a currency-based economy in colonial Guatemala (and in many colonial contexts) consisted of demanding tribute/taxation in the currency that colonial officials controlled and wanted to institute (see Forstater 2005). Spanish colonial taxation and tribute, when demanded in currency, led to the immediate valorization of said currency through the implicit or explicit threat of force if the currency was not acquired and the tribute or tax paid with it (see Graeber 2011, pp. 49–50). This monetized economy would in turn bring markets into existence (or in the Maya case, transform extant pre-Hispanic markets; for evidence of markets in pre-Hispanic Mesoamerica, see Braswell 2010; Braswell and Glascock 2003; Brumfiel et al. 1980; Dahlin et al. 2007; Feinman and Garraty 2010; Halperin et al. 2009; Millhauser et al. 2011; Nichols et al. 2002; Rodriguez-Alegria 2008; Rodríguez-Alegría 2002; Rodriguez-Alegria et al. 2003; Shaw 2012; Sheets 2000; Vargas et al. 2009; Zeitlin and Thomas 1997) as a "side effect" of the new found need to exchange subsistence and cash crops, manufactured goods and/or labor to acquire currency (Graeber 2011, p. 50; MacLeod 1983, p. 191).

However, it is critical the threat of violence and imprisonment as an extraeconomic factor underwriting the establishment of the currency economy and the emergence of markets/antimarkets not be downplayed. In opposition to the claims by Adam Smith, markets did not spring up of their own accord as "free" institutions facilitating trade and exchange; rather as Graeber (2011, p. 50) argues the emergence of markets is inextricably entangled with the unequal power of the state and/or other institution(s) to enforce "tax policies designed to create markets where they had not existed before" (see also Forstater 2005, p. 53). This genealogy of markets emerging with the "state" or other governing institution—paralleling the process in colonial Guatemala (Larson and Wasserstrom 1983, p. 50)—provides greater clarity to the assertion made by De Landa (1997, p. 48) that what are termed markets, are in fact always one form or another of antimarkets, and thus not unique to "capitalism", as they emerge in various contexts through the capacities afforded by the manipulative effects of unequal power relations on markets and other institutions facilitating the exchange of things across space.

Indeed, the Aztec period (CE 1150–1519) economy in the Valley of Mexico provides an example of a pre-Hispanic Mesoamerican antimarket. Brumfiel et al. (1980, p. 466) argue that observed market intensification in the Aztec period, rather than emerging spontaneously as an optimal resource distribution system for the increasingly centralized, urban Aztec "state" was in fact intimately tied to the emergence of the centralized Aztec state.

The Aztec state intervened in this process through their ability to generate and circulate tribute in raw materials and manufactured/craft goods extracted under coercion from regional communities outside of the urban center. Brumfiel argues that the influx of tribute goods into the market improved "the ability of the market to provide a steady supply of nonfood items to rural households at reasonable prices, it created conditions in which peasants would sacrifice their economic autonomy for greater dependence upon commercial activity" (Brumfiel et al. 1980, p. 466).

Moreover, recent research has identified evidence of the active manipulation of markets by the Aztec state to increase the value of tribute acquired nonfood items such as obsidian. Rodriquez-Alegria argues that: "The Aztecs controlled obsidian outcrops in Pachuca in part to force people to purchase finished blades in markets, forcing the kind of exchange that kept the Aztec market system alive" (Rodriguez-Alegria 2008, p. 39). In this case, the extraction of tribute in obsidian raw material for circulation as finished tools came with tighter (military) control over the raw material sources of that obsidian, in a sense creating a monopoly for a critically important manufactured good. This form of pre-Hispanic primitive accumulation and antimarket operation provided the means for continued accumulation and growth through the unequal power relations that maintained unequal exchange and relations of production in favor of the Aztec state.

Indeed, cultivation and manufacture of durable and nondurable goods as tribute demanded of conquered communities has a long history in Mesoamerica (see Berdan et al. 2003, pp. 104–105), as the Aztec example provided above indicates (Brumfiel et al. 1980). In the highland Maya region, it was common for Kaqchikel Maya polities to control territory and communities on the Pacific coast and piedmont and demand tribute in various goods and labor, including cacao (Berdan et al. 2003, p. 105; Orellana 1995, pp. 40–41). Aguacatepeque appears to have been one such subjected community specializing in the cultivation, production and circulation of tribute crops in the Postclassic. A 1549 Franciscan missionary's account states that the "guardiania" of Alotenango (within which Aguacatepeque would have been located) was a cacaotale and anexo of the highland Iximche Kaqchikel confederation (Vázquez and Lamadrid 1944, pp. 111, 128).

This document implies that in the immediately pre-Hispanic Late Postclassic period, the community of Aguacatepeque—likely due to its location within a microclimate that would support cacao cultivation (see Robinson and Pezzarossi 2012)—served as a cacao-growing "outpost" for the highland Iximche Kaqchikel confederation. This role as a cacaotale would potentially have meant a specialization in the cultivation and exchange of cacao. As a result it is expected that a lack of other localized "multicrafting" activities common to the Maya household (Hirth 2009a, b) would be practiced at Aguacatepeque. In sum, it lays the groundwork for considering that Aguacatepeque's prior experience as a tributary of the Iximche Kaqchikel, specifically in the cultivation of cacao as an exchange/tribute crop may have prepared the community to seize upon and take advantage of the production of another prized crop in the colonial period (i.e., sugar) out of necessity.

In colonial Guatemala colonial antimarkets shared a "family resemblance" with Aztec and Kaqchikel Maya tribute systems and antimarkets in the "structurally similar" practices of coerced tribute, tax, and labor demands made of colonized populations, with parallel and "broadly comparable" effects (see Scott 1990, pp. x–xi). One particularly notorious antimarket in colonial Guatemala was the repartimiento de bienes that in combination with taxes and tributes demanded in currency drew in and entrapped Maya communities in unequal relations of production, exchange and debt (cf. Baskes 2005; Larson and Wasserstrom 1983). Briefly, the repartamiento de bienes has conventionally been defined as "a forced system of production and consumption driven by the coercive authority of Crown officials that was designed to draw reluctant Indians into the market at unfavorable terms" (see Baskes 2005, p. 187).

The repartimiento provided native communities with overvalued manufactured goods, cash, and subsistence crops and currency on credit to help with shortfalls and with paying tribute in kind and currency, with the expectation that the debt be repaid with large amounts of undervalued cash and subsistence crops at harvest time, to the benefit of the Crown officials. The power to manipulate these prices and "force" goods and credit on communities lay with colonial officials who constructed an "artificial market for their [colonist's] merchandise...[in order to] mobilize native labor" into currency generating production practices (e.g., wage labor, cash crop cultivation; Larson and Wasserstrom 1983, p. 62). The currency generated by this shift in native production practices would have provided the basic income with which native populations could increasingly engage local and regional markets for quotidian needs no longer met by local production practices.

Credit, and the associated cash crop production it supported and stimulated, became a way to acquire colonial currency controlled by Spanish colonists and became a necessity not as a result of invisible, spontaneous "market forces" or the desires of Maya populations, but rather through the operation of Spanish colonial policies that manipulated markets through unequal power relations and the threat or application of violence for noncompliance. As Baskes (2005) points out for repartimiento de bienes debt collection, Simpson (1959) details for tribute collection for the encomienda of Chimaltenango, and Borg (1986, p. 54) for head of household tributes; the threat of incarceration, beatings (or worse) for those who refused or were unable to cancel their debts and obligations created the force by which needs and necessities, and thus native production and consumption practices were reconfigured in colonial Guatemala.

The coerced production of tribute—both in kind, in currency, and in labor— of early Spanish encomiendas and the later labor drafts and currency-based taxation under the labor repartimiento policies, all played crucial roles in affording the repartimiento de bienes as a viable strategy for Spanish colonists to generate profits through unequal relations of production with native communities. Contrary to Baskes' (2005) naturalization of native communities need for credit to subsist and survive, the necessity of credit was itself an effect of power-laden, coercive Spanish colonial policies that appropriated native labor and time through onerous tribute demands in currency, labor, and agricultural cash crops for export and exchange.

Aguacatepeque was enmeshed within these policies and was subject to their various effects; however the community also provides insight into the localized responses to the constraints and opportunities of these coercive colonial policies and entanglement in their antimarkets. Documentary sources indicate that the community was made to produce agricultural subsistence crops and livestock (e.g., maize, honey, chickens), as well as tribute and taxes in currency in the seventeenth century (AGCA A3. Leg. 2316 Ex. 34167)[1] and serve as coerced wage laborers as part of the repartimiento (Sherman 1979, p. 203) for Spanish officials, local estate owners (AGCA A1. Leg. 5368 Ex. 45405) and in a sugar mill near Escuintla, Guatemala (AGI, Guatemala, 27, R. 1, N. 29)[2]. Thus, Aguacatepeque found itself needing to produce tribute in kind (mainly foodstuffs), as well as tribute in currency, twice per year (see Simpson 1959), and found itself drawn into the repartimiento as wage laborers by force and by the need to generate currency for taxes. Indeed,

---

[1] Archivo General de Centro America, Guatemala City, Guatemala; AGCA from this point forward.

[2] Archivo General de Indias, Seville, Spain; AGI from this point forward.

wage labor as part of repartimiento, while providing income, brought with it a suite of hardships (see Borg 1986, pp. 115–124) that contributed to the emergence of new dependencies that would transform production and consumption practices at Aguacatepeque.

At the same time numerous mentions are made of Aguacatepeque's involvement in uncoerced (or differently coerced if we consider economic need catalyzed by colonial labor demands as a form of coercion) cash crop production. The dispersed and sometimes indirect effect of tribute demands on native production practices is evident at Aguacatepeque, in a 1689 document by Fray Francisco de Zuaza, who mentions the community's cultivation of maize, cacao, and sugarcane, the last of which was used in the production of unrefined sugar loafs (rapaduras) produced explicitly for sale at market as a cash crop (Vázquez and Lamadrid 1944, pp. 57–58). A 1690 Tercio de San Juan (June 29) tribute tasacion for Aguacatepeque lists 72 full tributaries (or minimum of 144 people) from whom silver currency (182 tostones; representing 728 person days of repartimiento labor) , maize, chickens, and "miel" (honey) was requested, but not sugar or sugar products (AGCA. A3.10 Leg. 1601, Exp. 26391, Folio 161), supporting the contention that the sugarcane cultivated and processed was not directly turned over for tribute but for sale at market.

By 1740, Aguacatepeque was still cultivating sugarcane and producing "panelas" (similar to rapaduras) "from which they pay their tribute" (Crespo 1740, p. 9). Again, sugarcane cultivation continued not as a direct tribute crop, but as a cash crop with which to acquire currency to pay tributes and taxes currency. Indeed, operation and success of the "great numbers of little sugar mills" found in Maya communities provided an alternative supply of sugar and sugar products (such as melada and alcoholic chicha) presumably to Maya, castas and Spanish colonists alike, which contributed to declining sugar and sugar product prices in the local economy, to the growing anxiety of Spanish colonial observers (de Fuentes y Guzmán and de Santa María 1969, p. 316; Hill 1992, p. 122).

Sugarcane cultivation and processing probably provided an additional source of income through the sale and exchange of illicit fermented beverages (chicha) and distilled spirits (de Fuentes y Guzmán and de Santa María 1969, p. 316; Hill 1992, p. 122) through the "informal" economy constituted by Maya inter- and extracommunity exchange (see Lutz 1994, p. 153). Local officials were especially concerned with this brisk illicit trade in alcohol as it proved a threat to the local colonial administrations monopoly on wine and aguardiente de cana distribution and thus a hindrance to their ability to artificially elevate prices and increase profits (Lutz 1994, pp. 153, 306–157).

While Aguacatepeque was likely engaged in cacao cultivation in the Postclassic, in the colonial period, specialized cash crop cultivation came with a suite of divergent effects, perhaps due to the added colonial burdens of repartimiento labor and declines in community population, as archaeological research has shown an increasing reliance on the labor and goods of those outside of the community becoming critical to survival.

The cumulative effect of Spanish colonial antimarkets, structured by coercive practices like the repartimiento de bienes, repartimiento labor drafts, and wage labor was to catalyze shifts in community and household production practices at Aguacatepeque toward mixed cash and tribute crop production as a means of generating necessary income with which to pay tribute and taxes (see Larson and Wasserstrom 1983, p. 74). Indeed, the introduction of taxes and tributes and credit/debt payable only in tostones, reales, and pesos in colonial Guatemala became a central instrument of more tightly entangling native communities into colonial antimarkets and shifting relations of production (see Gasco 1997, p. 58) with the effect of fostering intensifying dependence on goods acquired through markets subject to colonial manipulations.

## 5.8  Market Dependence and Temporal Dispossession: Antimarket Effects

Considering the above discussion and drawing inspiration from Harvey's (2003) argument for "accumulation by dispossession" (an expansion of Marx's primitive accumulation) as a critical component of historic and modern "capitalist" formations, I argue the emergence of capitalist relations, or more accurately the development of market dependence as an antimarket effect in Colonial Guatemala—at least at Aguacatepeque—came about less through the dispossession of land, and more from the dispossession of native time and labor. This "temporal dispossession" served—as many documents attest—to take time away from Maya people to labor on their land for subsistence needs (see Sherman 1968, p. 8).

As a result, between labor and tribute, and/or cash crop production, access to land "outside of the market" (Wood 2002, p. 54) was seriously curtailed by coercive forces that required Maya people to labor for free, or for minimal wages and thus dispossess the community of time and labor necessary for their self-produced subsistence. These unintended effects or indeed intended effects as part of the repartimiento de bienes, would have had the capability of intensifying intraregional subsistence exchange—a critical aspect of the emergence of capitalism in Marx's model (Harvey 2010, p. 297)—yet not through the dispossession of land and means of production, but rather through the dispossession of time through coerced labor.

As a sixteenth century Spanish judge Alonso de Zorita commented about the coerced labor drafts of the repartimiento that took native people away from their homes for weeks at a time, with considerable impact on subsistence practices:

> There is another injury-and it is not a small one-that results from their journeys. Because the Indians are so few and the demands for their labor so numerous, each Indian is assigned many turns at compulsory labor. Moreover, contrary to what Your Majesty has ordered, the officials make the Indians go at the season when they should be sowing or weeding their fields, which are their sole wealth and means of support. (Borg 1986, p. 124; de Zorita 1963, pp. 214–216)

Aguacatepeque was particularly impacted by this process of increasing demands on the community's time and labor and its concomitant impact on local production.

In a petition from 1593 (Sherman 1979, pp. 203–204), Aguacatepeque's leaders expressed concern over the temporal dispossession that repartimiento labor in the capital would cause due to the distance between the town and Santiago where they were being summoned to. They appealed to the president of the audiencia on the basis of the value of their cacao tribute production, which they argued would be interrupted to the detriment of the audiencia's coffers.

A common effect of this temporal dispossession would have been to afford a greater dependence on markets and thus consumption to "make ends meet" from season to season, week to week, as native laborers were taken away physically to labor in Spanish fields and enterprises, or dispossessed of the time necessary to grow subsistence crops, due to the importance of intensively cultivating labor- and time-intensive cash crops to meet Spanish colonial tribute demands both in kind or in currency (see especially sugar production at Aguacatepeque). This temporal dispossession, distinct from an iconic "capitalist" relation of production, nevertheless produces a parallel capitalist "effect" on the community in the form of intensifying currency-generating production practices, in order to acquire the necessary "basic inputs" needed to live, work, and continue producing currency and crops for tribute and with which to acquire more basic inputs.

As a result, Aguacatepeque quickly came to be entangled with the types of practices that drove the emerging "capitalist" world economy—in this case cash crop production and market engagement/dependence for subsistence—yet it did so from a radically different footing than in Europe and other contexts. Aguacatepeque's participation in "coerced cash crop labor" (Wallerstein 1974, p. 91) and wage labor was structured by the overt coercion of colonial power relations. The developmental trajectory of the Guatemalan colonial context yielded a unique suite of antimarkets that clearly set it apart from Western European developmental scheme of capitalist practices in form, yet not entirely in terms of "effects."

Archaeological research at Aguacatepeque has yielded insight into the degree of market dependence that developed within the community in the colonial period, as well as the practices that diverged from the models of market dependence development and effects. Preliminary analysis of ceramics recovered from colonial contexts has yielded an assemblage that is predominantly comprised of market acquired ceramics. Ceramic analysis at Aguacatepeque has focused on the identification of distinct paste groups—seen as representing distinct paste recipes unique to disparate regional and/or local workshops—in circulation and use during the colonial period (see Orton et al. 1993; Roddick 2009). At present, ceramic paste groups have been microscopically characterized and ceramic sherds sorted by paste group and subjected to extensive attribute analysis (e.g., decoration, form, residue, lip type, etc.).

Some of these attributes are chronologically diagnostic, while others are spatially diagnostic, indicating ceramics produced in distinct communities dispersed across the Maya highlands. Previous ceramic elemental characterization work with INAA and documentary research has identified the provenance of ceramic types with diagnostic features identified at Aguacatepeque (see Fig. 5.2), including Amatle (Robinson et al. 1998), Chinautla Polychromes (Rice 1977; Wauchope 1970) and lead glazed coarse earthenwares and majolicas made in Santiago (see Rodriguez

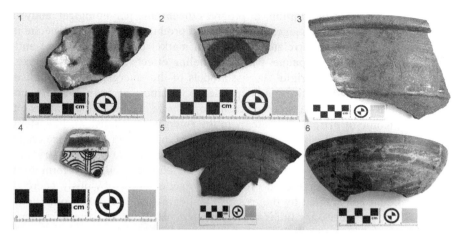

**Fig. 5.2** Sample of colonial period market-acquired ceramics from Aguacatepeque. **a, b** Guatemalan Majolica tableware. **c** Guatemalan lead-glazed coarse earthenware jar. **d** Mexican (Puebla) Majolica sherd. **e** Talc-slipped comal (highland/Pacific coast of Guatemala). **f** Chinautla polychrome bowl

Giron 2008; Sharer et al. 1970). Drawing on the cooccurrence of these diagnostic attributes with specific paste groups, it was determined, conservatively, that at least 65.9 % ($n = 1579$) of ceramic sherds recovered from colonial contexts were likely produced either in Santiago or in other highland Maya ceramic-producing communities such as Chinautla or near Chimaltenango and thus most likely market acquired. These findings represent a drastic change from the precolonial contexts excavated at Aguacatepeque, as all precolonial contexts (Late Classic and Postclassic in date) yielded an assemblage made up of only 25.4 % ($n = 235$) nonlocal, market-acquired sherds (see Pezzarossi and Escobar 2012).

Moreover, a Shannon–Weiner diversity index was calculated for all ceramics analyzed and converted to "true diversity figures" or effective species figures (Jost 2006), which provide a more direct metric of diversity of ceramic paste types present in colonial vs. precolonial contexts. Precolonial contexts yielded a true diversity figure of 25 effective paste groups, while colonial contexts yielded only 20 effective paste groups, indicating a 5-paste-group difference in the ceramic assemblages, which amounts to the colonial contexts being only 80 % as diverse as the precolonial contexts. This result, in tandem with the increase in market acquired wares, indicates that the colonial period population at Aguacatepeque was becoming more dependent on market-acquired wares produced by fewer, perhaps more centralized ceramic producers located in Santiago or elsewhere. I argue that these changes are linked to broader shifts in agricultural production and labor stimulated by colonial tribute demands and antimarket effects. These results are preliminary and will be checked against the result of in-progress neutron activation analysis on all recovered paste groups that will provide further empirical grounding for claims of disparate paste groups and vessels as nonlocal in origin. In addition, in-progress diachronic palynological analysis will provide insight into changes in agricultural production at Aguacatepeque in the colonial period that correlated to shifts in market dependence. These anti-market effects at Aguacatepeque, while paralleling effects in capitalist contexts, conspicuously break with rigid Marxist models of the emergence of capitalism through market-based practices and dependence in important ways. While Aguacatepeque did engage in the "coerced cash crop" mode of production Wallerstein defines as iconic of peripheral contexts in the emerging capitalist world system, it did so outside of Spanish tribute demands in currency and in subsistence crops. Thus, cash crop production—at least according to available documentary evidence—at Aguacatepeque appears as a strategic "choice" perhaps informed by precolonial cacao exchange crop production practices (yet obviously coerced, structured, and constrained by the exercise and demands of colonial power) intended to acquire necessary funds for tribute, potentially avoid excess frequently harsh wage labor and thus facilitate survival, community persistence, and "residence" (Silliman 2001) in the colonial world.

Moreover, market dependence that developed out of the temporal dispossessions catalyzed by the above, took its own form at Aguacatepeque. Documents mention the continued production of subsistence crops (e.g., maize, beans, and chiles) at the community indicating at least a measure of autonomy in quotidian subsistence. Market dependence is instead visible archaeologically through the analysis of ceramic artifacts, as colonial contexts at Aguacatepeque display a much elevated dependence on nonlocal market acquired goods likely bought in part from colonists and clergy (see Herrera 2003, p. 40; Paredes and Romero 2008, pp. 85–86) who were responsible for the tribute and labor demands that produced the antimarkets that set in motion these broader shifts and local changes in Aguacatepeque's production, consumption, and material practices.

Simply put: capitalism—as an entity—did not catalyze these changes. Rather the changes in practice at Aguacatepeque that mirror and parallel practices and relations iconic of capitalism are present as the effects of policies, practices, institutions, and processes backed by unequal power that gave rise to unequal and coercive relations of production (i.e., colonial antimarkets). These effects simultaneously bear a striking familial resemblance to and diverge from late "capitalist" contexts across the globe as well as noncapitalist contexts, and yet retain a unique historical trajectory that highlights similarities in development and effect in order to make contexts cross-comparable in terms of the impact of unequal power on those subjected to it.

## 5.9   Conclusions

The unique suite of production and consumption practices carried out at Aguacatepeque highlights the character and texture of one of the effects of antimarkets specific to colonial Guatemala and its Maya communities. Market dependence for subsistence needs and/or "circulating capital" (Braudel 1979, p. 242) when coupled with market/cash crop cultivation can be expediently interpreted and explained as a product of Aguacatepeque's engagement with and shift toward capitalism and "modernity." However a more complicated story emerges when we consider the precolonial roots of prized crop production, "primitive accumulation," and market manipulation and dependence (as in Aztec and highland Maya tribute demands for example) that place these practices and processes (albeit in changed form) well outside the exclusive purview of Spanish colonization and capitalism. By continuing to excavate these histories and the stubborn strata of abstractions that overlay them, we quickly encounter the "actual details" of history (De Landa 1996) that bring into relief the insufficiency of shift-based monolithic models of history (see Frank 1991; Gaitan-Ammann 2011, p. 147; Mielants 2007, p. 11). Indeed, this insufficiency is made manifest at Aguacatepeque, where "capitalist" practices, with precapitalist histories, afforded by colonial power and primitive accumulation coexisted alongside "feudal" and precapitalist/pre-Hispanic practices in an anachronistic, model-busting milieu.

The archaeology of capitalism and especially the archaeology of capitalism and colonialism in Latin America, and elsewhere, requires the reorientation of conceptual and analytical approaches away from top–down models and toward the "archaeology" of context contingent historical development of unequal relations of production and accumulation and the various and variable entanglements of historical processes, colonial power, and global economies that spawned manifold effects for those subalterned to them. The focus on antimarkets taken up in this chapter is an attempt to address both the persistent problem of defining and analyzing capitalism and the difficulties of investigating the development and influence of capitalism or capitalist effects in colonial or other "noncapitalist" contexts. In particular, the Mesoamerican historical context provides an important *longue duree* perspective on capitalist/antimarkets effects by highlighting the presence of parallel antimarket formations and effects in a decidedly "precapitalist" context. Reorienting analyses of capitalism around antimarkets, the engines that drive and make possible the relentless accumulation of capital through unequal relations of production and effects brings into sharp focus the presence and influence of power in structuring historic and modern economic formations and material conditions of life.

In sum, this chapter has—in a necessarily incomplete and preliminary manner—drawn on documentary and archaeological evidence to sketch out the interdigitated nature of colonial power and "capitalist" (anti)market-based material practices in colonial Guatemala and San Pedro Aguacatepeque in particular. The archaeology of San Pedro Aguacatepeque aids in this discussion by providing a case study for analyzing the unique assemblage of forces and actors (see De Landa 2006) that contributed to the development and unfolding of the unique hybrid of Maya, feudal, colonial, capitalist, and antimarket relations and practices that constituted the experience of "modernity" for one Maya community in the Pacific piedmont of Guatemala through their various effects. By focusing on the uneven contours of power in economic articulations, attention is drawn to the role colonial power played (and imperial power plays) in entangling colonized and subalterned populations in emerging global economies and the "system" of antimarkets undergirding them.

Archaeologies of capitalism, opened up into the archaeology of antimarket effects, can provide critical insight into the divergent developmental trajectories of parallel economic processes, antimarkets, and their effects on the material practices and daily lives of those subjected to them (something Braudel argued was out of reach of traditional history). In the process, a more inclusive consideration of the heterogeneous assemblage agents, actants, practices, and technologies that afforded unequal relations of production and their effects emerges, unveiling the causal forces historically ascribed to the capitalism. This chapter has attempted the incipient steps to uncovering what analyses and discussions of capitalism have papered over in Spanish colonial contexts through the identification of the forces directly responsible for the capitalist effects that Aguacatepeque weathered, adapted, and why influenced by in colonial Guatemala.

# References

Baskes, J. (2005). Colonial institutions and cross-cultural trade: Repartimiento credit and indigenous production of cochineal in eighteenth-century Oaxaca, Mexico. *The Journal of Economic History, 65*(1), 186–210.

Beals, R. (1967). Acculturation. In M. Nash (Ed.), *Handbook of Middle American Indians* (Vol. 6, pp. 449–468). Austin: University of Texas Press.

Berdan, F., Masson, M. A., Gasco, J., & Smith, M. E. (2003). An international economy. In G. C. Smith & F. Berdan (Eds.), *The Postclassic Mesoamerican world* (pp. 96–108). Salt Lake City: University of Utah Press.

Borg, B. E. (1986). Ethnohistory of the Sacatepequez Cakchiquel Maya, ca. 1450–1690. PhD Dissertation, University of Missouri, Columbia.

Braswell, G. E. (2003). *Highland Maya polities. The Postclassic Mesoamerican world* (pp. 45–49). Salt Lake City: University of Utah Press.

Braswell, G. (2010). A dynamic approach to ancient maya economy. In C. P. Garraty & B. L. Stark (Eds.), *In Archaeological approaches to market exchange in pre-capitalist societies* (Vol. 2010, pp. 127–140). Salt Lake City: University of Utah Press.

Braswell, G., & Glascock, M. (2003). The emergence of market economies in the ancient Maya world: Obsidian exchange in terminal classic Yucatán, Mexico. In M. Glascock (Ed.), *Geochemical evidence for long distance exchange*. Westport: Bergin and Garvey.

Braudel, F. (1979). *Civilization and capitalism, 15th–18th century. Vol. 1, The structures of everyday life*. Berkeley: University of California Press.

Braudel, F. (1984). *Civilization and capitalism: 15th–18th century. Vol. 3, The perspective of the world*. London: Collins.

Brumfiel, E. M., Brown, K. L., Carrasco, P., Chadwick, R., Charlton, T. H., Dillehay, T. D., & Sanders, W. T. (1980). Specialization, market exchange, and the Aztec state: A view from Huexotla (and comments and reply). *Current Anthropology, 21*(4), 459–478. doi:10.2307/2742060.

Chiapello, E. (2007). Accounting and the birth of the notion of capitalism. *Critical Perspectives on Accounting, 18*(3), 263–296.

Coronil, F. (2007). After empire: Reflections on imperialism from the Americas. In A. L. Stoler, C. McGranahan, & P. C. Perdue (Eds.), *Imperial formations* (pp. 241–274). Santa Fe: School for Advanced Research Press.

Crespo, A. (1740). Relacion Geografica del Partido de Escuintla Boletin del archivo general del gobierno Guatemala: A.

Croucher, S. K., & Weiss, L. (2011). *The archaeology of capitalism in colonial contexts: Postcolonial historical archaeologies*.New York: Springer.

Dahlin, B. H., Jensen, C. T., Terry, R. E., Wright, D. R., & Beach, T. (2007). In search of an ancient Maya market. *Latin American Antiquity, 18*(4), 363–384.

De Landa, M. (1996). Markets and anti-markets in the world economy. In S. Aronowitz, B. Martinsons, & M. Mensen (Eds.), *Technoscience and cyberculture*. London: Routledge.

De Landa, M. (1997). *A thousand years of nonlinear history*. New York: Zone Books.

De Landa, M. (2006). *A new philosophy of society assemblage theory and social complexity*. London: Continuum.

Deleuze, G., Guattari, F., & Massumi, B. (2005). *A thousand plateaus: Capitalism and schizophrenia*. Minneapolis: University of Minnesota Press.

Feinman, G. M., & Garraty, C. P. (2010). Preindustrial markets and marketing: Archaeological perspectives. *Annual Review of Anthropology, 39,* 167–191.

Forstater, M. (2005). Taxation and primitive accumulation: The case of colonial Africa. *Research in Political Economy, 22,* 51–64.

Frank, A. G. (1967). *Capitalism and underdevelopment in Latin America: Historical studies of Chile and Brazil*. New York: Monthly Review Press.

Frank, A. G. (1991). Transitional ideological modes: Feudalism, capitalism, socialism. *Critique of Anthropology, 11*(2), 171–188. doi:10.1177/0308275x9101100206.

de Fuentes y Guzmán, F. A, & de Santa María, C. S. (1969). *Obras historicas de Don Francisco Antonio de Fuentes y Guzman* (Vol. 1). Madrid: Ediciones Atlas.

Funari, P. P. A., Hall. M., & Jones. S. (1999). Introduction: Archaeology in history. In P. P. A. Funari, M. Hall, & S. Jones (Eds.), *Historical archaeology: Back from the edge* (pp. 1–20). London: Routledge.

Gaitan-Ammann, F. (2011). A life on broken China: Figuring senses of capitalism in late nineteenth-century Bogota. In S. K. Croucher & L. Weiss (Eds.), *The archaeology of capitalism in colonial contexts: Postcolonial historical archaeologies*. New York: Springer.

Gasco, J. (1997). Consolidation of the colonial regime: Native society in Western Central America. *Historical Archaeology, 31*(1), 55–63.

Graeber, D. (2011). *Debt: The first 5000 years*. Brooklyn: Melville House Publishing.

Halperin, C. T., Bishop, R. L., Spensley, E., & Blackman, M. J. (2009). Late classic (A.D. 600–900) Maya market exchange: Analysis of figurines from the Motul de San José Region, Guatemala. *Journal of Field Archaeology, 34*(4), 457–480. doi:10.1179/009346909791070745.

Harvey, D. (2003). *The new imperialism*. Oxford: Oxford University Press.

Harvey, D. (2010). *A companion to Marx's capital*. London: Verso.

Hauser, M. (2011). Uneven topographies: Archaeology of plantations and caribbean slave economies. In S. K. Croucher & L. Weiss (Eds.), *The archaeology of capitalism in colonial contexts: Postcolonial historical archaeologies*. New York: Springer.

Herrera, R. A. (2003). *Natives, Europeans and Africans in sixteenth-century Santiago de Guatemala*. Austin: University of Texas Press.

Hill, R. M. (1992). *Colonial Cakchiquels: Highland Maya adaptations to Spanish rule, 1600–1700*. Fort Worth: Harcourt Brace Jovanovich.

Hirth, K. (2009a). 1 Housework and domestic craft production: An introduction. *Archeological Papers of the American Anthropological Association, 19*(1), 1–12. doi:10.1111/j.1551-8248.2009.01009.x.

Hirth, K. (2009b). 2 Craft production, household diversification, and domestic economy in Prehispanic Mesoamerica. *Archeological Papers of the American Anthropological Association, 19*(1), 13–32. doi:10.1111/j.1551-8248.2009.01010.x.

Ho, K. (2005). Situating global capitalisms: A view from Wall Street investment banks. *Cultural Anthropology, 20*(1), 68–96. doi:10.1525/can.2005.20.1.068.

Horning, A. J. (2011). Subduing tendencies? Colonialism, capitalism, and comparative Atlantic archaeologies. In S. K. Croucher & L. Weiss (Eds.), *The archaeology of capitalism in colonial contexts: Postcolonial historical archaeologies* (pp. 65–85). New York: Springer.

Jost, L. (2006). Entropy and diversity. *Oikos, 113*(2), 363–375.

Laclau, E. (1971). Feudalism and capitalism in Latin America. *New Left Review* I/67, May-June 1971.

Larraz, P. C. y. (1958). *Descripcion Geografico-Moral de la Diocesis de Goathemala* (Vol. 2). Guatemala: Sociedad de Geografia e Historia de Guatemala.

Larson, B., & Wasserstrom, R. (1983). Coerced consumption in colonial Bolivia and Guatemala. *Radical History Review, 1983*(27), 49–78.

Lokken, P. (2004). A maroon moment: Rebel slaves in early seventeenth-century Guatemala. *Slavery and Abolition, 25*(3), 44–58.

Lutz, C. (1994). *Santiago de Guatemala, 1541–1773: City, Caste and Colonial Experiance.* Norman: University of Oklahoma Press.

Luxemburg, R. (2003). *The accumulation of capital.* London: Routledge.

MacLeod, M. J. (1973). *Spanish Central America: A socioeconomic history, 1520–1720.* Berkeley: University of California Press.

MacLeod, M. J. (1983). Ethnic relations and Indian society in the province of Guatemala ca. 1620-ca.1800. In M. J. MacLeod & R. Wasserstrom (Eds.), *Spaniards and Indians in southeastern Mesoamerica: Essays on the history of ethnic relations* (pp. 189–214). Lincoln: University of Nebraska Press.

Marx, K. (1990). *Capital: A critique of political economy* (Vol. 1). London: Penguin.

Mielants, E. (2007). *The origins of capitalism and the "rise of the West".* Philadelphia: Temple University Press.

Millhauser, J. K., Rodríguez-Alegría, E., & Glascock, M. D. (2011). Testing the accuracy of portable X-ray fluorescence to study Aztec and colonial obsidian supply at Xaltocan, Mexico. *Journal of Archaeological Science, 38*(11), 3141–3152. doi:10.1016/j.jas.2011.07.018.

Millon, R. F. (1974). When money grew on trees a study of cacao in ancient Mesoamerica. PhD, Columbia University, New York. http://worldcat.org/z-wcorg/database.

Mitchell, T. (2002). *Rule of experts: Egypt, techno-politics, modernity.* Berkeley: University of California Press.

Nichols, D. L., Brumfiel, E. M., Neff, H., Hodge, M., Charlton, T. H., & Glascock, M. D. (2002). Neutrons, markets, cities, and empires: A 1000-year perspective on ceramic production and distribution in the Postclassic Basin of Mexico. *Journal of Anthropological Archaeology, 21*(1), 25–82. doi:10.1006/jaar.2001.0389.

Orellana, S. (1995). *Ethnohistory of the Pacific coast.* Lancaster: Labyrinthos.

Orton, C., Tyers, P., & Vince, A. (1993). *Pottery in archaeology:* Cambridge: Cambridge University Press.

Paredes, J. H., & Romero, L. A. (2008). La Ceramica Tipo Chinautla del Convento de Santo Domingo. In Z. Rodriguez Giron (Ed.), *Investigaciones Arqueologicas en el Convento de Santo Domingo, Antigua Guatemala* (Vol. 2 Los Materiales Arqueologicos). Guatemala: Asociacion Tikal.

Pezzarossi, G., & Escobar, L. (2011). *Proyecto Arqueologico San Pedro Aguacatepeque, Alotenango. Informe Preliminar No. 1, Primera Temporada 2010.* Guatemala City: Instituto de Antropologia e Historia de Guatemala.

Pezzarossi, G., & Escobar, L. (2012). Reporte Preliminar de las Excavaciones en San Pedro de Aguacatepeque. Paper presented at the Simposio de Arqueología de Guatemala XXVI, Guatemala City.

Pezzarossi, G., & Escobar, L. (2013). *Proyecto Arqueológico San Pedro Aguacatepeque, Alotenango: Informe Preliminar no.2, Segunda Temporada 2011.* Guatemala City: Instituto de Antropología e Historia de Guatemala.

Pugh, T. W. (2006). Cacao, gender and the Northern Lacandon god house. In C. L. McNeil (Ed.), *Chocolate in Mesoamerica: A cultural history of cacao* (pp. 202–223). Gainesville: University Press of Florida.

Quijano, A. (2000). Coloniality of power and eurocentrism in Latin America. *International Sociology, 15*(2), 215–232. doi:10.1177/0268580900015002005.

Reents-Budet, D. (2006). The social context of Kakaw drinking among the ancient Maya. In C. L. McNeil (Ed.), *Chocolate in Mesoamerica: A cultural history of cacao* (pp. 202–223). Gainesville: University Press of Florida.

Rice, P. M. (1977). Whiteware pottery production in the Valley of Guatemala: Specialization and resource utilization. *Journal of Field Archaeology, 4*(2), 221–233.

Richard, F. G. (2011). "In [Them] We Will Find Very Desirable Tributaries for Our Commerce": Cash crops, commodities, and subjectivities in Siin (Senegal) during the colonial era. In S. K. Croucher & L. Weiss (Eds.), *The archaeology of capitalism in colonial contexts: Postcolonial historical archaeologies*. New York: Springer.

Robinson, E. (1990). *Reconocimiento de los Municipios de Alotenango y Sumpango, Sacatepequez*. La Antigau: CIRMA.

Robinson, E., & Pezzarossi, G. (2012). Los Mayas del Clásico Tardío en la Región del Valle de Antigua: Defensa y Agricultura en las Tierras Altas de Guatemala. Paper presented at the XXV Simposio de Investigaciones Arqueologicas en Guatemala 2011, Guatemala City.

Robinson, E., Wholey, H., & Neff, H. (1998). La tradición ceramica Flesh Ware en las tierras altas centrales y costa del Pacifico de Guatemala. Paper presented at the XI Simposio de Investigaciones Arqueológicas en Guatemala, Guatemala City.

Roddick, A. (2009). Communities of pottery production and consumption on the Taraco Peninsula, Bolivia, 200 BC–300 AD. PhD Dissertation, University of California, Berkeley.

Rodríguez-Alegría, E. (2002). Indigena Ware: Spain to valley of Mexico. In M. Glascock (Ed.), *Geochemical evidence for long-distance exchange* (pp. 13–31). Westport: Greenwood Publishing Group.

Rodriguez-Alegria, E. (2008). Narratives of conquest, colonialism, and cutting-edge technology. *American Anthropologist, 110*(1), 33–43.

Rodriguez-Alegria, E., Neff, H., & Glascock, M. D. (2003). Indigenous ware or Spanish import? The case of Indigena ware and approaches to power in colonial Mexico. *Latin American Antiquity, 14*(1), 67–81.

Rodriguez Giron, Z. (Ed.). (2008). *Investigaciones Arqueologicas en el Convento de Santo Domingo, Antigua Guatemala* (Vol. 2 Los Materiales Arqueologicos). Guatemala: Asociacion Tikal.

Scott, J. (1990). *Domination and the arts of resistance: Hidden transcripts*.New Haven: Yale University Press.

Sharer, R., Ashmore, W., & Hill, R. (1970). *The pottery of Antigua Guatemala*. Guatemala City: The Hispanic American Project.

Shaw, L. (2012). The elusive Maya marketplace: An archaeological consideration of the evidence. *Journal of Archaeological Research, 20*(2), 117–155. doi:10.1007/s10814-011-9055-0.

Sheets, P. (2000). Provisioning the Ceren household. *Ancient Mesoamerica, 11*(2), 217–230.

Sherman, W. L. (1968). Abusos contra los Indios de Guatemala (1602–1605). Relaciones del Obispo. *Cahiers du monde hispanique et luso-brésilien, 11*, 5–28. doi:10.2307/40849719.

Sherman, W. (1979). *Forced native labor in sixteenth-century Central America*. Lincoln: University of Nebraska Press.

Silliman, S. (2001). Agency, practical politics and the archaeology of culture contact. *Journal of Social Archaeology, 1*(2), 190–209.

Simpson, L. B. (1959). A seventeenth-century encomienda: Chimaltenango, Guatemala. *The Americas, 15*(4), 393–402.

Smith, M. E., & Berdan, F. (2003). *The postclassic Mesoamerican world*. Salt Lake City: University of Utah Press.

Stern, S. J. (1988). Feudalism, capitalism, and the world-system in the perspective of Latin America and the Caribbean. *The American Historical Review, 93*(4), 829–872. doi:10.2307/1863526.

Stern, S. J. (1993). Feudalism, capitalism and the world-system in the perspective of Latin America and the Caribbean. In F. Cooper, F. E. Mallon, S. J. Stern, A. F. Isaacman, & W. Roseberry (Eds.), *Confronting historical paradigms: Peasants, labor, and the capitalist world system in Africa and Latin America* (pp. 23–83). Madison: University of Wisconsin Press.

Tsing, A. L. (2005). *Friction: An ethnography of global connection*. Princeton: Princeton University Press.

Vargas, R. C., López, V. A. V., & Martin, S. (2009). Daily life of the ancient Maya recorded on murals at Calakmul, Mexico. *Proceedings of the National Academy of Sciences, 106*(46), 19245–19249.

102                                                                    G. Pezzarossi

Vazquez, F., & Lamadrid, L. (1937). *Crónica de la provincia del Santísimo nombre de Jesús de Guatemala de la orden de n. seráfico padre San Francisco en el reino de la Nueva España/ compuesta por Francisco Vázquez; con prólogo, notas e índices por Lázaro Lamadrid.* Guatemala: [s.n.].

Vázquez, F., & Lamadrid, L. (1944). *Crónica de la provincia del Santísimo nombre de Jesús de Guatemala de la orden de n. seráfico padre san Francisco en el reino de la Nueva España de la Orden de N. Serafico Padre San Francisco en el Reino de la Nueva Espana* (Vol. 2). Guatemala City: Tipografía nacional.

Voss, B. L. (2012). Sexual effect: Postcolonial and queer perspectives on the archaeology of sexuality and empire. In B. L. Voss & E. C. Casella (Eds.), *The archaeology of colonialism: Intimate encounters and sexual effects* (pp. 11–28). Cambridge: Cambridge University Press.

Wallerstein, I. M. (1974). *The modern world-system.* New York: Academic Press.

Wallerstein, I. (1991). Braudel on capitalism, or everything upside down. *The Journal of Modern History, 63*(2), 354–361. doi:10.2307/2938489.

Wauchope, R. (1970). Protohistoric pottery of the Guatemala highlands. In W. R. Bullard (Ed.), *Monographs and papers in Maya archaeology* (Vol. 61). Cambridge: The Peabody Museum.

Wood, E. M. (2002). The question of market dependence. *Journal of Agrarian Change, 2*(1), 50–87. doi:10.1111/1471-0366.00024.

Zeitlin, J. F., & Thomas, L. (1997). Indian consumers on the periphery of the colonial market system: Tracing domestic economic behavior in a tehuantepec hamlet. In J. Gasco, G. C. Smith, & P. Fournier-Garcia (Eds.), *Approaches to the historical archaeology of Mexico, Central and South America.* Los Angeles: The Institute of Archaeology, University of California.

de Zorita, A. (1963). *Life and labor in ancient Mexico: The brief and summary relation of the Lords of New Spain.* New Brunswick: Rutgers University Press.

# Chapter 6
# Ek Chuah Encounters the Holy Ghost in the Colonial Labyrinth: Ideology and Commerce on Both Sides of the Spanish Invasion

Susan Kepecs

## 6.1  Introduction

From the Mesoamerican Late Postclassic through the end of the Early Colonial Period,[1] the Maya of northern Yucatán used religious ideology to control the processes of production and commerce, much as the Spaniards used Christianity to drive the New World search for gold and spices. To date, most studies of Maya ideology have been culture historical, and focused on sacred beliefs. Here, my point of departure is world systems theory (Wallerstein 1974). This perspective, borrowed from the field of historical sociology, allows me to understand how Late Postclassic elites manipulated ideology to legitimize the prosperous exchange system that crisscrossed much of Mesoamerica (Kepecs 2003; also see Smith and Berdan 2003), and to recognize the continuing use of religious symbols to drive the native economy throughout the long first century of Spanish rule.

The Spaniards imposed Christian doctrines on the Maya and usurped a great deal of indigenous production and trade. In response, the natives adapted elements of European iconography to their own ends, and commerce itself became an ideology of resistance to Spanish rule. Below I lay out the elements of the world systems framework that I used to come to these conclusions, and then describe the native ideology of commerce before and after the advent of Spanish administration. I draw

---

[1] The Mesoamerican Late Postclassic runs roughly from 1200 AD to the Spanish invasion in 1521. The Early Colonial epoch ended in the late seventeenth century, when the native population was at its lowest point and Spain's Hapsburg rulers were in decline. The Late Colonial period, beginning in the eighteenth century, was marked by stark changes including increased piracy on behalf of other European nations and the advent of Bourbon rule in Spain. Of course, these administrative shifts do not correspond 1:1 with the temporal shifts we observe in the archaeological record. My arguments in this chapter do not rely on the material indicators and chronological details of this disjunction, but I have addressed that issue in other works (Kepecs 1997, 2005, 2013).

S. Kepecs (✉)
Department of Anthropology, University of Wisconsin-Madison,
Madison, WI 53706, USA
e-mail: smkepecs@wisc.edu

© Springer International Publishing Switzerland 2015                                    103
P. P. A. Funari, M. X. Senatore (eds.), *Archaeology of Culture Contact and Colonialism in Spanish and Portuguese America*, DOI 10.1007/978-3-319-08069-7_6

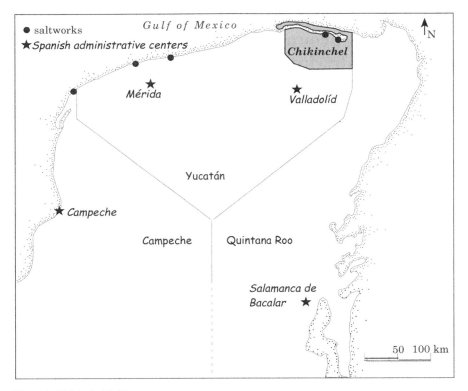

**Fig. 6.1** Chikinchel in Yucatan

on a broad literature from across Mesoamerica in general and Yucatan in particular, and show how my own archaeological and ethnohistoric data from Chikinchel (Fig. 6.1), a protocolonial or transitional era native territory (Roys 1957) some 2500 km² in Yucatan's northeast coast, where I have been working since the mid-1980s, fits into and amplifies the larger picture.

### 6.1.1 World Systems Theory

World systems are fundamentally economic, built on what Annales historian Fernand Braudel (1986, II, p. 582) called "the miracle of long distance exchange"— the wider the circulation network, the more profitable it becomes. Thus, world systems involve the production of surplus goods for exchange, and they depend on the exploitation of one social class by another across the interacting world[2]—the

---

[2] Today the world system is global, but when world systems theory is applied to premodern cases "world" simply refers to any given configuration of polities engaged in regular, sustained economic interaction (e.g., Chase-Dunn and Hall 1991; also Kepecs and Kohl 2003).

"simple division of labor across political boundaries" that defines Wallerstein's famous model (1974).

Elite accumulation is the major incentive for the creation, expansion, and continuation of world systems linkages; at the world systems scale accumulation depends not only on labor but also on investments in infrastructure and technological development in diverse areas such as manufacture, communications, transport, established exchange routes, international markets in which to transfer surplus goods, and ideology (Gills and Frank 1991). This last factor generally manifests as nationalist or religious cults that legitimize the system. When the various *structures of accumulation*—including the *ideological infrastructure of accumulation*—are regularly shared across political borders, they merge to varying degrees.

International airline alliances are a good modern example of shared transportation infrastructure; the logos on the planes vary, as do some of the commercial offerings inside airports, but there is a great deal of similarity in air travel all across the world. Ideological infrastructure, in the context of world systems accumulation, is an example of Marxist false consciousness. It exists to impress upon traders, consumers, and workers the religious and social importance of commerce; the Protestant work ethic, which helped build today's capitalist system, provides a case in point. If an ideological infrastructure of accumulation existed in the Late Postclassic Mesoamerican world, which was composed of many economically interacting polities (see Kepecs and Kohl 2003), I would expect to find symbolic messages located strategically at key centers of exchange across the macroregion, where they would be seen by merchants and buyers; such messages also would appear at major sites of production. Of course, symbols can spread for noncommercial reasons; thus, there must be acceptable reasons for interpreting these symbolic messages as indicators of world systems production and exchange.

## 6.2   The Late Postclassic Mesoamerican World System

There is a great deal of evidence for world systems exchange in Late Postclassic Mesoamerica. From Spanish accounts (Landa, in Tozzer 1941; de Sahagún 1975/1569), we know that currency was in use everywhere—cacao was most common, but cotton mantas and copper axe monies also were in play. Money is a technique for accumulation (Braudel 1986, I, p. 442, 477)—one that emerges when exchange is regular and sustained. Money allows fixing the value of an item according to predetermined prices set by outside parties. It replaces face-to-face barter, in which worth is calculated by the involved individuals' need or desire for the items being exchanged.

We know a fair amount about the archaeological distributions of durable goods produced and sold in the Late Postclassic Mesoamerican world system, which include obsidian, copper bells, and fine ceramics (e.g., Andrews 1983; Braswell 2003; Coggins and Shane 1984; Hosler 1994; McKillop and Healy 1989; Milbrath and Peraza 2003; Sabloff and Rathje 1975; Smith 1990; and see Smith and Berdan 2003). We also know how these goods were transported; Spanish sources (e.g.,

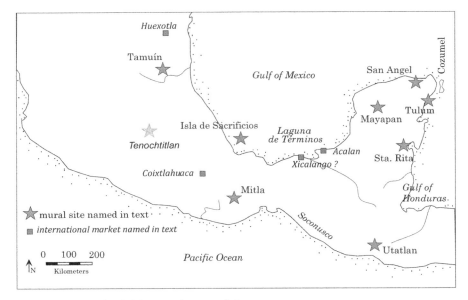

**Fig. 6.2** Late Postclassic Mesoamerican mural sites

Cortés 1988/1522, p. 390; Díaz del Castillo 1984, pp. 29–31, p. 497; Chamberlain 1948, p. 117; Edwards 1978; Thompson 1951, 1970, p. 153) describe Maya long-distance canoe traders plying the coast from the Gulf of Mexico to the Gulf of Honduras (Fig. 6.2). Professional merchants criss-crossed the inland routes of the Maya speaking world, and caravans of Aztec pochteca carried merchandise on their backs from the highlands to international markets in the mountains and on the coast (e.g., Berdan 1988; Roys 1943, pp. 51–52). While durable goods from this exchange—obsidian, copper bells, and luxury ceramics—remain in the material record, documentary sources (Landa, in Tozzer 1941; de Sahagún 1975/1569; Scholes and Roys 1948) provide ample descriptions of trade in perishable lowlands products, especially cacao, cotton, and salt.

Evidence of infrastructure for the large-scale production of some of these goods cements the picture. The Spaniards described indigenous cacao plantations on the humid coastal plains surrounding the international markets on the Gulfs of Mexico Honduras, and Soconusco, on the Pacific (e.g., Berdan 1996; de la Garza et al. 1983, II, p. 429; Gasco 2003, 2005; Landa, in Tozzer 1941, p. 94; Millon 1955; Orellana 1995; Pérez Romero 1988); hand irrigation and ditched fields that served as irrigation canals were among the technologies used to boost crop yield. Since the sweet chocolate beans could be grown elsewhere along the coast, the proximity of these intensively farmed fields to international markets was no accident.

Obsidian was mined intensively in the Late Postclassic. Complex networks of pits, shafts, and tunnels at two volcanoes—Pachuca in the central Mexican highlands (Pastrana 1992, 1998; Pastrana and Fournier 2011) and Pico de Orizaba in

Veracruz (Stocker and Cobean 1984)—are associated with large Late Postclassic components. Ixtepeque, in highland Guatemala, also a key obsidian source in this period, is less well studied, but archaeologists (Cobean et al. 1991) report quarries there.

Built infrastructure at the great salinas of Chikinchel on the northeast Yucatan coast (Andrews 1983; Eaton 1978; Ewald 1985; Kepecs 1997, 1999, 2003, 2005, 2007, 2013, 2014) was in use from the Epiclassic Period (beginning ca. 650 AD) through the seventeenth century. In what follows, I consider how the Late Postclassic Maya used the ideological infrastructure of accumulation in Chikinchel and elsewhere to drive the production and exchange of surplus goods; later, I show how the natives manipulated Christian ideology to suit their own ends while resisting Spanish domination through their own partly clandestine system of production and trade.

### 6.2.1   The Late Postclassic Ideological Infrastructure of Accumulation

In the Mesoamerican Late Postclassic world system, the ideological infrastructure of accumulation was painted prominently on the walls of public buildings—temples and "palacios"—at strategic points along the macroregional exchange routes of the period. The best documented examples (see Fig. 6.2) come from Mitla, on the Oaxacan route that crossed the mountains to the international market at Coixtlahuaca (Miller 1989, 1995); Tamuín, in the Huasteca on the Río Pánuco near the Gulf of Mexico (Du Solier 1946); Isla de Sacrificios on the Veracruz coast (Nuttall 1910); Utatlán, on the obsidian route that crossed the Guatemalan highlands (Wallace and Carmack 1977); Mayapán, the Late Postclassic political–economic hub of western Yucatan until its demise around 1450 AD (Milbrath et al. 2010); Tulum and its neighbor, Xelha, on the Caribbean coast of the Yucatan peninsula (Lothrop 1924; Miller 1982), and Santa Rita (Lothrop 1924; Miller 1982; Quirarte 1982), on Chetumal Bay, which linked the northern Maya lowlands with the points south. The buildings housing murals at Isla de Sacrificios and Santa Rita, still standing early in the twentieth century, are now destroyed, so it is logical to assume that additional but unrecorded Late Postclassic murals also have vanished.

The academic literature is replete with the esoteric and cosmological significance of these highly symbolic mural paintings, but their significance was not simply devotional; they clearly were meant to be seen and to function as a lingua franca for traveling merchants (Taube 1992, p. 90). Numerous elements beyond these strategic locations point to their commercial purpose. With world systems theory as my point of departure, I propose that the religious message in the murals served, in the manner of Marxist false consciousness, to sanctify the pursuit of commerce and to spur the production of surplus for exchange.

Scenes with deities and symbols linked to the planet Venus predominate. The plumed serpent (called Quetzalcoatl by the Aztecs, Kukulkan by the Maya)

S. Kepecs

dominates the murals at Mitla, Isla de Sacrificios, and Utatlán; at Tamuín, a line of Quetzalcoatl's priests marches across the wall. Quetzalcoatl is the king of Venus symbols. According to myth, a personage by this name died and ascended to heaven as Venus, the morning star.[3] And glyph-like symbols for Venus—specifically "ray signs" and "wasp stars" (Miller 1982, 1989)—are common to Late Postclassic mural paintings across Mesoamerica (Fig. 6.3).

In the previous archaeological period, the Epiclassic/Early Postclassic, ca. 700–1150 AD, when Tula (in the central highlands) and Chichén Itza (in northeast Yucatan) were the dominant economic cores in the Mesoamerican world system (Blanton et al. 1992; Kepecs 2007; Kowalski and Kristan-Graham 2007), the plumed serpent and the planet Venus were linked to military cults (Ringle et al. 1998), but as both Octavio Paz (1987) and Gordon Willey (1976) wrote many years ago, war and trade are the twin faces of intergroup economic relationships. And at Tula and Chichén, the military orders of the plumed serpent probably spurred trade and production in two ways: by inspiring crusades for god and loot, and through the public threat of force, to keep workers in line (Hirth 1989; Kepecs 2005, 2007; Kepecs et al. 1994).

Willey (1976) described in detail how the plumed serpent cult was reformulated in the Late Postclassic, adapted to the ideology of an ascendant class of merchants. Quetzalcoatl/Kukulkan was not a trade got per se. But in the Aztec city of Cholula, merchants sacrificed slaves and prepared great banquets in his honor (Duran 1972, pp. 128–139). Kukulkan was the patron saint of Paxbolonacha, the merchant king of Acalan, an international market in Chontal Maya territory on the Campeche coast (Scholes and Roys 1948, p. 57).

To the pro-trade plumed serpent we can add the Late Postclassic Mesoamerican trade gods proper, above all Ek Chuah[4] (God M) of the northern lowlands Maya (Fig. 6.3) and the Aztecs' Yacatecuhtli. Both Yacatecuhtli and Ek Chuah are (usually) black. They have long noses and carry merchants' packs supported with tumplines. Both are associated with militarism, with night fire ceremonies for protection on the road, and with cacao (e.g., Taube 1992; Thompson 1966). The pochteca toasted Yacatecuhtli with a cacao beverage (de Sahagún 1975/1569, IX, p. 501). In the northern Maya lowlands, merchants honored Ek Chuah in the month of Muan (the name of the month refers to a type of screech owl), sacrificing dogs with cacao-colored spots in *rejolladas* (sinkholes) planted in cacao, and carrying home cacao seeds as symbolic souvenirs of the ceremonies (Landa, in Tozzer 1941, p. 164). The association of God M with the Moan owl also is shown in the Madrid Codex, which contains an image of the deity wearing this bird as a headdress (Villacorta and Villacorta 1977, p. 442). It is worth noting that the Epiclassic/Early Postclassic military orders of Tula and Chichen Itza engaged in ritual wars—so-called

---

[3] "Venus as the morning star" refers to the planet's heliacal rising, when the planet can be seen in the morning sky. Venus has a synodic cycle of about 584 days. The planet can be seen in the morning sky for 247 earth days before it cycles behind the sun (the superior conjunction) and later appears in the evening sky until the inferior conjunction from which it emerges again as the morning star.

[4] "God M" is the designation for this merchant deity in the Maya codices.

**Fig. 6.3** Wasp star, ray signs, Ek Chuah, and glyph T680. Ek Chuah and T680 adapted from the Dresden and Madrid Codices. Originally published in the 1981 edition of *The World of the Ancient Maya*, written by John S. Henderson. Used by permission of the publisher, Cornell University Press

ray sign        wasp star        ray sign

Ek Chuah

Glyph T680

"shell-star" events, marked on the stone monuments of this period with glyphs of this name—that frequently occurred in the month of Muan (Miller 1986, p. 37; Schele and Miller 1986, p. 214). Reflecting this military heritage, Ek Chuah often carries a warrior's lance.

Ek Chuah (God M) and Yacatecutli also share a number of characteristics with God L of the Maya codices. God L, from southwest Yucatan and Veracruz, has roots in the Classic period, but like God M and Yacatecutli he is black, and he carries a merchant's pack. God L always is accompanied by a Muan owl (Taube 1992, pp. 84–85; Thompson 1970, p. 307), recalling the northern Maya merchants' ceremonies during the month of Muan.

Like Quetzalcoatl/Kukulkan, Ek Chuah and God L are associated with Venus, the morning star (Taube 1992; Thompson 1970). In Yucatec, "Ek" means black, but also "star" and "Venus" (Schellhas 1904, p. 37; Closs 1978, pp. 152–153). Ek Chuah's glyph, which epigraphers call T680 (Fig. 6.3), probably is a symbol for the planet Venus. And finally, spotted dogs like the ones sacrificed at Ek Chuah's festivals were linked to the cycles of Venus, possibly to direct the planet on its journeys across the skies (Closs 1978).

All of these seemingly small details, taken together, provide support to the notion that Yacatecutli, Ek Chuah, the plumed serpent, and other Venus symbols, displayed in mural paintings located along major commercial arteries, served as the ideological infrastructure of accumulation across the Late Postclassic Meso-american world system. Nevertheless, the economic organization of the partici-pating regions differed, as was also the case in the fifteenth-century Old World. In China, and to some degree in the Aztec empire, the economy was subject to cen-tralized political authority (Blanton 1985). On the other hand, the petty kingdoms of medieval Europe and the independent city states of northern Yucatan were small and weak, which facilitated unregulated economic competition (Kepecs 1997, 2003, 2005; Kepecs and Kohl 2003; Kepecs and Masson 2003). The elites who participated in the Late Postclassic Mesoamerican world system manipulated the partly merged ideology of commerce in ways appropriate to their own eco-nomic systems.

## 6.2.2   The Late Postclassic Ideology of Commerce in Yucatan

Based on what remains of the murals, the Yucatan Maya of the Late Postclassic—whose political–economic organization was closer to that of medieval Europe and more like capitalism than that of the Aztecs[5] (Kepecs 2003, 2005, 2013a)—had the richest concentration of commercial symbolism in Mesoamerica. Wasp stars and ray signs are abundant in the mural paintings at Tulum and Santa Rita, and solar discs with ray signs are common to both Santa Rita and Mayapan (Milbrath et al. 2010), and some symbols at the latter site probably represent Kukulkan (Milbrath et al. 2010). Taube and Gallareta Negrón (1989) reported a Late Postclassic mural painting of the plumed serpent at San Angel, near the north coast of Quintana Roo.

Ek Chuah/God M—frequently represented in the Late Postclassic modeled an-thropomorphic incensarios of Yucatan—is central to two mural scenes at Santa Rita, surrounded by ray signs and wasp stars (Taube 1992, p. 91, Fig. 91b). At Tulum, stucco masks adorning the outer front corners of Structure 16 (Miller 1982, plate 31) have eyes in the shape of glyph T680, an identifier of God M; not coinciden-tally, these masks are topped with plumed serpent headdresses.

In the mural paintings inside the buildings at Tulum, the deities Chac and God K appear, surrounded by ray signs and wasp stars (Lothrop 1924; Miller 1982; Taube 1992). Chac and God K are not merchant deities. Marilyn Masson (2003) suggests that the Tulum mural scenes may be related to ascensions to the throne. Neverthe-less, these multifaceted deities, with their ray signs and wasp stars, are spread along the coastal route, obviously meant to be seen by merchants and consumers who visited international markets on the east coast of the Yucatan peninsula. On the island of Cozumel, merchants who came from afar—especially from the lands of "Xicalango and Tabasco" (see Fig. 6.2)—visited a sanctuary with a talking oracle—a priest hidden inside a huge clay image of Ix Chel, usually cast as the goddess of

---

[5] The Aztec empire was composed of many city states; these polities, spread across the highlands and parts of the coastal plains of Veracruz and Chiapas (see Berdan et al. 1996), retained consider-able political autonomy, but forcibly paid tribute to the rulers of the Aztec capital, Tenochtitlán, in the Basin of Mexico.

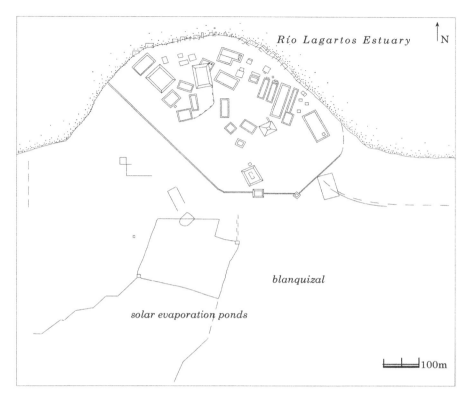

**Fig. 6.4**  Map of Emal

childbirth and the moon (de la Garza et al. 1983, II, p. 187; Roys 1957, p. 154; Tozzer 1941*n* 500).

Whatever else these mythical personages from the codices represented, I suggest that they also blessed commercial activities. The mere locations in which they appear served the purpose  of elite accumulation, and the messages these gods bore were systemic. International merchants would have returned to their homelands with this directive: to trade is divine, and to produce for commerce is, at least, a moral and spiritual obligation. The evidence from Chikinchel (Kepecs 1997, 1999, 2003, 2005, 2013b) supports this argument.

### 6.2.3   Salt and Sacred Murals in Late Postclassic Chikinchel

The hypersaline Río Lagartos estuary runs the length of Chikinchel's coast. Throughout the pre-Hispanic epoch, the Maya harvested salt from this "arm of the sea," most notably at the site of Emal (Fig. 6.4), a walled complex of ruined, small-scale

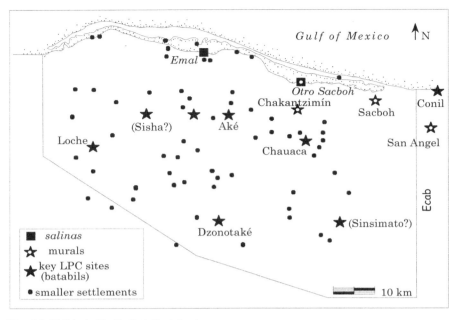

**Fig. 6.5** Chikinchel in the Late Postclassic

elite structures from which I collected impressive quantities of nonlocal ceramics, the remains of ancient macroregional exchange. Salt-encrusted mudflats surround the settlement. Today, eroded, rough-cut stone divisions stretch across 25 ha of crusty mud—the remains of a system that likely once was much larger. Despite their fragmentary condition, these features resemble modern solar evaporation systems, which divide large natural pools into successively smaller units through which brine is channeled to speed evaporation. Today the white crust is thin, but when Emal was in use canals probably were used to flood the ponds with estuary waters.

While the ceramic sequence at Emal spans the Classic through Late Postclassic periods (beginning ca. 250 AD) through the transitional period, a second pre-His-panic site with remains of solar evaporation features 20 km east—Otro Sacboh—is essentially Late Postclassic.[6] During this final pre-Hispanic period, both Emal and Otro Sacboh were supported, in terms of administration, labor, and agricultural pro-duce, by substantial centers situated 10–12 km inland. Each of these inland sup-port sites—Aké and Chauaca (Fig. 6.5)—consisted of a monumental architectural core surrounded by vast expansions of common settlement. Data from regional and full-coverage surveys at and around these inland centers (Kepecs 1999) indicate

---

[6] Ceramics indicate that Otro Sacboh and Emal were in use through the transitional period, though the archaeological and documentary records both indicate that Emal was by far the more important of the two at this time.

**Fig. 6.6** The Guardians of the Sands and the Guardians of the Sea

substantial population during the Late Postclassic. Based on very conservative archaeological population estimates for this period and historical descriptions of technologically traditional salt production at Emal, I calculate that a minimum annual dry-season salt harvest at each site in the Late Postclassic would have netted between 3500 and 5000 metric tons[7] of pure white salt (Kepecs 2003, 2005, 2013b).

Some Chikinchel salt circulated in northeast Yucatan's regional markets, but the briny diamonds of the sea also traveled across much wider networks (Kepecs 1997, 2003, 2005). The Books of Chilam Balam essentially are colonial-era chronicles[8] kept by native priests, written in Yucatec, in European script, and laid out in metaphors that prevented those Spaniards capable of reading the native language from grasping the texts' full meaning (Chuchiak 2010; Edmonson

---

[7] In 1605, the Emal saltworks produced 50,000 fanegas (ca 5750 metric tons) of salt. I used an account from the mid-nineteenth century (in Ewald 1985), still based on nonmechanized technology, to estimate how much labor a harvest of this size might require. According to this account, five workers could produce 20 fanegas of salt in a 1-day shift. A fanega is roughly a bushel and a half in size, and weighs about 115 kg (Andrews 1983, pp. 137–138). Thus 500 workers divided into 100 groups could collect 2000 fanegas per shift, or 60,000 fanegas in an intensive 30-day dry-season harvest. Even if 500 laborers worked half as hard in pre-Hispanic times, they still could produce 30,000 fanegas (close to 3500 metric tons) in a season. San Fernando alone easily could provide this number of workers in the Late Postclassic, and workers from the five smaller nucleated sites nearby, all with Late Postclassic ceramics, would have contributed significantly to overall population.

[8] The texts in the Books of Chilam Balam, written, copied and added to over the course of colonial rule and into the nineteenth century, contain heterogeneous texts; prophesy, astronomy, astrology, medicine—even Christian doctrine, as appropriated by the Maya, are included—but fundamentally the Chilam Balams are historical documents about Maya life in the colonial period (Hanks 2010).

1982, 1986). The Chilam Balams reveal that on the eve of the Spanish invasion, the governors of Emal were members of the powerful Chan lineage. The Chans of Emal had a strong alliance with the Chans of Uaymil, on the peninsula's east coast (Fig. 6.6). In the Chilam Balams, both groups were called "the guardians of the sands, the guardians of the sea" (Edmonson 1982, p. 35, 1986, p. 212; Roys 1973, p. 156), and complementing the salt enterprise at Emal, the Chans of Uaymil specialized in building large trade canoes (Roys 1957, p. 159). Early sixteenth-century Spanish explorers described such canoes, some large enough to hold 40 men, piled high with salt and traveling along the coast to the international markets on the Gulfs of Mexico and Honduras, where it was exchanged for cacao (Díaz del Castillo 1984, p. 497; Landa, en Tozzer 1941, p. 94)—in other words, for money. From the ports of trade on the Gulfs, Chikinchel's salt traveled deeper into the complex trade networks of the Late Postclassic, arriving even at such distant locations as the major Aztec highland markets of Huexotla and Coixtlahuaca (Kepecs 2003).

At Emal and Otro Sacboh, as well as at their inland support centers, ceramics mark this perishable exchange. Late Postclassic Fine Orange wares from the Gulf of Campeche—Matillas and Cunduacán—as well as the distinctive, near-fine paste "true" Tulum red from the peninsula's east coast (Kepecs 1998, 1999, 2003, 2005) were relatively abundant across these sites. From recently destroyed shrines or temples at Otro Sacboh and two additional sites in its vicinity (see Fig. 6.5), I also registered fragments of blue and black-painted plaster, most likely the remains of Late Postclassic mural paintings (Kepecs 1999, 2003, 2013b). This find is not anomalous; the site of San Angel, with its mural painting of the plumed serpent (Taube and Gallareta Negrón 1989), is only a day's walk east. The presumed murals at Chikinchel sites would have been seen by canoe traders filling their boats with salt, and by legions of seasonal saltworkers.

The murals alone probably would not motivate workers; the social relations of labor would have been key. We know that powerful Maya merchants commonly possessed slaves and serfs on the eve of the Spanish invasion (Chi, in Tozzer 1941, p. 231; Roys 1943, p. 34). While there is no concrete evidence of salaried labor, we know that goods were paid for in cacao (e.g., Landa, in Tozzer 1941; Millon 1955; Pérez Romero 1988; de Sahagún 1975/1569), and there is some evidence that prices were fixed (Chi, in Tozzer 1941, p. 231; Oviédo [Book 8, Chap. 30, quoted in Tozzer 1941, p. 98]; Thompson 1956). Thus it is not entirely unreasonable to speculate that monetary compensation was a reward for work in the highly commercialized economy of the Late Postclassic. However, to support the hypothesis that the ideology of this period served to facilite elite accumulation, much as the Protestant work ethic spurred the growth of the capitalist system, what is most crucial is simply evidence that the Yucatan Maya believed in the sanctity of commerce. The ways in which the natives dealt with the changes wrought by Spanish colonialism supply that evidence.

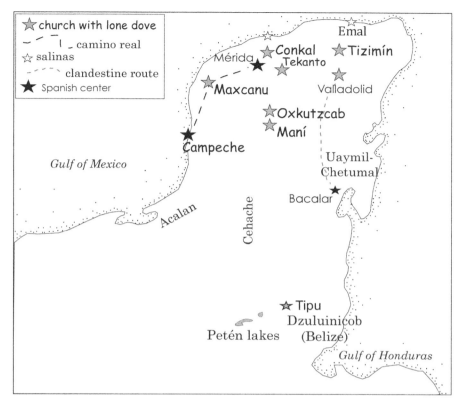

**Fig. 6.7**  Native Trade Routes and Churches with Doves

## 6.3   The Maya and the World System of the Sixteenth and Seventeenth Centuries

In the sixteenth century, Spain, at the top of the new transatlantic world system it had created, incorporated Mesoamerica into its domain. In pursuit of wealth the soldiers of European expansionism usurped the vast pre-Hispanic world system with firearms, beasts of burden, galleons, and insatiable demands on native labor. They quickly took possession of the international market areas on the Gulfs of Campeche and Honduras, and coopted indigenous transportation technology by demanding canoes and paddlers in tribute. Between 1540 and 1544, they established four centers on the Yucatan peninsula: Campeche, on the west coast; Merida, their provincial capital, in the northwest; Valladolíd, in the northeast; and Salamanca de Bacalar, on the east coast near Chetumal Bay (Fig. 6.7). Excessive tribute levies of cotton cloth, salt, ceramics, and more (e.g., de la Garza et al. 1983: I and II; Paso and del Troncoso 1905/1572–1589, 1939/1572–1589; Scholes and Roys 1948)—compounded by the toll on manpower reaped by foreign microbes—heavily undermined the indigenous regional economy, while fattening the purses of Spain and Yucatan's Spaniards.

The Maya, under pressure to produce food, chickens, cotton cloth, and utilitarian wares for the Spaniards as well as for their own consumption, abandoned the manufacture of sophisticated pottery and the erection of stone temples adorned with painted murals. Yet they mustered the time and energy to mount resistance on multiple fronts. In colonial contexts, subordinated groups develop practices—tax evasion, flight, and false compliance—that that contradict the rules of the power-holders (Scott 1990, pp. 4–5, p. 14). In the realm of religion, the colonized often adopt the dominant ideology superficially, using it to manipulate the new authorities and to hide indigenous practices. Such "hidden transcripts" are acts of resistance (Scott 1990, p. 68, pp. 86–87) as surely as armed rebellion. The information I lay out below, taken from the archaeological record, Christian iconography, and the Books of Chilam Balam, reveals that the Maya were masters of the hidden transcript, evading the Spaniards, trading behind their backs, and appropriating the Holy Ghost, especially when represented by a lone dove, to symbolize the ideology of indigenous commerce. The Maya also advocated outright rebellion—sometimes, through the voice of the Holy Ghost. This is not at all surprising given the close pre-Hispanic link between war and trade. But while the two manifestations of inter-group interactions were largely diachronic in the pre-Hispanic epoch, in the chaos of the colonial period they often merged.

In the sixteenth and seventeenth centuries, the Maya and the Spaniards participated in a complicated web of economic relations (e.g., Jones 1982, 1983, 1989, 1998; Roys 1957; Scholes and Roys 1948). During the civil congregaciones of the 1560s, the Spaniards tried to force the natives to resettle in towns under colonial control. Spanish markets were established in these towns to prevent the newly-subjected citizens from traveling in search of goods they did not produce at home (de Cogolludo Bk 5 Cap 19, 1957, I, p. 303). Yet, the Spaniards reported that the natives showed little interest in these stores, reportedly purchasing only machetes and a few Spanish trinkets (Farriss 1984, p. 45, 156).

That does not mean that the Maya had abandoned their predilection for commerce, or that congregación policies aimed at keeping the natives in place were successful. Trade outside the Spanish sphere was forbidden, but the Maya engaged in a production and exchange system that defied Spanish authority (see Scholes and Roys 1948, p. 245). The great macroregional trade routes and international markets of the Late Postclassic were destroyed, but in the 1579 *Relaciones Histórico-Geográficos de la Gobernacion de Yucatan* (de la Garza et al. 1983, I and II) several encomenderos in the Merida[9] district wrote[10] that native merchants carried cotton

---

[9] Yucatan was divided into two main administrative districts, Merida (the provincial capital, in the western portion of the peninsula) and Valladolíd, the secondary administrative center in the east.

[10] See de la Garza et al. 1983, I, p. 82, 149, 218 for examples.

mantles, wax and honey to Mexico and Honduras, returning to the peninsula with colored wool embroidery yarns, indigenous clothing, and cacao. However, the great majority of Spanish observations focused on indigenous exchange between the northern lowlands of Yucatan and the unconquered refuge zone to the south (see Fig. 6.7)—the Guatemalan Peten Lakes district and the territory of Cehache (the deep southern interior of modern Campeche). Of course, native wealth contracted significantly; Spanish demands, plus the ever-increasing flight of northerners to the southern refuge (Farriss 1984), drastically curtailed the scale of production for the Mayas' own economic ends. But long-distance exchange routes across the Maya-speaking world traversed indigenous political boundaries,[11] facilitating a reduced version of world systems accumulation among indigenous elites.

The Spaniards were aware of this shadow economy—much of what we know about it comes from Spanish reports—though they did not try to stop it, perhaps because to some degree it fed the official coffers. Grant Jones (1989, p. 106) suggests that some of this illegal trade allowed northerners to procure sufficient quantities of forest products to meet excessive Spanish tribute demands. Nevertheless, long distance exchange for tribute goods probably was minimal, since all items common in the tribute lists of 1549 (Paso and del Troncoso 1939/1572–1589, Vols. V and VI) and the *Relaciones* of 1579 (de la Garza et al. 1983, I and II)—maize, beans, hens, cotton mantas, and sometimes salt, beeswax, honey, pottery, and rope—were locally available in northern Yucatan, and long-distance overland transport costs would have been prohibitive.

### 6.3.1   Ek Chuah Encounters the Holy Ghost

The havoc wreaked on native production by Spanish demands and diseases went hand in hand with the devastating effects of Spanish religious zeal on the ideological infrastructure of native commerce. No other theme, argues Maya historian John Chuchiak (2002, p. 152), loomed as large in Spanish thought as the extirpation of indigenous religious practices. Like the native economy, the ideological infrastructure of indigenous commerce contracted but did not disappear. Through Spanish documents, Chuchiak (2002) traced incidents of idolatry throughout the colonial period. The trade gods—the plumed serpent, Ek Chuah, God L—are not among the deities named in the reports Chuchiak summarizes.

Nevertheless, Ek Chuah persisted in multiple media. The Maya of Yucatan produced codices in native script well into the eighteenth century (Chuchiak 2010); all of those books now are lost, but images of Ek Chuah likely were contained therein given his relative prominence in the Madrid Codex,[12] the largest and most impor-

---

[11] Beneath the Spanish provincial governor, the indigenous city states in Yucatan remained in place, though certain functions increasingly were intersected by Spanish administration (e.g., Chuchiak 2010; Restall 1997).

[12] There is no systematic, quantitative study of deities in the surviving codices, but by my count (Kepecs 1999) Ek Chuah is represented a noteworthy 29 times in the Codex Madrid.

tant pre-Hispanic source on the Late Postclassic Yucatecan deities (Taube 1992, p. 3). Several obscure statements in the Chilam Balams may refer to Ek Chuah (see Edmonson 1982, p. 61; Roys 1973, p. 151, 186). The stone frame around the doorway to the sacristy of the colonial church at Ichmul de Morley is decorated with dogs and cacao plants, carved by indigenous hand and recalling Ek Chuah's festivals in the Late Postclassic period.[13] Sir Eric Thompson (1977) reported crudely made incensarios with simple modeled heads in Uaymil and Chetumal, which bordered Uaymil to the south,[14] as well as throughout the southern refuge. A few of these incensarios from Chetumal display characteristics of Ek Chuah. Because these in-censarios bear close but degenerate resemblance to the painted and modeled an-thropomorphic incensarios of the Late Postclassic, Thompson concluded that they were colonial in date. Their distribution, and the fact that despite certain similarities they differ markedly from nineteenth-century Lacandon "god pots" found in parts of the colonial-era refuge zone (Palka 2005, p. 194, Fig. 11.5), further supports this temporal placement.

The trade god also appears in Spanish churches (Fig. 6.7), though his identity there was veiled, providing a classic case of recombinant patterning.[15] Fray Bar-tolomé de Las Casas (in de Cogolludo, Libro 4 Capitulo 6, 1957, I, p. 190; Tozzer 1941, p. 107 *n* 495), writing in mid-sixteenth century, tells us that for the Yucatan Maya the Holy Ghost represented the deity Ek Chuah. Although Las Casas did not lay out the reason for this symbolic merging, as a mnemonic device, it is completely logical—the image of the Holy Ghost, especially when he appears solo, usually consists of a dove—a bird, like the Moan owl associated with Ek Chuah and God L, set against the sun—a morning star, like the heliacal rising of Venus. Possibly the Maya even linked the two in some way—the Quiché Maya word for Venus trans-lates as "person who carries the sun on his back" (Miller 1982, p. 89).

I do not want to imply that all colonial examples of the Holy Ghost-as-dove in Yucatan represented Ek Chuah. At the Franciscan Church of San Bernadino,

---

[13] While this carved stonework is undoubtedly colonial, the Ichmul religious complex grew by ac-cretion; without excavation it is impossible to tell to which building phase the sacristy door frame belongs (R. T. Alexander, personal communication, June 3, 2013). The Franciscans erected a solid stone mission here around 1571. A small stone church "with three or four cells" was added in 1588, but it is unclear whether any of that original structure remains. Most of the religious complex still standing at this site dates to the mid-late eighteenth century (Bretos 1992, pp. 142–144).

[14] The borders of these native territories are speculative; Jones (1989) disagrees with Roys (1957), who I follow here.

[15] A number of terms in the anthropological literature refer to the kind of cultural reformulation this example represents. Earlier in this chapter I have used the term "reformulation," though an-thropologists are searching for a more academic turn of phrase. Older terms like "syncretism"— and even Fernando Ortíz' "transculturation," preferred by many Latin American scholars—are problematic, in that, to varying degrees, they imply a unilineal direction of sociocultural change (from the dominant or "conquering" culture to those "conquered"). Today a number researchers (i.e., Zeitlin and Palka 2013), following Watanabe 1990) prefer the concept of "recombinant pat-terning," which refers to the process of recombining attributes of multiple symbols according to the active community's structural principles. In this case, the active community is indigenous.

constructed in 1552 in Valladolíd, the dove appears in murals on both the Gospel and Epistle sides of the nave. Both murals, painted by native hand in the sixteenth century, depict the dove within the context of the full Trinity, with the bird at the top, surrounded by angels. Art historian Kate Howe (2002, and personal communication 2004) writes that the mural on the Gospel side is conventional, but the one on the Epistle side has clear native overtones. Howe proposes that for the natives, the dove in this mural represented the white hawk—the sací—for which the pre-Hispanic town that became Valladolíd was named. The dove's message in this instance may have been largely one of identity—"this town is still ours." Thus, the San Bernadino mural seems to be a somewhat separate example of how the natives manipulated Christian art for their own ends. Nevertheless, the pre-Hispanic deities often were multifaceted; while the bird at San Bernardino may have stood for Valladolíd's indigenous name, it also might have represented Ek Chuah.

It is important to note that the San Bernardino example is early. Since Las Casas was aware of the Holy Ghost as Ek Chuah when that church was built, the association must have begun not long after the Spaniards began setting up their administration in the 1540s. Yet, as noted above, images of Ek Chuah remained in use for some time, especially in areas where Spaniards were few. It may have taken a while for the Christian dove recombination to spread. In any event while Yucatecan churches generally grew by accretion, most of the artwork I discuss here dates to the seventeenth century and would have functioned as ideological infrastructure of native accumulation only for a 100 years or so before native trade trickled to a halt with the Spanish conquest of the southern refuge in 1697.

The emiprical evidence is far from sufficient to speculate that all Early Colonial doves in Yucatecan Christian iconography represented Ek Chuah, but the lone dove on the disc of the sun, without the extraneous information of the Trinity, is most easily tied to the trade deity. In Catholic churches around the globe the lone dove sometimes adorns the baptristy, and occasionally it is found on the undersides of canopies overhanging pulpits. In Yucatan only a few examples are known today, though some likely are lost or hidden under many coats of whitewash (Fernando Cuauhtemoc Garcés Fierros, personal communication 2004). Yet, all of the colonial images of the lone dove that exist today, which were painted or carved by indigenous artists, are located on indigenous trade routes.[16]

It would not have been difficult for the Maya to spread the word that the dove stood for Ek Chuah. When mass was officiated in Latin by Spanish clergy it meant little to the Maya, and men of the cloth were few; they relied heavily on their native

---

[16] There is one additional image of the lone dove, similar to the one at Maní, painted in the sacristy at San Augustín Tekantó, in north-central Yucatan; the Tekanto dove dates to the nineteenth century, though the monastery that is part of the religious complex there is sixteenth century, and the dove may be painted over earlier examples (Garcés Fierros, personal communication 2004). If the Tekando dove is indeed a copy from the sixteenth or seventeenth century, it, like the other examples cited in this study, fits my hypothesis. Cristobal Sánchez, encomendero of Tekanto in 1579, claimed that the natives engaged in trade, carrying cotton mantas, wax, honey, and salt "a México y Honduras y a otras partes de donde traen cacao y ropas para indios" (de la Garza et al. 1983, I, p. 218).

assistants—the maestros cantores—who performed numerous functions, including reciting a modified liturgy when no priest was available (Farriss 1984, pp. 335–336). Thus the Maya had a fair amount of freedom within Christian religious spaces. Officially forbidden to use their own temples, they took advantage of the Spanish churches to broadcast a key hidden transcript: trade remains divine.

The Spanish colonial religious complex at Maní, built at the Late Postclassic site of that name, provides a detailed case in point. In the Late Postclassic Maní was ruled by merchant kings of the Xiu lineage, who hosted annual festivals in honor of the plumed serpent (Landa, in Tozzer 1941, pp. 157–158). Maní was the first native town to receive a Spanish mission, which was dedicated to San Miguel Arcangel in 1549. Upon discovering that the Maya were carrying out clandestine rituals in Maní and elsewhere in the late 1550s, Bishop Diego de Landa set out to punish the apostates. In 1562, at the Maní mission, he presided over a brutal inquisition and auto-da-fe involving the flagrant public whipping of native idolators accompanied by the burning of idols and probably books (Landa, in Tozzer 1941, pp. 76–80; Tozzer 194, n 340, pp. 76–78). Yet, idolatry—with attendant persecution on the part of the Church—continued (e.g., Chuchiak 2002), and native merchants from Maní continued to trade. They plied exchange routes into the Cehache region and beyond to the Peten Lakes district of Guatemala, carrying salt, cloth, knives and machetes—the last two items often bought at Spanish markets—deep into the interior. On their return trips to Yucatan they carried forest products, including wax, honey, and copal[17] (Scholes and Roys 1948, pp. 184, 244–246). Maní merchants also traveled to Chetumal, where they exchanged northern goods for cacao grown farther south (Roys 1957, p. 164; 1962, p. 34; and see below for more details).

On the vaulted ceiling of the baptistry at Maní, which contains recently restored seventeenth-century murals, sits a splendid example of the lone dove (Fig. 6.8a). A lone dove carved in wood on the underside of the canopy over the pulpit at the church of San Francisco in Oxkutzcab (Fig. 6.8b), also governed by the Xiu, dates to the seventeenth century as well. Like their kin from Maní, the Xiu of Oxkutzcab traded with apostate groups deep in the interior (Scholes and Roys 1948, p. 245).

Very similar doves adorn the pulpit canopies in the colonial churches of San Francisco de Assis in Conkal, San Miguel Arcangel in Maxcanu (Fig. 6.8c), and the Three Kings in Tizimín (Fig. 6.8d).[18] Conkal, ruled by a member of the Pech lineage, possessed several moderately productive salt beds on the northwest coast (Roys 1957, p. 44). The Spaniards exploited this resource, but the natives likely did,

---

[17] While a certain amount of these southern goods may have been for Spanish tribute, as Jones suggests, copal resins are collected from various kinds of trees, and differs in color and form; in northern Yucatan resins usually are collected from gumbo-limbo trees; in Guatemala, pines—rare in the north—are common. Honey is highly variable from region to region. Thus much of this exchange likely was predicated on procuring goods with distinct properties for native ritual or medicinal purposes.

[18] At all of these churches, the dove also appears on the ornate retablos behind the altars, in the context of the Holy Trinity.

**Fig. 6.8** Images of the Lone Dove, (**a**) Maní, restored image, S. Kepecs; (**b**) Oxcutzcab, S. Kepecs; (**c**) Maxcanu, new copy of original, S. Boucher; (**d**) Tizimín, recent restoration, S. Kepecs

too; they had kin in the southern refuge. A Pech noble, evidently a descendant[19] of the mid-sixteenth-century ruler of Chuburna, a neighboring town, was the mayor of a Cehache refugee settlement in 1604 (Roys 1957, p. 43; Scholes and Roys 1948, p. 505).

Maxcanu is located on the Camino Real, the only road between the colonial cities of Campeche and Merida. In the Late Postclassic the Camino Real linked the Campeche coast with the important towns of Mayapan and T'Ho. It became a crucial route for the Spaniards, but the Maya continued to use it in the colonial epoch (Jones 1989, pp. 167–168).

Tizimín, for its strategic location between Emal and Sací, was a key node on a crucial inland route that veered southeast (see Fig. 6.7) from Sací (Valladolíd) to Uaymil and Chetumal.[20] And the natives of Uaymil—Chans, whose kin ties with the Chans of Emal were deep—maintained close contact with their kin and other groups in Chetumal and farther south, in the territory of Dzuluinicob (today Belize),

---

[19] The sixteenth-century ruler of Chuburna and the seventeenth-century alcalde of the Cehache refuge settlement bore the same name: Antonio Pech.

[20] This route would have been less important in late pre-Hispanic times, when canoe transport was common, but it likely was in use in the Late Postclassic and in any event surely pre-dates its appearance on the first modern map of the peninsula, drawn in 1734 (Antochiw 1994, Plate XXIX). Prior to the eighteenth century, this route may have been hidden from the Spaniards; it is not the Spanish route Jones (1998, p. 130, Map 8) calls the southern section of the Camino Real, which runs from Merida to Chetumal Bay and runs west of the Valladolíd/Chetumal road.

where Spanish presence was very weak and where the Maya of the town of Tipu possessed lush cacao orchards through the first several decades of the seventeenth century (Jones 1982, 1983, 1989, 1998; Thompson 1977; de Villagutierre Soto-Mayor 1983/1701). Cacao still was used as currency, by Spaniards and Maya alike; thus in the Early Colonial period as in the Late Postclassic, though to a lesser degree, the salt-for-cacao trade enriched the Chans of Emal.

### 6.3.2   Salt, Ek Chuah, and the Lone Dove at Emal, Chikinchel

The Spaniards wanted what the Chans of Emal possessed. In the 1550s the foreigners set up a small port, Río Lagartos, near the mouth of the eponymous estuary, and appropriated the salinas. By the 1570s Spanish ships from Cuba and Honduras carrying wine, olive oil, and other merchandise arrived frequently at Río Lagartos, returning home loaded with salt (Molina Solís 1988/1904, I, p. 105, 135, 303). The Spaniards also shipped Chikinchel salt (via Veracruz) to Mexico City, where some was consumed at Spanish tables, though most was sent overland to the highland silver mines for use in the process of extraction (Andrews 1983, pp. 14–15; Semo 1973, pp. 141–146). Annual salt harvests were considerable; in 1605, the Spaniards harvested 5750 metric tons from the Río Lagartos estuary, using native labor and technology (Andrews 1983, pp. 136–137; Ewald 1985).

The written record—at least the published sources and the Archivo General del Estado de Yucatán—reveals nothing about how many Spaniards actually lived in Chikinchel in the Early Colonial period, or how they administrated salt production. Most preferred the safety of their stronghold at Valladolíd. In Chikinchel, archaeological evidence of Spanish activity is stronger at Río Lagartos than elsewhere, and except for a few olive jar fragments there are no non-native artifacts at Emal, 30 km east of the port, that pre-date the eighteenth century (Kepecs 2013b). The Spaniards must have depended on native allies to supervise labor for the salt harvest, which led to divided loyalties. The Maya themselves pointed this out; references to pro and anti-Spanish factions at Emal appear frequently in the Chilam Balam of Tizimín (Edmonson 1982, p. 36 *n* 617, 37 *n* 655, 1986, p. xviii, pp. 141–142, p. 151, 157; and see Kepecs 2005; Roys 1973).

Despite internal factionalism, Emal retained tremendous significance in the indigenous world. Through the Late Postclassic period and the colonial epoch, the Maya divided time into a repeating sequence of thirteen 20-year cycles called katuns. The indigenous authors of the Chilam Balam of Tizimín (Edmonson 1982) noted that the katun was seated at Emal four times during the first 140 years[21] of the Spanish epoch—a total of 80 years, spanning more than half of the Early Colonial period. Though katun seatings implied ritual clout (Edmonson 1982; Rice

---

[21] Katun numbers are preceded by the title "Ahau," meaning "lord," much as we traditionally designate years with designation "A.D."—anno Domini, "in the year of our lord." According to the Chilam Balam of Tizimín the katun was seated at Emal (Edmonson 1982) in 13 Ahau (1520–1539), 11 Ahau (1539–1559), 5 Ahau (1599–1618), and 1 Ahau (1638–1658).

**Fig. 6.9** Crude Colonial-
Period Incensario from
Chikinchel

and Rice 2005), Emal's importance was not just symbolic. In the Early Colonial period, indigenous population there and on the inland support tier remained fairly substantial—archaeologically, roughly half the size of its Late Postclassic counterpart (Kepecs 2005, 2013b) but still sufficient to harvest over 5000 metric tons of salt per season without need to import workers from elsewhere on the peninsula (see footnote 7).

But salt production and trade was the Chans' inheritance, and to some degree allegiance to the Spaniards must have been the public face of a hidden transcript. Blood ties apparently were thicker than the rewards of working for the foreign over-lords, because the pro-Spanish natives at Emal did nothing to prevent their rebel brothers from harvesting the briny diamonds of the Río Lagartos estuary to exchange for cacao with their kin in Uaymil and points south. I recovered fragments of crude incensarios (Fig. 6.9), identical to the ones Thompson (1977) reported in Uaymil and across the refuge zone, at two inland support settlements in the vicinities of Emal and Otro Sacboh, as well as at one site in Chikinchel's southern interior.

Through this exchange, which largely evaded the vigilance and control of the Spaniards, the channels of communication remained open and rebellions took shape. In November, 1546, the Great Revolt broke out across eastern and southern Yucatan (Fig. 6.10)—the territories (as defined by Roys 1957) of Sotuta, Cochuah, Cupul, Tases, Chikinchel, and Uaymil (Bricker 1981, p. 19; Chamberlain 1948, pp. 240–249; de la Garza et al. 1983, II, p. 244; Farriss 1984, p. 18). It was tribute-paying time when the uprising occurred (Brinton 1882, pp. 189–259; Kepecs 2005). Some months later the Spaniards managed to control the situation in most of the region, but the rebels in Chikinchel resisted and continued to provoke other groups (Chamberlain 1948, p. 249). Rumors of uprisings still were circulating in Chikinchel

**Fig. 6.10** Native territories
in the Great Revolt

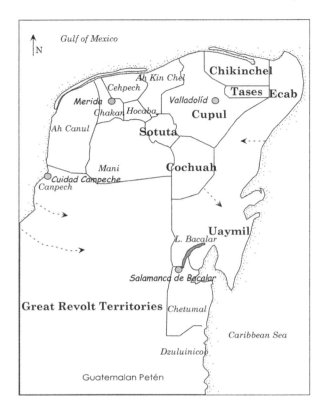

in 1579 (de la Garza et al. 1983, II, p. 91, 245). And in 1597, a talking oracle—like
the one at Late Postclassic Cozumel visited by traveling merchants—claimed to be
the Holy Ghost, commanding audiences in Sotuta (Reed 1964, p. 134). If the Holy
Ghost in this case was speaking for Ek Chuah, no doubt his words inflamed new
sentiments against the dominant economy.

Among the Chans of Emal and Uaymil (Jones 1983, pp. 78–80, 1989, pp. 18–
19), resistance simmered into the seventeenth century. Nine decades after the Great
Revolt—at the start of Katun 1 Ahau (1638–1658), which was seated at Emal—the
Chans orchestrated a new and bloody rebellion that spread across eastern Yucatan
from Chikinchel to Uaymil/Chetumal and south into Dzuluinicob (de Cogolludo
Lib. 11 Cap 12; Edmonson 1982, p. 141, 1986, p. 213; Jones 1989; Roys 1973,
p. 157; and see Kepecs 2005). The triggers that sparked the Chan rebellion differed
north to south, but economic factors were the common thread; in the south, excessive Spanish demands for cacao (Jones 1983, pp. 78–80, 1989, pp. 18–19) as well as
increasing missionary incursions into the refuge zone were the keys, and it was tax
time again in Yucatan when the war broke out (Edmonson 1982, p. 141).

The Chan war was the beginning of the end. In its aftermath the pro-Spanish
faction at Emal gained strength, occasioning the descent of the tumpline chiefs
(the merchants) and the guardians of the sands, the guardians of the sea, and new

taxes were imposed (Edmonson 1982, pp. 141–142, 1986, pp. 211–212). Emal is not referenced specifically in the following katun, 12 Ahau (1658–1677), though in general "the sole God" (Christianity) was installed; the merchants were beaten down and the warriors fled to the forest (Edmonson 1982, p. 149). Emal reappears in 10 Ahau (1677–1697), when *the dove was burned at the edge of the sea* (Edmonson 1982, p. 151, 1986, p. 220).

## 6.4  Epilogue

The burning of the dove is the last reference to the native economy I have found for the colonial period. During the second half of the seventeenth century the native population reached its nadir, and Spain's Hapsburg rulers were extremely weak. A century after the dove was burned, when Bourbon Spain instituted "comercio libre," salt production boomed at Celestun (see Ewald 1985, pp. 195–196). But only clandestine harvests—by pirates, and small groups of Maya or mestizos remaining in Chikinchel—occurred at the Río Lagartos salinas (Kepecs 2013b). Just a few sherds of eighteenth-century Mexican majolicas and British shell-edged pearlware, if the latter dates to the early end of this ware's manufacture, mark activity at Emal and its main inland support center, Aké, during this period.

Mexican Independence brought rapid change. In the 1840s Yucatan's salinas were privatized; bourgeous speculators with world market ties moved in and harvested "estimable quantities" (Serrano Catzín 1986, pp. 37–38) of Emal's diamond-like salt. Yet if there was a settlement here during the first half of the nineteenth century, it consisted only of perishable structures; sherds of transfer wares from England and Puebla, popular in Yucatan especially during the first half of the nineteenth century (Burgos Villanueva 1995), are the only archaeological evidence I have of this commercial growth (Kepecs 2013b).

Despite their long silence, the region's remaining Maya did not take the new wave of capitalist invaders calmly; the embers of the dove, burned at the edge of the sea over a century and a half earlier, still smoldered. A text from the first part of katun 11 Ahau (1842–1848)—the final written link to the ancestral Chans of Emal—prophesized that guns would be seen in the region, *and the sea will burn* (Edmonson 1982, p. 191).

In 1847, war broke out again. Two hundred years after the Chan uprising, the Caste War (Fig. 6.11) was launched by a new oracle—not the Holy Ghost, but a talking cross—in the town of Tepich, in July, 1847. The uprising shook the entire peninsula. Despite regional variations and academic debates over the role of land pressures occasioned by the dominant (white) class in sparking the revolt (see Alexander 2004, pp. 16–21), the ultimate cause was economic. Once the rebels had seized control over the east and much of the south, Caste War leader Jacinto Pat (in Rugeley 2001, pp. 51–52) wrote that if the whites wanted peace, they had to divide the peninsula in equal parts among themselves and the natives. This would be the

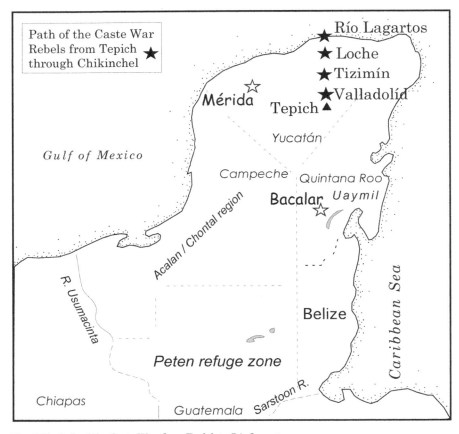

**Fig. 6.11** Path of the Caste War, from Tepich to Río Lagartos

indemnification for 300 years of economic subjugation—the countless contributions and taxes the Maya had forcibly paid.

The rebels tore through the region's white strongholds, burning churches and
wreaking havoc on the towns. They reached Loche and then Río Lagartos in June,
1848. I have no evidence one way or the other that Emal was similarly sacked
(Kepecs 2013b), though the Caste War effectively ended salt production on the Río
Lagartos estuary for another 30 years.

**Acknowledgments** I would like to thank the editors of this volume, Pedro Paulo A. Funari and
María Ximena Senatore, for their kind invitation to contribute this work. This chapter is a revised
and much extended version of a paper presented at the Segundo Congreso Internacional de Cultura Maya in Mérida, Yucatán, in 2005, co-authored with my colleague Sylviane Boucher at the
Instituto Nacional de Antropología e História, Centro Regional Yucatán, Mérida. Her invaluable
contributions to that paper have made their way into this one, as have those of other researchers
who kindly shared information for the 2005 endeavor: Master Restorer Fernando Chahuhtemoc
Garcés Fierros of INAH-CRY, independent art historian Dr. Kate Howe, and Dr. Rani T. Alexander
at the Department of Sociology and Anthropology, New Mexico State University. Without all of

them, this chapter would not exist. However, the bulk of the research for this chapter is my own, as are all opinions and interpretations contained herein. I take full responsibility for any and all errors of fact or interpretation.

# References

Alexander, R. T. (2004). *Yaxcabá and the caste war of Yucatan: An archaeological perspective.* Albuquerque: University of New Mexico Press.

Andrews, A. P. (1983). *Ancient Maya salt production and trade.* Tucson: University of Arizona Press.

Antochiw, M. (1994). *Historia Cartográfica de la Península de Yucatán. Centro de Investigación y de Estudios Avanzados del I. P. N., Grupo Tribasa.* México: Gobierno del Estado de Campeche.

Berdan, F. F. (1988). Principles of regional and long-distance trade in the Aztec empire. In J. K. Josserand & K. Dakin (Eds.), *Smoke and mist, Mesoamerican studies in memory of Thelma D. Sullivan, BAR International Series 402 (ii)* (pp. 639–656). Oxford: B.A.R.

Berdan, F. F. (1996). The tributary provinces. In F. F. Berdan, R. E. Blanton, E. H. Boone, M. G. Hodge, M. E. Smith, & E. Umberger (Eds.), *Aztec imperial strategies* (pp. 115–136). Washington, DC: Dumbarton Oaks.

Berdan, F. F., Blanton, R. E., Boone, E. H., Hodge, M. G., Smith, M. E., & Umberger, E. (Eds.). (1996). *Aztec imperial strategies.* Washington, DC: Dumbarton Oaks.

Blanton, R. E. (1985). A comparison of early market systems. In S. Plattner (Ed.), *Markets and marketing, monographs in economic anthropology No. 4* (pp. 399–418). Maryland: University Press of America.

Blanton, R. E., Kowalewski, S. A., & Feinman, G. M. (1992). The Mesoamerican world system. *Review: Fernand Braudel Center, 15*(3), 419–426.

Braswell, G. E. (2003). Obsidian exchange spheres. In M. E. Smith & F. F. Berdan (Eds.), *The Postclassic Mesoamerican world* (pp. 131–158). Salt Lake City, Utah: University of Utah Press.

Braudel, F. (1986). *Civilization and capitalism 15th–18th century Vol. I: The structures of everyday life. Perennial Library Edition.* New York: Harper and Row.

Braudel, F. (1986). *Civilization and capitalism 15th–18th century Vol. II: The wheels of commerce. Perennial Library Edition.* New York: Harper and Row.

Bretos, M. A. (1992). *Iglesias de Yucatan.* SA de CV: Producción Editorial Dante.

Bricker, V. R. (1981). *The Indian Christ the Indian King: The historical substrate of Maya myth and ritual.* Austin: University of Texas.

Brinton, D. G. (1882). *The Maya Chronicles.* Brinton's Library of Aboriginal American Literature No. 1, Philadelphia.

Burgos Villanueva, F. R. (1995). *El Olimpo: Un predio colonial en el lado poniente de la Plaza Mayor de Mérida, Yucatán, y análisis cerámico comparativo. Colección científica.* México: INAH.

Chamberlain, R. S. (1948). *The conquest and colonization of Yucatán, 1517–1550* (Publication 582). Washington, DC: Carnegie Institution of Washington.

Chase-Dunn, C., & Hall, T. D. (Eds.). (1991). *Core/periphery relations in precapitalist worlds.* Boulder: Westview.

Chuchiak, J. F., IV. (2002). Toward a regional definition of idolatry: Reexamining idolatry trials in the Relaciones de Méritos and their role in defining the concept of Idolatría in Colonial Yucatan, 1570–1780. *Journal of Early Modern History, 6*(2), 140–167.

Chuchiak, J. F., IV. (2010). Writing as resistance: Maya graphic pluralism and indigenous elite strategies for survival in Yucatan, 1550–1750. *Ethnohistory, 57*(1), 87–116.

Closs, M. P. (1978). Venus in the Maya world: Glyphs, gods, and associated astronomical phenomena. In M. G. Robertson & D. C. Jeffers (Eds.), *Tercera Mesa Redonda de Palenque* (Vol. IV, pp. 147–165). Palenque: Pre-Columbian Art Research Center.

Cobean, R. H., Glascock, M. D., Stocker, T. L., & Vogt, J. R. (1991). High-precision trace-element characterization of major Mesoamerican obsidian sources and further analyses of artifacts from San Lorenzo Tenochtitlan, Mexico. *Latin American Antiquity, 2*(1), 61–91.

Coggins, C. C., & Shane, O. C., III. (1984). *Cenote of sacrifice: Maya treasures from the sacred well at Chichén Itzá*. Austin: University of Texas Press.

de Cogolludo, F. D. L. de (1957/1688). Historia de Yucatán, Tomos I y II. México: Editorial Academia Literaria.

Cortés, H. (1988/1522). *Cartas de Relación*. Cisalpino-Goliardica, Milan. de la Garza, M., A. L. Izquierdo, Ma. del C. León, and T. Figueroa (editors).

Díaz del Castillo, Bernál 1984 [1568] *Historia Verdadera de la Conquista de la Nueva España*. Sexta edición, Espasa-Calpe, S.A., Madríd.

Duran, F. D. (1972). *[16th Century]book of the Gods and Rites and The Ancient Calendar, translated and edited by Fernando Horcasitas and Doris Heyden*. Norman: University of Oklahoma Press.

Du Solier, W. (1946). Primer Fresco Mural Huaxteco. *Cuadernos Americanos,30*, 151–159.

Eaton, J. D. (1978). Archaeological survey of the Yucatán-Campeche coast. *Studies in the archaeology of coastal Yucatán and Campeche, Mexico* (pp. 1–67). Tulane (Middle American Research Institute Pub. 46).

Edmonson, M. S. (1982). *The ancient future of the Itzá: The book of Chilam Balam of Tizimín*. Austin: University of Texas Press.

Edmonson, M. S. (1986). *Heaven born Mérida and its destiny: The book of Chilam Balam of Chumayel*. Austin: University of Texas Press.

Edwards, C. R. (1978). Pre-Columbian maritime trade in Mesoamerica. In T. A. Lee & C. Navarrete (Eds.), *Mesoamerican communication routes and cultural contacts* (p. 199; papers of the New World Archaeological Foundation No. 40). Provo: Brigham Young University.

Ewald, U. (1985). *The Mexican Salt Industry 1560–1980: A study in change*. Stuttgart: Gustav Fischer.

Farriss, N. M. (1984). *Maya society under colonial rule*. Princeton: Princeton University Press.

de la Garza, M., A. L. Izquierdo, Ma. del C. León, and T. Figueroa (editors) 1983 [1579–1581] *Relaciones Histórico-geográficas de la Gobernación de Yucatán*. Vols I and II, UNAM, Mexico, D.F.

Gasco, J. (2003). Soconusco. In M. E. Smith & F. F. Berdan (Eds.), *The Postclassic Mesoamerican world* (pp. 282–296). Salt Lake City, Utah: University of Utah Press.

Gasco, J. (2005). The consequences of Spanish colonial rule for the indigenous peoples of Chiapas, Mexico. In S. Kepecs & R. T. Alexander (Eds.), *The Postclassic to Spanish-era transition in Mesoamerica: Archaeological perspectives* (pp. 77–96). Albuquerque: University of New Mexico Press.

Gills, B. K., & Frank, A. G. (1991). 5000 Years of world system history: The cumulation of accumulation. In C. C. Dunn & T. D. Hall (Eds.), *Core/periphery relations in precapitalist worlds* (pp. 67–112). Boulder: Westview.

Hanks, W. (2010). *Converting words: Maya in the age of the cross*. Berkeley: University of California Press.

Hirth, K. G. (1989). Militarism and social organization at Xochicalco, Morelos. In R. A. Diehl & J. C. Berlo (Eds.), *Mesoamerica after the decline of Teotihuacan AD700–900* (pp. 69–82). Washington, DC: Dumbarton Oaks Research Library and Collection.

Hosler, D. (1994). *The sounds and colors of power: The sacred metallurgical technology of ancient West Mexico*. Cambridge: MIT Press.

Howe, K. (2002). Accommodating the faithful: San Bernardino de Sena and the Franciscan program in sixteenth-century Yucatán. PhD dissertation, Florida State University, Tallahassee.

Jones, G. D. (1982). Agriculture and trade in the colonial period central Maya Lowlands. In K. V. Flannery (Ed.), *Maya subsistence: Studies in memory of Dennis E. Puleston* (pp. 275–293). New York: Academic Press.

Jones, G. D. (1983). The last Maya frontier of colonial Yucatán. In M. J. MacLeod & R. Wasserstrom (Eds.), *Spaniards and Indians in Southeastern Mesoamerica: Essays on the history of ethnic relations* (pp. 64–91). Lincoln: University of Nebraska Press.

Jones, G. D. (1989). *Maya resistance to Spanish rule: Time and history on a colonial frontier.* Albuquerque: University of New Mexico Press.

Jones, G. D. (1998). *The conquest of the last Maya Kingdom.* Redwood City, CA: Stanford University Press.

Kepecs, S. (1997). Native Yucatán and Spanish influence: The archaeology and history of Chikinchel. In S. Kepecs & M. Kolb (Eds.), New Approaches to Combining the Archaeological and Historical Records, pp. 307–330. Journal of Archaeological Method and Theory 4(3)–4(4).

Kepecs, S. (1998). Diachronic ceramic evidence and its social implications in northeast Yucatán, Mexico. *Ancient Mesoamerica, 9*(1), 121–137.

Kepecs, S. (1999). *The political economy of Chikinchel, Yucatán, Mexico: Adiachronic analysis from the prehispanic era through the age of Spanish administration.* Ann Arbor: University Microfilms.

Kepecs, S. (2003). Chikinchel. In M. E. Smith & F. F. Berdan (Eds.), *The Postclassic Mesoamerican world* (pp. 259–268). Salt Lake City, Utah: University of Utah Press.

Kepecs, S. (2005). Maya, Spaniards, and salt: World systems shifts in 16th century Yucatán. In S. Kepecs & R. T. Alexander (Eds.), *The Postclassic to Spanish-era transition in Mesoamerica: Archaeological perspectives* (pp. 117–138). Albuquerque: University of New Mexico Press.

Kepecs, S. (2007). Chichen Itzá, Tula, and the Epiclassic/Early Postclassic Mesoamerican world system. In J. K. Kowalski & C. Kristan-Graham (Eds.), *Many Tollans: Chichén Itza, Tula, and the Epiclassic—Early Postclassic Mesoamerican World* (pp. 129–150). Washington, DC: Dumbarton Oaks.

Kepecs, S. (2013). From salt to cocaine: Northeast Yucatan in the world system, ad 250–2013. In R. T. Alexander & S. Kepecs (Eds.), *For colonial and postcolonial change in Mesoamerica: Archaeology as historical anthropology.* In preparation.

Kepecs, S. (2014). Cuando chocan sistemas capitalistas: Una larga historia económica del rincón noreste de Yucatán. In S. Kepecs & R. T. Alexander (coord.), *El Pueblo Maya del Siglo XIX: Perspectivas Arqueológicas e Históricas—Keypads 2014* (pp. 103–124). México: Centro de Estudios Mayas, Universidad Nacional Autónoma de México.

Kepecs, S., & Kohl, P. (2003). Conceptualizing macroregional interaction: World-systems theory and the archaeological record. In M. E. Smith and F. F. Berdan (Eds.), *The Postclassic Mesoamerican world* (pp. 14–20). Salt Lake City, Utah: University of Utah Press.

Kepecs, S., & Masson M. (2003). Political organization in Yucatán and Belize. In M. E. Smith and F. F. Berdan (Eds.), *The Postclassic Mesoamerican world* (pp. 40–44). Salt Lake City, Utah: University of Utah Press.

Kepecs, S., Feinman, G. M., & Boucher, S. (1994). Chichén Itzá and its Hinterland: A world systems perspective. *Ancient Mesoamerica, 5*(2), 141–158.

Kowalski, J. K., & Kristan-Graham, C. (Eds.). (2007). *Twin Tollans: Chichén Itza, Tula, and the Epiclassic—Early Postclassic Mesoamerican World.* Washington, DC: Dumbarton Oaks.

Lothrop, S. K. (1924). *Tulum: An archaeological study of the East Coast of Yucatán* (Pub. 335). Washington, DC: Carnegie Institution of Washington.

Masson, M. (2003). The Late Postclassic symbol set in the Maya area. In M. E. Smith & F. F. Berdan (Eds.), *The Postclassic Mesoamerican world* (pp. 194–200). Salt Lake City, Utah: University of Utah Press.

McKillop, H., & Healy, P. F. (Eds.). (1989). *Coastal Maya trade* (Occasional Papers No. 8). Peterborough: Trent University.

Milbrath, S., & Peraza, L. C. (2003). Revisiting Mayapán: Mexico's Last Maya Capital. *Ancient Mesoamerica, 14*(1), 1–46.

Milbrath, S., Peraza, L. C., & Delgado Ku, M. (2010). Religious Imagery in Mayapan's Murals. The PARI Journal, a quarterly publication of the Pre-Columbian Art Research Institute. Volume X, No. 3, Winter, 2010. http://www.mesoweb.com/pari/journal/archive/PARI1003.pdf. Accessed 28 Sept 2014.

Miller, A. G. (1982). *On the edge of the sea: Mural painting at Tancah-Tulum, Quintana Roo, Mexico.* Washington, DC: Dumbarton Oaks.

Miller, M. E. (1986). *The murals of Bonampak,* Princeton: Princeton University Press.

Miller, A. G. (1989). Pre-Hispanic mural painting in the valley of Oaxaca, Mexico. *National Geographic Research, 4*(2), 233–258.

Miller, A. G. (1995). *The painted tombs of Oaxaca, Mexico.* Cambridge: Cambridge University Press.
Millon, R. (1955). When cacao grew on trees. PhD Dissertation, Columbia University, University Microfilms, Ann Arbor.
Molina Solís, J. F. (1988/1904). *Historia de Yucatán durante la dominación española Tomo I. Primera edición facsimiliar.* Mérida: Consejo Editorial de Yucatán A. C.
Nuttall, Z. (1910). The island of sacrifice. *American Anthropologist, 12,* 257–295.
Orellana, S. L. (1995). *Ethnohistory of the Pacific Coast.* Lancaster: Labyrinthos.
Palka, J. W. (2005). Postcolonial conquest of the Southern Maya Lowlands, cross-cultural interaction, and Lacandon Maya culture change. In S. Kepecs & R. T. Alexander (Eds.), *The Postclassic to Spanish-era transition in Mesoamerica: Archaeological perspectives* (pp. 183–201). Albuquerque: University of New Mexico Press.
Paso Y., & del Troncoso, F. (1905/1572–1589). Papeles de Nueva España, Madrid, Vols. I and IV.
Paso, Y., & del Troncoso, F. (1939/1572–1589) Papeles de Nueva España, Madrid, Vols. V and VI.
Pastrana, A. (1992). *Proyecto yacimientos de obidiana. Consejo de Arqueología Boletín 1991* (pp. 219–221). México: INAH.
Pastrana, A. (1998). *La explotación azteca de la obsidiana en la Sierra de las Navajas. Colección Científica, Serie arqueología.* Mexico City: Instituto Nacional de Antropología e Historia.
Pastrana, A. & Fournier, P. (2011). Early Colonial Obsidian Exploitation at the Pachuca Mines. Paper presented at the 2011 Meeting of the Society for American Archaeology, Sacramento, CA, in the symposium "Archaeological Approaches to Indigenous Post-Conquest Developments in New Spain and Central America: Papers in Memory of Thomas H. Charlton," organized by Patricia Fournier, Rani T. Alexander and Susan Kepecs.
Paz, O. (1987). Food of the gods. *New York Review of Books, 30*(3), 3–7.
Pérez Romero, J. A. (1988). Algunas Consideraciónes sobre el Cacao en el Norte de la Peninsula Yucatán. Tésis de Licenciatura en Ciencias Antropológicas, Universidad Autonoma de Yucatán, Mérida.
Quirarte, J. (1982). The Santa Rita murals: A review. In Aspects of the Mixteca-Puebla Style and Mixtec and Central Mexican Culture in Southern Mesoamerica. Middle American Research Institute Occasional Paper No. 4, Tulane University, pp. 43–60.
Reed, N. (1964). *The caste war of Yucatán.* Stanford: Stanford University Press.
Restall, M. (1997). *The Maya world: Yucatec culture and society 1550–1850.* Redwood City, CA: Stanford University Press.
Rice, D. S., & Rice, P. M. (2005). Sixteenth an seventeenth century Maya political geography in central Peten, Guatemala. In S. Kepecs & R. T. Alexander (Eds.), *En The Postclassic to Spanish-Era Transition in Mesoamerica: Archaeological Perspectives* (pp. 139–160). Albuquerque: University of New Mexico Press.
Ringle, W. M., Negrón, T. G., & Bey, G. J., III. (1998). The return of Quetzalcoatl: Evidence for the spread of a workd relition during the Epiclassic period. *Ancient Mesoamerica, 9*(2), 183–232.
Roys, R. L. (1943). *The Indian background of colonial Yucatán* (Pub. 548). Washington, DC: Carnegie Institution of Washington.
Roys, R. L. (1957). *The political geography of the Yucatan Maya* (Pub. 613). Washington, DC: Carnegie Institution of Washington.
Roys, R. L. (1962). Literary sources for the history of Mayapán. In H. E. D. Pollock, R. L. Roys, T. Proskouriakoff, & A. L. Smith (Eds.), *Mayapan, Yucatan, Mexico* (pp. 25–86; Publication 619). Washington, DC: Carnegie Institution of Washington.
Roys, R. L. (1973). *The book of Chilam Balam of Chumayel.* Norman: University of Oklahoma Press.
Rugeley, T. (2001). *Maya wars. Ethnographic accounts from nineteenth century Yucatan.* Norman: University of Oklahoma Press.
Sabloff, J. A., & Rathje, W. L. (1975). The rise of a Maya merchant class. *Scientific American, 233*(4), 72–82.
de Sahagún, F. B. (1975/1569). *Historia General de las Cosas de Nueva España. Anotaciónes y apéndices por Padre A. Ma. Garibay K.* México: Editorial Porrúa.

Schele, L., & Miller, M. E. (1986). *Blood of kings.* Fort Worth: Kimbell Art Museum.

Schellhas, P. (1904). *Representation of Deities of the Maya Manuscripts.* Papers of the Peabody Museum of American Archaeology and Ethnology, Vol. 4, No. 1. Cambridge, Harvard University.

Scholes, F. V., & Roys, R. L. (1948). *The Maya Chontal Indians of Acalan-Tixchel* (Pub. 560). Washington, DC: Carnegie Institution of Washington.

Scott, J. C. (1990). *Domination and the arts of resistance: Hidden transcripts.* New Haven: Yale University Press.

Semo, E. (1973). *Historia del capitalismo en México: Los orígenes 1521–1763. Décimosegunda edición.* Mexico: Ediciones Era.

Serrano Catzín, J. E. (1986). Apuntes sobre la industria salinera de Yucatán a mediados del Siglo IX. Tésis profesional para el grado de Licenciado en Ciencias Antropológicas, Universidad Autonoma de Yucatán.

Smith, M. E. (1990). Long-distance trade under the Aztec Empire: The archaeological evidence. *Ancient Mesoamerica, 1,* 253–169.

Smith, M. E., & Berdan, F. F. (Eds.). (2003). *The Postclassic Mesoamerican world.* Salt Lake City, Utah: University of Utah Press.

Stocker, T. L., & Cobean, R. H. (1984). Preliminary report on the obsidian mines at Pico de Orizaba, Veracruz. In J. E. Ericson & B. A. Purdy (Eds.), *Prehistoric quarries and lithic production* (pp. 83–96). Cambridge: Cambridge University Press.

Taube, K. A. (1992). *The major gods of ancient Yucatan. Studies in pre-Columbian art and archaeology No. 32.* Washington, DC: Dumbarton Oaks Research Library and Collection.

Taube, K. A., & Negrón, T. G. (1988). Survey and reconnaissance in the ruinas de San Angel Region, Quintana Roo Mexico. A preliminary report of the 1988 San Angel Survey. Project submitted to the National Geographic Society, Washington, DC.

Thompson, Sir J. E. S. (1951). Canoes and navigation of the Maya and their neighbors. *Journal of the Royal Anthropological Institute, 79,* 69–78 (London).

Thompson, Sir J. E. S. (1956). Notes on the use of Cacao in Middle America. Carnegie Institution of Washington Notes No. 128.

Thompson, Sir J. E. S. (1966). Merchant gods of Middle America. In A. Pompa (Ed.), *Summa antropológica en homenaje a Roberto J. Weitlaner* (pp. 159–172). Mexico City: Instituto Nacional de Antropológía e Historia.

Thompson, Sir J. E. S. (1970). *Maya history and religion.* Norman: University of Oklahoma Press.

Thompson, Sir J. E. S. (1977). A proposal for constituting a Maya subgroup, cultural and linguistic, in the Petén and adjacent regions. In G. Jones (Ed.), *Anthropology and history in Yucatan* (pp. 3–42). Austin: University of Texas Press.

Tozzer, A. M. (1941). *Landa's Relacion de las Cosas de Yucatán.* Translation Papers of the Peabody Museum, 18, Harvard.

Villacorta C., Antonio, J., & Villacorta C. A. (1977). *Codices Mayas (reproducidos y desarrollados). Sociedad de Geografía e Historia de Guatemala, Segunda edición.* Guatemala: Tipografia Nacional.

de Villagutierre Soto-Mayor, J. (1983/1701). *History of the conquest of the province of the Itzá* (Translated from the second Spanish edition; edited and annotated by Frank E. Comparato). Culver City: Labyrintos.

Wallace, D., & Carmack, R. M. (Eds.). (1977). *Archaeology and ethnohistory of the central quiché* (SUNY Albany Publication No. 1). New York: Institute for Mesoamerican Studies.

Wallerstein, I. (1974). *The modern world system.* New York: Academic Press.

Watanabe, J. (1990). From saints to Shibbloeths: Image, structure, and identity in Maya religious syncretism. *American Ethnologist, 17*(1), 129–148.

Willey, G. R. (1976). Mesoamerican civilization and the idea of transcendence. *Antiquity, 50,* 205–215.

Zeitlin, J. F., & Palka, J. W. (2013). Religion and ritual in post-conquest Mesoamerica. In R. T. Alexander & S. Kepecs (Eds.), Colonial and Postcolonial change in Mesoamerica: Archaeology as historical anthropology, MS, In preparation.

# Chapter 7
# Archaeology of Contact in Cuba, a Reassessment

Lourdes Domínguez and Pedro Paulo A. Funari

## 7.1 Introduction: Contact as a Long-Term Feature

Archaeology has long a tradition in Cuba. Andrés Poey probably marks the start of archaeological study in Cuba. Poey found in 1847 a fragment of a human mandible at the coast in Camagüey, beginning the study of prehistoric peoples in the Island. It is a very early endeavor, considering that it was several years prior to the publication of Darwin's *The origins of species*, in 1859. It was so amazing that it was delivered to the American Ethnological Society in 1855. By the end of the nineteenth century, archaeology was recognized in the scholarly world, so that soon after independence, the Montané Anthropological Museum was established, in 1902. The name of the museum honored Montané Dardé, a pioneer in a major archaeological dig at Maisí region and with studies of human remains from the Cienega de Zapata. As early as 1913 the University of Havana established anthropology courses (Berman et al. 2005, p. 43).

This early upsurge of archaeology is due to several reasons, not least the unique position of the island in-between the Western Hemisphere and Europe, being thus linked to both worlds and through them connected with Africa and the Near and Far East. It is no coincidence the fact that people from all those continents contribute to the diversity of the Cuban population today, including a majority of people of Mediterranean and African descent, but also native and East Asian people. Cuba has been inhabited for at least 6000 years, and in the first 5500 or so years the inhabitants were in contact not only with neighboring North and Central America and other Caribbean islands but also with distant South America (Cosculluela 1946), as attest

L. Domínguez (✉)
Oficina del Historiador de la Habana and Academia de la Historia, Havana, Cuba
e-mail: lourdes@cultural.ohch.cu

P. P. A. Funari
Departamento de História, IFCH, Unicamp Laboratório de Arqueologia Pública Paulo Duarte (LAP/Nepam/Unicamp) UNICAMP Cidade Universitária Zeferino Vaz, Campinas, SP 13083-970, Brazil
e-mail: ppfunari@uol.com.br

© Springer International Publishing Switzerland 2015
P. P. A. Funari, M. X. Senatore (eds.), *Archaeology of Culture Contact and Colonialism in Spanish and Portuguese America*, DOI 10.1007/978-3-319-08069-7_7

the linguistic studies of Arawak languages (Patte 2010). This means that for thousands of years the island of Cuba (111,000 km$^2$) has witnessed an intense contact with other areas, thousands of miles away, confirming in a way Clive Gamble's assertion about humans as walkers (and we add seafarers) in ongoing encounters and mix (Gamble 2003). If this is so for humans in general, it is more so in the case of Cuba for its continuous relations with worlds close by and far away.

In this chapter though, we will not deal with prehistoric contact, even if it is enticing in itself and one of us (Domínguez) has been working with this for several decades and producing relevant literature on the subject. This chapter deals with colonial encounters, but we decided to start with a digression on the first thousands of years of human settlement in the Caribbean island as way of stressing the deep-rooted mixed character of Cuban human settlement: cultural contact is not only a recent epiphenomenon of imperialism, but a genuine constituent of the Cuban way of life, as we shall see in this chapter. We will thus start with a theoretical discussion about the way Cuban scholars have been discussing cultural contact and how archaeologists have been using those discussions in a creative manner. We consider with Chris Gosden (2004) and Tim Murray (2004) that contact in colonial contexts is subjected to a series of issues relating to power relations and imbalances and more so in the modern era and that the archaeological study of contact is thus particularly complex. We will then discuss three subjects as case studies: male and female contacts in the colonial period, slave and free people relations, and ethnic and religious relations through bead analysis.

## 7.2   Cuban Society, Cultural Contact, and Social Theory

Cultural contact and interaction has been at the root of Cuban society since early colonial times, when natives of different linguistic groups mixed and interacted with Spanish colonists and then enslaved Africans from different corners of the continent. Spaniards came from different regions of the colonial power, sometimes even using different languages, notably Galician and Catalan. Spain was from the start multiethnic, for the unified monarchy of Castile and Leon and the constitution of a new kingdom of Spain kept the regional traditions in the form of fueros (privileges), including the use of languages and local mores. Despite changes over time, this multicultural character of Spanish society has always been distinctive, in opposition to centralization in other European countries (Funari 2006). Cuba was a main Spanish colonial center, gathering people from all over Spanish America, further fostering diversity. For several centuries, Cuba received people from all corners of the Spanish world and far beyond.

This unique cultural experience led Cuban social theory to propose also new interpretive frameworks. Fernando Ortiz (1881–1969) was a Cuban intellectual who framed the anthropological discussion about the mixed features of human contact, contributing to understanding Cuban society but also the whole theoretical issue relating to culture contact. Ortiz was a keen observer of everyday life and the thousand ways people mix and proposed a new concept for interpreting cultural contact:

> With the reader's permission, especially if he happens to be interested in ethnographic and sociological questions, I am going to take the liberty of employing for the first time the term transculturation, fully aware of the fact that it is a neologism. And I venture to suggest that

it might be adopted in sociological terminology, to a great extent at least, as a substitute for the term acculturation, whose use is now spreading. Acculturation is used to describe the process of transition from one culture to another, and its manifold social repercussions. But transculturation is a more fitting term. The real history of Cuba is the history of its intermeshed transculturations. First came the transculturation of the paleolithic Indian to the neolithic, and the disappearance of the latter because of his inability to adjust himself to the culture brought in by the Spaniards. Then the transculturation of an unbroken stream of white immigrants. They were Spaniards, but representatives of different cultures and themselves torn loose, to use the phrase of the time, from the Iberian Peninsula groups and transplanted to a New World, where everything was new to them, nature and people, and where they had to readjust themselves to a new syncretism of cultures. At the same time there was going on the transculturation of a steady human stream of African Negroes coming from all the coastal regions of Africa along the Atlantic, from Senegal, Guinea, the Congo, and Angola and as far away as Mozambique on the opposite shore of that continent. All of them snatched from their original social groups, their own cultures destroyed and crushed under the weight of the cultures in existence here, like sugar cane ground in the rollers of the mill. And still other immigrant cultures of the most varying origins arrived, either in sporadic waves or a continuous flow, always exerting an influence and being influenced in turn: Indians from the mainland, Jews, Portuguese, Anglo-Saxons, French, North Americans, even yellow Mongoloids from Macao, Canton, and other regions of the some-time Celestial Kingdom. And each of them torn from his native moorings, faced with the problem of disadjustment and readjustment, of deculturation and acculturation-in a word, of transculturation. (Ortiz 1995 [1940], pp. 97–98)

It is thus no mean task the fact that a Cuban scholar has contributed a new concept to interpret cultural contact, considering that Cuba was and still is a small country and not a rich one for that matter. Bronislaw Malinowski (1884–1942), the leading anthropologist, in his introductory words to the volume by Ortiz, emphasized the creative concept proposed by the Cuban polymath (Malinowski 1995). Recently, it has been stressed that "Ortiz, constructing a perspective from the periphery, viewed cultural boundaries as artifices of power traced precariously on the sands of history" (Portell-Vilá 1995, p. xv), proving that Ortiz's legacy is as vital as ever for social theory.

Furthermore, recent research has been confirming with archaeological evidence the main tenets of Ortiz's transculturation stand. This is clear in a recent sum up:

It is increasingly clear that the indigenous communities in Cuba were not a monolithic group that passively accepted the fate the Europeans chose for them. Rather, there must have been a diversity of indigenous populations, with different cultural backgrounds and adaptive strategies, who actively showed distinct responses to the presence of newcomers. (Martinón-Torres et al. 2007, p. 40)

It is now high time to turn to our case studies.

## 7.3  Male and Female Contact in Colonial Times

Gender relations are not often considered as part of contact archaeology, but there is no more evident contact than between males and females. Gender archaeology has been developing since the 1960s, not least due to the advances of women's rights and struggle for equality worldwide and in Cuba as well. Women were able to control their own bodies and to assert their own social role in society. In Cuba this gender revolution was also a result of the overthrow of Batista's dictatorship and the increased importance of women in society at large and in academia. Archaeology in Cuba as elsewhere was the preserve of men, as the discipline was associated to male testosterone and command. Since the 1960s, though, the discipline has opened up to women and in a few decades a majority of practitioners are women (Domínguez et al. 2009). This changed the discipline and the perception of male and female contact, as we shall see.

Women were for too long absent in the archaeological discourse. New evidence has changed this picture, particularly in relation to the early colonial period. It has been evident from the colonial sources that women were key participants in shaping the new colonial society. Spanish chronicles criticized native women for being lascivious, but what they reveal is that Spaniards were mating with native women and in a way accepting the leading role of women in male and female relations. In fact the matrilineal inheritance, accepted for several decades from the start of the colonial period, is rooted in native practices and reverses what was common in the Iberian Peninsula. Furthermore, this is more remarkable, if we consider that the colonists knew quite well that only the mother is always certain and the father is always uncertain (madre cierta, padre incierto).

The archaeological evidence solves this mystery. Late prehistory and early colonial evidence shows that women were represented as very powerful and the female genitalia were highlighted. It is probably not a coincidence the fact that similar late prehistoric archaeological evidence from the lower Amazon pottery also attest to the overwhelming predominance of female sexual features. It is difficult to avoid the conclusion that women played a very important social role and that in the early colonial women, most of them native, were able to keep this predominance, reversing the male and female relations brought with them by the Spanish colonists. The contact between colonizers and colonized, that is, male and female, were not one of a simple and direct submission, as previously thought, but one of resistance and even reversal of roles (Domínguez 2009, pp. 45–67).

## 7.4 Slaves, Freedmen, and Born Free

Cuban society was from the start a mix of people with different social status and different degrees of freedom, depending on the definition of freedom itself. Freedom is no natural concept, for it depends on specific historical conditions. Freedom in colonial context is even more complex a concept, for the colonial condition is always there parting people. Is it possible to be free in a colonial setting? The colonial power is always there saying to everyone in the colony that he or she is not really free. But then again, the colonist is freer than the enslaved captive, so that there are degrees of freedom, not absolute enslavement or freedom. The slaves were able to forge their own morals and traditions, all too clear in the material culture, as we shall see, so that freedom was perhaps more real for slaves than to born free, who maybe were always colonized in the eyes of the metropolitans (and in their own perceptions of themselves, as mere shadows of the colonial masters in Madrid).

Whatever the case may be, freedom has been at the heart of Cuban society for the last 500 years. Indians were enslaved in the first decades and there is archaeological evidence of native resistance and struggle for freedom. Native pottery was used as ordinary pots, even by colonists, even if imported wares were always also in use, particularly as a way of distinguishing those in contact with the colonial power and those excluded from such possibilities. However, the use of imported wares were not only a way of establishing who were important in the colony, in opposition to those using native wares, but who were also subaltern to metropolitans. A mixed situation, as revealed by the archaeological evidence.

Africans were enslaved early in the colonial period. It was profitable to enslave Africans, benefitting both European and African dealers. As put by Manuel Moreno Fraginals (1982) and Fernando Novais (1976), the colonial machine was responsible for the interest in enslaving and transporting Africans from their own lands to American plantations. In Cuba, Africans were early on a major cultural force in plantations, in major cities and towns, and in their own runaway settlements. In plantations, the overwhelming majority of people were Africans and/or their descendants, shaping social life in the countryside. African sociability was overwhelming and colonists were only too happy to join them in festivals and other religious and social activities. The material evidence from this colonial interaction is clear in pottery, metal wares, rings, necklaces, and much more.

The most important and unique contribution of Cuban archaeology to the study of slavery has been the study of resistance to enslavement, as we should perhaps expect coming from such a freedom-loving people as Cubans. Runaway settlements are always difficult to spot and study. They were originally built to escape detection by plantation raiders, so that they were always located in the most difficult places, such as swamps, hills, and bushes, described in colonial documents as lugares apartados (in documents in Latin, these are described as solitudo, where people are alone, or as per nemora, montes sylvas, saltos). Those runaway polities were described as palenques, a word possibly linked to swamps (palus, in Latin), to a place fortified with stakes (palus in Latin), in any case in use in Spanish to describe native and/or African settlements out of reach. This was the word of choice to refer to maroons in the Caribbean and the fact that it is a Spanish word stresses the colonial approach to those fugitive settlements. There were maroons all over the island, but in Eastern Cuba the hilly areas were particularly suitable for runaway settlers and most of the archaeological research have been carried out there.

Santiago de Cuba was the main center in the East and in the early seventeenth century, after a century of colonization, 12 % of the population were Indians and 36 % were Black slaves (La Rosa 2003, p. 37), probably most of them Africans. In the late eighteenth century, the slave population in Santiago de Cuba reached 29.07 %, in Bayamo 36.40 %, in Holguín 12.90 %, and in Baracoa 7.01 %. The acme of plantation slavery in the nineteenth century explains the fact that in the 1841 census there were almost as many slaves as free people in the colony. Large-scale attacks on eastern Palenques intensified in the mid-nineteenth century, with the setting up of slave-hunting militias. The archaeological fieldwork, including surveys and excavations enabled La Rosa (2003) and associates to propose a complex settlement analysis, including an elaborate communication network linking runaway slave settlements in the Sierra Maestra area, as well as in Mayarí and El Frijol mountains. The Calunga Stream and Calunga maroon show how archaeology may be useful for understanding a rebel community. Calunga is most probably a Bantu word referring "to be intelligent, clever, hence, a deity." It is a name warding off the evil feelings of the enemies of the maroon people. The settlement comprised several dwellings in manmade slope and leveled area. The archaeological fieldwork suggested the existence of very active rebel communities, facing a complex structure of colonial repressive apparatus.

## 7.5  Religiosity and Bead Analysis

Archaeology has moved a long way from shunning feelings as a proper archaeological subject and religiosity is at the forefront of this renewed interest in subjectivity (Whitley 2008). In Cuba, religiosity has been at the root of social life for centuries, and particularly so as resistance to colonial domination. Spanish colonialism was interested in economic profit, but it was also part of a crusade for converting heathen to the true faith, so that their souls could be saved. The Reconquista in the Iberian Peninsula aimed at expelling those infidels from the land, which it did in the late fifteenth century with the simultaneous expulsion of Muslims and Jews in the very same year Christopher Columbus reached the Caribbean, in 1492. Since early days of colonial rule, Cuba witnessed the building of churches and other institutions linked to the Church. However, material culture witnessed symbolic resistance from the start, as it is the case of early colonial settlements in Cuba and the presence of majolica, a Muslim invention which spread first throughout the Mediterranean and is ubiquitous in Havana. Some scholars consider that the popularity of majolica is not to be dissociated from the religious feelings of Muslims (and former Muslims or Mozarabs; and Jews) which precluded human images. Whatever the case may be, majolica spread fast in the New World and Mexican wares were soon very popular in several parts of the Spanish empire, including Cuba. East Asian wares were also imported.

Majolicas were not the only obvious material culture item attesting to mixed feelings in the island of Cuba. Natives and Africans would play a most relevant role in this as in many other aspects of Cuban society. Columbus erected 29 crosses in the New World, and the only one preserved is in the Parish church of Barracoa (Domínguez 2009, p. 142), as a way of imposing the colonizer's official religion. And indeed, this colonial move was so powerful that all the other religious feelings and expressions were affected by Catholic sensibilities, shaping up unique mixed religious sentiments. In excavations of early colonial sites, native talismans can be seen as witnesses to the mixing of elements (Domínguez 1995, p. 100).

Cuba is known for its African heritage and religiosity and this is particularly true in colonial material culture since the late sixteenth century and mostly in the late period. Even in the harsh conditions of plantations, slaves were able to forge their own material world, even if constrained by the conditions and influenced by or mixed with other cultural roots. Particularly poignant is the way slaves, but also mixed people and even the elites, used beads as a way of expressing their own understanding of fate, life, and spiritual forces. Santería (Brown 2003) is usually understood as syncretic religion, well in tune with a transculturation approach, as proposed in this chapter. Archaeology has contributed to understand bead necklaces as a most composite item, deeply embedded in native understanding of the spiritual world, but also addressing the feelings of people at the disposal of superior forces. Slaves were of course in such a position, but also poor people and women in general, including elite ladies, in such a patriarchal society at that time. Necklace beads attest to a unique blend of feelings of the subaltern in their quest for autonomy and freedom.

## 7.6   Concluding Remarks

Contact archaeology has proven very important for complex societies, such as the Cuban one. Indeed, Cuba has been at a crossroads since the earliest times, at the center of the Caribbean pool. During the long colonial centuries, contacts have increased even more, to the point that the Island is a perfect example of a society in a constant flux of interaction. Social theory developed in Cuba due to several reasons, not least to this unique rich and enmeshed cultural setting, but also to the love for freedom and against imperial rule. Archaeology has developed fast in the last few decades in the country and profited from social theory, dealing with complex subjects relating to gender relations, ethnicity, slavery, religiosity, and much more. This chapter is just an appetizer, encouraging fellow archaeologists to further exploring the avenues only hinted here.

**Acknowledgments**  We owe thanks to Chris Gosden, Gabino La Rosa, and Tim Murray. We mention the institutional support of the Cuban Academy of History (Academia de la Historia de Cuba), Havana Heritage Authority (Gabinete del Historiador de la Habana, Cuba), University of Campinas—Unicamp, Brazil, São Paulo Science Foundation (FAPESP), Brazilian Science Foundation (CNPq), and the Public Archaeology Laboratory, Unicamp, Brazil. The ideas are our own and we are solely responsible for them.

## References

Berman, M. J., Febles, J., & Gnivecki, P. L. (2005). The organization of Cuban archaeology context and brief history. In L. A. Curet, S. Dawdy & G. La Rosa (Eds.), *Dialogues in Cuban archaeology* (pp. 41–61). Tuscaloosa: The University of Alabama Press.

Brown, D. H. (2003). *Santería Enthroned. Art, ritual and innovation in and Afro-Cuban religion.* Chicago: The University of Chicago Press.

Cosculluela, J. A. (1946). Prehistoric cultures of Cuba. *American Antiquity, 12*(1), 10–18.

Domínguez, L. (1995). *Arqueología Colonial Cubana*. Havana: Editorial de Ciencias Sociales.

Domínguez, L. (2009). *Particularidades Arqueológicas*. Havana: Ediciones Boloña.

Domínguez, L., Funari, P. P. A., Carvalho, A. V., & Rodrigues, G. B. (Eds.). (2009). *Desafios da Arqueologia, Depoimentos*. Erechim: Habilis.

Fraginals, M. M. (1982). *Between slavery and free labor*. Baltimore: Johns Hopkins University Press.

Funari, P. P. A. (2006). Conquistadors, plantations, and quilombo: Latin America in historical archaeology context. In M. Hall & S. Silliman (Eds.), *Historical archaeology* (pp. 209–229). Oxford: Blackwell.

Gamble, C. (2003). *Timewalkers. The prehistory of global colonization*. London: Penguin.

Gosden, C. (2004). *Archaeology and colonialism: Cultural contact from 5000 BC to the present*. Cambridge: Cambridge University Press.

La Rosa Corzo, G. (2003). *Runaway slave settlements in cuba. Resistance and repression*. Chapel Hill: The University of North Carolina Press.

Malinowski, B. (1995). In Ortiz, F. (Ed.). *Cuban Counterpoint, Tobacco and Sugar* (pp. lvii–lxiv). Durham: Duke University Press.

Martinón-Torres, M., Cooper, J., Valcárcel Rojas, R., & Rehren, T. (2007). *Diversifying the picture: Indigenous responses to European arrival in Cuba, International Archaeology* (pp. 37–40). London: UCL.

Murray, T. (Ed.). (2004). *The archaeology of contact in settler societies*. Cambridge: Cambridge University Press.

Novais, F. (1976). *Portugal e Brasil na crise do antigo sistema colonial*. São Paulo: Hucitec.

Ortiz, F. (1955). Cuban counterpoint, tobacco and sugar (Del fenómeno social de la «transculturación» y de su importancia en Cuba, Revista Bimestre Cubana, 1940). Durham: Duke University Press.

Patte, M. F. (2010). Arawak vs. Lokono. What's in a name? In N. Faraclas, et al. (Eds.), *In a sea of heteroglossia* (pp. 75–86). Curaçao: The University of the Netherlands Antilles.

Portell-Vilá, H. (1995). *By way of prologue, Cuban counterpoint, tobacco and sugar* (pp. ix–lvii). Durham: Duke University Press.

Whitley, D. D. (2008). Religion. In H. Maschner, A. Baxter, & C. Chippindale (Eds.), *Handbook of archaeological theories* (pp. 547–566). Lanham: AltaMira Press.

# Part II
# Local Histories: Diversity, Creativity, and Novelty

# Chapter 8
# Dress, Faith, and Medicine: Caring for the Body in Eighteenth-Century Spanish Texas

Diana DiPaolo Loren

## 8.1  Introduction

During the eighteenth century, theories of disease and illness were intertwined with Christian doctrines regarding spiritual well-being, Spanish imperial understandings regarding race and dress of colonizer and colonized, and culturally distinct medicinal practices for treating physical and spiritual sicknesses. To explore these admittedly complex entanglements of bodies, souls, and clothing, I place the physical and spiritual body at the center of analysis. My intent is to obtain a fuller understanding of the concerns of bodily and spiritual care at the eighteenth-century Spanish presidio of Los Adaes. I consider how material culture (including clothing, amulets, and religious medals) embodied the multiethnic inhabitants of Los Adaes treated and covered their bodies through dress, practices of faith, and medicine.

## 8.2  Considering the Spanish Colonial Body

Contemporary theories of embodiment in archaeology provide a stable base on which to build an understanding of the materiality of Spanish colonial spiritual and corporeal bodies. Drawing influence by the work of phenomenologists, including Merleau-Ponty, Husserl, and Heidegger, and practice theorists such as Bourdieu and Giddens, archaeological theories of embodiment posit that it is through the body that a person experiences the world and forms a sense of self and identity (Crossland 2010; Joyce 2005, 2007; Kus 1992; Stig Sørensen and Rebay-Salisbury 2012). Briefly stated, lived experience—or "being-in-the-world"—is culturally specific, situated in a discourse of appropriate bodily action, so that experiences of the body

D. D. Loren (✉)
Peabody Museum of Archaeology and Ethnology, Harvard University,
11 Divinity Avenue, Cambridge, MA 02138, USA
e-mail: dloren@fas.harvard.edu

© Springer International Publishing Switzerland 2015                                           143
P. P. A. Funari, M. X. Senatore (eds.), *Archaeology of Culture Contact and Colonialism in Spanish and Portuguese America,* DOI 10.1007/978-3-319-08069-7_8

can only be understood in the context in which that body exists (cf. Crossland 2010, pp. 389–390; see also Joyce 2007). Materiality was integral to lived experience. Lived experience is constituted with and through material culture, leaving residues of experiences in texts, objects, and space (Crossland 2010; Gosden and Knowles 2001; Joyce 2005, 2007; Kus 1992; Miller 2005). In this perspective, the dressed and adorned body is viewed as a totality: physicality, health, and spirituality are constituted in daily practice with material culture (Fisher and Loren 2003; Loren 2010, 2013; Stig Sørensen 2006; Stig Sørensen and Rebay-Salisbury 2012).

This complex entanglement of the clothed and adorned physical and spiritual self was of personal and imperial concern in the eighteenth century. The body was at the heart of the colonial project and in this ideology, it was not just outward appearance that was important, rather the whole body. Race, gender, and status—all conferred from bodily appearance—were part of the daily concerns of empire, which marked, policed, and documented the activities of colonized and colonizer. Colonial empires shaped colonial bodies: physical and spiritual care, social and sexual interactions, and dress and language were just a few of the concerns of imperial powers who strove to maintain hierarchies of inclusion and exclusion (Loren 2001, 2007, 2008, 2010, 2013; Stoler 2009; Voss 2008). For example, dressing and adorning one's body in colonial New Spain was a means of communicating status, morality, gender, as well as health, religion, and honorable conduct in a colony concerned with measuring racial difference (Deagan 2002; Lipsett-Rivera 2007; Loren 2007, 2010).

Eighteenth-century European medicine was built on the belief that the body was composed of four humors: black bile, yellow bile, phlegm, and blood (Foster 1953). The cause of illness—such as pneumonia, influenza, smallpox, and tumors—was tied to the mechanical imbalances of the four humors. The classification of these imbalances differed in Europe. Some argued that "animism" (the soul) was at the heart of everything and disease was the soul's attempt to re-establish bodily order, while other physicians took the view that the body was a machine, and disease was the body's way of expelling foreign matter (Shyrock 1960). Balance was restored to the body through diet, prayers, bloodletting, purging, vomiting, and compounds ingested internally and applied externally (Foster 1953; Shyrock 1960). Surgeons were uncommon in northern New Spain, and pharmacies were rare outside of Mexico City. Most individuals compounded medicines and dosed themselves based on knowledge of folk medicine or sought treatment through priests and *curanderos* (healers) who used a combination of scientific knowledge, botanical ingredients, and prayers (Guerra 1976).

Physical health and spiritual salvation were closely connected in the eighteenth century. Caring for the sick was part of the Seven Corporal Works of Mercy (charitable acts of mercy for bodily needs) and carried out by priests (Guerra 1969). Tending to the medical needs as well as spiritual needs fell into the hands of priests as a part of their daily routine. This practice was spiritual and pragmatic: to save souls, the body must be healed. Members of the Jesuit and Augustinian religious orders ministered to people in remote regions of New Spain where access to doctors and surgeons was rare or nonexistent. Priests and religious missionaries wrote many of the first medical books in New Spain. For example, Jesuit brother Juan de

Esteyneffer's *Florilegio Medicinal*, published in Mexico in 1712, combined European medical knowledge with knowledge of indigenous herbs found in New Spain (Kay 1977). Produced for missionaries, the *Florilegio* was a sourcebook for the diagnosis and treatment of diseases, surgical methods, and the composition of common medicines. Prayers as well as novenas for preventing and curing disease were included in the *Florilegio* and other medical books (Guerra 1969, 1976).

Eighteenth-century folk medicine practice, practiced in concert with more formal medicine, drew from knowledge about the natural and supernatural world (Foster 1953; Graham 1976). While folk medicine was used for physical care (illness, childbirth, pregnancy), it was also used for curing *mal de ojo* (evil eye) and other ailments considered to be causes of illness, such as shame, fear, anger, envy, and longing (Foster 1953). Practitioners of *curandería* could be male (*curandero*) or female (*curandera*). Within New Spain, they were distinguished from priests because of their magical curative powers, which the *curandera* attributed to God (Graham 1976; Quezada 1991). *Curandería* was a hybridized healing practice, containing elements derived from both indigenous and Spanish cultures; a male or female healer prayed for spiritual cleaning and protection against evil spirits or the acts of a *brujo* (witch) who had the power to cast the *mal de ojo* and imbalance humors (Foster 1953).

Religious officials were often highly suspicious of the curative powers of the *curanderas*, and in some Spanish colonial contexts, these healers were persecuted and punished for idolatry and witchcraft (Quezada 1991). Knowledge of the body and humors as well as the kinds of performances involved with acts of curing differed between the two groups of healers. Franciscan healers dispensed medicine and spiritual advice, and quietly prayed over the bodies of the ill; while *curanderas* (both Native American and non-Native American), who also dispensed medicine and spiritual advice, did so through prayer, dance, and performance in more elaborate healing ceremonies (Foster 1953). In this context, caring for the body was embedded in social practice that recognized various ways and means of healing spirit and flesh.

## 8.3   Caring for Body and Soul at Presidio Los Adaes

Presidio Nuestra Señora del Pilar de los Los Adaes (16Na16) consisted of a presidio and mission community situated along the easternmost frontier of Spanish Texas, along the border of western French Louisiana. Established in 1721, its purpose was to defend New Spain from the French and to convert Caddo peoples. During its 50-year settlement, the Los Adaes community included Spanish and mixed-blood military personnel and families as well as civilian settlers from New Spain, French refugees, Caddo Indians, and some escaped African slaves from French Louisiana (Avery 1995; Loren 2007; Gregory 1984; Gregory et al. 2004; Pavao-Zuckerman and Loren 2012).

The presidio community functioned more as a trading post than fort and engaged both economically and socially with nearby French and Caddo Indians (Avery 1996).

Los Adaes was located 300 miles away from the nearest Spanish military outpost at San Antonio, but was just 15 miles from the French post of Natchitoches. Shipments of goods between Los Adaes and the metropole in New Spain were so infrequent that official regulations regarding intercolony trade were often ignored out of necessity (Avery 1995). Interactions between the Spanish and French often extended into the personal realm, as intermarriage, inter-racial, and interethnic sexual relations were common.

No surgeon or doctor was stationed at Los Adaes; rather, Franciscan priests ministered bodily health and spiritual wellness. In his 1767–1768 diary of his inspection of the Texas missions, Franciscan father Fray Gaspar José de Solís (1931, pp. 64–65) noted the destitute nature of Los Adaes and the important role of priests in attending to the physical and spiritual wellness of the community:

> This mission of Señor San Miguel de Cuellar de los Adays [sic] is situated in a dense forest of thick trees, pines, post oaks, pin oaks…The ministers (who only occupy themselves in ministering to all the white people of the royal presidio and ranches, of which there are some) suffer many needs, and even lack the necessary things. By the time that aid reaches them, which is given to them by the piety of the King, Our Lord (may God guard him), they have already suffered and had these experience…The people live on the corn and do not have any sown fields. The flesh of the bulls that is furnished them is very bad. All seed, such as corn, frijoles etc. is scarce. There is only an abundance of whiskey, with which they are provided by the French of Nachitos [sic] who are seven leagues from here. In regard to the organization of the mission, there is no Indian congregation, because although they are numerous they do not wish to congregate, and go to the presidio rather than to the mission. What has been and is a consolation, as I have been assured by the old men, since many of the first who came in to settle in this country are still living, is that all of the Indians, both men and women, old and young, send for the Father in the hour of death, wherever they may be in order that he may "echar el Horco Santo," that is administer the Holy Baptism, although it is suspected that many ask for it as a natural remedy for obtaining bodily health.

Solís' account indicates that while Franciscan priests living at the mission were responsible for ministering the Spanish colonists, Caddo members of the community commonly sought healing through priests. A number of different diseases and maladies impacted the population of Northern Spain during the eighteenth century, including dysentery, smallpox, and influenza, as known as *mal de siete días* or the sickness of 7 days (Foster 1953; Nava 1795).

*Curanderas* also played an important role in healing, but received less respect than Franciscan priests. Franciscan father Juan Agustín Morfí published his lengthy *History of Texas, 1673–1677* following an inspection tour of northern New Spain missions in 1776–1777. In his account, Caddo medicine men are described in unflattering terms as *curanderos*:

> The multitude of medicine men (curanderos) with which this nation is flooded, contribute powerfully to the maintenance of faith in these delights, little cunning being necessary to deceive a superstitious people, who, instructed in advance in their favor, believe without examination, whatever these imposters propose to them (quoted in Swanton 1942, pp. 223, emphasis in original).

Morfí followed this statement with a lengthy—and highly skeptical—description of healing practices, which included singing, dancing, prayers, and bloodletting, noting that in the end, some did attain relief from their ailments after treatment by the *curandero*.

## 8.4 Archaeology of Dress, Faith, and Medicine

Archaeological excavations at the site in the late twentieth century identified portions of the fort's walls, the location of the governor's house inside the presidio walls, three structures outside the presidio, as well as a possible blacksmith area and the remains of a kitchen (Gregory 1973, 1980, 1982, 1984, 1985). Overall, a complex assemblage of clothing and adornment artifacts as well as tools used for the construction and embellishment of clothing, such as spindle whorls, scissors, thimbles, and embroidery hooks, were recovered from the excavations. Additionally, each household context included a diverse array of clothing and adornment artifacts. For example, a structure referred to as the "Southeast Structure" was located southeast of the main presidio building and featured a large outdoor kitchen.

Artifacts of clothing and adornment recovered from 1982 excavations of the structure included scissors and pins used for the construction and mending of clothing, lead bale seals from bolts of cloth, a scrap of gold lace, a piece of blue-gray woven fabric, buttons used for fastening shirt sleeves, plain shoe buckles, rings, a green paste jewel from a ring or another piece of jewelry, an earring, several religious medallions, tinkling cones and assorted glass beads, as well as collar stays used in military coats (Gregory 1984). The combination of these artifacts of clothing and adornment suggest that occupants of the house creatively configured their dress by combining aspects of different fashions: European style, evidenced by the blue-gray wool, patterned shoe buckles, and military shirt collar ornaments, with aspects of Native American-style dress, evidenced by the glass seed beads and tinkler cones likely sewn onto buckskin clothing (Loren 2007, 2010). Similar combinations of artifacts found throughout the site also suggest that many inhabitants mixed different styles of clothing in daily life.

The clothing and adornment of the residents of Los Adaes were viewed as sloppy and haphazard by visiting colonial officials, such as Solís. Yet, some artifacts recovered from the site suggest meaningful manipulation of material culture items related to spiritual and physical well-being, such as religious ornaments, amulets, and medical practice.

### 8.4.1 Religious Adornments: Devotional Medals and Crucifixes

Crucifixes and other religious objects are the residues of religious proselytization in the New World. They are often worn as an embodiment of faith. In New World contexts, they often symbolized the reassurance that Christianity was accepted and maintained by colonial peoples in favor of other religions. Yet, how were Christian symbols worn and used in combination with other fashions at Los Adaes? Here, we must be aware of the limitations of functional categories as Christian symbols can indicate more than religious expression or conversion. The context in which a Christian symbol was worn is crucial; in different contexts, it may have simultaneously spoken to other issues such as ethnicity, status, or gender. Crucifixes and religious medals held certain meanings for baptized individuals, but rosary beads and other

**Fig. 8.1** Crucifix and two religious medals recovered from Los Adaes. (Photo by Don Sepulvado)

Christian symbols took on new meanings when combined with other items to purposefully and publicly negotiate self in the context of religious conversion.

Religious ornaments add to the dynamic fashion embodied at the presidio and indicate how religious adornments and amulets were used to promote physical as well as spiritual well-being. Religious objects recovered from Los Adaes excavations include a copper alloy crucifix, a medallion depicting the Holy Family with a drilled hole under a broken loop attachment, and a St. John of Matha medal (Fig. 8.1). St.John Matha was the patron saint of prisoners and slaves, significant in the light of conscripts at Los Adaes who came from Mexican jails, and introducing the possibility of enslaved African influences at the site. The crucifix and Holy Family medals were recovered from domestic contexts with other diverse items of clothing and adornment such as a gilt paste shoe buckle, tinkler cones, glass beads, and plain copper alloy buttons, which suggest that these religious symbols were incorporated into the creative fashions worn by Los Adaes residents. The St. John of Matha medal was recovered from a context that suggests a more nuanced use (Gregory et al. 2009) and is described below.

## 8.4.2   Amulets: Higas and Pierced Coins

Kathleen Deagan (2002, pp. 87–105) provides a lengthy list of amulets recovered from Spanish colonial sites, all of which were intended to protect the wearer from illness or to help the individual withstand or bring about certain bodily processes: teething, nosebleeds, hemorrhage, or conception. These practices of using protective adornments often derived from European homelands. At Los Adaes, the recovery of numerous metal *higas* and a pierced coin amulet suggest that residents employed amulets in their daily life (Gregory 1984; see also Deagan 2002, pp. 95–99). Items used as amulets or charms fall into two categories: those specifically made for protection (such *higas* to ward off the evil eye) and everyday items put into use as charms or amulets (such as pierced coins).

**Fig. 8.2** Copper alloy *higas*.
(Photo by the author)

**Fig. 8.3** Silver *higas*. (Photo
by Don Sepulvado)

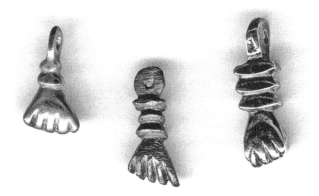

*Higas* (amulets in the shape of a fist with thumb placed between the index finger
and the middle finger, also known as *figas* or fig-hand) were employed to ward off
*mal de ojo* and other maladies (Hildburgh 1955). *Higas* and hand charms had roots
in Moorish traditions and were common throughout Spain and the Spanish New
World as a protective charm, especially important for babies. Made from coral, bone,
silver, and other metals, *higas* would have been worn as jewelry as earrings, on a
necklace, or pinned to clothing (Foster 1953). Based on historical documentation,
Gregory (1973, pp. 48–49, 177) argues that *higas* were also part of colonial horse
gear and were hung from the saddle as a form of protection. At Los Adaes, 24 *higas*
have been recovered from various locations in the presidial community, including
the area of the barracks, inside the south wall of the presidio (Gregory 1973, 1980,
1982, 1984, 1985). The majority of copper alloy *higas* shown in Fig. 8.2 are simple
or abstract in shape. Other *higas* recovered from the site were made from silver,
with holes for suspension, suggesting that they were worn as jewelry and attached
to clothing (Fig. 8.3). Additionally, silver is used as protection against the brujo
(Gregory, personal communication; see also Foster 1953).

**Fig. 8.4** Feature containing a wick trimmer, a red glass bead, St. John of Matha medallion, and an eggshell. (Photo credit Texas Beyond History)

Another potential amulet recovered from the excavations was a well-worn pierced coin (Gregory 1973, p. 167, 174). Coin charms were commonly used in many parts of Europe from the fourteenth through the nineteenth centuries as a form of countermagic, a touch piece or amulet worn to protect the wearer from sickness or sin; a practice was also followed by people of European and African descent living in colonial America (Davidson 2004; Hill 2007; Loren 2010; Wilkie 1995, 1997).

These items used to protect the body, oftentimes worn on the body itself, differ from religious medals or crucifixes in that they are not "used as intermediaries between their owner and a higher power" (Deagan 2002, p. 87). Rather, these items are invested with meanings and beliefs that imbue them with power, sometimes magical in nature but always protective of the physical and spiritual body.

### 8.4.3 Curandería

Gregory et al. (2009) postulate that based on a specific set of artifacts recovered from a cooking pit at the Southeast Structure, one of the house's occupants was a practitioner of *curandería*. In a cooking pit feature, a brass wick trimmer, egg shell fragments, and tubular blue and red glass beads were found in association with a St. John of Matha medal at the bottom of the pit (Fig. 8.4). Two knives, a small bundle of blue cloth, and a large metal vessel were located at the top of the feature. Gregory et al. (2009) argue that this unusual cluster was intentional and the result of folk medicine rituals. Foster (1953, p. 208–209) notes that in *curandería*, the most common form of divining and curing the evil eye in New Spain involved the use of a chicken egg, as the egg draws out the "eye" from the patient. Other items used by a *curandero* includes candles, pictures of saints, animal bones, herbs, and holy water (Gregory et al. 2009), items that closely resemble those recovered from the cooking pit.

Artifacts of clothing and adornment recovered from the Southeast Structure suggested certain fashion for inhabitants of the house who likely wore buckled shoes, tailored clothing, and beaded fabric as well as religious and secular jewelry. These artifacts suggest care taken of the body that was visual and tangible, the material embodiment of self (flesh and spirit) in an eighteenth-century community. The feature excavated and interpreted by Gregory and his colleagues add a particularly nuanced perspective of bodily care in colonial New Spain: how community members cared for one another through faith and healing.

## 8.5  Concluding Thoughts

In eastern New Spain, wellness and spirituality were rooted in the body. The combination of Catholic medals with secular items and amulets found at Los Adaes indicate how aspects of Catholicism and associated material culture were woven not only into worldviews and identities of people living at Los Adaes, but also the practices of adorning and protecting body and soul integral to constructing identities and safeguarding spiritual well-being. Franciscan priests viewed *curanderos* as transgressors of morality (Quezada 1991), but their knowledge and practice offered relief from many of the ailments suffered in New Spain. Historical narratives, such as those offered by Solís and Morfí, suggest that colonial peoples sought healing through priests and *curanderos*.

The use of both amulets and devotional medals for their prophylactic and curative powers does not suggest that *curanderos* were preferred over Franciscans, but rather, the use of different adornments represented embodied knowledge of practical action.

Interpretations of the physicality and materiality of the human body afforded by a perspective on embodiment bring attention to the corporeal predicament of colonialism. It focuses our attention on the relationship between people and things in a context where one's body—skin color, gender, health, dress, sexuality, and comportment—was described, scripted, and policed by colonial officials. It highlights intentional action meant to care and protect one's body by consciously dressing to include a *higa* and a devotional medal over or under clothing. The material strategies employed at this colonial community allowed the diverse community at Los Adaes to care for self and other, to embody self and maintain health from the skin outward.

**Acknowledgments**  The author would like to thank George Avery and Hiram F. "Pete" Gregory for the opportunity to examine the Los Adaes materials. It was Gregory's interpretation of *curandería* at the presidio that inspired my work on health and the body at Los Adaes and I am grateful for his continued insight. My larger study of colonial clothing and adornment, health, sin, and the body has benefited from discussions with Mary Beaudry, Trish Capone, and Christina J. Hodge.

# References

Avery, G. (1995). More friend than foe: Eighteenth-century Spanish, French, and Caddoan interaction at Los Adaes, a capital of Texas located in northwestern Louisiana. *Louisiana Archaeology, 22,* 163–193.

Avery, G. (1996). Annual Report for the Los Adaes Station Archaeology Program. Department of Social Sciences, Northwestern State University, Natchitoches.

Crossland, Z. (2010). Embodiment and materiality. In D. Hicks & M. C. Beaudry (Eds.), *The Oxford handbook of material culture studies* (pp. 386–405). Oxford: Oxford University Press.

Davidson, J. M. (2004). Rituals captured in context and time: Charm use in North Dallas Freedman's town (1869–1907), Dallas, Texas. *Historical Archaeology, 38*(2), 22–54.

Deagan, K. A. (2002). *Artifacts of the Spanish colonies of Florida and the Caribbean, 1500–1800, Vol. 2: Personal portable possessions.* Washington, D.C.: Smithsonian Institution Press.

Fisher, G., & Loren, D. D. (2003). Embodying identity in anthropology and archaeology. *Cambridge Archaeological Journal, 13*(2), 225–230.

Foster, G. M. (1953). Relationships between Spanish and Spanish-American folk medicine. *The Journal of American Folklore, 66*(261), 201–217.

Gosden, C., & Knowles, C. (2001). *Collecting colonialism: Material culture and colonial change.* Berg: Oxford.

Graham, J. S. (1976). The role of the Curadero in the Mexican American folk medicine system in West Texas. In W. D. Hand (Ed.), *American folk medicine: A symposium* (pp. 175–189). Berkeley: University of California Press.

Gregory, H. F. (1973). Eighteenth-century Caddoan archaeology: A study in models and interpretations. Doctoral dissertation, Southern Methodist University, Dallas.

Gregory, H. F. (1980). Excavations: 1979, Presidio Nuestra Señora del Pilar de Los Adaes. Office of State Parks, Louisiana Department of Culture, Recreation, and Tourism, Baton Rouge.

Gregory, H. F. (1982). Excavations: 1982, Presidio Nuestra Señora del Pilar de Los Adaes. Office of State Parks, Louisiana Department of Culture, Recreation, and Tourism, Baton Rouge.

Gregory, H. F. (1984). Excavations 1981–82, Presidio de Nuestra Señora del Pilar de los Adaes. Williamson Museum, Northwestern State University, Natchitoches, Louisiana.

Gregory, H. F. (1985). Excavations: 1984, Unit 227, Presidio Nuestra Señora del Pilar de Los Adaes. Office of State Parks, Louisiana Department of Culture, Recreation, and Tourism, Baton Rouge.

Gregory, H. F., Avery, G., Lee, A. L., & Blaine J. C. (2004). Presidio Los Adaes: Spanish, French, and Caddoan interaction on the northern frontier. *Historical Archaeology, 38*(3), 65–77.

Gregory, H. F., Avery, G., Galán, F. X., Black, S., Wade, M., Blaine, J. C., & Lee, A. L. (2009). Los Adaes: 18th-Century capital of Spanish Texas. http://www.texasbeyondhistory.net/adaes/index.html. Accessed 15 Nov 2013.

Guerra, F. (1969). The role of religion in Spanish American Medicine. In F.N.L. Poynter (Ed.), *Medicine and Culture* (pp. 179–188). London: Wellcome Institute of the History of Medicine.

Guerra, F. (1976). Medical Folklore in Spanish America. In W. D. Hand (Ed.), *American folk medicine: A symposium* (pp. 169–174). Berkeley: University of California Press.

Hildburgh, W. L. (1955). Images of the human hand as amulets in Spain. *Journal of the Warburg and Courtauld Institutes, 18*(1/2), 67–89.

Hill, J. (2007). The story of the amulet: Locating the enchantment of collections. *Journal of Material Culture, 12*(1), 65–87.

Joyce, R. (2005). Archaeology of the body. *Annual Review of Anthropology, 34,* 139–158.

Joyce, R. (2007). Embodied subjectivity: Gender, femininity, masculinity, and sexuality. In L. Meskell & R. W. Pruecel (Eds), *A companion to social archaeology* (pp. 82–95). Oxford: Blackwell.

Kay, M. A. (1977). The florilegio medicinal: Source of Southwest ethnomedicine. *Ethnohistory, 24*(3), 251–259.

Kus, S. (1992). Toward an archaeology of body and soul. In J.-C. Gardin & C. Peebles (Eds.), *Representations in archaeology* (pp. 168–177). Bloomington: Indiana University Press.

Lipsett-Rivera, S. (2007). Language of body and body as language: Religious thought and cultural syncretism. In S. Schroeder & S. Poole (Eds.), *Religion in new Spain* (pp. 66–82). Albuquerque: University of New Mexico Press.

Loren, D. D. (2001). Social skins: Orthodoxies and practices of dressing in the early colonial lower Mississippi Valley. *Journal of Social Archaeology, 1*(2), 172–189.

Loren, D. D. (2007). Corporeal concerns: Eighteenth-century casta paintings and colonial bodies in Spanish Texas. *Historical Archaeology, 41*(1), 23–36.

Loren, D. D. (2008). In contact: Bodies and spaces in the sixteenth- and seventeenth-century Eastern Woodlands. New York: Altamira.

Loren, D. D. (2010). The archaeology of clothing and bodily adornment in colonial America. Gainesville: University Press of Florida.

Loren, D. D. (2013). Considering mimicry and hybridity in early colonial New England: Health, sin and the body "Behung with Beades." *Archaeological Review from Cambridge, 28*(1), 151–168.

Miller, D. (Ed.). (2005). *Materiality*. Durham: Duke University Press.

de Nava, P. (1795). Letter to the Governor of Texas concerning the discovery of cure for "sickness of seven days." Bexar Archives 2S68, Roll 24. Dolph Briscoe Center for American History, University of Texas Austin.

Pavao-Zuckerman, B., & Loren, D. D. (2012). Presentation is everything: Foodways, tablewares, and colonial identity at presidio Los Adaes. *International Journal of Historical Archaeology, 16*, 199–226.

Quezada, N. (1991). The inquisition's repression of Curanderos. In M. E. Perry & A. J. Cruz (Eds.), *Cultural encounters: The impact of the inquisition in Spain and the New World* (pp. 37–57). Berkeley: University of California Press.

Shyrock, R. H. (1960). *Medicine and society in America, 1660–1860*. Ithaca: Cornell University Press.

de Solís, G. J. (1931). Diary of a visit of inspection of the Texas missions made by Fray Gaspar José de Solís in the year 1767–1768. *Southwestern Historical Quarterly, 35*, 28–76.

Stig Sørenson, M. L. (2006). Gender, things, and material culture. In S. M. Nelson (Ed.) *Handbook of gender in archaeology* (pp. 105–135). Berkeley: Altamira Press.

Stig Sørensen, M. L., & Rebay-Salisbury, K. (2012). Embodied knowledge. Refections on belief and technology. In M. L. Stig Sørensen & K. Rebay-Salisbury (Eds.) *Embodied knowledge: Historical perspectives on belief and technology* (pp. 1–8). Oxford: Oxbow.

Stoler, A. L. (2009). Along the archival grain: Epistemic anxieties and colonial common sense. Princeton: Princeton University Press.

Swanton, J. R. (1942). *Source material on the history and ethnology of the Caddo Indians*. Norman: University of Oklahoma Press.

Voss, B. L. (2008). "Poor people in silk shirts": Dress and ethnogenesis in Spanish-colonial San Francisco. *Journal of Social Archaeology, 8*(3), 404–432.

Wilkie, L. A. (1995). Magic and empowerment on the plantation: An archaeological consideration of African-American worldview. *Southeastern Archaeology, 14*(2), 136–157.

Wilkie, L. A. (1997). Secret and sacred: Contextualizing the artifacts of African-American magic and religion. *Historical Archaeology, 31*(4), 81–106.

# Chapter 9
# Uncommon Commodities: Articulating the Global and the Local on the Orinoco Frontier

Franz Scaramelli and Kay Scaramelli

## 9.1  Introduction

This chapter draws on archaeological and historical sources and oral tradition to provide a detailed account of the progressive structural engagement of the indigenous societies of the Middle Orinoco with the rest of the world (Fig. 9.1). Our discussion concerns certain products and practices that structured the relationships that evolved between the various sectors of the colonial societies of the Orinoco in different colonial and neocolonial contexts. We explore the commercialization of wild resources such as turtle oil, sarrapia (*Tonka beans*), traditional craft items such as shell beads (*quiripa*), and pottery, and the commoditization of indigenous subsistence staples, such as cassava (O'Connor 2009). These "uncommon commodities", as compared with the legendary commerce in cacao, coffee, cotton, sugar cane, and leather, have played a fundamental role in the regional history of the Middle Orinoco, which connects the Western Guayana Shield and the *Llanos* of Colombia and Venezuela. In this vast region, these local resources were fundamental items for exchange prior to and following European colonization. These industries, which were dependent on local expertise and raw materials, fostered productive relations and regimens of land tenure for local populations that profoundly influenced the articulation of local and global political economies in colonial and postcolonial contexts, shaping the societies and culture histories of the indigenous populations of the Orinoco up until the present. Although we cannot offer a detailed description of each product, we will refer to a few key commodities that illustrate those aspects that are particular to the Middle Orinoco, in contrast to colonial processes and forms of interaction that arose in other nearby geographical contexts. Our discussion will commence with the colonial period mis-

F. Scaramelli (✉) · K. Scaramelli
42 Atlantic Circle. Apt. 203, Pittsburg, CA 94565, USA
e-mail: fscarame@gmail.com

K. Scaramelli
Departamento de Arqueología y Antropología Histórica, Escuela de Antropología, Universidad Central de Venezuela, 1050 Caracas, Venezuela
e-mail: katasca@gmail.com

© Springer International Publishing Switzerland 2015                                    155
P. P. A. Funari, M. X. Senatore (eds.), *Archaeology of Culture Contact and Colonialism in Spanish and Portuguese America*, DOI 10.1007/978-3-319-08069-7_9

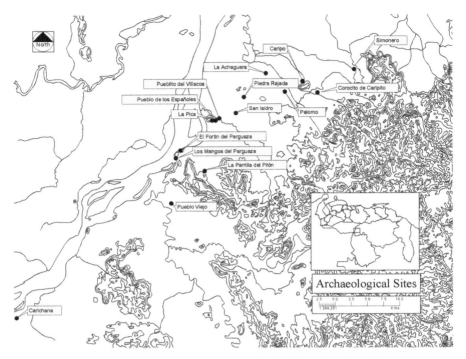

**Fig. 9.1** Map of the Middle Orinoco showing archaeological sites referred to in the text

sion system, their dependence on indigenous agriculture, and small-scale craft production using local resources (pottery, basketry, and shell beads). We continue with the commercial exploitation of natural resources with local technology (turtle oil), to finalize with a discussion of the nineteenth century sarrapia boom, which responded to international demand for aromatic species used in the cosmetic industry.

As a result of the commercialization of these products in the Middle Orinoco since the Colonial period, several local indigenous communities, such as the Mapoyo, the Eñepa, and the Piaroa, have developed an economy in which they complement their subsistence activities based on agriculture, hunting, and fishing, with cash cropping of certain products (maize, manioc) and seasonal, specialized gathering of wild forest products with a demand in the regional and international market. Whereas enslavement and annihilation came to characterize the rubber boom in the Upper Orinoco River, and slavery and other forced labor regimes were intimately linked to slavery and plantation economies along the Caribbean coast and the Antilles, the Middle Orinoco provides examples of social interaction on the periphery in which the Natives were often able to negotiate a greater degree of economic and social control compared with that prevailing in colonial centers.

Through insights derived from the material record, we will examine the ways in which indigenous societies entered into larger-scale relations of economic and political power, and the socio–cultural transformations they experienced through time. The commercialization of a variety of local products provides an opportunity to examine processes of commoditization of native material products, services, and labor associated with extractive industries. We highlight the interplay between productive and technological systems, the global demand for exotic materials and products, and the genesis of spatially anchored and ethnically defined economies. These aspects are all essential to the comprehension of the articulation between local and global structures of power and the variety of ways in which human societies have confronted situations of contact, colonization, and the multiple responses to the asymmetrical power structures these have entailed. We argue that the exchange of goods in the eighteenth century mission context, often in the form of trade partners, gift giving, and barter, foresees the emergence and amalgamation of new structures of value production and dependency in the course of activities involving the transformation of value through the gathering of native products and the production of agricultural surplus intended for sale. The colonial system fostered the exchange of merchandise that circulated through processes of advanced payments, debt peonage, and other forms of labor exploitation that led to increasing involvement in the market economy. Nonetheless, the nature of the products, the indigenous expertise involved in their exploitation, and the sporadic involvement in commercial transactions, as well as the continued maintenance of indigenous land tenure essential to subsistence farming, fishing, and hunting, led to a peculiar pattern of involvement and dis-involvement through time that played a key role in the redefinition of the modern indigenous groups inhabiting the region *vis a vis* the local *Criollo* sector (non-indigenous population born in Venezuela) and their insertion in the broader Venezuelan Nation-State. The analysis of these lesser known commercial transactions and their impact on ethnogenesis is an essential element in the attempt to transcend the static notion of culture and ethnicity that still finds echoes in the ethnographic literature, in which the diversity of historical trajectories of the indigenous groups and the dynamics of their engagement with western societies are all too often stereotyped as acculturative processes or simply ignored.

## 9.2 Analytical Framework

This analysis builds on previous regional studies of both mainstream and inland areas (Fig. 9.1), where an extensive occupational sequence ranging from pre-contact times through the present has been established (Scaramelli 2005, 2006; Scaramelli and Tarble de Scaramelli 2005a). This sequence provides a regional archaeological framework that has served as a baseline for a more comprehensive analysis of the consequences of Spanish colonial contact in the area (Scaramelli and Tarble de Scaramelli 2000, 2003, 2005a; Tarble de Scaramelli 2008; Tarble de Scaramelli and Scaramelli 2011, 2012). The identification and dating of local and imported artifacts provide the subdivision of the sequence into periods and phases recognizable in the archaeological record. We established five periods: (a) Late Pre-Hispanic 1400–1530; (b) Early exploration and contact 1535–1680; (c) Early Colonial 1680–1767; (d) Late Colonial 1767–1830; (e) Republican (1830–1930) (see Table 9.1).

**Table 9.1** Archaeological phase and associated artifacts in the study area

| Period | Phase | Dates | Sites | Constructions | Ceramics | Beads | Metal | Glass | Products |
|---|---|---|---|---|---|---|---|---|---|
| Prehispanic | Camoruco | 1200–1530 | Los mangos Simonero | Low habitation mounds Wattle and daub | Arauquinoid Valloid | Polished stone beads Bead polishers | None | None | Manioc Pottery Stone and shell beads Forest products |
| Early Colonial period | Pararuma | 1680–1767 | Pueblo de los Españoles (Nuestra Señora de los Angeles de Pararuma) Pueblito del Villacoa Fortín del Parguaza (San Francisco Javier De Marimarota) Piedra Rajada La Pica | Stone, wattle and daub and adobe buildings Wattle and daub | Salt glaze Olive jar Delft Bartmann (Bellermine) Faience Arauquinoid (San Isidro style) Valloid Caraipé Fine sand temper | Small "seed" beads Cornaline d'Aleppo faceted beads black beads with white and yellow appliqué (Dutch) Gooseberry Bead polishers | Forge Knives Nails Buckles Musket parts Lead bullets Harpoons Fish hooks Machete | Square gin bottles Onion shaped bottles Possible mirrors | Manioc Sugar cane Pottery Baskets and mats Shell beads Turtle oil |
| Late Colonial period | Pueblo Viejo | 1768–1829 | Pueblo Viejo La Pica | Stone, wattle and daub and adobe buildings | Pearl ware (English) Shell edge (1780–1820) Early hand-painted Annular ware: mocha (1756–1820) Boerenbont (Gaudy Dutch) Transfer print (1756–1820) Caraipé Fine sand temper Ground sherd | Drawn faceted "Russian" beads "White heart" Seed beads | Buckles Knives Coins (1812) Spear point | Square bottles Demi-johns Cylindrical wine bottles Engraved drinking glasses | Manioc Turtle oil Pottery |

**Table 9.1** (continued)

| Period | Phase | Dates | Sites | Constructions | Ceramics | Beads | Metal | Glass | Products |
|---|---|---|---|---|---|---|---|---|---|
| Republican | Caripo | 1830–1920 | Corocito de Caripito Palomo La Achaguera Caripito Piedra Rajada (re-occupation) Parrilla del Pilón Cueva Jacobero Cueva de Perez Cueva Pintada | No evidence Surface scatter | Pearl ware and White ware Shell edge Transfer print Stencil (1815–1835) Boerenbont (Gaudy Dutch) Annular ware Sponge stamped Ginger beer bottles (nineteenth century) | Very few small beads | Cans: Kerosene Gun powder Sardines and canned meat Thimble Medallion Spoons Knives Manioc graters made of punched tin cans Spear points | Bottles: Beer Wine Demi-johns Medicine Perfume Tonic | Manioc Maize Sugar cane Pottery Turtle oil Sarrapia |

The results of our archaeological investigations for the Colonial and Republican periods provide evidence for the foundation and subsequent development of the colonial mission frontier along the Villacoa River (Bolívar State, Venezuela)—where the Jesuits founded the mission of Nuestra Señora de Los Angeles de Pararuma in 1734 and, more extensively, the processes and transformations that took place in the area following the War of Independence. In the Orinoco, the Colonial Period brought about notable transformations in the landscape, indigenous settlement patterns, the use and construction of space, local productive activities, and in indigenous material assemblages. Here we will emphasize a limited set of transformations in productive activities involving novel forms of interface, and the formation of larger systems of relationships in which every group, including indigenous and colonizers, responded to values in action and strategies concerning value production, social insertion, and means of cultural control.

As part of a wider interest in the contextualizing of the native societies of the Orinoco within the process of western expansion, this study seeks to contribute to the growing body of research designed to understand the transformations experienced by the native societies as a result of European contact. Our contribution follows recent propositions concerning the examination of long-term contact histories, either in the form of historical archaeology and/or historical anthropology, involving the use of archaeological, historical, and ethnographic data (Funari 2006; Kirch and Sahlins 1992; Lightfoot 2005; Rodríguez-Alegría 2010; Schrire 1995; Silliman 2005; Voss 2005, 2008). Attention to this broad range of sources aims to disentangle some of the complexities of native socio–cultural dynamics within larger structures of colonial interactions. With a theoretical interest in colonial/postcolonial relations of economic and political power, our chapter incorporates aspects of contemporary approaches to explain the expansion of capitalism and the role of native cultures in shaping the forms of interactions.

In a desire to delve into the day-to-day interactions and negotiations that characterized the Native involvement in the colonial and post-colonial economies, we take up the classic, yet endlessly captivating topic of the role of material culture in colonial processes. We explore local and global interactions, as these unfolded in the Middle Orinoco, where indigenous and colonial agents sought to enhance value and exercise control over each other through the exchange of material goods. We adopt here a more peripheral, culturally oriented, practice-centered, and interactive perspective to focus on the role of native cultures as both a historical product and an agent (Dietler 1998, p. 299; Mintz 2010; Ortiz 1947; Sahlins 1988, 1996). We explore the articulation between local and global structures of culture and interaction and the mechanisms that have contributed to the development of structures of dependency and domination. We are also concerned with native systems and forms of cultural resilience. These dual dynamics are manifested in the interchange of goods, foodstuffs, technology, and manufactures, as these can be documented in written and artifactual sources. In particular, archaeological studies of colonial situations have shown the potential to illuminate a wide variety of processes and transformations, especially in frontier regions and in the hinterlands where documentary sources are limited both in scope and in viewpoint (Schrire 1995; Senatore 2003; Trigger 1984; Wilmsen 1989).

This study proceeds from the argument that these "uncommon commodities" have the potential to shed light on the progressive engagement of native societies with the western world. Our analysis allows us to follow the trajectory of certain commodities in the history of the Middle Orinoco, as they contribute to the transformations undergone by local indigenous societies. As this process is symbolically constituted and historically specific, we concentrate on colonial and republican examples of craft production and extractive industries to differentiate between various stages of contact and forms of involvement. We examine the role of certain goods and practices into native structures of interaction and systems of value, discussing the transformations in these systems, following the commoditization of certain native material products. These examples should not be conceived as independent or autonomous, but rather as intimately intertwined in the context of more general processes affecting indigenous cultures and societies.

## 9.3 Products of Contact in Colonial History

In the first part of the sixteenth century, European powers in what is today Venezuela became increasingly interested in long-term economic projects. Having abandoned their hopes of finding gold or silver and having depleted the pearl fisheries on the islands of Cubagua and Margarita, the Europeans turned their eyes to tobacco and sugar cane plantations and the exploitation of certain native products such as hard woods, spices, dyes, gums, and cotton. After the settlement of Caracas in 1567, new towns were founded in the Venezuelan Andes and the Caribbean coast. By this time, the basis of the colonial economy relied on agriculture and livestock production. Maize, sugar cane, and beef were domestic consumption staples; tobacco, cotton, and leather were among the more important exports. The prosperous agricultural districts of the Andean area, the western Llanos, and, notably, the fertile valleys around Caracas, La Victoria, Maracay, and Valencia produced a respectable surplus for exchange. In the early seventeenth century, cacao developed into a leading export in colonial Venezuela, while sugar cane and its products were mostly consumed on the local market (Molina and Amodio 1998). A considerable group of Spanish immigrants and Canary Islanders were attracted to the profitable business of cacao cultivation, and there was a large-scale demand for African slaves during the seventeenth and eighteenth centuries as the plantation economy prospered. Indigo and coffee became important export products in the late eighteenth century. Following 1728, the Guipuzcoana Shipping Company monopolized trade and imported wine, wheat, cloth, and steel from the mother country, Spain.

This conjuncture of different populations provided the framework for a social hierarchy in Venezuela. On the upper level of the colonial society, there was a small elite of Spanish-born colonists. The descendents of Spanish couples born in America (Creoles) occupied the second strata, above the Canary Islanders, who began to work in the colonies as wage laborers. Beneath these social groups, the racially mixed populations emerged as the largest sector of the Venezuelan population, who, by the late eighteenth century, constituted more than 50 % of the total population, followed by a large population of African slaves (c. 20 %). The indigenous population, in the northern coastal areas, decimated by disease, warfare, slavery, and compulsive colonial policies, comprised less than 10–15 % of the total population. The cacao plantation economy provided colossal profits to Spanish, Portuguese, and Dutch colonial entrepreneurs. As a result, thousands of African slaves were brought to the Antilles and Venezuela to work in the plantations in an unprecedented regime of forced production and exploitation.

Meanwhile, the immense majority of what is currently the hinterland territory of modern Venezuela remained relatively unsettled by the colonists. The Llanos of Colombia and Venezuela, and particularly the south bank of the Orinoco, and the Guayana Shield, continued to be well beyond the mainstream of the metropolitan life style. At the end of the seventeenth century, Jesuit, Capuchin, and Franciscan missionaries were commissioned to establish direct contact with the indigenous populations of the Orinoco region. Missionary intervention in this area was conceived as a major Catholic civilizing project aimed at incorporating indigenous peoples into the Spanish colonial structure. The missionaries were charged with the conversion of the native population and with the construction of the strategies for future settlement and economic extraction (Langer and Jackson 1995). In the Middle Orinoco, the Jesuits employed approaches that had proven effective in other areas. While military and religious strategies are well documented in the literature, less attention has been paid to more subtle strategies such as gift giving and trade, as these engaged populations across the colonial frontier.

Trade was a key mechanism that served to initiate and routinize the articulation between the colonizers and the native peoples. Trade also led to the acceptance or at least tolerance by certain indigenous populations of the newly founded missions in Orinoco. The more sedentary, agricultural indigenous societies of the Llanos (Plains) and the Orinoco, such as the Sáliva, the Achagua, and the Mapoyo were attracted to the Jesuit *reducciones* (mission settlements) by the lure of Western goods and protection from slaving incursions led by the Dutch and their indigenous allies. Although military coercion played a role in the establishment of the missions, the voluntary relocation of local communities was often encouraged through the distribution of coveted trade goods. Through offering trinkets and other exotic items, the missionaries were able to gain some acceptance among various indigenous factions (Gilij 1987; Gumilla 1944).

Foreign artifacts such as glass beads, scissors, knives, mirrors, cloth, steel machetes, and axes especially lured the indigenous peoples, who offered native products and exotic pets in exchange (Gilij 1987, II, p. 266). Initially, the indigenous groups seem to have been able to gain advantage through their proximity to the missionaries, but the role of the mission rapidly evolved far beyond the simple enticement through goods. Whereas the Natives were interested in European goods as a means to enhance social relations and as status symbols, in addition to their practical use as tools, the missionaries focused on their incorporation into Western institutions and value systems through a radical modification of indigenous economies and social organization. The desire for the acquisition of certain foreign items, which started in the form of barter, eventually engaged the indigenous societies of the Orinoco in an economic system with no precedent in the Orinoco. From the outset, the exchange of cassava, sugar cane, and other forest products in return for foreign manufactures already incorporated into indigenous structures of consumption, promoted the progressive involvement of the native population with the colonizers in a local economic system that relied on barter, rather than on coin. According to Gilij:

> It is not a cause for marvel, then, being so frequent this custom [barter] in the Orinoco that the Spaniards get used to this, also buying and selling in the manner they have found here. In this way canoes are bought, food and clothes are acquired, and houses are built... (…) …. He who hires rowers to navigate or hires someone to work in the fields, or for any other thing, establishes the number of axes, of yards [varas] of cloth, of mirrors, and of anything else the Indians request for their labor. (Gilij 1987, II, p. 100)

The conversion of value implied in the selling of labor and economic surplus paved the way to a more durable restructuring of traditional, social, and productive relations, hand in hand with a privatization of property, unknown prior to colonial intervention. In the short run, the incorporation of foreign technologies promoted changes in indigenous social relations of production and contributed to a reorientation of labor toward an increased production of items for exchange. The acquisition of machetes and metal axes may have facilitated an increase in the production of surpluses of some native products (cassava, fruits, hardwoods, *quiripa*, fish, and game, etc.) or the production of similar amounts of agricultural products within a shorter period of time. In either case, the value of certain products could be further invested in the acquisition of other desired items, a process ultimately conducive to the articulation of different economies necessary for the maintenance of the mission.

Even though the missions may have been used as trade posts, missionary reports emphatically negate the existence of marketplaces in the area.

> Under the pretext, then, of forging friendship between these savages [non-mission Indians in the forest] and the Spaniards and making them interested in the faith, they go there to trade with them taking from the reductions iron tools, cloths and things that are not found there, and bringing back curare and chica. Since there is no savage nation that does not have some singular manufacture and that does not have some friend among the reduced nations, all of them, and from all parts, and, usually privately, go to the forest to make exchanges. (Gilij 1987, II, p. 267)

It is interesting to note that Gilij refers to the process of exchange as a "borrowing" of goods. The borrowing was so common that the missionary became discouraged, talking about this practice as if it were a simple "permutation" of goods, that is, objects circulating among people that never really became the property of anyone— in the way that the missionary was trying to impose.

> Taken the aforementioned goods to the Orinoco, later they exchange them with the Christians for other things. The buyers exchange them once again for other things, and they change hands up and down, throughout the forest and along the river. I have seen shirts, pants and blankets that made the rounds of all the reductions, and were owned first by one and then by another. It is to no avail to tell them to keep for themselves their clothes and to exchange other things, because the men pay no attention to such warnings. (Gilij 1987, II, p. 268; our translation)

## 9.4    Uncommon Commodities in the Colonial Period

As the Jesuits struggled to establish a foothold in the Middle Orinoco region, they came to depend on indigenous knowledge and production for survival. The missions and forts that were established in the region were notoriously undersupplied with European goods, and missionaries made frequently admitted their dependence on local manufactures, foods, transportation, and construction materials. The highly seasonal tropical climate and relatively poor soils were not amenable to the plantation economies characteristic of the mountainous and coastal regions of Northern and Western Venezuela, nor were mining or textile industries viable under the local conditions. Nonetheless, several lesser-known local products and craft items figured prominently in the mission economy, including turtle oil, quiripa (shell beads), and locally manufactured pottery.

Locally produced pottery dominates the archaeological record throughout the Colonial Periods (see Fig. 9.2), leading us to propose that it was produced both for local consumption as well as for trade. Indigenous pottery was used in food preparation, service, and storage, thereby offering evidence of diet and commensality. At the same time, its role as a container allows us to infer the production and transportation of other commodities. In the Early Colonial Period (1680–1767), several local ceramic wares, distinguishable by their paste, manufacturing technique, color, and decorative modes were ubiquitous at the mission sites and fortresses. Bowls and platters were the dominant forms, suggesting their widespread use as cooking and serving vessels by both colonists and indigenous sectors (Fig. 9.3). Griddles and large pots used to ferment beer made from local roots and maize testify to

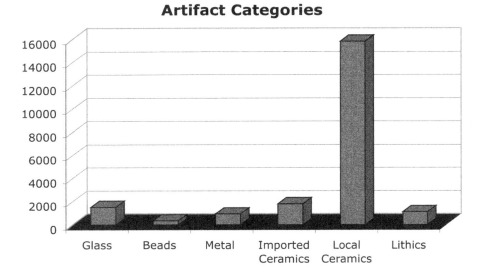

**Fig. 9.2** Relative frequency of artifact categories for the collection obtained at post-contact archaeological sites in the Middle Orinoco

**Fig. 9.3** San Isidro ceramics recovered at the San Isidro site (Early Colonial Period, eighteenth century)

the importance of local cultivars in the colonial setting. Gilij (1987) and Gumilla (1944), Jesuit missionaries who resided in the area between 1730 and 1767, refer to ceramic production and trade, especially in the hands of indigenous women residing in the missions (Gilij 1987, II, pp. 257–258; Gumilla 1944, I, p. 167). Pottery making is easily accommodated to the rhythms of other daily activities and to the agricultural cycle, thereby enabling the women to incorporate small-scale commodity production into their routine. This traditionally female activity, along with casaba production, discussed extensively elsewhere (Tarble de Scaramelli and Scaramelli 2012), may have provided the women a means to acquire other coveted trade goods, such as cloth, glass beads, or metal tools. At the same time, they maintained control of the knowledge of local clays and tempering materials, pigments used to decorate the vessels, resins used to coat them, and the techniques involved in the construction, drying, and firing of the pots.

Pottery was probably a trade item in pre-colonial times; the missionaries point to certain vessel forms made only by particular groups that were highly esteemed by others who acquired them through trade. Examples can be found in the double-spouted water jug, or *chirgua*, made by the Guamo, the flat-bottomed cooking pots used to render turtle oil made by the Otomaco, and the thin, red kitchen ware that was the specialty of the Tamanaco. According to Gilij, this ware was much sought after at his mission in La Encaramada (Gilij 1987, II, p. 257).

The colonists also encouraged the production of certain vessel types for their own use. They commissioned the production of *tinajas,* a small version of the indigenous beer fermenting pot, to use to keep drinking water cool (Ibid. 257). Although ceramic decoration declines notably, vessel form and production technique show considerable stability throughout the Colonial Period in the locally manufactured wares. This suggests that pottery production continued to be a small-scale, domestic activity, oriented primarily to the satisfaction of the needs of each household, with some surplus designated for sale or trade. Hand molded, locally made pottery is dominant at all archaeological sites in the Early and Late Colonial Periods.

Although local tableware was increasingly replaced by imported whiteware in the Republican Period, the water pot and the ceramic griddle, used to bake manioc or corn cakes, continued to be popular trade items throughout the post-contact sequence (Table 9.1). As cited by Torrealba (1987) (Torrealba: 6, my translation), in his *El Diario de un Llanero* (*Diary of a Cowboy*), indigenous potters supplied the Criollo population with pottery well into the twentieth century: "I'm going with my *compadre* Gregorio to Los Caballos, where he is going to order some pottery from the Indians, some six large *tinajas*, that can hold five hundred liters of water, two *budares* to cook bread [cassava cakes] four palms wide, some *búcaros*, *pimpinas* and a filter to use with charcoal."

The colonists also sought out other indigenous crafts that came to be incorporated into the material inventory of the emerging *Criollo* culture, such as woven hammocks and plaited mats. Evidence for their manufacture can be found in ceramic spindle whorls and fabric impressions on the bases of ceramic vessels. The spinning and weaving of cotton thread is an activity that Gilij attributes to women in the mission context (Gilij 1987), whereas basket weaving is the domain of the men. The Otomaco were famous for their woven mats, and according to Gilij (Gilij 1987, II, p. 261), "Indians, Spaniards and everyone sought them out". Further examples can be found in the colonist's dependence on indigenous agricultural production, hunting, and fishing, where the missionaries were forced to comply with the exigencies of the seasonal fluctuations in resources, and the need to permit the location of settlements in accord with appropriate farmland. This differs radically from other mission contexts, for example, in the Colombian Llanos, where textile industries (*obrajes*), based on indigenous labor, flourished along with extensive cattle ranching (Colmenares 1984) or the semi-industrial Capuchin mission system of the Lower Orinoco (Sanoja and Vargas Arenas 2005). This set the stage early on, in hand with the specialized gathering of resources for trade to be discussed below, for a pattern of insertion into the mercantile economy, to a certain extent on their own terms, without the resulting "acculturation" or "loss of culture" predicted by some models of cultural contact (Steward and Murphy 1977).

Another extraordinary example of an uncommon local manufacture that acquired exchange value during colonial times can be found in *quiripa*. These strings of freshwater shell beads, valued as body adornments and as status markers in the indigenous sphere, came to be used as a wide-spread medium for exchange in a colonial economy where money was scarce (Gassón 2000). In his detailed account of the rise and decline of the use of *quiripa* in the Orinoco region and beyond, Gassón emphasizes the appropriation of an indigenous item into the colonial exchange system, where, throughout the first half of the eighteenth century, they were used for barter, and even to pay debts, and taxes under a fixed rate. Although archaeological evidence of *quiripa* is notoriously absent, due perhaps to the acidic soils in most sites of the region, polishing stones and ceramic sherds with "U" shaped grooves, may have been used to polish the strands of beads after being chipped into shape, drilled, and strung. Glass beads of European manufacture eventually replaced *quiripa* as a key item in exchange lasting well into the twentieth century (Gassón 2000; Scaramelli and Tarble de Scaramelli 2005b), a clear indication of the resilience of indigenous value systems as opposed to a cash-based exchange system.

These craft items offered by the Indians for exchange in transactions with the colonists derived from indigenous knowledge of local resources, manufacturing techniques, and extended trade partnerships that were most probably present in pre-colonial times. The dependency on indigenous knowledge and goods gave some advantage to the local population, who could negotiate certain aspects of mission life to accommodate their needs to seek raw materials, and create the products using their own technology and chains of production. Gilij reports that the neophytes maintained secret trade partners in the interior, and, with the excuse of seeking out new souls for conversion, they would make incursions into non-colonized zones, taking with them axes, cloth, and other items of European manufacture that they had bargained for in the mission, to exchange them for resins, body paint (*chica*), and poisons (*curare*). On their return to the mission "they exchange them with the Christians for other things. The buyers again exchange them for others, and they go back and forth, up and down, from the thick forests to the river and back again" (Gilij 1987, II, p. 268).

An interesting aspect of the exchange of goods in the context of the mission at La Encaramada, where Gilij spent 18 years as a Jesuit missionary, can be found in his description of the attitude the neophytes had regarding his supplies of trade goods. Gilij describes his initial use of trade goods, including beads, knives, and other coveted items, in order to lure the Indians to settle at the mission. However, he found that he got very little in exchange, and that the Indians were forever referring to him as "stingy" and "tight-fisted" as long as he had any items in his stores. It was only after he came up with the idea of giving out all the goods, as soon as they came in, that he was able to make requests of reciprocity. This custom of "giving up front" may have been a precursor to the practice of "debt-peonage" that was so widespread in Republican times. It could be argued that this form of exchange was more amenable to indigenous exchange practices, where direct barter was not the desired practice, but rather, one in which the establishment of reciprocal obligations and the constant circulation of goods were at the center of the value system.

Turtle oil, a product derived through the processing of huge quantities of eggs collected on certain sandy beaches along the Middle Orinoco, was another important trade item. The exploitation of certain species of turtle that were found in great abundance in the Orinoco (especially *Podocnemis expansa*), formed an integral part of the seasonal resource cycle of multiple indigenous occupants of the region including the Atures, Saliva, Achagua, Otomaco, Guamo, Pumé, and Mapoyo (Meza 2013; Morey and Morey 1975). During the nesting season in the summer months (February–April), Indians and colonial entrepreneurs, gathered turtles for consumption and eggs for processing into oil. These *ferias* were reported to congregate up to 2000 people, at the height of the collecting season, and attracted people from near and far (Bueno 1965, p. 126). The Carib, for example, made annual incursions from the Guayana region to the Middle Orinoco to seek trade items, including slaves, curare, pigments, hammocks, and turtle oil. Turtle oil, a highly coveted item, compared in its qualities to olive oil by some missionaries (Gumilla 1944, I, pp. 305–306), was traded throughout the area, to Bogotá and as far as Guayana and the Island of Trinidad, where it was sold at increasingly higher prices (Gilij 1987, Vol. 1, p. 113). The oil was used by the Indians to rub on their bodies, often mixed with colorant, and to give sheen to their hair. The Otomaco also mixed it with fine clay and starch to form a special type of bread (Gumilla 1944, I, pp. 175–176). The colonists adopted it as cooking oil, and it had high demand as fuel for use in oil lamps (Gilij 1987, II, p. 193; I, p. 113). During the Republican period, it was used as a grease to maintain military arms and for lighting, until the introduction of kerosene (Meza 2013, p. 189).

The production of the oil involved indigenous expertise and labor. Before the nesting season, they posted guards at the beaches in order to ward off noisy intruders who would frighten off the turtles. Once they laid their eggs, the turtles tried to camouflage their nests with sand; nonetheless, the Indians used long, thin poles to locate the nests underground, and all members of the family joined in to dig up the eggs. Nearby, they installed canoes, cleaned out for the purpose, and filled with water. The turtle eggs were first washed and then transferred to other canoes, where the children would stomp on them to mix the yolks and release the oil. This was then skimmed off and poured into large cooking pots where the women heated it and impurities settled to the bottom. The clean oil was bottled, with a dose of salt to help preserve it, in *tinajas* or gourd recipients, ready to take back to the community or to be shipped off for sale (see Fig. 9.4).

According to documentary sources, the indigenous participants in these labors were able to later sell or exchange their oil for other items at the mission and in the hinterlands, indicating that they had considerable control over their product. Indigenous technology was utilized throughout the process: the knowledge of the turtle's nesting cycle, the expertise in rendering the oil, and the manufacture and utilization of the implements used in the process, such as canoes and ceramic pots and gourds for cooking and storing the oil. Nevertheless, Gilij points out that some Europeans, who were interested in the product, came to supervise the processing to guarantee the desired results (Gilij 1987, I, p. 112). Archaeological evidence for this process can be found in Early Colonial sites located in the area (Fig. 9.1) in the form

**Fig. 9.4** Turtle egg oil production during the eighteenth century . (Source: Gilij 1987, I, Plate between pp. 110–111)

of flat-bottomed ceramic pots, a specialty of the Otomaco mentioned earlier, that conform to the descriptions offered by the missionaries, and in the large jars that may have been used to store and transport the oil. Colonial agents, such as missionaries and commercial entrepreneurs, intervened in the process through the control of the access to the beaches, the oversight of the labors, and the establishment of the exchange rate for the sale of the oil. Although the Indians who produced the oil were compensated at low rates (1 real per jar, according to Gilij 1987, I, p. 113), they were able to sell it to other indigenous groups in the interior, and in this way, increase their profits.

During the Late Colonial period (1768–1830), after the expulsion of the Jesuits, Franciscan missionaries took over the supervision of the nesting grounds, and imposed new restrictions on access to the beaches. Mission Indians were given preference in the allotment of access to the nesting areas, and the missionaries supervised all transactions with external agents. Humboldt, who visited the area in the early nineteenth century, noted that the missionaries charged high prices for their trade goods, including metal tools used in fishing and agriculture, cloth, and other desirable items (Humboldt 1956, p. 293; Meza 2013, p. 115). He was also amazed at the huge quantity of eggs being processed for sale and was one of the first to comment on the potential decline of the population due to overexploitation.

## 9.5  Republican Flows in the Orinoco

The War of Independence between Republicans (Venezuelans) and Realists (Spanish) (1810–1830) marked the culmination of Spanish control in Venezuela. After years of pre-independence rebellions in the Caribbean and other parts of America, the emergence of liberal nationalistic movements led to the so-called Campaigns of Independence. The end of the Colonial period started a political process characterized by the formation of unstable independent nations that nonetheless found ways to rebuild legitimacy. While Spain was loosening ties with America, issues of social equality, emancipation, and abolition movements reflect the tensions inherited from the Colonial period. In a climate fraught by ideological quandaries concerning centralization and federalism, nationalism and popular sovereignty, the end of the Colonial period gave rise to the emergence of very strong charismatic leaders or *caudillos* and an extended period of unrest and warfare. No longer under the regulation of the Spanish Crown, the struggles for economic and political power associated with the federal wars made governments extraordinarily unstable. Questions about group interests and state building were intimately related to the need to redefine property and land tenure laws. Issues regarding individual private property and land tenure conflicts with indigenous communities, and the church were all at the forefront of the political debates. With the advent of new form of social relations between landowners and serfs, *hacendados* and peon, or patron–client relations were the historical outcome of asymmetrical links pervading the emerging postcolonial society.

Following the collapse of the Spanish colonial intervention in the Orinoco, those areas of savannah (Fig. 9.1) previously occupied by the missionaries became the territory of a very different social group composed of ex-mission Indians, free blacks, escaped slaves, *mestizos*, and *pardos*. Coming from different ethnic origins and cultural backgrounds, these populations coincided in the exploitation of the large population of feral cattle that had multiplied in the area since the time of its introduction in the sixteenth century (Montiel Acosta 1993). This multi-ethnic sector of the neo-native population, that came to be known as the *Llanero*, had played a crucial role in the Independence movement. Through the offer of legal titles to land, in return for their service as soldiers, many *Indios* and *Llaneros* had resolved to support the battle for "liberation". Nonetheless, following the war, the promises of land offered to the soldiers and the Indians never took place. The Republicans were in alliance with the aristocracy, but not with the lower ranks of the emerging colonial society; only the higher levels of the army were compensated with extensive lands. These owners immediately multiplied their holdings by buying up the papers for land promised to lower-ranked soldiers. As a result, a new wealthy sector of society obtained title to some of the traditional territories of the Indians in the Llanos of the Orinoco and the Western Llanos. During the early Republican Period, cattle ranching expanded, and the economy of Guayana was increasingly based on the exportation of cows, mules, and pigs, both for leather and for meat.

Indigenous groups who opted to stay in the lower Llanos found themselves caught up in the expansion of cattle ranching and the fencing off of private property (Rodríguez Mirabal 1992). Cattle exploitation constituted a productive system that was not compatible with the agricultural and foraging practices favored by the Indians. These required free access to large extensions of the region to cover their needs. Because cattle invaded most savanna areas of the Llanos of the Orinoco, including unfenced plots of land, the Indians used to "illegally" hunt cattle in retaliation. Eventually, this process led to a surge in interethnic hostility between Indians and Creoles that in some places of the Llanos took the form of outright rejection and massacres of the Indians. The introduction of cattle into the Llanos of the Orinoco initiated a profound change in economic and social relations, which ended up with the dichotomization of the natives into Indians (hunters, farmers, and foragers) and cattle workers (cowboys or *Llaneros*). Within the realms of their own properties, the owners of vast tracts of land (*hatos*) came to dominate the Western Llanos and the Orinoco, both politically and economically. In association with other sectors of the emerging Republican society, such as government officials and politicians, they promulgated laws that preserved their interests in the region as well as expanding into "unpopulated" indigenous areas to which they often obtained legal titles (Rodríguez Mirabal 1992).

Moreover, the progressive escalation of mono-cultivar intensive agriculture on the seasonally inundated floodplains, dedicated to commercial crops such as cotton and maize, resulted in the retreat of the indigenous groups from the riverbanks of the Orinoco, leaving these areas in the hands of the Creole population. This process played a primary role in the displacement of the indigenous populations inland and the restructuring of native productive relationships, settlement patterns, and regimes of property.

As a consequence of this expansion of the Llanero productive mode, indigenous native communities became marginalized into less attractive areas, unsuitable
for cattle ranching. Those groups who decided to adopt the new economic modes,
either as cattle ranchers, or in the exploitation of fluvial resources, did so at the
expense of their indigenous identity, as they were drawn to the closest towns of the
Middle Orinoco, such as Caicara del Orinoco, La Urbana, or Puerto Paez. Through
the adoption of Spanish and knowledge and skills associated with cattle ranching,
commercial fluvial agriculture, professional fishing, mining, and through intermarriage with Criollos, many of the indigenous people of the Middle Orinoco became
rural workers, dedicated to the export of meat, leather, and intensive agricultural
products. In order to pay less, the owners of the *hatos* (cattle ranches) exploited
the natives using patron client relations such as *padrinazgo* (Mitrani 1988, p. 162).
Through this process, however, by means of new standards of distinction, the
Indians who had grown up in the missions, as well as those born later in the *hatos*,
came to see themselves as different, sometimes even superior, to the neighboring
Indians, who were increasingly considered as backward, primitive, and irrational
(this process of identity transformation is constantly referred to by the local creoles
of the Orinoco).

In the meantime, the indigenous communities, particularly the Mapoyo, Eñepá,
and Piaroa (Uotjuja) employed an inland régime of dispersed settlement pattern
that has lasted until the present. Archaeological evidence for the dynamic changes
taking place in native social life during the Republican Period can be found in the
scattered remains of small habitation sites, consisting of a few habitation platforms and the ubiquitous domestic debris of imported whiteware, local pottery, tin
cans, glass bottles, and knives, fishhooks, gun powder flasks, and manioc graters
(Falconi 2003; Scaramelli and Tarble de Scaramelli 2005a; Tarble de Scaramelli and
Scaramelli 2011; Scaramelli 2006). Although the production of local pottery is very
limited when compared with previous periods, the presence of ceramic griddles in
every native settlement indicates that the production of cassava continued to be at
the core of indigenous domestic production (Tarble de Scaramelli and Scaramelli
2012). Manioc cultivation is maintained, and perhaps, even increases, as attested by
the large manioc griddles and the substitution of stone graters by perforated sheet
metal graters during the late nineteenth century (see Fig. 9.5).

The forests, savannas, and waterways of the Orinoco offered a variety of natural
resources that the Indians exploited seasonally both for their own consumption
and for exchange with the Europeans. Products ranging from fruits, roots, palm
fronds used for thatch, oils, dyes, poisons, gum, and resins, as well as insects, fish,
turtles, birds, feathers, and medicinal herbs were exploited according to seasonal
availability. Animals were hunted both for meat and skins, and hardwoods were
used in the construction of canoes, tools, arms, and buildings. As noted by Morey
and Morey, every indigenous group had its specialty items, some of which reflected
unique microenvironments, as in the case of the shafts used for blowguns, or the ingredients used to make *curare*, the famous poison used for darts. It was common for
families or even larger groups to set up temporary camps in order to collect different
items, either in the forest or on the banks of the Orinoco. The forest and the waterways were a source of supplies, either for personal use or for exchange. Through

**Fig. 9.5** Perforated sheet metal grater (late nineteenth to early twentieth century)

time, several products were in greater demand than others, and their exploitation produced a kind of boom, seen by the Indians as a means to cash or trade goods, beyond their usual subsistence activities. Among these we can mention cassava and sugar cane, cultivated as cash crops and the gathering of diverse forest species such as *sarrapia* (Tonka bean), palm fronds for thatch, copaiba, rubber, and other gums and resins. Turtle shells were used for buttons and deer, alligator, and jaguar were hunted for their skins, whereas exotic bird feathers were in high demand for their use in millinery fashion (Wickham 1988).

By the end of the nineteenth century, new sources of lighting became available, such as kerosene, and the market for turtle oil diminished. Nevertheless, turtle meat was highly coveted as food, and huge numbers of turtles were caught for local consumption and export. Labor came to be commoditized and the *caletereos* and *volteadores* (men employed to carry and turn over the turtles, for sale as meat or for the rendering of grease) began to receive salaries for their work. A brief, but unsuccessful venture in canning was also attempted, with the idea of exporting the turtle meat. Finally, following the drastic decline of the turtle population, strict governmental conservation measures were taken to protect eggs and young turtles in 1946, and, eventually, the prohibition of all forms of capture. As commerce in turtle oil decreased, new demands were arising for other local products.

## 9.5.1   Sarrapia and Sarrapieros

Sarrapia (*Dypteryx odorata*), or Tonka bean, as it is more widely known, has been a very important trade item in the Middle Orinoco, since the middle of the nineteenth century, as an element of the emerging global capitalist market system. With a growing demand in the rising world market of perfumes, sarrapia transformed the Guayana region into one of the key sources of product and labor supply. The commercialization of sarrapia was not solely the product of Europe's capitalist

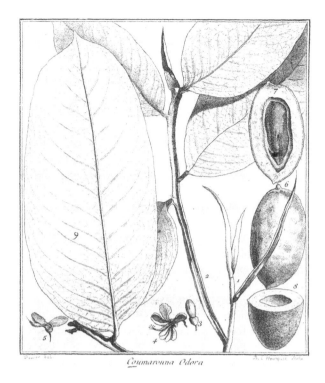

*Coumarouna  Odora*

**Fig. 9.6** Sarrapia (*Dypteryx odorata*) drawing from Fuseé-Aublet (1775)

aspirations and strategies, but was also shaped by indigenous agendas and strategies of action as they engaged in the sarrapia trade, in which they juggled the desire for cash and exotic goods with the struggle against alien forms of subjugation. In this particular case, sarrapia played an active role in the channeling of social relations and as a force in the cultural trajectory of the local groups.

The success of sarrapia in the perfume industry lies in the seductive power of its fragrance. It has a pungent, sweet, and rich aroma that evokes that of vanilla, almond, cinnamon, cloves, and even saffron, which blends well with the complexities of other scents including sandalwood, patchouli and lavender. Moderately toxic to human consumption, sarrapia has also been incorporated into different cuisines as an exotic seasoning with an engaging flavor. The sarrapia tree is a large rainforest tree that belongs to the legume family (see Fig. 9.6). It is native to South America, with a distribution that includes Brazil, Guyana, Colombia, Trinidad, and Tobago; nonetheless, Venezuela is one of the world's largest producers of sarrapia. The 12–15 m high trees are found dispersed in the high canopy rainforest south of the Orinoco and its eastern tributaries. The ripened fruit falls to the ground, where it is gathered between the months of February and April. The production of each tree is highly variable from year to year, but in general each tree produces 11–40 kg of seeds per season. The seeds contain approximately 3 % of coumarin, a glycoside with aromatic properties.

When the sarrapia seeds are fermented, these liberate coumarin in the form of white crystals that form a crust on the surface of the seed (Torrealba 2011).

The earliest references to sarrapia in South America can be traced back to the eighteenth century in French Guyana, when the fruit was first scientifically classified. It is only toward the end of the nineteenth century that comments on the growing commercial importance of sarrapia figure prominently in the historical sources (Chaffanjon 1986; Crevaux 1988; Michelena and Rojas 1989 [1867]; Spruce 1996; Wickham 1988). The naturalist Eugene André (1964) describes at great length the gathering activities of the sarrapia fruit, and it was he who first mentioned the *sarrapiero* (sarrapia worker) as an identity forged around the gathering of sarrapia. According to Fuentes Guerrero (Fuentes Guerrero 1980, p. 64), sarrapia was the most important commercial product in the Middle Orinoco region for decades, superceding rubber, copaiba balsam oil, and hardwoods, leading him to argue for the existence of an authentic "sarrapia epoch".

Recent historical and ethnographic research (Torrealba 2011) focuses on the origin and development of the sarrapia production in the Middle Orinoco and the labor system that developed as a result of its commercialization. According to Torrealba (2011, p. 162) there is only scant information on sarrapia production during the early nineteenth century, when it was small-scale, individual, and sporadic; both indigenous and Criollo peasants gathered the seeds to trade them to European merchants to be used in the flavoring of tobacco. The fruits and the seeds were used locally to scent clothing in Cumaná and Caracas. Sources vary in regard to the earliest date and the amount of sarrapia that was exported. It seems that it was locally commercialized in Guayana since 1832, but was first sold abroad in 1847. Between 1847 and 1855 the initial demand of sarrapia increased gradually, in cycles or intervals of commercialization, reaching 7698 kg exported in 1850. A second period of commercialization commenced in 1855. Hand in hand with the expansion of the fashion industry, perfume became one of the more important and profitable European commodities, with the coumarin derived from sarrapia as a key ingredient. In 1876 the harvest of sarrapia reached 108,862 kg, an unprecedented amount in the short history of its commercialization. After 1880, the price of sarrapia increased considerably and, during the first three decades of the twentieth century, Germany, France, Italy, Holland, Finland, Denmark, Sweden, and the United States were among the most important consumers of sarrapia in the emerging global market.

Since the beginning of the nineteenth century the commercialization of sarrapia was carried out with no governmental control, taxes, or intermediaries. This situation came to an end soon after the news about the abundance of sarrapia in Guayana and the commercial potential of the sarrapia came to be known in Caracas. Rumors about the chance to make a large profit encouraged a large number of fortune hunters and entrepreneurs, both from Venezuela and abroad, to head for the Orinoco looking for opportunities. In 1880, the commercialization of sarrapia reached its pinnacle and its exploitation became part of the government agenda, through the control of permits and taxes on the production.

Rapid changes took place among the Mapoyo and other indigenous groups of the Orinoco who became actively engaged in the production of sarrapia, and to a lesser extent balata and chicle, under the supervision of Creole merchants. Following the demise of the turtle oil trade, the gathering of forest products gave them a new opportunity to obtain the foreign commodities that had become indispensable to them, such as iron tools, coffee, sugar, and cloth. The process was carried out in the form of advanced payment, a form of debt peonage that has been considered by some as a form of modern slavery. Nonetheless, the sarrapia trade did not have the devastating effects on the local populations observed elsewhere, such as those associated with the rubber industry in the Upper Orinoco (Hill 1998; Scaramelli and Tarble de Scaramelli 2000, pp. 717–718). Despite the importance of the sarrapia production among peoples such as the Mapoyo, their productive activities continued revolve around fishing, hunting, and agriculture. The continued access to their traditional territories was essential to the success of this mixed economy.

Specific forms of labor mobilization, exchange, and consumption characterized the indigenous involvement in the sarrapia trade, subsumed under the system known, among the Mapoyo, as *estaciones sarrapieras* (sarrapia stations), which could be conceived of as a neocolonial trading post. As in the case of commercial trading posts, the purpose of these stations was the acquisition of raw material, obtained through indigenous labor, in exchange for foreign manufactures. A sarrapia station was basically a temporary warehouse, with adjacent living quarters and kitchen (Torrealba 2011). This warehouse was used to maintain or safeguard a large amount of foreign merchandise sufficient to supply the sarrapia gatherers during the gathering season: machetes, lanterns, knifes, canned food, cigarettes, sandals, and other articles of clothing. Canned sardines and meats were essential items in the whole system, as they provided supplies that could sustain the workers during the gathering of sarrapia, when fishing and hunting were not viable. The posts also functioned to protect the gathered product prior to its transport to the main ports of the Guayana region, particularly with Ciudad Bolívar, for export abroad. For this reason, the stations were generally located at the trailhead to the forested areas with abundant groves of sarrapia, and in the vicinity of the rivers to be used both for water supply and transportation. Muleteers, mules, and horses were used to transport the merchandise across the savanna, but special laborers were paid to carry the loads through the forest.

A number of peripheral sub-stations were located in the forest with high concentrations of the sarrapia trees. Each sub-post was supplied with merchandise by the central ones. In a similar way, each central post stored the seeds brought from the sub-posts. This dynamic and innovative system provided a link between the local and the global and its configuration synthesized the complex interplay between native knowledge, labor, and reciprocity, on the one hand, and redistribution and the global market, on the other.

The gathering of sarrapia was a collective, voluntary effort. No coercion was used to enforce indigenous participation in the production of sarrapia; nonetheless, foreign goods were used to entice the native population to partake in the gathering. The call to participate (*convocatoria*) was a key element in the whole process. The person in charge needed to have a highly regarded reputation and the moral authority and trustworthiness to convene other members of the indigenous

**Fig. 9.7** Nutting stone recovered from the Republican Period site, La Parrilla del Pilón (late nineteenth to early twentieth century)

communities, while at the same time having the savvy to deal with the Criollo and foreign dealers. Once it was decided to participate, and the negotiations as to price and payment were finalized, the gatherers set up camp (*rancherías*) in the forest, in the allotted area. The profit gained through the gathering was distributed in equal parts and individual labor was subordinated to the collective. As a family enterprise, men, women, and children participated in the gathering of the pods. Men were in charge of the gathering and carrying the heavy loads from the *rancherías* to the stations. Women and children helped with the gathering and the shelling of the fruits, achieved by placing the pod in a small depression on a rock (nutting stone; see Fig. 9.7), and striking it with another rock (this process was called *la pisada*). Huge quantities of shelled pods can still be found on the floors of caves in the forest used as sub-stations (Fig. 9.8), and the stone instruments used to shell the pods are frequent in the inventory of Republican period sites (Fig. 9.7). At the same time, tin cans, bottles, and other archaeological evidence belies the use of caves for temporary shelter.

At the height of the sarrapia boom, some gatherers began to be recognized as great *sarrapieros*. These were those who were able to negotiate the transactions, attract laborers, and gather large quantities of sarrapia during the season. This process led to a seasonal professionalization of the gathering that ultimately served to build a *sarrapiero* identity. Among the Mapoyo, this process ultimately served to construct an image that distinguished them from other local groups, both Native and Criollo. Although the cultural schemata of the indigenous group was challenged by their participation in the sarrapia business and the new forms of contact with foreigners, indigenous experience in the commercialization of the sarrapia did not bring to an end indigenous bonds and forms of solidarity.

Another aspect of the participation in the sarrapia industry that is visible archaeologically is its impact on the redefinition of space. The station system and the new forms of forest utilization required new forms of labor organization and spacial categorization. Toponyms arose to denote the sarrapiales: such as Jacobero, Cueva de Pérez, and Coloradito, at times named after personages that gained

**Fig. 9.8** Sarrapia deposits, Jacobero Cave

prominence in the industry. Even particular trees with known productivity were given a name. The Mapoyo, in particular, initiated a new form of seasonal settlement pattern, in which the more permanent settlements were located inland, in the savanna, near farmlands and fishing lagoons, while the temporary rancherías were set up in the forest during the gathering season.

## 9.6   Final Remarks

In the preceding pages, we have briefly discussed aspects of the material record aimed at exploring the role of certain commodities in local and global meeting points. The encounter with the missionaries in the eighteenth century set in motion a process that had profound effects on the indigenous societies of the region up until present time. Colonial intervention was part of a major project aimed at devising appropriate strategies for settlement and economic development of the region. With this agenda, the missionaries developed strategies that had proved advantageous in previous colonial experiences: they attempted to exert a pull on the local groups through a combination of visits to the hinterlands and gift giving. In this context, the encounter between two previously independent worlds was transformed into a situation of contact in which the components formed part of a wider system of interaction. In the analysis of these interactions, it is important to underline the contrast between colonial and indigenous strategies. In the Orinoco, exchange took place within opposing structures of interaction. These have to be analyzed as complex and reflexive processes of many conflicting strategies for exercising control and authority. For the colonists, power was based on the ability to obtain relations of dependency, as well as social and ideological forms of subordination. On the side of the indigenous societies, we have recurring forms of social relationships based on the power of gifts, flows, emphasis on the circulation and constant acts of sociability—or social inclusiveness. In this particular case, power and legitimacy were based on hospitality, kinship, and social action including the ability to create, mobilize, and expand reproductive forces.

It is known from historical sources that the missionaries took advantage of certain created 'needs' to seduce the neighboring indigenous populations into settling in or near the missions or towns in order to obtain native products and labor. This process provides a background for the analysis of later forms of native-colonist interaction that are crucial to the understanding of the uneven reproduction of social groups. Initial involvement of indigenous populations with the colonizers, and the processes associated with the commoditization of local products, services, and labor, played a role in the reorientation of native social and productive relations. In contrast to missionary claims of cultural superiority in the field of production and technology, the archaeological record provides evidence for limited changes of indigenous modes of production. Native knowledge of the territory, of the local resources, and the productive modes that were most appropriate to their exploitation, conferred the indigenous populations a strategic advantage over other sectors in the Middle Orinoco. Even though a number of foreign domestic animals and cultivars have been incorporated into the "traditional repertoire" of the Orinoco, the indigenous communities have maintained endogenous productive modes, with seasonal or limited participation in the economic "booms" related to specialized gathering, mining, or the sale of surplus agricultural produce. This, of course, is due in part to the maintenance of access to traditional agricultural lands and areas of resource exploitation, as well as the continuance of certain collective organizational and decision-making strategies (see Mintz 2010 for a discussion of the importance of these factors in the Caribbean). In contrast to mechanistic explanations of contact situations, in which the core determines the process experienced in the periphery, these productive modes illustrate aspects of native agency and their experience of the encounter in the Orinoco. In this region, different waves of colonial incursion, promoted by different agents and with different goals, led to successive booms and periods of intense interaction followed by periods of relative time-out. The latter confer the indigenous populations an opportunity to reconnoiter, readjust, and recuperate, in such a way as to face the next wave of extraction with greater experience and refined strategies, and a greater sense of historical consciousness (Fogelson 1989, pp. 133–147; Turner 1991). In analyzing peripheral colonial and neo-colonial situations such as these, we stress the importance of multidimensional contextual analysis for comparative purposes on a larger geographical scale. The examination of specific contexts of contact, with particular attention to Native mechanisms of control and capacities for social action, will eventually offer a more nuanced understanding of cultural and historical variations in contact situations.

**Acknowledgments** We are especially grateful to the Comunidad Mapoyo de El Palomo for their support, hospitality, and guidance in the field. We are particularly indebted to Capitán Simón Bastidas, Rosa de Bastidas, José Secundino Reyes, Victor Caña, José Alexander Caña, Petra Reyes, Mariana de Bastidas, Alexis Joropa, and Damasio Caballero and Anselmo Pino. Without their lively participation in our project this chapter would have been simply impossible.

# References

André, E. (1964). *Un naturalista en Guayana*. Caracas: Banco Central de Venezuela.

Bueno, O. F. M., & Ramon, P. (1965). *Tratado Histórico* (Vol. 78). Caracas: Biblioteca de la Academia Nacional de Historia.

Chaffanjon, J. (1986). *El Orinoco y el Caura. Relación de viajes realizados en 1886 y 1887 con 56 grabados y 2 mapas* J. Lecoin, transl. Caracas: Editorial Croquis.

Colmenares, G. (1984). Los Jesuitas: modelo de empresarios coloniales. *Boletín Cultural y Bibliográfico, 21,* 42–53.

Crevaux, J. (1988). Viajes por la America del Sur. In M. Á. Perera (Ed.), *El Orinoco en Dos Direcciones.* (pp. 121–333). Caracas: Ediciones Edime.

Dietler, M. (1998). Consumption, agency, and cultural entanglement: Theoretical implications of a mediterranean colonial encounter. In J. G. Cusick (Ed.), *Studies in culture contact: Interaction, culture change, and archaeology* (Occasional Papers) (Vol. 25, pp. 288–315). Carbondale: Center for Archaeological Investigations Southern Illinois University.

Falconi, M. (2003). *Arqueología del Período Republicano (1831-1940): Características del encuentro económico, social y cultural entre indígenas, criollos y extranjeros. Trabajo Final de Grado para optar al titulo de Antropólogo.* Caracas: Universidad Central de Venezuela.

Fogelson, R. D. (1989). The ethnohistory of events and nonevents. *Ethnohistory, 36*(2), 133–147.

Fuentes Guerrero, O. (1980). *Evolución Geohistórica de los Paisajes de la Sarrapia en la region del Caura.* Caracas: Universidad Central de Venezuela.

Funari, P. P. A. (2006). Conquistadors, plantations, and quilombo: Latin America in historical archaeological context. In M. Hall & S. W. Silliman (Eds.), *Blackwell studies in global archaeology: Historical archaeology* (Vol. 9, pp. 209–229). Malden: Blackwell.

Gassón, R. (2000). Quiripas and mostacillas: The evolution of shell beads as a medium of exchange in northern South America. *Ethnohistory, 47*(3-4), 581–609.

Gilij, F. S. (1987). *Ensayo de Historia Americana* . 3 Vols. A. Tovar, transl. Volume 71–73. Caracas: Biblioteca de la Academia Nacional de la Historia.

Gumilla, J. (1944). *El Orinoco Ilustrado.* 2 Vols. Bogotá: Editorial ABC.

Hill, J. (1998). Violent encounters: Ethnogenesis and ethnocide in long-term contact situations. In J. Cusick (Ed.), *Studies in culture contact: Interaction, culture change, and archaeology* (Occasional Paper) (Vol. 25, pp. 146–167). Carbondale: Southern Illinois University at Carbondale.

Humboldt, A. Von. (1956). *Viaje a las regiones equinocciales del Nuevo Continente* (Vols. III, IV). Biblioteca Venezolana de Cultura. Ediciones del Ministerio de Educación. Caracas.

Kirch, P. V., & Sahlins, M. (1992). *Anahulu: The anthropology of history in the Kingdom of Hawaii* (Vol. 1 and 2). Chicago: University of Chicago Press.

Langer, E., & Jackson, R. (Eds.). (1995). *The new Latin American mission history.* Lincoln: The University of Nebraska Press.

Lightfoot, K. G. (2005). *Indians, missionaries, and merchants: The legacy of colonial encounters on the California frontiers.* Berkeley: University of California Press.

Meza, E. (2013). *Aceite de Tortuga: Colonialismo, Agencia y Producción en el Orinoco Medio durante los siglos XVIII al XX. Trabajo Final de Grado.* Caracas: Universidad Central de Venezuela.

Michelena y Rojas, F. (1989). [1867] *Exploración oficial por primera vez desde el norte de la América del Sur.* Iquitos: Monumenta Amazónica.

Mintz, S. W. (2010). *Three ancient colonies: Caribbean themes and variations.* Cambridge: Harvard University Press.

Mitrani, P. (1988). Los Pumé (Yaruro). In J. Lizot (Ed.), *Los Aborígenes de Venezuela: Etnologia Contemporánea II* (Vol. 3, pp. 147–214). Los Aborígenes de Venezuela: Fundación La Salle.

Molina, L., & Amodio, E. (Eds.). (1998). *Técnicas y Tecnologías en Venezuela durante la época colonial* (Vol. 6). Quibor: Museo Arqueológico de Quíbor.

Montiel Acosta, N. (1993). *Etno Historia del Llanero en Barinas y Apure.* Caracas: Editorial Tropykos.

Morey, R. V., & Morey, N. C. (1975). Relaciones Comerciales en el Pasado en los Llanos de Colombia y Venezuela. *Montalbán, 4,* 533–564.

O'Connor, K. (2009). *Beyond "exotic groceries". Tapioca-cassava, a hidden commodity of empire. Commodities of Empire* (pp. 1–32). The Open University.

Ortiz, F. (1947). *Cuban counterpoint: Tobacco and sugar.* New York: Knopf.

Rodríguez Mirabal, A. (1992). El Regímen de tenencia de la tierra en los Llanos venezolanos: Figuras jurídicas, económicas y sociales. In M. E. Romero Moreno, (Ed.), *Café, Caballo y Hamaca: Visión Histórica del Llano,* (Vol. 47, pp. 105–119). Colección 500 Años. Quito: Abya-Yala Orinoquia Siglo XXI.

Rodríguez-Alegría, E. (2010). Incumbents and challengers: Indigenous politics and the adoption of Spanish material culture in colonial Xaltocan, México. *Historical Archaeology, 44*(2), 51–71.

Sahlins, M. D. (1988). *Cosmologies of capitalism: The trans-pacific sector of the world system.* Proceedings of the British academy, 1–51.

Sahlins, M. D. (1996). The Sadness of sweetness: The native anthropology of western cosmology. *Current Anthropology, 37*(3), 395–428.

Sanoja, M., & Vargas Arenas, I. (2005). *Las edades de Guayana. Arqueología de una quimera: Santo Tomé y las misiones capuchinas catalanas* (pp. 1595–1817). Caracas: Monte Ávila Editores Latinoamericana.

Scaramelli, F. (2005). *Material culture, colonialism, and identity in the Middle Orinoco, Venezuela.* Ph. D. Dissertation, The University of Chicago.

Scaramelli, K. L. (2006). *Picking up the Pieces: Ceramic Production and Consumption on the Middle Orinoco Colonial Frontier.* Ph. D. Dissertation, University of Chicago.

Scaramelli, F., & Tarble de Scaramelli, K. (2000). Cultural change and identity in mapoyo burial practice in the Middle Orinoco, Venezuela. *Ethnohistory, 47*(3-4), 705–729.

Scaramelli, F., & Tarble de Scaramelli, K. (2003). Caña: The role of aguardiente in the colonization of the Orinoco. In N. L. Whitehead (Ed.), *History and historicities in amazonia.* (pp. 163-178). Lincoln: University of Nebraska Press.

Scaramelli, F., & Tarble de Scaramelli, K. (2005a). Fundación y desarrollo de la frontera colonial en el Orinoco Medio (1400-1930). *Antropológica, 103,* 87–118.

Scaramelli, F., & Tarble de Scaramelli, K. (2005b). The roles of material culture in the colonization of the Orinoco, Venezuela. *Journal of Social Archaeology, 5,* 135–168.

Schrire, C. (1995). *Digging through darkness: Chronicles of an archaeologist. Charlottesville and London.* Virginia: University Press.

Senatore, M. X. (2003). Discursos Ilustrados y Sociedad Moderna en las Colonias Españolas de Patagonia (siglo XVIII). In P. P. A. Funari & A. Zarankin (Eds.), *Arqueología Histórica en América del Sur, los desafíos del siglo XXI.* Bogotá: Universidad de los Andes.

Silliman, S. W. (2005). Culture contact or colonialism? Challenges in the archaeology of native North America. *American Antiquity, 70*(1), 55–74.

Spruce, R. (1996). *Notas de un Botánico en el Amazonas y en los Andes.* Quito: Ediciones Abya-Yala.

Steward, J. H., & Murphy, R. F. (1977). Tappers and trappers: Parallel processes in acculturation. In J. H. Steward, J. C. Steward, & R. F. Murphy (Eds.), *Evolution and ecology: Essays on social transformation,* (pp. 151–178). Urbana: University of Illinois Press.

Tarble de Scaramelli, K. L., & Scaramelli, F. (2011). Generic pots and generic indians: The archaeology of ethnogenesis in the Middle Orinoco. In A. Hornborg & J. D. Hill (Eds.), *Ethnicity in ancient amazonia: Reconstructing past identities from archaeology, linguistics and ethnohistory,* (pp. 99–128). Boulder: University Press of Colorado.

Tarble de Scaramelli, K. L., & Scaramelli, F. (2012). Cooking for fame or fortune: The effect of european contact on casabe production in the Orinoco. In S. R. Graff & E. Rodríguez-Alegría (Eds.), *The menial art of cooking: Archaeological studies of cooking and food production,* (pp. 119–143). Boulder: University Press of Colorado.

Tarble, K. L. (2008) Coffee, tea, or chicha? Commensality and culinary practice in the Middle Orinoco following colonial contact. *Cuadernos de Arqueologia Mediterránea, 17,* 53–71.

Torrealba, A. J. (1987). *Diario de un Llanero*. 6 Vols. Vol. 1. Caracas: Universidad Central de Venezuela, Facultad de Humanidades y Educación, Instituto de Filología "Andrés Bello", Gobernación del Estado Apure.

Torrealba, G. (2011). *La Economía Política de la Sarrapia: Etnografía Histórica de las Actividades Extractivas entre los Mapoyo del Orinoco Medio, Venezuela*. Master's Thesis, Instituto Venezolano de Investigaciones Científicas.

Trigger, B. G. (1984). The road to affluence: A reassessment of early huron responses to european contact. In R. F. Salisbury & E. Tooker (Eds.), *Affluence and cultural survival*, (pp. 12–25). Washington, DC: American Ethnological Society.

Turner, T. (1991). Representing, resisting, rethinking: Historical transformations of Kayapo culture and anthropological consciousness. In G. Stocking (Ed.), *Post-Colonial situations: The history of anthropology* (Vol. 7). Madison: University of Wisconsin.

Voss, B. L. (2005). From casta to californio: Social identity and the archaeology of culture contact. *American Anthropologist, 107*(3), 461–474.

Voss, B. L. (2008). *The archaeology of ethnogenesis: Race and sexuality in colonial San Francisco*. Berkeley: University of California Press.

Wickham, H. A. (1988). Notas de un Viaje a través de la Selva. In M. Á. Perera (Ed.), *El Orinoco en Dos Direcciones*, (pp. 9–118). Caracas: Ediciones Edime.

Wilmsen, E. N. (1989). *Land filled with flies: A political economy of the Kalahari*. Chicago: The University of Chicago Press.

# Chapter 10
# Women in Spanish Colonial Contexts

Nan A. Rothschild

## 10.1 Introduction: Colonial Settings and Gender Roles

Colonial interactions always involve dominance, as well as the creation and elaboration of a hierarchy arraying racial and ethnic groups in relation to power. There is a gender element in this hierarchy; women were key players, although not consistent ones, in colonial settings (Stoler 2002; Cohn 1989; Comaroff 1985) but these roles are difficult to track as they vary over time within colonial contexts and also may vary from woman to woman. I contend that they were crucial no matter what the setting because they transformed many situations into domestic ones in which women were the dominant players. In these settings they mediated between the colonizers and the colonized.

Their roles were particularly crucial once the socio-biological categories dividing the European from the indigenous peoples were breached. Some famous examples are Pocahontas and La Malinche, but women played significant roles in many other less well-known contexts, mediating when captured or when they had chosen to connect to a European or African male. The creation of hybrid identities and ethnogenesis resulting from this breach had major impacts on community life and women became central to new community formations based on familial structures.

In this chapter, I will discuss some of the complexities of women's roles in Spanish colonial settings during the seventeenth to nineteenth centuries, primarily in the American Southwest, although I will also use occasional examples from other Spanish colonial contexts. First I will discuss colonial contexts broadly and consider the information sources (or archives) we have available. Then I will focus on New Mexico and, in particular, the settlement of San Jose de las Huertas and its descendant community, Placitas, making some comparisons with Santa Fe, the capital of the colony. I consider how women navigated colonial settings, how they were able to manipulate their own situations and exert agency. Colonial accounts often record men's activities; they are less likely to note women's. When women

N. A. Rothschild (✉)
Barnard College, Columbia University, 955 Lexington Ave, 6a, New York, NY 10021, USA
e-mail: roth@columbia.edu

© Springer International Publishing Switzerland 2015
P. P. A. Funari, M. X. Senatore (eds.), *Archaeology of Culture Contact and Colonialism in Spanish and Portuguese America,* DOI 10.1007/978-3-319-08069-7_10

are described, much of the existing commentary portrays the abuse to which many women were subject (Hackett 1937; Todorov 1984). There is no question that abuse was common, not only sexual abuse, but the Spanish endeavor appropriated many things (including food and other products) and labor from indigenous peoples. And in the American Southwest, where Pueblo women had traditionally held important roles in all aspects of culture (Parsons 1917), it must have been especially shocking to encounter Spanish men who perceived them as doubly disadvantaged, being female and indigenous. However, in spite of these attitudes and significant cultural misunderstandings about what women and men were supposed to, or not supposed to do, women were able to hold their own in many settings. I note that gender roles were not fixed over time and place; there was considerable variation. In this chapter, I focus on women but much of what I write about pertains to men as well (although their situations and particulars were often different). An important aspect of the definition of each gender role was its definition in opposition to the other one.

## 10.2   Differences

We know that there were clear differences in power between colonizers and colonized, but some discussion of colonial encounters has naturalized these categories and masked conflicting or variable intra-group interests among both groups—not all colonizers were equally committed to the colonial project. Subaltern groups are especially interesting in their modifications of existing conditions imposed on them, creating opportunities for access to power within supposedly powerless groups (Casella and Voss 2012) because of the many forms of entanglement—economic, political, material, sexual, and emotional—connecting people during colonial settlement. The last two factors are especially powerful in certain colonial situations—especially those involving Catholic colonizers such as the French and Spanish—but have somewhat less impact among British and Dutch colonizers at certain times (Rothschild 2003).

Another element that contributed to variation was the number and status of Spanish colonizers in the New World. The seventeenth century was marked by relatively few Europeans in the Southwest (mostly peninsulares, or those born in Spain; 1000–2400; Gutierrez 1991; Frank 1998), whereas the eighteenth century saw more intruders in the Southwest (up to 4800; Frank op. cit), including criollos (Spanish-born in the New World) and mestizos/Hispanos. The Pueblo population fell as the Spanish/Hispano numbers rose (Rothschild 2003, p. 62). The Bourbon reforms of the latter period also affected the modes of interaction among colonizer and colonized. And localities had very different constituencies and rules of behavior. A community such as eighteenth century Santa Fe had a stratified class structure, with elite, Pueblo peoples and some nomadic tribe members present at times, as well as Hispanos. The intersection of gender roles with race, ethnicity, and class led to variable expected behavior by category, but the statuses recognized in urban places were not relevant in smaller communities (Lutz and Restall 2005).

San Jose de las Huertas was a small community located to the south of Santa Fe as a buffer community to protect it from nomadic tribes (Atherton 2013; Rothschild 2003). Its identity evolved from genizaro to Hispano from 1765, when it was established, to 1826 and its composition was very different from that of Santa Fe. Atherton has shown that although there may have been status differences present within this settlement, they were dampened to serve the community's need to protect itself from marauding Navajos and others intent on stealing their domestic animals and sometimes children (2013).

The development of the mestizo/Hispano identity is meaningful in the Spanish southwest. Mestizaje today is valorized, but naturalized, and masks a great deal of variation, some of which is strongly linked to class differences and would have been present in the past. It was handled variably according to local circumstances and class rank. Once again, I believe that women were crucial in validating this identity. As noted, they were significant in settings to which they were removed (or to which they volunteered to go) because they centered community development. For example, San Jose de las Huertas is referred to as a genizaro settlement, meaning that the males in it had been captured by Spanish, served their time as indentured servants and then been freed. At that point, they could not return to their tribes and were landless, and thus were selected to protect the capital and given land by the governor. Who were the women in this settlement? Who would be willing to leave her family to form a bond with a foreigner (either Spanish or mestizo/Hispano)? Perhaps they were in the same position as men, perhaps they had become alienated from their families, unable to return; perhaps they had had an illegitimate child or become orphaned.

Whatever the reason for their settling in this community, once there, women did what they always did, by habit or habitus. They created a family, formed ties to relatives from neighboring settlements and the families formed the community. Carillo suggests that in the nineteenth century, the Hispano identity was established and marked by a specific form of blackware pottery (1997). Women were classically the potters in southwestern indigenous society, and although Hispano women are not known as potters, and we do not know why this particular form of pottery was produced, it is likely that they were its producers.

## 10.3   Information Sources

One of the important elements of this chapter involves the difficulties in understanding both men's and women's behavior, because of the limitations of our information sources. These derive from a variety of what I consider archives. The term archive is normally used to describe a wide range of written documents that are associated with governance, especially in colonial situations. In this chapter, I will also consider several other archival forms: The physical bodies of the colonized reveal the direct effects of contact in the form of new work load requirements imposed on subjects and new dietary habits. Archaeology offers another archive, the material culture associated with colonial lives, highlighting otherwise unseen aspects of these lives. Taylor (2003) has written of performance as a separate archive, in which individuals curate details that would otherwise be lost (Rothschild 2008). I will examine the exterior of bodies and their clothing as performance. And finally, oral history provides a view offered by descendants of the colonized, mediated of course by the recorder. None of these archives is either complete or unbiased; each has a "story" or point of view. Each is different in a number of salient ways from the others: the recorders differ, the kinds of designations indicating categories differ, and each was intended for a particular audience. Some are created by officials, some by the people themselves.

Several anthropologists examining post-colonial phenomena have deconstructed archives (Dirks 1992; Stoler 2002; Taylor 2003) rightly asserting that they are neither as reliable nor neutral as sources of data as had once been assumed. They can also be seen as objects that are able to produce knowledge of the colonized place. They objectify individuals and groups, recording them according to specific parameters: ethnic or racial identities, social statuses, or as economic resources. These attributes, ephemeral and subjective, once created, leave traces and acquire an existence that is independent of the things/people themselves and are used, at the time and later, by colonial government agents and scholars, as if the attributes were real (Rothschild 2008). Although they give the appearance of solidity they are fragile, susceptible to external pressures. As Stoler notes, archives are processes, experiments in governance. "They shape the regularities of what can be said" (2002, p. 96).

The major chapter archives to be considered in this discussion are church records (defining important attributes of parishioners, noting gender, age, ethnicity, and marital status), censuses, a court case from the inquisition and an inventory of the possessions of an elite woman, wife of the governor of Santa Fe in the late seventeenth century. I also briefly discuss casta paintings for their emphasis on hybridity in the colonial context.

## 10.3.1 Archives: Census and Church Records

Record-keeping in New Mexico varied from one community to another, but the categories employed were fewer than those in Mexico or other parts of Spanish America. Age and gender are recorded, especially at life cycle events. A census taken in New Mexico in 1750 was supposed to classify residents by one of the following categories: S (Spanish), C (Coyote—offspring of a Mestizo man and an Indian woman), L (Lobo—black man and Indian woman), Mu (Mulatto—a black person and a white one), Ca (Castizo—child of a Spanish and a Mestizo), I (Indian), M (Mestizo), or N (Negro) (Bustamonte 1989). It is intriguing that in the census of Santa Fe, in 229 households, only 3 people were given any designation, and that was Indian; they were recorded in the first household listed, that of Don Manuel Saenz de Garvisu. No other ethnic identifiers were used although some people were listed with no last names. In the same 1750 census, at the Villa of Albuquerque, with 191 households, more detail was offered. S and C were frequent, Mu was used fairly often, and M, L, and N were rare. I was used for a few individuals who were clearly servants and one Chinese woman is listed. At the end of the Albuquerque census, the recorder noted 500 "gente de razon" and 200 Indians (Olmsted 1981).

I have looked at two different sets of records from smaller communities, one from the pueblo of Pecos and the other, from a Hispanic community, San Jose de las Huertas. In both places, archives were maintained in church records, recording the crucial events of baptisms, marriages, and deaths. San Jose de las Huertas in Placitas, New Mexico, was occupied between 1765 and 1826. Heather Atherton and I conducted field research there from 2000 to 2003. The archival record includes church records from San Felipe, the nearest Catholic church; information exists from the 1760s to the early nineteenth century. There were few baptisms recorded in the eighteenth century; the only ethnic status noted was "español/a" and everyone was thus categorized. An interesting development occurred between April 1805 and October 1807; 13 of 24 baptisms recorded (more than 50 %) were described as mulattoes, with a few Spanish, Indians, and undesignated births being recorded. Since it is unlikely that there was a mulatto migration into the Las Huertas area, I imagine that a new priest, who was unused to babies with brown skins, must have come to the church. After this period, the priest returned to not labeling people or referring to them as Spanish (with two members of other Indian groups (Papago, Apache) noted). Names reveal both French and Spanish ancestry for some of the population. Marriage records at las Huertas contained no ethnic identifiers, and a few of the dead were referred to as "Spanish." A census, undertaken in 1803–1807, lists 62 families, by name and age with no labels. The term "coyota" was used occasionally, although it is unclear whether its meaning here was the same as in Albuquerque. The only distinction unique to women was the occasional note of either "Legitimate" or "Natural" birth, the latter referring to an unmarried mother (Atherton and Rothschild 2010).

Archives from Pecos, near Santa Fe, from the late seventeenth to the early nineteenth century, recorded members of local or neighboring Indian groups (such as Comanche, Picuris, Navajo, and Apache) and also noted: Español, mestizo, mulato, lobo, coyote (which seems somewhat elastic and included the offspring of Spanish plus Indian as well as mestizo and Indian), chino (Indian plus mulato), and genizaros (Christianized and Hispanicized Plains or other Indians). Pecos was following the Spanish system and recording local and other Indian groups as well as those with mixed blood, while in Las Huertas, it must be assumed that everyone was a variant of mestizo, but was given the honorific title of "Spanish." Single mothers were also recorded at Pecos (Levine 1999). It is sadly clear that information provided by such records is not very reliable because many census-takers did not record it or did so variably.

In addition to these written archives, we have other painted records that are unique to Spanish colonial situations, recording the Spanish concern with racial mixture in the form of casta paintings. These apply to Mexico rather than New Mexico, but I discuss them briefly to highlight the impact on the colonial system of inter-racial marriage. As noted, gender identity is closely linked to others: class, race, ethnicity, and caste. The last three were created through the powerful forces of sexual and emotional ties that leave material traces on the body and create amazing colonial variability in Spanish colonial contexts through the processes of mestizaje, creolization, hybridity, and ethnogenesis (Voss 2012, p. 11). The production of biologically different-looking individuals endangers imperial control. Many observers assumed that Spanish men instigated sexual encounters, mostly without anticipating consequences. However, Ramon Gutierrez, a historian who writes about this encounter believes that both women and men used their sexuality for different purposes at times: "they gave their bodies to persons they deemed holy, in order to partake of their supernatural power" and "Pueblo women cooled the passion of the fierce fire-branding Spanish katsina through intercourse...to...domesticate the malevolence of these foreign gods" (Gutierrez 1991, pp. 50–51).

### 10.3.2  Archive: Casta Paintings

These often depict men of a "higher" status paired with a woman in a "lower" category. An interesting element of these paintings is how women who had the same "label" (e.g., Indio) were dressed differently according to the casta of their male partners (wearing pearls and a fancy dress when with an Español, or wearing torn garments with a Negro or Mestizo). Design elements on clothing, the settings of the scene, and other attributes also vary (Gaitan-Ammann and Rothschild 2009). We may perceive these pairs in terms of the sexual exploitation of women, but they may also be seen as a path to higher status for women, a form of mobility.

## 10.4  Ethnicity and Classification

Ethnic identities were a subject of interest to the Spanish crown in New Spain during the entire period of their rule. Spanish Colonial authorities created two tiers, Spanish and Indio (indigenous); each was meant to have its own hierarchy and they were to live in separate places. These ideal schemes were difficult to maintain. In early days, it was believed that this physical separation would protect Indians from imagined abuse by Europeans and Africans, but by early seventeenth century, it had become a mechanism to control natives and mixed peoples (Carroll 2005, p. 251). People in different categories had varied rights and responsibilities; documentary accounts clearly describe the racialized system of social categories imposed on colonized subjects. The Spanish believed in "purity of blood," thus the ideal was for members of a given group (Spanish/white, Indian, or African) to marry within their own group (Katzew 2005, p. 40).

However, as intermarriage became a fact, the casta system was created in the mid seventeenth century (Carrera 2003, p. 36) in an effort by authorities to create order, control what they saw as dangerous racial mixing and reaffirm Spanish superiority. Mestizos as well as other categories that breached these two tiers were seen as agents of chaos (Mills and Taylor 1998, p. 324). The casta system consisted of a set of 16 slots in a table of identities; where an individual belonged depended on his/her parents. It only included those of mixed blood; Spanish/European, Indians, and blacks were excluded. It has been suggested (op. cit) that this system suited the Bourbon desire for scientific order and resonated with the Enlightenment, but it was also meant to define socially subordinate positions for indigenous people and enslaved Africans (Levine 1999, p. 92). The intriguing aspect of the system is that it was largely theoretical; many of these categories were little used. Those who did the classifying were either state functionaries or clergy; rarely would they have had access to individual genealogical histories, and thus they would have used simpler criteria to classify people: appearance, dress, language, style, or "calidad" (Boyer 1997). These were more accessible than specific genealogical details and also allowed for some manipulation by those wishing to alter their rank. The incentive to create these boundaries of difference is reinforced by the fact that the state had an urgent need to rule all peoples (marked by whatever differences of culture, language, and biology) in a given territory within one system (Voss 2012, p. 13). In New Spain, both racial mixing and social factors contributed to status and influenced each other: illegitimacy, impure blood, poverty, and criminality were all considered as lowering status. Similarly, one's status could be raised by marriage, honor, wealth, purity, legitimacy, and adherence to legal codes of behavior (Carrera 2003, p. 37), almost regardless of skin color.

## 10.5   Women's Mobility

In situations of racially mixed unions, it is clear that the mother determined the infant's status directly. Women's mobility was enabled in several ways. In the Southwest, they had economic power as the sellers or traders of products essential to colonizers, from food to household goods such as ceramics (Rothschild 2003). At times, conversion to Christianity (Tarble de Scaramelli 2012, p. 143) offered women increased status within the colonial system and access to European goods. Sexual connections created a potential attachment to a European man, enabling increased access to desirable European things and there was no stigma attached to pre-marital sexual liaisons in some ethnographic settings (Rothschild 2003; Loren 2012). Once women had access to these goods they had the ability to assume, through their clothing and accessories, a position different than one they were born into, since ethnic status was sometimes based on appearance. The body tells a different story than the written record does; it performs a lived history which is not subject to colonial authority and control (Gaitan-Ammann and Rothschild 2009).

Solange Alberto (Mills and Taylor 1998) offers an interesting account of Beatriz de Padilla, a mulatta who lived near Guadalajara, Mexico and was the mistress of a priest and other significant Spanish men. She notes that Padilla had freedoms denied to European women. She was able to talk to whomever she pleased, to move through the community freely, to dress as she wished, and even to define herself racially (as a morisca rather than a mulatta (op.cit, p. 184)). However, these freedoms did not grant her immunity from persecution; she was accused of witchcraft and murder, but ultimately acquitted. At that time, her property which included clothing (petticoats, Spanish skirts, and a cloak) was returned to her.

## 10.6   Colonial Power and Archaeology

Archaeological research plays a vital role in unpacking the variability of empires, seen both in their internal construction and in the differences among them (Casella and Voss 2012). As Gosden and Knowles note, archaeology is essential in understanding the colonial past "because all colonial relations were constituted with material culture" (Loren 2010, p. 93). I think we must include the physical body as an element of material culture and also consider how it was dressed (or not); a highly significant aspect of colonial societies. Administrators of these units were very cognizant of appearances. "Any weaknesses…through improper dress or actions of colonial subjects reflected weaknesses of the ruling empire" (Hall in Loren 2010, p. 22).

## 10.7   The Body

The role of women's bodies is one of the most important elements of this complex picture and is a unique site for understanding the colonial experience. Accounts have often focused on the corporeal exterior, serving as both a natural and a social symbol. Several issues are relevant here: the distinction (or lack thereof) between the physical and the social or cultural body (Rothschild 2007), the depiction of the body as a fragile entity, and the differences between external views of the body and those held by its owner. It is important, but difficult, to disentangle the physical and social aspects of bodies. As Burke notes, "the material body is often in plain sight, but the social body, as an artifact of the self and a canvas for identity, is both indispensible and invisible" (1996, p. 4). Archaeologists are privileged to have access to data from the body's interior, but these data must be analyzed in a frame beyond the biological, incorporating the physical body into a social context.

It is sometimes said that women have been "determined by their bodies" (Conboy et al. 1997, p. 1), their identity constructed by men as passive, fragile, and helpless, especially in regard to reproduction and associated phenomena (ibid.): clearly an external definition of women. Several forms of discourse, notably within visual anthropology, have considered the representation of the body. Brenda Farnell writes of changes in the perception of bodies, from relatively superficial appraisals, which merged the biological and cultural aspects of the body as an object (Farnell 2012, pp. 137–138), to later approaches, inspired by Foucault, which separated these elements. Meskell has criticized those approaches to the body that prioritize the body's exterior; she suggests that Foucauldian notions have established a discourse in which "power relations are mapped on the body as a surface" to be analyzed as a display (Meskell in Gilchrist 1999, p. 73.). Phenomenology focused on lived experience but still viewed the body as static (Farnell 2012, p. 151). Today, there is a greater tendency to perceive the body as a moving agent in a spatially organized world of meanings "as a biocultural resource for the dynamic expression of self, personhood, and identity (Farnell 2012, p. 151)." The presentation of the self can reflect expectations and/or be a political/social statement at the same time.

## 10.7.1   Archives: The Skeleton

The interior of the body as a part of material culture, accessed through skeletal remains provides information that is not otherwise available through any other means. Although the internal body is invisible, it offers socially relevant information to which archaeology is privileged to have access. Important data on disease, illness, physical stress, work load, and demography have been developed through these analyses. Colonial powers are known to have manipulated the colonized through new labor assignments (men in the Southwest were required to undertake farming and house construction, both of which had previously been women's work; Rothschild 2003, p. 139). Other effects came through enforced subsistence change which alters diet. Meredith Linn (2002, 2003) analyzed data from a series of site reports in order to demonstrate the effects of Spanish colonialism in North America. She discusses a wide range of impacts, including the devastation of total demographic collapse in some cases, due to a combination of epidemic disease, dietary stress, and the cruel exploitation of bodies for labor. Colonial encounters altered the body's physical structure, as seen in bone hypertrophy and remodeling as a result of work load, the development of rugged muscle attachments related to new assigned tasks, and osteoarthritis developed because of forced labor. A study of pre-colonial and post-colonial skeletons from Pecos, New Mexico, for example, indicates a decline in women's humeral strength while an increase in that of men as a result of the Spanish policy, which shifted the major task of agriculture from women to men (Linn 2003, p. 7).

In another Spanish colony in California, an analysis of diet from isotopes (strontium and nitrogen; c 3–4; op. cit, p. 11) shows that foragers' bodies in California demonstrate the long-term effects of colonialism (Linn 2002, p. 12, 15). They were healthier prior to missionization than after it, apparently due to a decrease in consumption of marine plants. Missionaries focused subsistence tasks on herding and agriculture and presumably discouraged the gathering of marine resources and fish. These studies offer other insights: evidence of disease, reflected in decreased fertility, bone lesions, and dental enamel defects (hypoplasias and other dental indicators) from childhood nutritional stress. However, Linn concludes that the greatest impact on health comes from enforced social change instituted by the Spanish: their policy of population aggregation, which promoted susceptibility to epidemic disease; relocation, and the enforced shift from foraging to agricultural production. Those indigenous people who remained the healthiest were those who lived in small groups, were mobile and had a dispersed settlement pattern, and managed to eat nutritiously but also avoided intense or prolonged contact with the colonizers (op. cit.).

## 10.8 Covering the Body

Issues of embodiment are connected to the clothing that covers the body. Loren (2010, p. 29) writes of the importance of clothing in defining deliberate political statements within colonial settings, in which individuals choose certain elements from each culture to display, combining beads, coins, and European fabrics with traditional elements. The prevalence of sumptuary laws in colonial settings reinforces the power of specific items as signals because they are forbidden to indigenous women (Rothschild 2003). It was not only women who chose to represent mixed statuses, but they seem to have been more frequent than men in participating in these activities (ibid.). Clothing is a form of visual media and is "simultaneously and variously produced by and productive of particular, multiply constituted ideas of who one is, must be, and would like to be" (Dudley 2011, p. 169). Dress not only expressed the person but also impacted the observer. However, as Loren notes, dress was more than superficial; it represented a woman's self-image, either established or desired. (2010, p. 9). Several studies of colonial encounters offer examples of the manipulation of clothing by women (Cohn 1989; Comaroff 1985) as well as the impact of wearing certain kinds of clothing on its wearers."Our bodies and the physical objects around us, including cloth and clothing, share qualities that determine the nature of our interactions with and perceptions of those other objects" (Dudley 2011, p. 170). Clothing is a complex part of visible culture. "…How clothing is worn, how the body shapes it, and notions of dress as a 'social skin'" are significant, as is the perception of clothing by others (Turner in Dudley 2011, p. 49). Hair style is another important aspect of dress and is discussed below.

It is important to try to tease out the differences between the exterior of the body and its interior, as it is also crucial to distinguish between an assigned status and a self-selected one. To what degree does the external reflect embodiment, and to what degree is it simply a shallow representation of a mixture of elements that mirror certain expectations? What is the role of habitus in influencing dress? Much of a person's appearance is a signal. The color of the skin and other physical traits combine with clothing and ornaments to present a certain image, but those who prioritize phenomenology over semiotics see dress as a form of social knowledge (Gilchrist 1999, p. 72) and as a "discursive daily practice of constructing and reconstructing one's identity in a social landscape" (Loren 2010, p. 93). Thus, the exterior is most often a genuine presentation of the embodied self.

## 10.8.1   Archive: The Body as Performance

Although we have little evidence from San Jose de las Huertas of the dress of women there, we have written accounts from Santa Fe of elite goods belonging to both men and women: Italian velvet, Chinese silks, lace, satin hats, fancy slippers, and a pearl headdress are recorded by Cordelia Snow (1993 in Rothschild 2003, p. 190). Apart from a few gilt buttons, there are no archaeological traces of these goods. Knowing living conditions in the seventeenth-century Santa Fe, it is difficult to imagine women wearing these items. However, an amazing document records the clothing of the wife of the Governor of Santa Fe, Bernardo López de Mendizábal, who was in power from 1659 until 1662, when he and his wife were arrested by the Holy Office of the Inquisition (González and Levine 2010, p. 179). When Doña Teresa de Aguilera y Roche (the only woman in New Mexico ever tried before the Inquisition; she was charged with alleged Jewish practices) was brought out of her house, a notary described her dress in great detail:

> She put on a doublet of blue fabric, and beneath that a scarlet damask corset, a blouse of Rouen linen embellished with silk tufts. Then she put on a red petticoat with five tiers of silver tips, and an underskirt…of the coarse cloth of this land, bracelets of coral, strings of beads, a thick braid of beads of blue and other colors and false pearls. (González and Levine 2010, p. 189)

In her account, Doña Teresa also described many items of clothing and jewelry she had given to the new governor, including "a black dress of moiré satin, a hooped petticoat, a hooped skirt of blue finely woven Holland linen silk, a scarlet cloak with blue point lace and embellished with silver" (ibid.). She wrote detailed accounts in her own defense, carefully laying charges against those who testified against her, and was ultimately acquitted of practicing Judaism (which apparently had been based on the fact that she bathed and changed bed linens on Fridays (op. cit. 207). What is interesting here, however, is the significance and elaboration of her costume, clearly a performance of her status.

We know that cloth was also an important good for Pueblo people. Cloth has been described as distinctively women's wealth and property (Weiner 1976; Weiner and Schneider 1989) and there are wills from Santa Fe, Colombia from the sixteenth and seventeenth century in which women often described their textile possessions in great and loving detail (Gaitan-Ammann and Rothschild 2009). However, in the indigenous Southwest, weaving was a male activity and some cloth was apparently woven in kivas (Webster 1997, pp. 46, 213). There was great demand by the Spanish for Pueblo cloth for all kinds of uses. As Spanish interest in Pueblo cloth increased, certain changes occurred. The manta, a traditional form of textile, was demanded in increasing quantities during the mid-seventeenth and into the eighteenth century as a form of tribute. As a result of these requirements, a dual-gendered production system developed in which men continued to weave while women and children and older family members worked in fiber preparation; women also did some weaving when needed (Webster 1997, p. 213). This situation offers an interesting exception to the idea that cloth was women's product and property.

## 10.8.2   Archives: Archaeology

It is very difficult to recover gender-based information from archaeological contexts. Nothing recovered from San Jose de las Huertas could be associated with a
specific gender, and the examination of a series of colonial sites (mostly Hispano)
in the Rio Grande area yielded no evidence of male or female-specific tools. One
cannot assume that stone tools were used only by men (Rothschild 2003, p. 180) or
that manos and metates were only used by women. It is likely that pottery was made
by women, but no production sites were found as most of it was made by Pueblo
women and traded for (op. cit. 185). It was even hard to separate Hispanic from
indigenous sites in the Rio Grande valley after the Pueblo Revolt; the assemblages
reflected cultural blending and the use by Hispanos of stone tools when they had no
access to iron (op. cit, p. 167).

Gender data did emerge from mortuary contexts at the site of Hawikku (in existence during colonial times) in western New Mexico. Howell and Kintigh (1996)
were able to demonstrate that women did have access to elite positions, especially
during the second of three time periods identified, but that female access to leadership declined after Spanish contact (Howell 1995, pp. 143–144). Needless to say, it
is rare to find these distinctive data in archaeological deposits.

## 10.8.3   Archive: Oral History

A Works Progress Administration (WPA) project recorded women's (and some
men's) stories from Las Placitas, New Mexico, a community whose members were
descended from the occupants of the archaeological site of San Jose de las Huertas.
They were recorded between 1938 and 1942 by an American woman, Lou Sage
Batchen, through interpreters (one of whom was a 12-year-old boy), which obviously would have had an impact on some elements of the tales (Rebolledo and
Márquez 2000). A few other stories were recorded from a different, nearby contemporary village by Annette Hirsch Thorp.

These tales offer significant information about the remembered lives of parents
and grandparents. Many of the story-tellers were elderly women, in their 70s and
80s, although some were younger and men were also interviewed. The village had a
story-telling tradition, which passed on local history and curated memories of past
customs. Batchen started with the list of the 21 founding families of San Jose de
las Huertas and focused on their descendants; she was very aware of genealogical
connections and many names such as Gurule and Trujillo keep recurring. She interviewed some people more than once. These wonderful documents provide a great
deal of information: on illness and curing, sad or traumatic events, and the activities
of witches, but others told of dances and weddings, trading and cooking practices,
and ceremonies and the minutiae of daily life.

The information on hair style and dress is particularly interesting with respect to
performance. Accounts pertaining to dress are minimal. The interviewer usually describes what the interviewee is wearing: "she dresses in cheap gray or black calico"

(op. cit, p. 96), and occasionally mentions dressing for a special event. An intriguing tale notes that a bride who had been known not to be a virgin was not allowed to wear a veil or carry flowers when she married (op., cit, p. 249).

The significance of long hair for both genders emerges in one story. Hair has traditionally been a signal of women's status for Pueblo peoples (Rothschild 2003); it is clear that it must be considered as part of performance and bodily presentation, although it is not accessible to archaeologists. In Las Huertas, married women wore their hair long in a knot on top of their heads, whereas unmarried women wore a single braid and men wore two braids. It was believed that short hair was a sign of criminal behavior (for a man) or the loss of virginity (for a woman; Rebolledo and Márquez 2000, p. 264). One story tells of Paquita, a young woman who was romantically attracted to a young violinist, an unworthy mate, and thus failed the virginity test when she was betrothed to Juan. In response, the village demanded her hair be cut. Juan decided to marry her anyway and thus his hair was cut; both remained in the village as outcasts, as did their children. When the Mexican government ordered the abandonment of the site in 1823, Paquita, Juan, their children, and spouses fled to the mountains, let their hair grow, and re-entered a new community, fittingly named Socorro, where they were accepted as respectable members (op. cit, p. 268). Subsequently, hair length became less important for men because after the Civil War, some men returned without braids and villagers had contact with short-haired American explorers. Thus, elements of these stories reveal the early stages of modernity and its associated changes in materiality.

Although there may be factual issues with respect to some of the stories, the image of women that emerges is most interesting for this chapter. They were active, authoritative, and rose to whatever challenges they faced. The editor of the volume, Tey Diana Rebolledo, suggests that the stories reveal resistance to traditional gender roles (2000, p. xvi). Women worked hard but were proud of their abilities in, for example, building their houses (Rebolledo and Márquez 2000, pp. 12, 128). When there were no males around, the women and girls did "outside" work (farming) as well as their normal domestic chores (op. cit, p. 20). Women were not afraid to live alone (op. cit, p. 4), although it was difficult at times (op. cit, p. 10). They were entrepreneurs and in charge of household finances (op. cit, p. 42), and filled the important roles of curer and midwife. These stories describe enterprising women, brave women (op. cit, pp. 119, 259), and also some women who wanted pretty things (op. cit, p. xlix).

Most marriages were arranged, but at times lovers, persevered (op. cit, p. 249). The stories address the dominance of men and the ways in which young women sometimes gave in to their fathers' wishes about marriage partners, but occasionally were able to have their way, even if it meant waiting until their father had died (op. cit, p. 95). Brothers did not have the power over their sisters that fathers did. Many tales recounted both brave and wastrel men. In one story from a different Hispano community, a woman showed up her lazy husband by taking his place on the buffalo hunt; when she came home in triumph, he killed her (op. cit, p. 86). Although the stories have very different outcomes and morals, the dominant message in these intriguing accounts is of the power, energy, and adaptability of women.

## 10.9   Conclusion

In this short chapter, I have tried to recreate a picture of the complexities that surrounded women in colonial New Mexico under Spanish rule. Although circumstances varied widely according to social rank, ethnicity, race, and local factors, making experiences tremendously different, certain elements define the discourse. Women were effective agents in all situations, finding their own sources of power, even though they could not always escape male domination.

This is borne out through the various archives that yield different components of information allowing us to piece together a somewhat more complete picture. Some status designations were defined by officials on paper (or in paint), whereas, human skeletal remains reveal the gendered impact of colonial rule. The discourse represented by the presentation of self in dress and hairstyle is particularly significant in revealing hybridity and women's autonomy. Oral historical accounts from Placitas offer the most recent accounts and the most concrete details of life, including important evidence of resistance to authority, whether it was colonial or male.

Women's power is due to their central positions in domestic situations, within which men lived. Their ability to mediate was a particular strength in hybrid or ethnogenetic contexts. Voss highlights Deagan's 2001 comment that "it was within… households and in women's domestic activities, that the social transformation of identity in the imperial colonies began, leading ultimately to the end of empire" (Deagan in Voss 2012, p. 22). And Voss states "the archaeology of interethnic colonial households powerfully reveals that…the intimate encounters between colonized and colonizer generated far-reaching cultural and political effects"; the importance of sexuality was a foil to colonial ambition (ibid.). It is within the minutiae of daily life that the conflictual edges of intercultural contact are abraded and new cultural formations established.

## References

Atherton, H. (2013). Community formation in the Spanish colonial borderlands: San José de las Huertas, New Mexico. PhD dissertation, Columbia University.

Atherton, H., & Rothschild, N. A. (2010). *Material manifestations (or not) of ethnic identities*. Society for American Archaeology meeting, St. Louis, MO.

Boyer, R. (1997). Negotiating calidad: The everyday struggle for status in Mexico. *Historical Archaeology, 31*(1), 64–72.

Burke, T. (1996). *Lifebuoy men, lux women: Commodification, consumption and cleanliness in modern Zimbabwe*. Durham: Duke University Press.

Bustamonte, A. (1989). Espanoles, castas y labradores: Santa Fe Society in the Eighteenth Century. In D. G. Noble (Ed.), *Santa Fe: History of an Ancient City* (pp. 65–78). Santa Fe: School of American Research Press.

Carillo, C. M. (1997). *Hispanic New Mexico pottery: Evidence of craft specialization, 1790–1800*. Albuquerque: LPD Press.

Carrera, M. M. (2003). *Imagining identity in New Spain: Race, lineage and the colonial body in portraiture and casta paintings*. Austin: University of Texas Press.

Carroll, P. J. (2005). Black-native relations and the historical record in colonial Mexico. In M. Re-stall (Ed.), *Beyond black and red: African-native relations in colonial Latin America* (pp. 245–267). Albuquerque: University of New Mexico Press.

Casella, E. C., & Voss, B. L. (2012). Intimate encounters: An archaeology of sexuality within co-lonial worlds. In B. L. Voss & E. C. Casella (Eds.), *The archaeology of colonialism: Intimate encounters and sexual effects* (pp. 1–10). Cambridge: Cambridge University Press.

Cohn, B. S. (1989). *Colonialism and its forms of knowledge: The British in India. Princeton Stud-ies in Culture/Power/History*. Princeton: Princeton University Press.

Comaroff, J. (1985). *Body of power, spirit of resistance: The culture and history of a South African people*. Chicago: University of Chicago Press.

Conboy, K., Median, N., & Stanbury, S. (Eds.). (1997). *Writing on the body: Female embodiment and feminist theory*. New York: Columbia University Press.

Dirks, N. B. (1992). *Colonialism and culture. Comparative studies in society and history book series*. Ann Arbor: University of Michigan Press.

Dudley, S. (2011). Material visions: Dress and textiles. In M. Banks & J. Ruby (Eds.), *Made to be seen: Perspectives on the history of visual anthropology* (pp. 45–73). Chicago: University of Chicago Press.

Farnell, B. (2012). Theorizing "the Body" in visual culture. In M. Banks & J. Ruby (Eds.), *Made to be seen: Perspectives on the history of visual anthropology* (pp. 136–158). Chicago: University of Chicago Press.

Frank, R. (1998). Demographic, social and economic change in New Mexico. In R. H. Jackson (Ed.), *New views of borderland history* (pp. 41–71). Albuquerque: University of New Mexico Press.

Gaitan Ammann, F., & Rothschild, N. A. (2009). Post-ethnicity and intra-ethnicity. Paper pre-sented at 2009 Meeting, Society for Historical Archaeology.

Gilchrist, R. (1999). *Gender and archaeology: Contesting the past*. London: Routledge.

González, G.T.E., & Levine, F. (2010). *In her own voice, Doña Teresa Aguilera y Rocha and Intrigue in the palace of the Governors, 1659–1662. In All Trails Lead to Santa Fe, An An-thology Commemorating the 400th Anniversary of the Founding of Santa Fe, NM in 1610* (pp. 179–208). Santa Fe: Sunstone Press.

Gutierrez, R. A.(1991). *When Jesus came the Corn Mothers went away: Marriage, sexuality and power in New Mexico, 1500-1846*. Stanford, CA: Stanford University Press.

Hackett, C. W., Jr. (Ed.). (1937). *Historical documents relating to New Mexico, Nueva Vizacaya and approaches thereto, to 1773* (Vol. 3). Washington, DC: Carnegie Institution.

Howell, T. (1995). Tracking Zuni gender and leadership roles across the contact period in the Zuni region. *Journal of Anthropological Research, 51*, 125–147.

Howell, T., & Kintigh, K. W. (1996). Archaeological identification of kin groups using mortu-ary and biological data: An example from the American Southwest. *American Antiquity, 61*, 537–554.

Katzew, I. (2005). *Casta painting: Images of race in eighteenth-century Mexico*. New Haven: Yale University Press.

Levine, F. (1999). *Our prayers are in this place: Pecos Pueblo identity over the centuries*. Albu-querque: University of New Mexico Press.

Linn, M. (2002). *Marred bones: The physical consequences of Spanish contact upon the native populations of North America*. MS at Columbia University, Human Skeletal Biology.

Linn, M. (2003). *Patterns of diet and activity: Fleshing out the native American demographic col-lapse*. MS for Columbia University, Human Skeletal Biology.

Loren, D. d. P. (2010). *Archaeology of clothing and bodily adornment in colonial America*. Gain-seville: University Press of Florida.

Loren, D. d. P. (2012). Fear, desire, and material strategies in colonial Louisiana. In B. L. Voss & E. C. Casella (Eds.), *The Archaeology of colonialism: Intimate encounters and sexual effects* (pp. 105–121). Cambridge: Cambridge University Press.

Lutz, C., & Restall M. (2005). Wolves and sheep? Black-maya relations in colonial Guatemala and Yucatan. In M. Restall (Ed.), *Beyond black and red: African-native relations in colonial Latin America* (pp. 185–221). Albuquerque: University of New Mexico Press.

Mills, K., & Taylor, W. B. (1998). *Colonial Spanish America: A documentary history*. Wilmington: Scholarly Resources.

Olmsted, V. L. (1981). *Spanish and Mexican censuses of New Mexico, 1750–1830*. Albuquerque: New Mexico Genealogical Society.

Parsons, E. C. (1917). Notes on the Zuni, parts I and II. Memoirs of the American Anthropological Association, no. 19 and 20.

Rebolledo, T. D., & Márquez, M. T. (Eds.). (2000). *Women's tales from the New Mexico WPA: La Diabla a Pie*. Houston: Arte Publico Press.

Rothschild, N. A. (2003). *Colonial encounters in a native American landscape: The Spanish and the Dutch in North America*. Washington, DC: Smithsonian Institution Press.

Rothschild, N. A. (2007). Colonized bodies, personal and social. In D. Boric & J. Robb (Eds.), *Past bodies: Body-centred research in archaeology* (pp. 135–144). Oxford: Oxbow Books.

Rothschild, N. A. (2008). *Archived anxieties: The creation of race in colonial archives*. Paper presented at Theoretical Archaeology Group, Columbia University, NY.

Stoler, A. (2002). *Carnal knowledge and imperial power: Race and the intimate in colonial rule*. Berkeley: University of California Press.

Tarble de Scaramelli, K. (2012). Effects of empire: Gendered transformations on the orinoco frontier. In B. L. Voss & E. C. Casella (Eds.), *The archaeology of colonialism: Intimate encounters and sexual effects* (pp. 138–155). Cambridge: Cambridge University Press.

Taylor, D. (2003). *The archive and the repertoire: Performing cultural memory in the Americas*. Durham: Duke University Press.

Todorov, T. (1984). *The conquest of America: The question of the other*. New York: Harper and Row.

Voss, B. L. (2012). Sexual effect: Postcolonial and queer perspectives on the archaeology of sexuality and empire. In B. L. Voss & E. C. Casella (Eds.), *The archaeology of colonialism: Intimate encounters and sexual effects* (pp. 11–28). Cambridge: Cambridge University Press.

Webster, L. D. (1997). The effects of European contact on textile production and exchange in the North American Southwest: A Pueblo case study. PhD dissertation, University of Arizona, Tucson.

Weiner, A. B. (1976). *Women of value, men of renown: New perspectives on Trobriand exchange*. Austin: University of Texas Press.

Weiner, A. B., & Schneider, J. (1989). *Cloth and human experience*. Washington, DC: Smithsonian Institution Press.

# Chapter 11
# Material Culture, Mestizage, and Social Segmentation in Santarém, Northern Brazil

Luís Cláudio Pereira Symanski and Denise Maria Cavalcante Gomes

## 11.1 Introduction

The city of Santarém is located in the state of Pará, Brazil, in the confluence of the Amazonas and the Tapajós rivers. It was built over a Tapajó indigenous village. This group occupied a vast region of the lower Amazon river, being extinct in the eighteenth century (Nimuendaju 1948). Some scholars have studied the deleterious impact of the European conquest over the lower Amazonian indigenous groups in the sixteenth and seventeenth centuries, detaching factors as the demographic reduction caused by epidemics, slavery, and the forced mixing of ethnic groups promoted by the missionaries (Roosevelt 1991, 1992). Nevertheless, there is still an absence of archaeological research focused on the consequences of the cultural contact between Europeans and Amerindians in this region during the eighteenth and nineteenth centuries.

The present paper aims to be an initial effort to fill this gap, focusing on the material culture recovered on three households of Santarém occupied during the eighteenth and nineteenth centuries. The assemblages are composed of distinct technological sets, including locally made artifacts and imported objects. During this period, distinct socio–cultural groups lived in the city, including Portuguese, Portuguese–Brazilians, Amerindians, Africans, and mestizos. The material analyzed, therefore, is informative of the cultural exchanges among these groups. These exchanges involved the affirmation and negotiation of social, cultural, and gender identities in the interior of the domestic spheres as well as in the wider urban space. If, by one side, these settings were marked by segmentation and hierarchy, on the other, mixtures and hybridization also characterized the daily life of these groups.

L. C. P. Symanski (✉)
Departamento de Sociologia e Antropologia, Universidade Federal de Minas Gerais,
Belo Horizonte, Brazil
e-mail: lcsymanski@yahoo.com.br

D. M. C. Gomes
Departamento de Antropologia, Museu Nacional, Universidade Federal do Rio de Janeiro,
Quinta da Boa Vista s/n, São Cristóvão, RJ 20940-040, Brazil
e-mail: denisecavalcante@yahoo.com

© Springer International Publishing Switzerland 2015
P. P. A. Funari, M. X. Senatore (eds.), *Archaeology of Culture Contact and Colonialism in Spanish and Portuguese America*, DOI 10.1007/978-3-319-08069-7_11

## 11.2   The Historical Context

The seventeenth century consolidated the Portuguese colonization in the Amazonia, through the building of fortresses, the expulsion of other European invaders, and missionary activity.

The first reference of the region of Santarém and its big indigenous village was done by Carvajal (1941), during the travel of Francisco de Orellana to Amazonia from 1540 to 1542. In 1639, Cristobal Acuña (1941) described the site as a place of imprisonment of Tapajó Indians. A few decades later, in 1661, a Jesuitic reduction was established in this area (Gomes 2002, p. 155). Besides the local Tapajó population, this reduction received Amerindians from distinct regions of Amazonia, which resulted in a multiethnic indigenous population. Its economy was based on the extraction of forest vegetal products, such as cocoa, vanilla, urucu, Brazilian nut, salsaparrilla, and clove. In 1697 the Portuguese Crown built, on the top of a hill located to the east of the village, the Fortress of the Tapajós river, which became one of the major defensive posts in the Amazonia (Betendorf 1909, p. 470).

In 1755 the Portuguese Crown founded the General Trade Company of Grão-Pará and Maranhão, with the major goal of commercializing the Amazonian products in Europe. This was also the beginning of African slavery in Amazonia. In 1759, as a result of a reformist politics of colonization headed by the Marques de Pombal, the indigenous slavery was prohibited in the Portuguese America, and the Jesuits were expulsed from Portugal and its colonies. The Jesuitic reductions were transformed in villages and the inter-racial marriage between Amerindians and white colonizers started to be stimulated as a strategy to integrate the Amerindians in the civilization (Oliveira 1988, pp. 83–88).

In the middle of the eighteenth century the village of Santarém was described as comprising two spatially segregated population groups, the Portuguese and the Amerindian. This division was kept during the next century, when several travelers described it. During this time, the city was spread between the Fortress of the Tapajós river and the Main Church, built in 1761 (Fig. 11.1). The indigenous village was located to the west, beyond the church (Daniel 2004, p. 397).Spix and Martius, two

**Fig. 11.1** Image of Santarém painted by Hercules Florence in 1977. In the *background* is the main church and the indigenous village in the *west*

German natural scientists who visited Santarém in 1819, informed about the population composition. According to them, around 2000 people lived in the urban center, and 2000 more in the district, which involved an area of 15 square leagues. There was a large number of white men, some of them married to indigenous women. This predominance of white men is explained by the authors as due to the stimulus that lower class Portuguese received from the Crown to immigrate to the region, to work in plantations using the easily available indigenous labor (Spix and Martius 1981, p. 99).

A few years later another European traveler, the French Hercules Florence, visited Santarém, describing the five groups who lived in the region: whites, Amerindians, mamelucos (people with mixed African and Amerindian ascendence), mulatoes, and negroes. One half of the white people was born in Portugal. He observed that negroes and mulatoes composed a minority group in the province, due to the late introduction of African slavery in the region (Florence 1977).

In the middle of the 1870s the Lieutenant of the Imperial Army, Rufino Luiz Tavares, described Santarém as the most populous and commercial city in the province of Pará. The city then received all sort of European and North American imports, coming from the port of Belém, the capital of the Province of Pará. It exported, in change, rubber, cocoa, fish, beef, leather, salsaparrilla, Brazilian nuts, copaiba oil, and clove. Tavares estimated the houses in the city to be in 300s. The upper classes lived in two floor houses. The city population composed of 1837 free people and 467 slaves (Tavares 1876, p. 12).

## 11.3   Cultural Meetings, Identities, and Material Culture

As exposed above, Santarém was the setting of cultural encounters practically since the beginning of the European colonization in Amazonia. In the sixteenth and seventeenth centuries these encounters promoted ethnocide, forced reallocation of indigenous populations, and ethnogeneses. New cultural configurations, thus, started to be formed as a product of the exchanges between Portuguese, Portuguese–Brazilians, Amerindians, mestizos, and, in a lower scale, Africans. Multiple identities emerged from this process, which cannot be purely reduced to the colonizer–colonized dichotomy.

In historical archaeology, the thematic of cultural encounters was, during a long time, approached through the traditional model of acculturation developed in the culturalist North American anthropology during the first half of the twentieth century (Cusick 1988). This model was based on a view of cultures as circumscribed entities, characterized by a specific set of features, which included from the technology to the cosmology, named cultural traits. In the archaeological studies this process was investigated considering the gradual substitution of a native material culture by that one produced by the colonizers (Cusick 1988, p. 131). This model presents obvious fails, which concern, primarily, to the equalization of artifacts with cultures, so that changes in the first ones directly reflected changes in the last ones.

In the last decade, studies in contexts of multicultural interaction brought about a growing perception that composite identities emerge as a result of the negotiations between the local agency and the colonial structures (Stein 2005, p. 28). In

historical archaeology it was the studies in contexts of African occupation, mainly in plantations, that made archaeologists search for models that could explain
the emergence of new cultural configurations involving, on one side, the African
cultural diversity and, on the other, the exchanges and mutual influences between
this diversified group, the Europeans, and the Amerindian populations. Scholars, thus, start to adopt the correlate models of creolization, transculturation, and
ethnogeneses (Delle 2000; Ferguson 1992; Singleton 1998). These models consider
the cultural exchanges between distinct groups and societies as bidirectional, so
that Euro-descendant groups are as much impacted by these exchanges as African-
descents and indigenous groups. In the same way, the adoption of the colonizers'
material culture by the colonized populations is not seen as indicating a passive
adoption of the cultural features of the first ones, since the last ones can use these
items according to their own cultural references, giving to them new uses and meanings that can have little, if any, identification with those original meanings given by
the colonizers (Ferguson 1992; Howson 1990; Wilkie 2000).

On the other side, scholars influenced by post-colonial theory have considered
that the hybridism that characterizes the emergence of colonial identities challenges
the conception of culture itself as a circumscribed entity, which determines the behavior of its carriers (Gruzinski 2001, p. 48). According to Gosden (2001, p. 243),
this hybrid nature of colonial cultures makes it clear that all participants in this configuration, as much the colonizers as the colonized, will have some kind of influence
on the structures of power, domination, and resistance that arise from this configuration. This fact turns it more complex to use dichotomies like colonizer/colonized and
dominant/dominated. Aligned with this perspective, Gruzinski (2001, pp. 48–52)
adopts the notion of mestizage to refer to the mixtures that occurred in the Americas,
since the sixteenth century, between human beings, imaginaries, and lifeways, as a
product of the contact between Amerindians, Europeans, Africans, and Asians. According to him, this process is as much objective, being observed in several kinds of
sources, as subjective, implying the consciousness that these past actors had about
what was going on. This consciousness can be expressed "…in the manipulations
that they dedicated themselves, in the constructions elaborated, as well as in the discourses and condemnations formulated by them" (Gruzinski 2001, p. 62).

This recognition of colonial configurations as products of the agency of all actors
involved in this process is, indeed, a great advance over the theoretical models that
highlight only the perspective of the politically dominant (Orser 1996; Funari et al.
1999). Nevertheless, it must be taken into account that such a position risks minimiz-
ing the brutal impact of colonialism over the native populations, underestimating the
fact that these populations did not have the choice of avoiding the conquest, rather they
were, after all, victims of this process. Among the deleterious consequences of this
process in the Americas, Hill (1998, p. 166) highlights the demographic collapses, the
forced reallocations, the slavery, the epidemics, and the ethnic recruitment. Therefore,
asymmetrical power relations between the actors involved in cultural contact situations
must be considered in all circumstances. Material culture has a determinant role in this
process, as Gosden (2004, p. 03) affirms, since the power emanates from the colonial
centers much more through the artifacts and practices related to them than through the
economic or military superiority. In colonial contexts this material culture challenges
the traditional values impacting everyone involved, not only natives but also colonizers.

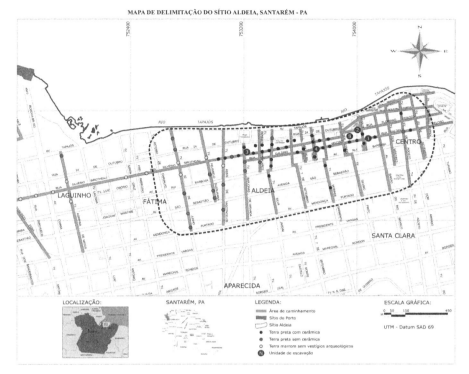

Fig. 11.2  Plan of Santarém indicating the unities 2, 4, and 8

## 11.4  The Archaeological Context

Denise Gomes carried out the first systematic excavations in the urban site of Aldeia, in Santarém, in 2008 and 2010 (Gomes, 2006, 2008, 2010). The goal was to understand the processes of formation of the pre-colonial site, with special attention to ceremonial contexts related to the Tapajó pottery. The excavation comprehended 8 spatially distinct areas, located in 4 domestic backyards, 2 commercial establishments, and 2 wastelands. In each area was excavated a unity measuring $2 \times 2$ m, totalizing 32 m$^2$ of excavations, which extended between 1 m and 2.50 m deep. The unities 2, 4, and 8 revealed, in their upper layers, a dense historical occupation, expressed in the thick archaeological upper layers, presenting sherds of tin-glazed earthenwares, refined earthenwares, glasses, pottery made by wheel, and coiled low-fired pottery. This historical component was a product of domestic activities of the eighteenth- and nineteenth-century households that existed in these areas.

The unities 2, 4, and 8 are located in the backyards of downtown houses (Fig. 11.2). Both presented trash pits composed of tin glazed wares, refined earthenwares, coiled low fired earthenwares, wheeled earthenwares, glass, and iron artifacts. The unity 4 is located in the boundaries between downtown and the neighborhood named Aldeia. It also presented a trash pit with historical material from the eighteenth and nineteenth centuries. The trash pits in these three unities were filled with dark soil. Under and around these features there were evidences of the pre-colonial Tapajó component, represented by concentrations of pottery sherds.

These pits represent a feature designed to dispose the domestic garbage of the residences, also found in the city of Porto Alegre and other urban contexts of the nineteenth century in Brazil, being related to the hygienic ideology (Symanski 1998, pp. 154–164; Tocchetto 2005, pp. 252–298). Similar features were excavated, in Santarém, in 2011, demonstrating the existence of indigenous pits for domestic garbage.

## 11.5 Households, Material Culture, and Social Hierarchies

Travelers accounts point to remarkable changes in material life and social practices of Santarém's elite during the second half of the nineteenth century. In 1819, Spix and Martius described the city houses as predominantly built of adobe and white painted. They were composed of numerous rooms, being usual multifamilial composites. The backyards had a detached kitchen, as well as isolated rooms for the house laborers, a function predominantly exerted by Amerindians and rarely by negroes and mulatoes. The domestic furniture was also very modest, represented by wooden chairs and cotton hammocks installed in the living rooms (Spix and Martius 1981, pp. 98–99).

In the second half of the nineteenth century, many of those houses had given space to two and three pavement houses, strongly built with stone wall or adobe (Bates 1944, pp. 7–9). These houses presented living rooms that contained a sofa and a set of sophisticated wooden chairs, painted in gold, and arranged in the form of a square. The chairs arrangement composed a traditional pattern in the nineteenth century living rooms in urban Brazil (Kidder 1941, p. 189; Reis Filho 1995, p. 128; Symanski 1998, pp. 81–82). Bates also observed the presence of several commercial houses, which sold British, French, German, and North American products.

According to Bates (1944, p. 11), during this period, white Portuguese and Brazilians composed the most numerous group in Santarém. This group was composed of traders, cattle farmers, cocoa and rubber planters, civil and military authorities. Bates described these elite as emulators of fashions and customs from the court, as a result of the steamship navigation in the Amazonas river, which had started in 1853.

Indeed, Bates' description of the visit rooms of Santarém houses as presenting furniture typologically similar and in the same spatial organization to that found in the elite houses from the biggest Brazilian urban centers during this period, suggests that the owners of the houses tried to adopt similar sociability practices common among the elites of those urban centers. These elite were then influenced by a Western European ideal of domesticity initially adopted in the city of Rio de Janeiro during the 1820s (Queiroz 1978, p. 58; Lima 1999). Nevertheless, the archaeological record, as will be further discussed, suggests that this cultural influence was balanced

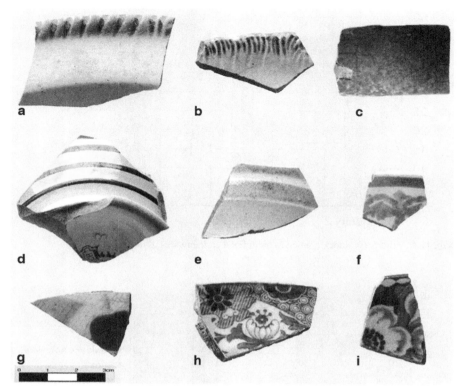

**Fig. 11.3** Refined earthenwares representative of Miller's Index (1980). Minimally-decorated: **a** shell edged green, **b** shell edged blue, **c** blue spatterware, **d** dipped ware, polychromic banded, **e** dipped ware, blue banded, **f** cut sponge; hand painted, **g** peasant style; transfer-printed, **h** unidentified floral pattern in blue, **i** unidentified floral pattern in cobalt blue

in the local sphere by some more traditional lifeways kept by these groups, indicating that the ideal of domesticity was not uniformly adopted, but subjected to some kinds of selective incorporation and even amalgamation with local practices and traditions.

The comparison of refined earthenware assemblages from the unities 2, 4, and 8, using both Miller's Economic Scale (the CC Index) (Miller 1980, 1991) and morphological variables point to significant differences in these households' material life, probably related to socioeconomic status, cultural practices, and gender (Fig. 11.3).

Regarding the CC Index, unities 2 and 8 presented a larger proportion of hand painted and transfer print wares in comparison with the more peripheral unity 4, indicating that the inhabitants of the two former houses invested in domestic items of higher economic value than those ones from the last house (Fig. 11.4). The presence of a porcelain saucer and an ornamental porcelain object in the unity 8 are other indications of this higher investment, since porcelain wares had the highest economic value among the ware categories.

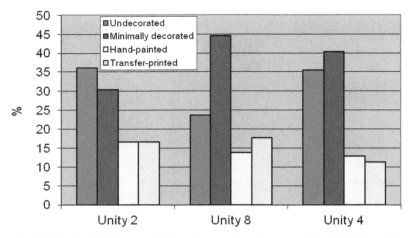

**Fig. 11.4** Miller's CC Index applied to the refined earthenwares of unities 2, 8, and 4

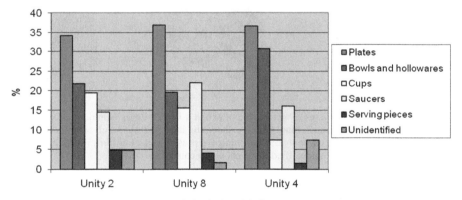

**Fig. 11.5** Refined earthenwares morphological variability. Unities 2, 8, and 4

The morphological variability also indicates clear differences in the use-patterns of refined earthenwares. These differences point to a more sophisticated material behavior in the households 2 and 8 (Fig. 11.5). These two unities not only presented a higher proportion of tea wares, but also a more balanced distribution between cups and saucers. Unity 4, in turn, presented a strong disproportion between cups and saucers favoring the saucers, indicating that these last pieces had been much more intensely used than the former ones, and thus must have been subjected to multiple uses, differently from the unities 2 and 8, where saucers must have had only a specific use: to support cups. The presence of tea pots in these two last assemblages is other indication of a functional segmentation regarding tea (and probably other hot beverages) consumption.

The higher proportion of serving pieces in the unities 2 and 8 is another indication of higher expenses with refined earthenwares, since serving pieces are much more expensive than those ones used to consume food, like plates and bowls. This pattern also indicates the segmentation of meals, through the exposition of foods and beverages on the table in specific containers, whereas in the unity 4 the foods were directly served from the low-fired local earthenwares, where they had been prepared. In addition, there is a very clear distinction in the bowls' popularity in these assemblages. Bowls are pieces used predominantly in the consumption of soups and stews. The unity 4 indicates a preference for this kind of meal, whereas in the unities 2 and 8 apparently the consumption of solid foods, probably using cutlery, was also significant, at least in special occasions. This discussion will be retaken further.

The higher socioeconomic status of the households 2 and 8, therefore, is expressed by the site locations in the upper class city region, in the use of more expensive wares, and in the higher complexity in the use-patterns of these pieces. Nevertheless, it must be noted that these assemblages do not indicate typical bourgeois lifeways, similar to those ones that were spreading in urban Brazil during the nineteenth century, which are archaeologically characterized by the presence of expensive tea and dinner sets in transfer print refined earthenwares and in porcelain. These Santarém elite-households assemblages, on the other side, did not present dinner or tea sets, and only a very low frequency of porcelain. This modest material behavior, thus, must be understood considering the local scale sociability practices.

The austerity in the domestic material life that characterizes these Portuguese and Portuguese-Brazilian Santarém households is probably related to the gender dimension. The Portuguese immigration to Brazil in the nineteenth century was strongly marked by the male predominance, well noticed by Spix and Martius (1819) and Florence (1977) in Santarém. In his classic book Casa Grande e Senzala (Mansions and Shantytowns) Gilberto Freyre (2004) already noticed that those areas in Brazil colonized by Portuguese couples had a much stronger European influence than the other ones (like Santarém) where Portuguese men espoused local women.

## 11.5.1  Mestizage, Foodways, and Material Ambiguities

In Santarém mixed households, composed by Portuguese men and indigenous or mestizo women, were very usual as attested by the high number of people classified as mameluco—a regional skin color classification for people of mixed European and indigenous ascendance. In northern Brazil the biological mestizage process was intensified since 1755, when Marquise of Pombal prohibited indigenous slavery and promoted a legislation that stimulated the marriage between the white and Amerindians, aiming to integrate the last ones in the civilization (Oliveira 1988, pp. 83–88). Florence (1977, p. 329) gave the following description of Santarém mestizos:

The mamelucos class is born from the inter-breeding between white men and indigenous women. Following habits more or less indigenous, they have a clearer skin color. Their language, however, is the same. In general women are very silent (…). They carry, around their necks, necklaces and gold relics, a metal that also shines in their ears, as well as in their long black tresses. They are always barefooted.

Mixed households were, indeed, very usual in Hispanic America, and the same must have occurred in Portuguese America, principally in northern Brazil, where the indigenous component was demographically dominant still in the nineteenth century. Archaeological research in Hispanic-American households has revealed that the evidences related to women agency, regarding household management, food processing, cooking, and pottery production, are predominantly represented by Amerindian or mixed, Euro-African-Amerindian, features (Deagan 2003, pp. 7–8). Souza (2002) observed a similar situation in eighteenth century households assemblages of Ouro Fino, a gold mining village in Goiás, Central Brazil. In this case, low-fired earthenwares, used by enslaved women to cook food in the kitchen spaces, presented incised decoration with Western African influence, whereas men used decorated tin-glazed earthenwares in the houses' sociability areas.

In Santarém households, these mixtures, beyond the nuclear family, also included the co-resident domestic laborers, who were almost exclusively indigenous in the early nineteenth century (Spix and Martius 1981, pp. 98–99). These domestic laborers lived in isolated quarters in the houses' backyards. In this sense, the archaeological record of the households under study, rather than an exclusive product of the white, Portuguese and Portuguese Brazilian component, is, in fact, the product of multiple group practices, which included white men, indigenous or mestizo wifes, whites and/or mestizo sons and daughters, and indigenous or mestizo domestic laborers. In this caldron, bodies and practices interbreed, resulting in an ambiguous archaeological record, indicative of practices and aspirations of European and indigenous influence.

Similar to Hispanic-American colonial households, locally-made low-fired earthenware, almost exclusively coiled, made according to indigenous technology, is an omnipresent material category in Santarém households, representing, in the households studied, between 9 and 12 % of the domestic ceramic assemblages (Fig. 11.6). Bates (1944, p. 42) described this local pottery production in the middle of nineteenth century, observing that it was made with white clay, from a source located to the east of Santarém. An antiplastic was added to this clay, called caraipé, made of the ashes from the crust of a siliceous tree (Licania turuiva).

This pottery artisanal production was an exclusive female occupation, just like the domestic activities of food processing and cooking. Although both the manufacture and antiplastic technologies used in this pottery production are indigenous, it must be noted that they represent a choice made during the historic period, since Santarém pre-colonial pottery present very distinctive characteristics. In this last case, the antiplastic applied to the clay was cauixi, sponge spicules of riverine water, mixed with crushed sherd (Gomes 2002, 2008; Guapindaia 1993).

Although there is no evidence pointing to a household production of low-fired earthenware in these sites, the manipulation of these pieces was, indeed, done by

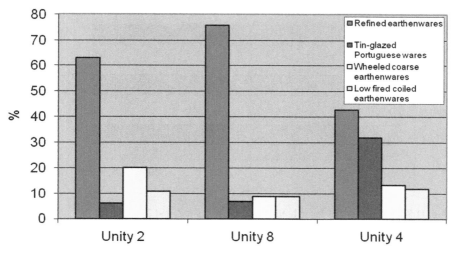

**Fig. 11.6** Earthenware categories (refined earthenware, tin-glazed Portuguese ware, wheeled coarse earthenware, low-fired coiled earthenware). Unities 2, 8, and 4

**Fig. 11.7** The four most popular ware types in Santarém households: **a** coiled low-fired earthenware pan, decorated with a fingered thread close to the rim, **b** storage vessel sherd in wheeled coarse earthenware, **c** tin-enameled Portuguese earthenware, **d** refined earthenware, green shell edged

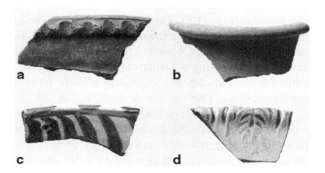

indigenous or mestizo women, in the backyard kitchens. Cook pans represent the most popular shape in these assemblages. These pans usually have as decoration just a narrow fingered or entailed thread, applied close to the rim (Fig. 11.7).

As can be seen in Fig. 11.6, wheel made pottery is also present in the assemblages, in proportions varying between 8.7 and 20 %. Differently from low-fired coiled earthenwares, wheeled pottery was made in specialized factories, and can be indicative of regional, or even national, interaction spheres. These pieces are mostly in storage jars shapes. There is, thus, a well established functional dichotomy between artisanal coiled low-fired earthenware cooking pans and factories wheeled pottery, used to store liquids and foods.

Other characteristic of these assemblages is the high popularity of hollow wares, mostly bowls, which are related basically to the consumption of soups and stews. As discussed, these shapes are more popular in the unity 4, which apparently suggest a

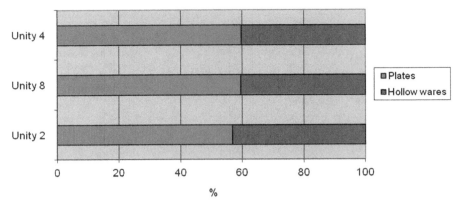

**Fig. 11.8** Proportion of plates to hollow wares. Unities 4, 8, and 2

greater emphasis in the consumption of boiled foods in this house. However, when the frequencies of plates and hollow wares are contrasted in the three unities, it indicates that this last category represents around 50 % of food consumption wares in all the cases. This data indicates that the consumption of boiled food was very intense in Santarém (Fig. 11.8). This high proportion of hollow wares disagrees with the morphological variability usually verified in Brazil nineteenth century urban contexts, where flatwares, basically plates, tend to dominate over the other functional categories, indicating a higher consumption of solid foods, generally eaten with cutlery in individual plates, consonant with the individualist ideology of industrial capitalism (Lima 1999; Symanski 1998, p. 208; 2002).

As Appadurai (1981, p. 494) reminds, foodways consist in a basic component of individual and group identity, which can serve as much to build social relationships based on equality, intimacy, and solidarity, as to sustain relationships characterized by hierarchy, distance, and segmentation. It must be taken into account that even individuals and groups materially deprived have the possibility of making choices concerning the preparation and consumption of foods, which makes the foodways domain a fundamental locus of identity, conformity, and resistance (Smith 2006, p. 480). In the case of Santarém, the great proportion of hollow wares in all the unities studied evidences the maintenance of traditional foodways, based on the consumption of soups and stews, directly taken from these pieces, without using cutlery. These foodways had roots both in the Portuguese peasant society of the Ancient Regime and in the Amazonic indigenous societies.

In Western Europe of the Ancient Regime, stews constituted the peasants essential meal (1998, p. 593). The same was true for the Portuguese peasants. In colonial Brazil, Cascudo (1983, p. 593) observes that stews, consumed in bowls, arrived together with the Portuguese colonizers. In the case of the indigenous amazonic societies, though roasted food dominated, boiled foods were also of usual consumption, particularly the porridge prepared with manioc flour and the meat and fish stews (Cascudo 1983, p. 149). Stews are still very popular in the traditional amazonic culinary, as is the case of tacaca, a shrimp boiled meal prepared with manioc.

Therefore, the high proportion of hollow wares in Santarém households point to an interesting convergence of Portuguese and indigenous foodways, in which boiled foods acted as a common denominator, linking very distinctive cultural universes. Gruzinski (2001, p. 48), when discussing the issue of mestizage in colonial America, criticizes the trend to polarize two blocks usually seen as impermeable: the victimized Amerindians and the villain Europeans. According to him, this dichotomy immobilizes and simplifies a very complex reality, insofar as it disregards the exchanges between these groups, and, moreover, the role of those intermediary individuals and groups, who had the ability of transiting between these two blocks. He affirms that mediatory spaces had an essential role in the colonization process, because these are the spaces where new ways of thought can emerge and develop. These ways of thought have the ability to transform and criticize the authenticity of both heritages—European and Amerindian. In the case of Santarém, the archaeological record indicates the kitchen as one of these major mediatory spaces. It was in the kitchen that the indigenous and mestizo women, supervised by housewives—most of these last ones also mestizos—processed and cooked food. These meals, in turn, were prepared in low-fired local earthenware pottery that had been made by other indigenous and/or mestizo women. Therefore, all these women acted as intermediary agents in this cultural exchange process that resulted in the rich northern Brazilian culture, which has in the culinary, one of its more remarkable features.

Groover (1994), in his study of multicultural households in a frontier context in South Caroline (USA), noticed that the socially visible material culture, represented by the architecture and the artifacts used in formal meals, reflected the colonizers' traditions, whereas the low visibility material culture tended to exhibit a synthesis of cultural traditions, involving African and Amerindian agents. In Santarém, as already discussed, most of the low visibility material culture, like the low-fired earthenware pans, is linked to female acting spheres, principally in the kitchen spaces. These pieces, therefore, show as much culinary and cultural mixtures, as segregation, the frontiers between domestic living spaces and kitchen, between men and women, and between whites and non-whites.

One would expect that these inequalities in the domestic space could also have been expressed in the foodways domain, with house owners favoring solid meals eaten in individualized plates, using cutlery, according to the bourgeois habits spread in Brazil at the time, instead of the more traditional boiled meals. In this case, this situation should be materially attested by a possible dichotomy between more expensive—porcelain or transfer printed—plates, used by house owners, and cheaper—white and minimally decorated—bowls, used by house laborers. However, in the assemblages studied, these two tableware functional categories presented little differences in terms of economic value, suggesting that the consumption of both, solid and boiled meals, was generalized between these two sociocultural groups (Fig. 11.9). This convergence in the foodways domain point to a possible ambiguity in the domestic sphere power relations, since it apparently suggests, following Appadurai (1981, p. 496) propositions, an effort to the maintenance of social relations based on equality, intimacy, and solidarity, rather than the hierarchy, distance, and segmentation that truly marked the relationships between the white house owners and the indigenous or mestizo house laborers.

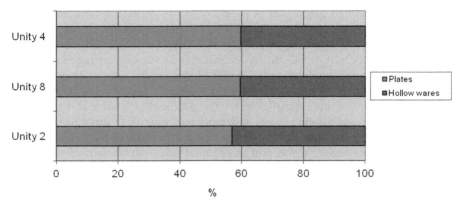

**Fig. 11.9** Miller's Index plates and hollow wares. Unities 2, 8, and 4

## 11.5.2 Inequalities and Cultural Choices

Although the similarities between the Santarém household assemblages suggest the conformation of a culturally mestizo local elite, some other evidences call attention to the maintenance of socio-cultural boundaries practiced as much in the interior of the domestic spaces as among them.

The domain of the major meals, predominantly done using cheap tableware, apparently does not express hierarchy and segmentation, nevertheless, the social inequalities in these households are more clear-cut in the domain of the teawares. Contrary to the dinner, a male domain, the social consumption of tea became, in the seventeenth century Europe, a female domain, having its own rules and etiquettes. In the eighteenth century Rio de Janeiro the elites and middle social segments incorporated the tea social consumption, which became, like in Europe, a sphere of female acting, although executed according to some local rules and habits (Lima 1997).

In Santarém households teawares are the domestic items that presented the highest social visibility, being the pieces of highest economic value present in the assemblages (Fig. 11.10). In the unity 8 this trend appears to be less clearly expressed because the porcelain teawares present in this assemblage are not included in the graph data. This higher significance of teawares demonstrates that frontiers in social practices between house owners and house laborers—or more probably between housewives and female house laborers—are more evident in this domain than in the dinner.

The differences among the assemblages, in turn, suggest that the occupants of unity 4 kept more conservative practices and cultural references than those ones who lived in the unities 2 and 8, which can be indicative of a stronger indigenous influence in that household. This is manifested by the presence of a manioc toaster, made using indigenous technology but presenting a decorated pattern of historical times. The antiplastic applied in this piece was cauixi—the sponge spicules of riverine water that characterized the pre-colonial Tapajó pottery industry. This piece

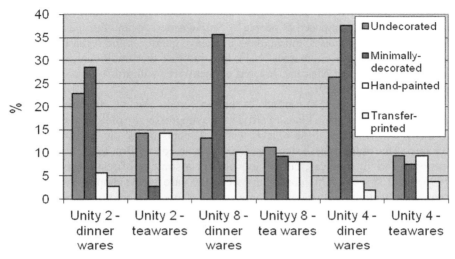

**Fig. 11.10** Miller's Index dinner wares and teawares. Unities 2, 8, and 4

**Table 11.1** Proportion of cut sponge to dipped banded refined earthenwares

| Unity | Cut sponge (%) | Dipped banded (%) |
|---|---|---|
| 2 | 0 | 4.9 |
| 8 | 0.8 | 4 |
| 4 | 5.9 | 5.9 |

was used to prepare manioc flour, a very typical indigenous food served as an accompaniment of all kinds of food among the amazonic indigenous people (Cascudo 1983, p. 104). It is possible, therefore, that the people who lived in the unity 4 kept some elements of an indigenous ancestral memory, linked to the preparation of manioc flour in toasters still made according to the local pre-colonial tradition. This same pattern was also found in two other unities more recently studied, the unities 5 and 7.

In the unity 4, refined earthenwares presented a higher proportion of cut sponge and dipped banded decorated hollow wares (Table 11.1).

Regarding the dipped wares, Otto (1984, p. 65) observes that pieces presenting this type of decoration had a particular appeal to traditional populations, like African agricultural peoples and enslaved African-Americans. Indeed, hollow wares presenting this decorative pattern are common in African-American sites in the United States and Caribbean. In the same way, cut sponge decorated wares also had a similar appeal among some traditional populations in North America. Cabak and Loring (2000, p. 23) notice that these refined earthenwares are very popular in the sites of Labrador that were occupied by the Inuit during the second half of the nineteenth and the beginning of the twentieth century. They have noted also that, in a sample of more than 500 historical sites around the Savanna river, southeast of the United States, earthenwares decorated in that way are extremely rare, except in the site Rancho Punta de Agua, in Tucson, Arizona, which was occupied by a mixed household, composed of people of Native American and European heritage. For the Brazilian contexts, the findings in a slave quarter in the Água Fria plantation, in Chapada dos Guimarães (MT), also indicate that traditional populations, in this case, enslaved Africans, favored earthenwares with this type of decoration (Symanski, 2006, p. 229).

Kearney (1996, p. 158) reminds us that, in certain contexts, the utilitarian and economic values of some kinds of artifacts are suppressed by the signal value given to them, which makes these objects active elements of identity affirmation. According to the author, these symbols, when consumed, reaffirm the consumer class identity, who, in this way, consumes value as a strategy of resistance (Kearney, 1996, pp. 168–169). This could have been the case of the dipped ware and cut sponge of the unity 4. By having a more aesthetic appeal for traditional populations, it is likely that indigenous and mestizos who lived in this unity privileged these earthenwares over those ones favored by the Portuguese-Brazilians, as the transfer-printed wares, which expressed Western European aesthetics and values. These earthenwares, therefore, may represent the mestizo world view of the occupants of the unity 4, which could be expected in a mixed household, owned by a Portuguese man married to an indigenous woman. By choosing earthenwares decorated in this way, which were used to consume meals cooked in ceramic vessels of indigenous influence, these individuals could be reinforcing values that were very distinctive from those ones expressed by colonizers' worldview.

## 11.6   Final Remarks

Two opposite domains, the first expressing conflict and difference, and the other ambiguity, mixtures, and mestizage, are simultaneously expressed in Santarém's domestic material culture. In the households studied, teawares represented the most socially visible items, which presented the highest economic value. Locally-made low-fired earthenware, in turn, were located in the less visible domain, that one of domestic female labor related to the preparation of meals in the spatially segregated kitchens.

Differences are also noted between the elite households (unities 2 and 8), and the more peripheral one (unity 4). People who occupied the first ones were more concerned in having more expensive domestic items, like porcelain pieces, European transfer-printed refines earthenwares, teawares, and serving pieces, whereas those ones living in unity 4 kept a larger number of cheaper, white, and minimally decorated, refined earthenwares, with a higher proportion of bowls. Thus, distinct values and identities were expressed through the use of material culture in these households, values linked, on one side, to a Portuguese-Brazilian elite and, on the other, to a group who kept more traditional indigenous and mestizos references.

It must be noted that ambiguity is an omnipresent characteristic in these households' material culture. It is particularly expressed in the great popularity of hollow wares, related to the consumption of boiled meals, in the three unities studied. These pieces seem to have been indiscriminately used by all groups who composed this society, whites, mestizos, Amerindians, house owners and employers, men and women, in a fusion, conducted by indigenous and mestizo women, between the Portuguese and indigenous culinary traditions. Besides the consumption of imported, European items, this population also produced new artifacts, that emerged from the exchanges between Amerindians, Portuguese, and, in a lower scale, Africans. This was the case of the locally-made low-fired earthenwares, used to process and cook food, present in significant numbers in the three households studied. In this sense, both European imported wares and locally-made wares were used to negotiate, as well as to affirm, contrasting and ambiguous identities.

The concept of mestizage seems to express very well the processes of cultural contact and identities fusion that occurred in Santarém during the eighteenth and nineteenth centuries. This approach, rather than victimizing Amerindian and African populations, highlights their agency capacity in front of the colonial power. Moreover, it tries to reveal the role of those cultural brokers who transited between these two apparently impermeable spheres and, in this way, had the ability to connect these opposite worlds, creatively extracting from the conflicts, differences, exploration, and resistance inherent to these cultural encounters, a new world.

# References

Acuña, C. (1941). Novo descobrimento do Grande Rio das Amazonas. In C. Leitão (Ed.), *Rojas, Carvajal & Acuña. Descobrimentos do Rio das Amazonas*. São Paulo: Companhia Editora Nacional.

Appadurai, A. (1981). Gastro-politics in hindu South Asia. *American Ethnologist, 8*(3), 494–511.

Bates, H. (1944). *O naturalista no Rio das Amazonas*. São Paulo: Companhia Editora Nacional.

Betendorf, J. (1909). Chronica da missão dos padres da Companhia de Jesus no Estado do Maranhão. *Revista do Instituto Histórico e Geográfico Brasileiro, 72*.

Cabak, M., & Loring, S. (2000). A set of very fair cups and saucers: Stamped ceramics as an example of Inuit incorporation. *International Journal of Historical Archaeology, 4*(1), 1–34.

Cascudo, L. C. (1983). *História da alimentação no Brasil*. Belo Horizonte: Itatiaia.

Carvajal, G. (1941). Relação do novo descobrimento do famoso Rio Grande que descobriu por grande ventura o Capitão Francisco de Orellana. In C. Leitão (Ed.), *Rojas, Carvajal & Acuñã, Descobrimentos do Rio das Amazonas* (pp. 11–19). São Paulo: Companhia Editora Nacional.

Cusik, J. (1998). Historiography of acculturation: An evaluation of concepts and their application in archaeology. In J. Cusik (Ed.), *Studies in culture contact—interaction, culture change, and archaeology* (pp. 126–145) Carbondale: Center for Archaeological Investigations.

Daniel, J. (2004). *Tesouro descoberto no máximo Rio Amazonas*. Rio de Janeiro: Contraponto.

Deagan, K. (2003). Colonial origins and colonial transformations in Spanish America. *Historical Archaeology, 37*(4), 3–13.

Delle, J. (2000). The material and cognitive dimensions of creolization in nineteenth-century Jamaica. *Historical Archaeology, 34*(3), 56–72.

Ferguson, L. (1992). *Uncommon ground: Archaeology and early African America, 1650-1800*. Washington, D.C.: Smithsonian Institution Press.

Florence, H. (1977). Viagem fluvial do Tietê ao Amazonas de 1825 a 1829. São Paulo: Museu de Arte de São Paulo Assis Chateaubriad.

Florentino, M., & Machado, C. (2002). Ensaio sobre a imigração portuguesa e os padrões de miscigenação no Brasil (séculos XIX e XX). *Portuguese Studies Review*, 1:58–84.

Freyre, G. (2004). *Sobrados e mucambos*. São Paulo: Global Editora.

Funari, P., Hall, M., Jones, S. (1999). Introduction: archaeology in history. In P. Funari, M. Hall, S. Jones (Eds.) *Historical archaeology: back from the edge* (pp. 1–20). London: Routledge.

Gomes, D. M. C. (2002). *Cerâmica arqueológica da Amazônia: vasilhas da coleção Tapajônica do MAE-USP*. São Paulo: Edusp/Fapesp/Imprensa Oficial.

Gomes, D. M. C. (2006). Identificação de sítios arqueológicos da cultura Santarém na área central da cidade de Santarém, PA. Final report presented to IPHAN.

Gomes, D. M. C. (2008). Relatório da etapa de campo relativa à escavação do Sítio Aldeia—Santarém, PA. Projeto, de Pós-Doutorado: Cronologia e contexto cerimonial da cultura Santarém. Partial report presented to IPHAN, 2008

Gomes, D. M. C. (2010). Análise das Sócio-cosmologias amazônicas pré-coloniais. Partial report presented to FAPESP, 2010. Unpublished.

Gosden, C. (2001). Post-colonial archaeology: Issues of culture, identity, and knowledge. In I. Hodder (Ed.), *Archaeological theory today* (pp. 241–261). Malden: Blackwell Publishers.

Gosden, C. (2004). *Archaeology and colonialism: Cultural contact from 5000 BC to the present*. Cambridge: Cambridge University Press.

Groover, M. (1994). Evidence for folkways and cultural exchange in the 18th century South Carolina. Backcountry. *Historical Archaeology, 28*(1), 41–64.

Gruzinski, S. (2001). *O pensamento mestiço*. São Paulo: Companhia das Letras.

Guapinda, V. (1993). Fontes históricas e arqueológicas sobre os Tapajó: a coleção Frederico Barata do Museu Paraense Emílio Goeldi. Recife: Universidade Federal de Pernambuco, Master thesis.

Hill, J. (1998). Violent enconters: Ethnogenesis and ethnocide in long term contact situations. In J. Cusick (Ed.) *Studies in culture contact—interaction, culture change, and archaeology* (pp. 146–171). Carbondale: Center for Archaeological Investigations.

Howson, J. (1990). Social relations and material culture: A critique of the archaeology of plantation slavery. *Historical Archaeology, 34*(2), 78–91.

Kearney, M. (1996). *Reconceptualizing the peasantry: Anthropology in global perspective*. Boulder: Westview Press.

Kidder, D. (1941). *O Brasil e os brasileiros*. São Paulo: Companhia Editora Nacional.

Lima, T. (1997). Chá e simpatia: uma estratégia de gênero no Rio de Janeiro oitocentista. *Anais do Museu Paulista: História e Cultura Material, 3*, 93–129.

Lima, T. (1999). El huevo de la serpiente: una arqueología del capitalismo embrionário en el Rio de Janeiro del siglo XIX. In A. Zarankin & F. Acuto (Eds.), *Sed Non Satiata—teorial social em la arqueología latinoamericana* (pp. 189–238). Buenos Aires: Ediciones del Tridente.

Miller, G. (1980). Classification and economic scaling of 19th. century ceramics. *Historical Archaeology, 14*, 1–40.

Miller, G. (1991). A revised set of CC Index values for classification and economic scaling of english ceramics from 1787 to 1880. *Historical Archaeology, 25*(1), 1–25.

Nimuendaju, C. (1948). Os Tapajó. *Boletim do Museu Paraense Emílio Goeld, 10*, 93–106.

Oliveira, A. (1988). Amazônia: Modificações sociais e culturais. Boletim do Museu Paraense Emílio Goeldi. *Série Antropologia, 4*(1), 65–115.

Orser, C. (1996). A historical archaeology of the Modern World. New York: Plenum Press.

Otto, J. S. (1984). *Cannon's point plantation—1794-1860 living conditions and status patterns in the Old South*. Orlando: Academic Press.

Queiroz, M. I. P. (1978). *Cultura, Sociedade rural e sociedade urbana no Brasil*. Rio de Janeiro: Livros Técnicos e Científicos.

Reis Filho, N. G. (1995). *Quadro da arquitetura no Brasil*. São Paulo: Editora Perspectiva.

Roosevelt, A. (1991). Determinismo Ecológico na Interpretação do Desenvolvimento Social Indígena da Amazônia. In W. Neves (Ed.), *Adaptações e diversidade do homem nativo da Amazônia*. Belém: Museu Paraense Emílio Goeldi.

Roosevelt, A. (1992). Arqueologia amazônica. In M. Cunha (Ed.), *História dos índios do Brasil* (pp. 53–86). São Paulo: Companhia das Letras.

Singleton, T. (1998). Cultural interaction and african-american identity in plantation archaeology. In J. Cusick (Ed.), *Studies in culture contact—interaction, culture change, and archaeology* (pp. 172–189). Carbondale: Center for Archaeological Investigations.

Smith, M. (2006). The archaeology of food preference. *American Anthropologist, 108*(3), 480–493.

Souza, M. (2002). Entre práticas e discursos: a construção social do espaço no contexto de Goiás do século XVIII. In A. Zarankin & M. X. Senatore. *Arqueologia da sociedade moderna na América do Sul—cultura material, discursos e práticas* (pp. 63–86). Buenos Aires: Ediciones del Tridente.

Spix, J., & Martius, C. (1981). *Viagem pelo Brasil 1817-1820*. Belo Horizonte: Itatiaia.; São Paulo: Editora da Universidade de São Paulo.

Stein, G. (2005). Introduction: the comparative archaeology of colonial encounters. In S. Stein (Ed.), *The archaeology of colonial encounters—comparative perspectives*, (pp. 3–32). Santa Fe: School of American Research Press.

Symanski, L. (1998). *Espaço privado e vida material em Porto Alegre no século XIX*. Porto Alegre: Edipucrs.

Symanski, L. (2002). Louças e auto-expressão em regiões centrais, adjacentes e periféricas do Brasil. In A. Zarankin & M. X. Senatore (Eds.), *Arqueologia da sociedade moderna na América do Sul–cultura material, discursos e práticas* (pp. 31–62). Buenos Aires: Ediciones del Tridente.

Symanski, L. (2006). *Slaves and planters in Western Brazil: material culture, identity and power*. Doctoral dissertation, Gainesville: Department of Anthropology, University of Florida.

Tavares, R. (1876). *O Rio Tapajoz*. Rio de Janeiro: Typhographia Nacional.

Tocchetto, F. (2005). Joga lá nos fundos!: sobre práticas de descarte de lixo doméstico na Porto Alegre oitocentista. *Arqueología Suramericana, 1*(1), 49–75.

Wilkie, L. (2000). Culture bought: Evidence of creolization in the consumer goods of an enslaved bahamian family. *Historical Archaeology, 34*(3), 10–26.

# Chapter 12
# Modernity at the Edges of the Spanish Enlightenment. Novelty and Material Culture in Floridablanca Colony (Patagonia, Eighteenth Century)

Maria Ximena Senatore

## 12.1 Introduction

The Spanish occupation of the Patagonian Atlantic coast in the late eighteenth century was part of the process of adding new spaces to the Modern Western World, within the frame of colonial expansion. *La Nueva Colonia y Fuerte de Floridablanca* was settled as part of the project of colonization designed by Charles III. This settlement—2000 km away from the Rio de la Plata Viceroyalty headquarters—was inhabited by about 150 people and was active for only 4 years, from 1780 to 1784.

Floridablanca meant the creation of novelty, setting new boundaries for the Modern World. It was a population trial put into practice by the Spanish Enlightenment of the eighteenth century for which reason, order and utopic thought played remarkable roles (Senatore 2007). Floridablanca also appears as the novelty among the ruptures and continuities in the coming about of the Patagonian landscape. The area chosen for this settlement had not been used before for colonial purposes but was inhabited temporarily by the Tehuelche indigenous group (Fig. 12.1).

The purpose of this chapter is to understand how the material and social dimensions of novelty became articulate in the everyday practices in Floridablanca.

## 12.2 Modernity and Novelty

Modernity is not—and never was—either spatially or temporally homogeneous (Thomas 2004, p. 3). Nevertheless, it brought about changes, which transformed ideas and standpoints about the world and produced conceptual schemes inherent to

M. X. Senatore (✉)
IMHICIHU Instituto Multidisciplinario de Historia y Ciencias Humanas CONICET Consejo
Nacional de Investigaciones Científicas y Técnicas, Universidad Nacional de la Patagonia
Austral & Universidad de Buenos Aires, Argentina, Cornelio Saavedra 15 5th Floor, C1083ACA
Ciudad Autónoma de Buenos Aires, Argentina
e-mail: mxsenatore@gmail.com

© Springer International Publishing Switzerland 2015                                    219
P. P. A. Funari, M. X. Senatore (eds.), *Archaeology of Culture Contact and Colonialism
in Spanish and Portuguese America,* DOI 10.1007/978-3-319-08069-7_12

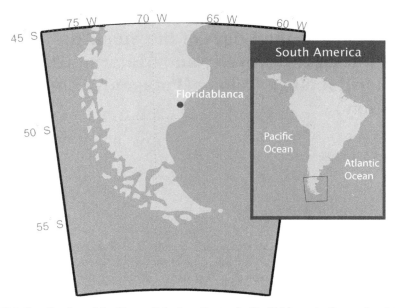

**Fig. 12.1** Localization of La Nueva Colonia y Fuerte de Floridablanca in Patagonian Atlantic Coast

modern society. This can be interpreted as the creation of a new social order, based on new institutions and bearing a new rationale (Giddens and Pearson 1998). It may mean a chronological division from the human experience related to industrialization and capitalism (Kumar 1988; Giddens 1990) but it is characterized by a peculiar philosophical frame and specific ways in which people operate socially (Giddens 1991; Thomas 2004). Modern thought includes and explains everything in terms of a rationale which is unique and which at the same time eliminates the possibility of any other perspective which could lead to a different interpretation of things (Bauman 2007).

The idea of novelty appears as a central aspect of what defines modernity. The term modern refers to an Age presenting a strong relationship to the past as well as appearing as the result of a transition from the old to the new (Habermas 2004). Modernity keeps a dialogue with the past, which is loaded with tension and confrontation. Enlightenment thinkers saw the past as a period inferior to the present, as a time in which reason had been weakly developed (Thomas 2004). By the eighteenth century, there was a growing sense that human beings were bringing about progress, transforming their own conditions of existence by their own actions and the implication of this was not only that the future would be unfamiliar, but that the past would have been unlike the present (Thomas 2004, p. 31). In Appadurai's words "Whatever else the project of Enlightenment may have created, it aspired to create persons who would, after the fact, have wished to have become modern" (Appadurai 2005, p. 1). Hence, modernity implies change, order, and a new relationship past-present and novelty may have taken different social and material shapes and ways in the different contexts of the colonial world.

Studying modernity implies understanding the complex and multiple ways in which the varied axes of social organization—which are still in force in our contemporary societies—were modeled in time and space. The claim here is that understanding the peculiarity of some specific colonial contexts will allow us to approach the complexity of the shaping of the modern world by following the multiple courses it took (Senatore and Zarankin 2002).

## 12.3   New Society in Multiple Shapes

The peculiar characteristics of the plan for the colonization of the Patagonian coast in the late eighteenth century show it as one of the experiments in search of a new type of society inspired in the ideals of Spanish Enlightenment (Senatore 2005). Thus these trials of "new societies" were meant to find solutions to the social problems present in Spain in the late eighteenth century. These problems were basically privileges and land in *manos muertas* that is in the hands of those who did not use them for productive purposes.

The Patagonian plan followed the ideas of Spanish Enlightenment thinkers and previous experiences that had been put into practice in the early eighteenth century in Sierra Morena and Andalucia inside the Iberic Peninsula (Senatore 2007). The pillars of this ideal society were agriculture as the main source of wealth and the mononuclear patriarchal family as the unit of social structuration.

Rigorous planning preceded the creation of the "new society". This planning consisted of different stages and was displayed in great scale. As Thomas (2004) states, in modern projects abstract thought is often considered to precede action and thought and action are conceived as separate events. For instance the planning of towns and the organization of societies is composed in theory before being put into practice, and that is one of the reasons why Utopian thinking is so distinctive of modernity (Bauman 1992, p. xv).

As regards the Patagonian project, the profile of the settlements was determined a priori. The recruitment of the settlers was organized and supervised by the Spanish Crown. The Real Orden of 1778 expressed the intention of sending poor Spanish farming families who would develop permanent bonds to the soil. A recruiting campaign was implemented in the northern Spanish regions (Galicia, Asturias and Castilla and León). Interested families signed an agreement with the Spanish Crown. Conditions stated included lodging, means of production; land ownership, seeds and a daily ration of food in exchange for being sent to the Patagonian new settlements. The agreement included "Subjection to destination" that is settler families were not allowed to abandon the settlement by their own will, but only by permission of the local authorities (Senatore 2005). As a result, the families were all hired under strict terms of equality.

Even though Spanish families formed the main component of the colonizing agents, other social groups were present as well. Some other people were hired in the Viceroyalty of Rio de la Plata under different hiring conditions: they were sent with the sole purpose of helping with the building of the facilities and the setting to work of the new settlement. This was a heterogeneous group of men, which included *Funcionarios* (Crown officers including the Superintendents who were the Head of the colonies, accountants, surgeons, and priests), *Tropa* (Troops from Infantry and Artillery of Buenos Aires), *Maestranza* (working men including carpenters, blacksmiths, barrel makers, lantern makers, caulkers, and laborers among others), and even *Presidiarios* (convicts) who were serving their sentence and who were given building tasks. The crews of the ships carrying goods for the settlement lived temporarily onboard in the natural ports near the settlements.

The three settlements, which formed part of the colonization, plan resulted in very different stories and configurations. Their shapes, developments and duration were different, as well as the kinds of relationships established with the same native Tehuelche groups. Floridablanca and Carmen de Patagones had a basically agricultural profile and a heterogeneous population whereas the Fuerte San Jose had a defensive profile and a solely military population. Floridablanca was abandoned and destroyed 4 years after its foundation as it was considered too costly to keep and useless for agricultural purposes. Carmen de Patagones has continued its life up to the present day and the Fuerte San Jose was moved on several occasions and finally abandoned after 60 years of existence as the result of an attack of the native population during which its facilities were destroyed.

The study of the ideas and ideals within which this population plan was framed shows us the social order underlying the design of the new colonies (Senatore 2007). Furthermore, the different ways of putting the master plan into practice in each of the settlements shows the richness and complexity of the new social and material realities in the Patagonian coast. This paper is aimed at contributing to the understanding of that social and material heterogeneity from a specific standpoint based on the peculiarities of life in Floridablanca during its short existence.

## 12.4   Floridablanca as Ruptures

Floridablanca was designed and built from *tabula rasa*. From a conceptual point of view, the settlement might be interpreted as the creation of new material conditions which brought about ruptures in San Julian Bay. Within this specific frame it would make sense to wonder how and why some specific forms of social interaction were developed instead of others. In other words, "The trick, of course, is to figure out, empirically and analytically, how some and not other signs and objects, identities and practices, circulated in the highly complex fields of exchange that composed colonial encounters—and why." (Comaroff and Comaroff 2006, p. 50).

The settlement of Floridablanca brought about ruptures in the development of the history of the Patagonian landscape and in the private histories of all the individuals who formed part of or were involved in the life of the colony. My interest is focused on understanding the social and material relationships built as a result

**Fig. 12.2** Virtual reproduction of the Floridablanca Colony. (Pablo Walker)

of those ruptures, within the frame of everyday life inside a colony that was active for only 4 years. The ruptures involved material, social, and temporal dimensions.

The Spanish settlements in Patagonia consisted of material spaces in constant transformation and growth. Building was started from the foundations, and continued permanently and contemporarily to the arrival of the inhabitants. In the case of Floridablanca, for instance, the building continued until a few months prior to its abandonment. In addition these structures worked as fixed points in space, highly visible and distinct, consisting of architectural structures mainly made of clay, rocks and showing tiled roofs of considerable size. Floridablanca consisted of a square, a fort, a hospital, houses, a bakery, stockyards, and a blacksmith's forge. While the settlement was active, metals and tiles were produced locally but many objects such as raw materials, food, animals and plants arrived on vessels, which moved along the coastline. This meant that buildings, new animals, cultivated land, orchards, and the temporary presence of vessels were only the most noticeable examples of visual ruptures (Fig. 12.2).

Floridablanca put together people who did not know one another previously and were total strangers to one another. The San Julian Bay was originally populated temporarily by moving Tehuelche groups, which included men, women, children and elderly people. The Spanish colonization project consisted of the settlement of the "newly arrived" by means of the movement and relocation at great scale of individuals coming from different places and different in age, gender and previous experience. The main component of the colonizing agents were farmer families coming from different villages in different regions of Castilla and Leon, or soldiers and officers coming from Infantry and Artillery Regiments in Buenos Aires. In addition to the diversity of places of birth, the diversity of ages among the settlers— ranging from newly born babies to people in their sixties—should also be considered as well as the life experience the military men had acquired in previous projects or military campaigns.

The inhabitants of the colony were summoned because they were considered useful to the development of the settlements (Senatore 2007). This implied the co-existence of these people's previous experience, diversity of interests, callings and fortunes. Farmers, carpenters, builders, surgeons, bleeders, servants, and others brought some previous learning and experience in a profession, craft or labor. As did convicts serving their sentences in Floridablanca, in their case vagrancy, drunkenness, desertion, theft were also part of their private experience as were their years of previous confinement. These individuals show that taking part in the Patagonian experiment was not a choice for them as it was for others.

The individuals, who conformed the population of Floridablanca, fluctuated in time. Among the "newly arrived" the farmer families were "attached to their destination" which meant that they had to stay in the colony forever, whereas part of the working men took turns in the Viceroyalty headquarters in Buenos Aires, Floridablanca and other Patagonian settlements. On the other hand, the Tehuelche groups occupying temporarily the San Julian area were permanently moving. These people did not move all at once but in certain seasons all the adult men moved away leaving behind women, children and elderly people in tent camps for several months.

New forms of social heterogeneity, spatial reconfiguration, temporal fluctuation and material irruption shaped the dimension of the ruptures and the creation of new conditions in the San Julian Bay.


## 12.5 "Novelty" in Everyday Life Practices

Novelty is defined as the quality of being new, original, or unusual. Some synonyms are originality, newness, freshness, unconventionality, unfamiliarity, unusualness, difference, imaginativeness, creativity, (creativeness,) innovation, modernity, a break with tradition.

How can novelty in the everyday practices in Floridablanca be studied? My proposition is to do so as from different material practices. Thus the relationships and practices born from the objects consumed, the new unknown objects and the objects preserved were evaluated. The aim is to explore the heterogeneity of social practices within the settlement and try to understand the multiple individual and group choices and decisions made in everyday situations. The standpoint proposed here is centered on the exploration of particular contexts. The focus is put on the housing spaces occupied by the different individuals who were part of Floridablanca. Different questions are posed and the choices and decisions made according to the specific housing contexts in the settlement analyzed. Therefore the idea of a homogenous response on the part of the Spanish colonizing group is left aside and there appears the possibility of understanding differences and similarities in the multiple choices that arose.

Everyday life appears as a highly interesting field to understand the relationship between the colonial structures and the agency of individuals. The theory of social structuring (Giddens 1984) is a frame that allows us to link actors and structures within a nondeterministic frame. Social structures depend on everyday practices and interaction routines among the social actors (Bourdieu 1977). Likewise, actors depend on structures to create the possibility of action. Individual actors will be confronted with a great variety of opportunities and limitations, in order to act in different ways. Within this frame it is interesting to explore the social and political implications of the most mundane activities and practices. Hence, the permanence of traditional ways as well as the implementation of new ways or the development of variations may appear with a variable degree of deliberate action and significance for the actors involved.

## 12.6   Archaeology and the Housing Contexts in Floridablanca

The aim of the project "Archeology and History in the Spanish Colony of Floridablanca" has been to study the social structuration in the colony. The empirical basis for this work has been a large and rich documentary corpus kept in historic archives in Argentina and Spain together with the archaeological information produced in the site during almost for 10 years of fieldwork (Senatore 2000). That means of topographic and geophysical explorations and extensive diggings in different areas of the settlement reaching 150 m$^2$ (Fig. 12.3).

The diggings included areas that were built by the Spanish Crown as part of the population project as well as areas built and financed by private individuals. The core of Floridablanca was built around a central square. The fort, the hospital, the bakery and the blacksmith's forge were the official buildings built around it. Two blocks of nine family houses were built in addition to the- former, one of which was not completed before the abandonment of the settlement. The structures, which did not belong in the official plans, were placed farther away from the square but they followed the general design of the settlement. These were used for living purposes except for one, which also worked as a *Pulpería*.

The integration of both historical and archaeological research has allowed us to link the social categories in Floridablanca with the housing contexts there. The Crown officers, the *Maestranza*, the *Tropa* and the *Presidiarios* lived in the fort. The houses were occupied by the farmer families who had come from Spain to their Patagonian destination. The Crown both built and financed the building of those houses that were granted to each farmer family as part of the initial equality terms offered. The design was identical in all cases. The house stood for the mononuclear, patriarchal family unit thought of as a productive unit as well as the basis of the social structuration in Floridablanca.

The diggings in Floridablanca included different housing contexts. These included a house belonging to a farmer family (Fig. 12.4). It was one of the nine houses built by the Crown—ASII6—and a structure attached to it built by the initiative of its inhabitants. Three sector S of the fort were also dug: the NW sector where the

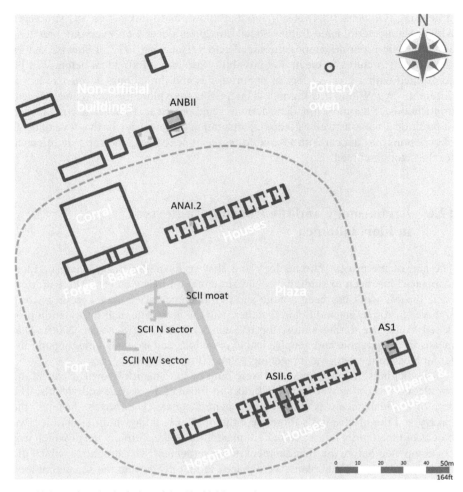

**Fig. 12.3** Archaeological plan of the Floridablanca site

bastion and a number of rooms for the military population were built, the west sector where the hierarchical personnel of the colony lived and a dumping structure that was placed in the perimetral moat of the fort (Fig. 12.5). Outside the official structures two sectors were dug which corresponded to houses built by private people: these were a soldier's house classified ANBII and a structure working as house and general grocery and drinking store built by a convict-ASI.

Comparative analyses were developed aiming at studying the differences in everyday practices in the different housing contexts of the settlement (Senatore et al. 2008). Within this frame it is possible to pose questions as regards the material dimensions of novelty in the everyday life of different housing contexts in Floridablanca.

**Fig. 12.4** House of Spanish family excavation view

**Fig. 12.5** Fort of Floridablanca excavation view

## 12.7    Novelty and Material Culture

I am interested in exploring novelty as part of choices and decisions made by individuals in everyday life in Floridablanca. That is linked to how individuals used material culture to negotiate new identities in colonial worlds (for interesting papers in this topic See Loren 2001; Voss 2008; Beaudry 2006; among others). The acquisition of new objects derived from consumption practices, together with the incorporation of unfamiliar or unknown objects as well as the keeping and exhibition of certain personal items were evaluated. The heterogeneity of possibilities for each individual or social group or housing context in the settlement was also evaluated.

One of the ways of studying novelty is consumption. To study consumption is to study cultural practices beyond economic interactions (Silliman and Witt 2010). Historical archaeologists have studied consumption from diverse and interesting perspectives and approaches (Miller 1987; Spencer-Wood 1987; Cook et al. 1996;

Mullins 2003; Silliman and Witt 2010; among others). Here, I explore consumption as a choice. But it is choice constrained by a variety of factors (Silliman and Witt 2010, p. 49). The meanings that people give to consumer goods engage with their sense of identity and how they relate to others (Silliman and Witt 2010, p. 49)

"What is unknown" is shaped in the clash between continuities and ruptures in the San Julian Bay. In this sense, the study of stone artifacts offers an interesting way to evaluate the relationship between the newly arrived people in Patagonia and unknown objects. Silliman worried about the negative tendency in archaeological analysis and representation of prioritization of the origins of artifacts over their multiple uses and meanings (Silliman 2010, p. 30). He agreed with Loren on the idea that a useful approach requires looking at the formation of ethnicity through specific material practices rather than the assignment of ethnicity through general categories of material culture (Loren 2000, p. 90; Loren 2008 in Silliman 2010, p. 36). Following this ideas, we must bear in mind that in this paper the stone artifacts are not considered native artifacts but "unknown objects".

Another interesting means of studying novelty in Floridablanca is the study of the objects that were part of the personal history of individuals, which therefore connect the present, and the past of the newly arrived. We then focused on the objects the travelers owned before the trip and which they chose to keep and carry with them. The studies of personal artifacts, as a class of material culture, demonstrated their great potential for examining individual lives particularly along the lines of gender, ethnicity, class, age (Loren 2000; Loren and Beaudry 2006; Beaudry 2006, among others). The use of personal artifacts also reflects individual choice as well as the norms and expectations of the broader society. The set of choices is restricted by the available materials and by the assessed set of options for an individual (White and Beaudry 2009, p. 213) in a specific social and historical context.

## 12.8   New Things and Consumed Objects

Floridablanca was a marginal context fully dependent on being supplied by towns belonging to the Viceroyalty. For the colonial administration eyes, the availability of new goods was restricted and limited to what was sent by the Crown. Thus for the official records, the universe of possibilities of choice was limited to the objects and supplies sold in the *Almacén de Floridablanca* (Crown Store). Even though nobody denies the existence of informal transaction the analysis of official consumption was considered an interesting line to become familiar with part of the consumption practices in Floridablanca.

The Administration of the Colony left records of all the official transactions that took place. These documents—called *Registros de Contaduría* (Accountancy Records)—showed monthly records of what was purchased by every one of the inhabitants in Floridablanca. The analysis of those records was developed as a part of a graduate thesis within the frame of the main project (Bianchi 2002). In this chapter, I interpret part of the results obtained there to analyze the consumption practices as different ways of relating to novelty for the different individuals in Floridablanca.

The Accountancy Records show the variety of products that were sold. These were food, alcoholic drinks, tobacco and clothing (pieces of garment and raw materials).

The analysis of the existing data on each individual item bought—price and date—gave us a detailed record of the consumption practices of the settlers. All this information was gathered and worked statistically, bearing in mind two aims. One of them was to find similarities and differences in consumption practices among the different individuals, this meant what, how much and how frequently they purchased goods. The second aim was to evaluate the choice of goods as regards preferences, that is to say which items were consumed and by whom.

The results of the analysis of consumption practices showed that there was a group of individuals that was clearly distinguishable from the others as regards consumption practices. This group was not homogeneous in the selection of goods but it was so as regards consuming practices. That is to say, they stood out as a group because they consumed a lot of goods of a great variety, whereas the rest of the inhabitants of the settlement consumed little and in a homogeneous way.

As regards their choice of goods, it is interesting to remark that this group purchased a lot of clothing articles or raw materials to be used to make garments. They acquired items having to do with personal appearance such as clothing. Their consumption practices indicate that they renewed their personal appearance much more frequently than the other settlers. Furthermore, by buying raw materials to make new garments they opened the possibility to combinations, which were not available in readymade garments. Thus, they could show clothing variations and combinations different from the ones presented by the rest of the population.

It is interesting to notice that this differentiated social group was formed by single men who were the part of the *Maestranza*, the army men and the higher officers of the Crown. Basically, the group consisted of members who carried some kind of hierarchy within those social categories, that is to say the high rank military officers, the master of *Maestranza*, and the higher rank Crown officers (*Funcionarios*). They lived exclusively inside the fort. For these men, novelty was shaped in as much we consider their consumption practices as a distinctive rhythm of renewal of their personal appearance.

## 12.9  New Unknown and Unfamiliar Objects

Lithic artifacts were part of the Patagonian landscape for ages. They were manufactured, used, and made to circulate and discarded in wide areas of the Patagonian coast before, during and after the settlement of Floridablanca. Yet, they were a novelty for many of the "newly arrived" in Patagonia as part of this Spanish colonization Project: probably never seen before, bearing strange shapes made of unknown raw materials and with unusual purposes. Yet the Tehuelche people who inhabited the Patagonian barren plains habitually used these lithic objects and the study of those elements in colonial contexts is frequently associated with studies of cultural contact.

In Floridablanca the first studies started from a binary perspective with the purpose of learning the role of material culture in the process of relationship building between the inhabitants of Floridablanca and the Tehuelche people. We studied how this meeting was materially built (Sanguinetti et al. 2004). The analytic lines chosen to approach the problem focused on how the way in which groups and individuals displayed on the land related to the flow of goods, resources and favors or services between them. The official discourse was analyzed from documentary sources—administrative records, diaries, and reports—and a first approach was made to the studies of material culture specifically focused on the analytic inclusion of definite surface contexts, located in areas adjacent to the settlement where associations of European and indigenous materials concentrated. The next step was to evaluate the contemporaneity of the archaeological contexts and it was proved that the lithic artifacts recovered in the housing contexts of the settlement were similar and perfectly comparable to those recovered from the areas identified as Tehuelche camps existing while the colony was active. Later, the interethnic relationships in San Julian area were studied as part of a doctoral thesis (Buscaglia 2009). In this chapter, I interpret part of the results we have obtained in all those papers already mentioned.

I assume that stone objects were unknown to most of the newly arrived in Floridablanca; nevertheless their incorporation to everyday life inside the settlement was not homogeneous. The study of the presence and characteristics of lithic objects in the different archaeological contexts of the site have brought about interesting results. The Fort stands out from the rest of the housing spaces for the frequency and continuity of lithic objects found as well as for the time of acquisition. Stratigraphy proved that the lithic elements there were found at a greater temporal depth than in the other archaeological contexts. This is true from the start and keeps on through all the occupation. It is important to remark that the Fort was the only housing space where not only the formatized tools were identified but also the waste of the manufacturing new instruments or the reuse of them were found, which means that these objects were used inside the Fort. This means, the incorporation of ready-made objects, but also the dynamics and contemporaneity of ways of manufacturing them. It is also important to remark that the lithic artifacts in the Fort are the only ones, which present no variation as compared to those found in sites prior to Floridablanca. This marks a contrast with the results of the diggings in other housing contexts inside the settlement which present not only low frequencies of these artifacts but also variations in raw materials—incorporating glass for instance, in technological features or even in the morphology of the artifacts.

The Fort appears as a particular space in Floridablanca where the unknown objects, which imply continuities with the San Julian space, are present in everyday life. Similar results were found in the analysis of consumption of animal species developed in two graduate thesis developed in the frame of the major project (Bosoni 2010; Marschoff 2004). The Fort appeared different from the other housing contexts. There, a more frequent consumption of Patagonian local species (i.e. guanaco) was found as compared to the consumption of farm animals (i.e. cows and pigs) brought to breed. As regards lithic artifacts not only the artifacts are present in the Fort but also traces of the processes of their manufacturing and renewal. If we consider time we can say that the unknown as an expression of novelty was present from the very start of the settlement. That is to say that in this place individuals established an early and immediate relationship with what was unknown and new.

## 12.10   Displayed and Preserved Personal Objects

These were the artifacts for personal use that were defined as those personal items that people chose, used and displayed as individuals (Deagan 2002, p. 5). What role did these objects for personal use play in the new context of social interaction? What role did these objects play in the first moments of interaction among people of different origins, with different life experience or unlike personal, work, or status histories? Following these questions the participation of artifacts of personal use in the communication of identities was studied. The analysis of this group of objects was performed for an undergraduate thesis (Nuviala Antelo 2008). Special attention was devoted to the identities marking relations between the past and the present of people: institutionalized identities, which fed back the order and social categories present in the colonizing project (Jenkins 1992, p. 24); "historized" identities prioritizing personal histories or trajectories (Goffman 1959) or the biography of the individual (White 2005) and identities of apparent status, which established new ways of introduction among people (Jenkins 1992). In Nuviala Antelo's work, comparisons were set as regards the construction/displaying of identities among the different housing contexts in the settlement. Objects of personal use coming from the different dug areas were studied (Fig. 12.6). The models of non-verbal communication were used as a frame and for their study the spaces in the settlement were divided in social networks which were as wide as the Fort or as reduced as the monofamiliar housing unit (following Wobst 1977).

The objects for personal use were analyzed as from qualitative aspects, that is, to say the type of objects used. Thus the presence and diversity of these objects was compared in all their categories and types as well as the raw materials they were made of. Another line of analysis was focused on measuring the visibility of these objects according to variables such as morphology, size, color and shine. The analysis also included the study of the presence of design in the pictures appearing on the objects.

General tendencies were observed in the different housing contexts in Floridablanca. Inside the Fort, the objects for personal use were widely used as a way to communicate personal identities as contrasted to the housing context. Results showed that the elements discarded in the Fort were of a greater diversity and variety of categories. High visibility and the presence of designs on them contrasted notably with the objects found in the other domestic spaces in Floridablanca.

The Fort presented very interesting aspects as regards the negotiation of identities expressing a link between past and present. The first thing to emphasize is that the display of identities linked to the biography of individuals or their personal

**Fig. 12.6** Artifacts of
personal use recovered in the
Fort excavations

history or traditions was not relevant here. In the first place, we identified the
communication of identities, which placed the individual in the present time in a
relational scheme. That is to say the display of institutionalized identities (those
placing the individual inside a group) and status identities (those differentiating him
within the same group) the latter is the identification of practices interpreted as the
construction of "apparent identities" (Canavese 2003). This was observed as from
the recurrence of certain techniques and raw materials such as cheap coatings imi-
tating a real gold or silver coating. This was linked to different situations in colonial
America in which as participants in new social situations individuals reinvented
themselves and showed a status different from the one they had in their place of
origin (Nuviala Antelo and Senatore 2009).

It is important for the purpose of this chapter to emphasize the practices that
show the different ways the individual inhabiting the Fort had of relating to what
was new in contrast to those of the rest of the population. The Fort worked as a
semipublic place where individuals showed themselves as preferring certain aspects
in identity communication/construction leaving aside their individual histories and
their past. Their practices reinforced their new appearance and prioritized their
relationship with the present.

## 12.11   Final Words

In previous papers I proposed Floridablanca as part of the projects of the Spanish
Enlightenment (Senatore 2005, 2007). With this purpose I focused on understanding the multiple ways in which the different and sometimes contrasting ideas of

the Spanish Enlightened thinkers were put into practice. In the Patagonian project families prevailed as colonizing agents and agriculture as the main means of progress. But the project also summoned other individuals, who had nothing to do with agricultural activities and were outside the family structure. Not considered by the great ideas these individuals participated actively in the creation of Floridablanca as a new social reality.

It is to these individuals that our questions about novelty as part of everyday life in Floridablanca take us. Through the study of material culture I detect practices which involve particular ways of relating to "what is new". For instance "unknown objects" are immediately incorporated to everyday life. "What is new" is shown through a distinctive rhythm in the renewal of personal appearance. In consumption practices as well as in the ways of using personal goods a different man privileging the present seems to have appeared.

Those individuals constituted the segment of population showing the highest mobility rates. The relief system established by the Crown maintained them in Floridablanca as long as they proved useful to the development of the settlement. As opposed to the farmer families they were not attached to their destination and were allowed to abandon the colony according to their own interests. Most of these individuals moved about answering their own will and convenience. They were single men who had previously acquired experience in everyday life in other contexts of the colonial world. These individuals' everyday life and their interacting practices may be related to the idea of cosmopolitanism. That is to say "...ways of living at home abroad or abroad at home –ways of inhabiting multiple places at once, of being different beings simultaneously, of seeing the larger picture stereoscopically with the smaller." (Pollock et al. 2000, p. 587).

Here my aim was only to ask about novelty in everyday life and enquire about the heterogeneity of practices of colonizing agents in Floridablanca. This allowed me to take distance from the essentialized visions present in colonial discourse (Liebmann 2008). I understand that the peculiar ways in which individuals, objects and spaces articulated with one another show configurations that are only understandable when analyzing specific and particular social contexts. Thus, the identification of certain everyday practices in the interplay of different analytic scales can contribute to understand the heterogeneity and complexity of a context like Floridablanca colony always within the frame of the vast and diverse colonial world (Gosden 2004, Funari et al. 1999, Rothschild 2003).

Thus, there is an intention of accepting the plurality of the parties involved in colonial interaction fields, aiming at leaving aside dichotomist as well as essentialized visions, in Dube's own words (2002, p. 198) "...critical discussions of cultures and pasts have also challenged the analytical binaries of modern disciplines, interrogating essencialized representations of otherness and questioning abiding representations of progress that are variously tied to the totalizing templates of universal history and the ideological images of Western modernity".

**Acknowledgment**  Universidad de Buenos Aires currently provides funding for the research project "Una arqueología de las narrativas históricas en el sur de Patagonia y Antártida". UBACyT 2011-2014 20020100100433. I would like to thanks Lorena Connolly.

# References

Appadurai, A. (1986). *The social life of things*. Cambridge: Cambridge University Press.
Appadurai, A. (2005). *Modernity at large. Cultural dimensions of globalization*. Minneapolis: University of Minesota Press.
Bauman, Z. (1992). Intimations of Posmodernity. London: Routledge.
Bauman, Z. (2007). *Modernidad Líquida*. Buenos Aires: Fondo de Cultura Económica de México.
Beaudry, M. C. (2006). *Findings: The material culture of needlework and sewing*. New Haven: Yale University Press.
Bourdieu, P. (1977). *Outline of a theory of practice*. Cambridge: Cambridge University Press.
Bianchi, M. (2002). *Organizar la Diferencia. Prácticas de consumo en Floridablanca*. Graduated thesis, Universidad de Buenos Aires.
Bosoni, C. (2010). *Entre lo dicho y lo hecho. Prácticas productivas en Floridablanca. (Patagonia, siglo XVIII)*. Graduate thesis, Universidad de Buenos Aires.
Buscaglia, S. (2009). *Relaciones de poder y dinámica interétnica desde una perspectiva histórica y arqueológica, Bahía de San Julián, Pcia. de Santa Cruz (siglo XVIII)*. Doctoral thesis, Universidad de Buenos Aires.
Canavese, G. F. (2003). Ética y estética de la civilidad barroca. Coacción exterior y gobierno de la imagen en la primera modernidad hispánica. *Cuadernos de Historia de España, 78*(1), 167–188.
Comaroff J., & Comaroff, J. (2006). Taking stock. A response to Turgeon and Creignton. *Archaeological Dialogues, 13*(1), 49–53.
Cook, L. J., Yamin, R., & McCarthy, J. (1996). Shopping as meaningful action: Towards a redefinition of consumption in historical archaeology. *Historical Archaeology, 30*(4), 50–65.
Deagan, K. (2002). Artifacts of the Spanish Colonies of Florida and the Caribbean 1500-1800. Volume 2: Portable Personal Possessions. Washington and London: Smithsonian Institution Press.
Dube, S. (2002). *Introduction: Colonialism, modernity, colonial modernities. Neplanta View from the South 3.2*, 197–219. (Special Issue Critical Conjunctions Foundations of Colony and Formations of Modernity). Durham: Duke University Press.
Funari, P. P. A., Jones, S., & Hall, M. (1999). Introduction: Archaeology in history. In P. P. A. Funari, S. Jones, & M. Hall (Eds.), *Historical archaeology. Back from the edge* (pp. 1–20). London: Routledge.
Giddens, A. (1984). *The constitution of society. Outline of the theory of structuration*. Cambridge: Polity Press.
Giddens, A. (1990). *The consequences of modernity*. Stanford: Stanford University Press.
Giddens, A. (1991). *Modernity and self identity: Self and society in the late modern age*. Cambridge: Polity Press.
Giddens, A., & Pierson, C. (1998). *Conversations with Anthony Giddens. Making sense of modernity*. Stanford: Stanford University Press.
Goffman, I. (1959). *The presentation of the self in everyday life*. Garden City: Doubleday Anchor Books.
Gosden, C. (2004). *Archaeology of colonialism: Cultural contact from 5000 BC to the present*. Cambridge: Cambridge University Press.
Habermas, J. (2004). Modernidad: Un proyecto incompleto. In N. Casullo (Ed.), *El debate modernidad-posmodernidad* (pp. 53–63). Buenos Aires: Retórica Ediciones.
Jenkins, R. (1992). Social Identity. London: Routledge.
Kumar, K. (1988) *The rise of modern society. Aspects of the social and political development of the west*. Oxford: Basil Blackwell.
Liebmann, M. J. (2008). Introduction: The intersections of archaeology and postcolonial studies. In M. J. Liebmann & U. Z. Rivzi (Eds.), *Archaeology and the postcolonial critique* (pp. 1–20). Lanham: Altamira Press.
Loren, D. D. (2000). The intersections of colonial policy and colonial practice: Creolization on the 18th-century Louisiana/Texas frontier. *Historical Archaeology, 34*(3), 85–98.
Loren, D. D. (2001). Social skins orthodoxies and practices of dressing in the early colonial lower Mississippi Valley. *Journal of Social Archaeology, 1*(2), 172–189.

Loren, D. D., & Beaudry, M. (2006) Becoming American: Small things remembered. In M. Hall & S. Silliman (Eds.), *Historical archaeology: Studies in global archaeology* (pp. 251–271). Oxford: Blackwell.

Marschoff, M. (2004). *Prácticas alimenticias en Floridablanca*. Graduate thesis, Universidad de Buenos Aires.

Miller, D. (1987). *Material culture and mass consumption*. New York: Basil Blackwell.

Mullins, P. (2003). Ideology, power, and capitalism. The historical archaeology of consumption. In L. Meskell & R. Preucel (Eds.), *A companion to social archaeology* (pp. 195–214). Blackwell: Malden.

Nuviala Antelo, M. V. (2008). *Materializando Identidades en Floridablanca. Los artefactos de uso personal en la comunicación no verbal de las identidades (Patagonia, Siglo XVIII)*. Graduate thesis, Universidad de Buenos Aires.

Nuviala Antelo, M. V., & Senatore, M. X. (2009). *Materializing identity. Personal & non verbal communication in the Spanish colony of Floridablanca. Paper presented at 42 annual conference on historical archaeology*, Toronto.

Pollock, S., Bhabha, H. K., Breckenridge, C., & Chakrabarty, D. (2000). Cosmopolitanism. *Public Culture, 12*(3), 577–589.

Rothschild, N. (2003). *Colonial encounters in a native American landscape*. Washington, D.C.: Smithsonian Books.

Sanguinetti de Bórmida, A. C., Senatore, M. X., Buscaglia, S. (2004). Patagonia en los confines de la sociedad moderna. Fronteras materiales en Floridablanca (siglo XVIII). In *La Frontera: realidades históricas, sociales, políticas y mentales*, (pp. 69–84). Buenos Aires: IMHICIHU–CONICET.

Senatore, M. X. (2000). *Arqueología en la Nueva Colonia y Fuerte de Floridablanca. Plano arqueológico y espacio social*. Anales de la Academia Nacional de Ciencias de Buenos Aires T. XXXIV (2), pp. 743–753.

Senatore, M. X. (2005). Enlightened discourse, representations and social practices in the Spanish settlement of Floridablanca (Patagonia, 18th century). In P. P. A. Funari, A. Zarankin, & E. Stobel (Eds.), *Global archaeological theory contextual voices and contemporary thoughts* (pp. 265–281). Kluwer: New York.

Senatore, M. X. (2007). *Arqueologia e Historia en la Colonia española de Floridablanca (Patagonia, siglo XVIII)*. Buenos Aires: Editorial Teseo.

Senatore, M. X., & Zarankin, A. (2002). Leituras da Sociedade Moderna Cultura Material, Discursos e Práticas In A. Zarankin & M. X. Senatore (Eds.), *Arqueologia da Sociedade Moderna na America do Sul* (pp. 5–18). Buenos Aires: Colección Científica, Ediciones del Tridente.

Senatore, M. X. et al. (2008). Arqueología de las prácticas cotidianas en la colonia española de Floridablanca (Patagonia, siglo XVIII). In L. Borrero & N. Franco (Eds.), *Arqueología del Extremo Sur de Sudamérica* (pp. 81–117). Buenos Aires: DIPA-IMHICIHU-CONICET & Editorial Dunken.

Silliman, S. (2010). Indigenous traces in colonial spaces. Archaeologies of ambiguity, origin, and practice. *Journal of Social Archaeology, 10*(1), 28–58.

Silliman, S., & Witt, T. (2010). The complexities of comsumption: Easter Pequot cultural economics in eighteenth-century New England. *Historical Archaeology, 44*(4), 46–68.

Spencer-Wood, S. (Ed.). (1987). *Consumer choice in historical archaeology*. New York: Plenum Press.

Thomas, J. (2004). Archaeology and Modernity. London and New York: Routledge.

Voss, B. L. (2008). *The Archaeology of ethnogenesis: Race and sexuality in colonial San Francisco*. Berkeley: University of California Press.

White, C. (2005). *American artifacts of personal adornment, 1680–1820: A guide to identification and interpretation*. Lanham: AltaMira Press.

White, C. L., & Beaudry, M. (2009). Artifacts and personal identity. In T. Majewski & D. Gaimster (Eds.), *International handbook of historical archaeology*, (pp. 209–225). USA: Springer Science Business Media, LLC. doi:210.1007/978-0-387-72071-5_12.

Wobst, H. (1977). *Stylistic behavior and information exchange*. In C. E. Cleland (Ed.), *Papers for the director: Research essay in honor of James B. Griffin; Anthropological papers, 61* (pp. 317–334). Ann Arbor: University of Michigan, Museum of Anthropology.

# Part III
# New Realities and Material Worlds

# Chapter 13
# Basque Fisheries in Eastern Canada, a Special Case of Cultural Encounter in the Colonizing of North America

Sergio Escribano-Ruiz and Agustín Azkarate

## 13.1 Introduction: Subject, Aims, and Sources

In the late fifteenth century, an English expedition that was aiming to find an alternative route to Asia reached the easternmost part of Canada. They did not discover the Indies but rich marine resources, which enabled a thriving fish industry based on whaling and cod fishing to develop. The Basque sailors played an active role in the origins of this process, and they encouraged the establishment of temporary settlements on Canadian land[1]. The intermittent occupation of the coast sparked close cultural interaction with the various local societies from the Strait of Belle Isle and the Gulf of St. Lawrence; this interaction was of a different nature than in the majority of other known cases. This process culminated in the eighteenth century,

---

The original manuscript was written in Spanish and has been translated into English by "Traductores-Intérpretes GDS, S.L."

---

[1] This study generally focuses on sailors from the Peninsular Basque Country, namely those who came from the Iberian Peninsula, who were Castilian subjects during the studied period. For the sake of distinction, the Basques who were subjects of the French Monarchy will be referred to as continental Basques. On occasions, it will be difficult to distinguish one from the other, since the way in which they are named in written documentation is ambiguous and because it is difficult to identify differences using philological evidence or material culture elements.

---

S. Escribano-Ruiz (✉) · A. Azkarate
Cátedra Territorio, Paisaje y Patrimonio, Grupo de Investigación en Patrimonio Construido, GPAC (UPV-EHU), Centro de Investigación Lascaray Ikergunea, Avda. Miguel de Unamuno, 3, 01006 Vitoria-Gasteiz, Spain
e-mail: sergio.escribanor@ehu.es

A. Azkarate
e-mail: agustin.azcarate@ehu.es

© Springer International Publishing Switzerland 2015
P. P. A. Funari, M. X. Senatore (eds.), *Archaeology of Culture Contact and Colonialism in Spanish and Portuguese America*, DOI 10.1007/978-3-319-08069-7_13

although the two centuries that it lasted provide a different example of cultural encounter within the context of the colonization of North America.

This chapter aims to provide an overview of this historical episode, which illustrates the heterogeneous nature of the colonization of America. This vision has drawn from various disciplines such as Archaeology, History, Anthropology, Geography, and Philology. A range of sources of evidence are brought together in our account, such as archaeological remains, written documents, language, toponymy, cartography, or testimonies from people present at the time that the events took place. They have all been interpreted jointly as part of this study. We believe that this approach makes it possible to provide a general overview of a complex historical process, which we aim to characterize in the sections that follow.

## 13.2 From the Search for a New Route to the Indies to the English Colonization of Canada

### 13.2.1 The Historical Framework of Transatlantic Basque Fisheries

Canada was discovered in the early stages of the colonization of America, as a result of the interest that the major European monarchies had in finding routes leading to Asia, with the aim of establishing direct trade with their inhabitants. After the monarchies from the Iberian Peninsula monopolized the routes to Asia via Southern Europe, with the easternmost route corresponding to Portugal and the western one to Spain, the remaining European royal families had to explore other alternatives. Within this context, and spurred on by Christopher Columbus's journey, John Cabot secured funding in England for attempting to find a new route that would lead directly to the Indies and its sought-after products by navigating in a north-easterly direction (Menard 2006, pp. 207–208). Pursuing this target, the expedition Cabot led reached the Canadian coast in 1497. Comparisons with Columbus's voyage are unavoidable as Cabot also believed that he had arrived in Asia (Hanbury-Tenison 2010, pp. 219–220) and both are outstanding examples of the accidental nature of American colonization. It was not until the early sixteenth century when the Europeans realized that they had come across a continent of which they had no knowledge—some authors date this awareness to 1502 (Céspedes del Castillo 2009, p. 25), while others suggest a later date of 1524 (Menard 2006, p. 215). The events involving Christopher Columbus and John Cabot are an emphatic reminder that error and chance were key features in the beginning of the colonization of America[2].

---

[2] Both cases indicate that "casual" is a much more appropriate way to describe the process than "inexorable," a term which is often related to the colonization process, despite it tending to underestimate the capacity for action and the heterogeneous nature of the local societies, as occurs when the term is applied to the advance of capitalism (Funari et al. 1999, p. 7; Funari 2007, p. 5).

As has been demonstrated by excavations in the Viking settlement of L'Anse aux Meadows, dating to around the year 1000 (Nydal 1989), Cabot and his crew were not the first Europeans to touch land in Newfoundland. Nevertheless, the expedition led by John Cabot drew the attention of the other European countries and signaled the beginning of the European colonization of Canada. Soon after its arrival, from the year 1500, several Portuguese expeditions explored the Canadian coast. They attested to the truth of John Cabot's statements that there were plentiful fishery resources along those coasts (Ray 1994, pp. 23–24). Attracted by the explorers' tales, and in the face of indifference from the English, whose involvement in fishing in Newfoundland was very sporadic until the late sixteenth century (Pope 1986; p. 6; Menard 2006, p. 229), it is understood that Portuguese sailors began to explore Canadian fishing grounds almost immediately. This is at least what is suggested by the tithe that the King of Portugal levied on fish from Newfoundland in 1506 (Trigger and Swagerty 1996, p. 339), although it should be interpreted cautiously (Menard 2006, p. 227). There are records of several French campaigns around the same time in the Newfoundland fisheries, led firstly by sailors from Normandy and then from Brittany shortly after (Menard 2006, p. 227; Trigger and Swagerty 1996, p. 339). Although historiography has attempted to argue to the contrary (Azkarate et al. 1992, pp. 23–24), there is every indication that the Basque sailors arrived in Canada a little later.

The arrival date of the Basques to Canada almost completely monopolized historical studies on this subject until the late twentieth century, although it is now no longer a topic of discussion. Modern historiography accepts that interest from the Basques came later, and that they arrived after the English, Portuguese, and French (Huxley-Barkham 1987, p. 27; Azkarate et al. 1992, pp. 24–25; Trigger and Swagerty 1996, p. 339; Barkham 2000, pp. 54–55; Ménard 2006, pp. 228–231; Azpiazu 2008, p. 39). The earliest testimony to the presence of continental Basque sailors in Newfoundland dates back to 1512 (du Pasquier 2000, p. 25). The documentary sources do not mention journeys from the Basque Country to Newfoundland until 1531 (Barkham 2000, p. 55; Azpiazu 2008, p. 39). There are no known written records that talk about Basque expeditions to Canada until the previously mentioned dates, although they were frequently mentioned from that time onward. There is also no archaeological evidence to prove that the Basques were present before Cabot's expedition. Although it is clear that these journeys could have been made some time before they were mentioned for the first time in written form[3], currently

---

[3] This possibility is very likely because the first documented journeys seem to refer to previous experience and to describe an already familiar reality. The interpretation of the text from the year 1531, which both Michael Barkham (2000, p. 55) and Juan Antonio Azpiazu refer to, led the latter to suspect that the peninsular Basque sailors' whaling activity in Newfoundland could date back to the 1620s (Azpiazu 2008, p. 39–42). Michael Barkham accepts that they were involved in the fisheries in the same decade (2000, p. 55), although the type of documentation used is indirect. In any case, the use of a Basque-Algonquin pidgin, which had already been consolidated in 1540 (Bakker 1991, p. 157–158), seems to prove that the presence of the Basque sailors came early and was intense. The fact that the first known Galician journey intended for cod fishing in Newfound-

available information is not enough to consider the possibility that these trips dated back to the end of the fifteenth century or the first decade of the sixteenth century.

In contrast to what occurred further south, and in the majority of colonial cases, the land in the far north-east of America was shared by all the Europeans throughout the sixteenth century. Initially, no European country was determined to claim it as their land, and therefore, Canadian fishing waters were freely accessible to Portuguese, French, English, Spanish, Irish, and Dutch sailors (Menard 2006, pp. 231–235). Furthermore, developing fishing activities meant that it was necessary to occupy the Canadian coast seasonally; small settlements were built there with the structures needed to process cod or melt whale blubber. However, apart from these seasonal occupations that will be analyzed in further detail in the following section, several attempts were made to occupy the land permanently during the sixteenth century, although they were not strengthened until the early seventeenth century.

According to available information, the Portuguese were the first to attempt to establish a colony, in 1520, on the present-day Cap-Breton Island (Belanger 1980, p. 219; Menard 2006, p. 214). It seems that they did not give up their mission, since there were rumors years later, in 1568, of another possible attempt at colonization (Menard 2006, pp. 252–253). The French also tried to set up permanent colonies, with one of the most well-known examples being the attempt made between 1541 and 1542. Following orders from the French monarchy, Jacques Cartier founded Charlesbourg-Royal, although he abandoned it shortly after owing to the harsh winter conditions. Roverbal almost immediately founded it for the second time under the name France-Roy, but he too left the following spring (Menard 2006, p. 221). The English made an attempt a short time later, in 1583, when Humphrey Gilbert tried to colonize and collect taxes around St. John's on behalf of the English monarchy, although he had little success (Menard 2006, p. 233; Hanbury-Tenison 2010, pp. 249–252). It is thought that the Europeans were unable to bear the Canadian winter until John Guy established the Cupids colony (Newfoundland) in 1610 (Pope 1986, pp. 10–16) and the French founded Port Royal (Nova Scotia) in 1604 (Moore 1994, pp. 116–117). Following these settlement attempts, many more were made in the early seventeenth century. The English and French fought to colonize Canadian land until 1763, when the English prevailed and they definitively colonized the land.

## 13.3   Basque Transatlantic Fisheries, the Exploitation and Seasonal Occupation of the New Found Land

Diego Ribero, a cartographer sent to Newfoundland by the Spanish monarchy, said in 1529 that the Canadian fishing grounds were of little value and not held in high regard (Huxley-Barkham 1987, p. 28). Nevertheless, from 1530, and until at least

---

land was in 1517 (Menard 2006, p. 228) strengthens the hypothesis that the peninsular Basques were present on the Canadian coasts before 1531.

the seventeenth century, fishing along these coasts became one of the most important economic activities for the inhabitants of the Basque Country. The province of Gipuzkoa recognized it as such in 1563, when it declared that fishing in Newfoundland[4] was "the most important" (Azpiazu 2008, p. 25), or shortly after, in 1581, when it claimed that the province's economic activity was based on iron and sailing to Newfoundland (Azkarate et al. 1992, p. 19). Several decades on, the Government of Biscay also recognized it in a memorial written in 1654, which alluded to the importance of the fishing grounds for the Biscayans (Labayru 1967, p. 396). Over 20 Basque archaeological sites (Loewen and Delmas 2012, p. 221) provide material evidence of the importance that this economic activity had. Written documents and materials refer to an often underestimated experience in the context of the European colonization of America.

### 13.3.1  A Return Journey: Organization of the Expeditions, Types of Catch, and Their Sale

The type of fishing developed by the Basques in Canada required very complex organization and drew on expertise gained in fishing in Ireland and the Western Cantabrian Sea from the Middle Ages. Fishing expeditions to Asturias, Galicia, England, Ireland, or Canada were organized in the same way as commercial journeys, funded by business and ship owners of varying scales (Barkham 2000, pp. 45–46). The trips to Newfoundland required the highest amount of investment of all, since larger ships were needed, as well as provisions to last longer periods of time, more weaponry, equipment, and human resources. For these reasons, they had to develop funding systems, hiring conditions, and protection mechanisms, especially insurance (Azkarate et al. 1992, pp. 45–62). Despite this, the expeditions to Newfoundland were the most economically profitable (Barkham 2000, pp. 54–63), to such an extent that Basque fishing in Ireland almost completely ceased, as stated by Lope Martínez de Isasti in 1625 (1985, p. 154). Despite the complexity and high cost of the voyages, the sale of cod and whale blubber became one of the pillars of the Basque economy. Many of the ships that left the Basque coasts were mixed expeditions, although cod fishing and cetacean hunting were two distinct activities. The resources required, the areas in which they were carried out, the rules for sale, expertise, funding, and the length of seasons were all different, although they did sometimes coincide with each other. They will be addressed separately.

Whaling and blubber trade was noticeably dominated by Basques until well into the seventeenth century[5] (Huxley-Barkham 1979, p. 16). It seems that Basques

---

[4] It must be remembered that when the testimonies from the era refer to *Newfoundland*, they are speaking of Canada's Atlantic coast in general. More specific areas are distinguished within this category, such as the *canal de la Granbaya* (the present day Strait of Belle Isle) or the *costa de Bacallaos* (south of present day Newfoundland).

[5] Other sailors, such as the Normans, also became accustomed to hunting whales, although they ceased this activity in the thirteenth century (du Pasquier 2000, p. 15–16). Since the first Euro-

from the Southern Pyrenees were the first to become interested in whale hunting (Barkham 2000, p. 55), while for continental Basque sailors, this was a supplementary activity until at least the middle of the sixteenth century (du Pasquier 2000, pp. 35–38). It is also assumed that the Castilian subjects were those who specialized in whaling and built ships of greater tonnage to transport barrels containing blubber (Huxley-Barkham 1979, p. 14). Although the majority of whaling stations were concentrated on the northern coast of the Strait of Belle Isle (Azkarate et al. 1992, p. 73), where whaling activity was much more intense, it covered the entire Gulf of St. Lawrence, expanding up to the St. Lawrence River Estuary (Loewen and Delmas 2012, pp. 215, 236–237). We have testimonies from several privileged witnesses, such as de Isasti, who wrote about the Newfoundland fishing grounds in 1625. Lope Martínez de Isasti described the procedures performed after a whale had been hunted and how it was made into a product. He explains that if the whale was fresh, they kept it in brine to sell to the French, who would eat it. On the other hand, if it were old, they melted it in ovens to collect the blubber or oil, which was sold in Spain, especially in Navarra and Tierra de Campos, or was taken to different places in Europe, such as Flanders or England. de Isasti highlights lighting, the textile industry, or treating some illnesses as its possible uses[6] (1985, p. 155).

Archaeology has made it possible to document some of the infrastructure used for marketing whale blubber, which became a necessary element in daily life activities in some Basque ports during the Modern Age. Blubber was transported in wooden barrels and, once it had been unloaded in the Basque ports, was stored in special large clay jars in the docks, ready for distribution at a later date. Excavations in the Biscayan town of Lekeitio (Cajigas 1999) and in the Gipuzkoan city Donostia (Arkeolan 1998) have recovered a total of 25 jars used for this purpose. All the recorded jars are very similar in terms of their typological features, and their height, of over a meter, is particularly salient. The way in which they were laid out is also identical, as all the jars were found arranged in one place, some of which were placed next to each other neatly. In both cases, the space that the jars occupied was covered with earth, with only the rim visible (Fig. 13.1).

Unlike whaling, all the European expeditions destined for Canada were involved in cod fishing from the start. For this reason, the far east of Canada was known as the Tierra de Bacallaos (Land of Cod) in the early sixteenth century (Huxley-Barkham 1989, p. 3). By the seventeenth century, when Lope Martínez de Isasti wrote his work, Bacallao (Cod) was the name used to refer to the more specific place. He was referring specifically to the area in which the majority of the cod fisheries were concentrated (de Isasti 1985, p. 154), namely the southern and western coasts of Newfoundland (Huxley-Barkham 1987, p. 44). It is surprising that when addressing cod

---

pean whale hunting companies were created in the early seventeenth century (Romanovsky 1999, p. 19), the English, Dutch, and Danish were taught how to hunt whales by Basque sailors (du Pasquier 2000, p. 83–91; Alberdi 2012, p. 290). The main consequence was that the English and Dutch took control of the whale blubber market from the mid-seventeenth century, and it was impossible for the Basques to meet their lower prices (Aragón and Alberdi 2006, p. 101).

[6] His opinion on this issue is identical to the one expressed by Gipuzkoan historian Esteban de Garibay in 1571. For this reason, Selma Huxley-Barkham (1987, p. 41) suspects that Garibay is the source from which de Isasti has gathered some of his information. He does, fortunately, expand on it.

**Fig. 13.1** Jars used to store whale blubber recovered in Lekeitio (Biscay). *Left*: picture of the jars in situ (Photograph: Silvia Cajigas); *right*: one of the recovered jars on show in Bilbao. (Photograph: Santiago Yaniz. Arkeologi Museoa, The Archaeology Museum of Biscay)

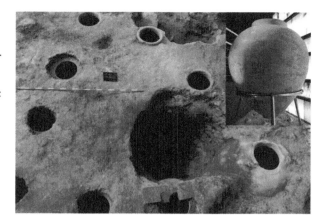

fishing, de Isasti does not describe this activity in detail, as he had done for whaling. Perhaps this is due to it being a more minor activity among Gipuzkoans compared with whale hunting. In contrast, he assured that ships went back loaded up with cod and that it was distributed all over Spain (de Isasti 1985, p. 154). Whatever, it is understood that the continental Basque fishermen, and not peninsular ones, were specialized in cod fishing (Huxley-Barkham 1979, p. 14). We are aware that most widespread fishing practice involved green or wet cod, which apart from being seasoned considerably was barely cured and did not keep well in Southern Europe (Grafe 2012, p. 60). There is not much mention of how the fishermen from the Basque peninsular prepared cod in Newfoundland, although the recovered statements referring to Spanish cod boats talk of green or wet cod (Rose 2007, p. 201). There is, however, evidence that suggests that they were involved in drying cod, a process which is estimated to have taken 50 days in Newfoundland[7] (Menard 2006, p. 127).

What is certain is that the Basque ports played an essential role in the cod trade and that, even after losing their dominance in Newfoundland, the Basques were the main cod providers in Castile (Grafe 2012, pp. 57–69). In addition, it may be stated that the products of Newfoundland were quickly accepted among the Basque population. In the middle of the sixteenth century, cod had already become one of the basic foods consumed in Bilbao (Grafe 2012, pp. 57–58) and whale blubber was also one of the most commonly consumed products (Labayru 1967, p. 283).

---

[7] The drying process was quicker on the Iberian Peninsula due to the warmer climate. For this reason, it is logical to suggest that some cod expeditions would have been able to compensate by fishing for less than 5 months and drying the cod in the ports of departure. In the case of the Basque sailors, it is most likely that they dried the cod on land, especially on mixed expeditions (cod and whale), since they had spent over 5 months in Newfoundland and they had to settle on land to melt the blubber. It is also possible that the Basque expeditions that were heading to Newfoundland to fish exclusively for cod did the same. de Isasti's testimony (1625) opens up this possibility. He mentions that the Gipuzkoan sailors would set off for *Cod* in March or April in order to return with plenty of cod in September or October, giving enough time for at least some of the cod to dry. The latest Basque sites to have been excavated, such as Hare Harbour in Petit Mecatina, make this seem feasible.

### 13.3.2  Occupation of the Land, Basque Settlements on the Canadian Coast

Fishing seasons required establishing settlements on the Canadian coast. It was not only necessary to settle on land in order to melt whale blubber, but also to prepare the cod. The place names used on Canada's Atlantic coast show that there was a strong Basque presence on the land. The maps drawn by Pierres Detcheverry or Denis de Rotis in the second half of the seventeenth century demonstrate that, even as late as then, many of the place names along the western Newfoundland coast that had originated from the Basque language, Euskera, had been preserved (Huxley-Barkham 1989, pp. 10–19). The maps in question only show a place name with a Basque origin for the Gulf of St. Lawrence (Babaçulho). However, many of these ports were used by Basque sailors and are mentioned in earlier documentary sources (Fig. 13.2).

The most recent overviews of archaeology relating to the Basque presence in Canada have quantified more than 20 Basque sites that have been excavated (Loewen and Delmas 2012, pp. 214–215). The majority of the work has focused on the excavation of whale stations located on the western coast of the Strait of Belle Isle, and the information that is available is therefore very unbalanced. The ovens and whale bone remains have helped to identify whale stations and have contributed to the study of them. The Red Bay whale station, which UNESCO named a World Heritage Site in 2013 and has been the focus of successive land (Tuck 1981, 1983, 1984, 1985, 1986) and underwater excavation campaigns (Grenier et al. 2007), is the most outstanding of all the whale stations where excavation has taken place. This and other studies have unearthed many material testimonies made by Basque fishermen, which have made it possible to characterize a whale station structure. The remains are concentrated in several sites that are spread out along Red Bay. The most noteworthy concentration is located in the northern half of Saddle Island, although significant structures have also been recorded on nearby islands, on the present-day Red Bay and to the west of it. A total of 14 tryworks used to melt whale blubber have been exhumed. The vast majority of them are of the same design, each with six furnaces. Several cooperages, middens containing food leftovers and wood, docks, piers, watch towers, and a cemetery with over a 100 graves have been recorded alongside the tryworks. The remains that have been found underwater correspond to woodchips, whale, and cod bones. The most remarkable vestiges that have been recovered during the underwater excavation campaigns are, however, the five sunken ships, three shallops, and all the related material culture. The remains that have been recovered during the above archaeological work amount to more than 500,000 objects of an extremely varied nature: coins, nails, work instruments, clothes, weapons, pottery[8], etc. (Loewen and Delmas 2012, pp. 226–228).

[8] We are involved in a study on Basque-Canadian pottery since 2008, in the framework of the TECNOLONIAL Project, *Technological impact in the Colonial New World. Cultural change in pottery archaeology and archaeometry*, funded by the Spanish Ministry of Science and Innovation (HAR2008-02834/HIST, 2008–2012) and the Spanish Ministry of Economy and Competitiveness

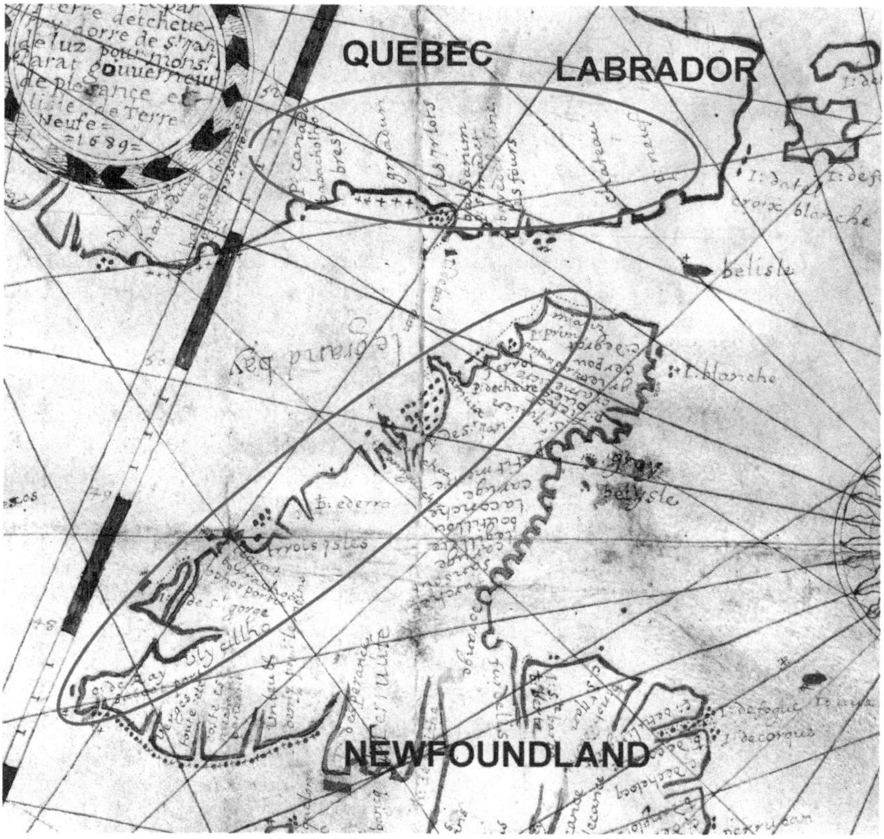

**Fig. 13.2** Map by Pierres Detcheverry (Bibliothèque nationale de France). A *blue circle* indicates the areas with the highest concentration of Basque place names and the ports mentioned in peninsular Basque documentation

The excavations that have taken place in the other whale stations situated in the Strait of Belle Isle confirm the Red Bay settlement pattern, although only one of them has been excavated extensively, namely the Stage Island station in Chateau Bay (Azkarate et al. 1992, pp. 109–160). This excavation reflects the Basque whale station model, which is distinguished by two main characteristics: (a) they are located on flat areas next to the coast and are characterized by the constant presence of tiles and whale bone remains, and (b) the existence of specific related built structures, namely ovens for melting blubber always found alongside docks and cooperages. But, moreover, Chateau Bay reveals interesting touches that add to this picture and offer a greater level of detail about the elements that have been

(HAR2012-33784/HIST, 2013–2015). For a brief overview, please see Barrachina and Escribano-Ruiz (2012).

described. One of its most distinctive characteristics is its stratigraphy, which is more complex than is usually found in Basque-Canadian sites, where the most common pattern is a single stratigraphical horizon (Loewen and Delmas 2012, p. 238). Stage Island's stratigraphy reveals a clear overlap of the successive occupations by the Basques, French, and English (Azkarate et al. 1992, p. 118). In addition, two phases have been recorded for the Basque period of occupation, one in the middle of the sixteenth century and the other continuing until the early seventeenth century; both are characterized by the presence of tryworks. There is a greater density of built structures in the second level: carpentry, store, and likely sleeping cabins. It is the only site in which the two latter structures have been recorded alongside the common tryworks and cooperages. Another of its unique characteristics is how extraordinarily well some of the structures have been conserved, such as the carpentry wooden walls (Fig. 13.3).

The Hare Harbour site, in Petit Mécatina (Quebec), is the third Basque site to have been excavated extensively in Canada and the only to be located outside the Strait of Belle Isle. It was occupied for the longest period of all the known Basque sites, in between the sixteenth and eighteenth centuries. This time frame has been identified based on the presence of Aragonese pottery dating to the sixteenth century (Fitzhugh et al. 2011, p. 112) and, among other items, a glass bead dated to between 1680 and 1730 (Fitzhugh 2006, pp. 61–62). Researchers have discovered two main occupation phases, the first involving whale hunting and the later one cod fishing, when occupation was more intensive (Fitzhugh et al. 2011, p. 123). Despite cod fishing being dominant, as proven by archaeozoological evidence, the occupation patterns are quite similar to those recorded in the mentioned whale stations. The settlement is formed by a type of rectangular kitchen, defined by a flagstone pavement with a large furnace, a cooperage, docks, and structures covered with tiles (Fitzhugh et al. 2011, pp. 104–109; Loewen and Delmas 2012, p. 244). However, it does also have unique characteristics, such as a lack of tryworks, the presence of coal production, a forge, or different pottery records than the rest of the peninsular Basque fisheries. The presence of a winter house attributed to the Inuit (Eskimos) is one of its unique features (Fitzhugh 2006, pp. 62–63; Fitzhugh et al. 2011, pp. 104–109), and it led to an episode of cultural interaction that will be covered in the following section.

## 13.4   Cultural Interactions Between Basque Sailors and Local Societies

One of the most distinctive features of the Basque fishing endeavor is the type of interaction that they had with the local populations. The settlements that have been mentioned previously and the nearby coasts were the backdrop to close cultural contact. On the whole, apart from some specific episodes, the relations between the Basques and the local societies on the Atlantic coast of Canada are considered to have been quite positive for both parts (Trigger and Swagerty 1996, p. 342). It

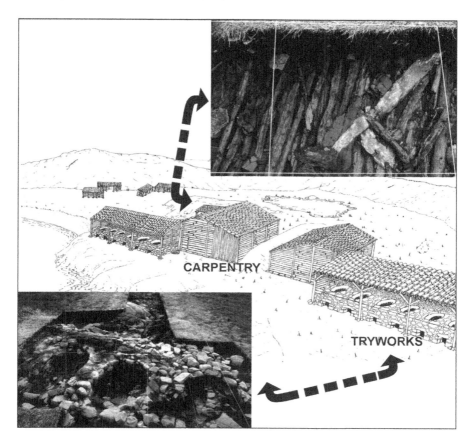

**Fig. 13.3** Hypothetical reconstruction of Xateo (Chateau Bay) and details of the documented structures. (Drawing: Julio Nuñez Marcén. Photographs: Agustin Azkarate)

cannot be ignored, however, that testimonies allude to apparent cannibalism and deaths that occurred while fighting with "savages." But, in general, the Basque sailors' impression of the native people whom they met on the Strait of Belle Isle was that they were intelligent and friendly (Huxley-Barkham 1980, p. 53). The Basques undoubtedly had closer cultural relations with the natives than the rest of the European cultural groups. There is a wide range of material and immaterial evidence, which confirms this and which will be summarized below.

The closest cultural contact that the Basques had was with the Mi'kmaq people (Micmac), the Innu (or Montagnais), and the Inuit (or Eskimos). Evidence of cultural hybridization has been preserved as a result of their interaction with these groups. It seems that they also had relations with the Beothuks, Iroquois of St. Lawrence, and other cultures, but the testimonies are scarce and the evidence suggests that the interaction was less intense. This reveals an interesting case of multicultural interaction and "middle-ground colonialism" (sensu Gosden 2008, pp. 101–135),

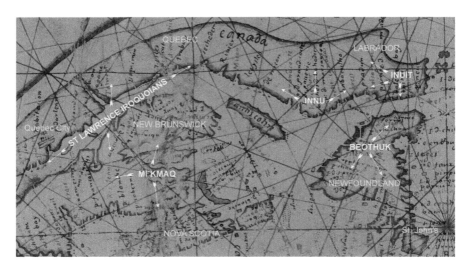

**Fig. 13.4** Map by Denis de Rotis, 1674 (Bibliothèque Nationale de France), on which the main native settlement areas are shown

which lasted throughout the time that the Basque venture continued in Canada. A short analysis of the evidence that has been preserved from each of the episodes of cultural encounters will now follow[9] (Fig. 13.4).

## 13.4.1 The Iroquois of St. Lawrence

Located in the St. Lawrence River area (Moussette 2009, p. 33), it has been suggested that the term Iroquois could be derived from the expression hildakoa, which means "the death" in Euskera (Bakker 2002, pp. 107–108). There is not much information about this society, and a large amount of what has been gathered is owing to descriptions by Jacques Cartier, who identified their location as being between actual Quebec City and Montreal. There are some specific testimonies about them, such as one from an Iberian-Basque sailor who confirmed their presence in the Strait of Belle Isle in 1542. According to this witness, the Iroquois of St. Lawrence were friendly toward them and had told them that they had killed around 30 of Cartier's men (Huxley-Barkham 1980, p. 53). Movement from their habitat to the Straits has been interpreted as proof that regular trade relations existed between the Basques and the French (Martijn et al. 2003, p. 192; Trigger and Swagerty 1996, p. 350). The

---

[9] These interactions provide very interesting examples of cultural contact; the interpretation of these contacts lies outside the scope of this study, which only aims to provide a general picture of the nature of the contact. The different types of interaction between the Basques and each of the cultural groups, and how each one unfolded, offer a rich base of information, which will be interpreted in future studies.

discovery of a piece of Iroquois pottery at Red Bay, under the collapse level of a Basque building (Moussette 2009, p. 31), seems to support such a possibility. However, it does not seem that the relations between them were very close because no linguistic evidence has been conserved to confirm that the Basque language had any effect on their language (Bakker 1991, p. 149). Furthermore, it is understood that the Iroquois of St. Lawrence were hostile toward the Basques on occasions and that they disappeared quickly (Huxley-Barkham 1980, p. 53), just before Basque fisheries extended to the St. Lawrence River estuary around 1580. Their disappearance is dated to the mid-sixteenth century, and it has been linked to various causes, such as European diseases (Trigger and Swagerty 1996, p. 366) or the tense relationships that they had with other local cultures (Moussette 2009, p. 36).

### 13.4.2   Beothuk

They lived throughout Newfoundland (Bakker 1991, p. 140; Moussette 2009, p. 33) and the north of the Strait of Belle Isle during the sixteenth century (Pastore 1990, p. 220). There is some evidence that supports the idea that they had contact with the European invaders. Some metal objects that were recovered from Beothuk sites in the North-East of Newfoundland have been interpreted as European artifacts used for trade, as a type of exchange or bartering (MacLean 1990). In a site in the Blanc-Sablon river area (Labrador), near Red Bay and which is associated with a possible Beothuk occupation, three characteristic pots of the Basque sites in Canada have been found, along with metal objects and whale bones (Moussette 2009, p. 38). Both cases evidence that there was direct contact (in the form of exchanges) and indirect contact (visits to European sites in winter) between the two groups. It does however seem that the contact was very limited, not very friendly and that the Beothuks abandoned the coasts, thereby avoiding the Europeans (Trigger and Swagerty 1996, p. 342). The Beothuks had to move to inland areas of Newfoundland due to the growing expertise in marine resource exploitation shown by the Mi'kmaqs, the French, the Inuit, and the Basques (Pastore 1990, p. 220). Obliged to hunt caribou, Beothuks disappeared in the nineteenth century (Pastore 1993, pp. 269–274). The contact that they had in this case is not considered to have been very intense, and no linguistic evidence has been preserved either to suggest that Euskera had an influence on their language (Bakker 1991, p. 149).

### 13.4.3   Mi'kmaq

The Mi'kmaqs were settled in the far south-west of the Gulf of St. Lawrence, and especially in New Brunswick and Nova Scotia (Bakker 1991, p. 140; Moussette 2009, p. 33). As a result of being located in this geographic location, it is thought that they had much greater contact with the continental Basque sailors than with the peninsular Basque sailors, as they frequented these coasts more often. The Mi'kmaq people seem to have been the Basque's main allies in the trade of skins (Bakker 2002, pp. 106–107). Another name for them, Souriquois, which would mean "the white one" in Basque, has been attributed to this relationship (Bakker 1991, p. 143). As a result of trade contacts, the linguistic hybridization mentioned previously occurred; it involved incorporating words and phrases from Euskera into their language, which was a variation of Algonquin. One of the most noteworthy examples of these linguistic borrowings is the Basque word, Adesquide, which means friend. The incorporation of the word friend shows that the Mi'kmaqs and the Basques held each other in high esteem[10]. This cultural hybridization also apparently was transferred to the material world, as demonstrated by the apparent presence of Basque symbols, such as the lauburu, in popular Mi'kmaq art (Bakker 2002, p. 106). It is surprising that this Algonquin group established themselves among the Basques and other local cultures. They obtained objects from the Basques and exchanged them, in return for local products such as skins, with other Algonquin groups in New England and Nova Scotia (Moussette 2009, p. 35). In this way, European products started to take on a role in the symbolic practices of many North American cultures. The objects' wide range of sensory characteristics gave them a very high symbolic value for some of the local cultures (Gosden 2008, pp. 105–107). It is, however, thought that their utilitarian value was higher for those cultures that were in direct contact with Europeans, such as the Mi'kmaqs (Trigger and Swagerty 1996, pp. 377–378).

### 13.4.4    The Innu (or the Montagnais)

The Innu, whom the Europeans named Montagnais, settled all along the northern shore of the Strait of Belle Isle in the sixteenth century (Bakker 1991, p. 140; Moussette 2009, p. 33). This location suggests that they had close contact with the Basque whale hunters. For this reason, it is thought that the Innu were behind a testimony from the early seventeenth century that reports collaboration with the local people in tasks involved in whale hunting (Martijn et al. 2003, p. 199). In addition, the Innu seem to be the protagonists of accounts by Basque fishermen who were interrogated by the Castilian monarchy about occupation attempts made by Cartier and Roberval. The testimonies described the contact that they had in 1537 in the port of Brest with some Indians who offered them skins in exchange for metal objects (Huxley-Barkham 1980, pp. 53–54, 1987, p. 58; Bakker 1991, p. 157). It is also assumed that the Innu were the better people that some other Basque sailors referred to in 1542, unlike other local cultures, which is a likely reference to the Iroquois of St. Lawrence (Huxley-Barkham 1980, p. 53). Lope Martínez de Isasti's testimony seems to confirm these suggestions. Referring to the Montagnais, he mentions three positive aspects relating to interaction with them: (a) they talked to the Basque sailors, (b) they warned them of the presence of the Inuit, and (c) they helped them to fish in

---

[10] This was not the case in other colonial contexts, in which there were doubts as to whether the native people were humans or they were considered to be exotic objects, slaves or even construction material (Todorov 2008, p. 184).

exchange for Basque products (1985, pp. 154, 164). All these references indicate that there was very close cultural interaction between them, which materialized, as in the case of the Mi'kmaqs, in a pidgin language. It is, however, not known for certain whether both pidgin languages could have shared the same common root (Bakker 1991, pp. 156–157). The borrowings that were preserved in each case are not the same, but some also had the same friendly tone as mentioned before. In Tadoussac in 1630, a member of the Innu culture called a French missionary *ania* (brother). The religious man was not aware that this name had come from Euskera, but he understood that it referred to a brother (Bakker 1991, p. 138). Once again, the fossilization of this word seems to have resulted from the positive nature of the interaction between the groups and supports the idea that this is an example of middle-ground colonialism.

### 13.4.5   The Inuit (or Eskimos)

The land area that has been attributed to the Inuit settlement is concentrated in the far east of the Labrador province, from the Strait of Belle Isle moving northward (Bakker 1991, p. 140). However, from the sixteenth century, they moved down to the Strait of Belle Isle (Pastore 1990, p. 221). The scarce objects associated with the material culture of the Thule, the ancestors of the Inuit, discovered in Red Bay (Tuck 1985, pp. 227–228), or the very few objects belonging to the Eskimos and linked to the Basque occupation, which were found in Chateau Bay, were a result of this moving southward. These pieces of evidence were, in the latter case, interpreted as being a result of the low-level influence that the whale hunters had had on the Inuit, who were supposed to visit the whale stations when they were not occupied by the Basques (Azkarate et al. 1992, p. 120). However, there is evidence that their influence in the Strait did increase. After the Chateau Bay whale station had been abandoned, a greater amount of Inuit artifacts made from whale and seal bones or stone was recovered (Azkarate et al. 1992, p. 240). At the Hare Harbour site, Petit Mecatina, there is also evidence pointing toward possible cultural interaction of a collaborative nature, whether involving Eskimo women or families working for the fishermen (Fitzhugh 2006, pp. 63–34), or as farmhands, hunters, or settlement guards in winter (Fitzhugh et al. 2011, p. 122). This range of evidence goes against the traditional view that the relationships with the Inuit were tense (Belanger 1980, pp. 126–128; Huxley-Barkham 1980, p. 54; de Isasti 1985, p. 154; Bakker 1991, p. 147; Martijn et al. 2003, p. 198). However, archaeology offers a vision of a more collaborative atmosphere, and there is linguistic evidence that also seem to support this idea[11]. Judging by the discoveries made in Hare Harbour, and considering that by the eighteenth century it was the Inuit who were trading with the Europeans (Bakker 2002, p. 106), it is very likely that the relationships between the Basques

---

[11] Although it has not been possible to demonstrate its existence in the present day, a document from the eighteenth century mentions that a Basque-Eskimo pidgin existed (Bakker 1991, p. 147–148).

and the Inuit had become more stable during the second half of the seventeenth century. There are also signs that hybridization occurred between the Europeans and Eskimos. Some specific discoveries, such as the iron copy of the Inuit fishing trident, kakivak (Fitzhugh 2006, p. 58), demonstrate that there was a fair knowledge of Inuit culture.

## 13.5   Final Remarks

The establishment of European fisheries in Newfoundland prompted the development of an intercontinental economy that was based on systematically exploiting North America's natural resources. The Basque sailors took part in this creative business, involving the local peoples in different ways. It all marked a very sudden change for those involved. The linguistic hybrid, which was used in the North-East of America until the mid-seventeenth century (Bakker 1991, pp. 157–158), is irrefutable proof of how close cultural contact was between the Basques and the local people. The fact that Euskera was the first language to have a real impact on other native societies, such as those from the North East of America (Bakker 2002, p. 105), strengthens this idea.

In addition, the linguistic evidence is accompanied by material elements. The presence of European objects that have been recovered from local sites has been interpreted as evidence of trade or exchange with the natives. For example, this is how the metal objects linked to the Basques that were found along the coasts of the Gulf of St. Lawrence, Newfoundland, Labrador, Acadia, Nova Scotia, and New Brunswick have been interpreted (Moussette 2009, p. 34). The majority of the whale stations that have been excavated have also revealed objects linked to the local societies (Moussette 2009, p. 38), which also indicates that there was close cultural interaction.

But besides this rich example of multiculturalism and cultural hybridization, the case study of the Basque fisheries allows us to delve deeper into the casual nature of early colonialism, underscores the random nature of its development, and stresses the importance that local population had in the development of the colonial process.

## References

Alberdi, X. (2012). *Conflictos de intereses en la economía marítima guipuzcoana. Siglos XVI-XVIII*. Bilbao: Servicio Editorial de la Universidad del País Vasco. http://www.ehu.es/argitalpenak/images/stories/tesis/Humanidades/XABIER_ALBERDI.pdf. Accessed 26 Sep 2013.

Aragón, A., & Alberdi, X. (2006). "… lleben… las colas a las varrigas de los bufos…": Balleneros guipuzcoanos en las "matanzas" de ballena de Galicia y Asturias durante los siglos XVI y XVII. *Obradoiro de Historia Moderna, 15,* 77–111.

Arkeolan. (1998). Excavaciones en la Bretxa. Donostia. *Boletín informativo semestral, 5,* 12–16.

Azkarate, A., Hernández Vera, J. A., & Nuñez, J. (1992). *Balleneros vascos del siglo XVI. Estudio arqueológico y contexto histórico*. Vitoria-Gasteiz: Gobierno Vasco.

Azpiazu, J. A. (2008). *La empresa vasca de Terranova*. Donostia: Ttartalo.

Bakker, P. (1991). Un pidgin vasco y amerindio. In P. Bakker, G. Bilbao, N. G. H. Deen, & J. I. Hualde (Eds.), *Basque pidgins in Iceland and Canada. Anejos del Anuario del Seminario de Filología Vasca Julio de Urquijo* (pp. 134–165). Donostia: Gipuzkoako Foru Aldundia.

Bakker, P. (2002). Amerindian tribal names in North America of possible Basque origin. In X. Artiagoitia, R. P. G. De Rijk, P. Goenaga, & J. Lakarra (Eds.), *Erramu boneta: Festschrift for Rudolf P.G. de Rijk. Anejos del Anuario del Seminario de Filología Vasca Julio de Urquijo* (pp. 105–116). Bilbao: Universidad del País Vasco.

Barkham, M. (2000). "La industria pesquera en el País Vasco peninsular al principio de la Edad Moderna: ¿una edad de oro?". *Itsas Memoria. Cuadernos de estudios marítimos del País Vasco,3*, 29–75.

Barrachina, C. P., & Escribano-Ruiz, S. (2012). Las producciones cerámicas vascas de época moderna: Un caso práctico de arqueología histórica. In J. Cascalheira & C. Gonçalves (Eds.), *Actas das IV Jornadas de Jovens em Investigaçao Arqueológica, JIA 2011* (Vol. I, pp. 219–224). Faro: Universidade do Algarve.

Belanger, R. (1980). *Los vascos en el estuario del San Lorenzo, 1535–1635*. Donostia: Auñamendi.

Cajigas, S. (1999). Manzana 2.1.1. (Lekeitio). *Arkeoikuska,1998,* 337–342.

Céspedes Del Castillo, G. (2009). *América Hispánica (1492–1898)*. Madrid: Marcial Pons.

Fitzhugh, W. W. (2006). Cultures, borders, and Basques: Archaeological surveys on Quebec's lower north shore. In L. Rankin & P. Ramsden (Eds.), *From the Arctic to Avalon. Papers in Honour of Jim Tuck* (pp. 53–70). Oxford: BAR International Series 1507.

Fitzhugh, W. W., Herzog, A, Perdikaris, S., & Mcleod, B. (2011). Ship to shore: Inuit, early europeans, and maritime landscapes in the northern gulf of St. Lawrence. In B. Ford (Ed.), *The archaeology of maritime landscapes* (pp. 99–128). New York: Springer.

Funari, P. P. A. (2007). Teoría e arqueología histórica: A América Latina e o Mundo. *Vestigios,1*(1), 51–58.

Funari, P. P. A., Jones, S., & Hall, M. (1999). Introduction: Archaeology in history. In P. P. A. Funari, S. Jones, & M. Hall (Eds.), *Historical archaeology. Back from the edge* (pp. 1–20). London: Routledge.

Gosden, C. (2008). *Arqueología y colonialismo. El contacto cultural desde 5000 a.C. hasta el presente*. Barcelona: Bellaterra.

Grafe, R. (2012). *Distant tyranny.Markets, power and backwardness in Spain, 1650–1800*. Princeton: Princeton University Press.

Grenier, R., Bernier M. A., & Stevens, W. (2007). *The underwater archaeology of Red Bay: Basque ship-building and whaling in the sixteenth century, 5 vols*. Ottawa: Parcs Canada.

Hanbury-Tenison, R. (2010). *The Oxford book of exploration* (2nd ed). Oxford: Oxford University Press.

Huxley-Barkham, S. (1979). Los balleneros vascos en Canadá entre Cartier y Champalain (siglo XVII). Boletín de la Real Sociedad Bascongada de los Amígos del País. *Año, XXXV*, 3–24.

Huxley-Barkham, S. (1980). A note on the strait of Belle Isle during the period of Basque contact with Indian and Inuit. *Etudes/Inuit/Studies,4*(1–2), 51–58.

Huxley-Barkham, S. (1987). Los vascos y las pesquerías trasatlánticas, 1517–1713. In S. Huxley (Coor.), *Los vascos en el marco del Atlántico Norte. Siglos XVI y XVII* (pp. 27–164). Donostia: Etor.

Huxley-Barkham, S. (1989). *The Basque coast of Newfoundland*. St. Johns: The Great Northern Peninsula Development Corporation.

de Isasti, L. M. (1985) [1625, 1850]. *Compendio Historial de Guipúzcoa*. Bilbao: Amigos del Libro Vasco.

Labayru, E. J. (1967) [1900]. *Historia general del Señorío de Bizcaya, Tomo IV*. Bilbao: La Gran Enciclopedia Vasca.

Loewen, B., & Delmas, V. (2012). The Basques in the gulf of St. Lawrence and adjacent shores. *Canadian Journal of Archaeology,36*, 213–266.

MacLean, L. (1990). Beothuk iron—Evidence for European trade? *Newfoundland Studies,6*(2), 168–176.

Martijn, C. A., Barkham, S., & Barkham, M. (2003). Basques? Beothuk? Innu? Inuit? Or St. Law-
    rence Iroquoians? The Whalers on the 1546 Desceliers map, seen through the eyes of different
    beholders. *Newfoundland Studies,19*(1), 187–206.
Ménard, C. (2006). La pesca gallega en Terranova, siglos XVI-XVIII. Tesis doctoral, Univer-
    sidad de Santiago de Compostela, Santiago de Compostela. http://dspace.usc.es/bitstre
    am/10347/2263/1/9788497508162_content.pdf. Accessed 26 Sep 2013.
Moore, C. (1994). Colonización y conflicto; la Nueva Francia y sus rivales. 1600–1760. In C.
    Brown (Ed.), *La historia ilustrada de Canadá* (pp. 115–206). Mexico D.F.: Fondo de Cultura
    Económica.
Moussette, M. (2009). A universe under strain: Amerindian nations in north-eastern North America
    in the sixteenth century. *Post-Medieval Archaeology,43*(1), 30–47.
Nydal, R. (1989). A critical review of radiocarbon dating of a norse settlement at L'Anse Aux
    Meadows, Newfoundland, Canada. *Radiocarbon,31*(3), 976–895.
du Pasquier, T. (2000). *Les baleiniers basques*. Paris: Editions S.P.M.
Pastore, R. (1990). Native history in the Atlantic Region during the Colonial Period. *Acadiensis,
    XX*(1), 200–225.
Pastore, R. (1993). Archaeology, history and the Beothuks. *Newfoundland Studies,9*(2), 260–278.
Pope, P. (1986). Ceramics from seventeenth century Ferryland, Newfoundland. M. A. Thesis, Me-
    morial University of Newfoundland, St John's.
Ray, A. (1994). El encuentro de dos mundos. In C. Brown (Ed.), *La historia ilustrada de Canadá*
    (pp. 21–114). Mexico D.F.: Fondo de Cultura Económica.
Romanovsky, V. (1999). *Le Spitsberg et les baleiniers basques*. Biarritz: Atlantica.
Rose, G. A. (2007). *Cod. The ecological history of the North Atlantic fisheries*. St. John's: Break-
    water.
Todorov, T. (2008). *La conquista de América. El problema del otro* (2nd ed). Buenos Aires: Siglo
    veintiuno editores.
Trigger, B. G., & Swagerty, W. R. (1996). Entertaining strangers: North America in the sixteenth
    century. In B. G. Trigger & W. R. Washburn (Eds.), *The Cambridge history of the native peo-
    ples of the Americas. Volume I. North America* (pp. 325–398). Cambridge: Cambridge Univer-
    sity Press.
Tuck, J. A. (1981). Field work at Red Bay, Labrador. Archeology in Newfoundland and Labrador
    1981. *Annual Report,2,* 56–67.
Tuck, J. A. (1983). Excavations at Red Bay, Labrador. Archeology in Newfoundland and Labrador
    1982. *Annual Report,3,* 95–117.
Tuck, J. A. (1984). Excavations at Red Bay, Labrador. Archeology in Newfoundland and Labrador
    1983. *Annual Report,4,* 70–81.
Tuck, J. A. (1985). Excavations at Red Bay, Labrador. Archeology in Newfoundland and Labrador
    1984. *Annual Report,5,* 224–247.
Tuck, J. A. (1986). Excavations at Red Bay, Labrador. Archeology in Newfoundland and Labrador
    1985. *Annual Report,6,* 150–158.

# Chapter 14
# The Spanish Occupation of the Central Lowlands of South America: Santa Cruz de la Sierra la Vieja

Horacio Chiavazza

## 14.1 Introduction

In the center of South America, a large-scale urban project was accomplished from scratch: the founding of Santa Cruz de la Sierra on February 26th, 1561. The documented motivation showed the benefits of such an environment for a settlement; benefits, which 40 years later, were gone back on, to fundament its compulsive desertion. Wrapped in the vicissitudes of European colonial policies on American territory, men and women (many of them coming from Asunción in the early years) who had founded the city of Santa Cruz de la Sierra in 1561 were forced to leave by the vice regal authorities between 1601 and 1604 (Còmbes and Peña 2013; Finot 1939).

During the interactions between Spaniards and natives, a change was registered, moving from conquest (promoted from Asunción as "advanced" and set in a context of good relations with local ethnic groups) to colonization; Santa Cruz de la Sierra became an "enclave" when the base in Asunción had to be moved because of the policy of permanent belligerence from the Charcas (Martínez 2013): "From an outpost into the rich land, it would become a frontier post, a defensive enclave against the Chiriguanos and a source of laborers for the haciendas and mines in the sierras" (Martínez 2013, p. 66). We understand that this meant that the city became a pivotal place among local ethnic groups "…on the border with two chiriguanaes provinces…," between the Andes and El Pantanal (Suarez de Figueroa 1586 in Còmbes 2013, p. 22).

These characteristics allow to inquire into the population organization experimented on different scales by the foundation of the town in the very heart of the South American continent. In the heart of and so far from everything… there lie the very reasons for settling and abandoning the place; constant dialectics of

H. Chiavazza (✉)
Departamento de Historia, Instituto de Arqueología y Etnología,
Facultad de Filosofía y Letras, Universidad Nacional de Cuyo, Centro Universitario,
Parque General San Martín, 5500 Mendoza, Argentina
e-mail: hchiavazza@gmail.com

© Springer International Publishing Switzerland 2015
P. P. A. Funari, M. X. Senatore (eds.), *Archaeology of Culture Contact and Colonialism in Spanish and Portuguese America*, DOI 10.1007/978-3-319-08069-7_14

colonization by means of cities that were populated and subsisted or were abandoned and/or relocated (Musset 2011; Hoberman and Socolow 1993).

By means of the archaeological excavations carried out with in our project, called Santa Cruz de la Sierra la Vieja" (from now on SCLV) in 2004–2007, we wanted to find the exact location of the city and typify the construction process taking into account its environment and its own structure. To that effect, we performed extensive and intensive prospection and excavations (E), both trial-excavations (E3, E4, E5, E6) and open-area ones (E1 and E2). The registered constructive contexts and the materials analyzed in general enabled to fundament that the foundation and growth of the city took place in that area and it also enabled us to advance some of its characteristics.

## 14.2   Santa Cruz de la Sierra in the History of the Spanish Conquest of South America

A strong heart in a weak body. In the sixteenth century the Spanish crown was stretching its domains beyond its breath. The anxiety of the body made the blood simmer. The enterprising personalities dared roam the unknown land in search of the promised riches that were both real and magnificent. More than 200 cities that were founded between Zacatecas and Buenos Aires in less than 100 years are a clear evidence of this dynamic (Fowler 2011; Romero Romero 1989). The stories of the "Amazonauts" reflect the anxiety, the vice regal consolidations, the need to quench that thirst, or at least to placate it with politics (Morales Padrón 1963).

The process of foundations in the area of the Rio de la Plata, in which the settling and later abandonment of Santa Cruz de la Sierra la Vieja (SCLA) between 1561 and 1604 is inscribed (Finot 1939), is based in this dialectic of anxieties and respites, ideals, and ideology. The rush of a tireless captain (Ñuflo or Nufrio de Chávez) and a group of men and women that had settled in Asunción (1537) and who firmly believed in their aspirations were the necessary ingredients to fulfill the aim to conquer, settle and, above all, after the failed attempts of the "great entry" of Martínez de Irala (1548), colonize.

This colonization is the answer to a stage that begins with Irala's death and the death of a generation of discoverers (1556). A second stage, this time of colonizers, with its indomitable strength, gave birth to a city that was powerful from its very foundation: Santa Cruz de la Sierra (1561). So far, that was what the Spanish newcomers desired. But their declared need to settle and conquer had a counterpart: one presented by those that were covered more than discovered (Dussel 1994). It has been clearly stated in other works that the lands that fell under the jurisdiction of SCLV were not empty (Còmbes 2013). A wide spectrum of ethnic groups, prominent for its variety, inhabited them and more important still, resisted them (Balza Alarcón 2001; Còmbes 2013; Métraux 1942; Susnik 1978). Thus, to speak of SCLV as an urban triumph on uninhabited lands seems a neocolonial excess, deeply involved in the construction of the present local identity, which is built on the systematic denial of any link with any Andean culture and which holds a vision of white, European supremacy, registered since the foundation and later migrations of an archaeological

**Fig. 14.1** Location of Santa
Cruz de la Sierra La Vieja
(SCLV)

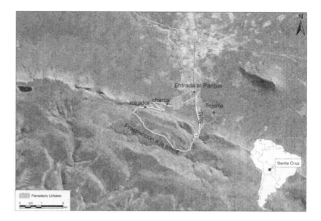

city constantly called upon to give meaning to the identity of Santa Cruz (see Pro-Santa Cruz Committee Management Plan as an example—Gandarilla 2004).

SCLV (located in the center-east sector of the present republic of Bolivia—17°52′6.54″ S—60°44″52.6″ W) lay on the side of the Serranía del Riquió and obtained its supply of water from the Arroyo Sutó (Fig. 14.1). In this way it secured its chances of success as a city amid the strong opposition from local peoples who, despite their massive incorporation as colonial forced laborers, in "encomiendas" or even as slaves, soon were able to repel the invasion. In fact, the nomadic nature of the city of SCLV was the result of two different kinds of pressure: one coming from the outside, in the shape of excessive ambition and its counterpart from the inside, a necessary resistance. The city was moved up to its actual site on the margins of the Rio Piraí. Thus, Santa Cruz became one of the nomad cities listed by Musset (2011). This fact generated a high-resolution archaeological record at the place of its first settlement.

## 14.3   Setting

The site is placed in the heart of South America, in the transition areas between Amazonía, and Chiquitano Monte and Dry Forest. The climate ranges from sub-humid to dry, with temperatures of 24 °C and a mean annual rainfall of 910 mm. The rainfall pattern is strongly seasonal with a wet period between November and March (155 mm) and a dry period between April and July (12 mm). The site lies within the Amazon basin and its main watercourse, the Arroyo Sutó (3 km from the site), has a low flow of water during the dry season. In the area, the Laguna Lateí is an excellent resource typical of the wetlands where more than 100 species can be found ranging from tall trees to grasses. Trees are centennial and signs of decay can be found such as dead trees both standing and fallen. Approximately some 70 species of animals have been recorded only in this area; mostly birds, rodentia, and in lesser numbers cervidae, felidae, canidae, dasypodidae, and myrmecophagoidea. Soils correspond to the Chaco-Beniana plains and 90 % are classified as unsuitable for agriculture (Muñoz Reyes 1980; Suárez Núñez del Prado et al. 2004).

## 14.4 Background

The area of Chiquitanía where SCLV was thought to lie was suggested by Cortés (1974) after making some field observations and stratigraphic crosssections in certain mounds. However, the author took it for granted that the coal and tiles found corresponded to what Enrique Finot had previously surveyed in documents (1939). Twenty years later, Sanzetenea (Sanzetenea and Tonelli 2003) carried out field surveys to support the creation of the National Historical Park of SCLV. In his excavations, he found evidence of what could be an urban structure but his manuscript does not detail or substantiate his conclusions. It only describes the materials and impressions that lead him to conclude that the archaeological remains corresponded to that of a city (although, as a whole, he attributes the diagnostic elements, ceramics, to native American typologies; Chiavazza 2013, p. 115). Until then and 30 years later, when we began our work in 2004, it was imperative to find empirical bases that showed that the records mentioned by these two authors in a brief note and a manuscript belonged to an urban site and that this site was, effectively, that of the Spanish foundation of SCLA in 1561. This was achieved after 3 years of work (Chiavazza and Prieto Olavarría 2006, 2007). On this basis, after our work was finished, local and Spanish archaeologists continued excavating and they even resumed the study of the objects that we rescued, recorded, and left in warehouses at the National Park. Their reports (Delfor Ulloa 2007 in Callisalla Medina 2012) confirm our hypothesis and theoretical and methodological framework after extending the excavations and increasing the collection of objects we obtained, even though they do not include the corresponding references in the background and they only mention "vessels discovered by Argentineans in 2004 and 2006" (Callisalla Medina 2012, p. 7) in the epigraph of an image.

## 14.5 Approach and Aims of the Urban Archaeological Work in SCLV

Historical inquiry in cities makes us face and resolve aspects directly related with social and political life. The material dimensions express the degree of conflict resolution produced in a medium that accelerated the contradictions, thus generating an urban culture. This is particularly relevant in cases when, as in Santa Cruz, urban phenomenon was imposed as a mechanism of domination (there were no cities prior to this foundation). Thus, from the analysis of the archaeological contexts, the situation aims at considering the turning point that the foundation of a settlement with evident colonial intentions meant to in the history of the Spanish conquest of South America. Nevertheless, from a strategic geopolitical continental scale, it did not reach fruition because of those same dynamic processes of Spanish imperialism; also taking into account local resistance that eventually caused the abandonment and move of the city. This means that, in context, the abandonment represented a triumph for the native peoples over the colonial project, with a noteworthy prec-edent in the failed campaign against the Chiriguanos, in which Viceroy Toledo him-self was repelled (1574). However, the price the natives paid for their victory was the consolidation of another urban settlement elsewhere and the strengthening of a colonial policy that continued during the stages of independence and republic and which eventually took its toll on the indigenous peoples.

We not only decided to excavate a colonial city but to delve into a failed process of colonial conquest and the success of indigenous resistance in an environmental context where the ruins of an ephemeral city represent the acceptance of colonial defeat.

In this way, we would focus on historical archaeological practices in the modern sense but under the category of historical criticism, for the inclusion of America to this dimension would, as we understand it, fall within the logical analytical results of a universal history (global), while actually it becomes a precedent in the theo-retical construction of a domineering West, even from the proposed neocolonial discourse (see Dussel 1994 for considerations from a contextual history).

The founding foundation of cities is part of "the birth of Modern Age conceived in European Medieval cities…" when Europe could face "the Other" and control it, defeat it, violate it; when it could define itself as an "ego" that discovers, conquers, colonizes the very Otherness of Modern Age (Dussel 1994, p. 8). Thus, by means of the foundation of new cities, Europe realized the colonization of South America. It would then be in the sixteenth century when Europe would achieve the status of global center (in the territory) and inaugurate Modern Age (in time).

The inquiry into SCLV from this theoretical viewpoint was centered in the analy-sis of all edited documents and bodies of historical works, and above all, of works on prospective and archaeological excavation on the site. These works aimed, in the first place, at detecting and limiting the site according to different scales, then at establishing the overall characteristics of the urban structure (streets and blocks), and finally, excavating sectors that, in theory, served to different purposes within the set, such as temples, yards, and rooms (Chiavazza 2010; Chiavazza and Prieto Olavarría 2006, 2007).

## 14.6   Scales of Analysis: Prospection and Excavations in SCLV

The work was organized round three spatial scales of work: territorial, urban, and structural units. The first one allows to consider the environment in which the city was inserted; the second one supposes the analysis of the shape of the city; and the third one dwells with domestic life within an urban context. In the first case, the landscape is dominated by a serranía (range of mountains), in sharp contrast with the plains that spread out from there, which enables us to understand the city as an enclave that, from the geopolitical point of view, had to be supported, and from there guarantee the control of resources such as water. The urban scale shows a rather irregular layout (in analysis) due to its position at the foot of the mountains and it is dominated by a nucleus formed by the "plaza" and the two churches of the city. The third scale allows to understand how the inhabitants of the city respond to differentiated identities. The cultural material abandoned shows elements (made by indigenous people or settlers) used and discarded in a multidimensional urban lifestyle.

Prospecting the land involved covering the ground and tracing our steps by means of GPS, following the paths. Vegetation and escarpments make it impossible to think of different paths. The urban layout was also traced by means of GPS, placing the given relation between mounds and depressions, probing by means of a bore, at regular intervals along transects and articulating the results with a topographical map of the set of blocks around the area known as "plaza." In this area six excavations were made.

## 14.7    Results

The general result showed a unique and widespread settlement with materials that corresponded with those used during the sixteenth century. This enabled us to confirm that there had been a colonial settlement from the sixteenth century in the site. It could be determined that it corresponded with that of the city of SCLV (an aspect that so far had not been possible to establish due to the lack of documentation). The characteristics of the settlement, the type of constructions, the distinctive layout, and the materials found allowed to support the correspondence of the site with the historic foundation. A radiocarbon dating gave $445 \pm 38$ years BP (URU0424) consistent with the only fragment of majolica (green) registered in the site (Chiavazza and Prieto Olavarría 2006, p. 53).

### 14.7.1    Walking the Land

Prospections showed that the chosen site fulfilled a strategic role in many ways. In the first place, the visual reference of the Riquió is important when considering its presence and relevance in a flat landscape. The city was founded at its foot, with the logical connotations in terms of a homogeneous, mountainous, and unknown landscape, difficult to "dominate" but that in this way it was controlled from its main height (Fig. 14.2). Thus, in the second place, we can see the importance that colonial tactics gave to strategy; the representation is put into practice when exercising domination.

**Fig. 14.2** Panoramic view from the viewpoints of Mount Riquió, to the south of the city. *Below* lies SCLV and to the *right* Mount Turubó

This high viewpoint that allows to keep greater visual control of the green plains is reached by accessible paths, and areas of wide visual control can be accessed quite fast. This fact is not only an advantage from the symbolical point of view but from the material one as well. In the strategy for subsistence, positioning the city at the headwaters of the Sutó creek guaranteed, in the third place, the satisfaction of the need for water in an environment with clear seasonal contrasts as regards its availability. Water abounds and is scarce at alternate times. The city is far enough from floods and near enough to satisfy the needs of its inhabitants.

> …the city gets its water from a creek that flows from some rocks, that exudes from them; it is about a wrist deep. In the wet season this creek flows into some lagoons four leagues away, more or less, and from these lagoons come so much fish (four species) that it can feed all of the inhabitants abundantly…. (Pérez de Zurita in Finot 1939, p. 184)

But even so, it is also documented that the creek did not provide enough water for the whole population and therefore holes in the ground were also made, which stored the water and we realized that they were used as an alternative source in the city (Fig. 14.3).

> … the locals … drink from hand-made troughs so that (rainwater) collects there and life goes on; and sometimes water is scarce and they kill each other for it…... (Pérez de Zurita circa 1586 in Finot 1939, p. 185)

Thus, from the colonial point of view, the city lies at a significant place, with a strategic view and can satisfy the needs in order to subsist. In many ways it resembles the model elaborated by Bernardo de Vargas Machuca in 1599 to establish cities in America almost 40 years later (Morse 2002, p. 280).

So far, SCLV looked like a colonial success on a local scale. However, in a world plagued with uncertainties, indigenous resistance and geopolitical requirements would attempt something against these virtues. Without a clear support for local strategies, these strengths eventually weakened the city. This took place when the city experienced isolation due to a different organizational scheme of the colonial

**Fig. 14.3** General view of a waterhole that can still be found on the second block to the east of the plaza and which stores rainwater

lands within the Viceroyalty of Perú on a macro scale. The once valued labor force, now depleted due to excesses (Còmbes 2013), became the armed force of a native resistance that would be impossible to dominate.

## 14.8 Archaeology of the City SCLV

The layout of the city is relatively regular, with perpendicular streets which form blocks. Very likely, the postdepositional processes, the growth of vegetation, the random construction of entrances, new agricultural fields, etc., distorted the original layout. However, there is an underlying irregularity in the layout and a not entirely orthodox planning. Because of its position so close to the mountains, the central axis, even if centered on the plaza, is tilted to one side because of the presence of the mountain side, close to which the city was built, giving protection and easy access to viewpoints wherefrom control the whole territory (Fig. 14.4). However, just opposite the "plaza" two mounds stand out; they are the remains of the Mercedarian and Jesuit temples the city had, keeping a structure consistent with the religious significance colonization had. López de Gomara said "…He who does not colonize, does not completely conquer, and if the land is not conquered, its inhabitants will not be converted…" (in Morse 2002, p. 283).

### 14.8.1 Structures and Urban Equipment

#### 14.8.1.1 Plaza and Streets

An open space of ca. 10,000 m², clearly differentiated, corresponds to the "plaza" that presented an area of bricked floor. An intrasite prospection was performed with

**Fig. 14.4** Map of the city and the land around it

a bore with a diameter of 10 cm at 10 m intervals along two perpendicular transects, each 400 m long. This enabled us to check an occupation layer between 80 and 100 cm deep in the mounds and check the interfaces between streets, buildings (debris), and floors. It is interesting to point out the existence of a layer of gravel at a depth of 40–50 cm that we have taken for the transition between streets and buildings in low sectors. This feature was found in the grids from the southern end in excavation 1 (at the most prominent mound which we believe is the Jesuit temple). Materials are very scarce in the depressions between the mounds (= streets) and increased at the mounds (= eroded buildings; Fig. 14.5)

These studies gave some degree of certainty to the preliminary description of the urban layout that has enabled to hypothesize a vectorial plotting not wholly regular of the urban layout (*sensu* Nicolini 2005). Besides, in stratigraphical terms, a difference in ground level between streets and buildings was detected, allowing to pose that in certain parts of the city, the buildings were mounted on previously built platforms (terraces) made of earth to raise the floor level and this feature can be related to the floods during the rainy seasons. However, not all buildings present this feature.

### 14.8.1.2   Temples

From documentary descriptions we know that there were two religious orders in the city following the presence of priests in a temporary church whose location has not been documented: the Mercedarios (ca. 1571) and the Jesuits (ca. 1587–1599) (Tomichá Chapurá 2013).

Based on the hypothesis that they were temples, we excavated two mounds, one to the north and the other to the west of the "plaza." It all seems to suggest that they were remarkable buildings that demanded a remarkable constructive inversion. We established excavation 1 (E1) on the northern mound. There, we observed the evident collapse of a roof and a tapia wall that could have supported it. This structure was at some distance behind the hypothetical façade line. A striking aspect of this

**Fig. 14.5** Topography and location of the excavations in the area of the "plaza" and nearby blocks

mound is that it develops from east to west and that toward the inside there is a hollow (probably resulting from processes of deflation or even plunder). Notwithstanding, the slopes are gentle and there were no stratigraphical variations that showed a process other than the burning down of the wooden structure (below the level of tiles and in contact with the tapia wall) and the collapse of the roof (above the level of burnt wood and the tapia wall).

For preservation purposes, this excavation did not go beyond the level of the tiles which was left uncovered and the excavation reached deeper levels just in places where its continuity was not observed (Fig. 14.6).

Working upon the hypothesis that it was a temple and based on the mound orientation, we carried out a trial excavation in the middle of the hollow, making it coincide with an inner and central sector of what could be the church. The aim was to detect floors (tamped down and/or tiled) and funerary evidence. In this way, we might establish on the one hand the level of the church floor, and on the other, its orientation according to the burials that were found (E4). The results were satisfactory. A human burial was detected which was positioned from west to east (head to feet) which we believe would confirm that: (1) The place corresponded to a church. (2) The positioning (façade–altar) would go from east to west, that is, side by side with respect to the "plaza" (as it has been documented in other colonial cities, Nicolini 2005). (3) The person buried there would be a priest (because of its positioning with the head towards the altar). (4) The level of the floor of this building was about 1 m

**Fig. 14.6** Tile level as a result of the collapse of the roof of the temple that we estimate belonged to the Jesuit order

above the level of the street and "plaza." This supposes a cambering (highlighting) of the building in the urban context and, at the same time, the use of mounds as foundations in construction. In view of these results, it can be interpreted that there was an attempt to highlight the building within the urban context and guarantee its integrity and functionality in the event of potential flooding.

To the west of the "plaza," we worked in order to understand the presence of a set of rocky blocks that could be observed lined up on the intermediate and upper sectors of a mound of middle height. However, this mound stands out for its position on higher land than the "plaza." We made four excavations which enabled us to establish the existence of another significant building although no traces of a roof could be observed. The meaningful aspect was the laying foundations with rocks put together with mud (Fig. 14.7). The basis of the foundation was above the level of what was considered to be the street.

This corroborated the use of mounds to build upon. Furthermore, to the northern sector, in the vicinity of the foundation, a hole was excavated on what could tentatively be labeled as a dumping ground (E5.3). There was a great variety of artifacts and fragments of ceramics in a carbonaceous matrix together with extremely degraded bones. In this case, some of the objects found cast some doubt about the place being a dumping ground. We have seen this kind of pits associated to foundations of temples (as in the Jesuit church in Mendoza; Chiavazza 2005) where objects appear suggesting a hypothetical meaningful aggregation. The excavated

**Fig. 14.7** Foundations of
the church attributed to the
Mercedarios (to the west of
the "plaza")

sector was named E5.3 and here the greatest variety of objects can be registered, together with a large amount of pottery and coal. Pellets, buttons, flint-stone, remains of a padlock and even a presumed "sucking stone" (pacifier) make us presume that in this place not only trash was dumped. This presumption is based on the fact that the so-called dumping ground was situated near the foundations of a temple, not toward the street but toward the inside of the possible cloister. There is also the possibility that those objects correspond to trash that was dumped during a period of time prior to the construction of the church that, we think, belonged to the Mercedarios Order. So these objects could have been dumped between 1561 and 1571 (before the Mercedarios were established). It is of significance to have found among the discarded objects some related to defense: pellets and flint stone, which were not easily available and more so, in such a conflictive context as Santa Cruz, they could have been highly valued. These pits could have been offering sites of a foundational nature in certain buildings, such as churches. Anyway, for the time being this is mere speculation.

### 14.8.1.3 Houses and Yards

According to some documentary data (Julien 2008), the early city had "… straw houses and staked fences and there was no other shelter…," there were no "…tapia walls nor tapia-fenced pens, they were made with sticks…." But 30 years after its foundation, toward 1590, houses were built after a pattern detected in other contemporary South American cities, e.g., Santa Fe (Calvo 2011).

Chambers and bedrooms were connected with the street through yards:

> …did not dare sleep in his/her bedroom that was in front of that chamber, but he/she went out to a room closing the door that led to his/her bedroom, and this room had a door that led to the yard that in turn, led to the street and another opposite it that led to a kitchen garden and on the other side there was another room that served as a pantry…. (Combès and Peña 2013, p. 262, underlined by us)

**Fig. 14.8** Excavation 2 with
the remains of the collapse of
a room with partition walls

They were even connected to areas destined to productive activities associated to
the houses:

> …It was taken out to a small pen away from the main house…. (Combès and Peña 2013,
> p. 262)

Although it is clear that constructions in general had no tile-roofs or bricks in most
parts:

> … bricks and tiles that many people from the city, attracted by the news, watched come
> out, that were thrown from that chamber, from an elevated corner where, they say, saw two
> shadows, not having in the house nor even in many neighboring houses brick or tile, using
> palm leaves, emptied, as tiles…. (Combès and Peña 2013, p. 263, underlined by us)

To the northwest of the "plaza," in the heart of a block, we proceeded to excavate an
area that we estimated was open but within the domestic realm (E3). This possible
yard did not show any traces of floor conditioning and the recovered materials were
extremely scarce. The excavation did not allow to distinguish features connected to
concrete uses or activities nor closures or specific separate places.

Excavation 2 (E2) contributed with significant data regarding the material characteristics of domestic life (Fig. 14.8). It was made in a room located in the inner
sector of a house situated to the east of the "plaza." It would comply with the room
pattern already documented.

This room had partition walls and charred remains and imprints of motacú palm
trees (whose leaves were traditionally used to roof houses) were found. The wood
imprints were attached to the charred clay plaster that lined the houses.

In terms of construction, because of the start of a sustained war against native
Chiriguanos, fortifications were needed. Thus, when Ñuflo de Chaves returned from
Charcas in 1566, "he found this city strong and protected, surrounded by tapia walls
and two walls high, houses and yards all built and a lot of food on the ground…"
(Service reports from Hernando de Salazar 2008 [1568], p. 176. In Martínez 2013,
p. 63). The finding of fragments of coat of mail, pellets, and flint stone supports
the evidence of the use of violence to maintain the colonial settlement in South

America. However, except for the area adjoining the rocky wall of the mountain bordering the city, we could not find other evidence of this kind of construction.

To sum things up we can mention that there were buildings on earth mounds, on top of which important buildings such as churches were founded. The Jesuit church had tiled roofs (E1), whereas the Mercedario one (E5) presented less material investment (but important rocky foundations). Correspondence between burial sites and temples was only registered in the case of the church we consider belonged to the Society (E4)[1]. With regard to domestic areas, we could observe building techniques such as partition walls (E2) creating rooms that led on to the streets (E6) or to inner yards surrounded by tapia walls (E3).

## 14.9   Life in the City: Some Documentary Evidence and Archaeological Material

The pieces recovered from the excavations do not present great diversity. Those made of earth and clay (constructive and ceramics) predominate. A striking aspect was the low frequency of findings related to subsistence (zooarchaeological and archaeobotanical). We relate this aspect to postdepositional processes. Notwithstanding, there are documents that mention products which the inhabitants valued as resources (Table. 14.1).

When it comes to subsistence, urban life was, according to the documentation, tough. In Table 14.1 it can be seen that agricultural products predominate in a city that has no supplies

> …and this land is so poor that it has no wheat, no wine, no oil, and to say Mass, they are brought from Perú, 120 leagues from Santa Cruz and the wine jug, that would be the equivalent to a pitcher or an arroba in Spain, costs 100 to 120 pesos, that here are yardsticks of cloth, because there is no other currency, each costing six reales, that would make 600 reales or more.
> (…)
> Instead of wheat bread, we eat bread made from maize, yucca and sweet potatoes, that are roots from this land that also produce wine; and yet people are healthy, thank the Lord, there is no physician in this place and some people are over 100 years old and, at the Society, no one has died in more than 13 years since we came, thank the Lord. The mettle of the land should help, although from September to March it is hot and it would be almost uninhabitable if Our Lord had not provided that rains are more common in this season; and so when they are late, we suffer from their absence in November with the sun on our heads and during the other season it is seldom cold; and that happens only when the south wind from the Pole blows, that is like the Cierzo in Europe, for this land lies on the Tropic of Capricorn. (Còmbes and Peña 2013, p. 271)

---

[1]  A documentary source presents a precise event; a Mercedario priest leaving his church towards the "plaza" heading to the west. This points to E5 as being that church. Therefore, taking into consideration the evidence found in E1, which is associated to a religious place, we ascribed it to the Jesuit church. The report from Callisalla Medina (2012) is not clear about this but the fact that he mentions the "gobernación of Santa Cruz de la Sierra La Vieja" even when evidence of Catholic burials has been found (Callisalla Medina 2012, p. 9) is striking.

**Table 14.1** Plant and animal resources mentioned in documents according to their origin (sixteenth and seventeenth centuries). (Sources: Pérez de Zurita in Finot 1939, pp. 184–186; Fernández 1896, p. 125; Knogler in Hoffman 1979, p. 166; Schmid in Hoffman 1979, p. 190)

| Plant resources | Animal resources | | | |
|---|---|---|---|---|
| Native and wild | Native and domestic | Introd. | Native | Introd. |
| Palm trees 1 | Maize 1 | Grapes 1 | Fish 1, 2, 3, 4 | Horses1 |
| Guava 1 | Beans 1 | Melon 1 | Hares 3 | Cattle |
| Pineapple 1 | Pumpkin 1 | Figs 1 | Wild boars 3 | |
| Granadillas | Peanuts 1 | Sugarcane 1 | Rats 3 | |
| Ambaiba (*Cecropia palmata*) 1 | Mates 1 (calabazos) | Rice | Mice 3 | |
| Lúcuma1 | Yucca | | Snakes 3 | |
| Tucumay (tarumá?) 1 | | | Monkeys 3 | |
| Cotton plant 1 | | | Bees 4 | |
| Garrobilla 1 | | | Birds 4 | |
| Dye roots 1 | | | | |
| Motaquí 2 | | | | |
| Bananas | | | | |

**Table 14.2** Existing indigenous people in SCLV (based on data from Còmbes 2013, pp. 30–31)

| Year | Indigenous | | |
|---|---|---|---|
| | Registered | Domestic repartimientos in urban area | Personal service in the city |
| 1561 | 30,000–60,000 | n/a | n/a |
| 1570 | 15,700 | n/a | n/a |
| 1584 | n/a | 9000 | 3000 |
| 1586 | n/a | 8000–3000 | n/a |
| 1587 | n/a | 10,000–20,000 | n/a |
| 1601 | 4000 | n/a | n/a |

Despite the previous account, due to droughts and lack of food, illnesses took their toll, and 30 years after the foundation of the city, deeply affected the population: "Around July of that year [1590], there was an outbreak of smallpox and measles that killed many people" (Còmbes and Peña 2013, p. 260).

In this context, documentary data clearly highlight the presence of indigenous "encomendados" both within and around the city, even when its numbers were dramatically decreasing (Table 14.2). This decrease in population in 40 years was very likely linked to illnesses due to feeding and subsistence problems.

In addition, the huge language diversity is remarkable. Six linguistic groups have been identified in Santa Cruz La Vieja: Arawak, Guaraní, Chiquito, Zamuco, Guaycurú, and Otuqui-Chiquito which are in turn, subdivided into more than 15 ethnic groups, without taking into account those that do not identify themselves with any definite tongue (Còmbes 2013, p. 22).

On an archaeological level and bearing in mind the pottery skills and the availability of clay, this diversity produced a local manufacture component with very

**Table 14.3** Summary of recovered objects during the excavations in Santa Cruz de la Sierra la Vieja (SCLV)

| Excav. | Material | | | | | | | | | |
|---|---|---|---|---|---|---|---|---|---|---|
| | Pottery | Bone | Metal and scoria | Glass | Lithic | Carbon samples[a] | Spindle | Organic | Wickerwork | Total |
| 1 | 157 | – | 2 | – | 1 | 18 | – | 4[b] | – | 182 |
| 2 | 2368[c] | 11 | 3[d] | – | | 83[e] | 1 | 9[f] | 2[g] | 2477 |
| 3 | 48[h] | 4[i] | – | – | – | – | – | – | – | 52 |
| 4 | 29 | 1[j] | – | – | – | – | 1 | – | – | 31 |
| 5.1 | 577 | 2 | 1[k] | – | – | 58 | – | – | – | 638 |
| 5.2 | 3 | 1 | – | – | – | 1 | – | – | – | 5 |
| 5.3 | 861 | 10 | 3[l] | 1[m] | 3[n] | 12 | – | – | – | 890 |
| 5.4 | 172 | 3 | – | – | – | 13 | – | – | – | 188 |
| 6 | 214 | 15 | – | – | – | 25 | – | – | – | 254 |
| Total | 4429 | 47 | 9 | 1 | 4 | 210 | 2 | 13 | 2 | 4717 |

[a] Samples of different weights
[b] Archaeobotanical indeterminate
[c] It includes 13 vessels whole or partially reconstructed
[d] Coat of mail, nail, and grater–percolator
[e] One sample of a charred wooden structure
[f] Leather and taquia (plant)
[g] Imprints on burnt lumps
[h] Lid on tile
[i] It includes an egg shell
[j] Human skeleton
[k] One button
[l] One lead pellet and one iron padlock
[m] Bead
[n] One flint stone, one quartz tassel or pacifier

diverse shapes and decorations both of indigenous and Spanish traditions. Only one fragment of majolica was found and registered at E1. This can be an evidence of the isolation that SCLV experienced, where exchanges were reduced to the essential. However, this can be revised in the future, when new excavations are performed or if we consider that we are in the presence of a situation of abandonment so that the imported pieces, which were greatly valued, were moved with the city. But it is remarkable the low frequency of these type of objects, which with greater or smaller quantities, generally appear in cities from this period.

## *14.9.1 Trends in Materials*

Pottery is the most abundant material in the site ($N=4429$) and it represents 93.8% of all the archaeological items recovered (Table 14.3).

It must be said that the presence of indigenous pottery pieces in all of the excavations is small. They do not present complete and clearly defined regional typologies but, according to some recent and general propositions (Callau and Canedo 2002;

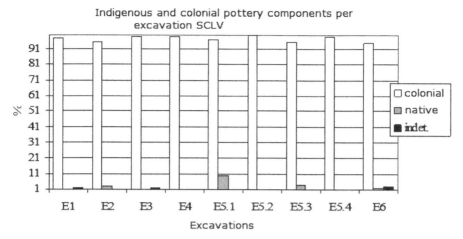

**Fig. 14.9**  Comparative tendencies of colonial and indigenous pottery artifacts

Requena and Callau 2006), it was possible to differentiate those pieces made following European techniques from those of local extraction (at least considering stylistic aspects in this first approach).

Excavation E2 deserves to be highlighted since there a context of departure was found, with whole vessels onto which a motacú roof and partition walls would have collapsed. This could be a domestic place for storing and processing (kitchen). The vessels present both colonial and indigenous typologies. They were found together with other utensils such as a copper percolator, abundant carbon remains, undetermined mineral scoriae, bone splinters, spindles, and traces of wickerwork (imprints of what could have been a rush-mat woven with fibers).

Regarding pottery, 54 % of the total amount was recovered in E2, in a context with a density of 88.5 archaeological elements per square meter. This density is only surpassed by the pit next to the foundations of the Mercedario building (E5,3) with 445 archaeological elements per square meter but that contained 19.5 % of the total pottery found. These two excavations also presented the greater diversity in terms of kinds of artifacts (Chiavazza 2010).

During the first detailed analytical assessment of the fragments, 27 types were defined according to microscopic aspects related to surface treatment, coloring, decoration, shape, and thickness. They were analyzed by means of a magnifying glass and different patterns of material as regards the matrix and the inclusions in terms of shape, color, size, and density (Chiavazza and Prieto Olavarría 2007, pp. 71–76) could be observed. This characteristic together with formal and decorative aspects enabled us to present two large typological groups (colonial or historical and indigenous or native). Even if the result presented a marked tendency toward typological diversity, it showed the predominance of handcrafts typologically related to the colonial group (Fig. 14.9).

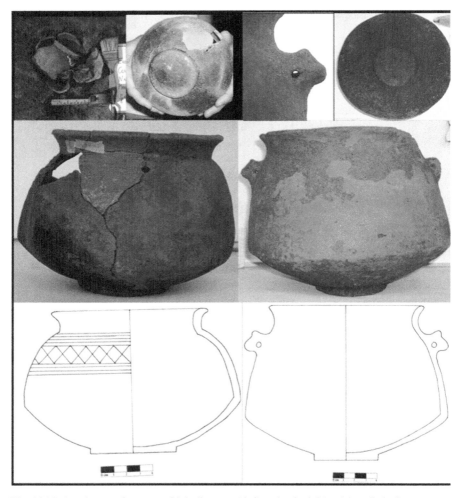

**Fig. 14.10** Specimens of pottery with indigenous (*left*) and colonial (*right*) stylistic features

   This would show that the numerous indigenous populations, with a strong traditional component as potters, was rapidly incorporated into the new pottery techniques not only from the point of view of design associated to new ways of storing, cooking, and consumption but also of decoration (Fig. 14.10). Pieces classified as belonging to indigenous tradition are found in lower numbers than colonial ones in this site when compared with other sites with components limited to the sixteenth century (e.g., Mendoza—Chiavazza et al. 2013; Ciudad Vieja in San Salvador—Fowler 2011). We do not rule out the influence of bias when sampling, generated by the choice of sites where to excavate.

## 14.10    Results and Conclusion

> …This road presents another difficulty, from the huge Guapay river to Santa Cruz, almost 50 leagues, there is no river or spring but lagoons of water from the sky, that one can drink from, so at times you cannot travel because of too little and at other times, because of too much (water). (Còmbes and Peña 2013, p. 259)

The nucleus of the city and the territory showed evidences that denote an urban process that grew for 40 years (according to documentation) because of its strategic position in the frontier during colonial disputes but that, when it was no longer useful to the geopolitical macro-regional interests, had to be abandoned. The discovery of new routes and the increase in costs for its upkeep, given the absence of the promised riches and the indigenous resistance, made it nonviable.

Archaeological excavations and the study of documents have allowed to confirm the existence of an urban settlement in this sector and that its chronology corresponds to the period comprised between the foundation and the abandonment of the city (1561–1604). From this information, an extensive outline of the urban process of foundation, growth, and abandonment of SCLV is proposed. Furthermore, the analysis of the correlation between mounds and depressions allowed to establish that they are related to the discontinuity between public (streets) and private (buildings) places. As regards artifacts, small general diversity was perceived which we understood could be the result of its short period of occupation and, above all, of a context of planned abandonment that involved moving many goods. This short period of occupation enables to define a stratified archaeological component, giving a high level of temporal resolution for an urban installment (it fulfills the expectation of excavating an intense and dense settlement but not older than 40 years). With regard to pottery artifacts, the lack of correspondence with the documented narration about a huge ethnic diversity inhabiting the city was striking, since this diversity is not reflected in the amount of pottery artifacts of indigenous origin found.

In short, we were not only excavating a colonial city but also having the difficult experience of the failed consolidation and, above all, a colonial defeat for the Conquistadores. Between 1561 and 1604, Modern Age laid its foundations in a city that could not settle down. This brought about a forced move to the west. On the site of its original settlement, the ruins emerge as the undisputed evidence of the decision to abandon it; which, to a certain extent, represents the acceptance of an indigenous victory according to the interpretation we offered to its makers. This proposition was clearly contradictory to the interests for its enhancement, where the monumentalization of the site aimed and still aims at the exaltation of the identity of Santa Cruz as counterpart to its belonging to Bolivia. The research has been productive, the interpretation can, naturally, be debatable; perhaps that is why our interpretation has not yet prospered.

# References

Balza Alarcón, R. (2001). *Tierra, territorio y territorialidad indígena. Un estudio antropológico sobre la evolución en las formas de ocupación del espacio del pueblo indígena chiquitano de la ex reducción de San José*. Santa Cruz: APCOB/SNV/IWGIA.

Callau, C., & Canedo, T. (2002). Manual de catalogación cerámica. Unidad de Turismo y Cultura, Prefectura de Santa Cruz. Bolivia.

Callisalla Medina, L. M. (2012). Investigación y musealización de Santa Cruz de la Sierra la Vieja en 2012. Gobierno Autónomo Departamental de Santa Cruz, Escuela taller de la Chiquitania del Plan Misiones, Gobierno Autónomo Municipal de San José de Chiquitos, DIAP PNHSCLV Dirección del Parque Nacional Histórico Santa Cruz la Vieja, Comité de gestión del Parque Nacional Histórico Santa Cruz la Vieja. COMAYO. Informe Manuscrito Final de Consultoria.

Calvo, L. M. (2011). Vivienda y ciudad colonial. El caso de Santa Fe. Ediciones Universidad Nacional del Litoral. Santa Fe.

Chiavazza, H. (2005). Los templos coloniales como estructuras funerarias. Arqueología en la iglesia jesuita de Mendoza. British Archaeological Reports. 1388. Londres.

Chiavazza, H. (2010). Colonización y Urbanismo en el Ambiente de las Tierras Bajas de Sudamérica durante el siglo XVI. Arqueología en Santa Cruz de la Sierra, Bolivia. In H. Chiavazza & C. Cerutti (Eds.), *Arqueología de ciudades Americanas del siglo XVI* (pp. 31–62). Mendoza: Editorial de la FFyL, UNCuyo.

Chiavazza, H. (2013). Arqueología de la Primera Santa Cruz de la Sierra. In I. Còmbes & P. Peña (Compilers), *Santa Cruz la Vieja (1561–1601)* (pp 109–146). Santa Cruz de la Sierra: Fondo Editorial, Gob Municipal Autónomo de Santa Cruz de la Sierra.

Chiavazza, H., & Prieto Olavarría, C. (2006). *Arqueología histórica en el corazón de Sudamérica: Santa Cruz de la Sierra la Vieja San José de Chiquitos*. Santa Cruz: Ed. Dirección de Turismo y Cultura de la prefectura de Santa Cruz.

Chiavazza, H., & Prieto Olavarría, C. (2007). Arqueología histórica en Santa Cruz de la Sierra la Vieja (II). Santa Cruz: Ed. Dirección de Cultura, Alcaldía de Santa Cruz de la Sierra.

Chiavazza, H., Prieto Olavarría, C., Zorrilla, V. (2013). Procesos sociales y ambientales en el sector urbano de Mendoza entre los siglos XIV-XVII. Actas del V Congreso Nacional de Arqueología Histórica. Tomo 2: 63-100. Editorial Academia Española. Alemania.

Còmbes, I. (2013). Santa Cruz Indígena. In I. Còmbes & P. Peña (Compilers), *Santa Cruz la Vieja (1561–1601)* (pp 15–32). Santa Cruz de la Sierra: Fondo Editorial, Gob Municipal Autónomo de Santa Cruz de la Sierra.

Còmbes, I., & Peña, P. (2013). *Santa Cruz la Vieja (1561–1601)*. Santa Cruz de la Sierra: Fondo Editorial, Gob Municipal Autónomo de Santa Cruz de la Sierra.

Cortés, E. (1974) El mito de las traslaciones de Santa Cruz de la Sierra o la interpretación, sociológicadesufundación, Jisunu n°1: 25–47. Academia de las Culturas Nativas de Oriente, Santa Cruz.

Dussel, E. (1994). 1492 El encubrimiento del otro. Hacia el origen del "mito de la modernidad". Ed. Plural, Universidad Mayor de San Andrés, La Paz.

Fernández, J.P. [1726] (1896). *Relación Historial de las Misiones de indios Chiquitos que en el Paraguay tienen los padres de la Compañía de Jesús*. Asunción: Biblioteca Paraguaya.

Finot, E. (1939). *Historia de la Conquista del Oriente Boliviano*. Buenos Aires: Librería Cervantes.

Fowler, W. (2011). Ciudad Vieja. Excavaciones, arquitectura y paisaje cultural de la primera villa de San Salvador. Secretaría de Cultura de la Presidencia, Editorial Universitaria. El Salvador.

Gandarilla, N. (2004). Prólogo. La gran decisión. In *La Creación del Parque Nacional Histórico Santa Cruz La Vieja* (pp. 6–10). San José de Chiquitos: Fundación Natura Viva. Editorial Imágen Gráfica.

Hoberman, L., & Socolow, S. (1993). Ciudades y sociedad en Latinoamérica colonial. Fondo de Cultura Económica.

Hoffman, W. (1979). *Las misiones jesuíticas entre los chiquitanos*. Buenos Aires: Fundación para la Educación, la Ciencia y la Cultura.

Julien, K. (2008). *Desde el Oriente. Documentos para la historia del Oriente boliviano y Santa Cruz la vieja (1542–1597)*. Santa Cruz: Fondo Editorial Municipal.

Martínez, C. (2013). Del Paraguay al piedemonte, de amigos a adversarios: Ñuflo de Chávez y los guaraníes en la conquista de Santa Cruz de la Sierra. In I. Còmbes & P. Peña (Compilers), *Santa Cruz la Vieja (1561–1601)* (pp. 33–66). Santa Cruz de la Sierra: Fondo Editorial, Gob Municipal Autónomo de Santa Cruz de la Sierra.

Métraux, A. (1942). The native tribes of eastern Bolivia and western Matto Grosso. *Bulletin 143*. Washington DC: Smithsonian Institution. Bureau of American Ethnology.

Morales Padrón, F. (1963). *Historia del Descubrimiento y conquista de América*. Madrid: Ed. Nacional.

Morse, R. (2002). El desarrollo urbano en Hispanoamérica colonial. In Economía y Sociedad. *América Latina en la época colonial, vol. 2*, pp. 273–306. Barcelona: Crítica. Cambridge University Press, Editorial Crítica.

Muñoz Reyes, J. (1980). Geografía de Bolivia. Editorial Juventud. La Paz.

Musset, A. (2011). *Ciudades nómadas del Nuevo mundo*. Mexico City: Fondo de Cultura Económica.

Nicolini, A. (2005). La Ciudad Hispanoamericana, medieval, renacentista y americana. Atrio. Revista de Historia del Arte. 10/11, pp. 27–36.

Requena, C., & Callau, O. (2006). Catálogo de San Carlos. Unidad de Turismo y Cultura, Prefectura de Santa Cruz. Bolivia.

Romero Romero, C. (1989). Fundaciones españolas en América: una sucesión cronológica. In *CEHOPU, La ciudad hispanoamericana: el sueño de un orden* (pp. 275–302). Madrid: Ministerio de Obras Públicas y Urbanismo.

Sanzetenea, R., & Tonelli, O. (2003). *Proyecto de Excavación Arqueológica y Puesta en Valor de Santa Cruz la Viexa*. Santa Cruz: prefectura de Santa Cruz de la Sierra (manuscrito inédito).

Suárez Núñez del Prado, S., Cuellar, B. A., & Montenegro, E. (2004). Documento. Parque Nacional Histórico Santa Cruz La Vieja. Fundamentos para su creación. Santa Cruz: Proyecto UTD-CDF-SC, 1988/San José de Chiquitos: Fundación Natura Viva.

Susnik, B. (1978) *Los aborígenes del Paraguay I. Etnología del Chaco boreal y su periferia (siglos XVI y XVII)*. Asunción: Museo etnográfico Andrés Barbero.

Tomichá Chapurá, R. (2013). Apuntes sobre la iglesia en la primera Santa Cruz. In I. Còmbes & P. Peña (Compilers), *Santa Cruz la Vieja (1561–1601)* (pp 67–82). Santa Cruz de la Sierra: Fondo Editorial, Gob Municipal Autónomo de Santa Cruz de la Sierra.

# Chapter 15
# Nautical Landscapes in the Sixteenth Century: An Archaeological Approach to the Coast of São Paulo (Brazil)

Paulo Fernando Bava de Camargo

## 15.1 Introduction

The initial contact between Europeans and indigenous peoples in Brazil occurred in the coastal area. As a result, we can imagine that the first buildings, structures and appropriations of elements from nature as components of euro-indigenous landscapes of the sixteenth century would be connected to the nautical needs required in that specific environment. Archaeological research related to the conquest and colonization processes should happen, preferably, in these coastal and bordering environments, including submerged portions of land and those connected to bodies of water.

However, we live in a different reality. Archaeological research about the initial contact between these populations experienced a significant development between the 1960's and the beginning of the 1990's. Despite the great uproar provoked by the fifth centennial of the arrival of Cabral's fleet (during the years prior to April, 22nd 2000), this type of study lost importance in the riverine-maritime archaeological setting along the coast of São Paulo.

The lack of refinement in the historical approaches regarding the subject of nautical themes adds to this situation. Contact is known to have happened in the coastal environment, including rivers and estuaries, but there is no precise perception that there is a determining relationship between the nautical equipment of these populations and the genesis of the occupation of the territory. In other words, a general claim that "the Portuguese arrived in caravels and disembarked in a Brazilian estuary" is not the same as affirming, "The Europeans came in ships and anchored in a determined bay, disembarking with small craft, at the beach". Each nautical action developed in this new territory depended on the purposes, the relationships established with the natives, the knowledge of local geography, and the available floating

P. F. Bava de Camargo (✉)
Department of Archaeology, Federal University of Sergipe, Samuel de Oliveira Square, Downtown, Laranjeiras, SE 49170-000, Brazil
e-mail: pfbavacamargo@yahoo.com.br

© Springer International Publishing Switzerland 2015
P. P. A. Funari, M. X. Senatore (eds.), *Archaeology of Culture Contact and Colonialism in Spanish and Portuguese America*, DOI 10.1007/978-3-319-08069-7_15

equipment. As a consequence, the results of this interaction determined the course of the conquest and colonization.

It is also overly simplistic and biased to mention in passing that the natives "used canoes", without ever trying to study the equipment involved in this action, the navigation techniques or the spaces created or maintained for the construction, protection and maintenance of these watercraft. After all, taking as an example a specific case, it is improbable that a Tupinambá warrior would not have a special zeal with his weaponry, including war canoes, which are always represented in the combat scenes represented in the original art by Hans Staden (1974). The natives' capability to threaten the new inhabitants or make them their new allies—with war skills that could be projected to other territories—was a determining factor to consolidate the European intentions in many regions of the new lands.

The main goal of this chapter is to understand which are the elements of the material culture that determine the 1500s landscapes regarding Euro-indigenous contact in the coast of São Paulo state, the region where I have focused my activities as a researcher until recently. In addition to this main goal, I propose an approach that can contribute to the construction of a broader historical-archaeological perspective of the contact.

## 15.2   Rightful Course/Route: The Appropriation of Geography

I start with the letter of Pero Vaz de Caminha addressed to King Dom Manuel, written in 1500. In it several aspects are highlighted: the first description of the Terra de Vera Cruz [Land of the True Cross], the first name given to Brazil; the first possible official contact between Europeans and natives in South America; the possession of territory already occupied, characterizing the first expropriation imposed on natives; and so on. There is, however, an unnoticed aspect: that the letter is also a report of events related to navigation.

The descriptions revealed the sea conditions and the existing needs of a large fleet that approached an unknown or poorly known territory. It involved, firstly, the identification of natural elements to the determination of landing and the appropriation of visual marks as reference points for coastal navigation.

> So, we followed our way, through this sea, until, Tuesday of the Easter Octaves, (…) which were the 21 days of April, (…) we came across some signs of land, which were a great quantity of long herbs, that the sailors called algae, like others that they give the name of rabo-de-asno[1]. And the following Wednesday, in the morning, we came across birds that they call fura-buxos[2]. (…) This same day, at the hours of vespers, we sighted land! First a very high rounded mountain, then another lower range of hills to the south of it; and plains, with large groves: to the high hill the captain gave the name—Pascoal [Easter mountain] and the land—Terra da Vera Cruz (Brasil, u.d.).

---

[1] Horsetail (*Equisetum sp.*).

[2] Popular name of puffins.

So, this procedure of nature's appropriation was repeated numerous times, until all the coastal territory was recognized by navigators. The case of São Paulo's coast is no different; toponyms are the first element relevant for archaeological research.

Usually, archaeological sites from the contact period are located, today, underwater or under numerous layers of urban occupation of coastal cities, some of them, true metropolises with busy ports. As a consequence, several vestiges are hard to get, demanding complicated logistics and urban management, including diving in polluted waters along with intensive ship traffic.

On the other hand, there were no significant changes in the 1500s toponyms. Although both native and European denominations of geographic elements lasted through the first centuries of colonization, the European names prevailed at the end.

In Cananéia, along the southern coast of the state of São Paulo—where I developed the research for my thesis and dissertation—as well as Monte Pascoal the visual mark is São João [Saint John] hill, in the past known as Candairó[3] (Almeida 1952, p. 9). Together with the island of Bom Abrigo [Good Shelter], it is one of the most important nautical geographic references in Cananéia, its denomination serving an explicit purpose. São João Batista [Saint John the Baptist] is known for, while still in his mother's womb, announcing the arrival of the Messiah[4]. Later, when he and Jesus were adults, there was the belief that João Batista was actually the Messiah. When, his disciples were in doubt about who was the truthful Messiah, João pointed to Jesus, and since then he became known for indicating the *Rumo Certo* [Rightful Route][5] so, the naming of a hill, visible from miles from practically all points of the lagoon-estuarine complex and surrounding maritime area, in an island with elevations that reach a maximum height of 20 m (average of 5–6 m), is significant.

This could be considered more a local fact than a pattern of navigators from the sixteenth century. But, if we pay attention to other references, there are indications of recurrent nominations of notable points with hagiology or biblical passages.

São Vicente, the first settlement of the São Paulo coast to become a village, in 1532, derives its name from Saint Vicente (from Zaragoza, Spain), which together with Saint Antonio were patrons of Lisbon, Portugal. The history of the veneration of the martyred remains of Saint Vicente is associated with nautical events. First, they tried unsuccessfully to bury the body in the sea soon after his death in the fourth century, since he was returned to the beach; later, between the seventh and eighth centuries some people from Valencia were fleeing from an attack by the Moors placed his body in a boat and took it to what is now known as the Cape of Saint Vicente, on the Portuguese coast. Later, during the reconquest of the Algarve in 1173, the remains of the martyr were placed in a ship destined for Lisbon, which was followed during the entire trip by two crows (Carillo 1613, pp. 110–115). Both

---

[3] This hill is 137 m high. Its function as a guide for sailors is increased by the Morrete [Little Hill] of Comprida [Long] island, which is 42 m high and is practically in front of the hill, on the opposite margin of the Pequeno [Little] sea.

[4] Luke, 1, p. 41–43.

[5] John, 1, p. 29–34.

the ship and the birds are represented in the city's coat of arms, which indicates the great importance of this event in the medieval genesis of Lisbon.

The same occurs with Santo Amaro, the neighboring island of São Vicente. Saint Amaro saved his cousin of drowning by walking on the water.

Saint John would be present in another bay entrance, important to the access to the *lagamar* [estuarine-lagoonal environment] of Santos, São Vicente and Bertioga. The fortification of Saint Tiago (another fisherman and sailor from Galilee, brother of John) was built in the opening of this bay, in the first decades of the sixteenth century.

It is possible to assert that these names were given because of the timing of the arrival of the sailors to those areas, or according to the devotion of the builder, normally accepted explanations. But, on the other hand, this type of naming, alluding to Christian passages related to water, was easily memorized by the sailors, most of whom were illiterate Catholics. They constituted a type of nautical itinerary based on religion.

Therefore, the concept of the arrival to a land from a watercraft would be very specific. The navigator does not arrive to the land when he disembarks, but when he sees it[6]—which could occur long before he places his foot on land—if it happens. The sailor-nominator would have some days to decide what would be the best name—sanctified or not—to designate a new land.

In the case of Monte Pascoal, despite its intrinsic connection with the commemoration of Easter upon the arrival of Cabral, its naming presents a certain ambiguity. Easter, in Latin *ressurectio*, in Greek *anastasis,* means resurrection or elevation, but *anastasis* also means the building above the rock-cut tomb of Christ on the Church of Holy Sepulchre in Jerusalem (Martins 2012, p. 104), a prominent and isolated/detached structure surrounded by the Church. There is the possibility that the naming of the elevation, instead of meaning the religious event, was related to the nautical function of the promontory, which was associated with the religious building related to the religious event. This inverse relationship was difficult to perceive from the letter written by Caminha, since he affirms: "From the seamanship and navigation I will not describe here to Your Highness, because I would not know how to do it, and the captains must have this responsibility".

Clearly, there are other names that do not allude to biblical passages or saints related to water or navigation in the South Central coastal Brazil, São Felipe, São Francisco, São Sebastião, and others. I do not argue that there was a deliberate plan to name all these geographical entities with nautical biblical references, but that this simple/basic association between the lives of saints and local geography could facilitate the charge of sailors. This, similar to some of the islands that were named according to their functionality or existing resources: do Mel [Honey], do Bom Abrigo [Good Shelter], Alcatrazes [Boobies, tropical sea birds of the genus *Sula*], dos Porcos [Pigs] (today, Anchieta), do Mar Virado [Churning Sea], among others.

---

[6] This specific relation becomes clear in the chronicle "Landfalls and departures" (The Mirror of the Sea) of the polish author Joseph Conrad (1857–1924), who for many years was a crewmember on commercial English ships.

Of course there is some relationship, not yet entirely understood, between religious understanding and the attribution of names to notable points along the coast. This relationship could be better understood if researchers, historians as well as archaeologists, approached the coastal environments not only as a physical interface between the land and the sea, but also as a mediator between societies and cultures.

## 15.3   Mooring, Anchoring and Landing

Mooring (lowering an anchor, allowing it to settle according to the winds and tides) and anchoring (lowering at least three anchors, leaving the ship practically immobile) were important parts of the process of preserving men and machines of the Conquest (Duran 2008). Nevertheless, they are fundamental activities, which deserve the highest attention from the sailors, because they are the heaviest equipment with which they work, as well as because they represent in many situations the only manner to prevent the loss of the ship.

Returning to Caminha's letter, it highlights the difficulty in anchoring Cabral's fleet:

> On this day, at vespers hours, we saw land! (…) He ordered them to drop the plumb-line. And they measured twenty-five fathoms; and at sunset, about six leagues from the shore, we dropped anchor in nineteen fathoms—a clean anchorage. There we lay all night. On Thursday morning we set sail and made straight for land, with the smaller ships leading, the water being seventeen, sixteen, fifteen, fourteen, thirteen, twelve, ten and nine fathoms deep, until half a league from the shore, where we all cast anchor in front of a river mouth. It must have been more or less ten o'clock when we reached this anchorage (…).

> On the following night, the wind blew from the southeast with rains that hunted the ships, and especially the captainship. On Friday morning, at eight more or less, at the advice of the pilots, the Captain raised the anchors and set sail; (…) And, sailing to the coast, about ten leagues of the site where we left, the smaller boats found a reef with a port inside, very good and very safe, with a very wide entrance. And they entered and lowered the sails. The ships arrived; and a little before sunset also lowered the sails, at around one league from the reef, and anchored at eleven fathoms. (…) On Saturday morning the captain set sail, and we entered through a wide and tall entry with five or six fathoms—a place so large, so beautiful and so safe, that could fit more than two hundred ships and boats (Brasil u.d.).

Adding to the inherent difficulties of the transoceanic navigation of that time, the safe anchoring of a powerful fleet, organized to install a fortified trading post (*feitoria*) in Calicute, India (Del Priore and Venâncio 2010, p. 16), was an extraordinary feat, so much that the area where this happened is known to this day as Porto Seguro [safe port], in Bahia. Still, not all points on the coast could serve as safe ports for large ships. And there are some that only offer safe harbor in certain periods.

On the island of Bom Abrigo, at the entry of the Cananéia bay, Pero Lopes de Sousa anchored. He was brother and one of the crewmembers of Martim Afonso de Sousa's fleet. Pero Lopes tells us that, stopping there on the 12th of August:

> Here on this island we stayed for 44 days: during which we never saw the sun; night and day it rained on us always with much thunder and lightning: on these days there was not

wind but from the southwest to the south. These winds gave us large storms and, so harsh as I never saw before. Here we lost many anchors, and broke many cables/ropes (Keating and Maranhão 2011).

Without doubt the fleet's situation would have been much worse if it had not been at the shelter of the Bom Abrigo, but since they anchored at seven fathoms—15.4 m— this could attest that they were not so close to the island, as nowadays the area of the anchoring is not that deep. It suggests the necessity to maintain a safe distance from the lands that could have people who are hostile to the intentions of the Portuguese *capitão donatário*[7], as well as the Spanish, who were predominant to the south of the São Vicente until the middle of the seventeenth century.

On the other hand, oceanographic data about the changes of the sea floor in the last centuries is lacking. Because oceanographic observations seek to understand the changes of the last decades using aerial photos and satellite images, oceanographic analyses also have data about sea dynamics over the course of thousands of years, obtained through geological cores. For the analyses of events and processes occurring over the course of hundreds of years, the main data are from nautical charts—more precise after the nineteenth century, or archaeological sites (Bavade-Camargo 2002). In other words, we cannot confirm if the Bom Abrigo harbor was deeper solely based upon the oceanographic information. Actually, archaeology will provide information to oceanography in order to understand the dynamic of sea floors in this temporal scale.

The anchorage of Bom Abrigo island presents an important underwater archaeological site (Rambelli 2003; Duran 2008; Guimarães 2010). Neither anchors nor grapnels from sixteenth century ships were found, but at least two anchors found there were Admiralty type (nineteenth–twentieth centuries), in addition to numerous whale bones (Guimarães 2010), remains of butchering in the island fishing depot, which operated between the second half of the eighteenth and the first decades of the nineteenth century (Duran 2008).

Whale bones were found in underwater excavation, but contrary to what one might imagine, they were not found buried beneath a thick layer of sediment (Guimarães 2010). This could indicate that this deposition, in the anchorage near the main beach of the island, was not so accentuated, allowing us to propose the hypothesis that the ships of the fleet of the Sousa brothers were not as close to Bom Abrigo.

The area from Cananéia island to the hill of São João, together with the mouth of the Olaria river, provides the best anchorage for large ships, with depths between 4 and 17 m and a sea bottom that allowed the anchor to be secured and released easily. It extends upon the waters of the Pequeno sea, and forms a bay with the mouth of the river that is protected from the southern winds, which does not happen in the sea in front of the city. Because of this, it is thought that the bay near the hill was the main anchorage of the settlement until at least the eighteenth century and that

---

[7] The recipient of a hereditary captaincy, the original Administrative division of the Brazilian colony.

a settlement was established in its surroundings in order to satisfy the needs of the crewmembers and ships.

Actually, the small bay formed by the hill and the river mouth is the largest anchorage of the island, principally for fishing boats, the largest that enter and leave through the main sound.

A frontispiece of the city drawn in 1776 indicates that it was based on the port of Cananéia. The perspective could only be obtained by someone who was in a boat of relatively large dimensions anchored near the point of the hill of São João.

If the mouth of the river was the anchorage, its margins and those of its tributaries would have been the preferred points for embarking and disembarking for the conquistador-colonizers. Perhaps they were also the preferred locations of the native and *sambaqui*[8] populations, since that region had less mangrove and mud, which complicates the simplest operations of loading, unloading, or anchoring.

The Olaria river was previously known as the Sambaqui river, demonstrating the importance of this type of archaeological site for the population, primarily in order to obtain lime. Today, at least one of these shell mounds remains—named Carijó—identified in the 1970–1980's (Garcia and Uchôa 1983 *apud* Calippo 2004). According to Calippo (2004), the establishment of this type of human settlement was more connected to the *restinga* environment, dominated by beaches, dunes, and sand. So, it is possible to deduce that the Olaria river and its tributaries provided better conditions for anchorage, even at the time of the European arrival.

Another factor influencing the deposition of fine sediments along the river margins is the anthropogenic actions that impede it. The non-fixation of the mangrove vegetation in some points of the bay/lagoon depends on the suppression of the plants by humans. It they are not removed, the plants form "traps" for the accumulation of more sediment, limiting the free access to the margins due to the growth of mangrove. In the estuarine-lagoonal region of Cananéia-Iguape, with the decline of importance of navigation for the common/daily movements of the population and laws of environmental protection, the plants are no longer cut, and the mangrove has proliferated, filling areas previously good for landing.

As a consequence, it is possible to think that the margins of the Olaria and other navigable routes were cleared from time to time, even during pre-Colonial times. This certainly occurred ruing recent times, as old photographs from the end of the nineteenth century up to the first decades of the twentieth century show a large quantity of canoes navigating in its margins (Bava-de-Camargo 2009). Until today, small boats cross its polluted waters, coming and going from the island's interior, the home of most of the fishermen.

In terms of written historical sources, there are three references to landing areas that are very significant. One of them mentions the port of Bugres[9], located along the old margins of the Ipiranga stream, a stretch of water influenced by the tides that is now an underground canal. In addition to canoes, it is believed that high tides would have allowed larger boats—*smacks, barges*—due to the demand of the

---

[8] Shell mound sites in Brazil are known as sambaquis.

[9] An ancient and derrogatory word used to designate natives/Indians in general.

houses situated in the oldest street of the city, Tristão Lobo (Almeida 1962, p. 215). The author, A. Paulino de Almeida, indicates that old nautical cables/ropes were found in these landing areas (Almeida 1964, pp. 443–444).

There is no evidence indicating the dates of operation of the port of Bugres, but the toponym offers a clue. "Porto dos Bugres" can indicate a port used by indigenous populations or a boarding area for Bugres, or in other words, an area for concentration and commercialization of captured Indians to be sold as slaves. John M. Monteiro writes that until 1630, many of the southern ports were involved with the Indian slave trade (1994, pp. 64–66). Cananéia was probably not an exception. Long before, Francisco de Chaves promised Martim and Pero Lopes de Souza during their first stay in 1531 that he would return from the interior with 400 slaves loaded with gold and silver (Keating and Maranhão 2011). Much more than pointing to the existence of mineral wealth in the interior, the promise indicated that obtaining slaves in great quantities was a common practice for the Portuguese Chaves.

The naming can refer to two things, since the manipulation of familial and intertribal indigenous relations by the Europeans stimulated the capture of natives by natives. The coastal Carijós[10] were important allies of the Portuguese in this commerce during the sixteenth century, until the Portuguese began to enslave their own allies by the first decades of the seventeenth centuries (Monteiro 1994).

This ancestral port (Bugres) had lost its importance by the eighteenth century. We can deduce this from documentation referring to the construction of two bridges of stone and lime above the Ipiranga in 1739 (Almeida, 1964, p. 496), which would have partially impeded its navigation, at least upstream from them, right at the original urban center of the settlement.

Still dealing with the navigation in the interior of Cananéia island, it is near the confluence of the Ipiranga and the Olaria that we find the origin of the Poço do Barco [Boat's Well] story. In the second stretch of the river, from the mouth to the interior, well south of the Figueira's [*Ficus* genus tree] esplanade, the depth increased. This was the area where a ship would have been sunk intentionally to escape a pirate. Following the danger, the boat would have been raised along with its treasure (Almeida 1952). This history or story reinforces the idea of systematic navigation in the vicinity of the Olaria/ Ipiranga complex.

## 15.4   Shipyards and Safety

Other landing areas were associated with nautical emergencies, such as in the case of the Sousa brothers' fleet in the summer of 1532, a few days before arriving in São Vicente:

> Tuesday January 8th at dawn we were at the margins of land; and at noon we saw the river on the northeast of Cananéia (…) Since I noticed that we could not put into port at the island of Cananéia: at sunset we came up to her land.

---

[10] Indians from the Tupi Guarani linguistic branch.

Wednesday 9th of the same month we had some large leak in the ship that gave us great work. Here in this island we stayed until Wednesday January 16th, departed with Southwest winds, always with a lot of leakage, which was not carried by the two pumps (Keating and Maranhão 2011).

It is possible that the Armada had remained in Bom Abrigo island for some days without success in repairing the damage to the ship, since it continued to leak until São Vicente.

However, could they have repaired their boats in the Cananéia region if they wanted? Would they have had the necessary knowledge, adequate space for pull the ship up on to the beach, wood for repairs, running water and workers? It is worth noting that the armada had built, 18 months earlier, in Rio de Janeiro, two brigantines each with 15 seats, paddles and sails (Keating and Maranhão 2011). These were small watercraft in comparison to ships and some caravels, but still with sizeable dimensions.

At the foothill of São João, sailors could make the repairs. It was such a good location that a shipyard existed in the location between the end of the eighteenth century and the first half of the nineteenth century.

In 2007, a survey was made at the educational and research base belonging to the Institute of Oceanography from the University of São Paulo (Instituto Oceanográfico—USP). The survey located the shipyard of the Sargeant-Major Joaquim José da Costa, one of the precursors of the so called "second phase" of the naval construction of Cananéia[11]. The ships' production in the old village was so significant that it was described by Martim Francisco Ribeiro de Andrada (1805), in a derogatory way, as the "carpenters' homeland" (Andrada 1977, pp. 191–192).

The continuation of its function as an area for naval construction and repair, from the eighteenth century up to today for storage and maintenance of the Institute's boats, points to the probability that it served as an area of nautical services also before this period. In addition to this hypothesis is the existence at the base of a source of potable water very close to the beach, and the recovery of remains of at least one ceramic utensil, with ungulate decoration, probably from the pre-colonial period. Also, a fragment of a corrugated urn found out of its original context reinforces our assertion (Bava-de-Camargo 2008).

Going back to Sousa's route, it is believed that it happened under reckless conditions of their floating equipment until São Vicente due to the need of the fleet to arrive with haste to what would become the first village of the captaincy. Maybe the most important question in this case is not the possibility of naval repair or construction being done in a locality, but the security of the conditions in which both could occur. The freshwater brigantines of the sailor brothers were built near a fortified house (Keating and Maranhão 2011). From the perspective of military logistics, the builders were protected by a palisade and by the ships' artillery. In this way, it is not reasonable to think that Martim Afonso's fleet and floating fortifications could

---

[11] The first phase would be marked by the construction of the ship Cananéia (1711) (Almeida 1965, p. 466). This phase would have initiated and ended with the same ship, since another watercraft of the same dimension was probably never built in the area.

be stranded for repairs without the protection of land artillery, which could not happen in Cananéia.

The same brigantines, agile, fast and with small draft were used by the Sousa brothers to contact the Cananéia inhabitants. It is not clear if the larger ships entered the Trapandé Bay or Mar Pequeno, where they would be at a disadvantage in case of clashes. Those were not clear Portuguese dominions, but the focus of the power of the Bacharel de Cananéia, an exiled Iberian who became a local potentate. It is important to highlight that a few years later in 1534, the Spaniard Rui Mosquera would leave that region to attack the village of São Vicente (Azara 2002). Due to this, it would not be a good idea to put one of the fleet's ships in a shipyard, leaving the expedition vulnerable in a region that would take almost a century to become a true Portuguese possession.

Along the same line of precautions against enemies, Caminha reports a strategy for disembarking without becoming helpless to terrestrial attacks organized within the dense Atlantic forest of the southern part of the state of Bahia:

> In the afternoon the Captain-Major left in his skiff to spend time with all of us and with the other captains in their boats around the bay, in front of the beach. But nobody disembarked, because the Captain did not want it, notwithstanding the beach being empty. We all only left the boats—in a large islet located in the bay and that during low tide is very empty. However it is surrounded by water, so nobody can reach it unless swimming or with a boat (Brasil u.d.).

At the Recôncavo Baiano, some archaeological sites resulting from port activities in rocky crowns were recently discovered (Bava-de-Camargo and Nascimento 2012). Some could be associated with the first or second century of the conquest/colonization.

Revisiting the route of the Sousa brothers, when the fleet arrived in São Vicente, one of the first tasks was to repair the boats.

> Tuesday [January 22nd] in the morning I went in a fleet's boat to the west side of the bay and found a narrow river, in which the boats could be corrected, by being well sheltered from all winds and in the afternoon we put the boats inside the bay because of the south wind. Since we went inside the distinguished captain ordered a house to be built on land for keeping the sails and shrouds. Here in this port of São Vicente, a boat was pulled up on to the beach (Keating and Maranhão 2011).

Where could this have occurred? Probably in the area properly named "Porto das Naus" [Nau's Port], on the continental portion of São Vicente, or in other words, on the opposite side of the Tumiaru port, situated in the island of the original location of the settlement, but with very small dimensions.

The protected and recently excavated archaeological site (Lima 2011) named Porto das Naus is, in reality, the area where in 1580 the sugarcane mill of Jerônimo Leitão was built. It is undebatable that in order to carry the sugar production, the watercrafts had to land at the sugarmill port, or at the *trapiche*, a term that refers both to the production unit and to the warehouse that is projected into the water until it reached depths amenable to the draft of the ship as can be seen in cities from Sergipe and Recôncavo Baiano (Bahia).

If that area was occupied earlier by Martim Afonso de Sousa's shipyard, it will be difficult to assert without underwater archaeology research. However, similar to what occurs in Cananéia, it is probable that an area where shipyards are located nowadays might have been previously used by others, since not all parts of the coast allow for the construction of these structures. And, in that area, between São Vicente and Praia Grande, there have been shipyards for small ships still in operation since at least the 1930s (Tribuna em São Vicente 1960).

At the time of Martim Afonso and also until later, consensus was reached that the area was favorable for shipyards. The religious and studious friar Gaspar da Madre de Deus from the 1700's cites an interesting portion of a document from the 1500's reporting the concession of the area near Porto das Naus to Jerônimo Leitão. The friar says: "Martim Afonso ... gave in such land to the Council *about a hundred meters*[12] for pulling the ship up on to the beach (because at the time it seems that they were run aground there" (Madre-de-Deus 1975, p. 50).

The discussion brought about by the historian-friar is centered around which types of ships could be landed at Porto das Naus and surrounding areas. Friar Gaspar asserts that only small watercraft—but not too small—could easily reach the place, but not by the inlet of São Vicente. In fact that area was reserved for smaller ships. Nevertheless, friar Gaspar forgot that Pero Lopes navigated the entrance of the estuary and surrounding areas before with a skiff evaluating the possibilities of the inlet, deciding at the end it was feasible. And he had done it.

## 15.5  Shipwrecks

Other times, unexpected naval occurrences became shipwrecks, such as what happened to the lead ship of Martim Afonso on the coast of Uruguay in 1531. Just after the rescue of castaways by the rest of the fleet, a camp was established whose goal it was to recover all possible parts of the ship's hull, particularly metal utensils (Keating and Maranhão 2011).

Besides this incident, located south of the coast in which we focus our interest, many other accidental wrecks occurred in the south-central coast of Brazil in the sixteenth century. These include ships from the fleets of Solis (SC, 1516), Caboto (SC, 1526), Cabeça de Vaca (SC, 1541), Sanabria (SC, 1551), Salazar (SP, 1553, which carried the German mercenary Hans Staden), the supposedly Spanish ship *La Provedora* (SC, 1583), among others that we do not know about as well as others that produced survivors mentioned in reports from chroniclers and sailors.

Survivors camps' resulted from these shipwrecks, some of which lasted for years, having been occupied by tens or hundreds of people. One of them would

---

[12] "Tiro de arco em roda", from the original text. An ancient measurement vaguely determined by an arrow shot with parabolic trajectory.

be from the brigantine[13] *San Miguel,* part of Sanabria's unlucky fleet, in which the aforementioned Hans Staden was a passenger. The German tells us that after six months of preparing the ships for an expedition to the river Plate, the brigantine shipwrecked at the port, situated in some point of the Southern bay of Santa Catarina's island. According to João Sanches, one of the major sailors of the expedition, the ship was lying on one side of the bilge[14] (Staden, 1974), or in other words, it was put on one of its sides, allowing the grounding and the recovery of part of its cargo and pieces of its structure, similar to Martim Afonso's lead ship.

The preparation for the trip to river Plate lasted almost seven months before the sinking and after the disaster, according to the German soldier:

> During two years we stayed in unoccupied/deserted areas and were in constant danger. (…) At the beginning the savages brought us enough provisions, while they received from us a lot of merchandise in return. Afterwards the majority left for other regions (Staden 1974, p. 64).

From this description it is clear that the castaways lived near the sunken ship for some time, during which they built a camp. For their survival, they depended on the ship's booty to exchange for food and other resources from the land. From the perspective of the material culture it would be expected that this dynamic would have formed an archaeological context where the remains from the dilapidated ship along with a relatively temporary settlement, with European and native resources, would be present.

The complex of archaeological sites located at the Cedro [Cedar] hill and its underwater surroundings, at the Palhoça municipality in the metropolitan region of Florianópolis, Santa Catarina State, corresponds to this expectation. According to surveys done both on land as well as underwater, ancient unstructured remains of a very deteriorated shipwreck, as well as historical and pre-colonial elements were found in the location. It should be highlighted that the shipwreck was only researched because a whole Guarani bowl was identified during the excavation of a trench for underwater electrical cables (Duran et al. 2010)[15].

## 15.6   Alliances, Dissensions, and Settlements

The arrival and settlement of Europeans along the Brazilian coast depended during all the sixteenth century on the establishment of amicable relationships with some indigenous groups. At the end of the century, all the advantages were on the side of the Europeans' and the Brazilian settlers, who enslaved even their native allies.

These amicable relations also were necessary to obtain provisions and to placate the fear that Europeans had in relation to the natives—in larger numbers—as well

---

[13] Patacho, in Portuguese, a two-masted sailing ship with square rigging on the foremast and fore-and-aft rigging on the mainmast. Enc. Britannica online, http://www.britannica.com/EBchecked/topic/79499/brigantine. Accessed 27 Oct 2013.

[14] Deitado de través, from the original text.

[15] Publication of CRM results from this extremely important archaeological complex is expected, which will certainly contribute to the study of the contact history between such distinct civilizations.

as in relation to their continental neighbors. The Sousa brothers dismissed the idea of making the existence of Cananéia official to the Portuguese empire. This could also be related to the loss of armed forces—40 archers and 40 harquebusiers—during Pero Lobo's expedition, which left Cananéia in 1531 (Keating and Maranhão 2011). It is alleged that the expedition was surprised by an attack in the territory now belonging to the state of Pará, but it is not known who the assailants were. We only know the result, but not the entire scheme.

With this we return once more to hill of São João. An elevation visible from a radius of many kilometers also allows an excellent view from it of the prominent waters and land. From the top of the hill one had a privileged view of Bom Abrigo island, Itacurussá point, the estuary entrance of Cananéia, Trincheira's beach, and Cardoso's island, which would facilitate the monitoring of all maritime traffic in the region. So much so that many times during history when conflicts seemed imminent, lookouts were established on the elevation (Bava-de-Camargo 2002).

On the other hand, being visible or allowing the view of a great extension of land caused opposite effects to people that would not like to be seen or who would prefer to keep themselves as far as possible from the site. It is only possible to imagine that at the beginning of the colonization in the sixteenth century when several groups fought for the area, the hill demarcated a settlement from which some should keep their distance. Along the same lines, a hypothesis for the foundation of Marataiama – the first Cananéia—at Comprida island, an area lacking rocks and clay for construction and without potable water most of the year, centers in the fact that the ancient Portuguese-Native settlers could not occupy the better and most wanted area due to the fact that it was to exposed to enemy attacks or to the settlement of enemies.

Oral information on the location of funerary urns in downtown Cananéia similar to ones found in the neighboring city of Iguape (Scatamacchia 1993, p. 157), along with ceramic fragments with corrugated decoration found during archaeological survey done at the port of Bacharel in 2007, reveal that in fact there was an occupation with a strong presence of natives at the original nucleus of the settlement. Would these indigenous vestiges have kept European settlers away from Cananéia's current downtown until the sixteenth century? This is very difficult to affirm without an underwater survey of the area surrounding the port of Bacharel, since there are strong indications that the marine dynamics had eroded and submerged the occupation prior to the eighteenth century at that specific location (Bava-de-Camargo 2009)[16].

Due to all this, the construction of settlements had to be extremely well planned. And yet, several of them were moved to positions distinct from the original. Besides Cananéia, Paranaguá (PR) moved from Cotinga island to the margins of the Itiberê river (Brasil 1959). And, Iguape was transported from Icapara, a site near the mouth of the Ribeira river, to its current location, close to the meandering portion of the same river closer to the Pequeno sea, allowing faster and more secure

---

[16] Since the first settlements of São Paulo's coast faced the sea and catered to the needs of the sailors, these put them at the mercy of the maritime dynamics. Madre-de-Deus (1975) and Marques (1980) present the case of São Vicente, whose first village was engulfed by a cataclysmic marine event (we cannot say a Tsunami, at least in this portion of the Atlantic) in 1541, forcing the relocation of the village.

communication by land, between the river and the sea (Scatamacchia 2003, with previous references).

The need for good mooring places—draft for large watercrafts, seabed with good holding[17], and shelter from strong winds—also promoted, perhaps not settlement changes, but provoked a strong decrease in population in some and dominance of others. This was probably one of reasons for the creation of Santos and the decline of São Vicente as a center for colonizing interests.

This could also be the case of Ubatuba. According to its definition, Ubatuba could signify both "group of wild canes"—plants—as well as "group of canoes" (Tibiriçá 1985, p. 116). According to Hans Staden, there is a higher propensity to understand the Tupi term as an 'area of many canoes.'

It is interesting to suppose how many canoes this would be. Hans Staden describes a common expedition by the Tupinambás against the Tupiniquins[18] and its Portuguese allies. According to the German, in August 14th 1554, now sitting in the region of the state of Rio de Janeiro, "38 canoes, each one filled with more or less 18 men" left from Ubatuba (Staden 1974, p. 124). Years later, in 1563, the Jesuit José de Anchieta writes that the combat operations of the Tupinambás before the Iperoig Peace involved 200 canoes or more, each one armed with around 20, 25, or even up to 30 warriors. They would not navigate as a fleet, but in groups in order to attack the Portuguese and allies guerrilla style (Anchieta 1933, p. 203). A large quantity of boats united for a period of strong warlike conditions.

Going back to the attack of August 1554, in the way of the Portuguese-Tupiniquim lands they camped in a site also named Ubatuba, this one in São Paulo's territory. According to Staden, "there were strong winds" (Staden 1974, p. 125). The wind, in August (wintertime), came from the South and they were not sheltered from it because the camp was temporary. On the other hand, this wind was favorable to the way the Tupinambás fought, since they navigated slowly to the South. However, after combat they came back as quickly as possible to the North, helped by the stern southern winds.

Would it be possible that they were camped where the Ubatuba municipality is located today? Its port is unsheltered from protection against southern winds. That would explain Staden's report. The partial shelter of ships against this wind is possible at the Grande [Big] river of Ubatuba, but there is some danger in traversing its inlet. Of course, the canoes could be kept at the beach, but what would be the real need of a "maritime" Native village to occupy a location that is clearly inferior in environmental terms, in a region where there were other more favorable places for human settlement, sheltered from the southern and eastern winds, this latter of which are less common but more destructive? Would not it be naïve to think that these maritime warriors kept their war canoes in systematic form at the beaches, exposed and susceptible to deformations caused by strong sun and cold rain? It seems that a settlement could have been there—maybe not a very important one—but contemporary Ubatuba developed there because there was a better connection of that

---

[17] Fundo de boa tensa, from the original.
[18] Tupinambás, Tupiniquins and Carijós are ethnic groups belonging to the Tupi Guarani linguistic branch.

low area with the route to the Paraíba valley, up the mountains. Although coastal natives also communicated with the valley groups, who were also Tupinambás, this need to shorten routes as much as possible, even to occupy a less favorable site, only appeared with Europeans, with their need to transport cargo and merchandise.

At least one place where a village or human settlement existed during the contact period was identified and studied by D. Uchôa, M. Scatamacchia, and C. Garcia, during the 1980's. Some artifacts of European origin were recovered, among them glass beads (Scatamacchia and Uchôa 1993). It seems, however, that the site corresponded to only one of the many villages that existed in the region. Among them were those belonging to Cunhambebe and Pindobuçu, important chiefs at the time when the priests Anchieta and Nóbrega signed the Iperoig Peace, celebrated between Portuguese and Tupinambás in 1563 (Porchat 1993, p. 76). Observing this geography of occupation from a nautical perspective, only the zones sheltered from the South and East winds could have supported an agglomeration linked to large nautical activities. Such a place would be nearby the current port of Ubatuba, built during the 1940's (São Paulo 1941), but today without any official movement of cargo. For the same reasons, the marinas at Itaguá beach are located in the area. The archaeological site of Itaguá is a short distance from the beach, but it communicates with the coast through the Lagoa [Lagoon] river, a tidal river, navigable at least during high tide. However, it is a small site and could have been built in an area where the natives were already trying to better protect themselves from invaders/exchange partners.

Anyway, there are strong elements that indicate the preference for the Itaguá region for the construction of villages sheltered from winds. Perhaps the presence of barriers provided by the high hills added to the mouth of the Acarau river and allowed the agglomeration of several canoes in the area. The *sambaqui* of Tenório, another important archaeological site for understanding the coastal occupation of São Paulo state, is located a few hundred meters to the south on the beach of the same name. Although there is no relation with the contact period ($1875 \pm 90$ years BP, according to Lima 1999–2000), several flaked and semi-polished hammerstones (80, a significant number for a site of less than 300 m²) were found outside funerary contexts, indicating their use in daily activities (Scheel-Ybert et al. 2003, p. 124) such as the construction of nautical materials (canoes, paddles, among others). Since Tenório's beach is absolutely unprotected from southern winds, we can suppose that some nautical activity related to *sambaqui* groups occurred along the Acarau river, in direction of the Itaguá river, during winter months.

## 15.7  Final Considerations: Markers of Ownership and Oblivion

Finally, in a categorical manner, the colonization also translated in markers of colonization, concrete signs of ownership. For the sailors of the fleet of Pedro Álvares Cabral, "the Cross was then planted, with Your Majesty's arms and blazon on it, which had before been fastened to it, and they set up an altar by its side" (Brasil u.d.). This temporary ownership marker was later substituted by another, made of stone.

In the same manner, at the point of Itacurussá island in the Cananéia region, Martim Afonso placed a stone marker when he passed through the region. This marker was recovered at the beginning of the twentieth century and today is part of the exhibit at the noble room of the Instituto Histórico e Geográfico Brasileiro.

Its significance transcends all that was said until them, because it is not a diaphanous element of the landscape. It is a distinct manifestation of ownership; the clear division of Tordesilhas. No sailor entering the Cananéia inlet could avoid seeing it.

There is no historian or archaeologist that does not take the marker into account in their research. It is the epitome of the European presence, in particular, of the Portuguese in Brazilian territory. Also, it is a contact point between History and Archaeology with the sea and the maritime, because its function is only justified to signal the ownership to boats and sailors; and, all the knowledge generated from it has to take into account, as a consequence, the marine side of the society.

Metaphorically, it is a pattern of knowledge. But the marker also indicates the distance of Brazilian researchers from the questions related to the material life on board and the intrinsic needs of navigation and its goals. The Itacurussá marker is not unique, although it is the only one to be seen.

Researchers forget that there is another inlet in the estuarine-lagoonal area of Cananéia. It is the Ararapira inlet, but is difficult to pass and is only suitable for small boats. However, it is an entrance to Cananéia and an entrance for the Portuguese empire overseas. In this way it would be necessary to alert the sailors who transpose it that they were entering dominated lands. It is believed that this marker could possibly be the one that is located today at the underwater portion of the sambaqui Cachoeira Pequena or Mirim, on Cardoso island, identified (2002) during the Master's research of F. Calippo (2004) and G. Rambelli's PhD (2003, p. 77).

And again, metaphorically, this drowned marker, or the absence of any mention to it, demonstrates the difficulty of most researchers in transcending the dominance of land-centered views that built History or Archaeology.

**Acknowledgment** I would like to thanks Daniela Magalhães Klokler (Federal University of Sergipe, Brazil), Dave Mehalic (Coronado National Forest, USA) for the translation of the original article and Leandro Domingues Duran (Federal University of Sergipe, Brazil) for the important comments e suggestions.

# References

Almeida, A. P. (1952). História da navegação no litoral paulista. *Revista do Arquivo Municipal, 153,* 3–10.
Almeida, A. P. (1962). Memória Histórica de Cananéia (V). *Revista de História, 25*(51), 192–217.
Almeida, A. P. (1964). Memória Histórica de Cananéia (VII). *Revista de História, 28*(58), 483–504.
Almeida, A. P. (1965). Memória Histórica de Cananéia (X). *Revista de História, 31*(64), 453–477.
Anchieta, J. (1933). *Cartas, informações, fragmentos históricos e sermões do padre Joseph de Anchieta*. Rio de Janeiro: Civilização Brasileira.

de Andrada, M. F. R. (1977). Jornais de viagens pela capitania de São Paulo e Diário de uma viagem mineralógica. In P. Marcelino. Cleto et all. (Eds.), *Roteiros e notícias de São Paulo Colonial* (1751–1804). São Paulo: Governo do Estado.

Azara, F. (2002). Descripción e historia del Paraguay y del Río de la Plata. Alicante: Biblioteca Virtual Miguel de Cervantes. http://www.cervantesvirtual.com/obra/descripcion-e-historia-del-paraguay-y-del-rio-de-la-plata-0/. Accessed 10 May 2013.

Bava-de-Camargo, P. F. (2002). *Arqueologia das fortificações oitocentistas da planície costeira Cananéia/ Iguape, SP. São Paulo*. Unpublished M.Sc. dissertation. Faculdade de Filosofia, Letras e Ciências Humanas, Museu de Arqueologia e Etnologia, Universidade de São Paulo.

Bava-de-Camargo, P. F. (2008). Prospecção Arqueológica na Base Costeira do Instituto Ocean-ográfico da USP em Cananéia, Estado de São Paulo. *Revista do Museu de Arqueologia e Etnologia, 18,* 323–330.

Bava-de-Camargo, P. F. (2009). *Arqueologia de uma cidade portuária: Cananéia, séculos XIX–XX*. Unpublished PhD thesis. Museu de Arqueologia e Etnologia, Universidade de São Paulo.

Bava-de-Camargo, P. F., & Nascimento, L. A. V. do. (2012). Programa de diagnóstico e prospecção arqueológica subaquática do gasoduto de transferência de gás natural do Terminal de Regas-eificação da Bahia (TRBA) São Francisco do Conde, Bahia. Relatório de encerramento de campo. Porto Seguro: Acervo, 2012. Report on file.

Brasil. (u.d.). Ministério da Cultura. Fundação Biblioteca Nacional. Departamento Nacional do Livro. A Carta de Pero Vaz de Caminha. http://objdigital.bn.br/Acervo_Digital/Livros_eletro-nicos/carta.pdf. Accessed 10 May 2013

Brasil (1959). *Enciclopédia dos Municípios Brasileiros*. Rio de Janeiro: Instituto Brasileiro de Geografia e Estatística.

Calippo, F. R. (2004). *Os sambaquis submersos de Cananéia: um estudo de caso de arqueologia subaquática*. Unpublished M.Sc. dissertation. Museu de Arqueologia e Etnologia, Universi-dade de São Paulo.

Carrilllo, M. (1615). Historia del glorioso san Valero, obispo de Çaragoça: con los martyrios de san Vicente, santa Engracia, san Lamberto, y los innumerables martyres de Çaragoça; con un Catalogo de todos los prelados, obispos, arçobispos y abades del reyno de Aragon. Zaragoza: Ivan de Lanaja y Quartet. http://books.google.com.br/books?hl=pt-BR&lr=&id=H8K5ouNANK4C&oi=fnd&pg=PA1&dq=vida+santo+%22s%C3%A3o+vicente%22+zaragoza&ots=JYzJHVZMgN&sig=M93BoUxhHXuDWd_sG_A8_X7By44#v=onepage&q=vicente&f=false. Accessed 01 Sept 2013

Del Priore, M., & Venancio, R. (2010). *Uma breve História do Brasil*. São Paulo: Planeta do Brasil.

Duran, L. D. (2008). *Arqueologia marítima de um Bom Abrigo*. Unpublished PhD thesis. Museu de Arqueologia e Etnologia, Universidade de São Paulo.

Duran, L. D., Bava-de-Camargo, P. F., Calippo, F. R., & Juliani, L. (2010). O Naufrágio das Nozes (Palhoça, SC): um estudo de caso de Arqueologia de contrato no Brasil. *Vestígios. Revista latino-americana de Arqueologia Histórica ,7,* 1–20.

Guimarães, R. S. (2010). A arqueologia em sítios submersos: estudo do sítio depositário da en-seada da praia do Farol da ilha do Bom Abrigo-SP. Unpublished M.Sc. dissertation. Museu de Arqueologia e Etnologia, Universidade de São Paulo.

Keating, V., & Maranhão, R. (2011). *Diário de navegação-Pero Lopes e a expedição de Martim Afonso de Sousa (1530–1532)*. São Paulo: Terceiro Nome.

Lima, T. A. (1999–2000). Em busca dos frutos do mar: os pescadores-coletores do litoral Centro-Sul do Brasil. *Revista Usp, 44,* 270–327.

Lima, R. (2011). Arqueólogos encontram vestígios da Era do Açúcar. O Estado de São Paulo, 15 July 2013. http://saovicentenamemoria.blogspot.com.br/2011/07/arqueologos-encontram-vestigios-da-era.html. Accessed 05 Aug 2013.

Madre-de-Deus, G. (1975). *Memórias para a História da capitania de São Vicente*. B. Horizonte: Itatiaia/ Edusp.

Marques, M. E. A. (1980) *Apontamentos Históricos, Geográficos, Biográficos, Estatísticos e Noti-ciosos da Província de São Paulo*. Belo Horizonte: Itatiaia/Edusp.

Martins, M. C. (September-December 2012) Itinerário de Egéria ou Peregrinação de Etéria: Pontos de uma edição crítica. *Revista Philologus, 54,* 100–114.

Monteiro, J. M. (1994). *Negros da terra: índios e bandeirantes nas origens de São Paulo.* São Paulo: Companhia das Letras.

Porchat, E. (1993). Informações históricas sobre São Paulo no século de sua fundação. São Paulo: Iluminuras.

Rambelli, G. (2003). *Arqueologia subaquática do Baixo Vale do Ribeira, SP.* Unpublished PhD thesis. Museu de Arqueologia e Etnologia, Universidade de São Paulo.

São Paulo. Secretaria de Viação e Obras Públicas (1941). *Obras de melhoramentos dos portos de S. Sebastião e Ubatuba.* São Paulo: Diretoria de Viação.

Scatamacchia, M. C. M. (2003). Arqueologia do antigo sistema portuário da cidade de Iguape, São Paulo, Brasil. *Revista de Arqueología Americana, 20,* 81–100.

Scatamacchia, M. C. M., & Uchôa, D. P. (1993). O contato euro-indígena visto através de sítios arqueológicos do Estado de São Paulo. *Revista de Arqueologia, 7,* 153–173.

Scheel-Ybert, R., Eggers, S., Wesolowski, V., Petronilho, C. C., Boyadjian, C. H., DeBlasis, P. A. D., Barbosa-Guimarães, M., & Gaspar, M. D. (2003). Novas perspectivas na reconstituição do modo de vida dos sambaquieiros: uma abordagem multidisciplinar. *Revista de Arqueologia, 16,* 109–137.

Staden, H. (1974). *Duas viagens ao Brasil.* B. Horizonte: Itatiaia/Edusp.

Tibiriçá, L. C. (1985). *Dicionário de topônimos brasileiros de origem Tupi.* São Paulo: Traço.

Tribuna em São Vicente, A. (1960). Clube de Regatas Tumiaru-55 anos de glórias ao município de S. Vicente. A Tribuna, 22 Dicember, p. 16. http://www.novomilenio.inf.br/sv/svh061b.htm. Accessed 26 Sept 2013.

# Chapter 16
# Fort San José, a Remote Spanish Outpost in Northwest Florida, 1700–1721

Julie Rogers Saccente and Nancy Marie White

## 16.1 History of Fort San José

In 2013, the "Viva Florida" celebration commemorated the 500th anniversary of the Spanish arrival in the state of Florida. Juan Ponce de León landed on the Atlantic coast in April 1513, naming the land "La Florida" after the rich landscape and flowery Easter season. His search for adventure and treasure was the first documented entrance of Europeans into what is now the USA. He was followed by many more explorers, including those who ventured into the Gulf of Mexico. But they did not enter northwest Florida's Apalachicola delta region (Fig. 16.1). Then came colonists and missionaries, until the Atlantic coast had a string of missions that also extended into the interior. By the mid- to late seventeenth century, Mission San Luis, in modern Tallahassee, was a major Apalachee Indian and Spanish center and supplier of goods to St. Augustine on the Atlantic and to Cuba (Hann and McEwan 1998). The port for Mission San Luis was at San Marcos (St. Marks) on the Gulf. At modern Pensacola, to the west on the Gulf, a 1719 presidio followed earlier settlement (Bense 1999). However, geographically in between these centers, the great, resource-rich delta area of the Apalachicola valley was ignored by the old-world intruders. Only a handful of Spanish goods filtered into aboriginal protohistoric sites (White 2011) until the Spanish established a short-lived lookout-type fort in 1701 and then the sturdier Fort San José in 1719 on St. Joseph Bay. The fort was located at the very tip of the barrier peninsula across from the mainland, in what is today Gulf County, within the T. H. Stone Memorial St. Joseph Peninsula State Park

J. R. Saccente (✉)
Next Generation Cultural Services, Inc., 1251 Lakeview Road, Clearwater, FL 33756, USA
e-mail: jhrsaccente@gmail.com

N. M. White
Department of Anthropology, University of South Florida, 4202 E. Fowler Ave. SOC107, Tampa, FL 33620, USA
e-mail: nmw@usf.edu

© Springer International Publishing Switzerland 2015
P. P. A. Funari, M. X. Senatore (eds.), *Archaeology of Culture Contact and Colonialism in Spanish and Portuguese America*, DOI 10.1007/978-3-319-08069-7_16

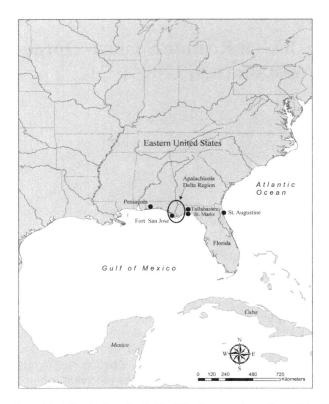

**Fig. 16.1** Location of Fort San José on the Gulf of Mexico coast in northwest Florida

and across the bay from the modern town of Port St. Joe (Fig. 16.2). Fort San José (official state site number: 8Gu8) is the only identified Spanish colonial site in the entire Apalachicola Delta region and was the only known Spanish occupation on the coast between Tallahassee/St. Marks and Pensacola.

There is historic documentation of this fort, and its location was verified by archeology in the 1960s. Hale Smith of Florida State University was invited by local landowners farther down the peninsula to investigate a prehistoric site, but when a girl showed him a piece of Spanish pottery from the tip of the peninsula, he forgot about the first site and immediately went to dig the fort. Unfortunately, he never reported his work, though his materials are still curated at Florida State. The University of West Florida later did a survey of the area (Benchley and Bense 2001). Recently a large private collection of artifacts from the fort was made available to us at the University of South Florida by a collector who obtained it 40 years ago and valued his artifacts enough to construct a small building in the back of his house to hold them all. In addition, local historian Wayne Childers has done work on Spanish archives in Mexico pertaining to the region. His 2001 *History of T. H. Stone Park, St. Joseph's Peninsula*, and other works provide great background and details about life at the fort.

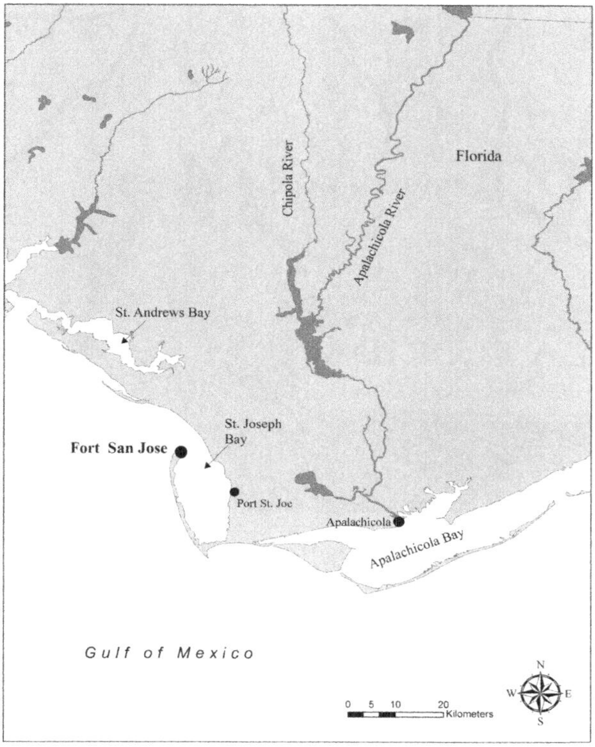

**Fig. 16.2** Location of Fort San José on the St. Joseph Peninsula, with modern towns of Port St. Joe and Apalachicola

Since Florida became the first region of North America north of Mexico to be invaded by the Spanish (Cabeza de Vaca et al. 1993 [1542]; Clayton et al. 1995; Wood 1989, p. 51), numerous exploratory expeditions passed by or stopped at the St. Joseph Peninsula. The bay appears early in history as the Spanish developed some awareness of their territory. It is first shown by name on the famous 1584 map by Abraham Ortelius (Fig. 16.3). The exact circumstances of why the bay was named St. Joseph are so far unknown, though many other saints' names were given to islands and bays in the region, possibly commemorating the date of first recording. The 1718 French map by Jean Beranger (Fig. 16.4) is the most detailed historic document we have found that shows the St. Joseph Peninsula. This map was created just 1 year before Fort San José was established near the tip of the peninsula. The location where the small Spanish lookout was established in 1701 is called "Pointe aux Chevreuil" (Deer Point). This tiny settlement lasted only a few months, but apparently set the foundations for the establishment of Fort San José about 18 years later.

St. Joseph Bay is 5–8 km wide and is a salty, nonestuarine lagoon. It offers a deepwater port, as opposed to the shallow Apalachicola Bay, which is approximately

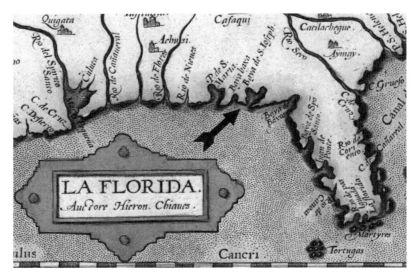

**Fig. 16.3** Excerpt from the La Florida map by Abraham Ortelius (1584); adapted from the original, courtesy of Diana Zaragoza; *arrow* indicates "Baya de S. Ioseph"

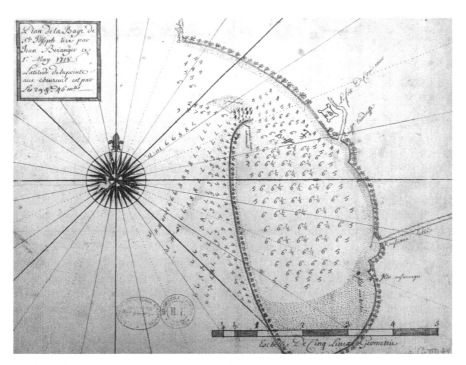

**Fig. 16.4** Excerpt from the Plan de la Baye de St. Joseph by Jean Beranger (1718); adapted from the online Newberry Library Cartographic Catalog; the tip of St. Joseph Peninsula is labeled "Pointe aux Chevreuil"; across from it on the mainland is "Le forte De Crève coeur" (the French Fort Broken-heart or Heartbreak) shown on a stream labeled "Ruisse l'au dousse" (freshwater creek)

**Fig. 16.5** Photo of Fort San José location today, with white sand beach, native pines and palms, and St. Joseph Bay in the right background

56 km by ship, east of St. Joseph Bay. Access to a deepwater port made St. Joseph Bay an ideal location for the Spanish with their heavy ships. Thomas Hutchins, explorer and mapmaker, visited the St. Joseph Peninsula in the late 1700s and described the bay as an excellent harbor in which the best place to anchor was just within the peninsula, opposite from the ruins of Fort San José. Hutchins warned against bringing boats too close to the shore as the bay becomes very shallow in these areas (Hutchins 1968, p. 85).

The shoreline of the St. Joseph Peninsula is constantly reworked by waves and currents, including seasonal storms and the occasional hurricane, which reveal material evidence of the fort on the beach and in the water. Because of the dynamic nature of the shoreline, any structural evidence of the fort is not apparent, and the only remaining physical evidence of the site are the artifacts that wash out (Benchley and Bense 2001). The dynamism of this environment would have affected anyone trying to settle there (Davis 1997). The site today is pristine white sandy beach that is used for recreational purposes (Fig. 16.5) and has won awards for its beauty.

Settlers obtained both aquatic and terrestrial species to supplement provisions supplied by the Spanish Crown. Aquatic resources are available seasonally and are restricted to saltwater species found in St. Joseph Bay and the Gulf of Mexico. Saltwater fish found in St. Joseph Bay include Spanish mackerel, bluefish, redfish, speckled trout, and flounder (Hubbell et al. 1956). Shellfish such as whelk, conch, and scallop would have been seasonally harvested from the bay, and their use by prehistoric people is reflected in numerous prehistoric occupation sites in this area (White 2005). Some of the fish that would have been present in great abundance in the 1700s include cod, grouper, and red mullet (Hutchins 1968, p. 86).

The first Spanish occupation of St. Joseph Bay in 1701 was by Mexican, Spanish, and Portuguese soldiers and sailors, as well as some of the local Chacato Indian population. The inhabitants brought with them skills they learned in their various professions; they included a shoemaker from a family of shoemakers in Mexico

City, weavers, and a stonecutter (Childers 2001, p. 8). What apparently led most of them to St. Joseph was not a thirst for adventure or even employment but rather the need to make reparations for a criminal past that for many included, murder and thievery.

Construction details of the Spanish lookout on the peninsula and a small garrison on the mainland are unknown. A large banner with Spain's coat of arms was reported to have been flown from a pole and seen far out to sea to alert the passing ships to the location of the entrance of the bay (Childers 2001, p. 8). Childers (2001, p. 7) speculates that houses probably consisted of small huts made from pine poles thatched with palm, materials being used in Pensacola and readily available in the St. Joseph Bay area. Such houses would typically have a hearth in the middle of the room and a smokehole opened in the roof. There were two churches established, one for the soldiers and another for the Chacato Indians. The churches were called St. Joseph and Our Lady of Guadalupe, respectively.

The exact date of the Spanish withdrawal from the first outpost at St. Joseph Bay is unknown. Weddle (1991, p. 374) states it was abandoned after a few months due to lack of provisions. Faye (1946, p. 177) believes the final withdrawal was in 1704 under orders of the Mexican commandant at St. Joseph Bay. The Spanish did not visit St. Joseph for at least the next 13 years as far as we know. Other than possible visits by native groups moving through the area, no other settlements are recorded here either from this time.

In early 1718, to the west in French territory, Jean-Baptiste Le Moyne, Sieur de Bienville (the founder of Mobile, Alabama) was ordered to occupy St. Joseph Bay (Weddle 1991, p. 208, 216). Bienville knew from the onset that the Spanish claim to this area would not be the only problem with occupying this site. He noted to the Navy Council that the entrance to the bay was very wide and could not be easily defended. Once inside the bay, there was no shelter for the vessels. Additionally, the soil was sandy, with no streams or rivers flowing into the bay, and Bienville commented that the drinking water was very bad here (Childers 2001, p. 13).

By May 1, 1718, the French had constructed, on the mainland opposite the tip of the peninsula, a fort with four bastions garrisoned by a company of 50 men (Faye 1946, pp. 185–186; Weddle 1991, p. 208, 216). The exact location of this French fort has yet to be verified archeologically. Beranger (Fig. 16.4) shows "Le forte De Crève Coeur" ("Broken Heart" or "Heartbreak" Fort) on the mainland across St. Joseph Bay, just opposite the point of the peninsula (Weddle 1991, p. 208). Our attempts to locate this French fort have turned up no evidence so far, though it was probably located adjacent to the only small freshwater stream in the area. St. Joseph Bay is more saline than the Gulf of Mexico because hardly any freshwater streams flow into it. European settlers would have wanted to be near fresh water.

Spanish response to the new French fort did not take long. Captain Juan Manuel Roldan, the acting governor of Pensacola, was notified of a French ship anchored inside St. Joseph Bay and sent scouts and then finally went himself to tell the French to leave. After Bienville presented his apprehensions about continuing to occupy St. Joseph to the colonial council in July of 1718, they decided unanimously to abandon and burn Fort Creve Coeur and leave St. Joseph Bay (Childers 2001, p. 14;

Hann 2006, p. 172). By August 20, 1718, the French were gone, having stayed there only 2 months.

While the French were packing their bags and setting fire to their fort, the Spanish were preparing to reoccupy St. Joseph Bay on the sandy beach of the peninsula. The Council of the Indies in Madrid considered the French issue at St. Joseph Bay a sign that the Spanish needed to strengthen their hold on the Gulf (Faye 1946a). On March 29, 1719, 800 men belonging to four companies arrived from Veracruz and Pensacola to occupy St. Joseph Bay under the command of Don Gregorio de Salinas Varona (Childers 2001, p. 15). Salinas picked the St. Joseph Peninsula for the location of this new fort, since his prior experience at Santa Rosa Island showed him that forts surrounded by water were easily defensible (Weddle 1991). This location was also ideal as a deepwater port, since the depth of the channel running into St. Joseph Bay drops to at least 9 m, making this port easily accessible for large ships. It is a good strategic location; however, it has a lack of readily available fresh water and the barrier formation of constantly shifting soft sands changes shape with every storm. The Spaniards constantly ignored this last point and were often rebuilding settlements around Pensacola and elsewhere which they had built on barrier islands.

After Pensacola fell to the French, Fort San José became the most important Spanish occupation in the Florida panhandle for the next 3 years. By 1720, the fort was mostly completed and its presence apparently deterred a French fleet of four warships and a storeship that had anchored just outside of the harbor of St. Joseph Bay from attacking (Childers 2001, p. 17).

Historical documents from Spain's archives translated by Childers (2001) suggest that Fort San José was modeled after standard Spanish construction plans. It had four sides and at least two bastions. The French priest, Pierre Charleviox saw the fort in May of 1722 and described it as "built only of earth but … well lined with palisades and defended with numerous artillery." (Charleviox 1761, p. 345). There were officer's quarters, a chapel, a powder magazine, storehouses for military equipment and rations, a guardhouse or living quarters for the common soldiers, and lodging for the officers within the northern part of the fort. Fort San José's floors were covered with ladrillos, red clay tiles, many of which were recovered during the excavations and some of which still wash up today on the shore of the site, visible in the clear bay water. But remains of the fort itself are gone, beyond some depressions amid the white dunes.

At the end of the War of the Quadruple Alliance, Spain demanded the return of Pensacola, and after much negotiation, a treaty was passed on March 27, 1721. Bienville received orders to hand over Pensacola to the Spanish on April 6, 1722. The desire of Spain to reinforce its foothold in Pensacola is the very reason the occupation at San José was so short-lived, as the orders also called for the abandonment of Fort San José. By early 1723, Fort San José had been dismantled and its people and resources moved to strengthen Pensacola (Childers 2001, p. 30). Of those residing at Fort San José, at least 179 soldiers and sailors, 24 forced laborers, an unknown number of women and children, and an unknown number of Indians, said to be Tocobaga and Apalachee, moved to Santa Rosa in Pensacola, according to historical correspondence from Spanish Lieutenant Colonel Alejandro Wauchope to the Viceroy in 1723 (Childers 2001, p. 30). The remaining residents of Fort San José were transported to Veracruz (Bense 1999).

The abandonment of Fort San José marked the end of the Spanish presence in the Apalachicola delta region. When the Spanish had returned to Pensacola Bay, they resided at Presidio Santa Rosa in Pensacola from 1722 to 1752. Santa Rosa was located on a barrier island, and after a devastating hurricane, its population was relocated to the mainland in 1752, where they resided at the Presidio San Miguel (Clune and Stringfield 2009; Bense 1999). By 1763, the Spanish had abandoned this settlement to Great Britain.

## 16.2 Archeology of Fort San José

Who was at Fort San José? Documents indicate a rich social and multicultural mix. There were priests, Spanish officers with their families, Mexican convicts, and even Mexican prostitutes sent by the church (!) to keep the men company (Childers 2001). There were also native Americans and apparently lots of Southeastern Indians. Though ethnicity is not always easily inferred from the material record, each of these peoples left portions of the archeological evidence.

We studied a total of 2851 artifacts (weighing 72,541 g) from Fort San José, representing all the known extant material culture from the site, including private and state-owned collections. The most dominant artifact type in the assemblage by number is historical European–American ceramics, followed by aboriginal ceramics and brick and mortar (Table 16.1).

Aboriginal ceramics make up 25 % of the total artifact assemblage by number. Only 5 % of the aboriginal pottery was able to be classified by established ceramic

**Table 16.1** Artifacts recovered from Fort San José by category, with percentages of the total assemblage by number and weight

| Type | N | Percentage | Wt (g) | Percentage |
|---|---|---|---|---|
| Aboriginal ceramics | 704 | 24.69 | 7216 | 9.95 |
| Historical European–American ceramics | 1070 | 37.53 | 20,830 | 28.71 |
| Indeterminate clay | 5 | 0.18 | 260 | 0.36 |
| Metal | 390 | 13.68 | 5286 | 7.29 |
| Glass | 95 | 3.33 | 1990 | 2.74 |
| Ground stone | 5 | 0.18 | 1594 | 2.2 |
| Brick and mortar | 525 | 18.41 | 34,640 | 47.75 |
| Historical lithics | 11 | 0.39 | 75 | 0.1 |
| Pumice | 4 | 0.14 | 33 | 0.05 |
| Fauna | 14 | 0.49 | 132 | 0.18 |
| Shell | 28 | 0.98 | 485 | 0.67 |
| Total | 2851 | 100 | 72,541 | 100 |

**Fig. 16.6** Aboriginal pottery from Fort San José. 2 Ocmulgee Fields Incised, Lamar Complicated-Stamped (*Top, left to right*); 2 Lamar Plain, sand-tempered, notched, and incised with an appliqué rim (Lamar?) (*Bottom, left to right*)

types (Deagan 1987; Noël Hume 1962; White 2009; Willey 1949). These types include Ocmulgee Fields Incised, Lamar Plain, Lamar Complicated-Stamped and Leon Check-Stamped with folded, punctated rims, and unique pottery such as a sand-tempered rim with a notched appliqué strip below the rim in a Lamar form but also unusual parallel-line incisions (Fig. 16.6).

None of the aboriginal ceramics are from the original natives. The late prehistoric indigenous people here had a material culture called Fort Walton, characterized by temple mounds and large villages, representing powerful chiefdoms (Marrinan and White 2007; White 2011). But they became extinct by around 1700 from the disruption and disease brought by the Spanish. It is unclear which other Indians moved into the empty land of the Apalachicola delta region, or where they came from, since these ceramic types at Fort San José are not Fort Walton but could have been made by Apalachee, various groups of Creeks, or other historical Indians. These peoples may have been fleeing the destruction of the Spanish missions by the English and their Creek Indian allies who moved south from Georgia to bring intensified violence and extinction of Florida's native peoples.

Thirty-eight percent of the Fort San José assemblage is ceramics imported by the Spanish, the majority of which is majolica. These types include El Morro, coarse earthenware, Guadalajara Polychrome, and kaolin pipes (Fig. 16.7). Majolica (37.9 % by number) is the most common imported ceramic ware, followed by olive jar (23.3 %), much of it made in Mexico (Fig. 16.8). The abundant presence of majolica shows the efforts by the Spanish to maintain traditional practices, but the high numbers of native wares suggest that the Indians who were around were intensively interacting with the fort's inhabitants and probably living there.

A wide variety of metal artifacts came from Fort San José, representing multiple artifact classes, including various activities, arms, and clothing. The metal

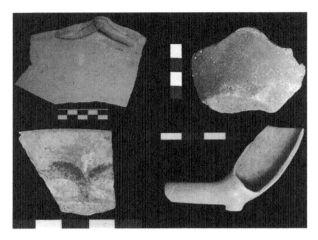

**Fig. 16.7** Imported Spanish ceramics from Fort San José. El Morro ware rim, coarse earthenware (*Top, left to right*); Guadalajara Polychrome, kaolin pipe (*Bottom, left to right*)

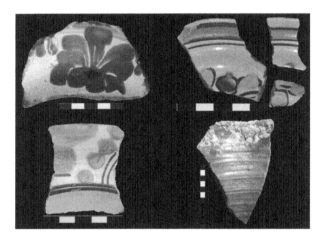

**Fig. 16.8** Majolica and olive jar sherds from Fort San José. Puebla Blue-on-White majolica, Abo Polychrome majolica (*Top, left to right*); San Luis Polychrome majolica, olive jar (encrusted with barnacles) (*Bottom, left to right*)

objects reveal a lot about the occupants' everyday lives. The abundance of specimens in the arms group (46 % of the metal by number) supports the interpretation of the site's function as a military settlement. Daily chores such as woodworking and forest clearing are represented by an axe head, and hand-rolled lead net weights indicate fishing activities. These items also reflect the self-sufficiency of the residents, which would have been important at this small and mostly isolated fort. Pestles represent kitchen activities; a pestle fragment recovered from Fort San José is nearly identical to the one pictured by Spaniard Diego Velázquez in

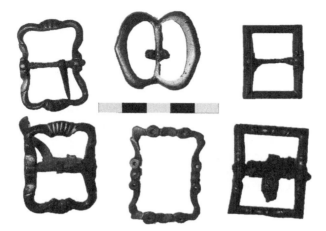

**Fig. 16.9** Metal buckles from Fort San José

his 1618 painting "Old Woman Cooking Eggs" and to another one displayed in the Mary Rose Museum in Portsmouth, England, among other items recovered from the Tudor ship that sank in 1545.

Personal metal items at the fort include those owned by high-status individuals, such as the numerous beautiful buckles (Fig. 16.9) and an engraved pocket knife handle. The buckles have a variety of designs and are all made of brass. Buckles were used on belts, straps, hats, stocks, and shoes. Noël Hume states that shoe buckles do not typically occur at American sites prior to 1700 and that they would be rare after 1815 (Noël Hume 1991, p. 86). One buckle (Fig. 16.9, top center) is a plain, figure-8 type that was common in the first half of the seventeenth century and continued in use until the early eighteenth century (Noël Hume 1991, p. 87).

The historical documents describe illegal trade with the French, and the ornate belt buckles that are not standard Spanish military issue suggest that interaction with other groups was definitely occurring. Since trade with the French was officially prohibited, this could be counted as smuggling. Most of the valuable personal items were probably carried away when the site was abandoned.

Other metal objects include nails, which were the only architectural metal items recovered. The small number of nails ($N = 37$) supports the interpretation that any salvageable architectural items were taken to Pensacola when Fort San José was dismantled (Childers 2001, p. 22). Metal items in the arms group include 63 pieces of lead shot and three cannonball fragments. This artifact group makes up the largest portion of the metal artifacts.

The historical records tell us about fabulous parties and wedding celebrations that occurred at Fort San José (Childers 2001). The glass artifacts, especially gin case bottles, support the interpretation that there was certainly some recreation. Gin case bottle fragments made up 73 % of the glass. This type of bottle is often referred to as a "Dutch Gin" bottle. It was one of the most common bottles used in the first half of the seventeenth century and continued to be popular through the nineteenth century (Beare 1965, p. 62; Noël Hume 1991). One dark olive-green bottle base was from a vessel that was free-blown and shows the pontil scar with a stamp in the shape of two crosses. Glass makes up 3.3% of the total artifact assemblage. All of the glass found at Fort San José represents the kitchen artifact group. None of the glass was identified as window glass.

One metate, two manos, and two pestles of stone were recovered from Fort San José. There is no way to determine if they were used by the native, Spanish, or Mexican residents. Manos and metates were staples of food preparation for all three groups. All of the ground stone represented here is basalt. Based on both the raw materials and the artifact styles of these five artifacts, an association with Mexican native traditions is most probable.

Building materials that were recovered from Fort San José are ladrillos (bricks), oyster shell mortar, tabby, and just one piece of concrete. Brick and mortar make up 18.4% of the assemblage by number and 47.8% by weight. Ladrillos are flat bricks made of unglazed coarse earthenware and are found throughout Spanish colonial sites in Florida, although they are relatively absent from St. Augustine (Deagan 1987, p. 124). They were imported, often as ballast in the bottom of ships, and were sometime made on-site. Ladrillos were typically made by masons rather than potters (Deagan 1987, p. 124). They are variable in size, and those found at Fort San José range from 29 to 30 cm in length and 14 to 18 cm in width. Ladrillos at Fort San José are larger than those found at Santa Rosa in Pensacola (Deagan 1987, p. 125).

Oyster shell mortar and tabby (a mixture of sand, shell, and lime) were used for building construction and would have been used in between timbers or as flooring. Oysters are not found in St. Joseph Bay because the water is too salty, but an abundance of oyster shell would have been found in the Apalachicola Bay, 56 km (35 miles) by ship to the east of the fort.

Four pieces of pumice have been recovered from Fort San José. Pumice is a porous, lightweight, volcanic rock that is formed from quickly cooling lava that, when hardened, shows holes where the gas bubbles were expelled during volcanic eruption (Hassan 2008). Pumice can be used to make concrete and as an abrasive. It does not occur naturally in the region, but has been found in at least 30 archeological sites throughout Florida, including at least two in the panhandle, near Pensacola and Tallahassee (Kish 2006; Wheeler 2006). The closest sources to Fort San José are the Lesser Antilles island arc and Mexico (Wheeler 2006, p. 191). Veracruz, Mexico, is one source of pumice; it was the place of origin for many of the supplies and people sent to Fort San José. Kish (2006, p. 231) has studied the original sources of pumice found in Florida and believes that, rather than human activity, pumice was brought to Florida via the Florida Loop Current within the Gulf of Mexico and the Florida Current flowing in the Florida Straits between the Florida Keys and Cuba. Pumice occurring in the Florida Panhandle could have traveled there in the Florida Current, which is restricted to deep water except near the panhandle, where this current has a limited near-shore presence.

## 16.3   Summary Analysis of Fort San José

At first, the short 4-year occupation of Fort San José seems almost inconsequential compared with the large, more longstanding Spanish fortifications and settlements on either side of it at Pensacola and Tallahassee during the great European struggle for control of the Gulf Coast. But a lot happened there during its brief existence, and what Fort San José really shows us is intent. The Spanish had no desire to make this spot only a brief waypoint for displaced Spaniards and fleeing Indians. The effort put into establishing a fort exactly where the Spanish thought the French wanted one as well, the amount of both everyday and fancy goods shipped to this fort, and the presence of families and homes, all represent Spain's strong assertion that the Gulf Coast was under its control. Despite Spain's lack of an inland presence in this delta and its horribly inadequate geographical knowledge of the land it claimed, there was no intent to let the territory go.

But the history and archeology of Fort San José show that intent quickly turned to desperation and then withdrawal. The fort was abandoned in 1723, apparently because it was too remote and too much trouble and expense to continue to support. It was dismantled and any usable material was taken to Pensacola to strengthen the fortifications there. Such a process is evidenced by the material record, since furniture, arms, military objects, and personal items make up a very small amount of the artifact assemblage (only 3.3 % for all these categories combined). A small amount of architectural remains (22 %) is present and almost all is broken and would not have been usable at Pensacola. The activities group makes up 47 % of what was left at Fort San José, the majority of which is the aboriginal pottery and broken olive jars, also not very useful for strengthening Pensacola. St. Joseph Bay was not significantly resettled until American merchants established the short-lived port town of St. Joseph well over a century after the departure of the Spanish.

Fort San José could have been a major center of Spanish Gulf coast dominance. It was established for international and very political reasons and inhabited by a very socially and ethnically diverse population. The history and archeology of this remote settlement indicate that its placement was a strategic move by the Spanish, however it failed, and that even the smallest of outposts can play an important role in the larger stage of globalization, immigration (or in this case colonization), and transformation.

**Acknowledgments** We thank Port St. Joe's historian–archeologists, Herman Jones and Wayne Childers, as well as the St. Joseph Bay State Buffer Preserve for their major contributions to this research.

## References

Beare, N. (1965). *Bottle Bonanza: A handbook for glass collectors*. Florida: Hurricane House Publishers.

Benchley, E. D., & Bense, J. A. (2001). Archaeology and history of St. Joseph Peninsula State Park. Phase I investigations. University of West Florida Archaeology Institute Report of

Investigations, No. 89. Submitted to the Bureau of Archaeological Research, Division of Historical Resources, Florida Department of State, Tallahassee.

Bense, J. A. (Ed.). (1999). *Archaeology of colonial Pensacola 1750–1821*. Gainesville: University Press of Florida.

Beranger, J. (1718). Plan de la Baye de St. Joseph. Electronic document, http://biblioserver.com/newberry. Accessed 4 Jan 2010.

Cabeza De Vaca, A. N., Favata, M. A., & Fernández, J. B. (1993) [1542]. *The account: Alvar Núñez Cabeza De Vaca's Relación*. Houston: Arte Público Press.

Charleviox, Pierre-François-Xavier de. (1761). *Journal of A Voyage To North-America*. Undertaken by Order of the French King. Containing the Geographical Description and Natural History of that Country, Particularly Canada. Volume II. Electronic document, http://openlibrary.org/books/OL24344100M/Histoire_et_description_générale_de_la_Nouvelle_France. Accessed 11 Mar 2012.

Childers, R. W. (2001). History of T. H. Stone Park, St. Joseph's Peninsula, Florida. In E. Benchley & J. Bense, Archaeology and History of St. Joseph Peninsula State Park. Phase I Investigations. Appendix I. University of West Florida Archaeological Institute Report of Investigation No. 89, Pensacola.

Clayton, L., Knight, V. J., & Moore, E. C. (Eds.). (1995). *The De Soto Chronicles: The expedition of Hernando de Soto to North America in 1539–1543*. Tuscaloosa: The University of Alabama Press.

Clune, J. J., Jr., & Stringfield, M. S. (2009). *Historic Pensacola*. Gainesville: The University Press of Florida.

Davis, R. A. (1997). Geology of the Florida Coast. In A. F. Randazzo & D. S. Jones (Eds.), *The geology of Florida* (pp. 155–168). Tallahassee: University Press of Florida.

Deagan, K. (1987). *Artifacts of the Spanish colonies of Florida and the Caribbean, 150–1800 Volume 1: Ceramics, glassware, and beads*. Washington, DC: Smithsonian Institution Press.

Faye, S. (1946). The contest for Pensacola Bay and other Gulf Ports, 1698–1722, Part I. *The Florida Historical Quarterly, 24*(3), 168–195.

Hann, J. H. (2006). *The Native American World beyond Apalachee, West Florida and the Chattahoochee Valley*. Gainesville: University Press of Florida.

Hann, J. H., & McEwan, B. G. (1998). *The Apalachee Indians and Mission San Luis*. Gainesville: University Press of Florida.

Hassan, G. (2008). Pumice. Encyclopedia of Earth. Environmental Information Coalition, National Council for Science and the Environment. Electronic document, http://www.eoearth.org/article/Pumice. Accessed 12 May 2012.

Hubbell, T. H., Laessle, A. M., & Dickinson, J. C. (1956). The Flint-Chattahoochee-Apalachicola-Region and their environments. *Bulletin of the Florida State Museum, Biological Sciences, 1*(1), 1–72.

Hutchins, T. (1968). [viewed 2012-03-11]. *A historical narrative and topographical description of Louisiana and West-Florida* [online]. Gainesville: University of Florida Press. http://ufdc.ufl.edu/UF00100327/00001/1j?search=joseph.

Kish, S. A. (2006). Geochemical and petrologic characterization of pumice artifacts from the Miami Circle Brickell Point archaeological site plus other sites in Florida-potential provenance locations. *The Florida Anthropologist, 59*(3–4), 209–240.

Marrinan, R. A., & White, N. M. (2007). Modeling Fort Walton culture in Northwest Florida. *Southeastern Archaeology, 26*(2), 292–318.

Noël Hume, I. (1962). An Indian ware of the colonial period. *Quarterly Bulletin of the Archaeological Society of Virginia, 17*(1), 2–14.

Noël Hume, I. (1991). *A guide to artifacts of colonial America*. New York: Vintage Books, Random House.

Ortelius, A. (1584). Additamentum to the Theatrum Orbis Terrarum: La Florida. Electronic document, http://www.lib.ua.edu/libraries/hoole/. Accessed 3 Jan 2010.

Weddle, R. S. (1991). *The French Thorn. Rival explorers in the Spanish Sea 1682–1762*. College Station: Texas A & M University Press.

Wheeler, R. J. (2006). Pumice artifacts from the Miami Circle. *The Florida Anthropologist, 59* (3–4), 191–208.

White, N. M. (2005). *Archaeological survey of the St. Joseph Bay State Buffer Preserve, Gulf County, Florida*. Report to the Apalachicola National Estuarine Research Preserve, East Point and the Division of Historical Resources, Tallahassee.

White, N. M. (2009). *Northwest Florida sorting guide*. Unpublished manuscript on file at the University of South Florida in Tampa and the Division of Historical Resources in Tallahassee.

White, N. M. (2011). Middle Woodland and Protohistoric Fort Walton at the Lost Chipola Cutoff Mound, Northwest Florida. *The Florida Anthropologist, 64*(3–4), 241–273.

Willey, G. R. (1949). *Archaeology of the Florida Gulf Coast. Smithsonian miscellaneous collections 113*. (Reprinted 1999). Gainesville: University Press of Florida.

Wood, P. H. (1989). The changing population of the colonial South: An overview by race and region, 1685–1790. In P. H. Wood, G. A. Waselkov, & Hatley, M. T. (Eds.), *Powhatan's Mantle Indians in the colonial Southeast* (pp. 35–103). Lincoln: University of Nebraska Press.

# Chapter 17
# Striking It Rich in the Americas' First Boom Town: Economic Activity at Concepción de la Vega (Hispaniola) 1495–1564

**Pauline Martha Kulstad-González**

## 17.1 Introduction

The Concepción de la Vega archaeological site is found in the central Cibao Valley of the Dominican Republic, on Hispaniola island. It was occupied from approximately 1495, when Columbus established a fort with that name in the area, until 1564, when its last remaining inhabitants moved to the shores of the Camú River after a devastating earthquake in December 1562. During the first half of its occupation it was the second most important city of the colony due to having one of the two official gold foundries on the island. By the mid-1510s, however, problems with the Native American workforce in the gold mines caused a crisis in the gold industry, and colonial authorities decided to change from a gold-based to a sugar-based economy, complete with a change of workforce.

According to historical records, when Concepción lost gold as its main source of income and could not switch to sugar production, the city became a ghost town, peopled by a few cattle ranchers. However, luxury items from the 1520–1550s found in the archaeological assemblage contradict this perception, and have prompted a more careful review of data linked to this site. Research into the economic activities at Concepción seems to demonstrate that other, alternate, social models were created on Hispaniola, different from the "official" model based on sugar production.

### 17.1.1 Labor/Social Divisions

To be able to understand the economic activities undertaken at Concepción, it is important to understand the division of labor within Hispaniola colony during the early contact period. This is due to the fact that the colony was conceived on an economic basis, and three different groups, originally from Africa, Europe, and the

P. M. Kulstad-González (✉)
EPS X-14398, 8260 NW 14th St., Doral, FL 33126, USA
e-mail: paulinekulstad@hotmail.com

© Springer International Publishing Switzerland 2015
P. P. A. Funari, M. X. Senatore (eds.), *Archaeology of Culture Contact and Colonialism in Spanish and Portuguese America,* DOI 10.1007/978-3-319-08069-7_17

New World, interacted with each other on an economic/labor basis, as opposed to the more familiar racial or cultural interaction we are accustomed to today.

The governors of Hispaniola decided to use a social class organization system based on what labor (if any) a person performed, as well as whether this labor was free or enslaved. The base for this classification was the Repartimiento labor system, in turn based on the Spaniards' interpretation of indigenous social hierarchy. According to Spanish chroniclers, the "Taíno Indians" they met on arrival divided their society into three major categories (Arranz-Márquez 1991):

- Nitaínos
- Trabajadores libres ("Free" laborers)—also known as Repartimiento Taíno
- Naborías

The *Nitaínos* were the Taíno nobles of the elite class. During the early contact period the Spanish considered the Nitaíno to be equivalent to the Spanish "lesser nobility" (Guitar 2001). These included the cacique (chief), the behique (healer/religious leader), and the tribe elders. Although the Nitaíno were an essential part of the colonial work system, they did not perform any manual labor. Their main function was to serve as intermediaries between the Taíno laborers and the Spanish authorities (Deagan 2004, p. 608).

The *Trabajadores libres* were the main worker group under the Repartimiento guidelines and corresponded to the Spanish nonelite class. They did not belong to one owner and were not private property (Cassá 1978, p. 44). They were under a cacique's jurisdiction and were mobilized from their native regions to gold mining regions, such as Concepción, to perform manual labor (Cassá 1978, p. 39, 41; Deagan 2004, p. 609). These laborers were assigned by groups to work for a particular Spaniard, but the government could reassign the workers to someone else at their discretion (Arranz-Marquez 1991). These workers were assigned and reassigned according to political nepotism in both 1510 and 1514 (Cassá 1978).

The last group, the *Naborías*, was made up of the servants of the Nitaínos. These were not under the jurisdiction of a cacique, or linked to a Taíno conglomerate (Cassá 1978, p. 53). A sub-group, the "Perpetual Naborías," captured Native American Indians who had rebelled against the Spanish, both from Hispaniola and from neighboring islands and territories (Cassá 1978, p. 53; Guitar 1998, p. 90), were essentially slaves. They were private property and could be inherited (Cassá 1978, p. 53).

This classification system was first instituted to organize Native American labor within the gold mining industry, but was later adapted to fit social and economic needs through the incorporation of Spanish class and slavery elements. This system was flexible, often adapting to changes in freedom laws during this early colonial period, but maintained the same basic labor structure when other economic industries, such as sugar and cattle, were introduced to the colony. The division of labor within this system eventually evolved to become the basis of the social hierarchy.

Specifically in Concepción, during the first period of occupation (1495–1514) the upper class was made up of Spanish elites and Nitaínos, followed by the nonelite category, most of which were Spanish, but also included the *Libertos*, or free people

**Table 17.1** Colonial social system 1495–1514

| Elite class | Spanish nobles |
|---|---|
|  | Nitaínos (Taíno noble class) |
| Nonelites | Spanish nonelite |
|  | Libertos (free Africans) |
| Slave class | Domestic African labor |
|  | Repartimiento Indians involved in urban labor |
|  | Amerindian and African field workers |

**Table 17.2** Colonial social system 1515–1564

| Elite class | Spanish nobles | |
|---|---|---|
|  | Spanish colonial officials | |
|  | Spanish clergy | |
| Nonelites | Spanish nonelite | |
|  | African Libertos | Free Taíno |
| Slave class | Ladino Africans in domestic setting | |
|  | Bozal Africans involved in urban work | |
|  | Amerindian and Bozal African field workers | |

of African descent. The Naboría class became the slave class with the incorporation of African slaves into the mix. Although at the bottom of the social pyramid, this class was not monolithic. The domestic African labor had the highest rank among the slaves, followed by the Repartimiento Indians involved in urban labor, with the Amerindian and African field workers at the bottom (Table 17.1).

During the second period of occupation (1515–1564), more specifically in 1542, the Repartimiento system was abolished and the Taíno became free (Fernandez-Alvarez 1975, p. 73). This meant that at the moment of the 1562 earthquake, Concepción's elite were mostly Spanish or mixed elite Taino/Spanish, followed by a nonelite group now made up of Spanish, a few Libertos and the rest of the Taíno. The slave class was composed of African domestic laborers, and Amerindian and African field workers (Table 17.2). It is important to note that the escaped Taíno, Amerindian, and Maroon ex-slaves, were not a part of this social classification system. They lived on the margins of organized society, but often interacted with the rest of society in a clandestine manner (Deive 1980; Larrazabal 1975).

## 17.2 Economic Activity at Concepción

Historical and archaeological records show that economic activities flourished at Concepción, both in rural and urban settings, before and after the gold production collapse. Gold was the city's main rural economic industry during the first period of occupation (1495–1514), but during the second period (1515–1564) sugar production and cattle ranching were attempted to maintain the same high standard of living offered by gold production. Large-scale urban economic activities included construction and government, while small-scale activities included clothing production, weaponry manufacture, blacksmithing, commercial activities, and street vending. While most of the workers involved in large-scale economic industries were men, women undertook many of the urban activities, especially clothing manufacture, and street vending (Deive 1980, p. 20; Landers 1999, p. 8; Larrazabal 1975, p. 13, 109). This division was particularly distinct among the African origin group (Larrazabal 1975, p. 110). The discussion to follow will present how these activities were carried out at Concepción, as well as identify some of the persons who undertook them.

## 17.2.1   Economic Activity: 1495–1515

When Columbus returned to Hispaniola on his second voyage, he planned to create an extractive factoría colony at La Isabela, which was to trade for gold with the native inhabitants of the island (Deagan and Cruxent 2002, p. 47), and attempt to produce cash crops (Guitar 1998, p. 203), including sugar cane (Ortiz 1947). Factorías were a type of settlement established in isolated locations to facilitate trade between two distant points (Deagan and Cruxent 2002, p. 8). These settlements often exploited raw materials not readily available in Europe, such as gold or spices (Incháustegui 1955, p. 53; Pérez-Collados 1992, p. 117; Pérez de Tudela 1954, p. 317–318). These settlements were backed by private capital, and led by an individual who hired artisans, craftsmen, and laborers to undertake the labor (Arranz-Márquez 1991, p. 27; Deagan and Cruxent 2002, p. 8). These types of trading posts had been used in the Mediterranean by several different countries since the mid-fourteenth century (Deagan and Cruxent 2002, p. 8).

Columbus was quite familiar with the Portuguese factoría model used in West Africa (Pérez de Tudela 1954). According to this model, the community leader would receive a license from the Portuguese crown to start his colony and funds to pay the workers' wages. In exchange, the Crown would receive one fifth of the profits generated. However, the Portuguese Crown did not assume political control over the territory in which the factoría was established (Deagan and Cruxent 2002, p. 8). These settlements were considered purely economic (Moya-Pons 1983, p. 13).

To make his factoría viable, Columbus depended on a supply of gold from the native Taíno Indians large enough to make the operation cost effective. In order to do this, he established a tribute (tax) system on the Taíno in 1495 (Charlevoix 1730, p. 110; Cassá 1978, p. 33; Deagan and Cruxent 2002, p. 62). Taíno communities had to pay one hawk's bell full of gold for each member of their community over 14 years of age every 3 months (Cassá 1978, p. 33; Charlevoix 1730, p. 110; Wilson 1990). Although the Taíno did process gold into artifacts before the arrival of the Spanish (Vega 1979), their method of production appears to have been too rudimentary to provide the amount of gold required. Columbus, however, insisted on tribute payment, and negotiated the tribute at 25 lbs. of cotton (Charlevoix 1730, p. 110), labor, or personal services rendered to the Spanish every 3 months in those places which could not pay in gold (Deagan and Cruxent 2002, p. 62).

The use of Taíno as labor, as opposed to mere providers of trade goods, created a colonial system different from a factoría. The model changed further when Spanish nonelite laborers left La Isabela to live in Taíno villages and forced the natives to work for them (Moya-Pons 1983, p. 12). This situation created a need to militarily guard all places where gold was found on the island (Cassá 1978, p. 33; Cohen 1997, p. 4). Eventually, a network of forts extended from Hispaniola's northern to southern coast to guard those places where gold had been found (Cassá 1978, p. 41).

Gold mineral and/or Taíno laborers must have been plentiful in the area around the Concepción fort in 1495, since Guarionex, chief of the Taíno settlement close to the fort, was the only ruler able to fulfill the tribute demands (Cassá 1978, p. 33; Moya-Pons 1978, p. 13). On the rest of the island, the failure of the tribute system brought down the Columbus regime, eventually leading to Columbus's destitution, and the appointment of Francisco de Bobadilla as governor (Pérez-Collados 1992, p. 161).

Under Bobadilla's governance, the Spanish monarchs claimed the right to control the land and its resources (Pérez-Collados 1992, p. 163). Spanish miners were granted licenses to extract gold, and were obliged to pay the government one-fifth of the gold profits earned (known as the *quinto*) (Deagan and Cruxent 2002, p. 201; Guitar 1998, p. 116). Until 1550, only Buenaventura (close to San Cristóbal on the south coast) and Concepción were permitted to smelt gold. As the northernmost Royal Foundry, Concepción received all the gold mined in the northern part of the island (Anghiera in Guitar 1998, p. 117).

In the Concepción area, as in the rest of Hispaniola, most of the gold discovered was placer gold (Guitar 1998, p. 127; Sauer 1966, p. 198), which is found by panning rather than digging. Gold panning on Hispaniola involved a mixed group of workers, including Taínos under *Repartimiento*. Each group of 10 mine workers was supervised by a servant, sometimes a free man of African descent (Guitar 1998, p. 125). Nonelite Spaniards worked as mining supervisors and overseers of several work groups (Guitar 1998, p. 126). Often a group of neighbors shared workers organized into compañías, also known as *cofradías* (Marte 1981, p. 401; Fernández de Oviedo in Rueda 1988; Patronato 1995, p. 60).

The mining extraction process involved several steps, similar to modern-day archaeological excavation. Gonzalo Fernández de Oviedo (Fernández de Oviedo in Rueda 1988, pp. 208–217) describes the process as follows: Gold was mined close to a water source. An area 18–20 steps in diameter would be staked out, with African slave and Perpetual Naboría (Amerindian) men clearing the surface of trees and rocks. Taínos under *Repartimiento* would then proceed to excavate, a hand-width at a time. The excavated soil would be taken by the Amerindian men to the panniers, sitting on the water banks. The panniers were mostly African and Amerindian women, who supposedly were better at spotting nuggets. The panniers would swirl the mud in flattened gourds called *bateas* until gold appeared. This process continued until bedrock was reached in the plot. The plot was then washed out to reveal possible gold veins. An average mining operation would have 50 workers: 10 panniers, 20 earth-carriers, and 20 diggers. The camp also included women cooks who mostly made cassava.

In spite of a fairly organized methodology, success in gold mining was by no means guaranteed. Various practices were instituted to improve findings. de Oviedo (Fernández de Oviedo in Rueda 1988, p. 150) records a practice followed by Christopher Columbus: The Taíno followed a religious ritual involving chastity and fasting previous to gathering gold, and Columbus believed the Spanish should also follow these principles, as well as confession and communion, before trying their luck. He refused to give gold licenses to those who did not comply. Many Spaniards protested, stating that their wives were in Spain (being involved with Amerindian women did not count), that they "died of hunger and had to eat roots" (manioc and many other Taíno staples are tubers or roots), and that the Church only required confession once a year. It is not known whether African and Amerindian workers were required to follow these guidelines as well. The recent discovery of a church within a mining camp in central Dominican Republic (Olsen 2013) may support this requirement.

This gold was kept until it was time for the "fundición," or smelting. This process was done twice a year at an official Casas de Fundiciones, one of which was at Concepción (Charlevoix 1730, p. 221; Anghiera in Guitar 1998, p. 117). The gold was received, smelted into bars and the *quinto* was taken by the Crown's *escribano de minas*—Melchor de Castro in Concepción (Marte 1981, p. 401). The rest went to the miner (Guitar 1998, p. 117).

The archeological assemblage at Concepción includes several items related to the gold industry: three metal molds, 13 hawksbells, 1 metal crusher and 2 pestles. There are also a large number of keys and lock fragments, indicating the need to safeguard valuables.

## 17.2.2   Urban Economic Activity: 1495–1514

Many of Concepción's urban residents made their living manufacturing clothing, weapons, smithing, or as merchants, domestic servants, or street vendors. These activities thrived due to the miners' gold earnings. All commercial transactions, according to Crown law, were to be conducted using money (Marte 1981, p. 401). These transactions are evidenced by the large numbers of coins that have been found at the site, both through archaeological excavation and looting (Abreu 1998; Stahl in Deagan 1999). Most of the coins stored at the site came from the first period of occupation, specifically from different periods of King Ferdinand's reign: the joint reign with his wife, the joint reign with his daughter, and a period ruling alone. Although this could be interpreted as being the moment when more coins were available, it must be noted that these are probably not truly representative of the total found at the site, but rather are the least attractive of the lot. The archaeological assemblage also includes two money weights. Historical evidence also records other kinds of commercial transactions and payment methods such as barter in unrefined gold, foodstuffs, used clothing (Marte 1981, p. 401; Patronato 1995, p. 55, 212), and credit transactions (Patronato 1995, p. 212, 265).

## 17.2.3   Construction Industry: 1495–1514

The large influx of settlers attracted by Concepción's gold created the need for a large number of buildings. The construction industry would have included not only those who put the buildings together, but also the designers and those producing the necessary materials (bricks, tiles, and nails) as well (Table 17.3). There is no evidence of any women involved in the construction industry (Deive 1989, p. 24; Larrazabal 1975, p. 13).

Most of the buildings at Concepción during the first period of occupation (1495–1514) were made of perishable materials, which were later replaced with masonry buildings during the second period (1515–1564). Currently there is no evidence that Spanish architects worked at Concepción, although the masonry fort was constructed by a Spanish "workers' brigade who knew about bricks, quicklime, and plaster," led by a man named "Zafra" (Palm 1952, p. 115), a very African-sounding name.

Taíno *Repartimiento* workers may have been involved in other aspects of masonry construction during this period, such as brick and tile-making and carpentry, as evidenced by the 1514 *Repartimiento* documents (Arranz-Márquez 1991; Guitar 1998, p. 150), which show Taíno assigned to nonelite Spanish tradesmen, such as master constructors Melchor Rendón and Pedro de Valera (Rodriguez-Demorizi 1971).

## 17.2.4   Government Employment: 1495–1514

Government employment was an important source of income for a large portion of Concepción's Spanish urban male population. This is in contrast to the non-Spanish inhabitants, most of which were involved in manual labor in the large-scale economic industries—gold and construction. The specific functions of government workers and many of their names are known thanks to the vast documents of the Spanish bureaucracy (Tables 17.3 and 17.4).

Most government jobs during this first period were reserved for the Spanish elite, many of which had previously been part of the Aragonese court in Spain. This included Miguel de Pasamonte, the colony's treasurer, who not only received a salary and a portion of the gold smelted (García 1906, p. 69; Casas in Rueda 1988, p. 98), but also used his position to receive many benefits, including more Taínos in the Repartimientos (Guitar 1998, p. 134; Moya-Pons 1983, p. 27). Government posts for the Spanish nonelite were limited to being constables and scribes (Benzo 2000).

Table 17.3 Inhabitants at Concepcion by Activity 1495–1514

| Activity categories | Inhabitants by activity | | | |
|---|---|---|---|---|
| Gold industry | *Miner*<br>Fernando de Alcantara<br>Sebastian Tapia<br>Lic. Lucas Vásquez de Ayllón | *Visitador*<br>Hernan Ponce de León[a]<br>Alonso de Porras<br>Diego Valdenebro | | |
| Food production | *Farm owner*<br>Juan de Robles | *Market gardener*<br>Hernando de Seña<br>(Peña)[b] | *Livestock raising* | |
| Architecture, construction and masonry | *Master constructor*<br>Melchor Rendon<br>Pedro de Valera | | | |
| Weaponry | *Crossbowman*<br>Diego Valdenebro<br>Gómez de Morón<br>Blas de Salamanca | | | |
| Clothing | *Tailor*<br>Cristóbal Avila<br>Francisco de Covarrubias | *Woolcarding*<br>Diego Diez | *Shoemaker* | |
| Transportation | *Blacksmith*<br>Pero Nisa | *Stable owner* | | |
| Religion | *Cathedral*<br>Archpriest of Concepción<br>Canon of Toro | *Monastery* | *Bishop's prebendary*<br>Blas Hierro | *Bishop*<br>Pedro Suarez de Deza |
| Government | *Treasurer*<br>Miguel de Pasamonte | *Alderman*<br>Juan Alburquerque<br>Rodrigo de Alcazar<br>Pedro de Atienza<br>Hernan Ponce de León[a]<br>Juan de Villoria<br>Juan Fernández de Guadalupe | *Notary*<br>Alonso Arce<br>Pero Perez<br>Vicente Lopez (public)<br>Cristóbal Rodríguez (translator) | *Constable*<br>Ruiz Gómez |

Table 17.3 (continued)

| Activity categories | Inhabitants by activity | | | |
|---|---|---|---|---|
| Government 2 | *Collector of Bienes de los Difuntos*<br>Pero Lope de Mesa[c] | *Residencia advisor*<br>Pero Lope de Mesa[c] | *Residencia judge*<br>Bachiller Alonso de Parada | *Procurator*<br>Hernán Ponce de León[a] |
| Government 3 | *Fort*<br>Juan de Ayala (fort mayor) (1495)<br>Miguel de Ballester (fort warden/mayor) (1497)<br>García de Barrantes (captain) (1497)<br>Gonzalo de la Rambla (soldier) (1497) | *Representative*<br>Rodrigo de Alburquerque<br>Hernán Ponce de León[a] | *Navigator*<br>Alonso Pérez de Almonte | |
| Health | *Apothecary*<br>Pedro Murcia[d]<br>Bachiller Francisco Hernandez[e] | *Physician*<br>Bachiller Francisco Fernandez[f] | *Barber*<br>Pedro Murcia[d]<br>Juan Ramirez | *Doctor*<br>Pedro Murcia[d]<br>Bachiller Francisco Hernandez[e]<br>Bachiller Francisco Fernandez[f] |
| Smiths | *Crown silversmith*<br>Rodrigo de Alcázar | *Locksmith*<br>Diego Rodrigo | | |
| Domestic labor | *Servant of Rodrigo de Villadiego*<br>Diego de Godoy<br>Gonzalo Martín<br>Ortiga de Herrera | | | |
| Commercial activity | *Merchant*<br>Rodrigo de Villadiego | *Market gardener*<br>Hernando de Seña (Peña)[b] | | |

a,b,c,d,e,f Each letter stands for a particular person, and each subsequent instance in the table indicates that it is the same person (Based on Arranz-Márquez 1991; Benzo 2000)

Table 17.4 Inhabitants at Concepcion by Activity 1515-1564

| Activity categories | Inhabitants by activity | | | |
|---|---|---|---|---|
| Gold industry | *Miner*<br>Hernando de Alcantara<br>Juan Martin de Xagua<br>Martin Callejas | | | *Livestock raising*<br>Diego de Ortega (cattle)<br>Alonso Martin (cattle)<br>Alonso Rodriguez (shepherd) |
| Food production | *Farm owner*<br>Garcia de Paredes (Estante) | | *Farm owners*<br>Juan Cobo<br>Gonzalo Gómes<br>Francisco de Hinojos<br>Alonso Rodriguez<br>Lorenzo de Cuellar[a] | Slaughterhouse |
| Architecture, construction and masonry | Master constructor | | | |
| Weaponry | *Sword maker*<br>Villadandro | *Crossbowman*<br>Gómez de Moróm | | |
| Clothing | *Tailor*<br>Cristóbal Davila Morales | *Shoemaker*<br>Pedro Pineda | | *Woolcarding* |
| Transportation | *Stable owner*<br>Juan de Villegas | *Mule driver*<br>Juan Martin de Trebejo | | |
| Religion | *Vicar-general*<br>Juan PérezCristóbal Deza[b]<br>Alvaro de León (Cathedral)[c]<br>Cristóbal de Zuazedo | *Sexton*<br>Francisco Toro<br>Juan Martin de la Fuente<br>Diego Martin<br>Lorenzo de Cuellar[a]<br>Juan Martin de la Fuente Sabz | *Cathedral*<br>Juan Cordoba (steward)<br>Luys de Morales (prebendary)<br>Jorge de Viguera (chantre)<br>Gonzalo Sanchez (presbyter)[d] | *Canon*<br>Alonso Martin (1520)<br>Alvaro de León (1526)[c]<br>Cristóbal Deza (1525)[b]<br>Alvaro de Castro[e]<br>Ruis |

**Table 17.4** (continued)

| Activity categories | Inhabitants by activity | | | |
|---|---|---|---|---|
| Religion 2 | *Apostolic notary*<br>Diego Sanchez Ruiz<br>Francisco de Soria | *Cleric*<br>Hernando de Camargo[f]<br>Juan de Gamarro[g]<br>Myllan Gutierre[h]<br>Blas López (Bishop's chaplain)<br>Juan de Santa Maria<br>Diego del Rio<br>Gonzalo Sánchez[d] | *Maestrescuela*<br>Antonio Márquez (1530) | *Dean*<br>Alvaro de Castro (1526–1532)[e] |
| Religion 3 | *Vicar-general*<br>Alvaro de León (Cathedral)[c]<br>Hernando de Camargo[f]<br>Cristóbal Deza[b]<br>Myllan Gutierre (Bishopric)[h]<br>Francisco de Mendoza<br>Juan Pérez<br>Cristóbal de Sabcedo<br>Jorge de Viguera<br>Gonzalo Sánchez (vicar)[d] | *Friars*<br>Fr. Antonio Pedroso (Franciscan)<br>Tomas de San Martin (Dominican) | *Inquisitor*<br>Marcos de Aguilar<br>Alvaro de Castro (commissary)[e] | *Various*<br>Sancho Cespedes (Archdeacon)<br>Juan de Santa Maria (Archpriest) |
| Government | *Governor deputy*<br>Juan Hurtado | *Alderman*<br>Pedro Castro<br>Francisco Ponce de León<br>Pedro de Atienza<br>Alonso Avila<br>Alvaro de Sieza | *Chief constable*<br>Antonio de Campos<br>Pero Lope de Mesa[i] | *Constable*<br>Juan de Zuñiga<br>Pedro Palomo[j]<br>Fordillo (executive constable) |
| Government 2 | *Notary*<br>Juan de Avila<br>Miguel de Gaviria (crown)<br>Martín Pérez de Landa (public)<br>Juan Soto (cublic)<br>Juan Ortiz (royal) | *Magistrate*<br>Lope Termiño de Velasco<br>Ruanyno de Velasco | *Mayor*<br>Juan Monegro<br>Francisco Orejón<br>Antón de Monegro<br>Francisco de Ocampo<br>Hernan Velázquez<br>Juan Mosquera | *Collector of Bienes de los Difuntos*<br>Francisco de Ocampo<br>Pero Lope de Mesa[i]<br>Hernando de Alcantara (will executor) |

**Table 17.4** (continued)

| Activity categories | Inhabitants by activity | | | |
|---|---|---|---|---|
| Government 3 | *Notary*<br>Juan Davila | *Court*<br>Antonio de Campos (appelate judge)<br>Pedro Palomo (public prosecutor)[j]<br>Pedro Sarmiento (public prosecutor) | *Residencia advisor*<br>Pero Lope de Mesa[i] | *Knight commander*<br>Alvaro de León[c] |
| Health | *Barber*<br>Pedro Palomo[j] | *Apothecary* | *Physician* | *Doctor* |
| Smiths | Silversmith | *Locksmith* | | |
| Commercial activity | *Merchant*<br>Villadandro<br>Juan Martín Callejas<br>Alvaro Castro and Morales (clothes)<br>Francisco Sánchez | *Salt*<br>Juan Martin de Trebejo | *Sugar mill*<br>Alonso Roman<br>Francisco Orejón | |
| Domestic labor | *Alvaro de Castro's servants*<br>Catalina Alpargas<br>Alonso Román<br>Pero Gómez<br>Pero Goncales<br>Pedro Valladolid<br>Juan de Gamarro[g]<br>Juan de la Fuente<br>Beatrizica: Lucayan woman<br>Catalina: Lucayan woman<br>Black woman attacked by Alonso Rodriguez | *Alonso Roman's servant*<br>Alonso Pastor | *Blas López's servant*<br>Juan de Orellana | |

a,b,c,d,e,f,g,h,i,j Each letter stands for a particular person, and each subsequent instance in the table indicates that it is the same person (Based on Arranz-Márquez 1991; Benzo 2000)

## 17.2.5   Clothing Production: 1495–1514

The production and repair of clothing was a widespread industry at Concepción, as it was in other colonial settlements (Deagan 2002). History records that these were manufactured, for the most part, from cloth imported from Spain (Patronato 1995, p. 136) since few ready-made new clothes were available (Patronato 1995, p. 212). At one point, the industry was affected by the gold boom wealth, creating a shortage in clothes and cloth (Patronato 1995).

Although sewing was an activity primarily undertaken by women at Spanish colonial sites (Deagan 2002), and 31 of pins and needles, as well as several thimbles have been recovered archaeologically at the site (Deagan 1999; Pimentel 1998), there is no historical evidence of their contribution to this economic activity. Only the men involved in this industry are mentioned, once again confirming the importance of using various avenues of inquiry to reconstruct a site's lifeways.

Among those men mentioned in relation to the clothing business is a wool-carding official, Diego Diez, present during the 1514 Repartimiento (Arranz-Márquez 1991; Benzo 2000). He did not receive any Taínos who could have served as apprentices (Arranz- Márquez 1991; Benzo 2000), as opposed to two nonelite tailors (Cristóbal de Avila and Francisco de Covarrubias) who received six Taíno apprentices through the Repartimiento (Arranz- Márquez 1991; Guitar 1998, p. 150) (Table 17.3).

Other clothing related items in the archaeological assemblage include 8 buckles, 7 buckle tips, a pair of scissors and 18 aglets (Deagan 1998). The different locations where these items were recovered could indicate more than one clothing store.

## 17.2.6   Commerce: 1495–1514

The Spanish mercantile system restricted colonial importation and exportation to trade with Spain through a monopoly established by Sevillian merchants (Deagan 1983, p. 19). This limiting system was based on the Treaty of Tordesillas which, in 1494, divided the Atlantic between the kingdoms of Portugal and Castile (Pérez-Collados 1992, p. 66). Based on a Papal Bull, this treaty gave Spain legal and religious jurisdiction over most of Spanish America (Tavares 1978, p. 103; Deagan 1983, p. 21). However, as the Protestant movement began to question Catholicism, Catholic hierarchy, and its close relation to the Spanish Crown, many questioned Spanish jurisdiction over the New World (Tavares 1978, p. 25; Guitar 1998, p. 264). With this in mind, France, Portugal, England, and the Netherlands undermined the Spanish mercantile system in the Caribbean, first through illegal trade, and later through piracy (Deagan 1983, p. 21; Haring 1964, p. 122).

At first on Hispaniola, when little local production existed, and large amounts of money were available, the mercantile system was advantageous on both sides of the Atlantic. This was especially true during the very prosperous Ovando government (1502–1509) (Deagan and Cruxent 2002, p. 208), and especially in gold-rich Concepción, where the miners looked to spend their earnings.

Only one merchant is identified at Concepción during this period, Rodrigo de Villadiego (Arranz-Márquez 1991). Although the 1514 *Repartimiento* documents do not specify the type of goods Villadiego sold, he was a *vecino* (Spanish landowner), and received 46 Taínos in the Repartimiento, suggesting that he commercialized at a relatively large scale.

## 17.2.7  Craft Production: 1495–1514

Several craft-related economic occupations can be identified at Concepción both through the historical and archaeological record. These crafts include crossbow and sword making, as well as different types of smithing. Unlike at La Isabela, where few metal tools were able to survive due to the unstable moisture and the salinity of the beachside soils (Deagan and Cruxent 2002, p. 247), a considerably large amount of metal artifacts are stored at Concepción.

Historical records show that three crossbow makers lived in Concepción during the first period (1495–1514) (Table 17.3)—Gómez de Morón, Diego Valdenebro and Blas de Salamanca (Benzo 2000). According to the 1514 *Repartimiento* records, both received 2 Taínos each (Arranz-Márquez 1991; Benzo 2000). Gómez de Morón continued to work in Concepción during the later years of its occupation, making him one of the few *vecinos* who lived at Concepción during both periods (Benzo 2000). Three crossbow arrows are present in the archaeological assemblage (Deagan 1998).

Blacksmiths and locksmiths were present at Concepción during both periods. According to historical records, gold, copper, and iron items were processed at Concepción (Guitar 1998, p. 210), but the copper and iron may have been imported from Spain. The origin of the latter two materials would have influenced the actions undertaken by the different smiths within the city. Documents record the names of Spanish blacksmith Pero Nissan and locksmith Diego Rodrigo, during this first period. Neither of these men were *vecinos*, but both received 2 Taínos in the 1514 *Repartimiento* (Arranz-Márquez 1991), probably as apprentices.

It is interesting to note that the archaeological assemblage contains a fair amount of vitreous enamel used in the elaboration of Spanish-style ceramics, but historical records do not contain the names of the artisans (Deagan 1998). It has been suggested that ceramics were produced by Native Americans at the Franciscan monastery on-site (Ugarte 1981). Further information is needed to identify the gender, origin, and class of these artisans.

## 17.2.8  Domestic Labor: 1495–1514

The great gold boom wealth allowed for widespread domestic labor at Concepción, including Spanish, Native American, and African servants. The archaeological assemblage needs to be examined more carefully to provide evidence of this activity.

Some glimpses as to their identities are available in the historical record. Two Spanish servants during this period are Diego de Godoy and Gonzalo Martin (Benzo 2000). Both worked for Rodrigo de Villadiego, the city's main merchant (Benzo 2000). It seems unlikely that many Spanish female servants were present at Concepción, given the small number of Spanish women who traveled to the New World during those years.

No historical evidence has been found to confirm that Taíno nonelite women worked as domestic servants in "Spanish" households at Concepción. Although it is commonly assumed that Taíno women provided domestic labor, this may not have been prevalent at Concepción, since there was a shortage of Taíno nonelite men for agricultural production, and the lack of a large-scale food production economic industry may have prompted the need for Taíno women to grow the native crops.

It is also possible that elite Taíno women from the *Nitaíno* class, married to Spanish *encomenderos*, had their precontact native servants present in the household. It would be interesting to see if these households had more or less Taíno influence than a household with Taíno servants, but headed by an elite Spanish wife. In 1514 half of the "Spanish" households at Concepción included Taíno women as wives and mistresses of the house (Benzo 2000). Further research is necessary to see "Spanish" households with a Taíno wife also had access to African slave servants. The amount of influence these non-Spanish women had on general household decisions, such as food preparation, is open to debate.

During Diego Columbus's first government (1510–1514) each of Concepción's inhabitants was allowed an African *Ladino* slave maid for domestic chores (Deive 1989, p. 20; Larrazabal 1975, p. 13). These Ladino maids had lived a portion of their life in Spain, spoke Spanish and were familiar with Spanish cultural traditions (Guitar 1998, p. 150).

However, not every Spaniard could afford an African slave. They were a luxury, and were used in an urban setting to safeguard the investment (Deive 1989, p. 20). There is reference to both male and female servants, but the vast majority were women. The *jornal* system (used by African slaves and their owners in Seville during this period), may have been instituted at Concepción. This system allowed slaves to live independently, in their own homes, in exchange for paying their masters a certain daily amount (Landers 1999, p. 16). The work could be assigned by the master, or could be done about town independently (Deive 1989, p. 20; Landers 1999, p. 16). This system was advantageous for both parties, since slaves would be relatively independent and had the possibility of buying their freedom, while the masters earned money without responsibilities for food, shelter, clothes, or medical care (Landers 1999, p. 16).

## 17.3 Economic Activity at Concepción: 1515–1564

While the first period was opulent, thanks to gold production, the second was made up of various attempts to replicate pre-1514 lifeways through different economic activities. The *Repartimiento* of 1514 marks the division between the two periods because this final distribution of gold workers at Concepción and on the rest of the island caused a loss in the social and economic mobility among those unable to have a large stable workforce engaged in producing wealth. Additionally, the *Cimarrón* uprisings (both Amerindian and African) caused a need to safeguard the slave population. The 1528 and 1544 Slave Ordenanzas limited the movement of African slave men to prevent their escape and their joining of the movement (Larrazabal 1975, p. 110).

### 17.3.1 Gold Production: 1515–1564

Many historians (see Floyd 1963, p. 68–69; Moya-Pons 1983, 1987) have assumed that gold became scarce at Concepción shortly after 1514, however a careful reading of sources (Marte 1981, p. 295, 368; Rodriguez-Morel 2000, p. 87) suggests that it was processed gold, rather than the mineral itself, that was scarce, due to the lack of a large, stable labor force able to undertake mining work. In fact, gold production on Hispaniola peaked in 1519 and 1520 (Incháustegui 1955, p. 126), and Concepción continued to be the main northern foundry until the mid-1540s (Rodriguez-Morel 2000, p. 106).

Several other factors seem to have contributed to this decrease in gold production. One was the mass migration of those *vecinos* who did not get Taíno workers assigned to them in 1514 (Moya-Pons 1983, p. 28). A second was the institution of the Jeronymite program to substitute gold for sugar as the main economic activity (Cassá 1978, p. 58). Another may have been the Cimarrón attacks on mining groups, to steal either their slaves or their gold.

Gold prospection continued, at a smaller scale, during this period, with an important difference—most prospecting was done on cattle ranching lands (Patronato 1995, p. 216, 220), probably as a means for protection. Another difference was that *cofradías* during this period were not allowed to roam the countryside, but rather had to return to the master's home every night to prevent slaves from escaping (Larrazabal 1975, p. 109). According to the 1528 *Ordenanzas*, these work groups had to be accompanied by a Christian foreman, who was either a nonelite Spaniard (Patronato 1995, p. 246), or possibly a *Ladino* slave (Larrazabal 1975, p. 107).

The Spanish Crown also undertook gold mining during this period, with the labor being carried out by African slaves rather than *Repartimiento* Taínos (Guitar 1998, p. 128). The Crown did not suffer from labor shortages, since it allowed itself access to a large number of slaves, but restricted licenses to private individuals (Guitar 1998, p. 128).

Historical accounts say that gold was no longer officially smelted at Concepción by 1547 (Rodriguez-Morel 2000, p. 106). However, it is possible that individuals may have illegally smelted gold on a small-scale, as had been done earlier at La Isabela (Deagan and Cruxent 2002, p. 186).

## 17.3.2   Failed Attempts at Sugar Production: 1515–1564

When Columbus came to set up his factoría in 1493, his second source of cash would be through the cultivation of certain crops, including sugar cane (Guitar 1998, p. 203; Ortiz 1947). However, he was unsuccessful in its production, as was Governor Ovando in 1503 (Rogozinski 2000, p. 51). Attempts to produce sugar continued, until it was produced commercially—for the first time in the New World—at Concepción de la Vega in 1506 (Concepción 1981, 1982; Ortiz 1947). The first sugar produced was similar to molasses (Guitar 1998, p. 206), but by 1512, crude presses, originally used in cassava bread production, helped make the product more crystalline (Ortiz 1947, p. 263; Guitar 1998, p. 206). The results must have been encouraging, because that same year, Concepción's Bishop Suarez de Deza, proposed to change the colony's main mode of production from gold mining by Taínos under the *Repartimiento*, to sugar production by African slaves (Moya-Pons 1978, p. 176).

As a member of the Dominican order, Deza supported the questioning of the Taíno working conditions by fellow monk Anton de Montesinos. He also saw the need to find a way to save them from extinction. At the same time, the colony needed to support itself economically, and a viable alternative had to be offered to gold production. Sugar, at that time, seemed the most promising. It had enjoyed high prices in Europe since 1510 (Moya-Pons 1974, p. 71), and Spain had previous experience with its production in the Canary Islands (Guitar 1998, p. 194), including the use of an African labor force familiar with Spanish language and culture (Ladino slaves). Another important advantage of sugar production was its sedentary nature, as opposed to gold prospecting, which required the mining teams to roam the countryside. By being sedentary, sugar production allowed a slave owner to have better control over possible slave escapes.

Bartolomé de Las Casas, another Dominican monk, championed Deza's ideas in the Spanish Court, and the Jeronymite government (1516–1519) instituted sugar production as part of their governmental plan (Incháustegui 1955, p. 127; Moya-Pons 1978). This plan included loans to *vecinos*, which came out of the Crown's gold *quinto* (Cassá 1978, p. 66; Moya-Pons 1978, p. 180), the elimination of taxes on mill equipment (Incháustegui 1955, p. 127; Ortiz 1947, p. 271–272), and foreclosure exemption for sugar mills (Cassá 1978, p. 67; Incháustegui 1955, p. 127; Wright 1916, p. 769–771). Concepción's early participation in the sugar industry is reflected archaeologically by a large number of broken ceramic sugar molds recovered from the site (Deagan 1998), and apparently used as construction aggregate due to their prevalence amongst discarded pottery.

Nevertheless, despite Concepción being the first to produce sugar commercially, history records production here as a short-lived failure (Guitar 1998, p. 206, 279, 326–329; Mira-Caballos 1997, p. 155; Rodriguez-Morel 2000, p. 50; Sáez 1994, p. 267–272). The reasons are uncertain. Some have suggested a lack of vecinos to carry out the venture. Records show members of Concepción's elite class during the first period, living in the south coast, close to Santo Domingo, and owning sugar mills during the 1530s and 1540s. There is some confusion as to whether the vecinos moved there because of geographical advantages for the sugar industry (rivers and ports) (Cassá 1978, p. 67; Concepción 1981, 1982), or whether the sugar industry was established in this area because the elite had already migrated en masse after the 1514 *Repartimiento* (Moya-Pons 1983, p. 31). Others have suggested that *Cimarrón* attacks on the roads made travel between cities unsafe, consequently making sugar marketing difficult (Guitar 1998, p. 262; Patronato 1995, p. 250).

### 17.3.3    Cattle Ranching (1515–1564)

Cattle ranching for the production of hides, with meat as a by-product, was a more feasible mode of production for Concepción than sugar after 1514, and especially during its last 30 years of occupation (1530–1562) (Moya-Pons 1978). It became the main economic industry at Concepción during the second period of occupation (García 1906, p. 114). Unlike sugar and gold production, cattle ranching required a smaller workforce (García 1906, p. 114), and hides, a non-perishable product, were easier to transport and sell (Cohen 1997, p. 8). Historical records show that cattle hides produced at Concepción were shipped to Spain (Marte 1981, p. 402), but it may be possible that some were part of the contraband trade (Deive 1989, p. 60).

Historian Frank Moya-Pons (1983, p. 51) had suggested that cattle ranching was an industry of last resort, undertaken by those "unable to migrate," and had no access to slaves. He describes what appears to be a small-scale, unorganized enterprise based on the hunting of wild cattle and pigs living in the Hispaniola wilderness (Moya-Pons 1983, p. 51). Other researchers (Cassá 1978, p. 63; Incháustegui 1955, p. 74; Patronato 1995, p. 17), however, seem to point to an organized, large-scale livestock industry. Cattle ranches, known as *hatos*, were owned by the Spanish elite, and were basically places where hides were processed (Patronato 1995, p. 56). Cattle was branded and left to run free, sometimes herded from pasture to pasture by workers, many of African descent. It is possible that many of these workers combined small-scale gold mining with cattle herding (Patronato 1995).

Officially, all hides were to be exported from Santo Domingo (Moya-Pons 1983, p. 52). The rest of the colony had to send live cattle to Santo Domingo and had them processed there, due to the high cost and dangers of traveling between cities (Moya-Pons 1983, p. 52). However, there is archaeological evidence that slaughterhouses existed in Puerto Real, on the northern end of the island, implying that hides could have been at least partially processed there (Deagan and Reitz 1995, p. 282). It is important to note that Puerto Real was under Concepción's political jurisdiction.

Regardless of how the cattle industry was undertaken, it was extremely lucrative. It is even believed that most cattle were killed only for their hides, wasting much of the meat (Deagan and Reitz 1995, Chap. 9; Moya-Pons 1983, p. 52). Some of the meat by-product was used to feed the workers living on the *hatos* (Cassá 1978, p. 63; Patronato 1995, p. 224), as well as those working in the gold and sugar industry (Moya-Pons 1983, p. 51). Concepcion's Dean Alvaro de Castro, for example, gave meat to gold prospectors on credit, to be paid at smelting time

(Patronato 1995, p. 265). It has been suggested that by the mid-Sixteenth century, the cattle ranchers had as much influence on colonial politics as sugar producers (Incháustegui 1955, p. 74).

### 17.3.4 Urban Economic Activities: 1515–1564

After 1514 there was considerably less money available in Concepción and it is quite possible that more products were paid through barter and through credit trans-actions. However, there is evidence of urban economic activities continuing in the city of Concepción itself, in spite of the failure of the gold and sugar industries.

### 17.3.5 Construction Industry: 1515–1564

During this period many of the buildings constructed out of perishable materials during the first period were reconstructed in masonry. Some were constructed with funds sent from Santo Domingo, as was the case for the public buildings (Marte 1981, p. 68, 86, 90), but some were constructed with private funds (Patronato 1995).

Unlike the first period when most construction workers were Taíno, during this period the construction workforce was probably composed of *Bozal* slaves (African slaves brought directly from Africa), given the changes which occurred in the over-all island workforce, although no historical or archaeological evidence exists at this point to confirm this. Historical documents do show that during the 1520s, Dean de Castro brought some carpenters from Spain to work on his properties (Patronato 1995, p. 238), and they may have used African workers for this task.

### 17.3.6 Government Employment: 1515–1564

During this second period there were fewer government positions due to the con-solidation of religious and political authorities of the colony into single one in Santo Domingo in 1524. Thanks to the records of Alvaro de Castro's trial, however, we know the names of many of the top city officials in the 1520s and 1530s (Table 17.4).

### 17.3.7 Clothing Production: 1515–1564

Four tailors and one shoemaker lived onsite during the second period (Table 17.4). It is interesting to note that the shoemaker, Pedro Pineda, was there during the later period, rather than during the more prosperous earlier period (Table 17.3 and 17.4). This is probably due to the fact that hides, and leather, would have been more plenti-ful and available.

Historical records show that native cotton was also used for clothing manufacture during this period (Sáez 1994). This cloth was produced by Taíno women (Deagan 2004, p. 609) as part of the Taíno tribute (Charlevoix 1730), and used to make the garments worn by the Taíno under the *Repartimiento* and African and Native American slaves (Sáez 1994). It appears Spaniards wore clothing manufactured in Spain. The wealthy wore new clothes, and the nonelites wore used clothing, mended onsite (Patronato 1995; Suarez-Marill 1998, p. 15).

## 17.3.8 Commerce: 1515–1564

By this second period (1515–1564), with the development of mainland settlements, Hispaniola was no longer a priority, and by the end of the first half of the sixteenth century, major shipping did not arrive on the island (Deagan 1983, p. 19). This was due to how shipping was organized through the *Casa de Contratación* (House of Trade) in Seville (Deagan 1983, p. 20). Goods were shipped twice a year to the colonies, and products were sent to Spain just as often, both times in large shipping convoys only stopping at Havana in the Caribbean (Deagan 1983, p. 20). Hispaniolan colonists had to ask for *sueltos*, or non-convoy ships, to receive goods from Seville (Deagan 1983, p. 19). Since sueltos were not profitable for the Sevillian merchants, few were sent (Deagan 1983, p. 19). The situation deteriorated further due to irregular scheduling of the convoys, hurricanes, shipwrecks, as well as the taxes added to already high prices (Deagan 1983, p. 20; Wright 1939, p. 341–43).

These changes, coupled with the workforce problems, caused a change in commercial activities at Concepción during this later period. Few people could afford to buy and maintain a slave (Larrazabal 1975, p. 39; Marte 1981, p. 401), prompting them to turn to other revenue-making activities that did not require slave labor, including the sale of items such as tools for the gold and cattle business (Patronato 1995, p. 212; Rodriguez-Morel 2000, p. 106–107), and clothes (Patronato 1995, p. 212, 213, 221).

In the rest of Hispaniola many colonists turned to contraband trade as a means to sell and buy needed products (Deagan 1983, p. 19). This trade, also known as *rescate* among the Spanish (Deagan 1983, p. 191), mostly involved the exchange of sugar and cattle hides to the French, English, Dutch, or Portuguese traders for European items and/or African slaves (Tavares 1978, p. 29; Guitar 1998, p. 264). Some of the items the Hispaniolans traded for included soap, wine, flour, cloth, perfume, nails, shoes, medicine, paper, dry fruit, iron, steel, and knives (Moya-Pons 1983, p. 44).

It is often assumed that contraband began to have a major influence in Caribbean commerce sometime between 1550 and 1580 (Deagan 1983, p. 21; Haring 1964, p. 122; Moya-Pons 1983, p. 53). If this were true, contraband would have had little influence on commerce in Concepción, since the city disappeared in 1562. However, contraband trade was at the center of the trial against Dean Alvaro de Castro, held in 1532.

Dean de Castro, in charge of the Concepción Cathedral, was accused of selling illegal African slaves, as well as being involved in the commerce trade in spite of being a "man of the Church" (Patronato 1995, p. 136). He evaded the restriction on being a merchant by not selling goods himself, but rather by owning a store run by Morales and a relative called Villandrés (Patronato 1995, p. 150). He sold tools for gold prospectors and for the cattle industry, as well as clothing (Patronato 1995, p. 212). He hired a tailor to sew and sell garments made from cloth which was destined for priests, and also sold a large amount of second-hand, ready-made clothes (Patronato 1995, p. 155). The ready-made clothes included capes, corselets, and pointed hoods (Patronato 1995, p. 213, 221). Castro also sold purple cloth to whoever could afford it, although it was supposed to be reserved for religious functions (Patronato 1995, p. 136). All of this merchandise could be bought on credit and paid in money, unrefined gold, or in clothing (Patronato 1995, p. 212).

Historical records also give the names of other merchants, such as Juan Martin Callejas and Francisco Sanchez (Benzo 2000). Unfortunately, there is no information about their shops or what these merchants sold. There were also non-Spanish merchants at Concepción—Juan Martin de Trebejo, a Portuguese man who sold salt, who drove mules (Benzo 2000), and Pero Diaz de Peravia, an Italian accused of being involved in the illegal slave trade (Benzo 2000; Patronato 1995).

While all of those identified as merchants with shops sold goods imported from outside the island, street vendors, often selling local products, also worked in Concepción's urban environment. Many, if not most, of these vendors were of African origin (Deive 1989, p. 20; Landers 1999, p. 8). These vendors could be free or enslaved, although it appears that, especially after 1544, most were African *Ladino* women, due to the restriction placed on African slave men's movements after the increase in *Cimarrón* activity in the 1530s and 1540s (Larrazabal 1975, p. 110).

In 1528 African *Ladino* women were allowed to sell vegetables on the streets and *plaza*s, but African men could only sell water and charcoal on the street, or sell livestock innards at the slaughterhouse (Larrazabal 1975, p. 110). African slave men were not allowed to sell clothing on the streets (Larrazabal 1975, p. 110).

The *Cimarrón* men often went into the towns to trade and buy goods, often stolen or captured during their roadside attacks (Larrazabal 1975, p. 110). Their clients were often African slaves (Larrazabal 1975, p. 110). Spanish authorities tried, through the Slave Ordenanzas (1528 and 1544) to eliminate this trade by limiting the items a slave could own, and in this way be able to identify escaped slaves, but were unsuccessful (Larrazabal 1975, p. 110).

## 17.3.9  Crafts: 1515–1564

Blacksmiths and locksmiths were present at Concepción during this period as well, and according to historical records, gold, copper, and iron items continued to be processed (Guitar 1998, p. 210). Blacksmiths were critical to all Sixteenth century towns, producing nails and fasteners, building hardware, iron tools, horseshoes and horse equipage, and domestic implements. Examples of all of these have been recovered archaeologically at Concepción, although it is not possible to determine which were produced locally and which were imported. The presence of a farrier is suggested by records of a stable owner, Juan de Villegas (Benzo 2000). Alonzo de Suazo, visiting the city in 1517, describes seeing at least 40 horses (Parry and Keith 1984, p. 274). Horseshoes and nails, bridle and bit pieces, axes and stirrups have been recovered archaeologically from Concepción (Deagan 1998).

No names of smiths are recorded during this period, but there is the name of a sword-maker—Villandro (Benzo 2000). It is possible that much of the smiting may have been undertaken by African *Libertos*, or even African *Ladino* men whose names were not recorded (Guitar 1998, p. 123; Landers 1999, p. 16). The fact that the name for the town's sword-maker is recorded (Villandro) suggest, however, that certain crafts (such as sword-making) were still reserved for Spaniards. There are 7 sword fragments in the archaeological assemblage, as well as 2 sword tips (Deagan 1998).

## 17.3.10   Domestic Labor: 1515–1564

Perhaps no other urban esconomic activity was as greatly affected by the decrease in gold production as domestic labor. Many of the Spanish who had servants before the 1514 *Repartimiento* could no longer afford them, and it appears that some undertook this type of labor to pay outstanding debts. This was the case for Alonso Roman, who became Dean Alvaro de Castro's servant (Benzo 2000). Castro was one of the few Concepción residents wealthy enough to maintain servants after 1514 (Benzo 2000). His servants included persons from several places, including indigenous women from the Lucayas (Bahamas) (Benzo 2000).

The composition of African servants changed drastically after 1526 when the importation of *Ladinos* from Spain was outlawed (Deive 1989, p. 32; Larrazabal 1975, p. 100). This made it difficult to procure African servants who knew Spanish language and customs. The Slave laws enacted in 1522, 1528 and 1544 required all slave servants to live with their owners (Larrazabal 1975, p. 110). These laws did not govern the movements of *Libertos*. It is possible that some of the African servants after this time may have been *Liberto* women who had gained their liberty through the *jornal* system.

## 17.4   Conclusions

Preliminary research into the archaeological assemblage at the Concepción de la Vega site seems to contradict the "official" history's depiction of a site, which went bust after a gold boom period. Research into lesser-known historical sources shows a place struggling to maintain its gold boom status through various means. It is interesting to note that the economic activity reflected in the historical record does not match the wealth in the archaeological record, leading to the possibility of "extra-official" sources of wealth, such as contraband in hides and/or slaves, much earlier than previously considered in the "official" historical record.

Research into these lesser-known sources also shows the existence of a less stratified, more fluid society at Concepción during the beginning of the Sixteenth century than is portrayed in Santo Domingo's sugar-based economic classification. This is particularly true for those of African descent, since most were not obligated to sleep in the same place every night, either due to their work or to their freedom status. This mobility has made it difficult to identify "African" elements in the Concepción archaeological assemblage, but at the same time, be a marker for a different type of interaction amongst the African-Indigenous-European origin groups.

# References

Abreu, H. (1998). Personal communication to Pauline Kulstad. Concepción de la Vega National Park. July 2008.
Arranz-Marquez, L. (1991). *Repartimientos y encomiendas en la isla Española*. Santo Domingo: Ediciones Fundación García Arévalo.
Benzo, V. (2000). *Pasajeros a la Española*. Santo Domingo: Amigo del Hogar.
Cassa, R. (1978). *Historia social y económica de la República Dominicana: introducción a su estudio: manual para estudiantes de educación secundaria y universitaria preliminar* (pp. 33, 39, 41, 44, 53, 58, 66, 67, 63). Santo Domingo: Editora Alfa y Omega.
Charlevoix, P. F. (1730). *Historia de la isla Española o de Santo Domingo* (Vol. 1, pp. 110, 221). Santo Domingo: Sociedad Dominicana de Bibliófilos.
Cohen, J. (1997). *Preliminary Report on the 1996 field season at Concepción de la Vega*. Project report submitted to the Dirección Nacional de Parques. Gainesville: Museum of Natural History.
Concepcion, M. (1981). *La Concepción de la Vega*. Santo Domingo: Editora Taller.
Concepcion, M. (1982). *La Concepción de la Vega: relación histórica*. Santo Domingo: Editora Taller.
Anghiera, P. M. d' (1998). In L. Guitar. Cultural genesis: relationships among Indians, Africans and Spaniards in rural Hispaniola, first half of the sixteenth century. Ph.D. dissertation, Vanderbilt University.
Casas, B. de Las (1998). In M. Rueda (Ed.), *Oviedo-Las Casas: Crónicas Escogidas* (p. 98). Santo Domingo: Ediciones Corripio.
Fernández de Oviedo, G. F. (1998). In M. Rueda (Ed.), *Oviedo-Las Casas: Crónicas Escogidas* (pp. 150, 208–217). Santo Domingo: Ediciones Corripio.
Deagan, K. (1983). *Spanish St. Augustine: The archaeology of a colonial Creole community* (pp. 19–21, 191). New York: Academic.
Deagan, K. (1998). *Reporte preliminar del análisis del laboratorio del Parque Nacional Concepción de la Vega, 1996–1997* (trans. from English by P. Kulstad). Gainesville: Museum of Natural History, University of Florida.
Deagan, K. (1999). *Cultural and historical resources at the Parques Nacionales Concepción de la Vega and La Isabela*. Final project report submitted to the Dirección Nacional de Parques. Gainesville: Museum of Natural History, University of Florida.
Deagan, K. (2002). *Artifacts of the Spanish colonies of Florida and the Caribbean, 1500–1800, vol. 2: Portable personal possessions*. Washington, D.C.: Smithsonian Press.
Deagan, K. (2004). Reconsidering Taino social dynamics after Spanish conquest: Gender and class in culture contact studies. *American Antiquity, 69*(4), 597–626.

Deagan, K., & Cruxent, J. M. (2002). *Columbus's outpost among the Taínos: Spain and America at La Isabela* (pp. 1493–1498). New Haven: Yale University Press.

Deagan, K., & Reitz, E. (1995). Merchants and cattlemen: Archaeology of a commercial structure at Puerto Real. In K. Deagan (Ed.), *Puerto Real: The archaeology of a sixteenth-century Spanish town in Hispaniola* (pp. 231–284). Gainesville: University Press of Florida.

Deive, C. E. (1980). *La esclavitud del negro en Santo Domingo* (pp. 1492–1844). Santo Domingo: Museo del Hombre Dominicano.

Deive, C. E. (1989). *Los guerrilleros negros: esclavos fugitivos y cimarrones en Santo Domingo.* Santo Domingo: Fundación Cultural Dominicana.

Fernandez-Alvarez, M. (1975) *Charles V: Elected emperor and hereditary ruler* (trans. from Spanish by J. A. Lalaguna). London: Thames and Hudson.

Floyd, T. (1973). *The Columbus Dynasty in the Caribbean.* 1492–1526 (pp. 68–69). Albuquerque: University of New Mexico Press.

García, J. G. (1906). *Compendio de la Historia de Santo Domingo.* Santo Domingo: Sociedad Dominicana de Bibliófilos.

Guitar, L. (1998). *Cultural genesis: relationships among Indians, Africans and Spaniards in rural Hispaniola, first half of the sixteenth century.* Ph.D. dissertation, Vanderbilt University.

Guitar, L. (2001). No more negotiation: Slavery and the destabilization of colonial Hispaniola's encomienda system. *Revista Interamericana, 29* (special issue).

Haring, C. (1964). *Trade and navigation between Spain and the Indies in the time of the Hapsburgs.* Gloucester: Peter Smith.

Inchaustegui, J. M. (1955). *Historia Dominicana. Tomo I.* Ciudad Trujillo: Impresora Dominicana.

Landers, J. (1999). *Black society in Spanish Florida.* Chicago: University of Illinois Press.

Larrazabal, C. (1975). *Los negros y la esclavitud en Santo Domingo.* Santo Domingo: J. D. Postigo.

Marte, R. (1981). *Santo Domingo en los manuscritos de Juan Bautista Muñoz.* Madrid: Fundación García Arévalo.

Mira-Caballos, E. (1997). *El indio antillano: repartimiento, encomienda y esclavitud (1492–1542).* Seville: Muñoz Moya.

Moya-Pons, F. (1974). *Historia colonial de Santo Domingo.* Santiago: UCMM.

Moya-Pons, F. (1978). *La Española en el Siglo XVI.* Santiago: UCMM.

Moya-Pons, F. (1983). *Manual de historia dominicana.* Santiago: Universidad Católica Madre y Maestra.

Moya-Pons, F. (1987). *Después de Colón: trabajo, sociedad, y política en la economía del oro.* Madrid: Alianza Editorial.

Olsen, H. (2013). Conference: Investigaciones arqueologicas en el primer campamento minero colonial de America, Pueblo Viejo, Cotui. Santo Domingo: Museo del Hombre Dominicano. 16 May 2013.

Ortiz, F. (1947). *Cuban counterpoint: Tobacco and sugar* (trans. from Spanish by H. de Oniìs). New York: A. A. Knopf.

Palm, E. W. (1952). La Fortaleza de la Concepción de la Vega. *Memoria del V Congreso Histórico Municipal Interamericano, 2,* 115–118 (Ciudad Trujillo: UASD).

Parry, J., & Keith, R. (Eds.). (1984). *The Caribbean. Volume II of the New Iberian World* (5 Vols). New York: Times Books.

Patronato De La Ciudad Colonial De Santo Domingo. (1995). *Proceso contra Alvaro de Castro 1532.* Santo Domingo: Patronato de la Ciudad Colonial de Santo Domingo.

Perez-Collados, J. M. (1992). *Las Indias en el pensamiento político de Fernando el Católico.* Borja: Centro de Estudios Borjanos.

Perez de Tudela. (1954). La negociación colombiana de las Indias. Revista de Indias, No. 55–56. Sevilla.

Pimentel, F. (1998). Personal communication to Pauline Kulstad. Concepcion de la Vega National Park. Oct. 1998.

Rodriguez-Demorizi, E. (1971). *Los domínicos y las encomiendas de indios de la Isla Española.* Santo Domingo: Editora del Caribe.

Rodriguez-Morel, G. (2000). *Cartas de los cabildos eclesiásticos de Santo Domingo y Concepción de La Vega en el siglo XVI*. Santo Domingo: Centro de Altos Estudios Humanísticos y del Idioma Español.

Rogozinski, J. (2000). *A brief history of the Caribbean: From the Arawak and the Carib to the present*. New York: Plume.

Rueda, M. (Ed.). (1988). *Oviedo-Las Casas: Crónicas Escogidas*. Santo Domingo: Ediciones Corripio.

Saez, J. L. (1994). *La iglesia y el negro esclavo en Santo Domingo: una historia de tres siglos*. Santo Domingo: Patronato de la Ciudad Colonial de Santo Domingo.

Sauer, C. O. (1966). *The early Spanish Main*. Berkeley: University of California Press.

Stahl, A. (1999). In K. Deagan. Cultural and Historical Resources at the Parques Nacionales Concepción de la Vega and La Isabela. Final project report submitted to the Dirección Nacional de Parques. Gainesville: Museum of Natural History, University of Florida.

Suarez-Marill, M. (1998). *Santo Domingo Colonial: sus principales monumentos*. (p. 15) Santo Domingo: Acción para la Educación Básica.

Tavares, J. T. (1978). *Piratas de America*. Santo Domingo: Editora de Santo Domingo SA.

Ugarte, M. (1981). Aparece en sitio de La Vega valiosa cerámica del siglo XVI. (p. 24) El Caribe, 5 Dic.

Vega, B. (1979). *Los metales y los aborígenes de La Hispaniola*. Santo Domingo: Ediciones Museo del Hombre Dominicano.

Wilson, S. (1990). Columbus, my enemy. *Natural History*, 44–49.

Wright, I. (1916). The commencement of the cane sugar industry in America, 1519–1538. *The American Historical Review, 21*, 755–780.

Wright, I. (1939). Rescates: With special reference to Cuba, 1599–1610. *Hispanic American Historical Review, 5*(3), 333–361.

# Chapter 18
# Brazil Baroque, Baroque Mestizo: Heritage, Archeology, Modernism and the Estado Novo in the Brazilian Context

Rita Juliana Soares Poloni

## 18.1 Introduction

The aim of this chapter is to discuss the question of mestiçagem—the Portuguese term for racial and cultural miscegenation—and its importance to the earliest ideas about Brazilian heritage. Two actors, the Brazilian modernist movement and the Estado Novo, will be highlighted as fundamental in shaping Brazilian concepts of national culture and heritage. Particular attention will be paid to the connections between the development of these concepts and archeology.

First, the appearance of discussions around mestiçagem will be traced in the context of the Brazilian modernist movement, particularly in the discourse that the influential figure Mário de Andrade constructed around the artist Aleijadinho as the main sculptor and emblem of Baroque Art from the state of Minas Gerais (Mineiro Baroque).

Second, the connections between archeology, modernism, and the development of the concept of heritage will be explored within the cultural milieu of the Brazilian Estado Novo. Particular attention will be paid to such concepts as culture and national heritage as well as to Baroque Art throughout the development of these ideas.

Finally, the importance of miscegenation or mestiçagem—both artistic and racial—will be underlined in the construction of a discourse about culture and national heritage. The reconstruction and images of the past during the Estado Novo period as well as the importance of heritage issues for archeology will be studied in connection with the State's demands.

R. J. S. Poloni (✉)
Pós-doc LAP/NEPAM—Unicamp, Rua Waldemar Santos Marques, 162, Jardim Santa Genebra, Campinas, São Paulo, 13080-310, Brazil
e-mail: julianapoloni@hotmail.com

© Springer International Publishing Switzerland 2015
P. P. A. Funari, M. X. Senatore (eds.), *Archaeology of Culture Contact and Colonialism in Spanish and Portuguese America*, DOI 10.1007/978-3-319-08069-7_18

## 18.2   Modernism, Culture, and Heritage in Brazilian Context

In Brazil, the first two decades of the twentieth century saw the first discussions about Modernism. Culminating at the Modern Art Week of 1922, the movement was to continue in the following decades, with one of its major concerns being the search of a Brazilian identity. Defenders of the idea of "Brazilianness" found two supporting pillars in the intellectual standing of Mário de Andrade and the defense of Baroque Art.

Before then, in the nineteenth century, Baroque Art had acquired rather negative connotations, its manner seen as excessively affected in comparison to the more splendid classical forms (Gomes Junior 1998, pp. 38–50). It was through Modernism that Baroque Art came to acquire new meanings in the early twentieth century. Disbelief in Europe and the Old Republic[1] in the aftermath of World War I as well as reflections on the need to build a future for the nation formed the basis for a new set of ideas in relation to Baroque Art. The Baroque artistic school was reinstated and connected to the ideas of "the popular" and the traditional, which were deliberately reinterpreted to create a sense of historical continuity for the nation and to signal the birth of "Brazilianness." Allegedly rooted in popular forms of aesthetic reinterpretation, "Brazilianness" constituted the country's connecting link to the universal and the modern (Nogueira 2005, pp. 181–195). Modernity being humanity's horizon, Mário de Andrade argued for Brazil's role in this common march as follows:

> …How may we concur to Humanity? Is it by being French or German? No, for that already exists in Civilization. Our stock must be Brazilian. The day we become completely Brazilian and Brazilian alone, humanity will have gained one more race, one more combination of human qualities. Races are musical chords … when we perform our own chord we shall then take part in the harmony of civilization…. (Andrade 1982; Nogueira 2005, p. 63)

Therefore, in order to become modern, it was necessary to turn to the past and present of the nation, to its popular history and traditions. Only by discovering a nation's history and culture and by trying to understand its peculiar intricacies would the country be able to harmoniously embrace the modern and the new—the future. The country's tradition, its past and history would therefore become its route to modernity and to the "harmony of civilization." At the heart of this notion of civilization was the defense of Baroque Art as a symbol of the birth of the Brazilian nation. This choice was as much a turn towards artistic and national difference as a choice to view the country from a closer perspective with respect to Western ideas of development by focusing on the art and architecture from the colonial period.

Among the modernists who most helped shape discourses about the peculiarity of the Brazilian Baroque, Mário de Andrade was especially renowned. His importance stems both from the texts he produced and the position he came to hold in the culture department in São Paulo. Andrade was an extremely skillful manufacturer

---

[1] The Old Republic *Republica Velha* was a period in Brazilian history between 1889 and 1930. The Old Republic saw the economic interests of elites overrule political questions. Coffee-planting oligarchs from São Paulo and Minas Gerais, alternately occupied the country's presidency.

of new meanings for Brazilian culture. His work on the Baroque Art of Minas Gerais (Barroco Mineiro) is intrinsically connected to the development of a cultural policy which was to have a great impact on national heritage.

Long before reaching this position in São Paulo's cultural establishment, Baroque Art was already of great importance to de Andrade's vision and discourse about Brazilian culture. The development of his thoughts on the subject can be traced to four texts entitled "Religious Art in Brazil," published in 1920 in the *Revista do Brasil*[2]. These thoughts were born of on-site observations of the local cultural heritage during a trip he took around Minas Gerais in 1919. Andrade's discourse on Barroco Mineiro dated the architectural movement's distinct national traits in the Brazilian colonial period (Gomes Junior 1998, pp. 54–55; Avancini 1998, pp. 111–115).

Sculptor Antônio Francisco de Lisboa "o Aleijadinho",[3] was particularly inspiring for Mário, who saw in this historic and artistic figure, the mulato genius of Brazilian architecture and art in general.

> Aleijadinho was thus, ultimately, also like this: only his creative strength, if often producing works of an incorrect realism, put a soul into each stone that he cut … All the religious art of Minas Gerais is in such a way imbued of his genius that one is under the impression that everything in it was created by him alone. That horrendous, miserable, short armless hunchback, who with his elbows clasped the tools which made stone explode. In talc stone he impressed the faces of his romans and made the flying smile of his archangels fly like butterflies until he turned the entire Minas into a single artist: himself! Had the sculptor of the prophets lived in another, more cultivated city and had he been instructed by the contemplation of ancient works he would no doubt have become one of the greatest. He'd have trained disciples, a school so magnificent as the genius his work gives away if observed attentively. But, barely a humble believer, having bought his own freedom with the few golden coins that the church paid, he lived chiseling his own dream of faith-the devotees and the infidel-giving the former all the love of his pity, stealing from the latter the beauty he could give them. (Andrade 1920, p. 106)

Identified alternately as a deformed artist who created in spite of his physical deficiencies and as a mulato who transcended his station by a cunning use of art, Aleijadinho became, in Andrade's interpretation of Baroque Art, a symbol of the defining traits of a quintessential Brazilian culture. In Aleijadinho's primitivism, Andrade saw the work of an undereducated artist who impressed upon an "expressionist", stylized, and imperfect interpretation of human forms. His art transformed an architectural movement, which had been European in origin, into a truly national style. The alleged "ugliness" of the artist's form was a new framework for

---

[2] Supplement of the newspaper *O Estado de São Paulo*.

[3] Antônio Francisco de Lisboa, "o Aleijadinho" (1738–1814) is the author of many baroque architectural, woodcarving, and sculpture pieces produced during the Brazilian colonial period in the present day's state of Minas Gerais. Little is known about his life or the exact number of his works, but he is reported have been the son of a Portuguese artisan, who would have taught him the first and most basic notions of design, architecture, and sculpture and an enslaved woman. The artist was nicknamed "o. Aleijadinho," a familiar term for a cripple, as he was struck by a mysterious illness at the age of 40, which left his arms and legs deformed. Still, he continued to work until the day he died, leaving a seemingly vast production (Martins 1939; Renault 1973; Vasconcelos 1979; Gomes Junior 1998).

his genius, which proposed an interaction between the popular and the erudite, thus founding a typically Brazilian work of art (Gomes Junior 1998, pp. 55–57; Avancini 1998, pp. 124–129).

During the following years, Andrade undertook several other trips around Brazil in a formative process that shaped his ideas about national culture. On these new trips, he had the chance to deepen and broaden his ideas about popular culture and folklore, which eventually encompassed "intangible" elements such as popular music. He would later have the chance to impress and materialize his ideas in the form of cultural policies implemented by the culture department of São Paulo (Nogueira 2005, pp. 99–175.)

### 18.2.1   The Department of Culture, the Historic, and Architectural National Heritage Service (SPHAN), and the Idea of National Heritage

The cultural policies implemented by Mário de Andrade at the culture department from the early 1930s included the defense of São Paulo's artistic and cultural heritage. This work eventually laid the basis for the most important heritage institution of the time: the Historic and Architectural National Heritage Service (SPHAN). The SPHAN was created in 1937 and was the predecessor of the present-day Institute for Historical and Archaeological Heritage (IPHAN)—Brazil's most important cultural agency. The Law 378 of January 1937 inaugurated the service and was a recognizable product of Andrade's philosophy. It defines heritage as follows:

**Article 1** National historic and artistic heritage consists of a set of movable and immovable items, extant in the country and whose observation is of public interest, whether through its links to memorable facts in the history of Brazil or for their exceptional archaeological, ethnographic, bibliographic or artistic (Nogueira 2005, pp. 239–240).

The difference between Mário de Andrade's idea of heritage and the one finally put in place by the legislation was that Andrade's concept was wide enough to include intangible heritage. However, during the time that Andrade worked for the institution until his death in 1945, the idea was never translated into specific policies.

When the SPHAN came into existence in 1937, it undertook heritage policies largely under the influence of Lúcio Costa, an important architect and a modernist who would later become involved in the construction of Brasilia. Costa was the director of SPHAN's Division of Studies and Recording from 1937 onwards. He was ultimately responsible for setting up the service's classifying criteria of Brazilian archeological heritage (Costa 1995; Londres 2001, pp. 87–101).

It is at this point that the overlapping of the concepts of archeology and heritage becomes particularly interesting. Despite fitting the very definition of national heritage word by word, SPHAN consistently left archeological heritage out of its focus, this point onwards. At this moment, it was the Baroque sets that attracted the discourses that were shaping around the ideas of identity and heritage.

On the other hand, the SPHAN began to record heritage in four inventory books, the compilation of which became a stimulus for the elaboration of a theoretical and methodological assemblage that defined an important part of the nation's past and identity. Despite a certain bureaucratization of the idea of heritage, the process allows us to track down the development of a certain discourse about the past through the choices it made about certain historical periods and the specific elements of material culture, which were considered noble and worthy of becoming symbols of the nation's history.

In this context, Baroque Art became a powerful symbol of the birth of the Brazilian nation, of its particularity and differentiation in relation to the metropolis. As shown below, the richness of the Brazilian nation was represented by its miscegenated, or mestiço, character in cultural and biological terms. Its values lay precisely in its poverty and its opaque meaning in relation to the original Baroque language and project. As we shall see, this reevaluation operated within the framework of the constituted power, the civilizing project that connected the young nation to Europe (Nogueira 2005, pp. 198–234).

## 18.3  The Magazine of National Historic and Artistic Heritage and Archeology

The fact that archeology was not the main focus of IPHAN's interests does not mean that the discipline was unaffected by the period's discussions or that it didn't have an impact on the archeological field. On the contrary, by understanding the several meanings that national heritage acquired at this point, we can reflect on the ideas of material culture that began to develop within the field of national archeology.

An analysis of materials published by the *Magazine of National Historic and Artistic Heritage and Archaeology* during the Estado Novo period can provide an overview of the discourses surrounding architectural and artistic national heritage in connection with Baroque Art. Also, comparisons can be made with other archeological publications of the same period. Although there is no exact correspondence between the year printed on the magazine cover and the time of the actual publication, the period between 1937 and 1946 represents a significant moment in the process of discourse formation around heritage. This period will be analyzed here as corresponding to the institutionalization of SPHAN, a bureaucratic phase that saw modernists concentrate on building discourses around cultural and national heritage.

In 1937, at the exact time of the magazine's first annual issue, an article entitled "A Contribution to the Study of the Protection of Archaeological and Ethnographic Materials in Brazil." In the article, author Heloisa Alberto Torres (1895–1977) discusses the protection of archaeological sites, museum collections, and the heritage of indigenous and "neo-Brazilian" communities in danger of extinction. This suggests the importance of archeological issues at that moment and their relevance to the construction of an official idea of national heritage and the institutionalization of the SPHAN (Torres 1937).

The first part of the article discusses the main problems surrounding the Brazilian archeological sites and some of the preventive methods used at that time. Indigenous issues and the northeast Brazil are the prevailing subjects as is the idea of the state's responsibility in the conservation of these sites. The second part is devoted to denouncing the looting of Brazilian museums, archeological collections, and other ethnographic materials, both indigenous and afro-Brazilian. Finally, the third part of the text, which deals with art and present-day populations, presents indigenous issues again, from the point of view of the need to protect the native.

Although, Heloísa Alberto Torres was a thorough student of marajoara culture among other issues, his work is largely guided by his personal interests with the discourse being indicative of the horizons of Brazilian archeology at the time. Although black and mestizo issues were not altogether lacking, they were not associated with archeological issues directly, but through an interest in museology. Elements such as fortifications, churches, and noble residences were excluded from the scope of heritage protection—the author's main concern in this text. Apart from that, the need to preserve archeological vestiges does not acquire nationalist connotations and neither does the search for symbols of "Brazilianness" present in the text's analysis of material heritage.

Other archeological texts in the magazine seem to follow the same trend. Of a considerably shorter length, the texts "Santarem Ceramics" published in 1939 (Estevão 1939) and "Amazonian Archaeology" from 1942 (Cruls 1942) were devoted to the subject of indigenous culture. While these texts recognize the importance of the material culture of the peoples being discussed, they do not approach the issues from a nationalist perspective. The preservation of national vestiges, sites, and indigenous populations is also a major concern, with concerns being expressed that SPHAN itself became more involved in these questions. Ceramic analysis is the main focus of these publications and authors do not have direct professional links with the service. All the researchers published here already enjoyed professional recognition and were well established before the foundation of SPHAN. They did not follow the modernist path of constructing a nationalist discourse around heritage.

By 1937, Heloísa Torres was already the director of the National Museum, while Carlos Estevão, author of the 1939 text, held the same position at the Emílio Goeldi Museum. Gastão Cruls, who wrote the 1942 text, was a well-known writer, who had participated in the Rondon Comission. His text "Amazonian Archaeology," the reader learns, was to be a part of the upcoming book *Hiléia Amazónica*—one of his great works. Their specific positions might explain why these authors withdrew from the discourses proclaiming the birth of national culture and heritage, espoused by modernists from the states of São Paulo and Minas Gerais.

## 18.4   Baroque Art in the Magazine of National Historic and Artistic Heritage and Archaeology

The *Magazine of National Historic and Artistic Heritage and Archaeology* presents other texts such as "Short Notes on Religious Art in Brazil" published in the 1938 magazine, "Decorative Painting in some of Minas' Ancient Churches," from 1939

(Jardim 1939), "The Architecture of the Jesuits in Brazil, from 1941" (Levy 1941) from the same year, which help us form a panoramic view of the discourse developed about the Brazilian Baroque of the period.

In the first text published in 1938, the peculiarities mentioned about Baroque Art as a specifically national artistic and architectural movement are still few. The birth of the so-called "Brazilian Baroque" is established in eighteenth century in Ouro Preto, São João d'ElRei, and Sabará areas. Among the specific traits the author mentions is the fact that an imbalance exists between the buildings' exteriors and their interiors, with the most splendorous phases for altars corresponding to simpler façades and vice versa.

The 1939 text is, on the other hand, more emphatic about the movement's specifically Brazilian characteristics. As a result of the work which the SPHAN had been doing to record this heritage, the author's preliminary results state a confirmation that "the underlying motivations that gave sense to that phenomenon are different from those present in Europe."

As the first different aspect, the author reminds us that when the movement started in the sixteenth century, Brazil was just a group of hereditary captainships with several extensions. Second, the eighteenth-century decadence of Baroque in Europe would have coincided with this school's heyday in Brazil. Also, the grandiose ornamentations of Brazilian Baroque would have lacked the counter-reformist purpose that characterized the movement in Europe. These would have been transplanted as a purely artistic tradition. Finally, the country's sheer architectonic poverty would have limited the creative horizons of Baroque artists, who, in most cases, limited themselves to seeking inspiration in extant churches and the available prints and old missal books.

Apart from this, the author highlights the power of fraternities and sodalities as well as their racial differentiation. White, black, and mulato fraternities, transformed into class institutions, limited the power of local parish priests and built their own private churches. This was encouraged by the absence of convents in the gold-mining area of Minas, a consequence of a metropolitan ban.

In this context, churches from Minas Gerais would have exhibited distinctive artistic riches that were closely linked to a strong racial difference. The richest churches were built by white fraternities and sodalities, while economic hardship would have caused lack of decorative splendor in other poorer churches.

The works of Aleijadinho feature prominently in this text too. The author's last few words are about the SPHAN's research on the Sabará church, whose pulpits are attributed to this sculptor. In his view, the fact that Aleijadinho uses different solutions to those canonized at his time cannot be attributed to artistic incapacity. This option could actually reflect the author's creativity and be a function of his artistic freedom.

What becomes clear from the analysis of this text is that the modernist and Estado Novista generation's reading of the Baroque period was permeated by the same intrinsic duality that has been highlighted in Mario de Andrade's discourse in the 1920s. Baroque Art's defects and insufficiencies seem to be at the very roots of its creative qualities. The Brazilian Baroque could have sprung up in a space kthat was poor, deprived of the strength of the state, and lacking its main ideological foundations and the great architectural and artistic works which could have inspired its artists.

It could have developed its strength only at a time when the worldwide Baroque school was already in decadence. Despite its apparent shortcomings, it would have been distant from the main centers of power, allowing it enough creative freedom to make it the landmark of national character.

Besides, the distinctive fact of miscegenation, whether in the form of a differential racial element or as a cultural byproduct of the colony, is emphasized as an important part of the idea of national culture.

The very same argument can be found in two texts from 1941, although in a more profound form. The first one "The Architecture of the Jesuits in Brazil" was written by the renowned architect Lúcio Costa. Costa begins by demystifying the idea of Baroque Art as decadent; something which could only be admired out of compassion. The style would have produced true works of fine art, the strangeness of which was the symbol of artistic renovation. First, the school should be considered, in the author's own words, a true artistic "Commonwealth," because of its duration. The Baroque movement spanned from the last phase of the Renaissance until the beginning of the nineteenth century, including Brazil. But it should also be considered a polyphonic movement in the light of the different tones it acquired wherever adopted. Thus, the Hispanic Baroque would be different from its Portuguese counterpart, for example. Even in a Brazilian context, the monuments and shrines from the early stages would have been more elaborate than those of the second period making the first set appear younger than the second, while the second set of Baroque production would appear more "primitivistic."

About the peculiar shrines of the two Jesuit Churches in São Paulo, Lúcio Costa gives the same argument that we had seen used to celebrate the Baroque from Minas: works carried out within Greco-Roman canons are not always the most esthetically valuable. Popular works and their power to disfigure erudite canons create new, spontaneous, and unseen works, and reveal creativity. Also, the work is quite detailed in its descriptions of all the different periods and components of Brazilian Baroque constructions.

Hannah Levy's text, entitled "On Three Theories of Baroque," is quite shorter, although considerably denser. The author discusses the work of Henrique Woelfflin, Max Dvorak, and Leo Balet, three main references in the theory of Baroque Art, which, in her view, would represent three different stances on this artistic movement's meaning within a broader context of the artistic field. So, while Henrique Woelfflin espouses the autonomy and independence of artistic transformations from history, Max Dvorak sees artistic innovation as the root of the transformation of ideas, especially philosophy and religion. Finally, Leo Balet sees transformations in the artistic domain as a consequence of all the other spheres of history.

According to Levy, only Leo Balet would have achieved full understanding of the Baroque. His explanation would be based on the effects of Baroque Art on social life and its need to exhibit itself and to advocate the endlessness of its own power. This would explain the impetuous movement that characterizes Baroque forms. Also, the deformation of natural forms would have been a way of showing excess power, the violation of nature being the ultimate expression of its dominion over reality.

If at first glance this way of explaining Baroque Art did not seem to support the previous discourse on the matter, the author solves the question by returning to Balet's historical argument. For her, the peculiarities of this school in Brazil would stem from the country's specificities and their impact on its cultural and artistic manifestations. These peculiarities would have adapted to reflect the reality of the country.

Both texts reveal a maturity and a deepening of discourses around the Brazilian Baroque (Gomes Junior 1998, pp. 64–76.) The first text's relevance lies in its authorship. However, Lúcio Costa's focus is on the first phase of the artistic school, which would disappear in 1759, when the Marquis of Pombal expelled the Jesuits from Brazil. Aleijadinho's work, made the birthmark of Brazilian culture by Mario de Andrade, corresponded to a later phase in the movement's history. Even then, some of the main arguments around Baroque Art are still present in the text. Both the celebration of the artistic school and that of works which escape the period's canons are present in the text. Therefore, Levy's text justifies the peculiarity of Brazilian Baroque on the basis of its historical specificity. This text, considered the first theoretical discussion of the Brazilian Baroque (Gomes Junior 1998, p. 69.) shows how the term began to acquire depth and richness in this period.

In the articles analyzed here, mestiçagem appears as an adaptation of artistic style to the country's situation, to its peculiar aspects. On the other hand, the idea of racial miscegenation or mestiçagem, which the figure of Aleijadinho comes to epitomize especially for Mario de Andrade, also appears in the magazine, in a perhaps more contained and reflexive form. In this respect, it follows the ideas set forth by the previous texts.

The texts "Contribution to the Study of Aleijadinho" (Andrade 1938), "The First Foreign Testimonies about Aleijadinho" (Franco 1939), and "Notes for the Recent Bibliography on Antonio Francisco Lisboa" (Martins 1939) look at the number of works attributed to the author, the first foreign descriptions of him and his physical deformation and the exact number of works that deal with him as a historical figure. They all set out to elucidate a number of myths about the author and to study him from a historical perspective. Even so, the peculiarity of Aleijadinho's work becomes significant in Alfonso Franco's reading of Eschwege and Saint Hilaire's account of them. For these authors, Aleijadinho's work would be disproportionate, lacking in taste, and poor. But these deficiencies should be forgiven in the face of the artist's very limited knowledge of the "civilized" world.

Therefore, the meaning of miscegenation or mestiçagem is stretched beyond the racial to incorporate cultural elements, and the sculptor would have been responsible for a specific reading of Baroque Art in the cultural atmosphere of the eighteenth-century Minas Gerais. "Brazilianness" is attributed to the whole school's cultural production in Brazil, and characterizes the form in which this historical period was envisaged by the modernist generation. They were responsible for instituting the standards which ruled over the choices and conservation criteria for national heritage. These parameters were subsequently adopted by the SPHAN and came to shape a range of discourses that became fundamental to several scientific areas and their readings of the Brazilian past.

Therefore, it is important to perceive the discourses about Baroque Art, not so much as accurate descriptions of a certain historical period but as a deliberate and successful attempt to create a typically national idea of art, architecture, and culture. These characteristics, which characterize the country's specificity, would stem directly from the power of the miscegenation of ideas and men.

## 18.5   Conclusions: Thinking the Discourse Around Miscegenation Within the Landscape of Mineiro Baroque

Homi Bhabha's book *The Location of Culture* (2007) tells us that in the colonial context, mimesis emerges as both the representation of difference and its refusal, and as a threat to normalized knowledge and disciplinary power. Such an imitation, "almost the same, but not exactly" breaks off from the dominant discourse and transforms colonial power into a partial and virtual presence (Bhabha 2007, pp. 130–131).

In this context, mimesis problematizes concepts such as race and culture which are at the very roots of the naturalization of the nation and thus marginalizes their monumentalization of history and power to become models. They therefore destabilize colonial power (Bhabha 2007, p. 132).

These questions reassert the fear that the mimesis demanded by the "Other" creates in the colonizer. The fear that it might become same, or that it may overcome the limits imposed on it by the colonial system.

In this sense, the role of miscegenation in the construction of an idea of national culture becomes particularly provocative. It would be precisely in its mimetic relation to the colonizer's culture, which is "almost the same, but not exactly" that Mineiro Baroque emerges as a symbol of "Brazilianness." Its withdrawal from the metropolis in both geographical and cultural terms transforms the Brazilian Baroque project into a masterpiece incarnated by the very figure of the mulato Aleijadinho—distorted, imperfect, ugly, and ignoble. But also, and for the very same reasons, these features make Aleijadinho's Baroque the work of a genius. It would precisely be the author's limited access to the cultivated artistic canons of the metropolis that would allow the author to develop a national version of the Baroque.

The choice of this approach transforms the colonizer's action into the very reason for the loss of his grasp over the colony. It is in the midst of prohibitions, of limitations, of the economic and cultural hardship that the colony is subjected to that national culture finds its birthplace. On the other hand, if the modernist discourse about the birth of art places the country in a challenging position in relation to the old metropolitan power, it does not move too far away from it, as it transforms a cultural expression, which was born in the context of colonial domination, into an exponent of Brazilian culture. Therefore, the type of mimesis proposed by Mineiro Baroque allows for the birth of "Brazilianness" without moving too far away from the artistic and architectural patterns promoted by the agents of "civilization."

Within this cultural milieu that brought about discourses of "Brazilianness," archeology was allocated quite a secondary role. Not only did the modernists, and later on the Estado Novo seem to keep away from archeology as a tool in the construction of the nation's history, but the scientific literature of the time also came to abandon such a project of nation-building. Not even the texts produced by the Magazine of the SPHAN vindicated archeological research in their rescue of the cultural history of "Brazilianness".

However, the fact that archeology kept far from the development of the idea of national culture does not make an analysis of these discourses irrelevant to archeology as a scientific field. On the contrary, the development of this discourse must be perceived as a historical and discursive construction, which influenced the images of the past and the material culture around the space and time framework of the Brazilian nation.

Therefore, rather than a description of the colonial world or of Baroque Art and Architecture, what the analyzed interpretations provide is the perception of how a certain discourse about the past was being constructed and the ensuing limitation of characters and elements of material culture that should be privileged, exalted, and preserved as part of the nation's history.

It is in this sense that an analysis of the colonial Baroque period in the discourses promoted during the first decades of the twentieth century becomes relevant. Science being a product of the present day's needs and questions (Kohl and Fawcett 1995; Díaz-Andreu and Champion 1996; Murray and Evans  2008; Voss and Casella 2012), the interests involved in the development of the idea of national culture shaped the vision of that historical moment. The construction of a discourse about the past acquires a political dimension and makes it possible to rethink the interpretation of material culture in other contexts. It also allows us to understand the development of a national discourse around the idea of mestiçagem or miscegenation in both its racial and cultural aspects and in direct connection with national identity. This allows an understanding of the discourse's political dimension and its importance as an element in the nation's identity.

# References

Andrade, R. M. F. (1938). Contribuição para o estudo da obra de Aleijadinho. *Revista do Serviço do Patrimônio Histórico e Artístico Nacional*.

Andrade, M. M. (1920). Arte Religiosa no Brasil. *Revista do Brasil*, *14*(54).

Avancini, J. A. (1998). *Expressão Plástica e Consciência Nacional na Crítica de Mário de Andrade*. Porto Alegre: Editora da Universidade/UFRGS.

Bhabha, H. K. (2007). *Da mímica e do homem: a ambivalência do discurso colonial* (In O Local da Cultura). Belo Horizonte: Editora UFMG.

Costa, L. (1941). Arquitetura dos Jesuítas no Brasil. *Revista do Serviço do Patrimônio Histórico e Artístico Nacional*.

Costa, L. (1995). *Lucio Costa: registro de umavivência*. São Paulo: Empresa da Artes.

Cruls, G. (1942). Arqueologia amazônica. *Revista do Serviço do Patrimônio Histórico e Artístico Nacional*.

Díaz-Andreu, M., & Champion, T. (Eds.). (1996). *Nationalismo and Archaeology in Europe*. London: UCL Press.

Estevão, C. (1939). A cerâmica Santarem. *Revista do Serviço do Patrimônio Histórico e Artístico Nacional*.

Franco, A. A. M. (1939). O primeiro depoimento estrangeiro sobre o Aleijadinho. *Revista do Serviço do Patrimônio Histórico e Artístico Nacional*.

Gomes Junior, G. S. (1998). *Palavra Peregrina: O Barroco e o Pensamentosobre Artes e Letras no Brasil*. São Paulo: Editora da Universidade de São Paulo.

Jardim, L. A. (1939). Pintura decorativa em algumas igrejas antigas de Minas. *Revista do Serviço do Patrimônio Histórico e Artístico Nacional*.

Kohl, P. L., & Fawcett, C. (Eds.) (1995). *Nationalism, politics and the practice of archaeology*. Cambridge: Cambridge University Press.

Levy, H. (1941). A propósito de três teorias sobre o Barroco. *Revista do Serviço do Patrimônio Histórico e Artístico Nacional*.

Londres, C. (2001). A invenção do patrimônio e a cultura nacional. In H. Bomeny (Ed.). *Constelação Capanema: intelectuais e políticas. Rio de Janeiro: Editora Fundação Getúlio Vargas; Bragança Paulista* (pp. 87–101). São Paulo: Editora Universidade de São Francisco.

Martins, J. (1939). Apontamentos para a bibliografia referente a Antônio Francisco Lisboa. *Revista do Patrimônio Histórico e Artístico Nacional*. Rio de Janeiro: IPHAN, N.º3.

Murray, T., & Evans, C. (Eds.) (2008). *Histories of archaeology: A reader in the history of archaeology*. Oxford: Oxford University Press.

Nogueira, A. G. R. (2005). *Por um Inventário dos Sentidos: Mário de Andrade e a Concepção de Patrimônio e Inventário*. São Paulo: Editora Hucitec/FAPESP.

Renault, D. (1973). O Retrato Imaginário do Aleijadinho. Revista Brasileira de Cultura. Rio de Janeiro: Conselho Federal de Cultura, Julho/Setembro, N.º17.

Torres, H. A. (1937). *Contribuição para o Estudo da Proteção ao Material Arqueológico e Etnográfico no Brasil*. Rio de Janeiro: Revista do Serviço do Patrimônio Histórico e Artístico Nacional.

Vasconcelos, S. de. (1979). *Vida e Obra de Antônio Francisco Lisboa: o Aleijadinho*. São Paulo: Plamipress.

Voss B. L., & Casella E. C. (Eds.). (2012). The Archaeology of Colonialism: Intimate Encounters and Sexual Effects. Cambridge: Cambridge University Press.

# Part IV
# Final Comments

# Chapter 19
# Narratives of Colonialism, Grand and Not So Grand: A Critical Reflection on the Archaeology of the Spanish and Portuguese Americas

Barbara L. Voss

*Archaeology of Culture Contact and Colonialism in Spanish and Portuguese America* defies summary or generalization. The rich and extensive collection of archaeological case studies in this book successfully disrupts the Grand Narratives of Spanish and Portuguese colonialism. In simple language, "narratives" are stories. They are representations created about real and imagined worlds, in which events are ordered in some way in time and space. Some researchers argue that making narratives is hard-wired into the human brain; in this view, story-telling is central to the evolution of human consciousness (Boyd 2010; Fireman et al. 2003; Gottschall 2012). These theories draw substantively on anthropological sources and archaeological evidence as well as psychological studies and cognitive research. Of course, these theories are also embedded in narrative: today, the tool-making human is increasingly supplanted by the story-telling human.

Critically, the narratives crafted about events and worlds are *not* those events or those worlds. This is not to say that the "real" does not exist—as philosophers of science such as Wylie (1992) have argued, evidence resists interpretation. The narratives that archaeologists craft about the past are meaningfully constrained by the sources we use. Still, it is too easy to misrecognize the narrative itself for the real. It is in fact this slippage between representation and the real that makes narratives so politically powerful, because stories shape perception of the world.

Perhaps the most important aspect of narrative is its social quality. Narratives rely on subject–object relations: I tell a story to you. Yet, even though the narrator holds a subject position of primary agency, the narrator cannot fully control the narrative: the meaning of the narrative is continually created by each reader or listener, in the context of the narrative's reception. So while it matters who tells the tale, it also matters very much who listens, and the circumstances under which the listening occurs (Barthes 1977). We can thus understand narratives as being continually

B. L. Voss (✉)
Department of Anthropology, Stanford University, Main Quad, Building 50, 450 Serra Mall,
Stanford, CA 94305-2034, USA
e-mail: bvoss@stanford.edu

© Springer International Publishing Switzerland 2015
P. P. A. Funari, M. X. Senatore (eds.), *Archaeology of Culture Contact and Colonialism in Spanish and Portuguese America*, DOI 10.1007/978-3-319-08069-7_19

generated through a complex array of conditions: the *positions* of the narrators and audiences; the *relationships* between the narrative and the events and worlds that it represents; and the *contexts* of the narrative's production, dissemination, circulation, performance, and reception.

Grand Narratives—a concept outlined and critiqued most famously by Lyotard (1984)—make special claims on position, relationship, and context in order to explain, rather than simply represent, the world. Grand Narratives establish their authority by positioning the world as knowable, the narrator as all knowing, and the audience as passive. Grand Narratives appeal to a desire for order and logic; they offer rational accounts of experiences and events that defy rationality. In the process, a Grand Narrative closes off alternative narratives or subsumes other narratives under itself. Yet, despite these attempts at closure, multiple Grand Narratives compete for legitimacy, and counter-narratives emerge to challenge them. This continual dispute among Grand Narratives exposes the contingency of their claims.

In the Spanish and Portuguese Americas, Grand Narratives have circulated since the beginning—perhaps even before the beginning—of the colonization of the Americas. Most notable of these is *La Leyenda Negra*, which explains the Iberian colonization of the Americas as the result of a barbaric and violent Iberian culture. Its counter-narrative, *La Leyenda Blanca* or *La Verdád História*, argues in contrast that Iberian colonial policies and practices included greater protections for native peoples than those of most other European nations (Juderías 1917). Since the exchanges between Bartolomé de las Casas and Juan Ginés Sepúlveda in the 1540s, the so-called "debate" about Spanish and Portuguese treatment of Native Americans and Africans has drawn attention away from European culpability for the events and outcomes of colonial projects. It is like asking whether it is better to be imprisoned or beaten by the police, without raising the question of whether the arrest itself is legitimate and warranted. Other closely related Grand Narratives and counter-narratives in the Spanish and Portuguese Americas include conquest, cultural evolution, indigenous complicity, indigenous resistance, and indigenous disappearance. What these Grand Narratives share is the way they close down, rather than open up, meaningful directions for research.

To these, anthropologists and archaeologists have added our own Grand Narratives. In particular, the focus on acculturation by English-speaking scholars during the past 50 years has generated a Grand Narrative that colonization is about cultural change, rather than violence, territorial appropriation, and economic exploitation. In Latin America, researchers have made global contributions to theories of social identity through models of hybridism, transculturation, and *mestizaje* (Funari and Senatore; Domínguez and Funari; Symanski and Gomes; Senatore; Poloni). Initially, both acculturation theory (Foster 1960; Herskovits 1938; Redfield et al. 1936) and transculturation research (Anzaldua 1987; Ortiz 1995) focused on the unequal power relations inherent to colonialism. However, the popularization of these theories often omits discussions of power, creating a new Grand Narrative of benign cultural and genetic mixing.

## 19.1   Crafting the "Not-So-Grand" Narrative: Approaches and Techniques

The editors and contributors to this important book present an array of approaches and techniques that resist the seduction and persistence of Grand Narratives. Diversification of the positions of the narrators—expanding who gets to tell the story—is one of the most common approaches to destabilizing Grand Narratives. This volume is no exception: Funari and Senatore have recruited scholars from former European imperial powers (Spain, Portugal, Netherlands) and from Latin America today (Brazil, Argentina, Cuba, Venezuela), as well as researchers from the United States, a settler nation whose borders encompass the northern reaches of Spain's former empire and which, in the present day, perpetuates neocolonialism in Latin America. Academic, government, NGO, heritage management, and museum perspectives are also presented together. The scholarship emerging from these diverse national and institutional affiliations exposes the positionality of the researcher/narrator and calls attention to the context of archaeological inquiry.

By publishing this volume in English, Funari and Senatore also challenge the positionality of the audience. Typically, "theory" in archaeology has flowed out from English-speaking countries, a trend recognized as intellectual imperialism (Curet et al. 2005; Funari et al. 1999). Latin American archaeologists rightly complain that archaeologists in the United States are largely monolingual and do not read the important scholarship being published in Spanish and Portuguese. This book hails English-reading archaeologists to attend to the important contributions of colleagues in Spanish- and Portuguese-speaking countries, reversing the flow of theory and innovation.

But it is not enough to simply expand the narrator and audience positions. Post-structuralist and post-colonial scholars have demonstrated that to disrupt the logical imperatives of Grand Narratives, we must also partition, fragment, multiply, negate, and refuse to close the narrative field (Aretxaga 2005; Barthes 1977; Bhabha 1984; Derrida 1973; Fanon 1977; Gilroy 2000). The "granular approach" (Senatore and Funari) adopted in this book unravels the Grand Narratives of colonization by drawing attention to the contradictions, particularities, and variety of experiences in the Spanish and Portuguese colonization of the Americas. The contributing authors offer a new suite of "not-so-grand" narratives to disrupt widespread assumptions, carefully exploring the tangles and complexities of specific times and places. These site-specific analyses resist generalization, fracturing colonial logics of universalism and interchangeability.

Thus, in place of the Grand Narrative of conquest, contributions to this volume reveal the use of bureaucratic and economic tactics to bind native communities to colonial projects through taxation and market dependence (e.g., Pezzarossi, Kulstad-González). Challenging the Grand Narrative of European colonial permanence and urbanism, archaeologists document short-term, abandoned, and "travelling" colonial settlements (e.g., Azkarate and Escribano-Ruiz, Senatore, Chiavazza, Saccente and White, Kulstad-González). In the face of the Grand Narrative of religious conversion, case studies show the appropriation and manipulation of Catholic symbolism for other purposes (e.g., Kepecs, Loren, Bava de Camargo) and document religious diversity (e.g., Domínguez and Funari). In place of the Grand Narrative of unidirectional change, nearly all the studies presented here document multidirectional exchange, including the impact of American colonization on Iberian culture (e.g., Teixeira et al., Escribano-Ruiz and Azkarate). Refuting the Grand Narrative of indigenous technological inferiority, several studies trace the continuance of pre-colonial technologies throughout the colonial periods, as well as the highly selective incorporation of introduced technologies into indigenous cosmologies and trade networks (e.g., Rodriguez-Alegría et al., Scaramelli and Scaramelli). Finally, in place of the Grand Narrative of benign culture change, studies presented here expose the exploitative dynamics involved in cultural translation, and the production of material ambiguity in colonial-era communities (Symanski and Gomes, Kulstad-González, Poloni).

Many of the studies in this book call attention to the Grand Narratives embedded in documentary sources, which themselves were produced within social contexts by colonial and indigenous narrators who sought to control perception of the world. Rothschild provides an insightful methodology that repositions documentary sources as only one of many archives, which, following Stoler (2002, p. 96), are then analyzed as experiments in governance. Kulstad-González re-evaluates sixteenth-century life in Concepción de la Vega, Hispaniola, where the presence of luxury goods belies records describing economic decline. Residents of the colonial settlement may have used official narratives of struggle and failure to draw attention away from "extra-official" economies involving contraband and enslavement. Likewise, Azkarate and Escribano Ruiz's investigation of the sixteenth-century *Sancti Spiritus* in Argentina exposes the "self-interested distortions" of colonial documents and instead reveals "*what was done.*" Similarly, Kepecs reanalyzes Mayan murals and codices and sacred Christian art in light of diachronic archaeological evidence; Senatore studies colonial records of the eighteenth-century Floridablanca in Patagonia to expose modernist logics of novelty and utopianism; and Bava de Camargo draws attention to the ideologies embedded in toponyms and place-markers in Brazilian maritime landscapes. These scholars demonstrate that colonial records are evidence more of colonists' self-perceptions and public projections than of factual history.

Additionally, this book challenges the relationship between Grand Narratives of colonialism and time. Narratives are chronological, and the starting and ending points of a narrative powerfully shape the narratives' meanings. Many chapters in this book shift the temporal frame back in time, to decades, centuries, and even millennia before Iberian exploration and colonization (e.g., Azkarate and Escribano Ruiz, Rodríguez-Alegría et al., Pezzarossi, Kepecs, Domínguez and Funari). By the time Europeans and their agents arrive on the scene, the narrative is already well underway. The "colonist" is no longer the main character of the story, and the events that unfold cannot be assumed to be caused by the colonists' actions. Other contributors extend the temporal frame far beyond the purported end of European colonialism in the Americas (Scaramelli and Scaramelli, Poloni), demonstrating the long-reaching effects of colonialism on the Americas, as well as the persistence of indigenous communities beyond colonization.

## 19.2 Power and Fragmentation

Overall, archaeologies of colonialism have tended to describe the colonial project as coordinated, strategic, and unified, while indigenous communities are portrayed as pluralistic, multilingual, and fragmented. As a counter-narrative to the Grand Narratives of indigenous passivity and disappearance, archaeologists have particularly emphasized the diversity of indigenous responses to colonization. The colonists themselves have received less scrutiny from archaeologists. The case studies in this book powerfully challenge this trend by tracing diversity *within* the colonial enterprise (e.g., Senatore, Loren, Rothschild, Kulstad-González).

There are reasons to be apprehensive about the "granular approach" used here. When taken to the extreme, emphasizing diversity and difference risks obscuring power by giving the impression that there was no coordinated or directed action. However, the studies presented in this book reveal, rather than conceal, the workings of power. For example, it is clear that there was no predetermined, unifying colonizing policy within either the Portuguese or Spanish empire. Rather, policy emerged through improvisation, failures, and re-assessment (Azkarate and Escribano-Ruiz, Senatore, Symanski and Gomes, Scaramelli and Scaramelli, Chiavazza, Bava de Camargo, Saccente and White, Kulstad-González)—what Saccente and White have poetically traced as a process in which "intent quickly turned to desperation and then withdrawl." Furthermore, those recruited to implement colonial plans, whether directly from Iberia or from existing settlements in the Americas, were themselves subject to the rule of empire, and lived under geographic, economic, social, and personal constraints (Domínguez and Funari, Rothschild, Senatore, Escribano-Ruiz and Azkarate).

Likewise, the researchers show that some indigenous communities responded forcefully to colonial incursions and demands (Azkarate and Escribano-Ruiz), and even maintained control of raw materials, labor, technologies, trade routes, and other economic assets, forcing colonists to collaborate or compromise in order to gain access (Rodríguez-Alegría et al., Kepecs, Scaramelli and Scaramelli). Others succumbed (Saccente and White), while still others maintained spaces of autonomy and ambiguity within delimited zones (Scaramelli and Scaramelli, Rothschild, Symanski and Gomes). However, even in these spaces of ambiguity, many indigenous communities were dispossessed of land, goods, and labor through exploitative policies, taxation, and direct force (Pezzarossi, Scaramelli and Scaramelli).

Thus, as Domínguez and Funari note, all residents of colonized spaces were subject to powers beyond their control, and experienced degrees of freedom rather than absolute freedom or absolute subjugation. This is shown especially to be the case in gender and sexual relations. Rothschild's study of the complexities of women's roles in New Mexico demonstrates that although women could not always escape male domination, they were nonetheless effective agents, finding their own sources of power. Kulstad-González shows that women in sixteenth-century Hispaniola were critical economic agents even as their labor was appropriated through hierarchies of gender, race, and rank. On the Texas frontier, Loren traces the care of the body to

promote physical and spiritual well-being. Saccente and White hint at the central-
ity of sexual labor to the colonial project, through discussions of female prostitutes
recruited by Church officials to frontier military settlements in La Florida. Finally,
Teixeira et al. return to the seat of colonial power to trace the gendered impact of
American commodities on daily life in Portugal: there, women—perhaps especially
nuns—were central to apothecary and confectionary uses of Brazilian sugar.

The studies in this book reveal practical experiences of domination, subjugation, and making do that challenge conventional theories of power: power cannot
be reduced to hierarchies of race, class, or gender; power does not follow post-
structuralist logics, such as those modeled by Giddens (1979) or Bourdieu (1977,
1980), in which power is enacted across multiple scales from practice to structure
and back again. Nor do the workings of power exposed in these studies resemble
the multidirectional, ever-present "capillary" flows observed by Foucault (1975) as
the hallmark of European modernity. The "unstable colonial world, manipulated by
many parties" (Rothschild) instead is one in which power operates through a broken, fragmented, and haphazard unfolding of events—even "casual… and random"
(Escribano-Ruiz and Azkarate). It is messy and excessive (Chiavazza); the efforts
of historical actors, both indigenous and colonial, to act for themselves and their
communities is continually destabilized by unpredictability.

Colonialism, Loren reminds us, is a "corporeal predicament." In this midst of
such instability, violence and risk thread through the fabric of daily life. The case
studies presented here all testify to the struggles—and failures—of both colonists
and colonized who created and inhabited contested and ambiguous zones. They did
so in ways that simultaneously reproduced and troubled prior systems of power and
inequality.

## 19.3   The Economic Turn

Many contributors to this book turn to economic analysis to trace the workings of
colonial power. As Pezzarossi notes, this is a substantive shift in the study of the
Spanish and Portuguese colonization of the Americas, which has largely been neglected in global studies of capitalism. The case studies presented here demonstrate,
however, that questions of colonial militarism, religious conversion, and cultural
change are all intertwined with economic relations.

The desire for profitable trade goods emerges as a primary motivation for colonial projects in the Americas, such as development of sugar production in
Brazil (Teixeira et al.), fisheries in Newfoundland (Escribano-Ruiz and Azkarate), cacao and sugar in Guatemala (Pezzarossi), gold and silver in Mexico
(Rodriguez-Alergría et al.), and turtle oil and other "uncommon commodities" in
the Middle Orinoco (Scaramelli and Scaramelli). Such colonial trade profoundly
transformed Europe and Africa as well as the Americas, pointing toward the need
for transatlantic analysis of archaeological materials (e.g., Teixeira et al., Escribano-
Ruiz and Azkarate).

There are four core contributions that this focus on economic relations makes toward advancing the archaeology of the Spanish and Portuguese Americas. The first is to highlight the role of individual and small-group merchants and capitalists as key actors driving large-scale changes in the colonial sphere. Intertwined with this is the symbiotic relationship between colonial institutions—the military, the church, and civil government—and these economic merchants and traders. As Pezzarossi points out through his discussion of anti-markets, the economic workings of colonialism depended on these institutions to control markets and concentrate economic power.

Second, the analyses presented here show that the ambitions of colonial military and church institutions were themselves heavily dependent on economic factors. For example, Saccente and White trace how the success or failure of military fortifications in La Florida depended on the extent to which the expense of maintaining defensive settlements could be defrayed through trade and local production. Similarly, Scaramelli and Scaramelli document how missionaries in the Middle Orinoco relied on trade to underwrite religious proselytizing.

Third, the long-term structures and practices of pre-colonial indigenous economies were significant factors in shaping colonization. Kepecs argues that indigenous elites appropriated colonial religious symbolism to maintain pre-colonial trade and exchange relations, transforming trade itself into a form of resistance to Spanish authority. Rodríguez-Alegría et al. demonstrate that economic factors were key to indigenous technological change, which is typically studied as an adaptive process: "the economic context in which materials became available to makers and users of tools, in which people manage labor, and in which people have differential access to the products that result from the use of one technology or another."

Fourth, the studies described here present a paradox: they demonstrate both the resilience of indigenous economies and the persistence of colonial structures that trapped indigenous populations in relations of dependency. Pezzarossi, in particular, notes that the economic entanglements between colonists and indigenous communities were formed within relations of inequality, including military force and market manipulation. Similarly, Scaramelli and Scaramelli trace how colonial missionaries' adoption of the indigenous practice of wealth redistribution and circulation, or "giving up front," led to debt peonage and other forms of labor exploitation and market dependence. Rodríguez-Alegría et al. note shared mutual interest among colonial and indigenous elites in economic transactions: "colonial strategies designed to create and perpetuate relations of dependency through enticement often articulated with the indigenous strategies intended at enhancing personal status and political power" (Rodríguez-Alegría et al.; see also Scaramelli and Scaramelli this volume).

This collection thus lays the groundwork for a new economic focus in the archaeology of Spanish and Portuguese colonialism in the Americas, one which steps away from rational-actor and free-trade models of commerce and instead emphasizes the structural inequalities shaping exchange between colonial and indigenous communities.

## 19.4 Closing Thoughts

There are many more things that could be written about this important book. Each chapter opened up new vistas and illuminated hidden corners of the history and archaeology of Spanish and Portuguese colonization of the Americas. The richly textured case studies draw scholars closer into the temporal and spatial scale of life as it was lived by those who enacted and experienced colonialism.

The next task ahead may be to bring these studies into conversation with each other through multisited research. Rodriquez-Alegría et al.'s examination of stone and steel tool use in central Mexico and the Venezuelan Orinoco, and Teixeira et al.'s study of the transformation wrought on Portuguese society by American commodities, begins to point toward the kinds of nonreductive multiscalar methodologies that can trace the particularities of daily life across time and space. Iberian colonization of the Americas was not Grand. However, it was extensive, enabling the creation and maintenance of structural inequalities across great distances. As Scott (1990) notes, such systems of power bear a "family resemblance" to one another, and so do the tactics used by those subject to domination. Having disrupted Grand Narratives, the studies presented here lay a new foundation for investigating the not-so-grand workings of colonialism.

## References

Anzaldua, G. (1987). *Borderlands/La Frontera: The new mestiza*. San Francisco: Spinsters/Aunt Lute.
Aretxaga, B. (2005). *States of terror: Begoña Aretxaga's essays*. Reno: Center for Basque Studies, University of Nevada.
Barthes, R. (1977). *Image/music/text*. New York: Hill and Wang.
Bhabha, H. (1984). Of mimicry and men: The ambivalence of colonial discourse. *October, 28,* 125–133.
Bourdieu, P. (1977). *Outline of a theory of practice*. Cambridge: Cambridge University Press.
Bourdieu, P. (1980). *The logic of practice. Translated by R. Nice*. Stanford: Stanford University Press.
Boyd, B. (2010). *On the origin of stories: Evolution, cognition, and fiction*. Cambridge: Belknap Press.
Curet, L. A., Dawdy, S. L., & La Rosa Corzo, G. (2005). *Dialogues in Cuban archaeology*. Tuscaloosa: University of Alabama Press.
Derrida, J. (1973). *Speech and phenomena and other essays on Husserl's theory of signs*. Evanston: Northwestern University Press.
Fanon, F. (1977). *The wretched of the earth*. New York: Grove Press.
Fireman, G. D., McVay, T. E. J., & Flanagan, O. J. (2003). *Narrative and consciousness: Literature, psychology and the brain*. Oxford: Oxford University Press.
Foster, G. M. (1960). *Culture and conquest: America's Spanish heritage. Viking Fund Publications in anthropology no. 27*. Chicago: Quadrangle Books.
Foucault, M. (1975). *Discipline and punish: The birth of the prison*. New York: Vintage Books.
Funari, P. P. A., Hall, M., & Jones, S. (Eds.). (1999). *Historical archaeology: Back from the edge*. London: Routledge.

Giddens, A. (1979). *Central problems in social theory: Action, structure and contradictions in social analysis*. Berkeley: University of California Press.

Gilroy, P. (2000). *Against race: Imagining political culture beyond the color line*. Cambridge: Harvard University Press.

Gottschall, J. (2012). *The storytelling animal: How stories make us human*. New York: Mariner Books.

Herskovits, M. J. (1938). *Acculturation: The study of culture contact*. New York: J. J. Augustine Publisher.

Juderías, J. (1917). *La leyenda negra: estudios acerca del concepto de España en el extranjero*. Barcelona: Editorial Araluce.

Lyotard, J.-F. (1984). *The postmodern condition: A report on knowledge*. St. Paul: University of Minnesota Press.

Ortiz, F. (1995). *Cuban counterpoint: Tobacco and sugar. Translated by H. De Onis*. Durham: Duke University Press.

Redfield, R., Linton, R., & Herskovits, M. (1936). Memorandum for the study of acculturation. *American Anthropologist, 38*(1), 149–152.

Scott, J. C. (1990). *Domination and the arts of resistance: Hidden transcripts*. New Haven: Yale University Press.

Stoler, A. L. (2002). *Carnal knowledge and imperial power: Race and the intimate in colonial rule*. Berkeley: University of California Press.

Wylie, A. (1992). *The interplay of evidential constraints and political interests: Recent archaeological research on gender. American Antiquity, 57*(1), 15–35.

# Index

15th century, 6, 28, 33
16th century, 3, 6, 19, 21–23, 28–30, 32, 34, 48, 59, 357
17th century, 6, 22, 23, 25, 26, 28, 30, 32, 33, 64, 161, 162, 184, 186, 188, 193
18th century, 3, 6, 21, 26, 28, 31–33, 69, 161, 166, 174, 187, 219, 221, 356
19th century, 6, 32, 169, 172, 174, 185, 187
20th century, 5, 6, 166, 174

**A**

Adaptation,
    mestiçagem, 347
    using technology, 53
Adaptationist models, 53, 54
Africans, 33, 317
    ethnic diversity in, 188
    heritage and religiosity, 138
    ivory trading, 34
    labor force, 329
    role in Cuban society, 138
    settlements, 137
    slave, 317, 326–328
    slaves, 35, 134, 137, 145, 161, 183, 315, 331–333
    social divisions amongst, 315
    trafficking of slaves, 34
Agency, 6, 183, 224
    cultural, 342

primary, 353
Agriculture, 156, 175, 191
    and fishing, 169
    and herding, 191
    and livestock production, 161
    commercial fluvial, 171
    in Patagonian project families, 233
    mono-cultivar intensive, 170
Aguacatepeque, 79, 80, 85, 91, 92, 94
    agricultural production at, 96
    antimarket effects, 93, 96
    archaeological research, 94, 95
    community, 86, 87, 90
    effects of capitalism, 96
    effects on, 81
    population, 95
    role in colonial market economy, 87
    tribute crops, 90
Aleijadinho, 339, 341
    works of, 345, 347, 348
Ambiguity, 49, 282, 357
Amerindians, 25, 28, 33, 61
    diet, 32
Anchoring, 283–285
Animals, 10, 21, 29, 32
    and cultivars, 178
    and plants, 223
    draft, 55
    exploitation of, 171
    in Patagonian era, 230
Antilles, 61, 156, 162
Antimarkets, 81, 82, 85, 94, 96

© Springer International Publishing Switzerland 2015
P. P. A. Funari, M. X. Senatore (eds.), *Archaeology of Culture Contact and Colonialism in Spanish and Portuguese America,* DOI 10.1007/978-3-319-08069-7

CPSIA information can be obtained at www.ICGtesting.com
Printed in the USA
LVOW05*1716031214

416970LV00001B/30/P